Dedication

We are proud to acknowledge our mentors, because we owe an incalculable debt to many teachers who encouraged us to pursue scientific psychology. In particular, we would like to dedicate this work to three outstanding psychologists who shared the fun and excitement of experimental psychology with us: **David A. Grant, William M. Hinton,** and **L. Starling Reid.** Each, in his own way, encouraged students to engage in sound psychological science. Their enthusiasm and wisdom led us into experimental psychology, and we hope our readers will find similar models to lead them in the same direction.

BRIEF CONTENTS

CONTENTS

ABOUT THE AUTHORS

David G. Elmes is a Professor of Psychology at Washington and Lee University, where he has taught since 1967. He earned his B.A. with high honors from the University of Virginia and completed his M.A. and Ph.D. degrees in psychology there. Dr. Elmes was an adjunct professor at Hampden-Sydney College, a research associate for a year in the Human Performance Center of the University of Michigan, and a Visiting Fellow of University College at the University of Oxford. At Washington and Lee, he co-directed the Cognitive Science Program and chaired the Department of Psychology for 10 years. Professor Elmes edited *Readings in Experimental Psychology* and *Directory of Research in Psychology at Primarily Undergraduate Institutions* and is coauthor of the eighth edition of *Experimental Psychology* (2005, with B. H. Kantowitz and H. L. Roediger III). Dr. Elmes has published numerous articles about human and animal learning, memory, and the sense of smell. The smell research received support from the National Institute of Environmental Health Sciences. He frequently referees papers submitted to technical journals and was a consulting editor for the *Journal of Experimental Psychology: Learning, Memory and Cognition* for several years. Professor Elmes has been active in the Council of Undergraduate Research, for which he has served as Psychology Councilor, Psychology Division Chair, and President. Professor Elmes is a Fellow of the American Psychological Society.

Barry H. Kantowitz is Professor of Psychology, Professor of Industrial and Operational Engineering, and past Director of the Transportation Research Institute at the University of Michigan, where he is Program Manager for a $16 million research project on human factors, safety, and telematics sponsored by the Federal Highway Administration. Previously he was Chief Scientist of the Human Factors Transportation Center of the Battelle Memorial Institute in Seattle. He received his Ph.D. in experimental psychology from the University of Wisconsin in 1969. From 1969 to 1987 he held positions as Assistant, Associate, and Professor of Psychological Sciences at Purdue University. Dr. Kantowitz was elected a Fellow of the American Psychological Association in 1974. He has been a National Institute of

Mental Health Postdoctoral Fellow at the University of Oregon, a Senior Lecturer in Ergonomics at the Norwegian Institute of Technology, and a Visiting Professor of Technical Psychology at the University of Lulea, Sweden. He has written and edited more than one dozen books. His research on human attention, mental workload, reaction time, and human-machine interaction has been supported by the Office of Education, the National Institute of Mental Health, NASA, the Air Force Office of Scientific Research, and the U.S. Department of Transportation. He served on the editorial boards of *Organizational Behavior and Human Performance* and *Human Factors*.

Henry L. Roediger III is the James S. McDonnell University Professor of Psychology and Dean of Academic Planning at Washington University in St. Louis, where he has taught since 1996. He received a B.A. degree in psychology from Washington and Lee University in 1969 and a Ph.D. in cognitive psychology from Yale University in 1973. He has taught at Rice University (1988–1996) and Purdue University (1973–1988) and spent 3 years as a visiting professor at the University of Toronto. His research interests lie in cognitive psychology, particularly in human  learning and memory. Dr. Roediger has published over 170 chapters, articles, and reviews, as well as two other textbooks: *Psychology* (coauthored with E. D. Capaldi, S. G. Paris, J. Polivy, and P. Herman) and *Experimental Psychology* (2005) (with B. H. Kantowitz and D. G. Elmes). He also co-edited *Varieties of Memory and Consciousness: Essays in Honour of Endel Tulving* (1989) and *The Nature of Remembering: Essays in Honor of Robert G. Crowder* (2001), as well as several other books. Dr. Roediger has served as editor of *Journal of Experimental Psychology: Learning, Memory and Cognition* (1984–1989) and *Psychonomic Bulletin & Review* (1994–1997). He is a consulting editor for nine journals, including the *Journal of Memory and Language: Memory,* the *Journal of Experimental Psychology: Learning, Memory, and Cognition,* the *American Journal of Psychology,* and *Psychological Bulletin.* He has served as President of the American Psychological Society, the Midwest Psychological Association, and the Experimental Psychology Division of the American Psychological Association. He was a member of the Governing Board of the Psychonomic Society for 5 years (Chair, 1989–1990). In 1994, he received a Guggenheim Fellowship and was elected a member of the Society of Experimental Psychologists. According to a 1996 study by the Institute of Scientific Information, Roediger's papers had the greatest impact (measured by their average number of citations) in the field of psychology for the 5-year period from 1990 to 1994. In 2005, Roediger was elected to the American Academy of Arts and Sciences.

PREFACE

Presenting you with the eighth edition of a book first published in 1981 gives us much pleasure. The book you are holding now differs radically from the first edition. We have tried to make revisions in response to numerous comments from students, professors, and reviewers, as well as our own changing ideas in teaching the research methods course. The popularity of the previous editions of this book has led to this eighth edition, which we hope you will find rewarding. As in the earlier editions, we present the methods of psychological science necessary to provide a solid understanding of what constitutes valid and reliable research. Regardless of whether you are a producer or a consumer of research, you must be able to evaluate and appraise it.

Organization

The first part of this book examines the basics of scientific psychology, the second part concerns basic research methods, the third part discusses advanced research topics, and the fourth and final part exposes the reader to the practice of scientific psychology. The first three chapters provide the groundwork for the rest of the material. In these chapters, we outline the rudiments of a research project, discuss the philosophy of science, and examine how to explore the literature of psychology. The second part includes three chapters concerned with basic research methods, and a single chapter overview of validity and reliability in psychological research. The final section has three chapters (ethics, interpreting results, and presenting reports) that may be read in any order and at any point the instructor deems most appropriate for the goals of his or her course. The appendices summarize descriptive and inferential statistics.

Pedagogical Features

Each chapter contains many features designed to improve comprehension and enhance interest. The *Opening Page* provides a summary of the upcoming chapter, alerts students to important concepts, and provides a convenient aid for review. The *Overview* introduces the substance of each chapter. *Concept Summaries,* which appear at the end of chapter headings, highlight important concepts and assist students with study and review. Most chapters include an *Application* section that demonstrates how some of the concepts discussed in the chapter can be used outside the laboratory setting. Several features appear at the end of each chapter: a point-by-point *Summary,* a list of *Key Concepts,* thought-provoking *Exercises,* and *Suggested Resources.* These features will help students derive maximum benefit from the contents of the chapter by reinforcing and extending students' understanding. The *Suggested Resources* include World Wide Web addresses for important links to research in psychology. They also point the reader to relevant chapters in Langston's (2005) *Research Methods Laboratory Manual.* The resources include selections from Wadsworth's *Workshops in Research Methods and Statistics.* A *Psychology in Action* section follows most chapters. These sections each present a project for students to undertake; we hope they will further students' interest in scientific psychology. The *Glossary* at the end of the book contains brief definitions of the *Key Concepts.* The inside covers of the book include summaries of valuable information of important concepts and methods for quick reference. As in earlier editions, many concepts receive more than one treatment, because repeated discussion of important ideas in separate parts of the text enhances understanding. We want to take advantage of the well-known benefits of distributed practice and varied rehearsal to maximize the efficiency of our readers' learning.

Changes New to This Edition

Users of the seventh edition will notice many changes in the eighth. The advice of our capable reviewers and editors, the suggestions of students, and our own experience have resulted in organizational and content changes. We have added emphasis on the role of technology in searching the literature, calculating statistics, controlling experiments, and simulating the environment. Further, as noted previously, the *Suggested Resources* at the end of each chapter include many new World Wide Web addresses for sites that contain important information about psychological research. In addition, readers of this book can visit the Wadsworth companion Web site for this book at http://psychology. wadsworth.com. We hope you visit this site not only to provide feedback but also to investigate resources other than those mentioned in the text. We have striven to make changes that are timely, interesting, pedagogically sound, and accurate. We have added numerous new references and several challenging exercises, and our examples reflect interesting research from a number of exciting areas of psychological research. Based on reviewers' suggestions, several new tables have been added to enhance the comprehension of the material. The chapter organization is new. Here we list the chapters in their new order, and we specify the content changes from the seventh edition.

The title of Chapter 1, *Overview of Psychological Research,* reflects the chapter's intent to provide a broad picture of what is involved in a research project. In addition to many new references and updated Web resources, there is an increased emphasis on how understanding the research process benefits students. We emphasize the importance of research skills for students' education and job placement. Chapter 2, *Explanation in Scientific Psychology,* includes new work on the philosophy of science. It explains how hypotheses are derived from generalizations, which are derived either from theory or from everyday experience. Gaggles of generalizations produce hordes of hypotheses. Chapter 2 includes an *Application Section* that discusses the importance of falsification in making inductive inferences.

At the suggestion of reviewers and readers, *Exploring the Literature of Psychology* now occurs early in the text as Chapter 3. New journals and search engines appear in the *Resources Section.* Data from an experiment concerned with cell phone use and driving helps illustrate how to read tabular information.

A new *Psychology in Action* section in Chapter 4, *Observations in Psychological Research,* examines remembering the 9/11 terrorist attacks. Several new references appear as well.

Relational Research, Chapter 5, still focuses on contingency and correlational research but now includes a discussion of regression in the context of predicting the initiation of adolescent sexual behavior. The section on cross-lagged panel correlation considers current research showing that childhood preference for violent TV is associated with violence and aggression in adulthood.

One of our strongest chapters, *Basics of Experimentation,* Chapter 6, considers interactions in the context of an experiment concerned with leadership styles.

Validity and Reliability in Psychological Research is now Chapter 7. Meta-analysis and effect size are new additions to this chapter. We also included more information concerning sampling and sampling procedures.

Chapter 8, *Experimental Design,* includes a meta-analysis study of stress in humans and received minor updates in the examples. The next chapter, *Complex Design,* received a thorough updating through the use of new examples.

Small-n Experimentation, Chapter 10, received an updated treatment of hyperactivity and the K-P diet. Memory dysfunction in dissociative identity disorders is illustrated by two recent experiments.

Chapter 11, *Quasi-Experimentation,* now has several contemporary examples of one-shot case studies. Two studies concern the effects of aircraft noise on the cognitive behavior of schoolchildren, and one quasi-experiment examines the effects of construction noise on students living in dormitories. As noted earlier, the final three chapters are written so that they can be read in any order and at nearly any time during the course.

Chapter 12, *Conducting Ethical Research,* presents the latest version (2002–2003) of the APA code of ethics for research with humans and animals. This chapter also includes a discussion of recent studies on plagiarism and the use of deception in research.

Changes to *Interpreting the Results of Research,* Chapter 13, include six new and recent references. These provide an interesting discussion of scale attenuation effects in the context of memory performance in people with brain damage. New work on cultural differences in personal space receives examination.

Chapter 14, *Presenting Research Results,* now considers how to prepare poster presentations. Several new references consider aspects of writing in scientific psychology. Revisions to the statistical appendices make them more accessible and include examples of using Excel and SPSS.

Acknowledgments

Writing a textbook requires authors to cooperate with readers and users of earlier editions and with editorial and production staff and to heed the sage advice of several capable reviewers. Many readers of the sixth edition and professors who assigned it have written us with valuable suggestions. As always, Vicki Knight, our editor, offered excellent advice and help.

The following reviewers helped us fine-tune several points for this edition: Susan Anzivino, University of Maine at Farmington; William Dragon, Cornell College; Michael Hall, James Madison University; Chris Koch, George Fox University; Louise Perry, Florida Atlantic University; and Pamela Schuetze, SUNY College at Buffalo. Reviewers of previous editions include: Nicole Anderson, Brigham Young University; Alfredo Ardila, Florida Atlantic University; Barbara Church, University at Buffalo; Jean Doerr, SUNY at Buffalo; Betty Edelman, University of Texas at Dallas; Amy Eischfield, The College of William and Mary; Michael Hall, University of Nevada, Las Vegas; Andrew Howell, Grant MacEwan College; Susan D. Lima, University of Wisconsin–Milwaukee; William Smotherman, University of Massachusetts, Amherst; and Marcel Voder, University of Illinois at Springfield. We appreciate the time and effort the reviewers spent to help us produce a better book.

Colleagues at our institutions provided advice and encouragement. David McCabe of Washington University in St. Louis provided valuable contributions. It is a pleasure to acknowledge the technical help of Stacy Henderson and Kendall Murphy. These two undergraduates helped in many ways with such skill and efficiency that this edition would still be in limbo without their fine assistance.

David G. Elmes
Barry H. Kantowitz
Henry L. Roediger III

Basics of Scientific Psychology

Part I focuses on most of the funda-
mentals of psychological research. The
first chapter provides an overview of
scientific psychology in the context of
a particular experiment. The second
chapter considers the ways in which
theories lead to organizing and explaining scientific facts. The third chapter
details how to explore the literature
of psychology.

Much of the material that an instructor might assign early in a course
on research methods, such as ethics
and writing about psychological research, appears briefly in Part I and in
detail in Part IV. Because the chapters
in Part IV can be read in any order, at
any time, during a typical course, in-
structors may assign them whenever
they choose.

CHAPTER 1

Overview of Psychological Research

Goals of Psychological Research
- Conducting sound research
- Critically evaluating research

Sources of Psychological Research
- Theories
- Practical problems

Sources of Research Ideas
- Observation
- Experts
- Literature search

Typical Steps in Research
- Get an idea
- Formulate a testable hypothesis
- Review the literature
- Conduct pilot research
- Complete the research
- Conduct statistical tests
- Interpret the results
- Prepare an article

"Musts" in Research
- Consider ethical issues
- Guard against researcher bias
- Construct operational definitions

In this chapter, you will participate in a demonstration experiment. Then you will discover that the focus of this book is on conducting sound research and critically evaluating the research of others. You will be introduced to the initial stages of the research process—getting ideas, formulating hypotheses, reviewing the literature, and conducting preliminary research.

"The overarching aim of education in psychology should be to communicate the understanding that scientific psychology offers ways of thinking and knowing that have great potential value of helping people to cope with the world's problems. . . . The fundamental goal of education in psychology is to teach students how to think as scientists about behavior" (Brewer et al., 1993, pp. 168–169). This quote, from a book published by the American Psychological Association (APA) (McGovern, 1993), defines our goal of helping you learn ways to understand why people and other animals behave as they do. **Behavior** is the fundamental factor that is measured in scientific psychology, and it includes activities such as eating food and recalling stories as well as the speed of responding, blood pressure, and other physiological indicators of thoughts and feelings.

Good psychological research can be very important. The astounding number of practical gains are too numerous to list, but include discoveries such as: improved methods of treating psychologically disordered people, better designs of vehicles to make them easier and safer to use, and new ways of enhancing the performance and happiness of workers. Just as important are scientific gains in psychological research. Scientific psychology is a relatively young science, having begun in earnest in the middle of the nineteenth century. Nevertheless, the 150 years of psychological research have resulted in a dramatic increase in the scientific understanding of behavior.

In this chapter, you will first participate in an experiment. Then we examine the course of psychological research by using the demonstration experiment as an example.

▶ An Investigation of Reading

To start your study of psychological research, we want you to take part in an experiment. We hope that your participation in this project will elicit the kinds of questions about research that psychology students and experimental participants often ask. We also will use the experiment to highlight many issues confronting researchers in psychology as they begin to study and use the methods of scientific psychology.

Introduction and Method

The design of the following demonstration experiment tries to decide whether aspects of reading and counting can occur automatically. You are a skilled reader, having spent 12 or so years of your life practicing this skill. You probably believe that reading words and enumerating objects are rational, deliberate processes. Are they? Do you have to think about reading and counting while doing them, or do these processes occur automatically, with little conscious effort? To find out whether reading can occur automatically, you will engage in a series of reading and counting tasks. The crucial part of the experiment is that the tasks differ in their requirements. The behavior you will measure is how fast you do each. One task is set up so that if reading occurs automatically, you will do that task more slowly than the others.

To participate in this experiment, you will need a clock or a watch with a second hand (a watch that records elapsed time in seconds will do), and you will need a pen or a pencil. You might want to do this experiment with a classmate, so you can accurately time each other. Your task is to read or count a series of digits or symbols as quickly and as accurately as you can. The digits and symbols are in a single column. You should start at the top and go to the bottom of the column without skipping any items. You will go through three different columns on three different pages. Be sure to do them in order. At the top of each page are directions—read them carefully, because the directions on each page are different. The phrase *Start Time* is also at the top of each page. If you are working alone and are using a clock or watch with a second hand, write down the exact time in minutes and seconds. Then start the task. If you are using a watch that records elapsed time, start the time and then begin the task. When you have finished the task on a particular page, either note your finishing time or stop your watch and write down the elapsed time. If you are doing this experiment with a classmate, have him or her time you as you go through each task. Your classmate then can serve as a participant, and you can do the timing for each task.

To begin the experiment, turn to page 26. Do not continue reading here until you have participated in the experiment.

Results and Discussion

What happened in the experiment? For each column of digits or symbols, figure out how long it took you to do the task. If you recorded elapsed time, this is straightforward. If you wrote down your start and finish times, calculate the time to go through the column by subtracting the start time from the finish time. When you compare the results of the three tests, you probably will find that naming the number of numbers (the last task you did) took the longest time and reading the digits took the shortest time.

When we conducted this experiment, we obtained the results shown in Figure 1–1. Students in our classes took an average of about 2 seconds longer to enumerate the pluses (the second task) than to read the digits (the first task). In the final task, naming the number of numbers, our students averaged about 6 seconds longer than when they simply read the digits. If you combine your results with those of your classmates, statistical procedures described in Appendix B will allow you to decide whether the differences in completion time among the tasks are large enough to be considered reliable ones worth considering.

An alternative way to think about the results is to examine how long, on average, it took people to respond to each item. Because there were 32 items

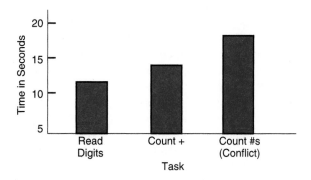

Figure 1–1   Results of demonstration experiment. The average time (seconds) that a class took to do each of the three tasks.

in each task, we can divide the mean time by 32 to find the average time per item. The students averaged .35 seconds to read a single digit, .43 seconds to count a row of pluses, and .57 seconds to count a row of numbers in the conflict task.

Time to read the columns is a measure of reading difficulty; the longer the time, the more difficult the task. Why is it difficult to name the number of digits when the response is different from the name of the digit? That is, why is it difficult to say "4" when you see 3 3 3 3?

To answer this question, we will outline a theory that seems to account for the results. Other researchers have found that people usually are slower in naming the quantity of digits when the names of those digits conflict with that quantity. Apparently, we automatically read the name of the digits as we enumerate the quantity. So, when we have to respond "2" when we see 3 3, we simultaneously have the responses "2" and "3" available, and because we cannot say two things at once, competition exists between the available responses.

You can think of this as a mental race between two processes that lead to different responses when you see 3 3. One process is naming the digits ("3"); the other is counting them and saying the number ("2"). Because the naming process is greatly practiced, it wins the race, and the naming response ("3") comes to mind before the correct counting response ("2"). Thus, there is response competition, because you must inhibit the faster naming response to permit the slower counting response to be spoken. Even if you try to ignore the names of the digits completely, you will discover that you are slower in counting numbers than you were in counting pluses (check the results of the second test you took). This outcome can be interpreted as showing that reading is an automatic process, because even when you try to avoid reading the numbers 3 3, you cannot completely suppress the response "3." Put another way, you cannot *not* read. Try looking at a word and not reading it.

▶ Goals of Psychological Research

You have just participated in a demonstration experiment that was supposed to show that reading occurs under some circumstances even when we do not want it to. You could ask at this point why people bother to engage in research, or why you are taking a course that focuses on research. Recall that our goal, and the likely goal of your instructor, is to help you think as a scientist about behavior. We are not alone in trying to achieve this aim. A survey of more than 650 departments of psychology in colleges and universities showed that about 90% either required or recommended some combination of courses in statistics and research design as part of their major program (A. J. Golden, personal communication, January 2, 1991). Furthermore, an analysis of the expected undergraduate psychology courses for admission to graduate programs in psychology showed that out of 1,554 departments, 66% either required or recommended a course in research methods and experimental design (Norcross, Hanych, & Terranova, 1996). Only statistics, at 88%, had a higher expectation than a methods course.

To become a scientist of behavior, you need to learn how to conduct sound research, and you need to learn how to evaluate the results of research. We examine each of these in turn.

Conducting Research

Science progresses when new facts lead to new theories. This progression begins with attempts to answer questions. Is reading a deliberate, reflective process? Not always, as our demonstration experiment shows. Scientific interest in reading is more than idle curiosity—it is curiosity guided by theories and data (facts). The finding that reading often does not require conscious attention must be considered by theories that attempt to explain some aspects of reading. For example, Cohen, Dunbar, and McClelland (1990) developed a theory of attention that tries to show how skilled reading develops. The theory predicts, for example, that highly practiced readers will be more disrupted by conflicts between reading and naming than will less fluent readers. Cohen and associates showed that this is the case, and their theory provides an account of the mechanisms underlying the effects of experience on automaticity. Thus basic research usually arises from curiosity and provides the data that allow the development of theoretical explanations.

Scientific progress is not only driven by basic questions and theories but is also motivated by practical problems. One aspect of the research by Cohen and his colleagues shows that automaticity in reading takes a substantial amount of practice. Some obvious practical issues include what amount of practice is needed for fluent reading and what the best way is to practice to become fluent. The application of scientific psychology to applied problems has had a tremendous impact on social welfare, and the development of improved ways to teach reading is no exception. The understanding of reading has benefited from attempts to determine its bases and solve some practical problems (Rayner & Pollatsek, 1995).

Obviously, psychological research is not exclusively practical or exclusively theoretical in its focus. Psychological research can have an impact on scientific explanation and the amelioration of applied problems. Many facets of human affairs involve psychological research, and a sample of careers using scientific psychology is summarized in the Application section.

CONCEPT SUMMARY

Research helps to

- provide scientific understanding
- solve practical problems

Evaluating Research

Although you have diverse opportunities for a career in psychological research, conducting sound research is not the only focus of a course concerned with research methods. The second focus of such a course, and of this book, is to help you evaluate the results of psychological research. Because the same research methods are used in many disciplines, much of the information you learn in this book about the logic of research will generalize to other fields, such as biology, sociology, and medicine. As an involved member of society, you will be influenced by psychological research. To be a careful consumer of research findings, you need to be able to consider carefully the soundness of the research.

We hope that you will acquire the ideas necessary to think critically about research. A **critic** makes an informed or reasoned judgment about the value of something. So, a **critical thinker** does not just find fault or criticize unfavorably. Rather, a critical thinker exercises careful judgment. Critical thinking is difficult. You probably accepted the results of the demonstration experiment without a second thought. Unfortunately, the design of the experiment does not permit an unequivocal answer to the original question.

Let us outline the principles of a good experiment and see how our experiment fails to meet those principles. In an ideal experiment, something is manipulated or changed, potential sources of influence are held constant, and some behavior is measured. The factor varied is called the **independent variable,** and the behavior measured is called the **dependent variable. Control variables** are those that are held constant. The researcher manipulates or changes the independent variable so that the effects of the different values or levels of the independent variable can be determined by changes in the

APPLICATION

Research Careers in Psychology

Many of you may view a course about psychological research as a necessary hurdle for a major in psychology but of little intrinsic interest. We hope that this book will convince you that psychological research is important and exciting. One reason that you may not be particularly interested in psychological research is that you are unaware of the important skills and habits of thought fostered by research. Walsh (2004) reports a wealth of information regarding job skills and other career-related information for psychology majors. In addition, she details much of the information required for going to graduate school.

The psychology major curriculum, especially research-related courses, provides a variety of job-related skills that are highly desirable to employers. According to Lorig (1996), research experience helps to hone skills such as teamwork, oral and written communication, analytic skills, and computer knowledge. In addition to the careers indicated here, Lorig provides a list of sample psychology-major employment options that includes personnel interviewer, probation officer, public health statistician, market researcher, and hospice coordinator.

The range of opportunities for a person with training in psychological research is surprisingly broad. Many of these areas require an advanced degree in psychology, but that is not always the case. In any event, almost all aspects of our lives need and use psychological research. Here is a list of some of the less obvious careers involving psychological research.

1. A police psychologist who serves as an expert witness on a variety of topics. The psychologist may do work on eyewitness testimony, profiles of criminals, and incentive programs for police officers.

2. A psychologist who does library and laboratory research on the causes of traffic accidents and evaluates safety programs. Or a psychologist who does the same kind of work but specializes in industrial or home accidents.

3. A research psychologist who specializes in population trends: migration, fertility, marriage, and the effects of population density. Federal, state, and local governments often need qualified psychologists to conduct such research.

4. A research psychologist who designs effective computer displays and user-friendly components and software. Such psychologists are in high demand throughout private industry.

5. A research psychologist who determines effective ways of increasing energy conservation. These researchers might study personality dynamics, or they might examine ways to teach people to conserve energy.

6. A research psychologist who tries to determine the brain mechanisms involved in alcoholism and drug addiction. Such a researcher is likely to work in a government hospital or hold an academic position.

(continued)

7. A research psychologist in human factors engineering who is interested in one or more of the following: urban transportation, military training, hijacking, equipment design, or the effects of fatigue on performance.

Further information about careers and graduate school may be obtained at:
American Psychological Association. *Non-academic careers for scientific psychol-*ogists. Washington, DC: American Psychological Association, (n.d.). Retrieved October 21, 2004, from http://www.apa.org/science/nonacad.html

Walsh, L. (2004). *Welcome to the pursuing psychology career page.* Retrieved October 5, 2004 from http://www.uni.edu/walsh/linda1.html

Lloyd, M. A. (1997, August). *Entry-level jobs for psychology majors* (online). Retrieved March 15, 2005, from http://www.psywww.com/careers/jobs.htm

dependent variable. In the demonstration experiment, the three tasks were the levels of the independent variable, and your time to go through the lists was the dependent variable. Control variables include the number of items on each of the three tests (32 in each), the numbers 1–4 of digits, pluses, and conflict items were equal, and the order in which you and your classmates went through the tasks was constant. The constancy of order is the problem, which we discuss next. A summary of the variables in experiments is presented in Figure 1–2.

To see how the constant order presents difficulties, you need to recognize that another variable that could influence the dependent variable should not vary with or contaminate the independent variable in an experiment. Because order and task varied together, they are confounded. **Confounding** here means that both the tasks and the order in which they were done varied together—order of the tasks and their nature were confused or confounded. The extra time taken in the third task may have resulted from fatigue or boredom rather than from the nature of the task. More likely, people did the tasks better as they went through them, which would underestimate the effect of the independent variable. In either case, order of task rather than the independent variable may have caused changes in reading time. Because of the confounding of

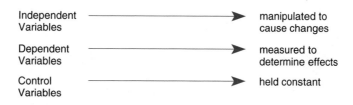

Figure 1–2 Variables in an experiment

task order and levels of the independent variable, the results of the experiment may not be interpretable. The confounding produces results that do not have **internal validity,** which means that they are not sound or true. When you conduct an experiment you want to be sure that the levels of the independent variable change behavior rather than a confounding variable. When you can be sure the experiment lacked confounding, then it would have internal validity (validity is discussed in detail in Chapter 7).

A critical view of the experiment questions the soundness of the results. A more careful research design would have different people go through the tasks in different orders, which would unconfound order and task. Alternatively, different groups of people would each be exposed to one task, so order of experiencing the tasks is not a consideration. When either is done, approximately the same results are obtained—the conflict task still takes longest to complete. Because you did not know that until now, you should have been skeptical of the results. As a rule, you should carefully evaluate research procedures so potential problems such as confounding may be identified.

An important time for you to think critically about research is when the results may have personal importance. Consider a hypothetical example. Suppose that in a few years, Doris, your child, is in the first grade. Her teacher calls you in for a conference and informs you that Doris has difficulty learning to read. The teacher then tells you that the school has several ways to provide remedial help. You and the teacher will choose what seems the best alternative to help Doris' progress. Can you make an informed judgment about the remedial reading methods? You probably are not an expert in teaching reading. Can you decide that one method shows more promise than another? What do you need to know? At least some parts of the answers to these questions require that you can critically assess the research and theory underlying the various programs.

Most of this book tries to help you identify problems associated with conducting sound research and develop the skills necessary to make informed judgments about the research process. You need to be able to identify weaknesses and to rectify them. Choosing a poor remedial reading program for your daughter could have dramatic effects—much more dramatic than her getting a mediocre grade in a required course. The need to understand psychological research will last your whole life, not just a single term of your undergraduate career.

CONCEPT SUMMARY

Critical thinking about research involves

- looking for design flaws such as confounding
- making informed judgments

▶ Sources of Research Ideas

We emphasize conducting and evaluating research. What constitutes a research project? The typical research project proceeds as shown in Table 1–1. It looks easy and straightforward, but it is not. You should know that the outline just presented is for the *typical* research project. Often, the sequence of events may be altered in a variety of ways. Consider one example. A veteran researcher may follow up on earlier experiments that she conducted by altering the independent variable in some way and then collecting data without getting the idea, formulating the hypothesis, and so on. In this chapter, we focus on the initial stages of a research project, and the rest of the book will complete the picture.

Observation

Science begins with observation, which is both a source of data and a source of ideas for further research. Look around with a critical eye, and you will likely generate a number of ideas for research. All you need to do is observe yourself, your classmates, your family, or even your pet. Then phrase your question so that you can make additional observations. Some typical questions might include: Do I study better in the library than in my dormitory room? Do students learn more in small classes than in large classes? Do students retain as much after studying with music on as without music? Do children work harder or less hard when given rewards such as candy? These and similar questions are easy to generate, and with some work, they can be turned into manageable research projects. Your native curiosity or the need to solve a particular problem will serve you well in developing ideas for research.

Experts

Both people, such as your professor, and textbooks, such as this one or your introductory psychology text, are usually good sources of research ideas. Often an idea presented in class or one that you read about will produce an

Table 1–1 Typical steps in research

1. Get an idea
2. Formulate a testable hypothesis
3. Review the literature
4. Conduct pilot research
5. Conduct the research
6. Analyze the results
7. Interpret the results
8. Prepare an article or presentation

The prudent researcher also considers ethical issues, guards against researcher bias, and uses operational definitions.

interesting idea. Once you are titillated by a problem, you should seek a consultant. Within a particular course, your instructor is the obvious choice. Beyond a particular course, you may try to get advice from someone whose competence and interest match what you are interested in exploring. Many faculty members will be delighted to discuss research with you. If you have read about an interesting research project, you can try writing to the author.

We designed this text to be a source of possible research projects. If you carefully answer the design-related questions that appear at the end of most chapters, the germ of a good research project may be lurking in one or more of your answers. Many of the questions derive from problems in actual research, so it is apparent that even experts do not conduct perfect research. Why not profit from their mistakes? At the end of many chapters, we point to the laboratory manual by Langston (2005), which contains thorough outlines of numerous interesting research projects. Another source of ideas in this book are the exercises presented at the end of each chapter in the Psychology in Action section. These exercises are usually easy to carry out. If you think critically about them, you will likely devise additional research projects.

Literature Search

Ideas frequently come from reading journal articles. Chapter 3 of this book considers how to read a journal article carefully. If you are going to be reading journal articles soon, we suggest that you read that chapter before you get into the technical literature. After reading several journal articles, you will soon have a longer list of possible experiments that you could perform.

To keep track of ideas generated from your critical reading of journals or textbooks, you should keep records of your research ideas. Most psychologists have some sort of index file containing information about the articles that they have read. On your file cards or in a computer file, you should have several kinds of information: authors' names, journals, article titles, and information about the procedure and results. It is probably best to supplement your article file with a file of research ideas. Most psychologists keep a file of such ideas, and you should too. Write down the reference that started you thinking, a short description of your idea for a project, and the date the idea occurred. You will find it interesting to go back through your files to see how your thinking about some topic has changed over time.

As your idea file gets larger because each article you read suggests at least one additional project to you, you are now confronted with another problem. At first an idea for any project was cause for celebration. Later the problem becomes one of deciding which of several ideas in your file should be tried. Some potential ideas will be eliminated because you do not have access to specialized equipment or special subject populations. Others will be too complicated or take too long to carry out. After paring down your list, you probably still will have more than one alternative. If each idea is equally practical and feasible, given your resources, our advice is to tackle the project you think would be most fun. Psychological research is interesting and exciting and often has important outcomes. However, interest, excitement, and importance will happen only if you do research (follow up on your idea file).

If you are unsure about what journals and other resources to examine for research ideas, you should refer to Chapter 3. For the moment, you should know that the computer search engine *PsycINFO* is a very effective tool for going through the technical literature. If your library does not subscribe to *PsycINFO,* other computerized searches may be available. The print companion to *PsycINFO* is *Psychological Abstracts,* and both contain abstracts of articles from almost all journals that publish psychological research. If you find an abstract of interest, you can then read the entire article for additional information. Chapter 3 also describes how to use *PsycINFO.*

CONCEPT SUMMARY

Sources of ideas include

- observation
- experts
- literature search

▶ Developing Testable Hypotheses

After you have developed an idea, you need to frame it in the form of a testable hypothesis. A **testable hypothesis** makes a statement about a presumed or theoretical relation between two or more variables (Kerlinger & Lee, 2000). According to Kerlinger and Lee, a testable hypothesis either states or implies that the variables are measurable. It also specifies the relation among the variables. Specifying measurements and relations sets the stage for the research project, because research requires that something can be observed and measured. Therefore, if a hypothesis is not testable, research on it is impossible.

Consider one of the ideas generated from observation that was considered earlier: Do I study better in the library than in my dormitory room? Is this a testable hypothesis? A relation is implied—better study in the library—but measurements are not specified. So, at this point, the hypothesis is not testable. How can you measure better study? One way would be to assess the outcome of study; namely, your grades on a test could be determined. Grades are observable and measurable, so they fit one of the criteria for a testable hypothesis. The reformulated question might become, Do I get better grades on tests after studying in the library than after studying in my dorm room? Because you might be interested in the generality of the research outcome, you can modify the initial question to develop the following hypothesis: Higher grades are obtained after studying in the library than after studying in the dorms. This hypothesis follows the guidelines, because it specifies both what will be measured and the expected relationship between study location and grades.

At this point, you might want to practice developing testable hypotheses. Take some of the ideas or questions you have and see if you can put them in testable form. Any research that you undertake requires a testable hypothesis, so now is a good time to practice generating them. If you do not have many potential ideas to consider, several are available in one of the exercises at the end of this chapter.

Many hypotheses cannot be tested, because they either do not include variables that can be observed and measured or do not specify relations among variables. Thus, scientific research cannot be used to study many moral and religious issues. Research can be used to assess a person's attitude toward abortion, for example, but it cannot address the issue of whether abortion in principle is good or bad. The broad statement "Abortion is wrong" specifies neither what is to be measured nor relations among measurable variables. Testable hypotheses about the positive or negative impact of abortion in particular circumstances are possible, but encompassing hypotheses about the moral value of abortion are not. Many questions that you generate may not be testable, because they fail to include observable and measurable variables. Scientific research can be used to study how people respond to colors, but it cannot address the question of whether your experience of the color blue is the same as someone else's experience of the color blue. *Experience* in this context cannot be measured, but response (behavior) can.

CONCEPT SUMMARY

Testable hypotheses specify

- how variables will be measured
- how variables will be related

▶ Reviewing the Literature

The next phase of the research process involves a review of the pertinent literature. Previously, we discussed using journals to obtain ideas. Now, we will consider another important use of journals—determining what is known about your hypothesis. A literature review will reveal whether your research hypothesis has been tested, and it will indicate important things for you to consider in developing your research project.

You do not want to reinvent the wheel. The idea about the effects of study location on grades probably is not novel. Therefore, you must find out whether someone else has already tested your hypothesis. Thousands of research articles about psychological hypotheses are published each year, so you will probably find many articles related to your hypothesis. Even if those articles do not match your hypothesis precisely, you will probably discover many details that will allow you to devise your own research project more efficiently. Chapter 3 takes you through a literature search, so we will not provide all the details here. As noted earlier, *PsycINFO* and *Psychological Abstracts* are valuable sources of information. In addition, the article or articles that led to your research question should be valuable as well. At the end of those articles, you will find a reference list, which provides a good place for you to start your search for additional information related to your question.

Suppose you wanted to test a hypothesis related to the demonstration experiment. We referenced an article concerned with the conflict effect by Cohen and others (1990). So, you might look up that article in the Reference section of this book and then go to the library to read it. You can read about the research they did and the theory they proposed. You can use their reference list as a source of additional articles for your literature search (they reference more than 70 research papers). One thing you will discover is that the conflict effect shown in the demonstration experiment is usually called the **Stroop effect,** after the person who first demonstrated the phenomenon (Stroop, 1935). Generally, you should read the primary source of a research phenomenon, so examine Stroop's paper. If you are interested in the Stroop effect, you will find a review of 50 years of research on the Stroop effect by MacLeod (1991) to be very helpful. He cites about 400 studies and summarizes them. For a person interested in the phenomenon, this journal article is an extremely important source of information.

Another efficient way to get background information is to examine the subject index of textbooks. If you look in the index of this book, you will find that the Stroop effect is discussed in two different places later in the text. In those discussions, you will find additional references that might be valuable to read. A particularly important article is the one by Windes (1968), who apparently was the first researcher to use a task similar to the one used in the demonstration experiment.

CONCEPT SUMMARY

To begin a literature search, use

- *PsycINFO*
- reference lists of relevant articles
- textbooks

▶ Conducting Pilot Research

Before undertaking a full-scale research project, you should do some preliminary research, which is usually called **pilot research.** A thorough literature search will help you devise a reasonable research plan, and help you figure out what kinds of material and apparatus you may need. However, you will probably find it necessary to try out various parts of your project. This is the purpose of pilot research.

In pilot research, you test a small number of participants to try to ensure that you have all the bugs out of your research procedure. You will find out whether your participants understand the instructions. You will learn how much time the experiment requires and whether the tasks you chose are too easy or too hard. You will be able to practice using the equipment and materials and to practice observing and measuring the behavior of interest.

Frequently, pilot research is used to assess the levels of the independent variable to make sure that they have an effect on the dependent variable. If one level of the independent variable is presenting the conflicting digits upside down, you should try this out on a few people to ensure that there is less conflict than when the digits are right-side up. Suppose you find that there is less conflict when the digits are presented upside down. Is that a foolproof sign that you have an independent variable that works? Probably, but it may not be the case. One difficulty with pilot research is that you test your procedure on just a few participants. For whatever reason, this small sample of people may not be representative of the population of people you are interested in testing. To find out whether your pilot data are a fluke, you need to conduct the full-blown project with several observations under each level of the independent variable. Although the small test sample is a problem, pilot research plays an important role in developing a sound research project.

CONCEPT SUMMARY

Conduct pilot research to

- refine the research procedures
- test the levels of your independent variable

▶ Some Pitfalls to Avoid

Several potential difficulties await the researcher. In addition to the possibility of confounding mentioned earlier, researchers need to worry about the ethicality of their research, whether they have inadvertently biased the results, and the reliability of their communication. Other potential pitfalls are detailed later.

Breaches of Ethical Practice

Ethical issues in psychological research receive a separate and detailed treatment in Chapter 12. The issues are so prominent, however, that we outline some of them here. The overarching issue involves the well-being of the research participants, whether human or animal. Scientists have an obligation to treat the objects of their work in an ethical fashion. Treating research participants ethically is a complex issue often involving pragmatic choices between the needs of the researcher and the needs of the participant. With human participants, the ethical questions seem to boil down to the so-called Golden Rule—the researcher should treat the participants as he or she would wish to be treated. Thus, physical and mental harm are avoided or minimized, confidentiality is not breached, and dishonesty and deception are not used.

Ethical issues surrounding the use of animals in research are complex and emotionally charged. As a major governing body for psychological research, the APA specifically bans cruel or negligent treatment of animals. That association has detailed guidelines that define what constitutes humane treatment of animals used in research. Furthermore, many federal and state agencies also have regulations governing research with animals. Nevertheless, some people oppose using animals in research. We examine some of the pros and cons in Chapter 12. Ethical issues facing a researcher are among the most important to be resolved while conducting a research project. You, as an ethical person and scientist, must consider these issues carefully.

CONCEPT SUMMARY

To conduct ethical research

- treat humans as you would like to be treated
- treat animals humanely

Biased Research

An ethical researcher does not present fraudulent results. Deliberate fraud of this sort is uncommon in science. However, **inadvertent researcher bias** is a problem of unknown magnitude. Just how often unplanned researcher bias occurs is difficult to determine, because many parts of the research process may be inadvertently contaminated. A scientist's political beliefs, for example, could result in an incomplete survey that assesses some attitudes and not others. This does not necessarily indicate deliberate bias but may merely represent the fallibility of the scientist. The scientist can think about only a limited number of things at a time, so the research designs will partially reflect his or her own preferences.

A famous example of faulty research design is the case of Samuel G. Morton, a well-known physician and scientist in the early and middle 1800s. He collected more than one thousand skulls of people belonging to different races. He believed that skull volume was indicative of intelligence. He used his collection of skulls to examine intelligence differences among races. He reported that whites were the most intelligent, African Americans were the least intelligent, and Native Americans were in between, a conclusion in perfect agreement with the prejudices of the time. It was not until 1978 that Stephen Jay Gould, a Harvard paleontologist, concluded, and from the very data reported by Morton, that there were no differences in skull size among the races. Gould showed that Morton had chosen his skulls in line with his expectations. For one group of blacks, he used an all-female sample, whereas for the comparison group of whites, he used an all-male sample. This comparison ignores the fact that male skulls tend to be larger than female skulls (Broad & Wade, 1982). One aspect of the Morton affair that should be kept in mind is that the scientific community of that time accepted his research as scientifically valid. Only under the scrutiny of contemporary scientists with different social beliefs was the biased design exposed. Thus, the questions asked by a researcher and the method he or she uses to answer those questions may be the result of the researcher's preconceptions about the problem. There are two solutions to this dilemma. First, researchers should be aware of their own underlying preconceptions (these preexisting notions are what philosophers of science call "paradigms") (Kuhn, 1962). Second, many scientists with different preconceptions should undertake a variety of attacks on a particular problem.

Another source of researcher bias derives from treating participants in a project differently over and above any *planned* differences in treatment. A substantial amount of evidence indicates that how the researcher treats the participants can have a profound effect on the results of the experiment (Barber, 1976). What measures can be taken to prevent a researcher from inadvertently influencing the outcome? Suppose you collected the data for Carver, Coleman, and Glass (1976) in their experiment concerned with fatigue suppression in hard-driving Type A personalities and more mellow Type B personalities. You know ahead of time that half your participants (Type A) might be prone to coronary heart disease. You record the exercise time on a treadmill as the participants are working at or beyond their maximum oxygen consumption. Would you be able to treat Type A and Type B people the same? Would subtle body movements or the tone of your voice clue the Type A people to take it easy so they do not overstress their hearts? (This is unlikely, because the Type A people were young—but they supposedly had the *potential* for coronary problems later in life.)

There are two ways to minimize this type of researcher bias. In the first place, the researcher must conduct the project as uniformly as possible for all participants. Uniformity can occur when the researcher carefully adheres to a **protocol**, which is a detailed list of the procedures and methods used to test each participant in the experiment. The only differences in treatment should be those that are introduced deliberately—independent variables, different questions in a survey, different observing times, and so on. Type A people must be treated exactly like those of Type B. This was done by Carver and colleagues, who even went so far as to eliminate the data on a participant who was acquainted with one of the data collectors.

A second way to minimize inadvertent differential treatment is to make the researcher *blind* with respect to potentially important attributes of the participants or the task. The experimenters in the study by Carver and associates did not know whether an individual was Type A or Type B, which diminished the chances of treating the Type A people differently on the treadmill. Furthermore, the participants did not know that the experimenters were interested in how long they stayed on the treadmill. When participants' behaviors are recorded in some way for later analysis, the people who score the recorded behavior often are blind to the treatment administered to a particular participant. In this instance, being blind to the treatment condition increases the likelihood that the scorer of the results will be objective and not biased by his or her expectations of what the results should be. If both the participant and the researcher are blind, we have what is called a **double-blind design.**

Double-blind designs are common in medical experiments that test the effectiveness of drugs. The experimental group is given the drug, and the control group is given a placebo substance. A **placebo** (the word is derived from a Latin word meaning "I shall please") is a pharmacologically inert substance (a "sugar pill") given to participants in a control group to deceive them. The control group, along with the experimental group, assume that they are receiving a real drug, so the expectations are the same for the two groups. Not only are the placebo participants blind, but so is the researcher. The researcher does not know who is receiving the placebo and who is getting the real drug. In the typical drug experiment, the substances have code numbers that cannot be deciphered by the person administering the drugs. However, someone knows who received the placebo and who received the drug. These precautions decrease the possibility of the control participants being treated differently than the experimental participants (apart from the drug, of course).

The personal attributes of a researcher also may bias the actions of the participants. The age, sex, race, and authority of the researcher may determine how the participants react. For example, a person in an interview is more likely to report sexual thoughts when the interviewer is of the same sex as the interviewee (Walters, Shurley, & Parsons, 1962). This kind of problem is solved if there is more than one researcher and each one follows the research protocol exactly. In your own research, you may not be able to enlist assistance from others. Therefore, you should try to treat each individual identically.

Strict adherence to procedure is important to minimize inadvertent researcher bias. This advice is particularly true when considering how data are recorded. Barber (1976) discusses several studies showing that data-recording errors do occur and tend to bias the results in the direction desired by the experimenter. Hence, in every condition for every participant, we must record data in the same way. This means that before the project is begun, we must define exactly what constitutes an acceptable datum.

Another potential researcher bias occurs in research with animals. When working with animals, a researcher must guard against **anthropomorphizing.** This term refers to the tendency to attribute human characteristics, especially thoughts and feelings, to animals. Anthropomorphism is sometimes obvious, as in "The dog loved and respected its master," and is sometimes not so obvious, as in "The rat was hungry, so it ate a lot." A similar problem arises in describing the thoughts and feelings of people belonging to technologically primitive cultures. An observer might attribute standard Western thought to such groups, as in "Their love of individual liberty conflicted with the socialist ideology of the tribal council." All of these examples are actually theoretical statements that may not be warranted based on the data. How do we define "love" in a dog? Does it mean the dog wagged its tail or came when it was called? What is hunger for a rat? These sorts of issues are examined in the next section.

CONCEPT SUMMARY

Control inadvertent researcher effects by

- following a protocol for uniform treatment
- using a double-blind design
- being alert for a placebo effect and anthropomorphizing

Reliability of Communication

We have discussed pitfalls in the research process resulting from ethical issues and experimenter bias. Assuming that you have effectively dealt with problems in these areas, another pitfall awaits you in conveying the results of your research to other scientists.

No serious discussion, scientific or otherwise, can progress very far unless the participants agree to define the terms they are using. Imagine that you and your date are having a friendly argument about who is the best athlete of the year. How do you define "athlete"? You both would agree about such common sports as tennis, swimming, and gymnastics, but what about more esoteric sports, such as frisbee throwing, hang gliding, and hopping cross-country on a pogo stick? Should practitioners of these activities be considered for your athlete-of-the-year award? Until this question of definition is answered, your discussion may just go around in circles.

Similar problems can arise in scientific discussions. Let us imagine that scientists in psychophysical laboratories in West Lafayette, Indiana, and Clayton Corners, Arkansas, are studying tail-flicking responses of the horseshoe crab to flashes of light. One laboratory finds that crabs give tremendous tail flicks, whereas the other lab finds that crabs hardly move their tails at all. The scientists are very concerned, and they exchange terse letters and autographed pictures of their respective crabs. Eventually, they discover the reason for the discrepancy. They were each defining the flash of light differently (their flashes were of different duration), although the brightness of the two flashes was similar. When they adjusted their flashes to be the same, both labs obtained the same results. This example is a little farfetched, because as we all know, crabs cannot autograph their pictures. Furthermore, all good psychologists know the importance of defining the stimulus exactly, so this confusion would probably not have occurred in the first place. This example does show, however, what *could* happen if scientists were not very careful about defining their terms.

Although social conversation and scientific discourse both require definitions, the requirements for scientific definition are more stringent. Terms that are perfectly adequate for ordinary conversation are usually too vague for scientific purposes. When you state that someone has a pleasant personality, other people have a good idea of what you mean, but when a psychologist uses the term *personality* in a technical sense, a great deal of precision is necessary. This important distinction between technical usage and common usage occurs frequently in psychology. It is all too easy to slip and use technical language imprecisely, especially in psychology. Words such as *information, anxiety,* and *fluency* have broad everyday meanings, but they must be precisely limited when they are used in a technical sense. The most common way of providing such technical meaning is by using an operational definition.

An **operational definition** is a formula for building a construct in a way that other scientists can duplicate. "Take the eye of a newt, the leg of a frog, three oyster shells, and shake twice" is an operational definition, although we may not know what is being defined. This recipe is easy to duplicate and so meets the major criterion for an operational definition. You can tell from the example that an operational definition need not make sense if it is clear and can be copied. In general terms, something is operationally defined when the procedures or operations used to produce and measure it are clearly specified. For instance, we might operationally define a construct called *centigrams* as the product of your height in centimeters and your weight in grams. Any scientist can easily determine the centigram score, so this is an operational definition. The ability to consistently use or observe something is an example of **reliability,** which is discussed in detail in Chapter 7. Of course, the centigram score probably could not be used for any important scientific purpose, but the potential utility of an operational definition is a separate issue from its clarity.

▶ Finishing the Research Project

After completing the preliminary stages outlined earlier and considering the pitfalls, you can now conduct the research, analyze and interpret the data, and then write a research paper. The remainder of this book focuses on these aspects of the research process. We hope you will be a critical reader and thinker, using the information we convey to conduct sound psychological research and to evaluate carefully the research of others.

Neither the practice nor the use of science is easy. The benefits that can be derived from scientific knowledge and understanding depend on critical and well-informed citizens and scientists. Unless you plan to hibernate or drop out of society in some other way, you are going to be affected by psychological research. As a citizen, you are a consumer of the results of psychological research, and we hope that the material discussed in this book will help to make you a more intelligent consumer.

Some of you, we hope, will become scientists. We also hope that some of you young scientists will focus on why people and animals think and act as they do. We wish you good fortune. Your scientific career will be exciting, and we hope that your endeavors will be positively influenced by the principles of psychological research presented in this text.

About a hundred years ago, T. H. Huxley, a British scientist, said: "The chessboard is the world, the pieces are the phenomena of the universe, the rules of the game are what we call the laws of Nature. The player on the other side is hidden from us. We know that his play is always fair, just, and patient. But we also know, to our cost, that he never overlooks a mistake, or makes the smallest allowance for ignorance."

Summary

1. One goal of psychological research is to provide scientific understanding about why people and animals behave as they do. Another goal of psychological research is to solve practical problems.

2. The goals of this book (and, likely, of your course) are to help teach you how to conduct sound research and to help you learn how to evaluate critically the research of others.

3. An experiment involves manipulating or changing the levels of an independent variable while trying to minimize the effects of confounding variables that may vary with the independent variable. Those factors that are held constant are called control variables. The behavior that is measured is called the dependent variable.

4. Research begins with observation, which is a source of data and ideas for research projects. Other sources of research ideas are journal articles and experts, such as your professor or your textbook.

5. Numerous journals report the results of psychological research. Sources for research ideas and background information include *Psychological Abstracts* and *PsycINFO*.

6. A testable hypothesis makes a statement about a presumed or theoretical relation between two or more variables. A testable hypothesis implies or specifies how the variables are measured.

7. Before undertaking a research project, you should do a literature search to find out whether your hypothesis has been studied. Becoming acquainted with the literature also will help you to design your project carefully and efficiently.

8. Preliminary research, called pilot research, usually is done before conducting a research project. The pilot research will help you refine your procedure, and it may help you to choose appropriate levels of your independent variable.

9. An ethical scientist treats research participants fairly and humanely.

10. Good research is often clouded by inadvertent researcher bias. A scientist's beliefs, attitudes, and scientific approach may bias the outcome of a research project. A careful researcher attempts to overcome this problem by strict adherence to a research protocol and other design tactics, such as the double-blind design.

11. A careful researcher operationally defines concepts by noting how they are produced and measured.

Key Concepts

anthropomorphizing (20)
behavior (3)
confounding (9)
control variable (7)
critic (7)
critical thinker (7)
dependent variable (7)
double-blind design (19)

ethical issues (17)
inadvertent researcher bias (17)
independent variable (7)
internal validity (10)
operational definition (21)
pilot research (16)

placebo (19)
protocol (18)
Psychological Abstracts (13)
PsycINFO (13)
reliability (21)
Stroop effect (15)
testable hypothesis (13)

Exercises

1. [*Special Exercise.*] (Some of the exercises at the end of chapters ask that you critique a research project in some way. You are provided with enough information in the question to answer it. If some procedural detail is omitted—for example, the time of day the research was conducted—you may assume that the detail is irrelevant. Base your discussion on the information provided.) Do you listen to music as you are studying? A large percentage of college students do. A substantial amount of research concerns the effects of music on people's ability to learn and remember. The research has generated an interesting controversy. Some researchers find that listening to music disrupts learning, and others report that music does not disrupt learning. Generate several testable hypotheses as to why music might or might not have a negative effect on learning. One thing you might consider is the type of music. One of the authors of this book never studied in his dorm room as a freshman because his roommate regularly played Ravel's *Bolero* during the evening.

2. Enter the term *aggression* into the keyword search of *PsycINFO*. Notice what happens. Examine the organization of abstracts on aggression, which helps the topical search be more manageable. Click on one of the hyperlinks that look interesting, and read a few abstracts. If you find an abstract of interest, do an author search using the last name of the author of the interesting abstract. Finally, determine whether your library contains the journal that has the full article of the abstract. If it does, you can read the entire article.

3. Transform each of the following problems or statements into at least two testable hypotheses:

   a. You can't teach an old dog new tricks.

   b. Eating junk food lowers your grade-point average.

   c. A penny saved is a penny earned.

   d. The best way to study is to cram the night before an exam.

   e. Out of sight, out of mind; or absence makes the heart grow fonder.

Suggested Resources

The following books contain additional information about the preliminary stages of the research process: Alsip, J. E., & Chezik, D. D. (1974). *Research guide in psychology.* Morristown, NJ: General Learning Press. Leedy, P. D. (1985). *Practical research: Planning and design.* New York: Macmillan.

The *Council on Undergraduate Research Quarterly* often contains articles related to jobs for holders of bachelor's degrees and articles related to graduate school. A very helpful issue for students in research courses is the September 1997 issue, in which articles address the issue of technology and the Internet in undergraduate research. A particularly useful article is: Koch, C. (1997). Learning the research process on the World Wide Web. *Council on Undergraduate Research Quarterly, 18,* 27–29, 48–49.

Web Resources

A substantial amount of career planning information is available in *JobWeb* (http://www.jobweb.com). The home page of the American Psychological Association (http://www.apa.org) has several links that you might find useful.

Psi Chi, the national honor society in psychology, has an excellent website. *Eye on Psi Chi* contains all sorts of pertinent articles, including information on careers and graduate school application. Check out: http://www.psichi.org/content/publications/home.asp

Wadsworth's *Statistics and Research Methods Workshops* has a section on "Getting Ideas for a Study." At: http://www.wadsworth.com/psychology_d/templates/student_resources/workshops/workshops.html

Laboratory Resource

The laboratory manual written by Langston (Langston, W. [2005]. *Research methods laboratory manual for psychology.* Pacific Grove, CA: Wadsworth) has several appendices that will help you in developing your research project. At the end of several chapters in this book, we indicate the relevant research projects that Langston recommends for the methodology under consideration.

The Stroop Effect

The original version of the Stroop test used color words such as *red* and *blue* printed in mismatching colors of ink. You could see if the same sorts of results occur in the color Stroop effect as occur in the number Stroop done in this chapter. You will need some index cards, colored markers, and a watch with a second hand (or some other way of measuring response times).

Suppose you have markers for four different colors (for example, red, blue, green, and yellow). Take 16 index cards, and put a bold line of color on each one—four cards should have a red stripe, four a blue one, four a green one, and four a yellow one. Next, write the words *blue, red, yellow,* and *green* with a black marker on index cards—four cards with each word. Finally, write the color words in a mismatching color (that is, *blue* in red ink); have four cards for each color word in mismatching ink. Your stimuli are now completed. The three decks you made correspond, respectively, to the naming, reading, and conflict tasks used in the number version of the Stroop task.

Shuffle each deck, and see how long it takes you to go through each one. You might want to do a careful mini-experiment. Test three different people with three different orders of the tasks: one gets *naming, reading,* then *conflict;* one gets *reading, conflict,* then *naming;* and one gets *conflict, naming,* then *reading.* Doing the experiment this way gets rid of the confounding of order with task that was present in the version of the Stroop test done in the chapter. If the entire class conducts this experiment, you could use all possible orders of three tasks several times, which would also mean that each task preceded and followed the other ones equally often. The relative difficulty of the three conditions should have been the same as in the number Stroop test.

Now you might consider some additional experiments that could be done using either version of the task. The Psychology in Action section for a later chapter also suggests variants of the Stroop task. Try to think of some interesting research to do without peeking at the later chapter. One thing you may have noticed when you did the number Stroop is that some mismatches between digits and quantity were more likely than others to slow down your naming time. Is this true for everybody or just you? Do most people have difficulty with the same mismatches, or do the difficult ones differ from person to person?

THE EXPERIMENT
DIRECTIONS: Name the numbers below aloud as fast as you can.

START TIME

_____

2
1
4
3
3
2
4
1
4
1
3
2
2
1
3
4
3
1
4
2
4
3
2
1
1
3
2
4
2
3
4
1

FINISH TIME   To continue the experiment, please go to the next page.

_____

ELAPSED TIME

_____

THE EXPERIMENT

DIRECTIONS: Count the number of +s aloud in each row as fast as you can.

START TIME

_____

```
+
+ + +
+ + +
+ +
+ + + +
+ +
+ + +
+
+
+ +
+ + +
+ + + +
+ +
+ + + +
+
+ + +
+ + + +
+ + +
+
+ +
+ +
+ + +
+
+ + + +
+
+ + + +
+ +
+ + +
+ + +
+ + + +
+
+ +
```

FINISH TIME   To continue the experiment, please go to the next page.

_____

ELAPSED TIME

_____

THE EXPERIMENT

DIRECTIONS: Count the number of digits aloud in each row as fast as you can.

START TIME

_____

2
1111
444
33
3333
222
44
11
4
11
3333
222
2222
11
3
444
3333
111
2
44
33
444
2
1111
3
1111
44
222
444
3333
2
11

FINISH TIME   You are through participating in the experiment. Please return to page 4.

_____

ELAPSED TIME

_____

CHAPTER 2

Explanation in Scientific Psychology

Why do people and animals behave as they do?

Research

- Arises from curiosity
- Solves basic and applied problems

Sources of Belief

- Authority
- Tenacity
- A priori assumptions
- Empiricism

Scientific Procedures

- Induction
- Deduction
- Strong inference
- Hypotheses

Scientific Theories

- Organize and predict
- Are parsimonious, precise, and testable

Scientific Data

- Illustrate psychological processes
- Demonstrate what can happen in controlled settings

How does science differ from other modes of understanding? What are some of the assumptions underlying the scientific method? How do psychologists use theory and data to explain behavior? We pursue these questions in this chapter by examining a social psychological phenomenon called social loafing. Because the answers to the questions provide a framework for the rest of the text, you need to understand what is meant by scientific explanation.

A scientist wants to discover how and why things work. In this desire, he or she does not differ from anyone else who is also curious about the world we inhabit. The casual observer may not feel terribly frustrated if some observation cannot be explained. For example, the nonscientist may simply accept that water always goes down a sink drain counterclockwise, or that individuals tend to work less hard in groups than when alone. However, the professional scientist has a strong desire to pursue an observation until an explanation is available or a problem is solved. By being unwilling to tolerate unanswered questions and unsolved problems, scientists use several techniques for obtaining relief from curiosity and developing explanations. Careful application of these techniques distinguishes scientific understanding from everyday understanding.

In this chapter, we introduce scientific explanation from the viewpoint of a working scientist—in particular, an experimentally oriented psychologist. To do so, we examine a series of research studies on social loafing. The purpose of the research is to understand why people work less hard in groups than when they work alone. Our discussion of scientific explanation leads to a consideration of aspects of the philosophy of science used for an understanding of behavior. Because abstract principles of science do not always make much sense when removed from specific topics, we relate the philosophy of science to research on social loafing. We intend to show how psychologists undertake to explain why people and animals behave as they do.

▶ Making Sense of the World

Social Loafing

A common observation—one you probably have made yourself on many occasions—is that people working in a group often seem to "slack off" in their effort. Many people in groups seem willing to let a few do the work. Bibb Latané, a social psychologist, noticed this tendency and decided to study it experimentally. Initially, Latané examined the research literature to see if any evidence existed for this phenomenon of people's working less hard in groups, which he named **social loafing.**

One of the earliest studies of social loafing was conducted by a French agricultural engineer (Ringelmann, 1913; see also Kravitz & Martin, 1986), who asked people to pull on a rope as hard as they could. The subjects pulled by themselves or with one, two, or seven others. A sensitive gauge was used to measure how strongly they pulled the rope. If people exert as much effort in groups as when alone, then the group performance should be the sum of the efforts of all individuals. Ringelmann discovered that groups of two pulled at only 95% of their capacity, and groups of three and eight sank to

85% and 49%, respectively. So, it is probably not just our imaginations when we notice others (and ourselves?) putting forth less effort when working in groups: Ringelmann's research provides us with a good example of social loafing.

Latané and his colleagues then performed a systematic series of experiments on the phenomenon (Latané, 1981; Latané, Williams, & Harkins, 1979). They first showed that social loafing could be obtained in other experimental situations besides that of rope pulling. They also demonstrated that social loafing occurs in several different cultures (Gabrenya, Latané, & Wang, 1983) and even holds for young children. Thus, social loafing is a pervasive characteristic of working in groups.

Latané related this work to a more general theory of human social behavior (Latané, 1981). The evidence from the experimental studies points to **diffusion of responsibility** as a possible reason for social loafing. People working by themselves think they are responsible for completing the task; when they work in groups, however, this feeling of responsibility diffuses to others. The same idea accounts for behavior in other group situations: If one of your professors asked a question in a class containing only two other people, you would probably feel responsible for trying to answer. However, if there were 200 other people in the class, you would likely feel much less responsible for answering. Similarly, people are more likely to help in an emergency when they feel the burden of responsibility than when several others are about who could help.

One possible benefit of such basic research into a phenomenon is that the findings may be applied later to solve some practical problem. A problem in American society is the declining productivity of the workforce. Although social loafing is, at best, only one factor involved in this complicated issue, Marriot (1949) showed that factory workers working in large groups produced less per individual than did those working in small groups. Thus, basic research that would show a way to overcome the problem of social loafing may be of great practical import. In fact, Williams, Harkins, and Latané (1981) found conditions that eliminated the effect of social loafing in their experimental situation. When individual performance (rather than just performance of the entire group) was monitored within the group situation, the individuals worked just as hard as they did when they worked alone. Certainly more research must be done, but simply measuring individual performance in group situations could help to eliminate social loafing and increase productivity. The proposed solution may seem simple, but many jobs measure only group performance, not individual performance.

Research on social loafing by Latané and others shows how an interesting problem can be studied scientifically and be understood. The research will, when carefully conducted, promote a better explanation of the phenomenon of interest than will simple observation of events and reflection about them. Let us now examine the nature of scientific explanations.

▶ Sources of Understanding

Fixation of Belief

Science and scientific psychology in particular are valid ways to acquire knowledge about the world around us. What characteristics of the scientific approach make it a desirable way to learn about and arrive at beliefs about the nature of things? Perhaps the best way to answer this question is to contrast science with other modes of fixing belief, because science is only one way that understanding is obtained.

More than a hundred years ago, the American philosopher Charles Sanders Peirce (1877) compared the scientific way of knowing with three other methods of developing beliefs. He called these the *authority, tenacity,* and *a priori* methods. According to Peirce, the simplest way of fixing belief is to take someone else's word on faith. A trusted authority tells you what is true and what is false. Young children believe what their parents tell them simply because Mommy and Daddy are always right. As children get older, they may discover, unhappily, that Mom and Dad are not always correct when it comes to astrophysics, macroeconomics, computer technology, and other specialized fields of knowledge. Although this may cause children to doubt some of their parents' earlier proclamations, they may not completely reject this method of fixing belief. Instead, some other authority may be sought. Religious beliefs are formed by the **method of authority.**

Long after children have rejected their parents as the source of all knowledge, they may still believe that the pope is infallible insofar as religious doctrine is concerned. Believing the evening news means that one accepts Dan Rather or some other news commentator as an authority. You may believe your professors because they are authorities. Because people lack the resources to investigate everything they learn, much knowledge and many beliefs are fixed by the method of authority. Provided nothing happens to raise doubts about the competence of the authority setting the beliefs, this method offers the advantages of minimum effort and substantial security. It is most pleasant in a troubled world to have complete faith in beliefs handed down to you.

Another method of fixing belief is one in which a person steadfastly refuses to alter acquired knowledge, regardless of evidence to the contrary. The **method of tenacity,** as it was termed by Peirce, is commonly seen in racial bigots who rigidly cling to a stereotype even in the presence of a good counterexample. Although this method of maintaining a belief may not be entirely rational, we cannot say it is completely without value. Bigots are still around and, somehow, manage to find a few others to share their beliefs. The method of tenacity allows people to maintain a uniform and constant outlook on things, so it may relieve them from a certain amount of stress and psychological discomfort. For people who have difficulty handling stress, the method of tenacity may be a reasonable way to try to understand the world.

The third nonscientific method discussed by Peirce fixes belief a priori. In this context, the term *a priori* refers to something that is believed without prior study or examination. In the **a priori method,** propositions that seem reasonable are believed. This is an extension of the method of authority. However, no one particular authority is being followed blindly in this method; rather, the general cultural outlook fixes belief a priori. People once believed the world was flat; and it did seem reasonable to suppose that the sun revolved around the earth, as does the moon. Indeed, the world does look flat if you are not in a spacecraft.

The last of Peirce's methods, the **scientific method,** fixes belief on the basis of experience. If we define scientific psychology (as well as science in general) as a repeatable, self-correcting undertaking that seeks to understand phenomena on the basis of empirical observation, then we can see several advantages to science compared with the methods just outlined. Let us see what we mean by **empirical** and **self-correcting** and examine the advantages associated with those aspects of science. First, none of those other methods relies on data (observations of the world) obtained by systematic observation. That is, the other methods do not have an empirical basis for fixing belief.

The word *empirical* is derived from an old Greek word meaning "experience." Having an empirical basis for beliefs means that experience rather than faith is the source of knowledge. Having one's beliefs fixed by authority carries no guarantee that the authority obtained data before forming an opinion. By definition, the method of tenacity refuses to consider data, as does the a priori method. Facts that are considered in these other modes of fixing belief are not ordinarily obtained by systematic procedures. For example, casual observation was the "method" that led to the ideas that the world was flat and that fish spontaneously generated from the mud each spring, as Aristotle believed.

The second advantage of science is that it offers procedures for establishing the superiority of one belief over another. Persons holding different beliefs not based on science will find it difficult to reconcile their opinions. Science overcomes this problem. In principle, anyone can make an empirical observation, which means that scientific data can be public and repeatedly obtained. Through public observations, new beliefs are compared with old ones—and old beliefs are discarded if they do not fit the empirical facts. This does not mean that each and every scientist instantaneously drops outmoded beliefs in favor of new opinions. Changing scientific beliefs is usually a slow process, but eventually, incorrect ideas are weeded out. Empirical, public observations are the cornerstone of the scientific method, because they make science a self-correcting endeavor and lead to scientific understanding.

While this view of science is enthusiastically accepted by most experimental psychologists, alternative views about the science of psychology have been expressed by a minority of behavioral scientists who have studied the philosophy of science (Slife & Williams, 1995, especially Chapter 6). Although psychology was originally regarded as a part of philosophy, most psychologists today have not studied epistemology and criticisms of the logical procedures embraced by science. Experimental psychology has decided that its methods make it scientific; indeed, this text is devoted to explaining these methods. While the authors of this text do not agree with most of these criticisms, such as the claim that science is limited by our ordinary habits and usage of language, it is important to think critically about the nature of science and its limitations. We will return to this issue at the end of this chapter.

> ### CONCEPT SUMMARY
>
> Methods of fixing belief include
>
> - authority
> - tenacity
> - a priori
> - scientific (empirical)

▶ The Nature of Scientific Explanation

Empirical observation and self-correction are the hallmarks of the scientific method. In this section, we examine how these work in science and scientific psychology.

Let us first step back and look at the social loafing research in a general way. Casual observation and some applied work suggested the problem area to be investigated. Laboratory experiments indicated some characteristics of social loafing and tested some predictions about its nature. Eventually, the data from the experiments suggested a solution to the practical aspects of social loafing. The same data also were related to diffusion of responsibility, a more general theory in social psychology. This summary captures how science typically works: Empirical observations based on either casual observations or more formal theories reveal something about those theories, which in turn can lead to further empirical work.

According to Harré (1983), this cyclical and self-correcting nature of science was first recognized by Sir Francis Bacon (1561–1626). Bacon is credited with being the leading force in the scientific revolution that began in the seventeenth century (Jones, 1982). Although Bacon's analysis seems somewhat primitive today, he anticipated several important aspects of modern science that we explore in detail.

Induction and Deduction

All approaches to science share certain basic elements. The most important of these are **data** (empirical observations) and **theory** (organization of concepts that permit prediction of data). Science needs and uses both data and theory, and our outline of research on social loafing indicates that they can be inter-linked in a complex way. However, in the history of science, individual scientists have differed about which is more important and which comes first. Trying to decide this is a little like trying to decide whether the chicken or the egg comes first. Science attempts to understand why things work the way they do, and as we will argue, understanding involves both data and theory.

Although Bacon recognized the importance of both data and theory, he believed in the primacy of empirical observations. Modern scientists also emphasize data and view progress in science as working from data to theory. Such an approach is an example of **induction,** in which reasoning proceeds from particular data to a general theory. The converse approach, which emphasizes theory-predicting data, is called **deduction.** With deduction, reasoning proceeds from a general theory to particular data. Because many scientists and philosophers of science have argued for the primacy of one form of reasoning over the other, we will examine induction and deduction in some detail.

Because empirical observations distinguish science from other modes of fixing belief, many have argued that induction must be the way that science should work. As Harré (1983) states, "Observations and the results of experiments are said to be 'data,' which provide a sound and solid base for the erection of the fragile edifice of scientific thought" (p. 6). In the case of social loafing, the inductive position would be that the facts of social loafing derived from experimentation produced the theory of diffusion of responsibility.

One problem with a purely inductive approach has to do with the finality of empirical observations. Scientific observations are tied to the circumstances under which they are made. This means that the laws or theories that are induced from them also must be limited in scope. Subsequent experiments in different contexts may suggest another theory or modifications to an existing one. So, theories that are induced on the basis of particular observations can (and usually do) change when other observations are made. This, of course, is a problem only if one takes an authoritarian view of ideas and believes in clinging tenaciously to a particular theory. Theories induced from observations are tentative ideas, not final truths. Changes in understanding that occur as a result of continued empirical work exemplify the self-correcting nature of science.

According to the deductive view, which emphasizes the primacy of theory, the important scientific aspect of the social loafing research is the empirical guidance provided by the formal theory of social loafing. Furthermore, the more general theory, diffusion of responsibility, provides understanding of social loafing. The deductive approach holds well-developed theories in high regard. Casual observations, informal theories, and data take second place to broad theories that describe and predict a substantial number of observations.

From the standpoint of the deductive approach, scientific understanding means, in part, that a theory will predict that certain kinds of empirical observations should occur. In the case of social loafing, the theory of diffusion of responsibility suggests that monitoring individual performance in a group

APPLICATION

The Importance of Falsification

Most students find the philosophical idea of falsifiability a difficult one to understand. Why is it important to try to disconfirm a hypothesis rather than simply to confirm that it is correct? The primary reason is because confirming evidence could be consistent with any number of hypotheses or theories, but disconfirming evidence will rule out some. Negative evidence usually provides more meaningful information than does confirming evidence.

To see how this works, consider the following problem from an experiment by Wason (1977). Wason presented his subjects with the series 2 4 6, which was supposed to illustrate a particular rule. The people in Wason's experiment were to discover the rule by generating sequences that Wason would confirm or deny as being consistent with the rule he had in mind. One plausible hypothesis is that the rule is any series of even numbers increasing by two. Wason observed that people showed a persistent bias in selecting sequences confirming that hypothesis. They generated sequences such as 8 10 12, 300 302 304, 620 622 624, and so on. Unfortunately, there are an infinite number of such strings, and although they confirm the theory of even numbers increasing by two, they are also consistent with other hypotheses. Could the rule be any numbers increasing by two, such as 3 5 7? Could the rule be even more general, such as any three ascending numbers? To test the last hypothesis, the subjects would have to suggest a sequence such as 8 7 6. Participants rarely generated sequences like the last one, even though it would rule out the previous two hypotheses. Furthermore, any three ascending numbers was the rule.

In ordinary human reasoning, the bias to confirm hypotheses is striking, even though it is not very productive. In scientific reasoning, the confirmation bias would limit scientific progress, because the bias would make self-correction unlikely. Why is there such a strong bias toward confirming hypotheses? Johnson-Laird (1988) notes that some confirmation is necessary, and he also notes that seeking ways to disconfirm a hypothesis is often difficult. Apparently, therefore, people take the easy way out and simply seek confirming evidence. If you are interested in pursuing this topic, Best (1999) reviews the large literature on reasoning and faulty reasoning.

should reduce the diffusion of responsibility. In turn, measuring individual effort should reduce the amount of social loafing that is observed. Experimental tests of this prediction confirm it, as we have seen.

But what do correct predictions reveal? If a theory is verified by the results of experiments, a deductive scientist might have increased confidence in the veracity of the theory. However, empirical observations are not final and can change. The tentative nature of scientific understanding means that verifying or confirming a theory is not enough. Popper (1961), a philosopher of science, has suggested that good theories, like good hypotheses (see Chapter 1), must be testable. The empirical predictions must be capable of tests that could show them to be false. This suggestion of Popper's has been called the **falsifiability view.** According to this view, the temporary nature of induction makes negative evidence more important than positive support. If data confirm a prediction, one cannot say that the theory is true. However, if a theory leads to a prediction that is not supported by the data, then Popper would argue that the theory must be false and should be rejected. According to Popper, a theory can never be proven; it can only be disproven. The importance of falsification is discussed in the Application section.

One problem with the deductive approach has to do with the theories themselves. Most theories include many assumptions about the world that are difficult to test and may be wrong. In Latané's work, one assumption underlying the general theory is that measuring a person's behavior in an experimental context does not change the behavior in question. Although this often is reasonable to assume, we will show later that people can react to being observed in unusual ways, which means that this assumption is sometimes wrong. If the untested assumptions are wrong, then a particular experiment that falsifies a theory may have falsified it for the wrong reasons. That is, the test of the theory may not have been fair or appropriate. One conclusion, then, is that the deductive approach by itself cannot lead to scientific understanding.

At this point, you may be wondering whether scientific understanding is possible if both induction and deduction are not infallible. Do not despair. Science is self-correcting, and it can provide answers to problems—however temporary those answers may be. Scientific understanding changes as scientists ply their trade. We have a better understanding of social loafing now than we did before Latané and his coworkers undertook their research. Through a combination of induction and deduction, science progresses toward a more thorough understanding of its problems. Figure 2–1 illustrates how induction and deduction join to produce understanding.

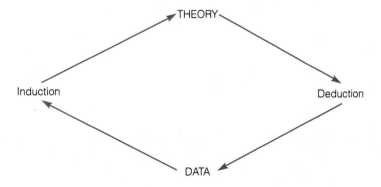

Figure 2–1 A theory organizes and predicts data. By means of deduction, particular observations (data) may be predicted. By means of induction, the data suggest organizing principles (theories). This circular relationship indicates that theories are tentative pictures of how data are organized.

By way of concluding this section, let us reexamine social loafing. Initially, positive experimental results bolstered our confidence in the general notion of social loafing. These results in turn suggested hypotheses about the nature of social loafing. Is it a general phenomenon that would influence even group-oriented individuals? Does it occur in the workplace as well as the laboratory? Positive answers to these questions are consistent with a diffusion-of-responsibility interpretation of social loafing.

In the next phase of the research, Latané and his colleagues attempted to eliminate other explanations of social loafing by falsifying predictions made by these alternative theories. In earlier work, they tested a particular person's effort both when alone and when in a group. They subsequently reasoned that under these conditions a person might rest during the group test so he or she could allocate greater effort to the task when tested alone. To eliminate the possibility that allocation of effort rather than diffusion of responsibility accounted for social loafing, they conducted additional experiments in which a person was tested either alone or in a group—but not in both situations. Contrary to the allocation-of-effort hypothesis, the results showed that social loafing occurred when a person was tested in just that one condition of being in a group (Harkins, Latané, & Williams, 1980). Therefore, they concluded that diffusion of responsibility was a more appropriate account of social loafing than was allocation of effort.

Note the course of events here. Successive experiments pitted two possible outcomes against each other in the hopes that one possibility would be eliminated and one supported by the outcome of the research. As Platt (1964) has noted, this eliminative procedure, which he calls **strong inference,** should, in the ideal case, yield one remaining theory (if the procedure of strong inference is used repeatedly). Of course, subsequent tests of the diffusion-of-responsibility theory might contradict it or add to it in some way. Thus, the theory might be revised or, with enough contradictions, rejected for an alternative explanation, itself supported by empirical observations. In any event, where we stand now is that we have constructed a reasonable view of what social loafing entails and what seems to cause it. The mixture of hypotheses induced from data and experimental tests deduced from testable hypotheses resulted in the theory that diffusion of responsibility leads to social loafing.

CONCEPT SUMMARY

The scientific method involves

- deduction—reasoning from general to specific cases
- induction—reasoning from specific to general cases
- strong inference—eliminating possible alternative explanations

▶ From Theory to Hypothesis

Theories cannot be tested directly. No single magical experiment will prove a theory to be correct or incorrect. Instead, scientists perform experiments to test hypotheses that are derived from a theory. But exactly what are scientific hypotheses, and where do they come from?

It is important to distinguish between hypotheses and generalizations (Kluger & Tikochinsky, 2001). A **hypothesis** is a very specific testable statement that can be evaluated from observable data. For example, we might hypothesize that drivers older than 65 years would have a higher frequency of accidents involving left turns across on-coming traffic when driving at night than do younger drivers. By looking at police records of accident data, we could determine, with the help of some statistics (see Appendix B), whether this hypothesis is incorrect. A **generalization** is a broader statement that cannot be tested directly. For example, we might generalize that older drivers are unsafe at any speed and should have restrictions on their driver's license, such as not being able to drive at night. Because "unsafe at any speed" is not clearly defined, this is not a testable statement. Similarly, the generalization does not define an age range for older drivers. However, it can be used to derive several testable hypotheses.

Figure 2–2 illustrates this process. Each generalization can produce more than one hypothesis. Only two hypotheses are illustrated in the figure to keep it simple, but a good generalization can produce a horde of hypotheses. For example, the aging-driver generalization could produce many hypotheses about different

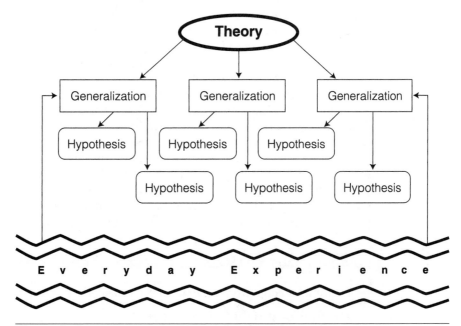

Figure 2–2 Gaggles of generalizations produce hordes of hypotheses.

kinds of accidents and behaviors that befall aging drivers: crashing into stopped vehicles, failing to signal for turns, driving on the sidewalk, backing up into objects, not keeping within their lane, and so on. These hypotheses could be tested by making observations in traffic, on closed test tracks (safer for the driving public if the generalization is true), or in driving simulators (safest for the drivers).

Now that we have explained that hypotheses come from generalizations, we can go on to the next question: Where do generalizations come from? Figure 2–2 shows there are two sources for generalizations. They can come from theory or from experience. While only three generalizations are shown in Figure 2–2, a good theory will produce a gaggle of generalizations. You may think that the aging-driver generalization comes from experience rather than from theory. You may have firsthand experience of being a passenger in a car driven by a grandparent, and that experience may have caused you to agree with the generalization. This is an inductive process (Figure 2–1) based on data, namely casual observation of the driving behavior of elderly citizens. Hypotheses derived from this inductive process are called *common-sense hypotheses*. While testing common-sense hypotheses was once frowned on in experimental psychology as being inferior to testing hypotheses derived from theory, there is currently a new appreciation of the value of common-sense hypotheses (Kluger & Tikochinsky, 2001).

Nevertheless, most psychologists prefer testing hypotheses based on theory. In this case, the generalization is formed deductively (Figure 2–1) from the theory. The aging-driver generalization could also be derived from theories of attention, perception, and decision making (Kantowitz, 2001). As we age, our ability to attend to multiple tasks decreases and our decision making becomes more conservative, often requiring more time to accomplish. So, elderly drivers might (a) have trouble seeing on-coming traffic at night, (b) have trouble attending to on-coming traffic while paying attention to in-vehicle devices like a radio or to a passenger, and (c) take a long time to decide whether a left-hand turn across traffic is safe, so that when they finally make the turn, it is too late and on-coming traffic cannot avoid hitting them. The advantage of a good theory is that it produces many generalizations. Theories of attention not only deal with aging drivers but make generalizations about many other practical situations, such as operating airplanes and nuclear power plants, to say nothing of more abstract predictions to be tested in laboratories. For example, many theories of attention would predict that talking on your cell phone while you are driving would be dangerous. However, common-sense generalizations are not productive, because even if they are correct, they do not create new generalizations. So, theories are more efficient in advancing scientific inquiry.

CONCEPT SUMMARY

Hypotheses come from generalizations. Generalizations are either

- inductive—derived from experience
- deductive—derived from theory

What Is a Theory?

Thus far, we have argued that scientific understanding is tentative: Incorrect theories are modified and additional information is gathered through empirical tests about the problem at hand. In this section, we focus on explaining theories.

A theory can be crudely defined as a set of related statements that explains a variety of occurrences. The more the occurrences and the fewer the statements, the better the theory. The law of gravity explains falling apples, the behavior of roller coasters, and the position of bodies within the solar system. With a small number of statements about the mutual attraction of bodies, it explains a large number of events. It is, therefore, a powerful theory. (This does not necessarily mean it is a correct theory, because there are some events it cannot explain.)

Theory in psychology performs two major functions: **organization** and **prediction.** First, it provides a framework for the systematic and orderly display of data—that is, it serves as a convenient way for the scientist to organize data. Even the most dedicated inductive scientist will eventually have difficulty remembering the outcomes of dozens of experiments. Theory can be used as a kind of filing system to help experimenters organize results. Second, it allows the scientist to generate predictions for situations in which no data have been obtained. As noted in Chapter 1, these testable hypotheses guide research. The greater the degree of precision of these predictions, the better the theory. With the best of intentions, scientists who claim to be testing the same theory often derive from the theory different hypotheses about the same situation. This unfortunate circumstance is relatively more common in psychology, where many theories are stated in a loose verbal fashion, than in physics, where theories are more formal and better quantified through the use of mathematics. Although psychologists are rapidly becoming equipped to state their theories more precisely through such formal mechanisms as mathematics and computer simulations, the typical psychological theory still is not as precise as theories in other sciences.

Let us see how the theory devised by Latané to account for social loafing stacks up with regard to organization and prediction. The theory of diffusion of responsibility organizes a substantial amount of data about social loafing. More important, the theory seems to account for a remarkable variety of other observations. For example, Latané (1981) notes that the size of a tip left at a restaurant table is inversely related to the number of people in the dinner party. Likewise, proportionately more people committed themselves to Christ at smaller Billy Graham crusades than at larger ones. Finally, work by Latané and Darley (1970) shows that the willingness of people to help in a crisis is inversely related to the number of other bystanders present. The entire pattern of results can be subsumed under the notion of diffusion of responsibility, which asserts that people feel less responsibility for their own actions when they are in a group than when they are alone. So, people in groups are less likely to help in an emergency, are less likely to leave a large tip, and so on.

Latané's theory also makes rather precise predictions about the impact of the presence of other people on a person's actions. In fact, one version of the theory (Latané, 1981) presents its major assumptions in terms of mathematical equations.

Theories are devised to organize concepts and facts into a coherent pattern and to predict the results of future research. Sometimes the two functions of theory—organization and prediction—are called *description* and *explanation,* respectively. Unfortunately, formulating the roles of theory in this manner often leads to an argument about the relative superiority of deductive or inductive approaches to science—a discussion we have already dismissed as fruitless. According to the deductive scientist, the inductive scientist is concerned only with description. The inductive scientist defends against this charge by retorting that description is explanation. If a psychologist could correctly predict and control all behavior by referring to properly organized sets of results, then that psychologist would also be explaining behavior. The argument is futile, because both views are correct. If all the necessary data were properly organized, predictions could be made without recourse to a formal body of theoretical statements. Because all the data are not properly organized as yet, and perhaps never will be, theories are required to bridge the gap between knowledge and ignorance. Remember, however, that theoretical explanation is tentative, because all the data will never be in. So, we have merely recast the argument between inductive and deductive views about which approach will more quickly and surely lead to truth. Ultimately, description and explanation may be equivalent. The two terms describe the path taken more than the eventual theoretical outcome. To avoid this pitfall, we refer to the two major functions of theory as organization and prediction rather than as description and explanation.

CONCEPT SUMMARY

A theory

- organizes data
- predicts new research

Intervening Variables

Theories often use constructs, such as intervening variables, that summarize the effects of several variables. Variables are discussed at great length in later chapters. Recall that in Chapter 1, we discussed independent and dependent variables. Independent variables are those manipulated by the experimenter. For example, not allowing rats to have any water for several hours would create an independent variable called hours of deprivation. Dependent variables are those observed by the experimenter. For example, one could observe how much water a rat drinks.

Science tries to explain the world by relating independent and dependent variables. **Intervening variables** are abstract concepts that link independent variables to dependent variables. Gravity is a familiar construct that accomplishes this goal. It can relate an independent variable, how many feet of height an object is dropped, to a dependent variable, the speed of the object when it hits the ground. Gravity also summarizes the effects of height on speed for all manner of objects. Gravity explains falling apples as well as falling baseballs. Science progresses when a single construct, such as gravity, explains outcomes in many different environments. By connecting concepts to independent and dependent variables, scientists attempt to make their theories empirical and testable. Diffusion of responsibility is an intervening variable connected to group size on the one hand and to individual behavior, such as work effort, on the other. If diffusion of responsibility were not measurable and producible, it would be a useless theoretical concept. Testable predictions concerning diffusion of responsibility can be made only if it can be varied (it is tied to an independent variable) and observed (it is tied to a dependent variable). The importance of testable concepts is considered further in the Psychology in Action section for this chapter.

Driver Workload You are tooling down Interstate 5 at peace and content with the world when suddenly a large tractor-trailer combination passes you. It seems as if the combination goes on forever—the cab has three large trailers attached behind it. Furthermore, the last trailer appears to be wobbling all over the roadway, although it never actually crosses the white line into your lane. You wonder if such large vehicles are safe. Can truck drivers really keep such a behemoth under control? Should there be a law against such big trucks sharing the highway with passenger cars?

Experimental psychology can help to provide a scientific answer to this question. Operator workload is an intervening variable that is very useful when asking practical questions about a person's ability to perform sustained jobs (Kantowitz & Casper, 1988). **Workload** relates the demands of the job environment to the capability of the human operator. If workload is too high, the job may be unsafe.

Figure 2–3 shows a direct and an indirect way to relate an independent variable, road geometry, to a dependent variable, tachometer reaction time (RT). Research conducted in a laboratory truck simulator (Kantowitz, 1994) showed that when professional truck drivers were required to read their engine tachometer, RT was influenced by road geometry (radius of curvature) and traffic density. Tight curves and dense traffic result in a longer RT to read the tachometer. The direct relationship uses only one arrow to link road geometry to tachometer RT. The results of the experiment could be used to build a mathematical formula that relates road curvature to RT. The indirect method

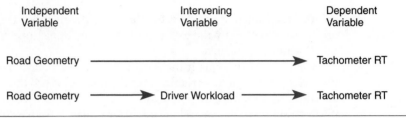

Figure 2–3 One set of variables

uses two arrows. The first arrow relates degree of highway curvature to driver workload, an intervening variable. When curvature increases, so does driver workload. The second arrow relates the intervening variable, driver workload, to tachometer RT. When workload increases, so does RT. Because the indirect method is more complicated, requiring an extra arrow, you might expect the scientist to prefer the direct method of explanation. Indeed, if the only scientific goal were to relate radius of road curvature to tachometer RT, you would be correct, because science prefers simple explanations to complex explanations. However, as we shall explain, the scientific goal is more general.

Figure 2–4 relates two independent variables, road geometry and number of trailers being towed, to two dependent variables, tachometer RT and heart rate variability. As workload increases, heart rate variability decreases (Kantowitz & Casper, 1988). Again, both direct and indirect explanations are shown. In Figure 2–4 direct and indirect explanations are equally complex. Each requires four distinct arrows.

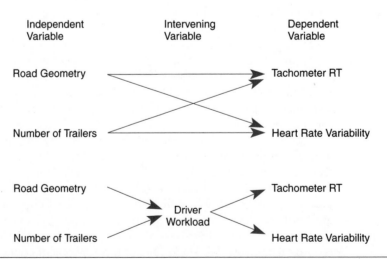

Figure 2–4 Two sets of variables

Figure 2–5 relates four independent variables to four dependent variables. Type of dolly is an independent variable. In the United States, most trucks use a type A dolly to connect the trailers. In Canada, a more expensive dolly (type C) is often used, because it is believed to offer superior control. Another goal of the study is to compare the effects of these two types of dolly and the level of traffic density on driver workload and driver behavior. Subjective ratings are a dependent variable often used to measure workload (Kantowitz & Casper, 1988). Steering wheel rate is also a dependent variable that refers to driver control movements of the steering wheel. Again, both direct and indirect explanations are shown. Now it is obvious that the indirect method is less complicated. It requires 8 separate arrows, whereas the direct method requires 16 arrows. So, as science tries to relate more independent and dependent variables, intervening variables become more efficient.

Intervening variables have yet another advantage. Workload, no matter how produced, should have the same effect on all dependent variables. This can be tested in experiments. If it is not true, we can modify the idea of a single intervening variable. Later chapters discuss this under the topic of converging operations.

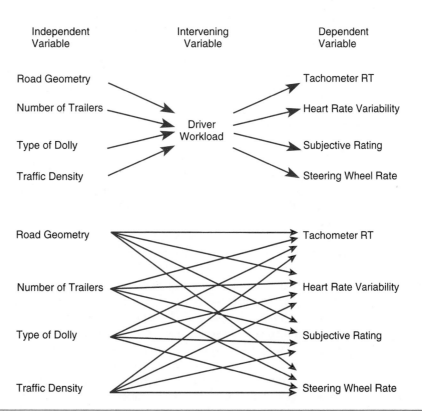

Figure 2–5 Four sets of variables

Evaluating Theories

The sophisticated scientist does not try to determine whether a particular theory is true or false in an absolute sense. There is no black-and-white approach to theory evaluation. A theory may be known to be incorrect in some portion and yet continue to be used. In modern physics, light is represented, according to the theory chosen, either as discrete particles called quanta or as continuous waves. Logically, light cannot be both at the same time. Thus, you might think that at least one of these two theoretical views must necessarily be false. The physicist tolerates this ambiguity (although perhaps not cheerfully) and uses whichever representation—quantum or wave—is more appropriate. Instead of flatly stating that a theory is true, the scientist is much more likely to state that it is supported substantially by data, thereby leaving open the possibility that new data may not support the theory. Although scientists do not state that a theory is true, they often must decide which of several theories is best. As noted earlier, explanations are tentative; nevertheless, the scientist still needs to decide which theory is best for now. To do so, there must be explicit criteria for evaluating a theory. Three such criteria are **parsimony, precision, and testability.**

One criterion was hinted at earlier when we noted that the fewer the statements in a theory, the better the theory. This criterion is called parsimony, or sometimes Occam's razor, after William of Occam. If a theory needs a separate statement for every result it tries to explain, clearly no economy has been gained by the theory. Theories gain power when they can explain many results with few explanatory concepts. Thus, if two theories have the same number of concepts, the one that can explain more results is a better theory. If two theories can explain the same number of results, the one with fewer explanatory concepts is to be preferred. Here you can see the relationship between theories and intervening variables. Constructs, such as diffusion of responsibility and workload, are intervening variables tied to several independent and dependent variables. The theoretical notion of diffusion of responsibility is parsimonious, because it accounts for substantial amounts of data, as seen in our previous discussion.

Precision is another important criterion, especially in psychology, where it is often lacking. Theories that involve mathematical equations or computer programs are generally more precise and, hence, better than those that use loose verbal statements (all other things being equal, of course). Unless a theory is sufficiently precise so that different investigators can agree about its predictions, it is for all intents and purposes useless.

Testability goes beyond precision and is the most important aspect of a good theory, as we have emphasized in this chapter and the previous one. A theory can be very precise and yet not able to be tested. For example, when Einstein proposed the equivalence of matter and energy ($E = mc^2$), nuclear technology was not able to test this relationship directly. The scientist places a very high value on the criterion of testability, because a theory that cannot be tested can never be disproved. At first, you might think this would be a good quality, because it would be impossible to demonstrate that such a theory was incorrect. The scientist takes the opposite view, as we noted in the discussion of falsifiability. For example, consider extrasensory perception (ESP). Some believers in ESP claim that the presence of a disbeliever is sufficient to prevent a person gifted with ESP from performing, because the disbeliever puts out "bad vibes" that disrupt ESP. This means that ESP cannot be evaluated, because only believers can be present when it is demonstrated. The scientist takes a dim view of this logic, and most scientists, especially psychologists, are skeptical about ESP. Belief in a theory increases as it survives tests that could reject it. Because some future test possibly may find a flaw, belief in a theory is never absolute. If a theory cannot logically be tested, it cannot be evaluated; hence, it is useless to the scientist. If it is logically possible but not yet technically feasible, as was once the case with Einstein's theory, then evaluation of a theory is deferred.

Foxes and Hedgehogs Roaming Through Psychological Theory

Research in experimental psychology tends to be organized by subfields. This approach is the way of the fox who knows many paths (Figure 2–6). Such was not always the case in the history of psychology. There were psychologists (e.g., James, 1890) who tried for a unified explanation of psychological phenomena. This is the way of the hedgehog who knows one big thing (Figure 2–6).

Both approaches face significant challenges. The dominant approach builds strong barriers between fields. Professors are hired within a field and

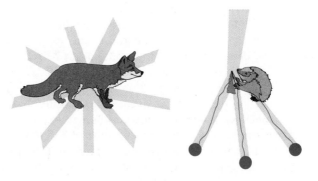

"The fox knows many things,
but the hedgehog knows one big thing."
–Archilocus

Figure 2–6 Segmented (Fox) and unified (Hedgehog) approaches to psychological theory

tend to have offices located by field of specialization, the better to fend off territorial thrusts from other subfields. Graduate students get trained by field, with appropriate course requirements, and this perpetuates the division. Even panels that evaluate grant proposals are organized by specialties. The new Ph.D who takes a job in industry is ill prepared for the cooperation across fields necessary to solve any important practical problem.

Recently, sympathy has been growing for a more unified (hedgehog) approach (Sternberg et al., 2001). These theorists try to knit competing theories together, stressing that the explanation role of theory is more crucial than the predictive role. Theory knitting is a worthy goal if it can be accomplished. However, the present divided system arose because earlier integrated theories were unable to span all of the subfields of psychology. Will the new hedgehogs knit better than the old hedgehogs?

CONCEPT SUMMARY

Good theories are

- parsimonious
- precise
- testable

▶ The Science of Psychology

Some students find it difficult to think of psychology as a science in the same sense that physics and chemistry are sciences. They believe that there are aspects of human experience, such as the arts, literature, and religion, that defy scientific analysis. How can the beauty of a Klee lithograph, a Beethoven sonata, or a Cartier-Bresson photograph be reduced to cold, scientific equation? How can the tender feelings of a first romance, the thrill of driving a sports car at 100 miles per hour, and the agony of a defeated football team be captured in the objective, disinterested fashion required by science?

Some psychologists, known as humanists, would answer these questions in the negative. These humanists, most often clinical and counseling psychologists, claim that to evaluate and test human feelings and experience objectively by traditional scientific methods is impossible. Even tough, "brass-instrument" experimental psychologists concur that the domain of science is limited. We cannot establish or refute the existence of God by scientific means any more than we could test gravity by theological methods. Science operates where it can test hypotheses (see Chapter 1). This does not mean that knowledge cannot be gained wherever science fears to tread—that is, by nonscientific means. Many important fields of human endeavor have yet to benefit from extensive scientific analysis—ethics, morals, and law, to name but a few.

However, most scientists believe that scientific analysis eventually might be usefully applied to many such areas. Much of contemporary psychology was regarded as the sole property of philosophy at one time. As psychological techniques improved, these aspects of human expertise and behavior moved into the realm of science, and now most psychologists believe that virtually all facets of human experience are fair game for the science of psychology. If testable hypotheses can be made, then scientific psychology can be used. Deriding scientific progress in psychology, as did one U.S. senator who criticized the National Science Foundation for supporting research on romantic love (Elmes, 1988), will not halt efforts to expand psychological knowledge. Although concern for the proper and ethical use of such knowledge is valid and important, ignorance is no solution.

Hard Science as a Model for Experimental Psychology

Psychologists can be arranged along a continuum according to how well they think physics and chemistry serve as disciplines for psychology to emulate. The "hard-shelled" psychologists think these older sciences are perfect models, whereas the "soft-shelled" psychologists believe that social sciences must find another model. Because we are experimental psychologists by trade, and because this book is intended as an experimental-psychology text, we tend to sample more from the hard-shelled end of the continuum.

All science has data and theory. What distinguishes among the different sciences, and among the subspecialties within a science like psychology, are the different techniques used. Astronomers do not need Skinner boxes any more than animal-learning psychologists need telescopes, yet both practice science. A learning theorist's memory drum is not intrinsically superior to a social psychologist's "aggression machine." Even the modern microcomputer of an information-processing psychologist does not guarantee better science, although it may improve the odds. Most of this text is devoted to explaining the techniques needed in psychological research today. Although the hard-shelled psychologist does have more refined techniques, this is in part because of selection of problems that are amenable to sophisticated analysis. As psychology subjects more and more of human experience and behavior to scientific analysis, it is only natural that initial techniques may be crude. At one time, this was true of hard-shelled psychology too. Having a hard shell should not preclude one from having an open mind.

Psychology and the Real World

Scientists in general, and psychologists in particular, have many reasons for pursuing their profession. We think it rather easy to prove that psychological research does serve humankind (see the Application section in Chapter 1). We would like to stress that we do not find service to humankind the only, or necessarily the major, justification for a career as a research psychologist. Many scientists investigate certain problems simply because they find them interesting. We have complete sympathy with a colleague who might state that he or she studies gerbils just because gerbils provoke his or her curiosity. It is true that certain studies are performed on animals because they are unethical or impractical to perform on humans—for example, studies of long-term crowding, punishment, drugs, and so on—but it is equally true that the behavior of animals is interesting in its own right.

As noted in Chapter 1, ideas for research come from both theoretical predictions and practical problems, and scientific research is often divided into two categories: basic and applied. **Applied research** aims at solving a specific problem—such as how to cure bedwetting—whereas **basic research** has no immediate practical goal. Basic research establishes a reservoir of data, theoretical explanations, and concepts that can be tapped by the applied researcher. Without this source, applied research would soon dry up and sputter to a halt unless applied researchers became, of necessity, basic researchers. It takes quite a while for a concept developed by basic research to find some useful application in society. Adams (1972) traced five socially important products to discover the impact, if any, of basic research. Although basic research accounted for 70% of the significant events, these events occurred 20 to 30 years before the ultimate use of the product. This long time lag obscures the crucial role of basic research, so that many persons incorrectly believe that basic research is not very useful to society. Often it is difficult to tell what basic research being done today will have an impact 30 years from now, but this inability to predict does not mean that we should stop doing basic research (Elmes, 1988).

Although the scientific quest for knowledge may be for one purpose only, usually basic and applied interests eventually intermingle in interesting ways, as demonstrated by the various kinds of research done on social loafing. Ringelmann's early observations of social loafing in the laboratory were also documented in the workplace (Marriot, 1949). A potentially useful way to improve group productivity then arose from the laboratory work of Latané and his colleagues, who found that individual performance assessment can reduce social loafing.

The division of research into basic and applied categories is common, but a far more important distinction is between good and bad research. The principles and practices covered in this text apply with equal force to basic and applied research. You can and should use them to evaluate all the psychological research you encounter, whether as a student, a professional psychologist, or an educated person reading the daily newspaper.

Are Experiments Too Far from Real Life?   Students of psychology typically demand a higher level of relevance in their psychology courses than they expect from other sciences. Students who are not at all dismayed that their course in introductory physics did not enable them to repair their automobile often are disturbed that their course in introductory psychology did not give them a better insight into their own motivations, did not cure their neuroses, and failed to show them how to gain eternal happiness. If you did not find such information in introductory psychology, we doubt that you will find it in this text either. If this seems unfair, read on.

The data that psychologists gather may at first seem unimportant, because an immediate relationship between basic psychological research and pressing social or personal problems may be difficult to establish. Naturally, people then doubt the importance of this research and wonder why the federal government, through various agencies, funds researchers to watch rats press bars or run through mazes.

The difficulty, however, is not with the research but with the expectations as to how "useful" research should be conducted. As noted by Sidman (1960, p. 27), people expect progress to occur by the establishment of laboratory situations that are analogous to real-life situations: "In order to study psychosis in animals we must learn how to make animals psychotic." This is off the mark. The psychologist tries to understand the underlying *processes* rather than the physical situations that produce these processes. The physical situations in the real world and the laboratory need not be at all similar, provided that the same processes are occurring.

Suppose we would like to know why airplane accidents occur or, more specifically, what the relationship is between airplane accidents and failure of attention on the part of the pilot and/or the air traffic controller. A basic researcher might approach this problem by having college sophomores sit in front of several lights that turn on in rapid succession. The sophomore has to press a key as each light is illuminated. This probably seems somewhat removed from midair collisions of aircraft. Yet, although the physical situations are quite different, the processes are similar. Pressing a key is an index of attention. Psychologists can overload the human operator by presenting lights faster than he or she can respond. Thus, this simple physical situation in a laboratory allows the psychologist to study failure of attention in a carefully controlled environment. In addition to the obvious safety benefits of studying attention without having to crash airplanes, there are many scientific advantages to the laboratory environment, as we will show in later chapters. Because failures of attention are responsible for many kinds of industrial accidents (see Tsang & Vidulich, 2003, for examples from aviation), studies of attention by use of lights and buttons can lead to improvements outside the laboratory.

By the same token, establishing similar physical situations does not guarantee similarity of processes. One can easily train a rat to pick up coins in its mouth and bury them in its cage. This does not necessarily mean, however, that the "miserly" rat and the miserly human who keeps coins under his or her mattress do so because the same psychological processes are controlling their behaviors.

You also should be aware of two important reasons for doing research, the purposes of which (at least initially) may not be directly related to practical affairs (Mook, 1983). One reason that basic research aids understanding is that it often demonstrates what *can* happen. Thus, under controlled conditions, it can be determined whether social loafing does occur. Furthermore, the laboratory affords an opportunity to determine the characteristics of social loafing more clearly than does the workplace, where a number of uncontrolled factors, such as salary and job security, could mask or alter the effects of social loafing (see Chapter 13).

A second reason for the value of basic research is that the findings from a controlled, laboratory setting may have more force than similar findings obtained in a real-life setting. Showing that the human operator can be overloaded in a relatively nonstressful laboratory task suggests that attentional factors are crucial for performance. Individuals could be even more likely to be overloaded under the stressful conditions of piloting large passenger planes in crowded airspaces.

If a researcher wants to test a theoretical prediction or apply a laboratory result in an applied setting, then real-life tests are required (Kantowitz, 1992a). There are strong limitations on applying basic research directly to a practical setting (Kantowitz, 1990). For example, despite the large amount of basic knowledge about workload, several cautions need be observed before applying this knowledge to truck drivers on the road (Kantowitz, 1992b). Similarly, installing a way of assessing individual performance to reduce social loafing in a group manufacturing situation without first testing in a manufacturing environment would be foolhardy.

This section has two morals. First, basic research is often closer to real life than may appear at first glance. Second, although applied research benefits from previous basic research, gaining this benefit in a practical situation is seldom easy. Additional testing and evaluation in the applied setting usually are needed.

CONCEPT SUMMARY

Good laboratory research

- examines psychological processes
- shows what can happen in a controlled setting
- may have more force than real-life research

One way to summarize the material presented in this chapter is to say that engaging in experimental psychology can be stimulating and enjoyable. The attempt to understand why people and animals behave as they do arises out of curiosity and the search for solutions to basic and applied problems. Although empirical procedures that rely on induction and deduction offer advantages compared with other methods of fixing belief, the advantages come with a cost. The cost is that theoretical explanations are always tentative, because alternative theories lead to the search for new data and new data provide the bases for modifications of existing theories. Paradoxically, the cost provides the scientific psychologist with a payment by helping to satisfy curiosity, at least temporarily, and by stimulating that curiosity into additional research and theory. Trying to answer questions about ourselves and animals is an exciting challenge. We hope that you are spurred by this challenge and are gratified by the application of sound psychological science to the understanding of behavior.

Summary

1. Scientific psychology is concerned with the methods and techniques used to explain why people and animals behave as they do. This curiosity may be satisfied by basic or applied research, which usually go hand in hand to provide understanding.
2. Our beliefs are often established by the method of authority, the method of tenacity, or the a priori method. The scientific method offers advantages over these other methods because it relies on systematic, empirical observation and is self-correcting.
3. Scientists use both inductive and deductive reasoning to arrive at explanations of thought and action.
4. Generalizations produce hypotheses.
5. A theory organizes sets of data and generates predictions for new situations in which data have not been obtained.
6. A good theory is parsimonious, precise, and testable.
7. Laboratory research is concerned with the processes that govern behavior and with showing the conditions under which certain psychological processes can be observed.

Key Concepts

applied research (50)	generalization (39)	precision (46)
a priori method (33)	hypothesis (39)	prediction (41)
basic research (50)	induction (35)	scientific method (33)
data (34)	intervening variable (43)	self-correcting (33)
deduction (35)	method of authority	social loafing (30)
diffusion of	(32)	strong inference (38)
responsibility (31)	method of tenacity (32)	testability (46)
empirical (33)	organization (41)	theory (34)
falsifiability view (37)	parsimony (46)	workload (43)

Exercises

1. List five statements that might be considered true. Include some controversial statements (for example, men have lower IQs than women) as well as some you are sure are correct. Survey some of your friends by asking if they agree with these statements. Then ask their justifications for their opinions. Classify their justifications into one of the methods of fixing beliefs discussed in this chapter.

2. Compare and contrast inductive and deductive approaches to science. Clarify your answers by referring to at least one branch of science outside experimental psychology.

3. Discuss social loafing research from the standpoint of strong inference.

4. Is it necessary (or even desirable) for experimental psychologists to justify their research in terms of applied benefits to society?

5. [*Special Exercise.*] In 1983, a researcher studied how three age groups felt about war. One group comprised 10-year-olds, a second group consisted of 35-year-olds, and the last group was made up of 60-year-olds. Marked differences in their attitudes about war were observed. There is an important confounding variable in this study. What is it? Speculate on the effects of this confounding with regard to the attitudes of each age group. (Hint: You might think about this question in terms of the generation gap.)

Suggested Resources

Further information about the nature of science and scientific psychology may be found in Kantowitz, B. H., Roediger, H. L., III, & Elmes, D. G. (2005). *Experimental psychology: Understanding psychological research* (8th ed.). Belmont, CA: Wadsworth.

Excellent discussions about the nature and importance of scientific psychology appear in these publications: Broadbent, D. E. (1973). *In defense of empirical psychology.* London: Methuen. Hebb, D. O. (1974). What psychology is about. *American Psychologist, 29,* 71–79. Sidman, M. (1960). *Tactics of scientific research.* New York: Basic Books.

For those of you who are particularly interested in the philosophy of science, we recommend these three books: Kendler, H. H. (1981). *Psychology: A science in conflict.* New York: Oxford UP. Mayr, E. (1982). *The growth of biological thought.* Cambridge, MA: Belknap Press. Slife, B. D., & Williams, R. N. (1995). *What's behind the research?* Thousand Oaks, CA: Sage.

 ## Web Resource

An entire course in experimental psychology can be found at http://step.psy.cmu.edu

Intervening Variables and Testability

One way to gauge the value of a theory is to determine its testability. Theories are testable to the extent that the concepts can be manipulated and observed. Hence, connecting intervening variables to independent and dependent variables is crucial for scientific progress. You can assess theories in psychology by how well they define their intervening variables. If you examine a dictionary of psychology, such as the one by Chaplin (1968, p. 356), you can assess a theory. For example, Freud defines personality as "the integration of the id, the ego, and the superego." The crux of the definition of the id is "that division of the mind, or psyche, which is the seat of the libido. From it (the id) arise the animalistic, chaotic impulses which demand gratification." Are the Freudian notions of personality and the id formulated as intervening variables? What are the independent variables? What are the dependent variables? Can you generate testable hypotheses from Freud's ideas?

Dollard and Miller (1950, p. 228), as well as many other experimentally oriented psychologists, believe that Freud's theories do not allow testability. The primary reason is because most Freudian concepts are hard to connect to independent and dependent variables. Dollard and Miller tried to rephrase many of Freud's concepts so that they were intervening variables that could be studied in an objective way.

To assess the scientific value of other theories, you might try examining some other concepts in a dictionary of psychology. Aggression and Sheldon's constitutional theory of personality are two entries worth exploring for intervening variables.

CHAPTER 3

Exploring the Literature of Psychology

How to Conduct a Literature Review

Use . . .

- *Psychological Abstracts*
- *Social Science Citation Index*
- *PsycINFO*

How to Read Research Reports

What to Look for in the . . .

- *Abstract:* What was done to whom; what was found
- *Introduction:* What the author proposes; the hypotheses tested
- *Method:* Dependent, independent, participant, and control variables; does the method test the hypothesis?
- *Results:* Do the results support or reject the hypothesis?
- *Discussion:* What conclusions are stated?
- *References:* Other reports you might read; are citations complete?

Suppose you developed an interest in the Stroop effect after participating in the demonstration experiment at the end of Chapter 1. You have developed a testable hypothesis about reading based on this demonstration experiment. Because the experiment showed that it is difficult not to read words, you reasoned that the conflict might disappear if reading were made difficult—say, by printing the materials upside down. Your hypothesis is: The time required to read lists with a conflict between the number of digits and their name will be less if the digits are presented upside down rather than right-side up. However, when you have a research idea, it is always possible that someone else has had the same idea and already done the experiment that you are considering. For this reason, you should do a literature search before running the experiment. A literature search will allow you to discover whether the experiment has been done and any "tricks of the trade" that might help you in designing your own experiment.

▶ How to Do a Literature Search

If you are unsure about what resources to examine to help refine your research ideas, refer to Table 3–1 to help you along. The table lists several general sources of information as well as journals with particular topical emphases. Perhaps the most important general resource is ***Psychological Abstracts,*** which contains brief abstracts of articles from almost all journals that publish psychological research. More will be said about abstracts later in the chapter, but typically they are short summaries (150 words or less) of the experiments in the article. After you have found an abstract of interest there, you can then

Table 3–1 Some important resources for psychological research

Topic area	Title of resource	Comment
Article titles	*Current Contents*	Several specialty areas
Author citations	*Social Science Citation Index*	
Article abstracts	*Science Citation Index*	
	Biological Abstracts	
	Ergonomics Abstracts	
	Index Medicus	
	MEDLINE/PubMed	
	Psychological Abstracts	
	PsycINFO	
Review articles	*American Psychologist*	
	Annual Review of Psychology	Book with chapter-length reviews
	Psychological Bulletin	
	Psychological Review	Often contains original studies
	Psychological Science	Also contains research articles
	Psychological Science in the Public Interest	Also contains research articles
	Psychonomic Bulletin & Review	Also contains research articles
Empirical articles	*American Journal of Psychology*	
	Animal Learning and Behavior	Some field studies
	Behavior Therapy	
	Behavioral Neuroscience	
	Canadian Journal of Experimental Psychology	
	Child Development	
	Cognitive Psychology	
	Cognitive Science	
	Developmental Psychology	
	Developmental Psychobiology	
	Human Factors	
	Journal of Abnormal Psychology	

(continued)

Table 3–1   *(continued)*

Topic area	Title of resource	Comment
	Journal of Applied Behavioral Analysis	
	Journal of Applied Psychology	
	Journal of Comparative Psychology	
	Journal of Educational Psychology	
	Journal of Experimental Child Psychology	Some field studies
	Journal of Experimental Psychology: Animal Behavior Processes	
	Journal of Experimental Psychology: General	
	Journal of Experimental Psychology: Learning, Memory, and Cognition	
	Journal of Experimental Psychology: Human Perception & Performance	
	Journal of Experimental Social Psychology	
	Journal of the Experimental Analysis of Behavior	Small-*n* experiments
	Journal of Memory and Language	
	Journal of Personality and Social Psychology	
	Learning and Motivation	
	Memory	
	Memory & Cognition	
	Neuropsychology	
	Perception & Psychophysics	
	Psychobiology	
	Quarterly Journal of Experimental Psychology	
Various research methods	*Behavior Research Methods Instrumentation and Computers*	Notes on apparatus and computers
	Psychological Methods	

find the entire article in your library or send a note to the author requesting a reprint of the article or additional information. The other resources listed in Table 3–1 have a variety of purposes, and we recommend that you familiarize yourself with each of the first seven general purpose resources and as many of the research journals as seem to be of interest to you. We have included only a small number of research journals in the table, but these few are among the most widely read in psychological research. Others emphasizing education, clinical problems, sociology, law, and industrial concerns can be ferreted out of your school's library.

Perhaps the most powerful method now available to search the literature is the **computerized literature search.** Most libraries provide access to computerized databases for literature searches of numerous subject areas. Many of these libraries also provide access to a psychological database called *PsycINFO*. *PsycINFO* is a reference service provided by the OCLC (Online Computer Library Center) FirstSearch service in conjunction with the American Psychological Association (APA). *PsycINFO* indexes more than 1,900 journals in psychology and related fields. The coverage presently extends from 1967 to the present (updated every week) and also includes historic records of articles going back to 1887. The reason this system is so powerful is that it can search its entire set of journals for articles that match a few key words that you provide (see the Psychology in Action section at the end of this chapter for a more detailed explanation). After specifying your search terms (key words), *PsycINFO* lists the titles and provides access to the abstracts of articles (along with source information) that match your search terms.

Although *PsycINFO* and other similar computerized search systems provide quick and easy access to a large number of journal articles, it is important to keep in mind that it may be helpful to supplement or even start your search with a simpler method. One of the most effective methods for doing a literature search is first to find a recent paper on your topic of interest (perhaps by looking through one of the sources listed in Table 3–1) and use the articles listed in it as a guide to the literature. In this way, you can benefit from the scholarly research of others and move on from there. Computerized databases are certainly powerful, but they are not necessarily complete. They may not index many book chapters, for example, and they may extend back only 30 years or so. Furthermore, unless you are already well versed in the terms used by psychologists, it is possible to use less-than-optimal search terms and so miss potentially important articles. Thus, it is still advantageous to look at the references others have cited, as either a supplement to your literature search or a first step.

An excellent method for discovering new findings uses the *Social Science Citation Index,* which can be searched either by computer or manually. By entering a critical or key reference, you can obtain a list of more recent articles that have cited your critical reference. Because these articles contain a discussion of your key reference, it is very likely that they are directly related to your topic of interest. This is an extremely efficient way to bring yourself up-to-date in some specific content area.

Once you have done your literature search and obtained the articles relevant to your research interest, the next step is to read the articles. Trying to read a psychology journal article for the first time can be a challenging experience. Researchers write articles for other researchers, so they use jargon and a terse writing style. These features aid communication among scholars in a particular field, because they can read short reports and understand them. However, such writing can be difficult to comprehend for students beginning their study of a field. The following section is designed to prepare you for your first encounter with the literature of experimental psychology. Because psychology is a science, progress is measured by the accumulation of knowledge in the various fields. Researchers spend a great deal of their time reading and writing journal articles in an effort to contribute to this accumulation of knowledge. Even if your career in psychology extends no further than this course, you will discover that critical thinking and writing skills are invaluable for living in a world that revolves around information. To help you become fluent in the art of reading research reports, we will describe the format and style most often used in journal articles. Then hints will be provided to help you become a critical reader, skilled at objectively evaluating an article. With some practice, you will be able to read psychology articles with relative ease.

▶ The Parts of an Article

The basic psychology article consists of seven parts: (a) title and author(s), (b) abstract, (c) introduction, (d) Method, (e) Results, (f) Discussion, and (g) references. Each part has an important function and is a necessary component of the article.

Title and Author(s)

The **title** gives you an idea of the contents of an article. Because titles must be short, the most common type of title states only the dependent and independent variables—for example, "The effect of encoding strategy on recognition memory for odors." Although this title is not particularly appealing, it conveys important information. The title and author(s) of each article typically occupy a prominent place in a given journal issue, such as the inside front cover, back cover, or first page.

As you continue to gain knowledge in a particular content area, you will become familiar with many researchers. You may start to pay attention to the authors first and then look at the titles. After you have read several articles published by the same **author,** you will grow in understanding of that writer's viewpoints and how they differ from those of other researchers.

So many psychology articles are published each month that no one has the time to read all of them. The table of contents is a first step to selecting those articles relevant to your own interests, but an even better decision can be made by consulting the abstract and the references of an article.

Abstract

The **abstract** is a short paragraph (120 words) that summarizes the key points of an article. According to the *Publication Manual of the American Psychological Association* (APA, 2001b), it should be "a brief, comprehensive summary of the contents of the article; it allows readers to survey the contents of an article quickly" (p. 12). The abstract is the best way to discover quickly what an article is about. A well-written journal abstract will convey the problem under investigation, the procedure used to explore the problem, the results, the conclusions, and the implications or applications of the research findings. This information provided in brief allows you to discover quickly whether a particular article warrants further reading. As you gain experience and become familiar with authors in the field, you will want to consult the references as well before making this decision.

Introduction

The **introduction** specifies the problem to be studied and tells why it is important. The author also reviews the relevant research literature on the topic. A good introduction also specifies the hypotheses to be tested and the rationale behind the predictions.

Method

The **Method** section describes in detail the operations performed by the experimenter. It is usually printed in smaller type to conserve space, but this does not mean it is an unimportant part of the article, to be quickly skimmed. The Method section should contain enough information so that another experimenter could replicate the study.

It is customary to divide the Method section into subsections that cover participants, apparatus or materials, and procedure. The **participant** subsection (also called the **subject** subsection traditionally and in some current journals; but current APA publication guidelines specify the use of the term *participant* instead) tells how many of the target population were enrolled, how they were selected (randomly, haphazardly, only the investigator's relatives, etc.), and who they were (college undergraduates taking introductory psychology, paid volunteers obtained by an ad in a newspaper, a particular strain of rats purchased from a supply house). The **apparatus** subsection is often not relevant and is not always included, but it describes any equipment used to test the participants. This subsection might include such details as the model number of a computer or the size of a conditioning chamber and is referred to as the **materials** subsection when questionnaires, written or videotaped sketches, and other similar means are used to test participants. If they are extensive, special materials may be placed in an appendix section, usually set in smaller type. The **procedure** subsection explains what happened to the participants and contains enough information so that someone else could repeat the study exactly as it was done.

Results

The **Results** section tells what happened in the experiment. It is unusual to find raw data or individual participants' scores reported in a journal article; instead, descriptive statistics are presented that summarize the data. Inferential statistics present the probability of whether the observed differences between the various experimental conditions were produced by random, or chance, factors. This information helps both the researcher and the reader to determine how confident to be that the independent variable(s) produced a change in the dependent variable. (See Appendices A and B for further explanation and review.) Both kinds of statistics are important and help psychologists to understand the outcome of an experiment.

Either tables or graphs may be used to describe and summarize data. In the typical **table,** such as Table 3–2, data and summarized data appear under various headings. These data are taken from an experiment designed to determine whether talking on a cell phone interferes with one's ability to drive a car (Strayer & Johnston, 2001). The authors hypothesized that talking on a cell phone would impose greater attentional demands than listening to the radio, and would disrupt driving performance to a greater degree. All participants completed the simulated driving task by itself (single task). Half of the participants also completed the driving task while talking on a cell phone, and the other half completed the task while listening to the news on a radio. Before you look at the data, you should first read the title of the table (the title generally appears immediately under or next to the words "Table *n*," where *n* refers to the number of the table). The title of the table should be explicit enough to tell you what sorts of data appear in the table.

The title of Table 3–2 tells you that it contains information about missed traffic lights as a function of the interfering task, whether it was listening to the radio or talking on a cell phone, and task condition, whether the participants were engaged in the interfering task (dual task) or simply driving (single task). Next, you should examine the headings and subheadings carefully. These will tell you about the conditions or variables that are relevant to the data in the table. For example, in Table 3–2 the headings include Interfering Task and Task Condition. So, you should look for data that show the proportion of errors in each of the four conditions. We see from these data that participants are generally more likely to miss traffic lights on the dual-task condition ($M = (.07 + .04)/2 = .055$) than under the single-task condition ($M = (.03 + .04)/2 = .035$). Finally, you should note that the effect of the dual task is greater when someone is talking on a cell phone (.07) than when listening to the radio (.04). The finding that there is a difference in one condition (dual task) but not another (single task) is called an *interaction* and is an important

Table 3–2   Proportion of missed traffic lights as a function of interfering task and task condition

Interfering Task

Task condition	Cell phone	Radio
Single task	.03	.04
Dual task	.07	.04

aspect of experimental data. Elsewhere in the text, we will spend a considerable amount of time discussing interactions.

You have not encountered any **figures** containing data in this chapter. Some data are shown in Figure 3–1. These are the results of an experiment conducted by Roebers and Schneider (2000). The experiment concerned children's eyewitness testimony. The participants watched a film depicting two children being robbed by a gang of boys. Three weeks later, the children answered a series of cued recall questions about the film. Some questions were neutral, in that they were phrased so that they did not suggest a specific answer (for example, How much did the boy have in his purse?). Other questions were misleading, in that they suggested an incorrect answer to the question (for example, Did the boy have 60 cents in his purse?). In Figure 3–1, we see the proportion of correct answers on the vertical axis, which is called the **ordinate,** while on the horizontal axis, which is called the **abscissa,** we have the two types of questions: neutral and misleading. Nearly all figures from any type of psychological research have a scale of the dependent variable (what is measured) on the ordinate. In figures from experiments, the independent variable (what is manipulated) is on the abscissa. Be sure to examine the labels on the ordinate and abcissa so that you know what data are plotted in the figure, then you can examine the data. In Figure 3–1, the heights of the bars tell you the mean proportion of correct answers for each of the question types, and you can see that the children answered fewer questions correctly (10% less) when the questions were misleading than when they were neutral.

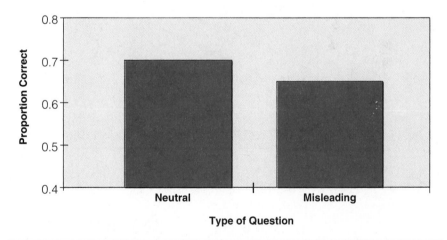

Figure 3–1 Mean proportion of correct answers on a cued recall test as a function of question-type. The dependent variable (correct answers) is on the ordinate, or vertical axis, and the independent variable (type of question) is on the abscissa, or horizontal axis. Note that subjects answered 10% fewer questions correct in the misleading condition (*M* = .60) than in the neutral condition (*M* = .70). (Data adapted from Roebers and Schneider, 2000.)

Figure 3–1 is a bar graph, and data from an experiment are plotted as bars when the levels of the independent variable are defined at the nominal level (that is, the conditions are qualitatively different and have different names, but they cannot be ordered on a quantitative dimension). A different way to plot data is shown in Figure 3–2. There, the data appear as points (circles or triangles) connected by lines (solid or broken). Curves such as these are drawn when the independent variable is measured on a scale other than a nominal scale, one in which an ordering of the measures is possible. In Figure 3–2, the abscissa represents the age of the children. Of interest is whether younger children are more susceptible to the misleading suggestions than are older children. A line graph like this one is used when the independent variable (for example, age) is ordered along a dimension. This figure has two sets of points: one for the neutral questions and one for the misleading questions. It is also conventional to connect data points with straight lines, unless you actually determine the equation for the curve that could pass through those points.

After you have examined the ordinate and abscissa, the parameters within the graph (that is, the labels for the different conditions—in this case, neutral and misleading questions), and any legend under the figure, you can then study

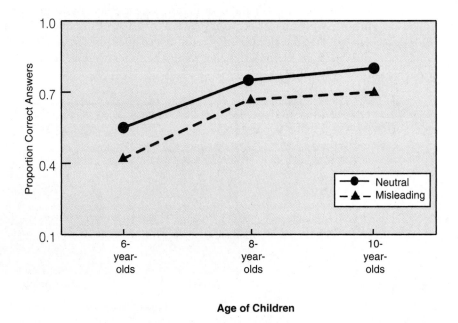

Figure 3–2   Mean proportion of correct answers on a cued recall test (the dependent variable on the ordinate) as a function of age (the independent variable on the abscissa) for neutral (filled circles with solid lines) and misleading questions (triangles with broken lines). Older children answered more questions correctly, but they were also affected by misinformation. (Data adapted from Roebers and Schneider, 2000.)

the data. Figure 3–2 clearly shows that older children answered more questions correctly than did younger children. However, all children in this experiment showed a suggestibility effect, not just the youngest children.

When you are trying to understand the data in a figure, be sure that you pay close attention to the scale of the dependent variable on the ordinate. Sometimes the scale can be misleading: An abbreviated scale with widely spaced numbers will tend to make differences appear more impressive, and a scale with numbers jammed close together will tend to make differences appear smaller. To see how this works, consider the following example.

Suppose that the number of murders in a city increased from 72 to 80 to 91 over 3 years. The next year, the mayor is running for reelection and is eager to show that the city has been safe for the last 3 years under her administration. So, her campaign workers draw up the graph shown in the left of Figure 3–3. By making the scale on the ordinate very long, they create the impression that the murder rate is fairly steady. In the same year, the city police are arguing that they need higher staffing levels. They want to show that the city is becoming more unsafe, so they depict the murder rate as increasing steeply by changing the scale, as in the right-hand graph of Figure 3–3.

The facts are shown accurately in both graphs. However, the left graph gives the impression that the murder rate is increasing very gradually, hardly worth worrying about. (Hasn't the mayor done a good job leading the city?) The right graph, on the other hand, creates the impression that the murder rate is increasing dramatically. (Don't we need more police?)

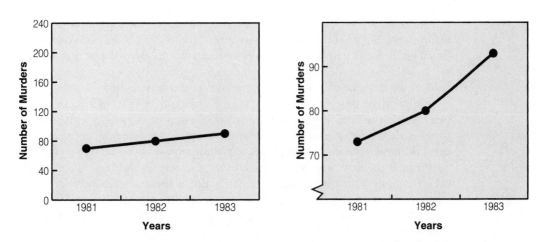

Figure 3–3 Variation in scales. Exactly the same data are presented in the two panels. However, the variation in scales on the ordinate causes the graph at the left to seem to show the murder rate to be increasing only slightly, whereas the one at the right seems to show the rate going up dramatically. Yet both graphs actually show the murder rate accurately—the difference is in the scale on the Y-axis. It is important to examine a graph carefully and note the scale of measurement, because scale changes can make small differences look large and vice versa.

These graphing techniques are common. In fact, there are exaggerated scales used in some of the graphs in this book to show patterns of results more clearly. You should always look carefully to see what the scale is in a graph. With experimental data, it is more important to determine whether a difference is statistically reliable than to determine whether the difference appears "large" when graphed.

Which way of graphing the results is right? In a sense, both are, because both can be argued to portray matters accurately. On the other hand, if statistical tests have shown a difference to exist between the two measures, then the graph on the right more accurately captures the relation between measures. Inferential statistics permit the assessment of whether differences that appear in the results, as on the right graph, are real and not the result of chance factors. Inferential statistics about the data appear in statements such as "$F(4,60) = 2.03, p < .05$." All this means is that the odds for obtaining by chance an F-statistic at least as large as 2.03 would be 5% if the experiment were repeated. That is, if the experiment were conducted 100 times, the results would be similar in at least 95 out of the 100 repetitions. There is no fixed rule for setting an appropriate level of significance—.05 (or 5 in 100) as opposed to .001 (or 1 in 1,000), for instance. It is up to the researcher to decide whether the odds are just right, too high, or too low. Depending on the import of your conclusions, you may require more (for example, .001) or less certainty (for example, .10, or 10 in 100) that what happened has not happened by chance.

Imagine the problem of a graduate-student admissions officer who has been told that resources at the university are extremely limited. It has been suggested that she discriminate against women in accepting students into the program, because they are believed to be less likely to finish. She would like to put such unsubstantiated notions to rest and so commissions a statistical analysis to test this hypothesis. Here odds of 5 in 100 to reject the null hypothesis that women are less likely than men to finish are too high, because the import is so great. A level of significance of 1 in 1,000 would be more appropriate.

Or, take the case of a breakfast-cereal company that wishes to include a prize inside the box. It performs a statistical analysis to decide which one of five potential prizes, all of which cost the same, is preferred by consumers. If there is any difference among prizes, the company wants to be sure to find the best one. If the firm is wrong and incorrectly selects a single one when in fact all are equally attractive, no great harm is done, because each prize costs the same. Here odds of 5 in 100 are too low. A level of significance of 50 in 100 might be more appropriate. The situation determines what the level of significance should be. Additional discussion of inferential statistics and the level of significance can be found in Appendix B.

In the Results section, the author's specific choice of words is important. Beware of such statements as this: "Although the data just barely missed reaching the proposed level of significance, it appears that a trend in the predicted direction did occur." This kind of statement should be approached with caution for several reasons. First, the word *trend* is a technical term: Existence of a trend can be determined only by an appropriate statistical test. Second, it implies that results that are significant go beyond a trend—that is, they are true and utterly reliable—and that failure to reach a prescribed level only means that "truth" is latent rather than explicit. This implication is false: Even significant results are reliable only in a probabilistic sense—for example, 95 times in 100.

Discussion

The **Discussion** is the most creative part of an article. Here an author is permitted to restate what the data show (if he or she so desires) and to draw theoretical conclusions. Most editors have firm standards for both the Method and the Results section, but the author is given greater latitude in the Discussion. In the words of the *APA Publication Manual* (APA, 2001b): "You are free to examine, interpret, and qualify the results, as well as to draw inferences from them" (p. 26). Keep in mind that research results are not incontestable truths and that experimental findings are relative to the context in which they are found. Freedom for the author requires caution from the readers.

References

References are found at the end of the article. In contrast to journals in other disciplines, psychology journals list full titles of referenced articles. This practice helps to tell the reader what the article is about. Furthermore, the references are valuable as a guide for related information. They can also be used as an index of the merit of the article. Articles should refer to the most recently published works in the area as well as to the most important previous publications. Furthermore, only articles cited in text should be included in the reference section. This is different from a bibliography, which includes as many relevant citations as is feasible.

▶ Checklist for the Critical Reader

In this section, we offer some hints that have helped us to become better consumers of the information presented in psychological journals. Our major suggestion is to avoid rushing through an article. Instead, you might deliberately stop after each section and write down the answers to the questions we shall list here. This can be difficult at first, but with practice, this process becomes automatic and requires little extra time.

Introduction

1. *What is the author's goal?* The introduction explains the reasons behind the research and reviews the earlier literature on the phenomena of interest. If one or more theories are related to the research, the

introduction gives the predictions the theories make. As with scientists in other areas, psychologists do not necessarily agree as to the underlying mechanisms and theoretical interpretations of behavior. Authors may present a particular theory that they think provides a useful explanation of behavior. Although authors may present more than one theory in the introduction, they will later demonstrate that not all of these theories help equally to predict and explain the obtained results. Try to figure out which of the several theories an author believes and which are slated for subsequent rejection.

2.   *What hypothesis will be tested in the experiment?* The answer to this should be obvious and stated directly within the Introduction section.

3.   *If I had to design an experiment to test this hypothesis, what would I do?* This is the key question for the introduction. You must try to answer this *before* continuing to the Method section of the article. Many experiments are done within the context of a systematic investigation of behavior to test and support a particular theoretical framework developed by the author. If the author has any skill as a wordsmith, once you have finished the next section, you are likely to agree with the method that the author has advocated in the article. A clever author will plant the seeds to this answer in the introduction itself; this practice makes it harder for you to state a method independently. Write down the major ideas for your method of testing the hypothesis.

Method

Compare your answer to question 3 with that of the author of the article. They probably will differ, if you have not peeked. Now answer questions 4a–c.

4a.   *Is my proposed method better than the author's?* Regardless of who has the better method, you or the author, this forced comparison will make you think about the Method section critically instead of passively accepting it.

4b.   *Does the author's method actually test the hypothesis?* The hypothesis is sometimes the first casualty, disappearing between the Introduction and Method sections. Always check that the method used is adequate and relevant to the hypothesis at hand.

4c.   *What are the independent, dependent, and control variables?* This is an obvious question and can be answered quickly. Listing the variables helps you avoid passive reading of the Method section. After you have resolved differences between your proposed method and the author's, answer the next question.

5.   *Using the participants, apparatus, materials, and procedures described by the author, what results would I predict for this experiment?* You must answer this on your own before reading the Results

section. To help yourself, review the hypothesis and the independent and dependent variables. You may find it impossible to predict a single outcome. This is not really a problem, because the author probably also had more than one prediction originally. He or she may have done some preliminary investigations to narrow down possible outcomes; alternatively, he or she may have been surprised by the results and had to rethink the introduction once the results were in. Draw a rough sketch illustrating the most likely outcomes you have predicted.

Results

Resist the temptation to skip the Results section. Sometimes you will interpret the results differently from the authors; thus, you should not rely solely on the Discussion's summary of the results. Read carefully whatever details are provided (such as the analyses used and any descriptive statistics reported), and examine all figures with attention to what is plotted on each axis. Compare the results with your predictions. If they are the same, go on to questions 7a–c. If not, answer question 6 before continuing on to the remaining questions.

6. *Did the author get unexpected results?* After some thought, you will reach one of two conclusions: Either your prediction was wrong, or the results are hard to believe. Perhaps the method the author selected was inappropriate and did not adequately test the stated hypotheses or introduced sources of uncontrolled variance, or perhaps these results would not be obtained again if the experiment were repeated. You might even try your own experiment. See if you can replicate the reported results.

7a. *How would I interpret these results?*

7b. *What applications and implications would I draw from my interpretation of the results?* Try to answer this question and question 7a on your own, before reading the discussion.

7c. *Can I think of another explanation for these results?* Even when the data are as predicted, there may be more than one reason why the results occurred as they did. You will often encounter multiexperiment papers in which the authors follow up their first experiment by doing additional experiments to eliminate alternate explanations. You might want to try thinking of a new experiment to test an alternative hypothesis.

Discussion

As mentioned earlier, the Discussion section includes the author's interpretation of the data in the form of conclusions. A good Discussion section brings the reader full circle in that it provides a narrative response to the question posed in the introduction. In addition, authors expand on their conclusions by offering insight regarding the applications and implications of the experimental results.

As a critical reader, you have constructed your own interpretation of the results. Compare the merits of your interpretation with the merits of the author's. Which one do you prefer? Answer questions 8a and 8b to help you critically assess both your own and the author's interpretation of the results. Answer questions 8c and 8d to help you think critically about possible future directions.

8a. *Does my interpretation or the author's best represent the data?* Because authors are allowed more latitude in the Discussion section than in other sections of a report, it is possible to find that an author has drawn conclusions that may not be warranted by the data. In other cases, authors draw conclusions that are largely appropriate and then proceed to extend these conclusions beyond what the data can support. The latter situation typically occurs when a researcher fails to recognize the limitations of the dependent variable.

8b. *Do I or does the author offer the most cogent discussion of the applications and implications of the results?* This question is secondary to the question posed in 8a. Nonetheless, you can gain valuable insight regarding the overall integrity of the research by considering this question. A researcher's responsibilities extend beyond that of conducting a tightly controlled experiment; he or she must also consider the rationale and theory that underlie the research. The extent to which an author demonstrates wisdom in identifying applications and implications of the results provides a good indication of the overall integrity of the research.

8c. *What questions are left unanswered?* No study ever answers all questions. It may be that you are left with general questions about the literature, or perhaps you were puzzled by some specific data point ignored by the authors.

8d. *What additional studies might I do?* It may be that you feel the author has not ruled out all possible explanations for the results, or you want to answer one of the questions you posed in 8c. You are back to question 3: If I had to design an experiment to test this hypothesis, what would I do? The research process never ends.

Checklist Summary

As you are reading your first article carefully, try to write down the answers to all eight questions. It is hard work the first several times, so do not be discouraged. The following is a typical psychological article. It has been analyzed according to the checklist summarized in Table 3–3.

Table 3–3 Questions for critical readers

Introduction

1. What is the author's goal?
2. What hypothesis will be tested in the experiment?
3. If I had to design an experiment to test this hypothesis, what would I do?

Method

4a. Is my proposed method better than the author's?
4b. Does the author's method actually test the hypothesis?
4c. What are the independent, dependent, and control variables?
5. Using the participants, apparatus, materials, and procedures described by the author, what results would I predict for this experiment?

Results

6. Did the author get unexpected results?
7a. How would I interpret these results?
7b. What applications and implications would I draw from my interpretation of the results?
7c. Can I think of another explanation for the results?

Discussion

8a. Does my interpretation or the author's best represent the data?
8b. Do I or does the author offer the most cogent discussion of the applications and implications of the results?
8c. What questions are left unanswered?
8d. What additional studies might I do?

▶ A Sample Journal Article

In this section, we have reprinted a short article from *Psychological Science* with sample answers to the checklist questions. The article is about the **Mozart effect,** the finding of improved spatial-temporal abilities after listening to classical music by Mozart.

Most articles are written for experts in a particular area, so the authors of a report assume that their readers have some knowledge of the topic under investigation. In addition, most journals set page limitations on articles, which means that some information may be missing or presented very tersely. The assumptions made by the authors and the brevity of many articles pose a problem for the novice reader. The novice may have to read other articles or textbooks to understand a particular report. To help you understand the following report, we present some background information.

The publication of a report on the so-called Mozart effect (Rauscher, Shaw, & Ky, 1993, 1995) attracted much publicity, even to the point of the governor of Georgia earmarking money for Mozart CDs in the budget. Hence, failures to replicate this effect are particularly disturbing. One factor may be the particular spatial-temporal task used as the dependent measure. To

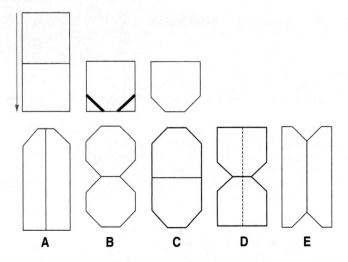

Figure 3—4   Practice Stanford-Binet paper folding and cutting item, from Steele, Bass, and Crook (From Steele, Bass, and Crook, "The Mystery of the Mozart Effect" in *Psychological Science, 10,* 367, figure 1. Copyright © 1999 Blackwell Publishing. Reprinted with permission.) Subjects see a hypothetical piece of paper undergoing a series of folds and cuts and then have to predict what the paper will look like when it is unfolded. For this example, the correct answer is C. In the Nantais and Schellenberg (1999) paper, the dependent measure is the number correct out of 34 of these items.

maximize the likelihood of replicating the effect, Nantais and Schellenberg (1999) used the exact same task as in the original paper. A sample task is shown in Figure 3—4. Subjects see a hypothetical piece of paper undergoing a series of folds and cuts and then have to predict what the paper will look like when it is unfolded.

The research question is whether performance on this spatial task will improve after listening to music composed by Mozart. Nantais and Schellenberg (1999) attempted to replicate this finding and then examined whether it generalized to other types of classical music and other complex tasks. Their report is brief. Now that you have some background information, you are ready to approach this article as a critical reader. To help you, we have placed checklist items at various strategic locations.

▼ ▼ ▼

The Mozart Effect: An Artifact of Preference

Kristin M. Nantais[1] and E. Glenn Schellenberg[2]
[1]University of Windsor, Windsor, Canada, and
[2]University of Toronto, Mississauga, Canada
(From Nantais & Schellenberg, "The Mystery of the Mozart Effect"
in Psychological Science, 10, *370–373. Copyright © 1999 Blackwell*
Publishing. Reprinted with permission.)

Abstract—*The "Mozart effect" reported by Rauscher, Shaw, and Ky (1993, 1995) indicates that spatial-temporal abilities are enhanced after listening to music composed by Mozart. We replicated and extended the effect in Experiment 1: Performance on a spatial-temporal task was better after participants listened to a piece composed by Mozart or by Schubert than after they sat in silence. In Experiment 2, the advantage for the music condition disappeared when the control condition consisted of a narrated story instead of silence. Rather, performance was a function of listeners' preference (music or story), with better performance following the preferred condition.*

Claims that exposure to music composed by Mozart improves spatial-temporal abilities (Rauscher, Shaw, & Ky, 1993, 1995) have received widespread attention in the news media. Based on these findings, Georgia governor Zell Miller recently budgeted for a compact disc or cassette for each infant born in the state. Reports published in *Science* (Holden, 1994), the *APA Monitor* (Martin, 1994), and the popular press indicate that scientists and the general public are giving serious consideration to the possibility that music listening and music lessons improve other abilities. If these types of associations can be confirmed, the implications would be considerable. For example, listening to music could improve the performance of pilots and structural engineers. Such associations would also provide evidence against contemporary theories of modularity (Fodor, 1983) and multiple intelligences (Gardner, 1993), which argue for independence of functioning across domains.

Although facilitation in spatial-temporal performance following exposure to music (Rauscher et al., 1993, 1995) is temporary (10 to 15 min), long-term improvements in spatial-temporal reasoning as a consequence of music lessons have also been reported (Gardiner, Fox, Knowles, & Jeffrey, 1996; Rauscher et al., 1997). Unfortunately, the media have not been careful to distinguish these disparate findings. The purpose of the present study was to provide a more complete explanation of the short-term phenomenon. Rauscher and her colleagues have proposed that the so-called Mozart effect can be explained by the *trion model* (Leng & Shaw, 1991), which posits that exposure to complex musical compositions excites cortical firing patterns similar to those used in spatial-temporal reasoning, so that performance on spatial-temporal tasks is positively affected by exposure to music.

On the surface, the Mozart effect is similar to robust psychological phenomena such as transfer or priming. For example, the effect could be considered an instance of positive, nonspecific transfer across domains and modalities (i.e., music listening and visual-spatial performance) that do not have a well-documented association. Transfer is said to occur when knowledge or skill acquired in one situation influences performance in another (Postman, 1971). In the case of the Mozart effect, however, passive listening to music—rather than overt learning—influences spatial-temporal performance. The Mozart effect also bears similarities to associative priming effects and spreading activation (Collins & Loftus, 1975). But priming effects tend to disappear when the prime and the target have few features in common (Klimesch, 1994, pp. 163–165), and crossmodal priming effects are typically weak (Roediger & McDermott, 1993). Moreover, it is far from obvious which features are shared by stimuli as diverse as a Mozart sonata and a spatial-temporal task.

In short, the Mozart effect described by Rauscher et al. (1993, 1995) is difficult to situate in a context of known cognitive phenomena. Stough, Kerkin, Bates, and Mangan (1994) failed to replicate the findings of Rauscher et al., although their use of Raven's Advanced Progressive Matrices rather than spatial tasks from the Stanford-Binet Intelligence Scale (Rauscher et al., 1993, 1995) to assess spatial abilities may account for the discrepancies. Whereas tasks measuring spatial recognition (such as the Raven's test) require a search for physical similarities among visually presented stimuli, spatial-temporal tasks (e.g., the Paper Folding and Cutting, PF&C, subtest of the Stanford-Binet; mental rotation tasks; jigsaw puzzles) require mental transformation of the stimuli (Rauscher & Shaw, 1998). In their review of previous successes and failures at replicating the Mozart effect, Rauscher and Shaw (1998) concluded that the effect is obtainable only with spatial-temporal tasks.

Our goal in Experiment 1 was to replicate and extend the basic findings of Rauscher et al. (1993, 1995). A completely computer-controlled procedure was used to test adults' performance on a PF&C task immediately after they listened to music or sat in silence. Half of the participants listened to Mozart during the music condition; the other half listened to Schubert. The purpose of Experiment 2 was to test the hypothesis that the Mozart effect is actually a consequence of participants' preference for one testing condition over another, the assumption being that better performance would follow the preferred condition. Control conditions in Rauscher et al. (1993) included a period of silence or listening to a relaxation tape, both of which might have been less interesting or arousing than listening to a Mozart sonata. Consequently, if the participants in that study preferred the Mozart condition, this factor might account for the differential performance on the spatial-temporal task that followed. In a subsequent experiment (Rauscher et al., 1995), comparison conditions involved silence or a combination of minimalist music (Philip Glass), a taped short story, and repetitive dance music. Minimalist and repetitive music might also induce boredom or low levels of arousal, much like silence, and the design precluded direct comparison of the short story and music conditions. Indeed, in all other instances in which the Mozart effect has been successfully replicated (see Rauscher & Shaw, 1998), control conditions consisted of sitting in silence or listening to relaxation tapes or repetitive music. In Experiment 2, our control condition involved simply listening to a short story.

Address correspondence to E. Glenn Schellenberg, Department of Psychology, University of Toronto at Mississauga, Mississauga, Ontario, Canada L5L IC6. E-mail: g.schellenberg@utoronto.ca

▲ ▲ ▲

Question 1. What are the authors' goals? The authors propose to replicate earlier studies (Rauscher et al., 1993, 1995) indicating that performance on spatial-temporal tasks improved after listening to pieces by Mozart. This goal is important given that others have failed to replicate the Mozart effect (for example, Steele, Bass, & Crook, 1999). In Experiment 1, the authors wanted to see whether the boost in performance was specific to music by Mozart or whether *any* classical music would similarly improve performance. In Experiment 2, the authors tested a possible alternate explanation for the Mozart effect—namely, that performance improves after participants do something that they enjoy.

Question 2. What hypotheses will be tested? The hypotheses are listed as questions to be answered before one can accept the validity of the Mozart effect: (1) Does performance on spatial-temporal tasks improve after listening to music by Mozart? (2) If so, does the effect occur following only Mozart's music? (3) Is the so-called Mozart effect simply the result of people having just done something that they enjoyed?

Question 3. How would I test these hypotheses? To show a Mozart effect, you would need to demonstrate that people's performance on spatial-temporal tasks was better if they had just listened to Mozart than if they had done some other task. Because some people have had difficulty replicating the Mozart effect, it would be best to use the same control task as used in the experiments by Rauscher et al.—namely, silence. You would then need additional groups of participants to test Hypotheses 2 and 3. To test Hypothesis 2, you would see whether a second group showed better performance on the spatial-temporal tasks if they had just listened to music by another classical composer than if they had simply sat in silence. You might think carefully about which composer's piece to choose for this second condition; you could imagine that you would be more likely to obtain the so-called Mozart effect in this condition if you chose a composer similar to Mozart (for example, from the same time period). Finally, to test Hypothesis 3, you would need another group whose performance on the spatial-temporal tasks would be examined following listening to Mozart and following completion of another enjoyable task. Sitting in silence for 10 minutes is not very enjoyable; instead, you could have subjects listen to a comedy monologue or a taped National Public Radio broadcast. If the subjects show no more improvement following Mozart than following the other entertaining soundtrack, you know that the effect has nothing to do with music per se. To buttress your argument that subjects' enjoyment of the intervening task was critical, you could ask subjects at the end of each task to rate how enjoyable it was and then look for a relationship between task enjoyment and ability to solve spatial-temporal problems.

▼ ▼ ▼

Method

Participants

We recruited 84 undergraduates: 56 for Experiment 1 and 28 for Experiment 2.

Apparatus and Stimuli

The first 10 min of Mozart's (1985, tracks 1–2) Sonata for Two Pianos in D Major, K. 448 (as in Rauscher et al., 1993, 1995) and the first 10 min of Schubert's (1985, track 4) Fantasia for Piano, Four Hands, in F Minor (D940) were digitally rerecorded from a compact disc onto a Power Macintosh computer using the SoundEdit 16 software program. Both pieces came from the same compact disc and were performed by the same two pianists. The sound quality was not adversely affected by the rerecording process (i.e., 16-bit sound files, sampling rate of 44.1 kHz). Stimulus presentation and response recording were controlled by a customized program created with PsyScope 1.1 software (Cohen, MacWhinney, Flatt, & Provost, 1993) installed on the computer. During testing, listeners received a stereo signal over lightweight headphones (Sony CD550) in a sound-attenuating booth (Eckel Industries).

The control condition in Experiment 1 consisted of sitting in silence for 10 min. In the control condition of Experiment 2, participants listened to 10 min of the short story "The Last Rung on the Ladder" (King, 1994), which was also rerecorded from audiocassette onto the hard disk of the computer. A short story was selected as an auditory stimulus that would be engaging without being overly arousing, much like music composed by Mozart.

Participants used a mouse connected to the computer to initiate a 10-min listening period and to record their responses on the subsequent PF&C task, which included 34 items (20 from the Stanford-Binet Intelligence Scale, 14 created for the experiment) that were scanned into the computer. Each item had an upper panel that showed a rectangular piece of paper and a series of folding and cutting manipulations, plus a lower panel with five possible outcomes. The relative difficulty of the items was determined in a pilot study in which 20 university students completed the entire set of items presented in random order. Following the pilot study, two 17-item subsets of equal difficulty were formed.

Design and Procedure

Each student participated in two conditions (music and control) on separate days within a maximum of 2 weeks. In both conditions, the task was administered after a 10-min listening period. In the music condition, participants listened to the Mozart or Schubert piece. Immediately afterward, each of 17 PF&C items was displayed on the computer monitor for a maximum of 1 min, and participants selected one of the five unfolded displays as the appropriate outcome. The 17 items were ordered from least difficult to most difficult. No feedback was provided. Sessions took approximately 25 min to complete.

In Experiment 1, half of the 56 participants listened to the Mozart piece in the music condition; the other half listened to Schubert. In Experiment 2, all 28 participants listened to Mozart in the music condition. Control conditions were identical to the music conditions except that during the listening period, participants sat in silence wearing headphones (Experiment 1) or listened to a short story (Experiment 2). For each participant, different subsets of 17 task items were used for the two testing conditions. Order of conditions was counterbalanced with order of subsets. After the second test session, participants in Experiment 2 were asked which condition (music or story) they thought was more interesting and which condition they preferred.[1]

[1]We did not pose the same questions to participants in Experiment 1 because we assumed that the vast majority would prefer listening to music over sitting in silence.

▲   ▲   ▲

Question 4a. Is my proposed method better than the authors'? Our methods are essentially the same, except that we suggested listening to a comedy monologue as the entertaining nonmusic control, whereas the authors used a recording of a short story. The authors also split the three groups over two experiments; an argument could be made that it would be cleaner to run all the subjects in the same experiment and thus avoid cross-experiment comparisons.

Question 4b. Does the authors' method actually test the hypotheses? Yes, we believe the method is appropriate. As indicated already, we would have preferred to avoid cross-experiment comparisons. Also, you should think about other ways to operationalize the preference factor. As the experiment was done, preference was determined by self-report, and subjects were assigned to conditions post-hoc based on their ratings. It would have been preferable to experimentally manipulate preference rather than having condition assignment depend on subjects' self-reported preferences.

Question 4c. What are the variables (independent, participant, dependent, control)? Independent variable: type of intervening task (in Experiment 1, Mozart, Schubert, silence; in Experiment 2, Mozart, story) and subject-reported preference. Participant variables: none. Dependent variable: number of items correct on the spatial-temporal test. Control variables: order of two tasks (counterbalanced across subjects).

Question 5. What do we predict? On the basis of Rauscher et al. (1993, 1995), we can predict that performance on the spatial-temporal test will be higher after listening to Mozart than after sitting in silence. In addition, we might predict that a similar effect will occur after listening to Schubert, because Mozart and Schubert are both classical composers. A more difficult prediction to make is that regarding the effects of listening to the short story. We find the authors' arguments compelling—namely, that any stimulating task may lead to an increase in performance.

▼ ▼ ▼

Results

Experiment 1

Means and standard deviations for the music and control conditions in Experiment 1 are provided in Table 1. A mixed-design analysis of variance (ANOVA) was used to examine performance as a function of condition (music or silence), musical piece (Mozart or Schubert), and testing order (first or second). A main effect of condition revealed that scores on the spatial-temporal task were higher after listening to music than after sitting in silence, $F(1, 52) = 15.16$, $p < .001$. Differences between conditions accounted for 20% of the within-subjects variance. A main effect of testing order (accounting for 8% of the within-subjects variance) indicated that performance improved from the first to the second session, $F(1, 52) = 6.20$, $p = .016$. None of the other main effects or interactions was significant.

Table 1   Mean number of items correct in Experiments 1 and 2

Experiment	N	Condition			
		Music		**Control**	
1	28	Mozart	12.75 (3.38)	Silence	11.89 (3.59)
	28	Schubert	12.36 (4.05)	Silence	11.04 (4.61)
2	28	Mozart	13.00 (3.80)	Story	12.93 (2.91)

NOTE: Standard deviations are given in parentheses.

In short, the Mozart effect reported by Rauscher et al. (1993, 1995) was successfully replicated in a completely controlled laboratory setting. More important, when a piece by Schubert was substituted for the Mozart piece used by Rauscher and her colleagues, an effect of equivalent magnitude was evident.

Experiment 2

Means and standard deviations for the music (Mozart) and control (story) conditions in Experiment 2 are provided in Table 1. An ANOVA that examined effects of condition (music or story) and testing order revealed a reliable order effect; performance improved from the first to the second testing session, $F(1, 26) = 4.31$, $p = .048$, and testing order accounted for 14% of the within-subjects variance. The main effect of condition was not significant (explaining less than 0.1% of the within-subjects variance) and did not interact with testing order. In other words, the Mozart effect disappeared when the control condition consisted of a story rather than silence.

The next set of analyses tested our hypothesis that performance would be a function of listeners' preference for the Mozart piece or the short story. Each participant considered his or her "preferred" condition to be more "interesting" as well, so participants' responses were treated simply as a preference factor (13 preferred Mozart, 15 preferred the story). Mean levels of performance as a function of listeners' preference are provided in Table 2. As predicted, overall levels of performance were better in participants' preferred condition ($M = 13.57, SD = 3.07$) than in their nonpreferred condition ($M = 12.36, SD = 3.56$), $t(27) = 2.94, p <$ .001 (one-tailed). An ANOVA with three factors (condition, testing order, and preference) confirmed that preference interacted with condition, $F(1, 24) = 5.02, p =$ .035. Whereas participants who preferred the Mozart excerpt scored significantly higher in the Mozart than in the story condition, $t(12) = 3.77, p < .001$, participants who preferred the story exhibited marginally better performance in the story than in the Mozart condition, $t(14) = 1.49, p = .079$ (one-tailed tests). Listeners' preferences accounted uniquely for 15% of the within-subjects variance. Participants who preferred the Mozart piece also scored marginally higher than other participants across conditions, $F(1, 24) = 3.09, p = .092$.

▲ ▲ ▲

Question 6. Did the authors get unexpected results? From our perspective, the results are not unexpected. From the perspective of Rauscher and associates and of other proponents of the trion model, the results from the story condition would be surprising. We did find one result surprising, albeit not the focus of the paper. We were intrigued by a main effect of *what* participants preferred on spatial-temporal reasoning; performance was overall better for people who preferred listening to Mozart to the story. Why do you think this would be?

Question 7a. How would we interpret the results? First, we would grant that the Mozart effect is replicable, at least when care is taken to use the exact procedures of Rauscher and colleagues. Second, we would argue that the Mozart effect is not specific to Mozart—and is not even specific to music. We would also note that the current experimental design does not allow conclu-

Table 2 Mean number of items correct in Experiment 2 as a function of listeners' preference

Preference	*n*	Condition	
		Mozart	**Story**
Mozart	13	14.62 (2.40)	13.23 (2.35)
Story	15	11.60 (4.29)	12.67 (3.37)

NOTE: Standard deviations are given in parentheses.

sions about the locus of the effect: Does listening to Mozart *help* performance, or does sitting in silence *hinder* performance? What experimental conditions would be needed to tease these two possibilities apart? Finally, even if it turned out that engaging in complex tasks helped performance, we still wouldn't feel like we were sure why this occurred or when to predict it. Would any complex task yield the same benefit, or would it have to be auditory? And what role does the preference variable play? How does this relate to mood? Would silence yield better performance than a detested task?

Question 7b. What applications and implications would we draw from our interpretation of the results? We would recommend that the governor of Georgia rethink the expenditure of state money on Mozart music for infants. We would have recommended that regardless of this new data, given that the Mozart effect is short term. However, the new data further suggest that (a) there is nothing special about Mozart over other composers, and (b) *any* stimulating task might have the same effect.

Question 7c. Can I think of any other explanations for the results? Yes. While the authors have nicely shown that the Mozart effect replicates, and that it also occurs with one other composer (Schubert) and one other complex task (listening to a story), we do not feel that the whole story has been told. As described in question 7a, we can think of numerous questions still to be asked. In our opinion, a major issue is whether the entertaining task *helps* performance or the silence *hinders* performance. We think it is a distinct possibility that subjects' performance in the silence condition would be impaired after the boredom of 10 min of silence. This remains to be tested experimentally.

▼ ▼ ▼

Discussion

The present study examined the effects of exposure to music on a subsequently presented spatial-temporal task. In Experiment 1, performance was better after participants listened to music composed by Mozart or Schubert than after they sat in silence. Although both pieces of music are relatively "easy listening" examples from the common-practice period, our finding makes it clear that the Mozart effect has nothing to do with Mozart in particular. Moreover, it seems likely that the effect would generalize to a wide variety of enjoyable pieces of music composed in the Classical (i.e., late 1700s; for example, Mozart, Haydn) or Romantic (i.e., early 1800s; for example, Schubert, Liszt) styles.

Indeed, this finding implies that a similar effect might be evident when any positive stimulus (musical or otherwise) is paired with a less engaging stimulus. We examined this possibility in Experiment 2 by substituting listening to a story for the silence (control) condition. Although performance in the Mozart and story conditions did not differ, listeners performed better following the condition they preferred. Thus, the spatial-temporal advantage reported by Rauscher et al. (1993, 1995) does not appear to be a consequence of listening to music per se. Rather, our results raise two possibilities. First, performance on spatial-temporal tasks may be enhanced after passive listening to a pleasant or interesting auditory stimulus. Second, decrements on such tasks may be the consequence of exposure to 10 min of a stimulus deemed to be relatively boring or unpleasant. Regardless, all previous findings of the Mozart effect (see Rauscher & Shaw, 1998)—in which a piece by Mozart has been paired with silence, a relaxation tape, or repetitious music—can be explained similarly.

Participants' preferences for one condition over another could have been accompanied by between-condition differences in mood or level of arousal. Although our lack of a direct measure of mood or arousal means that this proposal is speculative at the present time, it allows the seemingly enigmatic Mozart effect to be explained by well-known psychological phenomena. Emotional states consist of qualitative, cognitive aspects dependent on the context as well as quantifiable, physical aspects (Schachter, 1964), with mood associated with the former and arousal with the latter. In Experiment 1, positive mood states or elevated levels of arousal created by the music could have facilitated performance on the spatial-temporal task (Isen, Daubmann, & Nowicki, 1987).

Alternatively, negative moods or decreased levels of arousal caused by sitting in silence for 10 min may have had a detrimental effect (O'Hanlon, 1981), or both of these factors may have been operative. For example, many adults report using music as an agent of emotional change (Sloboda, 1992). In the laboratory, "happy" music induces happiness, whereas "sad" music produces sadness (Parrott & Sabini, 1990). Exposure to "elated" music tends to increase heart rate and systolic blood pressure; "depressing" music has the opposite effect (Pignatiello, Camp, Elder, & Rasar, 1989). Exposure to "happy" music also results in faster speed and greater persistence on various tasks (Kavanagh, 1987). Conversely, states of boredom and low levels of arousal are associated with poor performance on a variety of perceptual, cognitive, and motor tasks (O'Hanlon, 1981). Negative emotions may decrease the efficiency of information processing relative to positive affective states (Wyer & Srull, 1989), causing decrements in learning and performance (Boyle, 1983). Future research could test our speculation that participants' preferences are accompanied by changes in mood or arousal.

In sum, although listening to music composed by Mozart might contribute to improved performance on a subsequently presented spatial-temporal task, our results provide no evidence that the improvement differs from that observed with other engaging auditory stimuli that are equally pleasing to participants.

Acknowledgments—Funding for this research was provided by a grant awarded to the second author from the Natural Sciences and Engineering Research Council of Canada.

References

Boyle, G. J. (1983). Effects on academic learning of manipulating emotional states and motivational dynamics. *British Journal of Educational Psychology, 53,* 347–357.

Cohen, J. D., MacWhinney, B., Flatt, M., & Provost, J. (1993). PsyScope: A new graphic interactive environment for designing psychology experiments. *Behavior Research Methods, Instruments, & Computers, 25,* 257–271.

Collins, A. M., & Loftus, E. F. (1975). A spreading–activation theory of semantic processing. *Psychological Review, 82,* 407–428.

Fodor, J. A. (1983). *The modularity of mind.* Cambridge, MA: Bradford.

Gardiner, M. F., Fox, A., Knowles, F., & Jeffrey, D. (1996). Learning improved by arts training. *Nature, 381,* 284.

Gardner, H. (1993). *Multiple intelligences: The theory in practice.* New York: Basic Books.

Holden, C. (1994). Smart music. *Science, 266,* 968–969.

Isen, A. M., Daubmann, K. A., & Nowicki, G. P. (1987). Positive affect facilitates creative problem solving. *Journal of Personality and Social Psychology, 52,* 1122–1131.

Kavanagh, D. J. (1987). Mood, persistence, and success. *Australian Journal of Psychology, 39,* 307–318.

King, S. (1994). The last rung on the ladder (narrated by J. Glover). In *Graveyard Shift and other stories from Night Shift* [cassette]. New York: BDD Audio Publishing.

Klimesch, W. (1994). *The structure of long-term memory: A connectivity model of semantic processing.* Hillsdale, NJ: Erlbaum.

Leng, X., & Shaw, G. L. (1991). Toward a neural theory of higher brain function using music as a window. *Concepts in Neuroscience, 2,* 229–258.

Martin, S. (1994, October). Music lessons enhance spatial reasoning skills. *APA Monitor,* p. 5.

Mozart, W. A. (1985). Sonata for two pianos in D major, K. 448 (K. 375a) [Recorded by M. Perahia & R. Lupu]. On *Music for piano, four hands* [CD]. London: Sony Classical. (1992).

O'Hanlon, J. F. (1981). Boredom: Practical consequences and a theory. *Acta Psychologica, 49,* 53–82.

Parrott, W. G., & Sabini, J. (1990). Mood and memory under natural conditions: Evidence for mood incongruent recall. *Journal of Personality and Social Psychology, 59,* 321–336.

Pignatiello, M., Camp, C. J., Elder, S. T., & Rasar, L. A. (1989). A psychophysiological comparison of the Velten and musical mood induction techniques. *Journal of Music Therapy, 26,* 140–154.

Postman, L. (1971). Transfer, interference and forgetting. In J. W. Kling & L. A. Riggs (Eds.), *Woodworth & Schlosberg's experimental psychology* (3rd ed., pp. 1019–1132). New York: Holt, Rinehart and Winston.

Rauscher, F. H., & Shaw, G. L. (1998). Key components of the Mozart effect. *Perceptual and Motor Skills, 86,* 835–841.

Rauscher, F. H., Shaw, G. L., & Ky, K. N. (1993). Music and spatial task performance. *Nature, 365,* 611.

Rauscher, F. H., Shaw, G. L., & Ky, K. N. (1995). Listening to Mozart enhances spatial-temporal reasoning: Towards a neurophysiological basis. *Neuroscience Letters, 185,* 44–47.

Rauscher, F. H., Shaw, G. L., Levine, L. J., Wright, E. L., Dennis, W. R., & Newcomb, R. L. (1997). Music training causes long-term enhancement of preschool children's spatial-temporal reasoning. *Neurological Research, 19,* 2–8.

Roediger, H. L., III, & McDermott, K. B. (1993). Implicit memory in normal human subjects. In F. Boller & J. Grafman (Eds.), *Handbook of neuropsychology* (Vol. 8, pp. 63–131). Amsterdam: Elsevier.

Schachter, S. (1964). The interaction of cognitive and physiological determinants of emotional state. *Advances in Experimental Social Psychology, 1,* 49–80.

Schubert, F. (1985). Fantasia for piano, four hands in F minor D940 (Recorded by M. Perahia & R. Lupu). On *Music for piano, four hands* [CD]. London: Sony Classical. (1992).

Sloboda, J. A. (1992). Empirical studies of emotional response to music. In M. R. Jones & S. Holleran (Eds.), *Cognitive bases of musical communication* (pp. 33–46). Washington, DC: American Psychological Association.

Stough, C., Kerkin, B., Bates, T., & Mangan, G. (1994). Music and spatial IQ. *Personality and Individual Differences, 17, 695.*

Wyer, R. S., Jr., & Srull, T. K. (1989). *Memory and cognition in its social context.* Hillsdale, NJ: Erlbaum.

▲   ▲   ▲

Question 8a. Does our interpretation or the authors' best represent the data? The authors also mention the possibility that sitting in silence would impair performance. The authors mention a number of possible explanations for their data, but their end conclusion is fine and does not overstate their findings (reread the last sentence of their paper).

Question 8b. Do we or do the authors offer the most cogent discussion of the applications and implications of the results? The authors have a fine discussion, with an interesting section on the effects of mood on performance on cognitive tasks. We are less shy than the authors about making a recommendation to the governor of Georgia.

Question 8c. What questions are left unanswered? There are a number of unanswered questions. First, how generalizable is the basic effect? Nantais and Schellenberg replicated the Mozart effect following the procedure of Rauscher and associates exactly, but others have failed with slight variations. How interesting is an effect if it is tied to very specific procedural details? Second, a number of questions are left open regarding when the effect will versus will not occur, and why the effect occurs at all; see our answers to question 7a.

Question 8d. What additional studies might I suggest? Music is often used to manipulate mood (see the examples in the ethics chapter of this book). Do you think you would still get a Mozart effect if you used "sad" music? If not, what would that suggest about the role of positive mood in the occurrence of the so-called Mozart effect?

Summary

1. Before embarking on a research project, it is wise to do a literature search to detect what other researchers have done that is related to your proposed experiment.

2. There are seven parts to psychological journal articles: title and author(s), abstract, introduction, Method, Results, Discussion, and references.

3. The abstract is a short (120 word) description of the article.

4. The introduction describes the rationale behind the experiment.

5. The Method section describes the participants, materials, design, and procedures used by the experimenter.

6. The Results section contains a summary of the data collected in the experiment.

7. Proper interpretation of tables and figures is crucial to understanding the results of experiments reported in journal articles. The vertical axis of a figure is called the ordinate, on which the dependent variable is scaled. The horizontal axis of a figure is called the abscissa; in experiments, the independent variable appears on the abscissa.

8. The Discussion section is the part of the article in which the author can state the implications of his or her findings.

9. The References section contains a list of all papers referenced in the article.

10. The critical reader is able to answer such questions as: What hypothesis does this experiment test? How might this experiment have been done differently? What results would I predict for this experiment? How would I interpret the author's results?

Key Concepts

abscissa (63)
abstract (60)
apparatus (61)
author (60)
computerized literature search (59)
discussion (67)
figures (63)

introduction (61)
materials (61)
method (61)
Mozart effect (71)
ordinate (63)
participants/subjects (61)
procedure (61)
PsycINFO (59)

Psychological Abstracts (57)
references (67)
results (61)
Social Science Citation Index (59)
tables (62)
title (60)

Exercise

1. Your book has come with a subscription to *InfoTrac*, which allows you 24-hour access to many journal articles. Visit http://www.infotrac-college.com, and type in the passcode that came with your book. Then type in subjects of interest and see what articles appear. For example, try searching for the Mozart effect to read research related to the paper presented in this chapter.

Suggested Resource

Hints on using the World Wide Web for doing a literature search, as well as other aspects of research, can be found in Koch, C. (1997). Learning the research process on the World Wide Web. *Council on Undergraduate Research Quarterly, 18,* 26–29, 48–49.

Web Resources

An interesting online journal, *Psycholoquy*, which is sponsored by the American Psychological Association, can be found at http://www.cogsci.soton.ac.uk/psycoloquy

Another interesting online journal, *Undergraduate Journal of Psychology*, can be found at http://www.psych.uncc.edu/Journal.htm

A Literature Search

Suppose you become interested in the effects of emotion on memory. You have heard that emotion can upset one's ability to pay attention to ongoing events, and so it might also interfere with one's ability to remember events. However, you have also heard (and you believe from your own experience) that emotional events can be very well remembered. How can emotion have both effects at once? What might be going on?

To obtain answers to these questions, you decide to do a search of the psychological literature. You go to your reference librarian, who informs you that a good place to start is *PsycINFO*. At your school, as in many others, *PsycINFO* is available on the World Wide Web, which is a handy way to access information available through the Internet. After helping you to log on to the system, the librarian suggests that you begin searching the database using the name of a prominent researcher who works on this topic. Because you are new to the area and you do not know the name of anyone who researches this topic, you ask for another way to get started. The librarian points out that you can just do a "key word search" and moves on to help another person. You look at the screen, and you see a box with the label "key word" next to it. You guess (correctly) that this must be where you enter the topic you want to search for, but what key word should you use?

You decide to try "memory," so you take your mouse, click in the box, type it in, and click the "Start Search" button. You get a list of article titles, but you also notice that the output indicates 93,248 "hits"! A bit too much to review before dinner, you decide wisely. You notice that there is an "And, Or, & Not" option next to another box. You reason that by clicking the "And" option and typing in the term "emotion" in the second box, you will limit the hits to those articles having to do with both memory *and* emotion. This time you get 2,143 records, which is still a bit much. You spot the "Limits on Search" option and decide to limit the search to articles that were published between 2003 and 2005 and were written in English. This time you get 240 records. Finally, you decide to change the search terms to memory *and* emotion *and* attention. This time you get only 50 articles, a reasonable place to start. You click on the titles that look interesting to you, read the abstracts, and decide to print out (or download) some of the more interesting references so that you can obtain the actual article from your library.

Now suppose you have found an article from several years back that contains a theory attempting to explain why emotion sometimes helps memory but also why it sometimes hurts it. You might like to know more about the implications of this theory and whether it has held up under experimental scrutiny. One way to find out about this would be to find more recent articles that have cited this article. To do this, you would use *Social Science Citation Index* (SSCI); like *Psychological Abstracts,* it exists in both printed and electronic form. The electronic form is generally preferable, because it is more efficient (check with your reference librarian to see if it is available in electronic form). The SSCI allows you to enter an article's reference and find out who has cited that article. That way, you can find out about the recent developments in that area.

Basic Research Methods

Chapter 4
Observations in Psychological Research

Chapter 5
Relational Research

Chapter 6
Basics of Experimentation

Chapter 7
Validity and Reliability in Psychological Research

Part II considers the basic research methods that allow the research to answer the questions of what, when, and why. Observation procedures are especially good at determining what behaviors have occurred. Relational procedures permit predictions of when particular behaviors will occur. Experimentation allows the researcher to determine what causes particular behaviors.

CHAPTER 4

Observations in Psychological Research

Descriptive Observations Include
- Naturalistic observation
- Case studies
- Surveys

Descriptive Observations
- Provide a database for controlled research
- Are often very flexible
- Examine the ecological function of behavior

Descriptive Observations May Suffer from
- Researcher bias
- Participant reactivity
- Internal invalidity

This chapter examines observations in psychology. Descriptive observations provide a valuable database and may lead to an understanding of the ecological function of a behavior.

Science is an intellectual enterprise that builds cumulatively. From a scientific perspective, we know more about the world today than people have known at any other time in history. On the other hand, literature, art, and most other humanities may be different today than they were in ancient Greece, but we probably cannot say that these disciplines are in better shape or more accurately represent the world.

One primary reason that science cumulates is that scientists strive for the most accurate observation possible of the world. As we have stated, science is self-correcting in that scientists develop theories and hypotheses that allow prediction about what should happen under specified conditions. These ideas are then tested by comparing the predictions with carefully collected observations. When the observations differ drastically from predictions, scientists modify or abandon their theoretical conceptions. Much of the scientific enterprise concerns empirical observation: the collection of data on some particular aspect of the world.

Observers are fallible. Seeing should not be believing—at least not always. Often our perceptions fool us, as we can see by the way we perceive the optical illusions in Figure 4–1. We have all seen magicians perform seemingly impossible feats before our eyes, when we knew that we were being tricked by natural means. Such tricks demonstrate that direct perceptions can be inaccurate if we are not careful—and, sometimes, even if we are.

Scientists, being human, are also subject to errors of observation. Essentially, the research techniques employed by scientists—including logic, use of complicated apparatus, controlled conditions, and so on—are there to guard against errors of perception and to ensure that observations reflect the state of nature as accurately as possible. Even with our best methods and most careful techniques of observation, however, we can only approximate this ideal.

▶ Descriptive Observation Methods

The most obvious ways of making observations in psychology have description of behavior as their major purpose. **Descriptive observations** enumerate what behaviors occur and in what quantity and frequency.

In this chapter, we discuss four descriptive methods of gathering psychological data. One such method is **naturalistic observation,** which is the most obvious and, perhaps, the most venerable way of gathering data. Many people, such as bird-watchers, are amateur naturalists, but scientific naturalists, as we will see, are more systematic in their observations. For example, recent work has shown that male blue-throated hummingbirds have songs that consist of notes organized into five song units; males in a particular area tend to sing the same song units (Ficken, Rusch, Taylor, & Powers, 2000).

An additional classic way of obtaining descriptive information is the **case study.** Usually, a case study involves the detailed examination of one individual, but it also may involve a comparison of a small number of individuals. Case

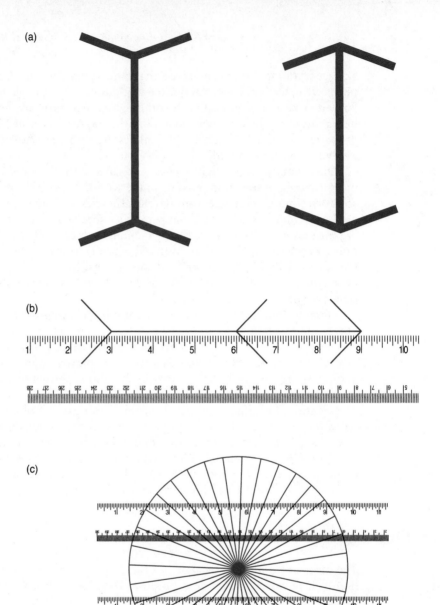

Figure 4—1 Visual illusions. (a) The Müller-Lyer illusion. The vertical lines are the same length but appear unequal due to the different directions of the fins in the two cases. (b) The illusion apparently distorts even an objective measuring device, the ruler, but close examination indicates that the ruler is not really distorted and that the lines are of equal length. These illusions are maintained although we "know," as in (b), that they cannot be so. (c) Our observations can suffer distortions no matter how careful we are. (Examples taken from Gregory, 1970, pp. 80–81.)

studies are especially effective when the topic of interest is either rare or idio-syncratic. One recent case revealed that when K. R., a 30-year-old mother of four, came to therapy, she had various counting rituals that severely hampered daily activities (Oltmanns, Neale, & Davison, 1999). During grocery shopping, for example, K. R. believed that if she selected one of the initial four items on a shelf, then one of her children would suffer dire consequences. She believed that selecting the second box of cereal would result in a disaster happening to her second child, selecting the third box would hurt her third child, and so on.

Similar to the case study is the **survey,** in which detailed information is gathered from a number of individuals. In a survey of drinking habits, Sim-mons (2000) found that beer is the alcoholic beverage that 43% of drinkers say they consume most often. There are strong age differences in alcohol pref-erence. Simmons reported that 50% of 18- to 29-year-olds claimed to drink mostly beer. On the other hand, Simmons reported that 46% of those older than 50 years said they drank wine most often, and only 27% said they regu-larly drank beer.

Another survey attempted to determine the sorts of memory problems suf-fered by elderly Americans (Lovelace & Twohig, 1990). Healthy, older adults with an average age of 68 years claimed that the most vexing memory prob-lem they had was an inability to remember someone's name. However, most of these respondents reported that memory difficulties had little effect on how well they could engage in daily activities. The Psychology in Action section at the end of this chapter considers how repeated surveys over extensive periods of time have been used to see what people remember about important public events, such as the terrorist attacks on the United States on September 11, 2001 (Talarico & Rubin, 2003).

Descriptive research plays an important role in psychology. These proce-dures provide a major part of the database that can lead to subsequent, more highly controlled research (Miller, 1977). Description of behavior is a neces-sary first step in understanding. A familiar example is Harlow's (Blum, 2002; Harlow, 1959) work on attachment and affection in infant monkeys. Before doing his experiments, Harlow needed to know what behaviors baby monkeys exhibited; he also needed to know some of the things they seemed to like (their soft blankets) and dislike (the wire floor of the cage). With this background in-formation, Harlow could attempt to explain the behavior via experimentation. Thus, we should not view description as somehow secondary or subordinate to experimentation because it lacks control. In the sense just mentioned, de-scription precedes experimentation. Now we examine the descriptive proce-dures in more detail.

Naturalistic Observations

One problem facing a person wishing to make naturalistic observations is de-termining what behaviors to observe. Human observers have a finite capacity to perceive and think about events. Although most of us can walk and chew gum at the same time, most of us cannot attend to and remember 20 different behaviors occurring over short periods of time. Thus, we must set a boundary on the range of behaviors that we plan to observe.

How do we delimit the range of behaviors to be studied? Part of the answer seems straightforward. If we are interested in human nonverbal communication, we observe it. However, this is not necessarily easy to do. In the first place, nonverbal communication is highly complex, which means that observers are faced with the same problem we started out trying to avoid. In the second place, examining nonverbal behavior presupposes that we already know some of the behaviors to describe. Obviously, we do not enter a research project devoid of all knowledge, which is especially the case when we are trying to test certain hypotheses. On the other hand, we do not begin description with all the answers. What usually happens is that we begin a series of studies in which successive projects rely on previous data to refine and delimit the field of inquiry. Let us consider some examples to illustrate how naturalistic observations are conducted.

Ethology Naturalistic research of interest to psychologists is perhaps most prevalent in the area of **ethology,** the study of naturally occurring behavior (often in the wild). Simply observing the behavior of animals or humans allows one to gain a global impression of the characteristics and range of behavior. However, one may soon desire more systematic observation. One way ethologists make more systematic observations is by identifying different categories of experience for the organism under study and then recording the number of times the organism engages in each behavior. These behaviors can be divided into large units, such as mating, grooming, sleeping, fighting, eating, and so on, or into much smaller units. For example, an **ethogram** of the various behaviors involved in the courtship pattern of a fish, the orange chromide, is shown in Figure 4–2. An ethogram is a relatively complete inventory of the specific behaviors performed by one species of animal. By counting the number of times that any specific behavior occurs, ethologists can begin to get some idea of the significance of the behavior.

A complete ethogram may be the ideal to attain but is unlikely in practice. Identifying and classifying all the behaviors associated with chromide courtship would be cumbersome if the observer did not have particular hypotheses in mind. Timberlake and Silva (1994) argued that observation categories should be designed to answer specific questions rather than to describe and classify behavior completely. They suggested further that observation categories should be unambiguous, so that the observer can easily judge that the behavior in question has occurred. If an observer is attempting a courtship ethogram, then he or she likely must consider several aspects of the organisms' behavioral repertoire. Assigning behaviors to categories should be set up so that it can be done quickly and without much chance for error.

If two observers consistently categorized behavior in the same way, then the behavior categories probably are clear and unambiguous. Often, two or more observers categorize the behavior of the same organism, and then their

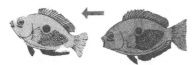

a. *Charging:* An accelerated swim of one fish toward another.

d. *Nipping:* An O-shaped mouth action that cleans out the (presumptive) spawning site.

b. *Tail Beating:* An emphatic beating of the tail toward another fish.

c. *Quivering:* A rapid, lateral, shivering movement that starts at the head and dies out as it passes posteriorly through the body.

e. *Skimming:* The actual spawning movement whereby the fish places its ventral surface against the spawning site and meanders along it for a few seconds.

Figure 4–2 Ethogram showing courtship pattern in orange chromide. An ethogram can be compiled for all behaviors of a species, or for only selected aspects of behavior. (From Drickamer, L. C., & Vesey, S. H. (1982). *Animal behavior: Concepts, processes, and methods* [p. 28]. Boston: Willard Grant Press.)

results are compared to check on the degree of agreement. **Interobserver reliability** measures whether two or more observers yield similar results when they simultaneously observe the same behavior (Martin & Bateson, 1993). The degree of interobserver reliability can be measured in several ways, but it is typically measured by a coefficient of correlation (see Chapter 5). High agreement between two observers would be shown by a high positive coefficient of correlation. Correlations usually have a maximum value of 1.00, and the accepted criterion for high interobserver reliability is when the coefficient is greater than 0.70 (Martin & Bateson, 1993).

Ficken and associates (2000) were able to characterize the songs of bluethroated hummingbirds. Further, they developed an ethogram of when female hummingbirds would sing. Clearly, the researchers had to be able to record and analyze the hummingbirds' songs. This is not a trivial undertaking. Obtaining accurate records in a natural habitat is difficult. For example, continuous vigilance usually is impossible, even with automatic recording apparatus. Additionally, both the apparatus and the observers may result in reactivity, which would spoil the measures. These are just a few of the challenges associated with naturalistic observation of animals.

Applying similar techniques to human behavior is even more difficult, because people do not usually appreciate having their every action noted by curious scientists. Barker and his associates (for example, Barker & Wright, 1951; Barker, 1968) were pioneers in applying methods of naturalistic observation to humans in a number of settings. Let us examine some naturalistic observations of humans.

Flashing Eyebrows   The famous ethologist of human behavior Eibl-Eibesfeldt (for example, 1970, 1972) has done a substantial amount of field research on human facial expressions. He and his colleagues traveled around the world taking pictures of facial expressions in a variety of contexts. Careful examination of the expressions indicated that many are similar across cultures, but some are not. In the process of examining facial expressions associated with people greeting each other, Eibl-Eibesfeldt discovered that most humans give a brief eyebrow flash. He went on to examine this phenomenon in detail.

Generally, the eyebrow flash is a brief (one-sixth of a second) raising of the eyebrows, which is accompanied by a slight smile and a quick nod of the head. The eyebrow flash has been observed in people of many cultures, including Bushmen, Balinese, and Europeans. However, some cultures seem to differ in their uses of the eyebrow flash. The Japanese do not use the flash, because in Japan, it is considered suggestive or indecent. Furthermore, Eibl-Eibesfeldt found that the flash occurred in other circumstances, such as in flirting and acknowledging a gift or service (that is, as a kind of thank you) in addition to greeting.

We can see from his work that previous observations suggested additional ones for Eibl-Eibesfeldt, and by delimiting his range of inquiry, he was able to garner substantial information about a common human behavior.

Testing Neonates   Another example of refinement comes from studies of newborn humans (neonates). What do neonates do, and what can we look for in their behavior? Most people think of neonates as being limited in their behavior. However, neonates can do more than eat, sleep, eliminate, and cry. All their senses are operative, and they possess a number of complex reflexes. Brazelton and his associates (for example, Lester & Brazelton, 1982) have spent many years refining a scale to assess the optimal performance of neonates in a variety of behaviors. Initially, the scale assessed reflexes (squeezing, blinking) and a few behaviors. Repeated observations of neonates from a variety of cultures and in a variety of situations led to changes, which in turn caused more changes. The resulting Brazelton Neonatal Behavioral Assessment Scale contains measurements of 16 reflexes and 26 behaviors. The reflexes are rated on a 3-point scale (low, medium, and high), and the behavioral items, such as responses to a pinprick and hand-to-mouth activity, are rated on 9-point scales.

Earlier observations had suggested that the level of arousal was very important in respect to the appearance and magnitude of certain behaviors, so the current scale indicates when the neonate should be assessed on the various behaviors. For example, responses to a pinprick are assessed when the neonate is asleep or quiet, but not when the neonate is alert or crying. Hand-to-mouth behaviors can be assessed during any state.

Brazelton and his coworkers have been particularly concerned with individual and cultural differences in development, and they have conducted a substantial amount of more controlled research to examine these differences. The controlled research would not have been possible had they not made the exhaustive series of observations that led to the development of the assessment scale.

▶ CONCEPT SUMMARY

- Naturalistic observation is refined by ethograms and by delimiting observation categories.
- Interobserver reliability assesses whether two or more observers agree on how to categorize naturalistic observations.

The Case Study

Another venerable form of inquiry in psychology is the case study. Freud's psychoanalytic theory arose from his observations and reflections on individual cases. In general, a case study is the intensive investigation of a case of some sort, whether of a neurotic patient, a spiritual medium, or a group awaiting the end of the world. An interesting case study of this last instance was provided by Festinger, Riecken, and Schachter (1956), who infiltrated a small group of persons who were awaiting the end of the world. The members thought themselves to be in contact with beings from another planet, who had communicated to one member that the destruction of the Earth was near. The group was expecting to be rescued by spacecraft before the catastrophe. Festinger and his colleagues were especially interested in the reactions of the group when the calamity did not occur. They observed that for many of the members of the group, belief in its delusional system actually increased rather than decreased after the predicted date of catastrophe had passed.

The case study is a type of naturalistic observation and is subject to all the disadvantages and the few advantages (to be discussed shortly) of that method. One chief disadvantage is that case studies usually do not allow firm inferences to be made about what causes what. Typically, all one can do is describe the course of events. Often, however, case studies provide implicit comparisons that allow the researcher to make some reasonable guesses as to what causes what. The case study of K. R., the compulsive counter mentioned earlier, revealed an exceptionally stern upbringing that involved rigid orderliness and severe punishment for sins and misdeeds. K. R.'s current family life seemed beyond her control—her children were unruly, and her husband suffered from a disabling illness. The therapist concluded that her rituals were an attempt to gain control and to be orderly (Oltmanns et al., 1999). We should consider this conclusion tentative, however, because we do not know what kind of person K. R. would have become had she had a more orderly childhood and less stressful family situation.

A type of case study that best attempts to minimize the difficulties of making inferences is the **deviant-case analysis.** Here the researcher considers two cases that bear a number of similarities and yet differ in outcome. For example, one twin brother might become schizophrenic, but the other does not. The researcher attempts to pinpoint, through a careful comparison of the two cases, the factors that are responsible for the difference in outcome. Such comparisons usually cannot be made, because comparable cases that differ in only one factor are rare. Furthermore, any conclusions drawn from this method cannot really be considered firm or well established, because the researcher can never be certain that he or she has identified the critical causes in the differing outcomes. These cautions notwithstanding, let us consider a case study reported by Butters and Cermak (1986) that illustrates how judicious use of the procedure can provide valuable information.

The study is about P. Z., a world-famous scientist who suffered from severe memory loss (amnesia) in 1981 after long-term alcohol abuse. He had extreme difficulty both in remembering new information and in recollecting past events and people. The latter memory deficit was easy to determine, because 2 years before the onset of amnesia, P. Z. had written his autobiography. When he was queried about the names and events mentioned in his autobiography, he showed a drastic memory deficit. P. Z.'s memory for these events was compared with the retention of a similar-aged colleague (the comparison person for deviant-case analysis) who did not have a history of alcohol abuse. The comparison case did not show a memory deficit as serious as P. Z.'s, so Butters and Cermak reasoned that the long-term alcohol abuse was an important causal factor in P. Z.'s amnesia. Furthermore, P. Z.'s memory deficit for new information was very similar to that shown by other people with a history of alcohol abuse. This latter technique of comparing the case's behavior with that of others is essentially an experimental one, and this procedure is emphasized throughout this text.

> ## CONCEPT SUMMARY

- Case studies suffer from an inability to determine what causes what.
- Deviant-case analysis compares two similar cases that differ in specific ways, which improves the inferential capabilities of case studies.

Survey Research

Case studies usually involve only a few participants, and often these individuals are not at all representative of the population at large. P. Z., for example, was both a brilliant scientist and an amnesiac. Often researchers want to obtain information on a large sample of people in a large geographic area, although the amount of information obtained from any one person is necessarily limited. The survey technique is little used in most areas of psychology, though it is familiar to most of you through its use in predicting elections and the like. With the precise sampling procedures now available, relatively few people can be queried and the results will nonetheless generalize well to the population at large.

Because the survey leads to results that are generally descriptive in nature, this method is not particularly popular with psychologists. Nevertheless, clever use of the method may allow contributions to some areas of psychology. The work by Lovelace and Twohig (1990) that was summarized briefly at the outset of this section is a good example. The older adults they surveyed reported that they relied very strongly on notes, lists, and other external memory aids to help them remember to do things. Furthermore, the older respondents claimed not to rely on various memory "tricks" such as mnemonic devices. The results reported by Lovelace and Twohig agree with other survey data (Moscovitch, 1982), which show that compared with younger people, older adults are much more likely to make lists and use date books and are less likely to resort to internal memory procedures, such as mnemonic devices. These results are provocative, because they suggest that older individuals are somehow aware that they may have some memory limitations, which they try to minimize by relying on external memory aids. However, more controlled research is necessary before that conclusion can be confirmed.

A crucial issue in survey research relates to the sample that is surveyed. The researcher wants the sample to be representative of the population for whom the questions are designed. So, for example, a researcher interested in people's reactions to earthquakes would sample from a population of people who had suffered from an earthquake. However, the problem still remains—does the sample surveyed present a reasonable picture of the population?

A large random sample is likely to be the surest way to have a representative sample. A **random sample** is one in which each person in the population has the same chance of being sampled (i.e., surveyed). We discuss sampling in more detail in Chapter 7. A complete analysis of sampling approaches can be found in Weisberg, Krosnick, and Bowen (1989).

▶ Advantages of Descriptive Observations

As noted earlier, descriptive observation is extremely useful in the early stages of research, when one desires simply to gain some idea as to the breadth and range of the problem of interest (Miller, 1977). However, descriptive observation does not allow one to infer how factors may be related. In some cases, there is no way to employ more controlled methods of observation; therefore, only descriptive ones are available. If you want to know how penguins behave in their natural habitat, you simply have to observe them there. Still, for most psychological problems, descriptive observation is useful primarily in defining the problem area and raising interesting questions for more controlled study by other means, especially experimental ones. For example, the case study by Festinger and his colleagues of the group predicting the end of the world helped lead to Festinger's (1957) cognitive dissonance theory of attitude change, which has been quite important in guiding social psychological research.

Descriptive techniques share features that make them very desirable scientific tools, especially when they are compared with controlled laboratory experimentation. Timberlake and Silva (1994) note that flexibility is a major asset of naturalistic observation. It can be inexpensive (only minimal equipment and other facilities often are required), and it is often convenient and relatively easy to do. When both of these possibilities are true, a prudent researcher supplements controlled procedures, such as experiments and tests, with direct observation of behavior.

Another feature of all descriptive procedures is that they typically try to understand interesting, naturally occurring behaviors. Often, then, descriptive procedures may have an ethological and ecological slant to them (Timberlake & Silva, 1994; Todd & Perlmutter, 1980).

In the present context, **ecological function** refers to the role that various behaviors play in adapting to the environment—what function they seem to serve for the organism. A good example of this approach in contrast to the standard experimental one can be seen in the work of Perlmutter and her associates (Perlmutter & Myers, 1979; Todd & Perlmutter, 1980). In controlled experimental settings, Perlmutter and Myers showed that the deliberate memory for lists of words is much worse for 3-year-olds than for 4-year-olds. However, the implicit memory of everyday events and actions that Perlmutter and Myers studied naturalistically show much smaller advantages for the older children.

Let us examine the naturalistic work on memory, because it illustrates many of the important features of such research. Todd and Perlmutter observed children of various ages individually in two 1-hour sessions. They carefully documented the spontaneous memory statements of the children, which were categorized according to their duration, frequency, and level of detail. Both the younger and older children recalled many novel events, such as a trip to the zoo, and many routine events, such as playing with particular toys. The major difference between the younger and older children lay in the ability of the older children to recall more events over longer retention intervals than the younger ones. In addition, the older children tended to recall more aspects of their internal states, such as happiness or fear, than did the younger children. To check on these children's deliberate memory, Todd and Perlmutter noted that it took the younger children about five times as many repetitions as the older ones to memorize a two-sentence rhyme. The latter finding contrasts to the much smaller differences in spontaneous memory for events and activities and agrees with the results of controlled studies on memory for word lists.

Several other features of Perlmutter's work should be noted here. First, interobserver reliability was very high in classifying the memories into the categories noted previously. Second, Perlmutter had the parents of the children corroborate the spontaneous memory claims. She found that the accuracy of both the younger and older children was very good according to the parents' determination. Obtaining corroborating evidence for the children's memories was very important as a source of control that Perlmutter and associates added to naturalistic observation. Third, the research illustrates both the flexibility and ecological function often associated with naturalistic observation. The researchers had a great deal of latitude in observing the children—they could merely sit and talk nonchalantly to them, or they could ask the children questions if they were being comparatively silent. The ecological aspect of the research is apparent in the nature of the spontaneous memories that the children reported: visits to zoos, a doctor's appointment, and the like. Such events are markedly different from the sorts of things that are usually studied in laboratory-based experiments on memory, especially when the children are asked to deliberately learn and remember the material. Note that ecologically relevant experiments are possible, but naturalistic observation in particular, and descriptive research in general, allows ecological functions to be studied with ease. This means that descriptive observations often have high **ecological validity**.

CONCEPT SUMMARY

Advantages of descriptive observations include

- being an important source of basic knowledge
- flexibility
- ethological approach
- ecological validity

▶ Sources of Error in Descriptive Research

The primary problem unique to descriptive observation is that it does not readily allow us to assess relations among events. An investigator might note that grooming behavior in free-ranging monkeys occurs at certain times, following five different prior conditions (such as eating). If one is interested in finding out which antecedent conditions are necessary to produce grooming, descriptive observation cannot provide an answer, because these antecedent conditions cannot be manipulated. For this, one needs an experiment.

APPLICATION

Difficulties of Observation

Direct observation may seem a straightforward and simple process: We open our eyes, look hard, and see what is there. However, the history of science is replete with examples of phenomena that have eventually turned out to be radically different from the way they were initially perceived. We consider two examples here, one from psychology and one from physics, to show that scientists must be continually vigilant for errors in their own observations.

Ivan P. Pavlov (1849–1936) was a Russian physiologist who won the Nobel Prize for medicine in 1904 for his work on how gastric juices operate during digestion. Pavlov also made important contributions to psychology by identifying and studying classical conditioning. When Pavlov began studying learning in dogs, he and his coworkers discovered they had a problem that had not been apparent when they had previously been concerned only with the digestive system. The difficulty lay in how to describe the behaviors they were observing. Pavlov describes the problem of studying conditioned reflexes:

> But how is this to be studied? Taking the dog when he eats rapidly, snatches something in his mouth, chews for a long time, it seems clear that at such a time the animal strongly desires to eat, and so rushes to the food, seizes it, and falls to eating. He longs to eat. . . . When he eats, you see the work of the muscles alone, striving in every way to seize the food in the mouth, to chew and to swallow it. From all this we can say that he derives pleasure from it. . . . Now when we proceeded to explain and analyze this, we readily adopted this trite point of view. We had to

deal with the feelings, wishes, conceptions, etc., of our animal. The results were astounding, extraordinary; I and one of my colleagues came to irreconcilable opinions. We could not agree, could not prove to one another which was right. . . . After this we had to deliberate carefully. It seemed probable we were not on the right track. The more we thought about the matter, the greater grew our conviction that it was necessary to choose another exit. The first steps were very difficult, but along the way of persistent, intense, concentrated thinking, I finally reached the firm ground of pure objectivity. We absolutely prohibited ourselves (in the laboratory, there was an actual fine imposed) the use of such psychological expressions as the dog guessed, wanted, wished, etc. (Pavlov, reprinted 1963, pp. 263–264).

A second problem is relevant to observation in all types of research. This is the issue of how much our conceptual schemes determine and bias what we "see." Pavlov's statement is eloquent testimony to the difficulty of establishing objective methods that would enable us all to see things in the same way. He had found it initially "astounding" and "extraordinary" that this difficulty existed and was surprised at the elaborate precautions needed to ensure objectivity. Philosophers of science have pointed out that our observations are always influenced by our conceptions of the world—if in no other way, at least by the particular observations we make (see, for example, Hanson, 1958, Chapter 2).

"Pure objectivity," to use Pavlov's phrase, is quite elusive, if not impossible. Objective and repeatable observation in science is an ideal to be approximated, but we may never be completely confident that we have achieved it. Nevertheless, we must make every possible step toward this ideal, which is what much of the technical paraphernalia of science is designed to help us with.

The problem of observations being unduly influenced by expectations is not, however, automatically overcome by the use of sophisticated equipment, as is evident in an illustration cited by Hyman (1964, p. 38). In 1902, shortly after X-rays were discovered, the eminent French physicist Blondlot reported the discovery of "N-rays." Other French scientists quickly repeated and confirmed Blondlot's discovery; in 1904, no fewer than 77 publications appeared on the topic. However, the discovery became controversial when American, German, and Italian scientists failed to replicate Blondlot's findings.

The American physicist R. W. Wood, failing to find N-rays in his own lab at Johns Hopkins University, visited Blondlot. Blondlot displayed a card to Wood with luminous circles painted on it. Then he turned down the room light, fixed N-rays

on the card, and pointed out to Wood that the circles increased in luminosity. When Wood said he could see no change, Blondlot argued that this must be because Wood's eyes were too insensitive. Next, Wood asked if he could perform some simple tests, to which Blondlot consented. In one case, Wood moved a lead screen repeatedly between the N-rays and the cards, while Blondlot reported the corresponding changes in luminosity of the circles on the card. (The lead shield was to prevent passage of the N-rays.) Blondlot was consistently in error, and often reported a change in luminosity when the screen had not been moved. This and other tests clearly indicated that there was no evidence for the existence of N-rays, despite their "confirmation" by other French scientists.

After 1909, there were no further publications on N-rays. The mistake was too much for Blondlot. He never recovered, and he died in disgrace some years later. We can see from this dramatic example that even with the sophisticated apparatus of physicists, errors of observation are possible and must be guarded against.

Sources: Hanson, N. R. (1958). Patterns of discovery. Cambridge: Cambridge University Press. Hyman R. (1964). *The nature of psychological inquiry.* Englewood Cliffs, NJ: Prentice-Hall. Pavlov, I. P. (1963). *Lectures on conditioned reflexes.* New York: International Publishers.

Descriptive observation may produce data that are deficient in other ways too. Scientific data should be easy to reproduce by other people using standardized procedures if these people doubt the observations or are interested in repeating them. Many descriptive methods, such as the case study, do not allow reproducibility; they are thus open to question by other investigators.

Another problem in descriptive approaches is maintaining as strictly as possible a descriptive rather than an interpretive level of observation—researcher bias. In the study of animals, the bias problem is sometimes one of attributing human characteristics to animals, or anthropomorphizing, which was discussed in Chapter 1. When you come home and your dog wags its tail and moves about excitedly, it seems perfectly natural to say that it is happy to see you. However, this is anthropomorphizing, and if one were engaged in descriptive observation of the scene, it would be inappropriate. Instead, one should record the overt behaviors of the dog with the least possible attribution of underlying motives such as happiness, sadness, or hunger.

Although Freud was not guilty of anthropomorphizing, his case studies are based entirely on such singular interpretations of the facts. Besides being non-reproducible, such cases suffer from the possibility that they could probably be used to prove any theory. Freud selected particular case studies and particular answers to the questions asked. Then he wove these "facts" into a previous conceptual system of his own devising, which means he could support his theory no matter how sloppy the methodology. This is not to detract from the creative flair and genius evident in Freud's system. However, he is certainly open to criticism in terms of the evidence on which it is based.

▶ Reactivity in Descriptive Research

In many areas of psychological research, we can view the reactions of the participants not only in terms of the project itself but also in terms of everyday social interaction. Suppose you are responding to a survey that asks you to estimate the number of times a day you think about sex. Go ahead and make a guess. Now, suppose you are asked the same question in a personal interview. Would your answer in the interview be the same as the one given in the survey? You might be reluctant to say, "I think about sex at least 15 times a day." On the other hand, writing "15" in response to a question on an anonymous survey might not bother you at all. In general, ordinary social interaction may put demands on a research participant that changes the way he or she reacts.

Weber and Cook (1972) used the phrase **subject (participant) roles** to highlight the important social and psychological factors that occur in research and may influence the results. As used here, *role* refers to how the participants perceive the research setting and how they then react to it. Because the perceived role may determine how the participants respond, unnatural responding, or **reactivity,** could occur and confound the results. We will consider several examples of reactivity and some possible solutions.

The term **demand characteristics** was at one time the standard way to refer to participant reactivity. The phrase was coined by Orne (1962) to highlight the pressure put on people participating in research. Orne emphasized the obedience of the participant to the researcher's demands. We believe that *reactivity* is a more general term to describe the roles that participants may adopt than is the phrase *demand characteristics*.

Naturalistic Observation   There are two general ways to guard against participants' reactions ruining observations: We can make unobtrusive observations, or we can take unobtrusive measures (Webb, Campbell, Schwartz, & Sechrist, 1981).

First, we will consider **unobtrusive observations.** Imagine that you are walking down a street in your hometown. Occasionally, you greet a friend (perhaps with a handshake, perhaps with an eyebrow flash). As your walk continues, a man with a large camera approaches and proceeds to take moving pictures of you every time you greet one of your friends. How are you likely to react to this attention? Quite likely, your mode of greeting people would change dramatically. (Have you ever noticed how spectators behave at sporting events when they know the television camera is on them?) Eibl-Eibesfeldt guarded against participant reactivity in his research by using a camera with a special sideways lens. This lens permitted him to aim the camera 90 degrees from the individual being observed; presumably, the individual would think that Eibl-Eibesfeldt was photographing something else. Thus, this person would not act abnormally to the presence of the observer and his camera; instead, the observed individual would act naturally, which is what Eibl-Eibesfeldt intended. The special camera lens allowed the researcher to observe without intruding on the person, which means that Eibl-Eibesfeldt used an unobtrusive observation technique.

In general, unobtrusive observations of people are likely to reveal more natural behavior than if the people are aware of being observed. In studying animals, researchers use unobtrusive observations whenever possible so that the behavior of interest will not be affected by the observer's presence.

Sometimes, however, either the participants themselves, the terrain, or some other aspect of the project demands close contact. In these situations, **participant observation** often provides a solution. For example, Fossey (1972) spent a great amount of time observing the mountain gorilla. The mountain gorilla lives in central Africa, and its habitat is threatened by human beings who are moving into that area. The mountain gorilla's natural habitat is in the mountainous rain forest, which makes long-range unobtrusive spying out of the question. Fossey was particularly concerned with the free-ranging behavior of the gorillas, so she decided to become a participant observer. This was difficult, because the gorillas are not tame. She had to mimic the gorillas so that they would become accustomed to her presence. She mimicked aspects of the animal's behavior, such as eating, grooming, and making weird gorilla-like vocalizations. As she said, "One feels like a fool thumping one's chest rhythmically or sitting about pretending to munch on a stalk of wild celery as though it were the most delectable morsel in the world. But the gorillas have responded favorably" (p. 211). It took several months for Fossey to gain the confidence of the gorillas, and she continued to live with and study the gorillas until her death in 1986. How would you like to act like a gorilla for 10 or 15 years?

Unobtrusive measures, in contrast to unobtrusive observations, are usually indirect observations of behavior. Unobtrusive measures are indirect because the *result* of the behavior, not the behavior itself, is being studied. Thus, instead of measuring behavior directly, we examine it after the fact by looking at what the behavior has accomplished. Instead of observing a student's studying activities, we examine his or her transcript. Instead of living with the gorillas, we look at their effect on the environment. Obviously, unobtrusive measures are not suitable for all questions being investigated (an unobtrusive measure of an eyebrow flash might be difficult), but for some, these measures are not merely good, they are the only ones that are feasible. Consider the question of graffiti in public restrooms. Who does it? What does the graffiti usually concern? A number of serious ethical questions (ethics are discussed in Chapter 12) would be raised if a researcher stood around in restrooms observing the patrons. However, the graffiti *topics* can be examined, and they can provide substantial information. Kinsey, Pomeroy, and Martin (1953) discovered that graffiti in men's restrooms was more erotic than graffiti in women's restrooms. Furthermore, they found more graffiti in men's rooms than in women's rooms.

Using unobtrusive measures is akin to a hunter following animal tracks or a police officer examining clues such as fingerprints. Tracks and clues are left behind and often allow us to infer things about the behavior that caused them. Recently, a popular psychological and anthropological unobtrusive measure has been to examine the garbage and other refuse that people discard. From the characteristics of the discarded objects, the observer attempts to understand some aspect of the behavior behind that refuse (for example, a discarded liquor bottle or love letter that has been thrown away could reveal information about behavior).

Case Studies   Case studies are individual histories, which means that much of the evidence in these studies is **retrospective** in nature. In other words, it comes from looking back into the past. Looking backward often causes problems. One difficulty is that the evidence may be inaccurate because of ordinary forgetting. We may not remember what our thoughts and actions were in nursery school because what has happened since then interferes with our memory of early events. Another difficulty with case studies is that participant reactivity may lead to **motivated forgetting.** Motivated forgetting refers to the active way in which humans reconstruct past experiences. People may distort their memories to match their current beliefs. For instance, a politician who has changed views on a controversial issue such as the death penalty may recall the former stance as having been much more moderate than it really was. Similarly, people may inflate their memory for positive events. A powerful example of this type of positive distortion could be seen in the memory of John Dean during the Watergate scandal in the early 1970s. Appearing before a congressional committee, Dean described personal conversations between President Nixon and himself. In these descriptions, he generally overestimated his role in the conversation and tended to exaggerate any praise bestowed on him by the president (Neisser, 1981). We know that John Dean's recollections were distorted because audiotapes of these same conversations have since been compared with the congressional testimony. The example of John Dean illustrates that an effective method for dealing with motivated forgetting is to obtain corroborating evidence from other sources. Unfortunately, such evidence may be difficult to obtain, and if other people serve as additional sources, then their memories are subject to the same problems.

Surveys, Interviews, and Tests   To the extent that other forms of descriptive research rely on retrospective reports, they face the same reactivity problems as case studies, that is, both ordinary and motivated forgetting. However, many of the responses on tests and surveys are not retrospective, and we instead face problems resulting from **response style** or *response sets*. Different people may have habitual ways of answering questions. These habits may result from how they view themselves or from the expectations of the researcher and society (more on this later). In general, there are three kinds of response styles: yea-saying or **response acquiescence,** nay-saying or **response deviation,** and **social desirability.** College-bound high-school graduates tend to respond no to the question "Do you use marijuana daily?" Does this answer reflect the true behavior of these people, or does the answer reflect the habitual tendency to say no (response deviation)?

On the other hand, the answer could be a socially desirable one, because marijuana is a controlled substance and many authorities frown on its use. The high-school graduates not heading for college tended to answer yes to this question twice as often as the college-bound (Bachman & Johnston, 1979). Is this yes response a true one, or does the answer simply indicate that these people are likely to acquiesce and say yes regardless of what the question is? Based on the answer to this one question, we cannot determine whether the answer is a true one or the result of a particular response style.

Edwards (1953, 1957) developed an interesting solution to the response-style problem, at least for certain kinds of descriptive research. In particular, Edwards suggested the use of a **forced-choice test** in which participants must choose between two alternatives of equal social desirability in a personality test. On Edwards' test, called the Personal Preference Schedule, the respondent has to select one of two activities or indicate which of two thoughts or feelings better reflects the characteristics of the respondent. For example, the respondent might have to choose between playing tennis or waterskiing. Although equal in social desirability, the two alternatives are hypothesized to be associated with different personality characteristics. Here waterskiing may be the more typical choice of extroverted individuals. The forced-choice technique decreases the influence of social desirability as well as eliminating the possibility of response acquiescence or response deviation.

Associated with the problem of response styles is one that is more difficult to cope with—the **volunteer problem.** Volunteer participants differ in a number of ways from potential participants who do not volunteer (Rosnow & Rosenthal, 1970). Volunteers tend to be more intelligent, better educated, more cooperative, better adjusted, and in greater need of social approval than nonvolunteers. These characteristics of volunteers could strongly influence participant reaction. The volunteer problem might also limit the generalizability of results in an experiment.

What the volunteer problem means in terms of your own research is that you have to be careful in sampling from the population of participants available to you. If your test or survey is boring and requires that the respondent go to extreme lengths to be cooperative, then the answers you get may be based on a biased sample of opinion (this is an example of selection bias). Those people willing to trudge through snow at 11:00 p.m. to the Psychology building will differ from those unwilling to do so. The problem is also serious, as Rosnow and Rosenthal point out, in opinion surveys that rely on volunteer mailings or phone-ins. What are we to make of the results of a magazine survey that relies on voluntary compliance of the readers? Alternatively, how about the radio survey that solicits calls from its listeners? In both cases, we do not know anything about the people who *did not* respond, nor do we know anything about the people who do not read that magazine or listen to that station. We can find out about the nonrespondents by expending a great deal of time and effort. Usually, this effort is not made.

There are three possible solutions to the nonrespondent problem, although none is completely satisfactory. First, you can get a **random sample** of the entire population that is available to you. This means that every potential respondent has an equal chance of being questioned. Of course, this assumes that all individuals in the population will participate if questioned. Second, you could give the nonrespondents some extra incentive to participate in your project. They could be offered money or be given detailed information about the research project. Since some potential respondents would be treated differently from others, the extra inducements might bias the results. Third, you could replicate your research with additional samples of potential respondents. Although your project may again be plagued with the same volunteer problem, this would be a good solution if the problems associated with volunteers and nonrespondents were not likely to recur in your **replication.**

CONCEPT SUMMARY

Descriptive observations may suffer from

- lack of reproducibility
- anthropomorphizing
- internal validity
- participant reactivity

Summary

1. The descriptive methods of observation include naturalistic observations, case studies, and surveys.
2. Ethology is the study of naturally occurring behavior that is often systematized by an ethogram, which categorizes a number of different behaviors.
3. The accuracy of naturalistic observation is often determined by measures of interobserver reliability, which assess how well two or more observers agree on how to assort behaviors.

4. Deviant-case analysis is a case-study procedure in which the researcher considers two cases that bear a number of similarities but differ in outcome.

5. Random sampling is probably the best way to obtain a representative sample for a survey.

6. Descriptive research often lays down the empirical foundation for subsequent, more controlled research. Furthermore, it tends to be more flexible than experimentation, and it can address important issues about the ecological function associated with particular behaviors.

7. Sources of error in descriptive research include anthropomorphizing and experimenter bias. Another difficulty relates to reactivity by the people or animals being observed. Human participants often adopt particular roles that could undermine the research when they know they are being evaluated.

8. Unobtrusive measures and unobtrusive observations attempt to minimize reactivity by measuring the traces of behavior (unobtrusive measures) or by concealing the measurement process from the individuals being observed (unobtrusive observations).

Key Concepts

case study (89)
demand characteristics (102)
descriptive observations (89)
deviant-case analysis (96)
ecological function (98)
ecological validity (99)
ethogram (92)
ethology (92)
forced-choice test (105)

interobserver reliability (93)
motivated forgetting (104)
naturalistic observation (89)
participant observation (103)
random sample (97)
reactivity (102)
replication (106)
response acquiescence (105)

response deviation (105)
response styles (105)
retrospective (104)
social desirability (105)
subject (participant) roles (102)
survey (91)
unobtrusive measures (103)
unobtrusive observations (102)
volunteer problem (105)

Exercises

1. Do a Web search on the term *ethology*. If your browser gives you reports that describe ethological analyses, find one that interests you and summarize its results.

2. Present some testable research hypotheses that cannot be studied in laboratory experiments. Indicate some alternative ways in which they could be studied.

3. [*Special Exercise.*] A researcher is interested in the extent of drug use among college students. She has the option of doing an anonymous survey, in which the students write down their answers, or a face-to-face survey, in which answers are given verbally. Each method has advantages and disadvantages—enumerate them.

Suggested Resources

An interesting article on the use and development of observational skills is Boice, R. (1983). Observational skills. *Psychological Bulletin, 93,* 3–29.

A detailed discussion of methodological problems and considerations in descriptive research can be found in the following two articles: Woolfolk, A. E. (1981). The eye of the beholder: Methodological considerations when observers assess nonverbal communication. *Journal of Nonverbal Behavior, 5,* 199–204; and Wildman, B. G., & Erickson, M. T. (1977). Methodological problems in behavioral observation. In J. D. Cone & R. P. Hawkins (Eds.), *Behavioral assessment.* New York: Brunner/Mazel.

Web Resources

Diverse sources on much of the information in this chapter can be found at: http://server.bmod. athabascau.ca/html/aupr/tools.shtml

Wadsworth's *Statistics and Research Methods Workshops* has a section on "Non-Experimental Methods," which has information on naturalistic observations and surveys. There is also a section devoted to "Surveys." At: http://www.wadsworth.com/psychology_d/templates/student_resources/workshops/workshops.html

Laboratory Resource

Chapters 1 and 2 in Langston's manual (Langston, 2005) consider naturalistic observation and survey research, respectively. The naturalistic observation research concerns humans defending parking spaces, and the survey research focuses on grade inflation in college.

Remembering the 9/11 Terrorist Attacks

Can you answer the following questions?

1. What time of day did you first hear the news of the 9/11 attacks?

2. Where were you?

3. What were you doing?

4. Who told you?

5. Who else was there?

6. How did you feel about it?

7. Can you describe at least three vivid details of the experience?

8. What did you do immediately after hearing the news?

Ask a few of your friends the above questions. Surveys usually relate to important and interesting problems. The questions above are an example.

You and your friends probably have very vivid memories of 9/11, and people typically have detailed recollection of the events and peripheral details of these so-called *flashbulb memories* (Brown & Kulick, 1977). Although flashbulb memories are dramatic and usually personally relevant, such memories are subject to error. Sources of error include talking and thinking about the event long after it happened. Your retelling may depend on your audience, and you will hear other versions of the same event. Examples of the effects of these appear in work by Schmolck, Buffalo, and Squire (2000), who examined memories of hearing the verdict in the O. J. Simpson trial. Compared with initial accounts, 15 months later only 50% of the details were accurate, and after 32 months only 29% were considered accurate. Many psychologists surveyed people about 9/11 right after the attacks on September 11, 2001. Follow-up surveys are ongoing, and the first reports are now being published (e.g., Talarico & Rubin, 2003). Interesting errors appear in the follow-up surveys.

Clearly, you would have difficulty repeating the survey of your friends as Schmolck and associates did theirs, especially because your survey was not done immediately after the attacks. However, you might consider ways that you could get corroboration about the answers you and your friends provided about the events of 9/11. For example, friends of friends could be interviewed (that is, the people listed in question 5) to see whether they can verify some of the assertions of the people you surveyed. Who would be the best person to corroborate your answers? If you and your classmates combine your data, you ought to examine the kinds of events that were most likely not to be corroborated. Are you obtaining results similar to those reported by Talarico and Rubin (2003)?

CHAPTER 5

Relational Research

Relational Research Attempts to
- Determine the relationships between variables

Relational Research Includes
- Contingency table research
- Correlational research

Relational Research Usually Cannot
- Provide strong internal validity

Caution Is Best Inferred from
- Experimental research

This chapter examines research that tries to assess the relationship between variables. Contingency tables examine how the frequency of observations change as a function of two nominal variables. Correlational research looks at both the magnitude and the direction of relationships. At the end of this chapter, we consider experimental observations from the standpoint of making causal statements about the effects of one variable on changes in another.

Scientists describe, relate, and experiment. In this chapter, we focus on **relational research,** which attempts to determine how two (usually) or more variables are related to each other. Typically, relational research does not involve manipulation of variables, as do experiments, so the data that are related are often called **ex post facto** data, which means *after the fact.* That is, the results that are related usually have occurred because of some naturally occurring events and are not the result of direct manipulation by an experimenter. The researcher categorizes or assesses the data and then probes for relationships. Often, the relationships allow the reasonably accurate prediction of one event when a correlated event occurs.

▶ Contingency Table Research

Much psychological research seeks to determine whether the outcome of one variable depends on the outcome of another (for example, Hurlburt, 1994). We will examine a particular research problem to illustrate one kind of relational research. Suppose that you want to determine the distribution of men and women in various major programs at your college. To examine this, you assess the frequencies with which women and men declare major programs and enter the outcome of your results in a contingency table. A **contingency table** is a tabular presentation of all combinations of categories of two variables, which allows the relationships between the two to be examined. An example of the development of a contingency table appears in Table 5–1.

Panel A of Table 5–1 shows the number of women majoring in various departments. More women are majoring in English than in any of the other departments listed. History has the fewest women majors. The number of men majors in the five departments appears in Panel B. Note that more men major in economics than in any other department. Psychology has the fewest men. Panel C illustrates the entire contingency table and adds some important information—the relative frequency of men and women majors. The overall figures for men (55.6%) and women (44.4%) are less than the nearly equal distribution of men and women in the entire student body (not shown in the Table). The relative frequencies for each cell in the table show the percentage of men and women in each major program. The contingency table illustrated in Panel C is referred to as a *two by five contingency table,* because it has two rows and five columns (not including the totals). Contingency tables have to have at least two rows and at least two columns. The convention is to present the number of rows, then the number of columns in the description, hence "2 × 5." A particular row-column combination is called a **cell;** for example, the cell entry indicating the percentage of women biology majors is 53.8%.

The percentages in the table clearly indicate that a relationship exists between a person's gender and his or her choice of major at this particular college. History and economics have proportionately more men than women majors, and the reverse is true for psychology, biology, and English. This kind of

Table 5–1   Development of a contingency table indicating some of the major programs chosen by men and women at a small liberal arts college

Panel A: The number of women majoring in five departments

		Major Program		
History	Psychology	English	Biology	Economics
22	42	51	28	26

Panel B: The number of men majoring in five departments

		Major Program		
History	Psychology	English	Biology	Economics
66	11	20	24	87

Panel C: A contingency table showing frequency and relative frequency in percentage of women and men majoring in five departments

Gender	History	Psychology	English	Biology	Economics	Total
Women	22	42	51	28	26	166
%	25.0%	79.3%	72.8%	53.8%	23.0%	44.4%
Men	66	11	20	24	87	208
%	75.0%	20.7%	28.2%	46.2%	77.0%	55.6%
Total	88	53	71	52	113	374
%	100.0%	100.0%	100.0%	100.0%	100.0%	100.0%

relationship indicates a lack of independence between gender and choice of major. If you wanted to statistically analyze the data in the table, you would probably use a **chi square test for independence.** The symbol is χ^2, and this test is often used to determine whether the data in a contingency table are statistically independent of each other. The data are statistically significant in this case (refer to Appendix B for a discussion of statistical significance). This means that we can be reasonably sure that major selection is dependent on the gender of the student, or in other words, that the two variables are not independent of each other, rather they are related to each other.

Now, let us examine an example of research using a contingency table analysis that has been published. In Chapter 12, we will discuss the research of Plous (1991), who surveyed animal-rights activists as well as some nonactivists at a large animal-rights rally. The number of activists and nonactivists answering one of his survey questions is shown in Table 5–2. To help interpret this 2×3 contingency table (again, ignore totals), the percentages also appear. Note that the nonactivists were much less likely than the activists to believe that psychological research caused as much animal suffering as medical research. So, there is a relationship between being an activist and one's view of the harmfulness of certain kinds of research. The two variables are not inde-

Table 5–2   A 2 × 3 contingency table adapted from data presented by Plous (1991)

Which kind of research causes more animal suffering?

Group	Psychological	Medical	Equal	Total
Activists	64	56	281	401
	16.0%	14.0%	70.0%	100.0%
Nonactivists	8	20	25	53
	15.1%	37.7%	47.2%	100.0%
Total	72	76	306	454
	15.9%	16.7%	67.4%	100.0%

pendent of each other. According to Plous, this relationship may explain why animal-rights activists have tried to disrupt animal research in psychology.

Contingency table research is widely used to investigate the relationships between variables measured at the nominal level (activist/nonactivist and type of research were the two nominal categories in the survey by Plous). The cell entries are usually frequencies (or relative frequencies), and almost always an individual can appear only in one cell. Thus, when people are repeatedly measured on a task, this type of research and the χ^2 analysis of it are inappropriate.

Participant reactivity can be a problem in contingency table research, especially when the participants have been interviewed or surveyed. Plous's work could have had reactivity, because he interviewed the participants in a face-to-face survey. However, not all contingency research need be obviously subject to reactivity. The data presented in Table 5–1 are completely ex post facto, so that the people who declared a particular major do not know that they have appeared in a particular cell of a contingency table. This at first may seem to be a big plus in favor of such research. However, you should be aware that the participants' reactivity is unknown in this particular example. The real problem is that they could have chosen a particular major for reactive reasons ("Mom wants me to be an English major"). There is no simple way to determine that sort of reactivity if you collate the data from statistics prepared by someone who simply notes who majors in a particular program. Thus, what often occurs in ex post facto research is that there is participant reactivity of an unknown magnitude and an unknown source. When researchers assess rather than manipulate, they often stay in the dark with regard to such possible confounding as reactivity.

> ## CONCEPT SUMMARY

> - Contingency research assesses the relationship between all combinations of categories of two variables.
> - A χ^2 test for independence can be used to assess the statistical significance of contingency table data.

▶ Correlational Research

The second sort of relational research considered in this chapter is called **correlational research,** and it allows the researcher to determine simultaneously the degree and the direction of a relationship with a single statistic. In Chapter 7, we indicate how coefficients of correlation are used to evaluate measurements and tests. Here we discuss how correlations can be used directly as a research tool for determining relationships and for predicting outcomes.

Woodzicka and LaFrance (2001) examined how women reacted to sexual harassment in a real or imagined interview, and the authors used correlational procedures to help them understand some of their results. Women who imagined the interview reported more anger than those who experienced the real interview, whereas those in the real interview reported substantially more fear than those who imagined the interview.

The women in the imagined interview reported that they would confront the harasser. What did women do when they were actually harassed? For those women in the real interview, Woodzicka and LaFrance were able to examine the correlation between feelings and actions. They found that self-reported anger (which was not very high, remember) was not related to confronting the harasser. On the other hand, they established that the greater the degree of fear reported by the women in the real interview, the less likely it was that they would confront or challenge their harasser. These results indicate a difference between the actual responses to harassment and the imagined responses. This discrepancy can lead to the idea that women are at fault when they fail to confront their harasser (Cohen & Cohen, 1993). Bystanders who have not experienced real harassment apparently fail to recognize the intimidating effect that fear has on behavior and, consequently, blame the victim for the problem.

It is often difficult to determine the causal variables in correlational research. We examine how to interpret the results of correlational research after we consider the correlation coefficient itself.

The Correlation Coefficient

There are several different types of **correlation coefficients,** but almost all have in common the property that they can vary from -1.00 through 0.00 to $+1.00$. Commonly, they will not be one of these three figures but something in between, such as $-.72$ or $+.39$. The *magnitude* of the correlation coefficient indicates the degree of relationship (larger numbers reflecting stronger relations), and the *sign* indicates the direction of the relation, positive or negative. Putting the appropriate sign in front of the correlation coefficient is necessary, because otherwise, one cannot know which way the two variables are related, positively or negatively. It is common practice, though, to omit the plus sign before positive correlations, so that a correlation of .55 would be interpreted as $+.55$. It is a better practice always to include the sign. An example of a *positive* correlation is the relation between lung cancer and smoking. As one variable increases, so does the other (though not perfectly; that is, the correlation coefficient is less than +1.00). There is also a documented *negative* correlation between smoking and another variable, namely, grades in college. People who smoke a lot have tended to have lower grades than those who smoke less (Huff, 1954, p. 87).

There are actually several different types of correlation coefficients, and which is used depends on the characteristics of the variables being correlated. We shall consider one commonly used by psychologists: **Pearson's product-moment correlation coefficient,** or **Pearson *r*.** Because this is only one of several, you should consult a statistics text to determine which is appropriate for your particular case.

Let us imagine that we are one of the many psychologists who devote their careers to the study of human memory. We hit upon a simple, intuitive idea concerning head size and memory: Information from the outside world enters the head through the senses and is stored there. An analogy can be made between the head, where information is stored, and vessels such as boxes, where all kinds of things can be stored. Based on such analogical reasoning, which is common in science, we make the following prediction from our knowledge of the properties of physical containers: As the head size of a person increases, so should the person's memory. More things can be stored in bigger boxes than in smaller boxes, and similarly, more information should be stored in larger heads than in smaller ones.

This "theory" proposes a positive correlation: As head size increases, so should memory. A random sample of the local population could be taken. The persons chosen could be measured on two dimensions: head size and the number of words they can recall from a list of 30, presented to them once, at the rate of 1 word every 3 seconds. Three hypothetical sets of results from 10 participants are presented in Table 5–3. For each individual, there are two

Table 5–3 Three hypothetical examples of data taken on head size and recall, representing (a) a positive correction, (b) a low (near-zero) correlation, and (c) a negative correlation

	(a) Head			(b) Head			(c) Head	
Participant	Size (cm)	Recall (words)	Participant	Size (cm)	Recall (words)	Participant	Size (cm)	Recall (words)
1	50.8	17	1	50.8	23	1	50.8	12
2	63.5	21	2	63.5	12	2	63.5	9
3	45.7	16	3	45.7	13	3	45.7	13
4	25.4	11	4	25.4	21	4	25.4	23
5	29.2	9	5	29.2	9	5	29.2	21
6	49.5	15	6	49.5	14	6	49.5	16
7	38.1	13	7	38.1	16	7	38.1	14
8	30.5	12	8	30.5	15	8	30.5	17
9	35.6	14	9	35.6	11	9	35.6	15
10	58.4	23	10	58.4	16	10	58.4	11
	$r = +.93$			$r = -.07$			$r = -.89$	

measures, one of head size and the other of number of words recalled. In addition, the two types of measures need not be similar in any way to be correlated. They do not have to be on the same scale. Just as one can correlate head size with number of words recalled, one could also correlate IQ with street-address number. Any two sets of numbers can be correlated.

The mathematical assessment of correlation coefficients is discussed in Appendix A. If you are unfamiliar with this material, you might review Box A–1, where the mathematical formula for *r* is presented. Pearson *r* is calculated for the data presented in column (a) of Table 5–3. Working through this example will help you to better understand the basis of correlation coefficients. Researchers seldom use the mathematical formula to calculate *r* by hand. Most researchers rely on computers or calculators to calculate correlation coefficients for them.

Graphical representations of correlations are called **scatter diagrams,** and the data in the three panels of Table 5–3 are presented in the three panels of Figure 5–1; head size is plotted along the horizontal, or X, axis (the abscissa), and number of words recalled is plotted along the vertical, Y, axis (the ordinate). The high positive correlation between head size and number of words recalled in panel (a) in Table 5–3 is translated into a visual representation that tilts upward to the right, whereas the negative correlation in panel (c) is depicted as sloping downward to the right. Thus, you can see how knowing a person's score on one variable helps predict (though not perfectly in these cases) the level of performance on the other. So knowing a person's head size in the hypothetical data in the (a) and (c) panels helps to predict recall, and vice versa. This is the primary reason correlations are useful: They specify the strength of relations and allow predictions to be made.

This last statement cannot be made about the data in panel (b), where there is essentially a zero correlation. The points are just scattered about, and there

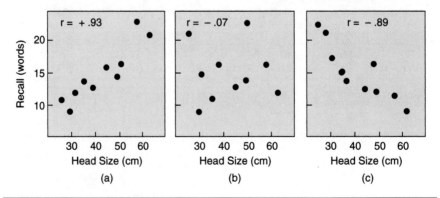

Figure 5–1 Graphical representation of the data in Table 5–3 showing the characteristic pattern of (a) a high positive correlation, (b) an essentially zero correlation, and (c) a strong negative correlation.

is no consistent relation, which is just what a low Pearson *r* reflects. Even in the cases where the size of the correlation is rather large, it will not be possible to predict perfectly an individual's score on one variable given his or her position on the other. Even with *r* = +.75 between head size and number of words recalled, it is still quite possible for a person with a large head size to recall few words, and vice versa. Only when the correlation is perfect (–1.00 or +1.00) will prediction of one score when given the other be perfect.

What do you think the real correlation would be between head size and recall for a random sample of the population at large? Although we have not actually done such a study, we think it quite likely that it would be positive. Willerman, Schultz, Rutledge, and Bigler (1991) conducted research on a related topic, the relation between brain size and intelligence quotient, or IQ. They found a correlation of +.51 between brain size and IQ in a sample of 40 right-handed white introductory psychology students. In a general review of the literature, Rushton and Ankney (1996) reported that data from several different studies show a correlation of +.44 between brain size and cognitive ability. A later study (Rushton, 1997) found a +.21 correlation between cranial size and IQ. Rushton concluded that only additional research could determine whether the correlational data could be interpreted as brain size causing differences in cognitive ability. What can we conclude from correlational studies? How can correlation coefficients be interpreted? We turn to this issue next.

Interpreting Correlation Coefficients   An important warning is always given in any discussion of correlation: The existence of even a sizable correlation implies nothing about the existence of a causal relationship between the two variables under consideration. *Correlation does not prove causation.* Based on one correlation by itself, one cannot say whether factor X causes factor Y, factor Y causes factor X, or some underlying third factor causes both. Let us consider some examples. Suppose we have found a correlation of +.70 between head size and recall of words in children. This is in general agreement with our theory that larger heads hold more information, but certainly other interpretations of this relationship are possible. It could be argued that the high positive correlation between head size and recall is mediated or produced by some third variable underlying both, such as age. We know that people's heads grow as they age and that recall also improves with age. Therefore, age (or one of its correlates) might actually be responsible for the large positive correlation we have found between head size and number of words recalled. In other words, the internal validity (internal validity is discussed in detail later in this chapter) of relational research is always suspect.

In correlational studies, we cannot conclude that any one factor produces or causes another, because a number of factors are likely to vary simultaneously with those of interest. In an experiment, we attempt to avoid this problem by directly manipulating one factor while holding all the others constant. If we are successful in holding other factors constant, which is very difficult to do, then the influence of the manipulated factor on whatever we are measuring can be directly attributed to the factor of interest. Recall that when two (or more) factors are varied at the same time, so that we cannot know whether one factor, the other factor, or both operating together produce some effect, we say that the factors are confounded. Confounding is inherent in correlational research and leads to the interpretation difficulties with such research. In the example of the correlation between head size and recall, we cannot say that variations in head size produced or caused differences in recall, because head size was confounded with at least one other factor: age.

In other cases, the relation between two factors may seem to allow a causal interpretation, but again, this is not strictly permitted. Some studies have shown a positive correlation between the number of handguns in a geographic area and the number of murders in that area. Proponents of gun control might use this evidence to support the contention that an increased number of guns leads to (causes, produces) more murders, but again, this is not the only plausible interpretation. It may be that people in high-crime neighborhoods buy handguns to protect themselves, or that some third factor, such as socioeconomic class, actually mediates both. We can see, therefore, that no conclusion is justified simply based on a moderate or even a high correlation.

Because correlations can be calculated between any two sets of scores, often even very high correlations are accidental and not linked to one another at all. There may be a very high correlation between the number of preachers and the number of pornographic movies produced each year since 1950, with both being on the increase. However, it would take an unusual theory to relate these two in a causal manner.

A high degree of correlation is given greater weight in cases in which obvious competing explanations from confounding factors seem less plausible. Most of the early evidence linking cigarette smoking to lung cancer was correlational. Yet the conclusion was drawn (over the protests of the cigarette manufacturers) in the 1964 U.S. Surgeon General's report that cigarettes were likely to lead to or cause cancer. This eventually led to warnings on cigarette packages and a ban on advertising cigarettes on television, among other things. The correlation was considered indicative of a causative relationship, probably because competing hypotheses seemed implausible. It appears unlikely, for example, that having lung cancer causes one to smoke more cigarettes (to soothe the lungs?).

More plausible, perhaps, is the possibility that some underlying third variable (such as anxiety) produces the relationship. In fact, Eysenck and Eaves (1981) argued that the correlation between lung cancer and smoking in humans is produced by personality differences. Certain personality types, according to Eysenck and Eaves, are more likely to smoke and to get lung cancer. Thus, they argued that the smoking/cancer correlation does not imply causation. We should mention, though, that the link between cigarette smoking and lung cancer has now been established by experimental studies with nonhuman animals, typically beagles. Most scientists disagree with the view of Eysenck and Eaves.

As another example of the pitfalls of the correlational approach, consider the negative relation mentioned previously between cigarette smoking and grades. More smoking has been related to poorer grades. However, does smoking cause poorer grades? This seems unlikely, and certainly there are ready alternative interpretations. Students with poor grades may be more anxious and thus smoke more, or more sociable students may smoke more and study less, and so on. No firm conclusions on the causal direction of a relation between two variables can be established simply because the variables are correlated, even if the correlation is perfect. As is true for the descriptive methods, the correlational method is very useful for suggesting possible relations and directing further inquiry, but it is not useful for establishing direct causal relationships. The correlational method is superior to descriptive methods, because the degree of relation between two variables can be precisely stated. Further, predictions can thus be made about the (approximate) value of one variable if the value of the other is known. Remember, the greater the correlation (nearer -1.00 or $+1.00$), the better the prediction.

Low Correlations: A Caution If high correlations cannot be interpreted as evidence for some sort of causal relation, one might think it should at least be possible to rule it out if the correlation is very low, approaching zero. If the correlation between head size and recall had been $-.02$, would this have ruled out our theory that greater head size leads to better recall? If the correlation between smoking and lung cancer had been $+.08$, should we have abandoned the idea that they are causally related? The answer: sometimes, under certain conditions. However, other factors can cause low or zero correlations and may mask an actual relationship.

One common problem is that of **truncated range**. For a meaningful correlation coefficient to be calculated, there must be rather great differences among the scores in each of the variables of interest; there must be a certain amount of spread or variability in the numbers. If all the head sizes were the same in the panels of Table 5–3 and the recall scores varied, the correlation between the two would be zero. (You can work it out yourself using the equation for r in Appendix A.) Suppose we looked only at the correlation between head size and recall in college students. It might be quite low, because the differences in head size and recall among college students might not be very great compared with the population at large. This could happen even though there might be a positive (or negative) correlation between the two variables if head size were sampled over a wider range. The problem of restricted range can produce a low correlation, even when there is an actual correlation present between two variables.

You might think that everyone would recognize the problem of truncated range and avoid it, but it is often subtle. At a college with very high admission standards, consider the problem of trying to predict success in college from SAT scores. The scores on the verbal and quantitative subtests can range from 200 to 800, with average (mean) performance of just less than 500. Imagine that mean scores at our hypothetical college are 800 on each subtest. The admissions officer at this college computes a correlation between combined SAT scores and freshman grades and finds $r = .00$, very small indeed. Her conclusion: SAT scores cannot be used to predict grades in college. The problem, however, is that the only scores considered are ones from a very restricted range, specifically all the same. People with low scores are not admitted to the college. Obviously, the truncated-range problem is very likely to be a factor here, or in any research situation involving a limited sample of subjects with homogeneous characteristics.

This example, where all the scores on one variable are the same, is obviously fictional. Bridgeman and associates (2000) looked at the correlation between SAT I scores and freshman grades both collectively and individually at 23 colleges and universities. When they adjusted scores for restrictions in range, they found that higher average SAT I scores predicted freshman grades somewhat better than lower average SAT I scores. The reason for this result is difficult to determine, but it may arise from the fact that grades receive higher emphasis at the more selective schools. Because psychologists often use homogeneous populations such as college students, the restricted-range problem must be carefully considered in interpreting correlations.

A final problem in interpreting low correlations is that one must be certain that the assumptions underlying the use of a particular correlation coefficient have been met. Otherwise, its use may well be inappropriate and lead to spuriously low estimates of relationship. These have not been discussed here, but it is imperative to check on these assumptions in a statistics book before employing Pearson r or any other correlation coefficient. For example, one assumption underlying Pearson r is that the relationship between the two variables is linear (can be described by a straight line) rather than curvilinear, as in the hypothetical (but plausible) relationship in Figure 5–2 between age and long-term memory. At very young ages, the line is flat. Then it increases between ages 3 and 16, where it again levels off until late middle age, where it drops slightly, until very old age, where it decreases at a greater rate (Howard & Wiggs, 1993). Thus, one can predict recall of words from age, but Pearson r will be rather low, because the relationship between the two variables is not linear. This could, of course, always be checked by plotting a scatter diagram, as in Figure 5–2. Low correlations, then, may not reflect that a relationship is absent but, rather, only that the assumptions of the particular coefficient employed have not been met.

Reactivity in Correlational Research   As mentioned in previous chapters, many of the participant reactivity problems found in descriptive research are also applicable to correlational research, because test results and survey data often provide the bases for correlations. In fact, demands on participants might be magnified in correlational research that involves two measures taken at the same time. Participants do not usually react passively to the inquiries of the researcher. Instead, they often try to figure out what is going on and re-

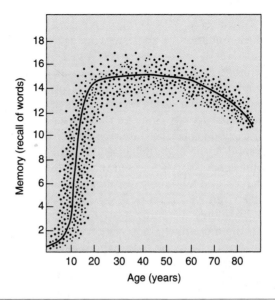

Figure 5-2   A hypothetical figure depicting a curvilinear relationship between long-term memory and age. Although memory is related to age in a systematic fashion, and one could predict recall by knowing age, Pearson *r* would be quite low, because the relationship is not linear.

spond according to their perceptions of the project and in ways that will make themselves look good to the researcher (Weber & Cook, 1972). For example, suppose you surveyed a college population about their sexual and religious attitudes. At the same time, you also asked them about their use of drugs. Most college students could figure out at least some of the purposes of the project, and consequently, their responses to the two sets of questions asked together might differ from their responses to either set asked alone.

Regression

In our fictitious study relating head size to word recall, we could have based the discussion around the prediction of one variable given the other. This use of the correlation coefficient is called **regression** (symbolized by *R* to distinguish it from *r*). Usually a researcher uses regression when there are many correlations available that involve several variables, each of which is correlated with a target independent variable that is to be predicted. This procedure with multiple variables is called **multiple regression**. Thus, in our head size/word recall study, we could also correlate age and intelligence with word recall. A multiple regression would then be done to see whether the three variables together (head size, age, and intelligence) would predict word recall better than each variable by itself.

Collins et al. (2004) report a regression analysis of their work on predicting the initiation of adolescent sexual behavior from watching sex on television. Over 1,700 adolescents (12 to 17 years of age) were interviewed on the telephone for baseline measures and then again one year later. During each interview, the adolescents reported on their sexual experience, their TV viewing, and more than a dozen other factors associated with the initiation of adolescent sexual activity. Some of these latter factors, called **covariates** because they too can influence the initiation of sexual activity, included family structure, parental supervision, religiosity, and the personality trait of sensation seeking. Collins and associates found that TV exposure to sexual content (both sexual behavior and talk about sexual activity) predicted the initiation of intercourse in the virgin participants, $R = +.47$, when they held constant the influence of the covariates. Thus the more the adolescents watched TV with sexual content, the more likely they were to initiate sexual intercourse in the following year. For those participants who had engaged in intercourse at the time of the first interview, Collins and associates found that viewing TV with sexual content advanced the level of their sexual activity, $R = +.37$. The remainder of our discussion of this research will consider only the data pertinent to the initiation of intercourse.

Many of the covariates by themselves also predicted the initiation of intercourse. Living with both parents was a negative predictor ($R = -.54$), as were close parental monitoring of TV viewing and religiosity. The trait of sensation seeking (Zuckerman, 1996) is characterized by thrill-seeking activities and the desire to take risks, and sensation seeking itself predicts initiation of intercourse ($R = +.60$).

Collins and her associates combined variables in several ways to see the predictions. They compared the predictability of intercourse initiation for those with high exposure to TV sexual content (at the 90th percentile) with those with low exposure (at the 10th percentile). At all ages studied (12–17 years), the high-exposure adolescents were twice as likely to initiate intercourse as were the low-exposure children.

The regression analyses in the research by Collins and her associates pinpoint the influence of viewing TV with sexual content. Although it is clear that TV sexual content alters the sexual behavior of adolescents, what is not so clear is the particular causal variables that underlie the initiation of intercourse in the teen years.

Complex Correlational Procedures

Does watching violent TV programs cause aggressive behavior? Eron, Huesmann, Lefkowitz, and Walder (1972) measured children's preferences for violent programs and the children's aggressiveness as rated by their peers. For these third-graders, Eron and coworkers found a moderate positive correlation, $r = +.21$, indicating that children who were more aggressive tended to watch more violent TV (and less aggressive children tended to watch less violent programs). How are we to interpret this positive correlation? Can we say that watching violent programs causes aggressiveness? The answer is no. To see why this is the case, all we have to do is turn our causal statement around. We could assert that being aggressive causes a preference for violent TV. We have no reasonable way to decide on the direction of causality, based on this one correlation coefficient. Causal statements are difficult, if not impossible, to make based on a single correlational study. Instead, researchers typically view correlational evidence as tentative until there is converging evidence from independent studies and a compelling underlying mechanism is identified.

The internal validity of correlational research may be enhanced by examining patterns of correlations. One technique is called the **cross-lagged-panel correlation procedure.** Eron and coworkers used it in a 10-year follow-up study of the same children in the "thirteenth" grade. They also used it in a recent project that examined aggression in adults who were initially interviewed in the mid-1970s (Huesmann, Moise-Titu, Podolski, & Eron, 2003). The designs of the two studies are summarized in the two panels of Figure 5–3.

The logic of the cross-lagged procedure is that the correlations along the diagonals will help us understand the direction of causation between the variables. Do aggressive people watch violent TV, or does watching violent TV produce aggression? If watching violent TV produces aggressive behavior, we would expect a small or null relationship between early aggression and later preference for violent TV (the dashed diagonals in Figure 5–3). We would also expect a positive correlation between an early preference for violent TV and later aggression (the thick, solid diagonals). The underlying assumption is that if one variable causes the other, the first (watching violent TV programs) should be more strongly related to the second (aggressiveness) later in time than when the second (effect) variable is measured at the same time as the first (causal) variable. The remaining correlations are of interest and may permit predictions, but they suffer from the inability to determine causation. In the 1972 project, 211 males were studied. Both males (152) and females (176) provided data for the 2003 report.

For the 1972 study, the correlation between a preference for violent TV and aggression was essentially zero ($r = +.05$). They obtained a relation between aggressiveness in the two grades ($r = +.38$), indicating that aggression is a somewhat stable trait. The cross-lagged correlation between aggressiveness in the third grade and preference for violent TV in the thirteenth was very small ($r = +.01$). On the other hand, the crucial cross-lagged correlation between early watching of violent TV and aggression in the thirteenth grade was positive and statistically significant, $r = +.31$. Similar results appeared in the 2003 report. The important cross-lagged correlation between watching violent TV in childhood and adult aggression was positive and significant for both males ($r = +.21$) and females ($r = +.19$). The crossed-lag correlation between childhood aggression and adult TV violence viewing was small for both males ($r = +.08$) and females ($r = +.10$).

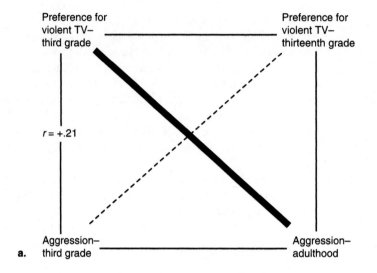

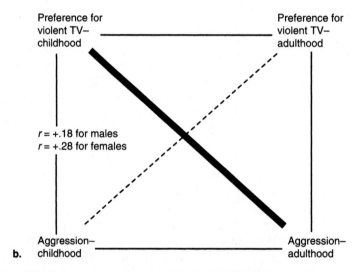

Figure 5–3   (a) The cross-lagged-panel correlation design used by Eron et al. (1972), who examined the correlations between a preference for violent TV programs and aggression as rated by peers. The diagonals indicate important cross-lagged-lagged correlations. The dashed correlation should be small. The solid one is expected to be positive and large. (b) The design used by Huesmann et al. (2003). Preference for violent TV programs was correlated with aggression. Subjects were first examined at ages 6 to 10 and then about 15 years later. Adult aggression was measured by self-reported incidents, ratings by another person (including spouses), and arrest records. The aggression index includes both physical and verbal aggression.

The cross-lagged-panel correlations in these studies, along with other complex analyses, led Eron and colleagues to conclude that childhood exposure to violent TV increases later aggression (also see Eron, 1982, and Huesmann, Eron, Lefkowitz, & Walder, 1973). This is just one example of how the cross-lagged procedure can aid in arriving at a solid explanation in correlational research. However, causal statements cannot be as strong as those derived from experiments, because the correlated variables have not been manipulated by the researcher. Clearly, many other variables contribute to aggressiveness.

The general strategy of the cross-lagged procedure, then, is to obtain several correlations over time and, based on the size and direction of the coefficients of correlation, determine what leads to what. The cross-lagged technique has the obvious drawback that the research project may be very time-consuming. Nevertheless, this method for determining causation from correlational research has been used with success in several problem areas. Several other statistical procedures are used to try to gain a better understanding of causation in correlational research. The techniques typically involve an examination of several relationships, not just a single correlation, and are described in numerous texts (see especially Cook & Campbell, 1979).

CONCEPT SUMMARY

In correlational research, correlation coefficients describe the strength and direction of relations, which permit prediction. Correlations have suspect internal validity because of

- the third-variable problem
- truncated range
- unknown direction of causation

The cross-lagged-panel correlation procedure enhances the internal validity.

Experimentation and Internal Validity

We have repeatedly cautioned you about incorrectly concluding that a correlation means causation. Causation is a controversial subject in science and philosophy, and we will now consider some of the issues. Owing to the influence of some philosophers of science, it has become unpopular among contemporary scientists to use the term *cause,* because the philosophical implications become frightfully complicated. Thinking too long about the cause of even a very simple event leads to an infinite regress of causes for that event. For this and other reasons, the term *cause* has dropped out of use in some circles (see the Application section on causation for further discussion).

In this book, we muddle through using the term *cause,* because its meaning is always limited. Experiments lead to causal inferences, because the independent variable is manipulated while all others are, in the ideal case, held constant. Whatever effect on the dependent variable that occurs in such cases has been caused by the factor that varied. Thus, we can say that when the Stroop experiment is conducted in such a way that confounding is minimized, changes in the levels of the independent variable cause changes in the dependent variable.

A more interesting point is that many factors that are experimentally varied are themselves quite complicated sets of independent events, any one of which could be the cause of an experimental effect. Time is a good example of such a variable. If we are interested in the effects of the length of time that one studies a persuasive communication on the amount a person's attitude changes toward the communication, we vary the amount of time people spend studying the message. Suppose we find an increase in attitude change with increases in study time when other factors are held constant? Can we say that time has caused an increase in attitude change? In a sense, this is true, but in a more fundamental sense, it is not. Presumably, some psychological process acting over time causes the attitude change. It is something correlated with time, but not time itself, because time is not a causative agent. If we leave a bicycle outdoors in the rain and it rusts, we do not say that time caused the rust; chemical processes acting over time caused it.

Usually, a manipulated variable is actually composed of a number of complex and interacting parts, any one or set of which may actually cause some effect. For this reason, it is sometimes said that experiments are only controlled correlations, because the variable manipulated is actually composed of a number of confounded parts. This is certainly an accurate characterization in at least some cases. Even so, we are far ahead of having a simple correlation, because we know the direction of effect. Take the example of how amount of time spent studying a persuasive communication affects attitude change. We could simply give the message to a number of people and let them read it for as long as they desired. We could time this for each person and then see how much the person's attitude changed. If we found a positive correlation, we would not know whether the time people spent studying the passage caused more attitude change or whether the more people decided to change their attitudes, the more they studied the passage to make sure they knew the facts. There are other possible reasons for the relationship too. In the experiment in which time is varied while other factors are held constant, however, we can say that more study time leads to (determines, produces, causes) more attitude change.

Experiments allow us to know the direction of the relation. This is their overwhelming advantage to correlations. They also inform us (which a correlation does not) that the causal factor is at least embedded in the independent variable and not some third outside factor. It is in this sense that they tell us about causes and are internally valid, at least in principle.

APPLICATION

Causation

If you generate a visual image of something you are trying to remember, you will retain it better if you simply repeat the information (Bower, 1972). The philosophical implications of *why* imagery enhances remembering can become extremely complicated. Thinking too long about the cause of even a very simple event can lead to an infinite regress of causes for that event. A regressive causal analysis of the effects of imagery might be as follows: Imagery causes better remembering than simple repetition. Why? Because imagery results in more associations than does repetition. Why? Because more protein molecules in the brain become active when imagery is used. Why? Because evolution determined the structure of the human brain. Why? Because . . .

In this book, we use the terms *cause* and *why* because their meanings here are always limited. Experiments can lead to causal inferences because one factor is varied while other factors are held constant, and we can say that the effect was caused by the factor that varied. In the typical psychology experiment, therefore, the immediate causes of an effect are determined. These immediate causes are called the **proximate causes** of an event and are to be distinguished from the **ultimate causes** (Mayr, 1982). Proximate causes derive from the immediate manipulations in an experiment (for example, instructions to the participants to use imagery or repeti-

tion). Ultimate causes are those that are supposed to stop the infinite regress of "why" and "because" as outlined earlier. One ultimate answer to our questions about imagery could be an appeal to evolution. Biologists argue that evolution is the ultimate cause behind all aspects of biology and therefore provides the physiological and genetic framework for ultimate causation in psychology (Mayr, 1982). According to such an analysis, imagery instructions would be the proximate cause of differences in retention, and evolutionary forces would be the ultimate cause for the effectiveness of those instructions. There are other possible ultimate causes (for example, a deity), and we could argue that something had to set evolution in motion (perhaps a "big bang"). Because of these possibilities, the distinction between proximate causation and ultimate causation may not be clear or relevant. Therefore, many people prefer asking "Under what conditions does imagery enhance memory?" instead of "Why does imagery enhance memory?" Likewise, instead of saying "Imagery causes better memory," some people prefer to say "Imagery may enhance [is an antecedent condition of, determines, or directly affects] memory." Because we generally will be talking about individual experiments, we will use the latter phrases interchangeably with *cause* and *why* where appropriate.

CONCEPT SUMMARY

Experiments are internally valid because the causal variables and the direction of causation are known.

Summary

1. Relational research attempts to show how two variables change together.
2. A contingency table is a form of research that looks at the frequencies of all combinations of categories of two variables.
3. The statistical reliability of a contingency table is often assessed by the χ^2 test for independence.
4. Usually, contingency tables assess the relationship between nominal variables.
5. Correlational research permits a determination of the strength and direction of relations among variables.
6. The internal validity of the correlational technique is suspect because of third-variable confounding, an unknown direction of causation, and sometimes a truncated range of scores on one or more of the variables. Clever use of regression analyses can enhance the prediction of certain outcomes.
7. The cross-lagged-panel correlation procedure can increase the internal validity of the correlational technique by showing the direction of causation.
8. Experimentation allows causal statements in principle, which means that experiments can be internally valid.

Key Concepts

cell (111)
contingency table (111)
correlation coefficients (114)
correlational research (114)
covariates (122)
cross-lagged-panel correlation procedure (123)

ex post facto (111)
multiple regression (121)
Pearson's product-moment correlation coefficient (Pearson r) (115)
proximate causes (127)

regression (121)
relational research (111)
scatter diagrams (116)
truncated range (119)
ultimate causes (127)
χ^2 test for independence (112)

Exercises

1. [*Special Exercise.*] A psychologist studied the remote memory of college graduates by seeing how many names of old television programs they could correctly recognize. The results indicated that there was no correlation between the graduates' intelligence-test scores and their ability to recognize the names of old programs ($r = +.07$). Assume that the procedure of memory testing was valid and that the age of the participants was not a problem. Can you think of some problems in this research that would prevent you from making a valid conclusion about the small r?
2. An illustration of how Pearson r is calculated for the data in column (a) of Table 5–3 is presented in Box A–1 of Appendix A. Work through this

example, and then calculate *r* values for the data in columns (b) and (c) of Table 5–3. Make sure that your *r* values are the same as those given at the bottom of Table 5–3.

3. The table here shows some fictitious data from a college admissions office. For 10 students, we have the scores from the verbal portion of their SAT as well as their freshman GPA. The GPA is on a 4-point scale, where F = 0, D = 1, C = 2, B = 3, and A = 4 points. Calculate the correlation coefficient between these two sets of scores. What might you conclude?

Student	Verbal SAT	Student GPA
1	471	2.00
2	403	1.50
3	510	2.25
4	485	2.00
5	575	2.25
6	445	1.75
7	400	2.50
8	590	3.25
9	560	2.50
10	555	2.75

4. [*Special Exercise.*] There are a number of potential methodological problems associated with relational research. Some of them are discussed in this chapter. What are these methodological problems, and how are they overcome?

Suggested Resource

An extensive discussion of research relating aggression to watching violent television can be found in Eron, L. D. (1982). Parent-child interaction, television violence, and aggression of children. *American Psychologist, 37,* 197–211.

Web Resources

Websites that describe relational statistical procedures are: http://www.mcgill.ca/course/ 204204b01 and www.prophet.bbn.com/statguide. General information about relational and other kinds of research can be found at: http://www.columbia.edu/~abm/6/design.html
Wadsworth workshops on nonexperimental approaches can be found at: http://www.wadsworth. com/psychology_d/templates/student_resources/workshops/workshops.html

Laboratory Resources

Langston's manual (2005) discusses relational research in Chapter 3. The major issue examined by Langston is the relationship between pet ownership and health. In Chapter 11, Langston discusses the problem of causal statements based on correlations. Langston, W. (2005). *Research methods laboratory manual for psychology.* Pacific Grove, CA: Wadsworth Group.

Amount of Sleep and Tension Headaches

This project is a variation of a research procedure used by Hicks and Kilcourse (1983). These researchers were interested in the relationship between the number of hours of sleep that participants got and the frequency of tension or migraine headaches the participants experienced. In a health survey, the researchers asked college students (a) to estimate the number of hours of sleep they usually got each night, and (b) whether they had tension or migraine headaches *often, sometimes,* or *never.* Hicks and Kilcourse found an inverse relationship between these two variables; that is, people with more headaches slept less than those with fewer headaches. The researchers' mode of categorizing the frequency of headaches and the amount of sleep naturally leads to a contingency table research design. The amount of sleep could be categorized as *inadequate* or *adequate.* Alternatively, you could categorize the amount of sleep along a ratio dimension (that is, the number of hours of sleep usually obtained).

An alternate way of conducting this research would be as a correlation design. To use a Pearson *r*, you would need to have two pairs of measures that are interval or ratio in nature. One way to do this would be as follows. You can modify the second question by asking: "Estimate the number of tension or migraine headaches you have each month." Ask 20 or so of your college acquaintances the modified question and the one concerning the estimated number of hours of sleep. Survey enough people so that you do not have a truncated range on one of your variables. Then calculate the *r* between these two variables. You can enhance the reliability of your results by combining your data with those of classmates. If you pool your data, make sure that you and the others doing the project are surveying different people. When your data are combined, you may wind up with a large number of participants, so you will find that MINITAB or some other statistical package will be helpful in calculating *r*.

To anticipate a later Psychology in Action project (see Chapter 11), you should collect some additional demographic data on your participants, such as age, gender, and year in school.

Hicks, R. A., & Kilcourse, J. (1983). Habitual sleep duration and the incidence of headaches in college students. *Bulletin of the Psychonomic Society, 21,* 119.

CHAPTER 6

Basics of Experimentation

Independent Variables

- At least two levels of a variable are manipulated to provide a standard of comparison. Interactions may occur when there are two or more independent variables.

Dependent Variables

- Specific behaviors are measured in an experiment.

Control Variables

- In the ideal experiment, all other variables are held constant.

Experimental Group or Condition

- The treatment group or condition that receives the level of interest of the independent variable

Control Group or Condition

- The group or condition that is untreated or receives a comparison (baseline) level of the independent variable

Possible Sources of Error

- Participant reactivity
- External validity

A tightly designed, well-conducted experiment is the goal of psychologists who attempt to answer the question of why we act as we do. This chapter considers the basic characteristics of a good experiment. The essential ingredient of an experiment is production of a comparison while holding other variables constant.

► Experimentation: An Example

Can you name:

A famous theme park in the heart of Copenhagen

The world's largest single rock in Australia

The main law court in London

The actress who played Hermione in *Harry Potter and the Prisoner of Azkaban*

The actress who played the grandmother in the *Sopranos*

The actor who played the President in the *West Wing*?

You probably were able to answer some of these questions and were utterly unable to answer others. Perhaps there were some questions whose answers you were not sure of but which you felt you might know. Indeed, the answer might be on the tip of your tongue. (Answers: Tivoli Gardens, Ayers Rock, Old Bailey, Emma Watson, Nancy Marchand, and Martin Sheen.)

The tip-of-the-tongue state has been much studied by experimental psychologists interested in human memory (Brown & McNeill, 1966). It occurs when you have partial knowledge of an answer and the feeling that you could recognize the answer if it were given to you. For example, Brown and McNeill discovered that when people said they were in a tip-of-the-tongue state, they could correctly identify the first letter of the answer 57% of the time, even though the entire correct answer could not be produced.

What kind of information might help elicit correct answers from people in tip-of-the-tongue states? The answer to this question has important implications for understanding how we encode and store information in memory. Brennen, Baguley, Bright, and Bruce (1990) performed an experiment to discover whether a visual picture aided recall in tip-of-the-tongue states. Their first experiment was very simple. They presented a list of 50 questions about television celebrities and noted when their experimental participants, 15 college undergraduates, reported they were in a tip-of-the-tongue state. On average, this happened 10.5 times per participant. Of course, some participants had only a few tip-of-the-tongue states and some had many (the range was 4 to 22 incidences), but on average, about 20% of the questions produced tip-of-the-tongue states. Once this state occurred, the experimenters either asked the question again or showed a picture of the face of the television personality. Results of this experiment are shown in Figure 6–1. Clearly, presenting faces did not help resolve tip-of-the-tongue states any better than did merely repeating the question.

One experiment by itself seldom satisfies experimental psychologists, so Brennen and others performed a second experiment both to expand their findings and to ensure that their initial results could be repeated. In this experiment, they doubled the number of participants to 30. They also added a new

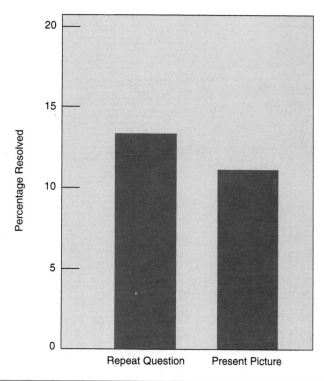

Figure 6–1 The results of the first experiment showing the percentage of tip-of-the-tongue states resolved as a function of the two conditions. (From T. Brennen, J. Bright, & V. Bruce (1990), "Resolving semantically induced tip-of-the-tongue states" in *Memory & Cognition, 18,* 339–347. Reprinted with permission.)

condition in which the person's initials were presented. So, now there were three experimental conditions: (a) repeat the question, (b) present a picture, and (c) present letter initials. Results of this second experiment are shown in Figure 6–2.

These results tell us two important things: First, repeating the questions and presenting a picture were equally effective. This means that the results of the first experiment have been repeated. Second, presenting letter initials was much more effective in resolving tip-of-the-tongue states than either repeating the question or presenting a picture. This result implies that memory information is stored in such a way that only the spelling of a name, and not a visual image, can aid memory retrieval in tip-of-the-tongue states.

This conclusion illustrates how experiments let us find the causes of behavioral events. In the first experiment, similar results for repeating the question and presenting a picture did not allow us to distinguish between these two possible causes of aided memory retrieval. In the second experiment, however, presenting letter initials did cause a memory improvement. How do experiments permit us to make such causal statements?

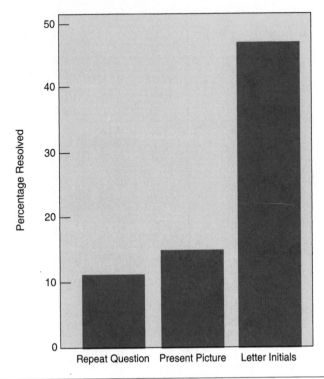

Figure 6–2   The results of the second experiment showing the percentage of tip-of-the-tongue states resolved as a function of the three conditions. (From T. Brennen, J. Bright, & V. Bruce (1990), "Resolving semantically inducted tip-of-the-tongue states" in *Memory & Cognition, 18,* 339–347. Reprinted with permission.)

▶ What Is an Experiment?

As discussed in Chapter 5, **experiments** are tests designed to arrive at a causal explanation (see Cook & Campbell, 1979). The conditions necessary for arriving at explanations were set forth in the nineteenth century by the philosopher John Stuart Mill (1843, reprinted 1930). The conditions he outlined provide a good definition of an experiment.

Mill argued that causation can be inferred if some result, X, follows an event, A, if A and X vary together and if it can be shown that event A produces result X. For these conditions to be met, what Mill called the **joint method of agreement and difference** must be used. In the joint method, if A occurs, then so will X, and if A does not occur, then neither will X.

Let us apply this reasoning to the experiment on tip-of-the-tongue states. Here the result X is a correct resolution of the tip-of-the-tongue state. The event A is presenting letter initials. Figure 6–2 showed that event A produced result X. Furthermore, if A is absent (for example, the question is repeated but no letter initials are presented), then result X is not produced. This is Mill's joint method of agreement and difference at work.

The situation even in this simple experiment is more complicated, however, because event *A* does not always produce *X*, and the absence of event *A* does not always fail to produce *X*. As shown by Figure 6–2, presenting letter initials did not resolve 100% of the tip-of-the-tongue states. Similarly, merely repeating the question does resolve tip-of-the-tongue states a small percentage of the time, and this small percentage is greater than zero. Thus, in practice most experiments do not show causality all the time for every single trial in the experiment. Instead, most experimental psychologists are content if event *A* produces result *X* more than some other event *B*. (The question of how much more is answered by statistical analysis, which is explained in Appendix B. For now, we ignore how much and only ask if there is any more *X* produced.)

So, a more complete statement of causality is that event *A* (presenting letter initials) produces more resolution of tip-of-the-tongue states (*X*) than does event *B* (repeating the question) or event *C* (presenting a picture). At first, you might incorrectly conclude that event *A* causes *X* a great deal and that event *C* causes only a little bit of *X*, but this would be wrong. Most experiments have within them a baseline condition that evaluates neutral events, such as the passage of time, that are not believed to have causal influence. For some event to exert causal influence on behavior, it must have a greater effect than the neutral baseline event. In this experiment, repeating the question is the neutral baseline event. Any small effect this might produce is not interesting by itself. Instead, this calibrates other events of potentially greater interest. For example, event *C* (presenting a picture) might be expected (from certain theories of memory) to produce a causal relationship with *X*. If the experimenters had omitted baseline event *B* (repeating the question) in Figure 6–1, they might have mistakenly concluded that event *C* caused *X*, because more than 0% of the tip-of-the-tongue states were resolved. As Figure 6–1 shows, however, event *B* was as effective as event *C*. Therefore, we conclude that no causal relationship exists between events *C* and *X*. This lack of a causal relationship inspired the experimenters to perform yet another study (see Figure 6–2) in which a causal relationship was obtained.

Experiments that fail to reveal any causal relationships are seldom published. Although the lack of a causal relationship where one might be expected as a result of theoretical reasons is important, it is even more important to show some causal relationship in an experiment. Failure to find any causal relationships could indicate a flaw in the experimental design (perhaps not enough participants were tested, etc.). Thus, finding at least one causal relationship in an experiment gives us some confidence that a failure to exhibit causality with some different event in the same experiment is more likely to be correct rather than to have happened because of some (unknown) deficiencies in the experiment itself.

The hallmark of an experiment is the production of a comparison by controlling the occurrence or nonoccurrence of a variable and observing the outcome. Boring (1954) noted that the concept of **control** in experimentation derives from the joint method of agreement and difference. One way we can view control is in terms of direct manipulation (*A* occurs or does not occur), which, according to the joint method of agreement and difference, leads to a basis for comparison (hence the term *control group,* as explained later). Control also suggests that we can eliminate alternative explanations of our results. Usually, control in experimentation is thought of in three ways: (a) There is a control condition for purposes of *comparison,* (b) the levels or values of the independent variable can be *produced,* and (c) the experimental setting can be controlled by holding certain aspects *constant* (for example, type of apparatus or method of measurement). These three types of control—comparison, production, and constancy—are crucial to the conduct of an experiment that will yield an explanation of why people and animals behave as they do. In fact, comparison, production, and constancy provide us with a definition of an experiment.

CONCEPT SUMMARY

An experiment occurs when a particular comparison is produced while other aspects of the situation are held constant.

In summary, producing comparisons, as Brennen and colleagues did, can allow us to rule out the possibility of a mere correlation between variables. Correct use of Mill's procedure can lead to causal statements.

▶ Advantages of Experimentation

Let us examine another research problem to illustrate the advantages of experimentation. One characteristic of modern life is that many of us are subjected to changes in atmospheric pressure during air travel. Furthermore, a substantial portion of the world's population lives at elevations between 2,000 and 10,000 feet. What this means is that many people are subjected to mild decompressions in barometric pressure. Are these decompressions hazardous, as so many other things are in the world today (such as pollution, pesticides, and food additives)? This question was the impetus for experiments conducted by Graessle, Ahbel, and Porges (1978). Early research indicated that greatly reduced barometric pressure (as occurs in altitudes greater than 10,000 feet) can retard both fetal and newborn development. Graessle and colleagues wanted to see whether lesser decompressions, more like those experienced during air travel, also affected the development of infants.

To study this problem, the researchers experimented with pregnant rats. The general procedure was to subject the rats to a series of mild decompressions similar to those experienced during air travel (around 6,000 feet) and then compare the growth and behavior of rats born to the mothers that experienced decompression with the growth and behavior of rats born to mothers kept at ground level (728 feet, in this instance).

Now for some particulars of their research. Pregnant rats were randomly divided into two groups: One group received seven daily decompressions for 20 days during pregnancy, and the second group was kept at ground level. Changes in pressure for the one group (up to a pressure equaling an altitude of 6,000 feet) lasted for about 20 minutes. These changes in pressure were gradual, simulating the sorts of changes that occur during air travel. Following birth, all infant rats were weighed daily and received periodic testing of their ability to grasp a thin wire, turn over (the righting reflex), move on an inclined plane, and climb (pull themselves up a thin wall when suspended by their forepaws).

The *independent variable* (what was varied) was atmospheric pressure, and the *dependent variables* (the things observed and measured) included the weight of the babies and the various behaviors just described. In Brennen's experiments, cuing condition was the independent variable, which had two levels in the first study and three levels in the second one. What was the dependent variable? At this point, we need to mention a third class of variables, the *control variables,* which the experimenter holds constant. In the decompression experiment, control variables included similar housing and feeding conditions for all rats at all times, identical testing procedures, and treated and untreated mothers of the same strain of rats. In Brennen's work, species, age, and persons to be identified were among the control variables.

Ordinarily we call the group of subjects that receives the independent variable the **experimental group;** the designation for the untreated subjects is the **control group.** (Note that a control group is not the same as a control variable. The meaning of "control group" will become clear momentarily.) In the decompression experiment, the decompressed mother rats and their babies represent the experimental group. The mothers and infants that were kept at ground level as a comparison or baseline group make up the control group. These labels (experimental and control group) make sense in that the control group receives a different treatment, and an examination of this group's behavior serves to indicate changes that would occur in the absence of the independent variable. Thus, the control group *controls* for changes that may occur whether or not any particular variable is introduced into the situation. The experimental group, of course, defines the experiment for us. The experimental group is the one that receives the treatment of interest—decompression, in this case. (Note that we are using Mill's procedure to arrive at an explanation.) Graessle and colleagues found that rats given decompressions before birth began to climb at a later age than the control animals and that the prenatally decompressed rats gained weight more slowly than the controls.

The results of the decompression experiment are intriguing and may have important practical implications. If you were interested in this topic, you might have considered the possibility of doing this experiment with pregnant human beings. The ethics of that tactic would be questionable without knowing in advance the effects of mild decompressions. That is why we do many types of experiments, especially preliminary ones, on animals. An alternative approach to the decompression problem might be to do the research **ex post facto,** which means selecting our participants after the fact. Thus, we could do a quasi-experiment (see Chapter 11). In quasi-experiments, the levels of the independent variable are selected rather than manipulated directly by the experimenter. We would find infants whose mothers had flown on airplanes during pregnancy. Then we would compare their development with that of infants whose mothers had remained at ground level during pregnancy. Other than the tedious job of identifying the participants in the first place (imagine trying to identify human participants ex post facto for this study), the major drawback to the research done ex post facto is a loss of control. As we will discuss later, it is very difficult to hold potentially relevant variables constant after the fact. In particular, we would be hard put to find two groups of participants whose only difference was that some had flown on planes prenatally and some had not.

We can conclude, therefore, that this animal study about the effects of mild decompression is more ethical, more economical, and better controlled than alternative research procedures. This experiment is not problem free, however. You might find it worthwhile to consider some of the difficulties associated with it. One obvious problem concerns generalizing from rat development to human development.

CONCEPT SUMMARY

- In an experiment, a particular comparison is produced while other variables are held constant.
- An experimental group receives the important level of the independent variable.
- A control group serves as the untreated comparison group or receives a comparison level of the independent variable.

▶ Variables in Experimentation

Variables are the gears and cogs that make experiments run. Effective selection and manipulation of variables make the difference between a good experiment and a poor one. This section covers the three kinds of variables that must be carefully considered before starting an experiment: (a) independent, (b) dependent, and (c) control. We conclude by discussing experiments that have more than one independent or dependent variable.

Independent Variables

The **independent variable** is manipulated by the experimenter. The brightness of a lamp, the loudness of a tone, the number of decompressions given to a rat are all independent variables, because the experimenter determines their amount.

Independent variables are selected because an experimenter thinks they will cause changes in behavior. Increasing the intensity of a tone should increase the speed with which people respond to the tone. Increasing the number of decompressions given to a mother rat may change the rate of development of her babies. When a change in the level (amount) of an independent variable causes a change in behavior, we say that the behavior is under control of the independent variable. Failure of an independent variable to control behavior, often called a **null result,** can have more than one interpretation. First, the experimenter may have incorrectly guessed that the independent variable was important, and the null results may be correct. Most scientists will accept this interpretation only reluctantly, so the following alternative explanations of null results are common.

The experimenter may not have created a valid manipulation of the independent variable. Let us say you are conducting an experiment on second-grade children and your independent variable is the number of small treats (chocolates, peanuts, or whatever) the children get after each correct response in some task. Some children get only one, whereas others get two. You find no difference in behavior between the two groups. Perhaps if your independent variable had involved a greater range—that is, if it went from 1 piece of candy to 10 pieces of candy—you would have obtained a difference. Your manipulation was not sufficient to reveal any effect of the independent variable. Or, perhaps unknown to you, the class had a birthday party just before the experiment started, and your participants' stomachs were filled with ice cream and birthday cake. In this case, maybe even 10 pieces of candy would not have shown any effect. That is why, in studies of animal learning in which food is used as a reward, the animals are deprived of food before the experiment starts. Thus, experimenters are careful to produce a strong manipulation of the independent variable. Failure to do so is a common cause of null results. Other common causes of null results are related to dependent and control variables, to which we now turn.

Dependent Variables

The **dependent variable** is observed and recorded by the experimenter. It depends on the behavior of the participant, which, in turn, is supposed to depend on the independent variable. The time it takes to press a switch, the speed of a worm crawling through a maze, and the age at which a rat climbs are all dependent variables, because they are observed and recorded by the experimenter.

One criterion for a good dependent variable is reliability (see Chapter 7 for a discussion of reliability in testing and measurement). When an experiment is repeated exactly—same participant, same levels of independent variable, and so on—the dependent variable should yield about the same score as it did previously. Unreliability can occur if there is some deficit in the way we measure the dependent variable. Let us say we want to measure the weight in grams of a candle before and after it has been lit for 15 minutes. We use a scale that has a spring that moves a pointer. The spring contracts when it is cold and expands when it is hot. As long as our weight measurements are taken at constant temperatures, they will be reliable, but if temperature varies while objects are being weighed, the same object will yield different readings. Our dependent variable is then unreliable. Generally, we want our measuring devices to be consistent, just as it is crucial for the observer to be consistent (as in following a protocol; see Chapters 1 and 4).

Null results can often be caused by deficits in the dependent variable even if it is reliable. The most common cause is a restricted or limited range of the dependent variable so that it gets "stuck" at the top or bottom of its scale. Imagine you are teaching a rather uncoordinated friend how to bowl for the first time. You know from introductory psychology that reward improves performance, so you offer to buy your friend a beer every time he or she gets a strike. Your friend gets all gutter balls so you drink the beer yourself. Thus, you can no longer offer a reward, which means that the unrewarded performance should decrease. Because it is impossible to do any worse than all gutter balls, however, you cannot observe any decrement. Your friend is already at the bottom of the scale. This is called a **floor effect.** The opposite problem, that of getting 100% correct, is called a **ceiling effect.** Ceiling and floor effects prevent the influence of an independent variable from being accurately reflected in a dependent variable (these effects are discussed in detail later).

A final source of null results is one associated with inferential statistics. The results of a statistical test (see Appendix B) may fail to reject the hypothesis that the experimental and control groups do not differ, when in fact they do. This failure to reject the null hypothesis when it should be rejected is called a **type 2 error.** The likelihood of committing a type 2 error increases as we lower the level of statistical significance, but the likelihood can be decreased by increasing the power (sensitivity) of the experiment (see Appendix B).

Control Variables

A **control variable** is a potential independent variable that is held constant during an experiment. It does not vary, because it is controlled by the experimenter. For any one experiment, there are more desirable control variables than can ever be controlled in practice. In even a relatively simple experiment (for example, requiring people to memorize three-letter syllables), many variables should be controlled. Time of day (diurnal cycle) changes a person's efficiency, and ideally this should be controlled. Temperature could be important, because your participant might fall asleep if the testing room is too warm. The time that has elapsed since a person's last meal might also affect memory performance. Intelligence is related. The list could go on. An experimenter tries to control as many salient variables as possible, hoping that the effect of uncontrolled factors will be small relative to the effect of the independent variable. The smaller the size of the effect produced by the independent variable, the more important it is to carefully control extraneous factors.

Holding a variable constant is not the only way to remove extraneous variation. Design techniques, which we shall discuss in Chapter 8, also control extraneous variables. However, holding a variable constant is the most direct experimental technique for controlling extraneous factors, and so we shall limit our definition of control variables to this technique. Null results often occur in an experiment because of insufficient control of these other factors—that is, they have been left to vary unsystematically. This is especially true in studies outside of laboratories, where the ability to hold control variables constant is greatly decreased. Remember, we call these unintended effects **confoundings,** because their influence confounds (or confuses) the proper interpretation of the results. An example of a confounded experiment is presented in the Application section.

Using Variables

In summary, a perfect experiment would have the dependent variable entirely controlled by the independent variable. In practice, this is not very likely. All experiments contain error, which can be defined as other (uncontrolled) influences that alter the dependent variable. The experimenter tries to cope with factors that influence the dependent variable in two ways. First, factors can be studied as independent variables. In many cases, independent variables of minor interest are created to minimize error. For example, if an experiment is performed by several people, an independent variable called Experimenter may be created to account for variation in the dependent variable associated with different experimenters. If this were not done, such potential variation might show up as error in the experiment. Second, factors can be held constant as control variables. Other variation in the dependent variable, not produced by independent variables or not held constant by control variables, is error. Experimenters strive to minimize error.

CONCEPT SUMMARY

- Independent variable is manipulated.
- Dependent variable is observed.
- Control variable is held constant.

Naming the Variables

Because independent, dependent, and control variables are so important, we have included some examples here for you to check your understanding of these terms. For each situation, name the three kinds of variables. Answers are provided at the end of this section.

APPLICATION

Confounded Experiments in Advertising

A major value of a tightly controlled experiment is that the results are unambiguous: You can be confident that the independent variable led to changes in the dependent variable. Your conclusion about the effectiveness of the independent variable depends on minimal effects of extraneous factors—confounding variables. An advertising campaign presented an incorrect conclusion because the intended independent variable (Pepsi versus Coke) was confounded with another variable.

In the advertisement, people were asked to choose between the two cola drinks. In one series Pepsi was in a cup labeled *S* and Coke in a cup marked *L*. Most people chose the drink in the *S* cup (Pepsi), so the conclusion was that cola drinkers prefer Pepsi. Is this a legitimate conclusion?

An experiment by Woolfolk, Castellan, and Brooks (1983) calls the advertising results into question. These authors reasoned that the labels on the cups may have had some influence on the choices made by the

people in the advertisement. This supposition is based on the knowledge that labeling of various kinds can have a strong effect on consumer behavior. As a first step in their research, Woolfolk and her associates determined that college students like the letter *S* better than the letter *L*. Then the researchers had other students choose between the colas presented in cups labeled *L* and *S*. In this experiment, unlike in the advertisement, the letters were the only independent variable, because the type of cola in the cups was held constant. For half the subjects, both cups contained Pepsi; and for the other half, both cups contained Coke. Regardless of the type of cola in the cups, the students preferred cola *S* to cola *L* in 85% of the cases. Thus, it is possible that the conclusion in the advertisement was confounded by the preference for certain letters and did not result from the preference for different colas. Let the viewer beware!

Woolfolk, M. E., Castellan, W., & Brooks, C. I. (1983). Pepsi versus Coke: Labels, not tastes, prevail. *Psychological Reports, 52,* 185–186.

1. An automobile manufacturer wants to know how bright brake lights should be to minimize the time required for the driver of a following car to realize that the car in front is stopping. An experiment is conducted to answer this. Name the variables.

2. A pigeon is trained to peck a key if a green light is illuminated but not if a red light is on. Correct pecks get rewarded by access to grain. Name the variables.

3. A therapist tries to improve a patient's self-image. Every time the patient says something positive about himself or herself, the therapist rewards this by nodding, smiling, and being extra attentive. Name the variables.

4. A social psychologist does an experiment to discover whether men or women give lower ratings of discomfort when they are one of six people crowded into a telephone booth. Name the variables.

Answers

1. Independent (manipulated) variable

   Intensity (brightness) of brake light.

   Dependent (observed) variable

   Time from onset of brake light until depression of brake pedal by following driver.

   Control (constant) variables

   Color of brake light, shape of brake pedal, force needed to depress brake pedal, external illumination, and so on.

2. Independent variable

   Color of light (red or green).

   Dependent variable

   Number of key pecks.

   Control variables

   Hours of food deprivation, size of key, intensity of red and green lights, and so on.

3. Independent variable

   Actually, this is not an experiment, because there is only one level of the independent variable. To make this an experiment, we need another level (say, rewarding positive statements about the patient's mother-in-law). Then the independent variable would be kind of statement rewarded.

   Dependent variable

   Number (or frequency) of positive statements about self.

   Control variables

   None. This is a poor experiment.

4. Independent variable

   Sex of the participant. (*Note:* This is not a true independent variable, because the experimenter did not manipulate it. This is a quasi-experiment.)

   Dependent variable

   Rating of discomfort.

   Control variables

   Size of telephone booth, number of persons (six) crowded into the booth, and so on.

More Than One Independent Variable

It is unusual in a psychology journal to find an experiment in which only one independent (manipulated) variable was used. The typical experiment manipulates from two to four independent variables simultaneously. There are several advantages to this procedure. First, conducting one experiment with, say, three independent variables is often more efficient than conducting three separate experiments. Second, experimental control is often better, because with a single experiment, some control variables—for example, time of day, temperature, and humidity—are more likely to be held constant than would be the case with three separate experiments. Third, and most important, results generalized across several independent variables—that is, shown to be valid in several situations—are more valuable than data that have yet to be generalized. Fourth, just as we need to establish generality of results across different types of experimental participants and settings, we also need to discover whether some result is valid across levels of independent variables.

Let us say we wish to find out which of two rewards facilitates learning geometry by high-school students. The first reward is an outright cash payment for problems correctly solved, and the second is early dismissal from class—that is, each correct solution entitles the student to leave class 5 minutes early. Assume that the results of this hypothetical experiment showed early dismissal to be better. Before we make early dismissal a universal rule in high school, we should first establish its generality by comparing the two kinds of reward in other classes, such as history and biology. Here subject matter of the class would be a second independent variable. It would be better to put these two variables into a single experiment than to conduct two successive experiments. This would avoid problems of control, such as one class being tested the week of the big football game (when no reward would improve learning) and the other class being tested the week after the game was won (when students felt better about learning).

When the effects produced by one independent variable are not the same across the levels of a second independent variable, we have an **interaction**. The search for interactions is a major reason for using more than one independent variable per experiment. This can be best demonstrated by example.

In an article titled "Fatal Attraction," the authors studied how college students selected a hypothetical political candidate for governor (Cohen, Solomon, Maxfield, Pyszczynski, & Greenberg, 2004). They were interested in the relationship between terror management theory and leadership style. Terror management theory states that human behavior is controlled by awareness of death, which can create overwhelming terror. We manage the anxiety associated with fear of death by several cultural worldviews, such as belief in an afterlife or achieving some version of immortality by having children, which make one's inevitable departure from this mortal clime seem to be less threatening. Leadership style refers to the interaction between leaders and followers. Charismatic leaders inspire their followers because of the magnetism of the leader's personality. This contrasts with relationship-oriented leaders, who emphasize the importance of mutual responsibility and cooperation between leaders and followers.

The study had two independent variables that manipulated awareness of death and leadership style. Mortality salience was manipulated by having half of the students answer two open-ended questions about emotions associated with the thought of your own death and what you think will happen to you after you are physically dead. The other half of the students received parallel questions about their next exam. Leadership style was manipulated by having all students read brief campaign statements. The charismatic statement stressed characteristics such as engaging in risky but calculated behavior and emphasizing the identity of the group as a whole:

> I will be the perfect governor for this state because I am committed to this state and this nation's future. . . . You are not just an ordinary citizen, you are part of a special state and a special nation and if we work together we can make a difference.

The relationship-oriented statement stressed treating followers respectfully and acknowledging and appreciating the efforts of followers:

> I will be the perfect governor for this state because I worry about the citizens' well being. . . . I know that each individual can make a difference. Everyone's contributions are recognized and appreciated.

Students then evaluated each candidate on a 5-point scale. Figure 6–3 shows the results of this evaluation for each of the two independent variables. Each independent variable is plotted separately. The relationship-oriented candidate was slightly preferred, but there was no difference between students who were asked questions about exams versus death.

Figure 6–4 shows that this interpretation is too simple. If, as Figure 6–3 implies, leadership has its own unique effect, then results should look like the two parallel lines in Figure 6–5 when the two independent variables are plotted on the same graph. Instead, the lines in Figure 6–4 are not parallel. This indicates an interaction between the two independent variables. The evaluation of each leader depends upon the salience of mortality, as predicted by terror management theory. When they are reminded of death, students preferred the charismatic leader. Charismatic leaders prosper in times of great distress. But when students were reminded of their next exam, which is far less stressful than death, the relationship-oriented leader was more desirable.

Now let us imagine that this experiment was performed in two separate parts. In the first part, only leadership style was varied and all students received a question about their next exam. The experimenter might have concluded that the relationship-oriented leader was always preferred. In the second part, only the kind of question (exam or mortality) was varied and only a relationship-oriented candidate was considered. The experimenters would have concluded that questions about exams increased the desirability of

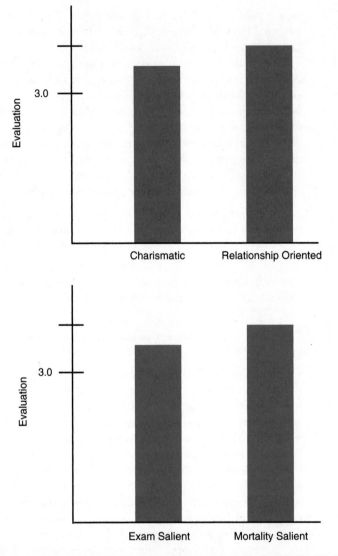

Figure 6–3 Effects on leadership evaluation of two independent variables. (Adapted from Cohen et al, 2004.)

relationship-oriented leaders. But as we know from Figure 6–4, this is incomplete. You can see that by doing the experiment in two parts, we would have lost important information.

Figure 6–4, which contains the actual results, shows an interaction. The effects of leadership style depend upon the kind of questions that preceded the evaluation. Questions that induced thoughts about death changed the preferred leadership style.

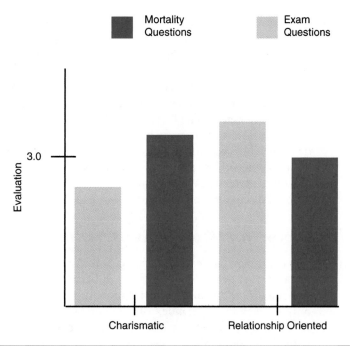

Mortality Questions   Exam Questions

Evaluation

3.0

Charismatic   Relationship Oriented

Figure 6–4   Effects of two independent variables on leadership evaluation. (Adapted from Cohen et al, 2004.)

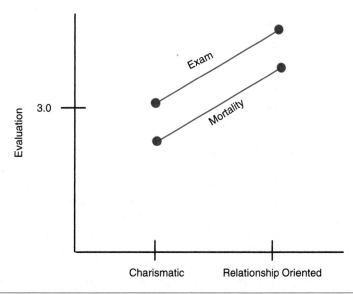

Evaluation

3.0

Exam

Mortality

Charismatic   Relationship Oriented

Figure 6–5   Fictitious data showing no interaction between the two independent variables.

Note that in order to make it easier for you to detect whether or not the lines are parallel, we have drawn Figures 6–4 and 6–5 as line graphs instead of bar graphs. When an interaction occurs, lines are not parallel. However, because the variables plotted on the horizontal axis are not continuous, technically they are better drawn as bar graphs, as in Figure 6–3.

In summary, an interaction occurs when the effects of one independent variable are determined by the levels of other independent variables. When interactions are present, we usually do not discuss the effects of each independent variable separately. Because the effects of one variable depend on the levels of the other variables, it makes sense to discuss interacting variables together. Interactions are an extremely important topic, so they will receive additional discussion in Chapter 9.

More Than One Dependent Variable

The dependent (observed) variable is used as an index of behavior. The experimenter must decide which aspects of behavior are relevant to the experiment at hand. Some variables are traditional, but this does not mean they are the only, or even the best, index of behavior. Take, for example, the behavior of a rat pressing a bar or a pigeon pecking a key. The most common dependent variable is the number of presses or pecks observed. However, the force with which a key is pecked can also lead to interesting findings (see Notterman & Mintz, 1965), as can the latency, or time to respond. Researchers can usually come up with several dependent variables that may be appropriate. Let us say we wish to study the legibility of the typeface that you are now reading. We cannot observe legibility, of course. What dependent variables might we observe? Here are some that have been used in the past: retention of meaningful information after reading text, time needed to read a fixed number of words, number of errors in recognizing single letters, speed in transcribing or retyping text, heart rate during reading, and muscular tension during reading. This list is far from complete.

Reasons of economy argue for obtaining as many dependent measures at the same time as is feasible. The truck driver workload experiment discussed in Chapter 2 (see Figure 2–5) uses several dependent variables. Nevertheless, the typical experiment uses only one or at most two dependent variables simultaneously. This is unfortunate, because just as the generality of an experiment is expanded by having more than one independent variable, it is also expanded by having several dependent variables.

One reason for not using several measures is that the results may be hard to interpret. Sometimes it may not be possible to determine whether the dependent variables are measuring the same thing or different things. Another reason more dependent variables are not used is that it is statistically difficult to analyze several dependent variables at once. Modern computer techniques make the calculations feasible, but many experimental psychologists have not been well trained in these multivariate statistical procedures and thus hesitate

> ## CONCEPT SUMMARY
>
> ### Variables in Experiments
>
> | Type | Operation | Example |
> | --- | --- | --- |
> | Independent variables | At least two levels of a variable are manipulated | Cue type; decompression |
> | Dependent variables | Particular behaviors are measured | Percentage resolved; infant growth and movement |
> | Control variables | Other variables are held constant | Strain of animals; general test environment |
>
> Multiple independent and dependent variables are important. An interaction occurs when the effects of one independent variable depend on the level of another independent variable.

to use them. Although separate analyses could be conducted for each dependent variable, this loses information in much the same way that separate analysis of independent variables ignores interactions. Because multivariate analysis is complex, we will not discuss it here. Nevertheless, you should be aware that it is often advantageous to use more than one dependent variable in an experiment.

▶ Possible Sources of Experimental Error

Reactivity in Experimentation

The problem of participant reactivity is not restricted to descriptive research. Research involving experimental procedures faces similar difficulties with reactivity. In fact, just telling someone that he or she is in a psychology experiment may cause reactivity problems. To illustrate, walk up to a stranger and say, "Please do me a favor by doing 10 push-ups." Repeat your request to several others. Then repeat the procedure, but this time say, "I'm doing a psychology experiment. Please do me a favor by doing 10 push-ups." The odds are that you will get very little compliance from the first group of people and very few refusals from the second group. People sometimes will do things in the name of science and experimentation that they will not ordinarily do

(Orne, 1962). In other words, experiments may not only examine behavior, they may produce it! Reactivity can be an important source of contamination in experimental data.

Orne (1962, 1969) noted that participants entering an experiment have some general notions of what to expect and are usually trying to figure out the specific purpose of the experiment. They are likely to believe that reasonable care will be taken for their well-being and that whatever the experimenter asks them to do will serve a useful purpose. Because many psychological experiments would provide uninteresting results if the true purpose were known, elaborate deceptions are often used to mask the goal of the experiment. However, as Orne points out, these might sometimes be rather transparent. At any rate, the general problem exists as to how the participant's expectations affect or determine her or his behavior in an experiment. Orne notes:

> Insofar as the subject cares about the outcome, his perception of his role and of the hypothesis being tested will become a significant determinant of his behavior. The cues which govern his behavior—which communicate what is expected of him and what the experimenter hopes to find—can therefore be crucial variables. Some time ago I proposed that these cues be called "*demand characteristics* of an experiment."
>
> . . . They include the scuttlebutt about the experiment, its setting, implicit and explicit instructions, the person of the experimenter, subtle cues provided by him, and, of particular importance, the experimental procedure (Orne, 1969, p. 146, italics added).

In this paragraph, Orne uses the phrase **demand characteristics** to refer to the reactivity of the participants. Orne's terminology is a commonly used alternative to *reactivity*.

Participant reaction may limit the generality of the results of an experiment, because if the results are produced by just the participants' perception of the experimental situation, they will not generalize to other situations. Often when people know they are being observed, their behavior is greatly affected. One famous case of this is the **Hawthorne effect,** named after the Western Electric Company plant at which an experiment was conducted on factors affecting worker productivity (Homans, 1965). Six average women workers participated in a longitudinal study of factors affecting the rate at which they assembled telephone relays. First, the baseline rate of producing relays was measured. Then the women were placed in a special test room, and after a period of adjustment to their new circumstances, they experienced a number of changes in their daily routine that were supposed to affect productivity. During one period of the study, rest pauses were inserted into their schedule, and later, the frequency of pauses was increased. During another period, their method of payment was changed, then during yet another, a light lunch was provided, and so on. The experiment lasted for more than a year, and the results were quite surprising. With few exceptions, no matter what changes were made—whether there were many or few rest periods, whether the workday was made longer or shorter, and so on—the women tended to produce more and more telephone relays. Although the reason for this change is difficult to determine (because a number of variables were confounded), that the women knew they were in an experiment, felt the special attention, and wanted to cooperate are likely candidates. The workers knew that the experimenters expected the changes in the working conditions to affect them, so they did. The women kept working harder and harder. (For a different interpretation, see Parsons, 1974.)

Because the changes in behavior apparently resulted from the fact that the workers were in an experiment and not because of the independent variables that were manipulated, we can say that the Hawthorne effect represents one kind of reactivity. Orne argues that to some extent, experiments with humans always have this feature built in. The person is an active participant interested in what is happening and is usually eager to help. Orne and his associates have done a great deal of research on demand characteristics in experimentation. Some of the most interesting studies deal with reactivity in hypnosis research.

Investigators have asked participants under hypnosis to do all sorts of things, often with notable success. One apparently well established finding is that participants under hypnosis can be led to perform various antisocial and destructive acts, such as throwing acid in someone's face and handling venomous snakes (Rowland, 1939; Young, 1952). Orne and Evans (1965) suspected that this might have owed more to the demand characteristics of the situation than to the effects of hypnosis. They asked participants to perform a series of dangerous acts, such as grasping a venomous snake, taking a coin from fuming acid, and throwing nitric acid in the experimenter's face. There were several treatment conditions: (a) participants who were under deep hypnosis, (b) participants who were told to simulate being hypnotized, (c) awake control participants who were not asked to simulate hypnosis but who were pressed by the experimenter to comply with the requests, (d) awake control participants who were not pressed to comply, and (e) people who were asked to perform the task without being made part of an experiment. The experimenter did not know which condition the participants were in, so as to minimize bias. The results are summarized in Table 6–1.

Table 6–1 Percentage of participants who performed dangerous tasks in response to requests by the experimenter

Participant group	Grasp venomous snake	Take coin from acid	Throw acid at experimenter
Real hypnosis	83	83	83
Simulating hypnosis	100	100	100
Waking control— pressure to comply	50	83	83
Waking control— without pressure to comply	50	17	17
Nonexperimental	0	0	0

From M. T. Orne & T. J. Evans, "Social control in the psychological experiment: Antisocial behavior and hypnosis" in *Journal of Personality and Social Psychology, 1*, 189–200. Copyright © 1965 by the American Psychological Association. Adapted by permission of the author.

As would be expected, people not in the experimental setting refused to carry out the antisocial tasks, but as other investigators had reported, a high percentage of hypnotized participants did carry out the tasks as instructed. However, *all* simulating control participants also performed the tasks, and even the nonsimulating controls, if pressed to comply, performed them to a large extent, which demonstrates the power of the experimental situation. Thus, hypnosis is not necessarily responsible for participants performing the antisocial acts. Rather, reactivity to the experimental situation, including the setting, the instructions, and the way participants think they are supposed to behave while under hypnosis, is sufficient to produce the antisocial acts. Perhaps people can be induced to perform antisocial acts under deep hypnosis, but current studies do not offer reliable evidence to support this idea.

Weber and Cook (1972) described various social roles that could influence behavior in a laboratory setting. These roles are similar to the response styles we discussed. Participants might adopt a **good-subject role** in accordance with the theory of demand characteristics put forth by Orne. A participant acting in a good-subject manner will do anything necessary to validate the experimental hypothesis. The **faithful-subject role** is one in which the participant attempts to be honest and faithful, even if he or she has some idea about the experimental hypothesis. The participant who exhibits a **negativistic-subject role** will attempt to sabotage or otherwise mess up the experiment (Masling, 1966, has called this the "screw you effect").

In an extensive review of the literature, Weber and Cook did not find much evidence that these roles played a significant part in the confounding of laboratory experiments. However, they did find some evidence for the importance of a fourth role—the **apprehensive-subject role** (also see Rosenberg, 1969). The apprehensive participant feels uncomfortable about being evaluated in an experiment, and because of this **evaluation apprehension**, the participant tries to respond in a socially desirable way. Weber and Cook summarized a number of studies that point to evaluation apprehension as an important potential source of confounding in experiments. Unfortunately, predicting exactly what kinds of behaviors will be elicited by evaluation apprehension is very difficult. For example, Weber and Cook report that in conformity studies, participants who have some idea about the purpose of the experiment tend to conform less than unaware participants (because of apprehension, the aware participants do not want to appear to be "sheep"). On the other hand, in learning studies in which better performance signifies a "better" participant, aware participants often perform better than unaware ones. Thus, it is hard to predict which changes in behavior may occur as a result of apprehension.

Countering the effects of reactivity in experimentation is often very difficult. Unobtrusive measures and observations may not work in a laboratory setting, because most people know they are in an experiment. Consequently, many psychologists do their experiments in a natural setting. This **field research** is similar to naturalistic observation, except that field experiments have a real or ex post facto independent variable. Going into the field, where people may be unaware that they are in an experiment, poses additional problems: Loss of control that is characteristic of laboratory experiments may exist, and unobtrusive measures may violate some of the ethical standards of research. Furthermore, as we will discuss in more detail later, field studies are not necessarily more externally valid than laboratory experiments. Dipboye and Flanagan (1979) found that field studies in industrial and organizational psychology generally involve a narrow range of participants, settings, and dependent variables.

One way to insert unobtrusive measures into laboratory experiments is to use **deception**. Deception can push reactivity in a particular direction so that the participant will respond naturally to the true independent variable. In a famous example of deception by Milgram (1963), participants were led to believe that they were giving shocks to a "learner" to improve the rate of learning. In fact, the shock apparatus was fake, and the learner just pretended to receive severe shocks. From the point of view of the participants, they willingly caused pain and suffering to another person. Many people regard this sort of deception as unethical (see Chapter 12).

Another way a researcher can try to control reactivity is to omit information about the experiment. For example, let us say that half the participants in a memory experiment receive special instructions on how to learn and remember. The other half of the participants do not receive these instructions; this group serves as a baseline for "natural memorizing." The experimenter might not tell the participants in the control condition that other participants were treated differently. Despite its usefulness, omitting information about the experiment can present ethical problems, particularly when the information is relevant to an individual's decision about whether to participate in the experiment. For instance, participants in a study on anxiety may not be told that the experimental procedure is likely to make them feel uneasy and nervous. Alerting them of possible reactions might induce those very reactions; however, withholding this information is deceptive. Deception by omission may be warranted in some circumstances; however, when it is used, we must be careful to maintain the dignity of the person being studied.

When we withhold some pertinent information from the participant, we say we are running a *blind experiment*. A good example is a study by Carver, Coleman, and Glass (1976), who examined the suppression of fatigue by Type A and Type B men, which was mentioned in Chapter 1. Type A people are aggressive and always strive to win in competitive situations, but they are supposed to be prone to coronary heart disease (Wright, 1988). Type B people are less aggressive and competitive and are less likely to have heart problems. Type A and B people were put on an exercise treadmill to see how long they would exercise relative to their maximum capacity. Carver and associates also got subjective estimates of fatigue from the participants. During the course of the experiment, the researchers made every attempt to remove any hint of competition—both against the clock and against other people's performance on the treadmill. In fact, the participants were told they would be removed from the treadmill after a predetermined time. In actuality, the time on the treadmill was determined by the participant, who indicated when he had had enough. Confronting the Type A individuals with evidence of competition might have enhanced their competitive drive, and the experimenters wanted them to become fatigued in the absence of any apparent competition. So, making the participant blind to the nature of the experiment seemed important. In this instance, the deception does not seem unethical. Carver and coworkers found that the Type A subjects worked longer on the treadmill than did their Type B counterparts. Despite the extra effort, the Type A subjects reported less fatigue than did the participants of Type B.

Another way to control reactivity is to conduct a **simulated experiment,** as Orne and Evans (1965) did in their hypnosis study. As mentioned earlier, they used people who simulated being hypnotized as well as people who were hypnotized. The logic here is straightforward. The demands of the situation are assumed to be the same for participants in both the experimental condition and the simulating control condition. If the experimental manipulation (hypnosis) is truly effective, then the behavior of the experimental group should differ reliably from that of the simulating group. Another approach to simulating an experiment is to tell simulating participants what the independent variable is and ask them what they would do in the experimental situation (Richman, Mitchell, & Reznick, 1979). If the results of the simulated experiment are highly similar to the results owing to the independent variable in the actual experiment, we can conclude that there are likely to be important reactivity factors contaminating the effects of the independent variable.

▶ External Validity of the Research Procedure

Another area in which problems arise in the design of a research project concerns its relation to what is often termed the "real world." We might ask whether our research has anything to do with why people and animals think and act as they do. Have we selected an object of study that is representative? Is our research setting one that will yield a valid answer to our fundamental question? In sum, is our research externally valid?

We alluded to some of these issues in Chapter 2. Several problems associated with external validity must be dealt with before a project is begun. In this section, we will detail the problems of participant representativeness, variable representativeness, and setting representativeness. We will also present some ways in which these problems can be handled.

Participant/Subject Representativeness

Basic research in psychology draws a large number of its participants from two populations: white rats and college students. Rats and other animals are often used because the scientist can control the heredity and environment of animals more easily (and more ethically) than that of humans. Also, rats and college students are readily available to most researchers. The justifications for using rats and college students are control, convenience, and ethics. The question remains: Are these organisms representative? Are data from these organisms pertinent to general statements about psychological processes? In other words, is there **participant/subject representativeness?**

Limiting your observations to these populations may present some problems. A major difficulty is **reversibility** (Uttal, 1978). In mathematics, reversibility refers to an attempt to determine the problem or equation from a solution. Consider the answer 7. Can we figure out what led to 7? Not without more information. The answer 7 could have come from $4 + 3 = ?$, $377 - 370 = ?$, $\sqrt{49} = ?$, How many days are in a week?, or any of an infinite number of other possibilities. The answer 7 is not reversible. Thus, given the answer 7 twice, there is no way to know whether the 7s arose from the same equation or different equations. Reversibility poses a similar problem in research. Just because a particular behavior is observed both in a rat and in a human, it does not follow that the underlying processes (the mathematical equation) are the same in both instances. For example, if we damaged a rat brain to understand how the human brain works, we have to assume that the brain processes in both species are the same (have the same equation). Physiological psychologists assume that the solution (the rat's behavior) is unique to a particular equation (the rat's brain) and that the equation is the same for rats and humans. Thus, by reversing the solution (damaging the rat's brain to eliminate a particular behavior), we arrive at the problem (what aspect of the brain controlled that behavior). In other words, damaging the rat's brain should lead us to understand how its brain controlled particular behaviors, and because we assume equivalence between the brain of a rat and the brain of a human, we further our understanding of human brain functioning.

The difficulty, of course, is the assumption of equivalence between rats and humans. The problem remains even if one ignores physiology and tries to generalize across species at the purely behavioral level, because the assumption of equivalence remains in whatever mechanism is hypothesized to account for the behavior. Harlow and colleagues summarized the dilemma this way: "Basically the problems of generalization of behavior between species are simple—one cannot generalize, but one must. If the competent do not wish to generalize, the incompetent will fill the field" (Harlow, Gluck, & Suomi, 1972, p. 716).

Despite the difficulties it poses, generalizing across species can lead to spectacular successes. In the nineteenth century, Gregor Mendel, a Czechoslovakian monk, determined the basics of genetics by studying garden peas. More recently, the discovery of neurotransmitters in the brain that function like opiate drugs was based on work concerned with neural transmission in the reproductive organs of rats. If we view the results of animal research as a model or analogy, then we recognize that our cross-species generalizations are always tentative. We may have to perform many tests on many species before we can come to strong conclusions.

The difficulties we have just examined also pertain to research that uses college students as participants. How representative are the results obtained from such studies? The answer to this question is vague; it depends on the purposes of the research and the boldness of the investigator. If we are concerned with processes that are likely to be shared by all humans, such as basic sensory processes or simple forms of learning and retention, we can be fairly sure that our data on college students will be representative of human beings in general.

A difficulty arises, however, when we are interested in complex psychological processes. Language, problem solving, and sophisticated memorizing strategies require that the participant possess characteristics that may not be common to everyone. We cannot limit our psychology to normal human adults living in Western cultures. Young children, Ibos living in Africa, and individuals with hearing impairments are likely to possess abilities different from those of the typical college student. Imagery may enhance memory in college students (Atkinson, 1975; Bower, 1972). Its success for young children, however, has limits (Tversky & Teiffer, 1976), and cross-cultural differences in the use of imagery exist as well (Cole, Gay, Glick, & Sharp, 1971).

Because of the limits in generalizability from easily available populations, it is sometimes necessary to seek out participants from special populations. For instance, if we are interested in whether the incidence of depression found in young people is the same for older persons, we must find a population of older individuals willing to participate in our study. Despite the convenience of the white rat and the college student, these populations alone cannot meet all research needs.

The moral here is that we should be careful in generalizing on the basis of a single sample of participants from a subset of the population at large. If we are too bold ("Imagery always aids memory, no matter who uses it"), we run the risk of being wrong. Again, if we view the college student as a model for psychological processes in the same way that we view the white rat as a model, we will recognize that some of our conclusions must be tentative. This is particularly true when basic research findings are used for applied purposes. The generalization should be tried out on the target population before a particular policy or practice is implemented. Time and effort would be wasted if, on the basis of Bower's (1972) work with college students, imagery training were instituted in a nursery school.

Variable Representativeness

We want our results to generalize across different participant populations. In the same way, we want our results to have **variable representativeness**—the ability to generalize across different experimental manipulations. For example, if a researcher were interested in whether background noise hurt reading comprehension, he or she might compare music with silence. If it were shown that noise and music both hurt comprehension relative to silence, the researcher would have an interesting finding; however, it would be premature to assume that the results would generalize for any kind of background noise. The results may have been unique to the kind of music chosen or to the particular volume at which the music was played. Likewise, the results may have been different if random environmental noises had been used instead of music. Further experimentation would be necessary to determine the generality of the effect of background noise. By using a wide range of independent variables to address a particular question, we can also get a better idea of how the variables we have chosen relate to the situation in the real world that we are trying to address.

Setting Representativeness

Perhaps the major issue associated with representativeness has to do with the setting. **Setting representativeness,** often called **ecological validity,** can be a serious problem in experimentation, where, by definition and through the imposition of control, the experimental setting is an artificial one. Neisser (1976, 1978, 1982), for example, questions the ecological validity of laboratory experiments, particularly those involving cognition and memory. He argues that psychologists have avoided studying natural memory in natural settings, which means that "the orthodox psychology of memory has very little to show for a hundred years of effort, perhaps because it has always avoided the interesting issues" (1982, p. 3). Neisser is correct in his concern for ecological validity, but as we shall see, he is incorrect in his indictment.

When considering the problem of ecological validity, we need to distinguish between **realism** and **generalizability** (Berkowitz & Donnerstein, 1982). Realism refers to whether the experimental setting bears a resemblance to the real world. Do the experiments involving rats learning in Skinner boxes resemble any learning situation in the real world? The answer, of course, is probably not. However, the critical question has to do with the importance of this mundane realism. As was true of the problem of subject representativeness, our concern with ecological validity should be with its relation to psychological processes. If we can demonstrate that the processes exhibited by rats in artificial settings are similar to the processes occurring in the real world, then we can say that realism is not a crucial threat to external validity. Thus, it follows that the ability of an experimental result to generalize to other situations is more important than its superficial resemblance to the real world. Various tests try to determine whether the processes observed in the laboratory are also the processes involved in settings representative of the real world. In Chapter 13, we will consider some other aspects of generalization, but for now, we will examine some direct tests of generalizability.

The strategy used to test the generalizability of experimental results is to repeat the observations in a natural setting—a field study. Obviously, studying memory in a classroom or decision making in a courtroom is less controlled than in the corresponding laboratory study. This is why laboratory experiments are conducted—to provide an internally valid causal statement about a psychological process. If we are going to try to generalize our results beyond the laboratory, we may need to conduct a less well-controlled field experiment. Before considering such tests of generalization, we should note that field studies do not necessarily permit broad generalization. As pointed out earlier, Dipboye and Flanagan (1979) found that a narrow range of participants, settings, and variables had been used in field studies done in industrial and organizational psychology. The tests should be varied and not just "natural."

Many applied psychologists have questioned the external validity of laboratory studies on decision making. A substantial amount of laboratory work has examined how people integrate many sources of information to arrive at a decision, and many sophisticated mathematical theories describe information integration (Anderson, 1981). Levin, Louviere, and Schepanski (1983) conducted a number of direct tests of the external validity of results from laboratory studies involving decision making, and they found excellent correspondence between the laboratory and the real world. They discovered that the choice of transportation to get to work, as well as choice of shopping location, are almost perfectly predicted by models derived from laboratory studies of decision making. They also report that several other behaviors in the real world coincide with results from strictly controlled experiments. These behaviors include gambling decisions, jury decisions, and occupational choices. Thus, laboratory studies of decision making may be contrived and artificial, but they also predict behavior in the real world.

What about Neisser's (1982) criticism of laboratory work in memory? Encouraged by Neisser's critique of memory, some memory researchers have abandoned their laboratories and begun to conduct their research in real-world settings. Their experiments often lack the strict experimental control of laboratory research, but adherents to what is called the "Everyday Memory movement" argue that what they lack in control is more than made up for by increased ecological validity. Banaji and Crowder (1989) responded strongly to Neisser's criticisms (and to the Everyday Memory movement in general) by arguing that he ignored the distinction between realism and generalizability. Hence, Banaji and Crowder point out that results derived from laboratory experiments may or may not generalize to a variety of situations, but they also point out that results derived from everyday memory experiments, despite their surface realism, still may or may not generalize to other situations. Because surface realism does not guarantee an increase in generalizability, Banaji and Crowder question whether the loss of experimental control is worth the increased (surface) realism of the everyday memory experiments.

Banaji and Crowder's (1989) article has stirred up considerable controversy among memory researchers. In fact, an issue of *American Psychologist* (January 1991, Volume 46) includes nine articles (pp. 16–49) discussing the various aspects of this debate. In contrast to the stereotype of the cold, objective scientist, some of the authors exhibit a great deal of emotion in addressing this topic. We recommend that you read some of these articles. Although the debate is specifically addressed to the study of human memory, the issues raised regarding ecological validity are quite general, and the same arguments would apply to almost any area of psychology.

In summary, surface realism in an experimental setting does not guarantee ecological validity. In fact, an experiment can be ecologically valid with little or no surface realism. Nevertheless, some researchers argue that experiments with surface realism are more likely to lead to results with high generalizability, but this argument remains controversial. In any case, it is generalizability rather than surface realism that determines whether an experimental procedure is ecologically valid.

> ### CONCEPT SUMMARY
>
> Your choice of
>
> - participants
> - variables
> - setting
>
> may all distort the underlying psychological processes. Generalization can be enhanced by using
>
> - different participants
> - different variables
> - different settings

Summary

1. The joint method of agreement and difference permits causal explanation by showing that result *X* occurs when event *A* occurs, and that result *X* does not occur when event *A* does not occur.

2. An experiment can be defined as the production of a particular comparison while other aspects of the situation are held constant. Thus, comparison, production, and constancy are the hallmarks of control in experimentation.

3. Independent variables are those manipulated by the experimenter. It is important to select appropriate levels of the independent variable to avoid null results.

4. The dependent variable is the behavior observed and recorded by the experimenter. A reliable dependent variable is consistent. You need to guard against the possibility of ceiling and floor effects on

your dependent variable by making sure that it does not have a restricted range of values.

5. A control variable is a potential independent variable that is held constant during an experiment. It is controlled to minimize confounding.

6. Using more than one independent variable is important in ensuring general results. When the effects produced by one independent variable are not the same across the levels of a second independent variable, we have an interaction.

7. Obtaining measures on more than one dependent variable can provide important information and increase the generality of results.

8. Reactivity often occurs in experiments. A famous example of reactivity is the Hawthorne effect, in which worker productivity improved throughout the course of an experiment, regardless of the experimental manipulations.

9. Invalid conclusions may be drawn from research if the participants, variables, or settings distort the underlying psychological processes.

10. Because experiments are well controlled, and therefore artificial, the ecological validity of experiments is often questioned. The crucial problem is not realism, but whether the experimental results generalize to other settings, which they often do.

11. Many field studies (experiments done in natural settings) show that the results of laboratory studies do generalize to the real world.

Key Concepts

apprehensive-subject role (152)
ceiling effect (140)
confounding (141)
control (135)
control group (137)
control variable (140)
deception (153)
demand characteristics (150)
dependent variable (139)
ecological validity (157)
evaluation apprehension (152)
experiment (134)

experimental group (137)
ex post facto (138)
faithful-subject role (152)
field research (152)
floor effect (140)
generalizability (157)
good-subject role (152)
Hawthorne effect (150)
independent variable (138)
interaction (144)
joint method of agreement and difference (134)

negativistic-subject role (152)
null result (139)
realism (157)
reversibility (155)
setting representativeness (157)
simulated experiment (154)
subject/participant representativeness (155)
type 2 error (140)
variable representativeness (156)

Exercises

1. [*Special Exercise.*] An experimenter examined the effects of LSD on complex learning in rats. One group of rats was given a very small dose of LSD—so small that it was unlikely to have any behavioral effects. A second group was given a large dose. Then both groups ran through a complex maze several times. The dependent variable was the number of errors the rats made before obtaining the food reward at the end of the maze. The large-dose group made 4.5 times as many errors as the small-dose group, and the experimenter concluded that LSD can negatively affect complex learning. Comment on the levels of the independent variable that were used. What other dependent variables could be recorded? Comment on the conclusion by the experimenter.

2. Define what an experiment entails. Your definition should include mention of independent, dependent, and control variables.

3. Design an experiment to determine the effect of sex of the person to be identified on tip-of-the-tongue states. Specify the levels of your independent variable, describe your dependent variable, and note important control variables.

Suggested Resource

Numerous experiments on a variety of topics can be found in Elmes, D. G. (1978). *Readings in experimental psychology*. Chicago: Rand McNally.

Web Resources

Several interesting links to many of the issues discussed in this chapter can be found at http://www.trochim.human.cornell.edu

The Wadsworth workshops consider experiments at http://www.wadsworth.com/psychology_d/templates/student_resources/workshops/workshops.html

Laboratory Resources

Langston (2005) considers a variety of ways of doing experiments on the Stroop effect in his chapter on basic two-condition experiments (Chapter 4). Langston, W. (2005). *Research methods laboratory manual for psychology* (2nd ed). Pacific Grove, CA: Wadsworth Group.

Preference for Cola Drinks

A good follow-up to the findings of Woolfolk and associates (1983) that were discussed in the Application section would be to do the taste-test experiment appropriately. Perform the experiment with unmarked cups (or at least cups that do not have markings that are visible to your participants). You will need some small paper cups and a supply of beverages (say, Pepsi and Coke, or perhaps Sprite and 7-Up). Allow each person to taste a small amount of each beverage and then indicate his or her preference. Make sure that your participants do not know the brand names of your drinks (and, of course, make sure they do not see you pouring the drinks into the cups). A Likert-scale procedure (see Chapter 7) could be used as an alternative dependent variable. If you use it, you will probably want to have your participants make judgments about each drink separately along some dimension (say, a goodness-of-taste dimension).

One thing you should try to do in this experiment is to make sure that half your participants taste Coke first, then Pepsi, and that the other half of your participants taste the beverages in the reverse order. This reversal of order is called *counterbalancing* and is used to guard against the possibility that the order of tasting the drinks has an effect on the dependent variable. Counterbalancing is discussed in Chapter 8.

CHAPTER **7**

Validity and Reliability in Psychological Research

Validity
- Predictive validity
- Construct validity
- External validity
- Internal validity

Reliability
- Test reliability
- Statistical validity and reliability

Measurement Procedures
- Psychophysics
- Psychometrics

Validity refers to whether a researcher measures or studies what he or she wants to measure. This chapter examines several types of validity. Reliability concerns the consistency of measures or observations, and this chapter also examines several ways of assessing reliability. Much of this chapter focuses on the reliability and validity of measurements, which means that the nature of measurement and measurement scales must be examined as well.

▶ Validity

Psychological observations provide scientific understanding by describing behavior, relating two or more behaviors, and explaining the causes of behavior via experiments. When do we know that our descriptions, relationships, and explanations are good ones? Good observations of any kind are valid. In the current context, **validity** refers to the truth of the observations. Because scientific truth changes with each new observation (see Chapter 2), it is probably safest to assert that validity and its converse, *invalidity*, "refer to the best available approximation to the truth or falsity of propositions" (Cook & Campbell, 1979, p. 37). The validity of descriptions, relations, and explanations can be considered in several ways: (a) predictive validity, (b) construct validity, (c) external validity, and (d) internal validity. Later, we will also examine statistical validity.

Predictive Validity

A common way of validating an observation or measurement is to check it against some criterion. A **criterion** is another measurement of behavior that serves as a standard for the measurement in question. Consider the SAT I, for example, which is used by colleges during the assessment for candidates for admission. Admissions officers want measures that predict some criterion behavior, and one such behavior that often is chosen is the grade-point average (GPA) during the freshman year of college. In general terms, criterion validity involves relating one aspect of a person's behavior, such as the SAT I score, to another measure of his or her behavior, such as the freshman GPA. If the relation between the test score and grades is strong, then we can predict one behavior when we know the other. This means that we have **predictive validity.** A correlation coefficient determines the degree of predictive validity (see Chapter 5 for a discussion of correlations).

The admissions officers hope that SAT I scores of applicants predict a later behavior, freshman GPA. The better the prediction, the greater the predictive validity of the predictor score, which is SAT I, in this case. Bridgeman, McCamely-Jenkins, and Ervin (2000) report that the current SAT I predicts freshman GPA about as well as earlier versions of the SAT. These authors also report that the SAT I predicts freshman GPA about as well as does high school GPA (another predictor score). A more accurate prediction of freshman GPA occurs when both the SAT I score and high school grades are combined as predictors than when either predictor is used by itself. This is an example of using multiple regression (see Chapter 5).

You should note that the criterion score determines how the predictor observation is valid. That is, freshman grades in college may be predictable by the student's performance on the SAT I. However, we cannot then infer that people with high SAT I scores are more intelligent than people with low SAT I scores. To make that kind of statement, we would have to predict intelligence test scores from SAT I scores. Thus, predictive validity does little to define a measurement except by limiting its predictive validity. The next sort of validity, construct validity, helps us define variables.

> ### ▶ CONCEPT SUMMARY
>
> Predictive validity relates one measure of behavior to another, criterion measure.

Construct Validity

Construct validity in a particular research project is the degree to which the independent and dependent variables accurately reflect or measure what they are intended to (Cook & Campbell, 1979; Judd, Smith, & Kidder, 1991). Consider the Stroop experiment from Chapter 1. Are the three levels of the independent variable in that experiment valid reflections of reading? Certainly, each task involves reading, so at least for this research project, we might safely assume that these are valid ways to test aspects of reading. What about the dependent variable—the time to go through the lists? Is it a valid measure of reading? Certainly, how smoothly and quickly one reads is a good indicator of reading; however, there are at least two ways in which our measure may be invalid. One source of invalidity is that some confounding variables other than the independent variable could have influenced reading times. We often label such confounding variables *extraneous variables,* because they come from outside the bounds of the planned investigation.

Reading aloud may involve processes that do not occur when people read silently to themselves, which means that we may not be measuring "reading" as we usually consider it. This sort of confounding could result in very low construct validity, because we believe we are studying reading when we are really examining something else. The task imposed on the participants—reading aloud—resulted in confounding and, perhaps, low validity. . . Let us consider an example of another sort of confounding that was associated with the way in which the participants were tested.

Katz, Lautenschlager, Blackburn, and Harris (1990) have argued that the SAT suffers from construct invalidity as a result of confounding. They found that people responded at better than chance levels (20%) on SAT reading questions in the absence of reading the passages. Because people did not have to read the passages to get correct answers, Katz and associates argued that the reading questions did not actually measure reading comprehension. Rather, these startling results seem to indicate either of two possibilities. First, the general knowledge and reasoning ability of the people could have allowed them to answer the questions correctly. Alternatively, information in the question allowed the people to determine the correct answer, because it was highly related to the information in the missing reading passage.

If Katz and associates are correct, then the usefulness of the reading comprehension portions of the SAT (and, by extension, of similar multiple-choice reading tests) may be minimal. Recently, Freedle and Kostin (1994) claimed to have evidence supporting the idea that the SAT reading tests measure comprehension. Through a series of analyses, they also found evidence suggesting that the structure of the questions can influence the degree of correct answers. In addition, however, Freedle and Kostin showed that subjects do use information in the passages to answer the questions. More important, the passage information plays a stronger role in responding correctly than do the questions themselves. Freedle and Kostin cautioned that although their results seemed to show some construct validity for the SAT reading passages, we still do not know precisely what the readers comprehend.

The Stroop test may have another confounding variable. If you had read the lists aloud as someone was timing you, you might have been somewhat nervous or apprehensive about being evaluated for your reading skill. This could have influenced your reading times in a number of different ways. Your apprehension may have led you to read faster and more accurately than usual so you would "look good." On the other hand, you might have been nervous and not performed as well as when you were not being timed by another person. Such reactivity by research participants is an important source of invalidity, and we discussed some ways to control it in Chapter 4.

Another threat to construct validity is random error. You or your partner may have misread the timing device, which could lead to a recording error in one or more of the conditions. This source of invalidity might be important in the Stroop experiment, because different participants might have used different modes of timing. Thus, the dependent variable might not be a valid measure of reading time, and the experiment would have weak construct validity.

These points lead us to be suspicious about the construct validity of almost any manipulated and measured variable in psychological research. The reasons appear in Figure 7–1. A variable could be composed of the construct of interest as well as confounding influences and error (Judd, 1991). The extent to which the other sources enter into observations determines the degree of

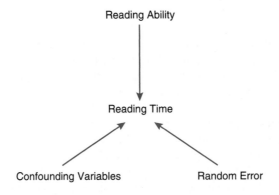

Figure 7–1   The composition of a variable could include the construct of interest and two sources of invalidity: confounding variables and error (modified from Judd, 1991).

construct validity. So, a prudent researcher tries to minimize construct invalidity by limiting the possibility of confounding and error.

We consider several ways of minimizing construct invalidity throughout the text, two of which we consider here. The first involves *operational definitions*. Recall that an operational definition is a recipe for specifying how to produce and measure a construct, such as reading. The conditions that produce the concept are carefully specified, and the ways in which the concept is to be measured are defined. A concept such as reading, therefore, becomes tied to the independent variables that produce it and the dependent variables that measure it. In this fashion, an operational definition is similar to good definitions of theoretical constructs (see the discussions of intervening variables and theoretical constructs in Chapter 2).

Although time was the dependent variable in the Stroop experiment, we need something besides an operational definition to ensure that we measure the behavior accurately. What we need is a protocol. Remember, a *protocol* is the specification of how the measurement and procedures are to be undertaken. Valid research adheres strictly to a protocol so that the behavior of all subjects is measured precisely, accurately, and in the same way under all levels of the independent variable.

Providing adequate operational definitions and following protocols do not guarantee construct validity, but they do help to minimize invalidity, especially invalidity owing to random error.

> ## CONCEPT SUMMARY

- Construct validity refers to the extent to which the variables accurately reflect or measure the behavior of interest.
- Operational definitions and protocols help minimize construct invalidity resulting from error.

External Validity

External validity refers to the extent to which one can generalize from the research setting and participant population to other settings and populations (Cook & Campbell, 1979). Observations with substantial external validity allow generalization to other situations and participant populations. Externally invalid observations are limited to the original research setting and population of participants. If, for example, small procedural changes eliminate a particular observation, that observation lacks external validity. This does not necessarily mean that the observation is completely invalid; rather, it means that it is limited to specific circumstances and so may be of less general interest.

Researchers hope that their observations represent general psychological phenomena. Thus, a prominent concern is **replication,** or whether the observations can be repeated under different circumstances. In the Stroop experiment done in Chapter 1, we would not be interested in those observations if they were true only for college students. We can be confident in the generalizability of the results to other participant populations, because replications of the experiment show that the ordering of the three conditions is the same for adults, high-school students, and college students.

A more serious threat to external validity relates to the experimental setting. The tasks do not seem representative of the kinds of reading that most people do. However, as we noted in Chapter 2 and will detail later, the important criterion is not how realistic the tasks are but whether they represent an important psychological process. The general way to determine the generality is to conduct replications that vary the nature of the task and materials. A substantial variety of tasks has been used to induce the kind of conflict seen in our version of the Stroop experiment, which means that our observations have some external validity.

CONCEPT SUMMARY

- External validity refers to the extent to which the observations can be generalized to other settings and subject populations.
- Replications help assess the generality of the observations.

Internal Validity

Recall that **internal validity** refers to whether one can make causal statements about the relationship between variables (Cook & Campbell, 1979). When observations are internally valid, the researcher can safely believe that one variable caused changes in another. If the observations are not internally valid, then the researcher is not able to make assertions about whether one variable caused another to change.

In principle, experimental observations permit causal statements. The experimenter varies the independent variable, which may cause changes in the dependent variable. Thus, we can say that a carefully conducted experiment is internally valid. In Chapter 1, we discussed the internal validity of the Stroop experiment when we introduced the topic of confounding. We noted that the validity of the experiment was suspect because the levels of the independent variable were confounded with the order in which they were experienced. This indicates that the results of that experiment may not be internally valid, because something other than the independent variable might have caused the observed changes in the dependent variable. Because scientists often strive to determine what causes what, the bulk of this text concerns how to make internally valid observations.

> ## CONCEPT SUMMARY
>
> - Internal validity concerns whether causal statements about the relationship between variables are warranted.
> - Confounding is a major threat to internal validity, because the causal variable(s) cannot be determined.

▶ Reliability

In addition to being valid, good measures or observations must be reliable. **Reliability** refers to the consistency of behavioral measures. Reconsider the research on social loafing discussed in Chapter 2. Clear answers about the nature of social loafing would be impossible if the measures of it, under the same conditions, were inconsistent. In fact, if the measures were not reliable, they would also be invalid, and it would be impossible to determine what was truly being measured.

You might suppose that several attempts to measure the same thing would yield the same numbers—unless, of course, someone made an error. However, variability is always present in a group of measures, even when they are measures of the same thing. The amount of variability determines the reliability of the measuring instruments and procedures. Highly variable measures indicate low reliability, and vice versa. The measurement "error" to which psychologists and statisticians often refer does not imply that someone made a mistake but, rather, that certain factors caused unpredictable variability in the data. Researchers try to reduce this variability and therefore to increase reliability by taking the measurements under the same conditions. Later, we will examine some statistical procedures associated with reliability.

Psychologists often use sophisticated equipment to enhance the reliability of observations and measurements. In particular, the digital computer plays a major role in controlling experimental manipulations and recording dependent variables. For example, suppose you wish to examine how quickly people can respond to pictures that they see for a very short period of time. A properly programmed computer can precisely control the presentation time of the pictures, and it can consistently provide an accurate measure of the response times. One can, for example, program a computer to display a picture for just a few milliseconds (thousandths of a second). If the program sets the display time for ten milliseconds, then that display time will be precisely replicated each time a picture is shown. Also, response times can be measured with millisecond resolution, which is impossible to do with stopwatches and difficult with many other kinds of apparatus. It is an understatement to say that the digital computer has markedly increased the reliability and precision of experimental control and measurement.

> ► **CONCEPT SUMMARY**
>
> Reliability refers to the consistency of the measures of behavior.

Types of Reliability

The reliability of the results of tests and other descriptive measures of behavior can be checked by taking measures under the same conditions on successive occasions. Under identical conditions of measurement, then, any variability in measurement must be caused by a real change in the measured quantity. If two measures of your height are 5'8" and 5'10", is this variability owing to error or to a real change in your height? The answer could be either, or both. However, the more similar the conditions—shoes worn, posture—the less likely you would be to attribute the difference to error. Also, the closer the two measures were in time, the less likely you would be to attribute the difference to a real change in stature. You have some notion of how quickly stature can change, or of the stability of a person's true stature.

Intelligence and other psychological processes are more difficult to measure than stature, however. It is also more difficult to develop a notion of their stability. Do they vary at all, or do they remain fixed throughout life? If they change markedly, can they do so within a week, a month, a year, or 10 years? If something changes, can we determine those factors that produce the change, or are the changes the result of unreliable measurement? These are questions that psychologists would like to answer; the answers require measurement. However, the alert reader will realize that we have now reasoned ourselves into a logical circle. Let us go around again, and try to get out.

Several measures of the same quantity will not, in general, exactly agree. This variability may be a result either of error or of a real change in the measured quantity. We cannot tell, without some additional assumptions, how much error is in our measurement. Thus, how can we ask whether a psychological process changes? A useful assumption—one that allows the logical circle to be broken—is that the measured quantity is stable over relatively short periods of time. (If a researcher measures your intelligence in the morning and then again in the afternoon under the same conditions, we can assume that any change results from measurement error rather than a real change in intelligence.) With this assumption, a psychologist can estimate measurement error and attempt to improve and specify the reliability of the measuring instrument.

We will examine test reliability in the context of the concept of intelligence. Many different theories of intelligence exist, and intelligence is difficult to measure. Some theorists postulate a number of separate mental abilities, perhaps more than a hundred (Guilford, 1967). Others believe that there is one mental ability and that although other, more specific, abilities may be isolated, they are less important. This primary ability has been described as "a capacity for abstract reasoning and problem solving" (Jensen, 1969, p. 19). To test for this ability, people try to solve collections of problems or tasks, generally within a specified time period. Then we compare the score that an individual achieves with those obtained by others. Before placing much confidence in an individual's score, however, we need to know how reliable it is. Would the individual achieve about the same score if we were to test him or her again the next day, or a week later? Because we do not believe that the underlying ability changes appreciably over so short a time, we attribute a large change in scores to measurement error, indicating unreliability in our test. This procedure of giving the same test twice in succession over a short time interval determines the **test-retest reliability** of a measure. A coefficient of correlation between first and second scores obtained from a large sample of individuals expresses the test-retest reliability. A high, positive correlation indicates high reliability.

Researchers use a slightly different procedure to avoid problems such as specific practice effects. This technique involves giving alternate or **parallel forms** of the test on the two testing occasions. Again, if correlations between first and second scores are high, they indicate reliability of the tests. Also, the equivalence of the two forms of the test can be determined in this way.

A third useful procedure evaluates reliability with a single test presentation. This technique provides **split-half reliability;** it involves dividing the test items into two arbitrary groups and correlating the scores obtained in the two halves of the test. If these correlations are high, the test is reliable. In addition, the equivalence of the test items is established.

CONCEPT SUMMARY

Test reliability is determined by the

- test-retest method
- parallel forms method
- split-half method

Statistical Reliability and Validity

Given a set of results, the methods of inferential statistics (see Appendix B) allow the **statistical reliability** of data to be assessed by showing how likely one is to obtain those results by chance. In an experiment, for example, inferential statistics can determine whether a difference obtained between conditions results from the operation of the independent variable or from chance factors. If the difference between conditions is great enough to occur by chance in less than or equal to 1 case in 20, then the researcher rejects the possibility that chance factors produced the result. Instead, the difference is accepted as evidence for a real or statistically significant effect of the independent variable. When we statistically analyzed the results of the Stroop experiment conducted in Chapter 1, we found that the differences were large enough to consider them reliable rather than the result of chance.

Sampling

Another statistical factor that influences the reliability of measures has to do with the number of observations. When we take measures of behavior, we rarely investigate the entire **population** that we could study (for example, all college students). Rather, we usually select a **sample** to measure, such as volunteer psychology students in our college. Generally speaking, the greater the number of observations in our sample, the more confident we can be that the sample reflects the characteristics of the population. If a sample of persons is asked about preference for candidates in an upcoming election, we can be more confident that the survey results reflect the population of voters if the sample consists of 100,000 people than if it contains only 100.

How a sample is determined also can affect the validity of the sample. Because a researcher studies only a sample of an entire population in a project, he or she needs to obtain a sample that accurately represents the characteristics of the population. Can you be sure that sophomores taking introductory psychology at your institution are representative of all sophomores in colleges? We consider aspects of sampling in Appendix B, and representativeness receives additional treatment later. For now, we want to emphasize random sampling and its relation to sample size. Recall that *random sampling* means that each member of a particular population has an equal chance of being in the sample. Unbiased random selection guarantees in the long run that the sample represents the population. This does not mean that a particular sample will be perfectly representative of the population and hence a perfectly valid sample of the population; that cannot be guaranteed. What random selection does mean is that you can make a statistical or probabilistic guess that the sample is representative of the population. When a research procedure has features that do not limit conclusions to the procedural details itself, then we say that the research has external validity. Random sampling should allow us to have a sample that represents a larger population, which means that the conclusions we draw may be externally valid. Let us see how this works.

You probably believe, intuitively, that large samples are more representative of the population than are small samples. You might expect, for example, that one unusual member of a small sample will distort your results more than if that deviant member were part of a larger sample. You can test this yourself by tossing coins. The more coins you toss (the larger your sample is of all coin tosses), the closer you get to seeing the ideal of 50% heads show up (Thompson & Buchanan, 1979).

The value of random selection is related to sample size in an interesting way. Kerlinger and Lee (2000) suggest that large sample sizes allow the effects of random selection to work. Very small samples are less likely to be representative of the population, because even random selection can yield a limited or biased sample if the sample size is very small. An unusual member of a small random sample can have unfortunate effects even when that individual was selected at random. Thus, a large random sample is likely to yield a more externally valid representation of the population than is a small one. Large samples dilute the effect of having selected an unusual individual.

Psychologists rarely attain the ideal of random selection, because it is extremely expensive and time-consuming to try to sample from an entire population, such as all college sophomores. Because individuals differ in many ways, we can often assume that the population of possible scores in a research project can vary randomly (Glenberg, 1988). If this is the case, then it is crucial that participants be assigned to experimental conditions on a random basis. In conducting an experiment on the effects of a brain operation on memory, it is necessary that the operation be the only difference between the operated and unoperated animals. Otherwise, random differences among the subjects could be confounded with the independent variable, and a clear answer to the research question might be unlikely. In this context, *confounding* refers to differences between groups that do not result from the independent variable. When an experiment has minimal confounding variables, then we say that it has internal validity, which allows us to make accurate conclusions about the effects of the independent variable on the dependent variable. Randomly assigning subjects to conditions can minimize differences attributable to the characteristics of the subjects.

Most statistical tests are sensitive to the size of the sample. That is, most tests are more likely to detect true effects of independent variables when the number of observations is large than when it is small. **Power** occurs when a statistical test can detect effects. The power of most statistical tests increases with increases in the sample size.

Random samples are expensive, because each individual in the population has an unbiased chance of being in the surveyed sample. If you wanted a random sample of all college students for a face-to-face interview, you might have to fly to Maine for one interview, then to Oregon for two, then to Indiana for several more, and so on. One way to simplify this problem is to use a **stratified sample,** which divides the population into smaller units, and random sampling is done from the smaller units. So, if 40% of the undergraduate students in the United States attend school in the northeast or in California, we would stratify the sample by region accordingly to make sure that the proportion sampled from an area reflects the population distribution. Stratifying a sample is handy when two or more groups within a population are part of the sample. If we were particularly interested in attitudes of male and female college students, for example, we might stratify based on gender. This might yield more accurate results than sampling from all college students and then breaking down that sample into groups of interest. There are several variations of the stratification procedure, each with its own strengths and weaknesses (see Weisberg et al., 1989). We note here that in large-scale surveys investigating national issues, researchers often combine probability sampling procedures such as the random and stratified techniques and their variants.

CONCEPT SUMMARY

- Statistical reliability determines whether findings are the result of chance.
- Random sampling helps ensure the external validity of a sample taken from a population.
- Large samples have power that increases the likelihood of detecting effects.
- Stratified sampling is a good alternative to random sampling.

▶ Meta-analysis

Finally, we discuss the technique of **meta-analysis,** which is a relatively objective technique for summarizing across many studies investigating a single topic. Often, when a particular topic is researched repeatedly, the results vary. In this case, the question becomes, is the phenomenon real or just the result of random error? Which results should you believe? Rotton and Kelly (1985), for example, performed a meta-analysis on the lunar-lunacy hypothesis, referring to a popular belief that the full moon causes aberrant or risky behavior. You may have heard claims that emergency rooms are busier when the moon is full. Some studies have found such a relationship between aberrant behavior and the moon, whereas many have not. What, then, is the truth of the matter? Rotton and Kelly, using the statistical methods provided by meta-analysis, found that the number of studies that observed a lunar effect was no more than would be expected by chance. Further, meta-analysis often involves a comparison of effect sizes (see Appendix B), and they found small effect sizes in data on lunacy hypothesis. Thus, when taken as a whole, no meaningful relationship between the moon and behavior can be observed in the research literature.

As such, no single experiment or study in isolation can give us a definitive picture of how things truly are. One could ask, for example, Does watching violence on television cause people to be violent? To answer this question, one could conduct a study that investigates this hypothesized relationship. However, even if we conduct a study that finds a relationship between television violence and violence in society, how can we be sure that the violence is really a result of television and not some other societal factor or extraneous variable? Worse yet, how can we be sure that our findings are legitimate and not the result of some quirk of the experimental procedure?

One way to approach this problem of external validity is to summarize across many studies, that is, to do a review of the research. As noted in Chapter 5, the effects of watching television are a highly studied variable. Psychology relies heavily on papers that review a particular area of research, both to answer better specific questions and to synthesize theories of psychological phenomena. If a given relationship replicates in many studies and under many conditions, one can be more certain that the observation is real, especially if the effect sizes are large. Unfortunately, the person reviewing can be just as fallible as any observer in a specific study. In fact, observer fallibility can be a greater problem here than in direct observation. Drawing conclusions across a large number of studies is a difficult and often subjective process that is susceptible to error and bias. The reviewer may favor his or her own belief over those of others and so demonstrate bias by selecting only studies that confirm this prior belief or expectation. In the last few decades, meta-analysis has gained popularity as a relatively objective method for summarizing across the results of many studies investigating the same topic.

To return to the question of violence on television and violence in society, a few meta-analytic reviews have attempted to answer this question by analyzing the results of the numerous studies conducted on this topic (Paik & Comstock, 1994; Wood, Wong, & Chachere, 1991). These meta-analyses found a consistent relationship between television violence and violent actions, although the size of this relationship varied depending on how violence was measured. Note, however, that many studies found that this relationship occurred in a laboratory setting. It is possible that these findings are limited to specific settings and measurements and do not generalize to society at large. A more recent meta-analysis by Anderson and Bushman (1997) compared laboratory studies of violence with studies conducted in more naturalistic settings. Their conclusion argues against the interpretation that laboratory studies do not generalize. Anderson and Bushman demonstrated that some of the same factors that produce violence in the laboratory also appear to produce it in society. Thus, in this case, the method of meta-analytic observation and analysis has helped to clarify the broader implications of a large and complex area of research.

As noted earlier, meta-analytic techniques use statistical methods not only to determine the validity of a particular observation across a large number of studies but also to evaluate the size of the effect or strength of that observation. Although an observation may be real—a variable may have a real effect—it could be difficult to detect under certain conditions. Perhaps other factors often interfere or overwhelm its detection because the effect of that specific factor is small, and so some studies find it, whereas others do not. On the other hand, even if an observation is reliable, it may be that the effect is too small to be of practical interest. A good example of this issue of the size of an effect comes from a meta-analysis performed on the effect of sodium (a component of salt) on hypertension (high blood pressure). Much research over the years has observed that sodium causes hypertension. Still, many studies have failed to find such a relationship. Some have argued that sodium is a factor that reliably causes hypertension in many adults, so sodium intake should be restricted to minimize the health risks associated with hypertension. Those who believe that sodium causes hypertension tend to cite studies that found such a relationship. Those who do not believe this cite studies that found no such relationship. Midgley, Matthew, Geenwood, and Logan (1996) conducted a meta-analysis on the relevant literature to make a more objective review of the research. They found that although decreasing sodium intake did, in fact, tend to decrease blood pressure, this decrease was on average quite small (3.7 mm Hg per 100 mmol/day of excreted sodium) and may be tiny compared with other factors. Such a relationship is equivalent to a large reduction in sodium intake having only a very small effect on blood pressure.

> ## CONCEPT SUMMARY

- Meta-analysis is a relatively objective statistical method for summarizing across the results of many studies investigating a specific topic.
- It can help to determine the external validity of a particular observation, its relative strength, and its consistency.

▶ Measurement Procedures

A brief summary of the previous chapters and the material considered thus far in this one might go like this: Theories and observations result in hypotheses that are testable by empirical observations that are reliable and valid. Measurement, the use of which determines the growth and progression of a science (Boring, 1961), is the underpinning of testable hypotheses as well as of reliability and validity.

Measurement is a systematic way of assigning numbers or names to objects and their attributes (we discuss measurement scales in the Application section). How dependent variables are measured has important implications for their validity and reliability, as we shall soon see. Recall that in the first chapter, we discussed *operational definitions,* and in the second chapter, we considered *intervening variables.* Both these ideas described how we link inputs (procedures that produce the concept in question) and outputs (how we measure or assess that concept). Intervening variables usually are more complex than operationally defined concepts, because the former tend to rely on several input and output variables rather than on just one or two. The complexity of intervening variables often leads to them being called **theoretical constructs.** This designation derives from the notion that the theory constructs the relationships among the numerous inputs and outputs that specify the intervening variables.

Our discussion of construct validity shows how conventional measures, such as reaction time, correct responding to SAT questions, and the like, can sometimes be called into question. Difficulties in interpreting dependent variables occur in many areas of psychology, because the contact between the behavior and the supposed underlying psychological process may not be easy to determine. Consider how psychological processes can be by our measures.

Schematic drawings of two theoretical constructs appear in Figure 7–2. The top portion has well-specified inputs, lights of differing intensities, and outputs, statements concerning how an observer perceives the light. We might call this construct *brightness*. The bottom portion of the figure illustrates a construct with less well-specified inputs, previous experience and genetics, but with precise outputs, statements regarding feelings of depression. We might call this construct *depression*. Scaling of concepts such as brightness is called **psychophysical scaling.** Concepts that receive psychophysical scaling usually relate inputs with a known physical dimension.

For example, a typical psychophysical experiment might relate what a person says about the detection of lights to the intensity of those lights. We can contrast psychophysical scaling to **psychometric scaling,** which applies when concepts, such as depression, are measured but usually do not have clearly specified inputs. Ordinarily, psychometrically measured constructs are only assessed and not produced. We assess a person's feelings of depression or his or

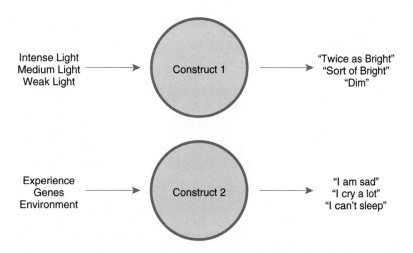

Figure 7–2   Defining two theoretical constructs (intervening variables) by specifying the inputs that produce them and the outputs that are used to measure them. Note that Construct 1 has better specified inputs than Construct 2.

APPLICATION

Measurement Scales

Measurement scales can have four properties (McCall, 1990), and the combination of these properties determines what is measured. Thus, these properties determine the validity of the scale.

All measurement scales have instances that are different from each other. This fundamental property, **difference,** means that some temperatures are colder (or warmer) than others, some people are male and some female, and so on. The other scale properties are not universal. Some scales can determine the **magnitude** of attributes. This means the scale can show that one attribute is greater than, less than, or equal to another instance of that attribute. Another property of attributes that some scales can determine is whether there are **equal intervals** between magnitudes. A final property of some measurement scales is a **true zero** point.

Psychologists use four measurement scales: (a) nominal, (b) ordinal, (c) interval, and (d) ratio. These scales are defined by which of the four properties of measurement they possess. **Nominal scales** measure only differences. **Ordinal scales** measure differences and magnitude. **Interval scales** possess the properties of difference, magnitude, and equal intervals. **Ratio scales** have all four properties of measurement scales (difference, magnitude, equal interval, and meaningful zero).

Nominal scales include ZIP codes, gender (male and female), and undergraduate major program. Each of these scales classifies you in some way, but they do not measure magnitudes in any obvious way. Thus, useful statistics, such as the arithmetic average, cannot be used to characterize nominal measures. Even assigning arbitrary numbers to major programs (Business 1, Psychology 2, and so on) would not legitimize the "average" major at an institution.

Ordinal scales include most Likert scales (discussed later in this chapter) and other ranked measurements, such as placement in a beauty contest or finishing order in a horse race. Where you finish in a beauty contest tells the magnitude of beauty, but it reveals little about the intervals between the ranks. The top two people in a ranking might be very close to each other, but the fifth and sixth people might be very far apart. Averaging numbers with unequal intervals is not legitimate. In fact, nominal and ordinal scales have special statistics (*nonparametric statistics,* which are described in the statistical appendices) that should be used with them.

Interval and ratio scales allow you to perform most mathematical operations on them, and ordinary inferential statistics (see appendices for *parametric statistics*) can be used on attributes measured at these levels. Most IQ measures and SAT scores are examples of interval scales, because adjacent values have equal intervals across the entire scale. The 10 units of difference between an IQ of 90 and an IQ of 100 are supposed to be the same as the 10 units of difference separating IQs of 110 and 120. Neither the IQ nor the SAT has a true or meaningful zero point, so they are not ratio scales. However, measures such as response speed and percentage correct are ratio measures, because you can exhibit zero speed or no correct responses. Note well that the measurement scale derives from the measuring procedure, not necessarily from the nature of the element measured. Temperature measured by the Kelvin scale has a true zero and is a ratio measure. The Fahrenheit and Celsius scales, however, do not have a true zero (these scales have no point for an absence of temperature), so they are interval scales. Finally, if we simply say that one thing is hotter than another, we are measuring at the ordinal level.

Behavioral data derived from different scales tell us different things, and the kinds of conclusions we can draw depend, in part, on the scale we use. If depression were assessed on an ordinal scale, it would not be proper to say that a person with a depression score of 8 on the scale was twice as depressed as someone with a depression score of 4. To make such a statement, we would have to measure depression on a scale that has a meaningful zero point and equal intervals between adjacent score values (a ratio scale). Knowing the type of scale being used to measure behavior is important. A summary of this information appears in Figure 7–3.

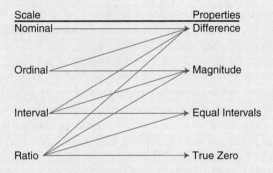

Figure 7–3 Measurement scales with their properties.

her level of intelligence. This assessment contrasts to manipulating the conditions under which they occur so that we can produce variations in them, as we can by changing brightness judgments by manipulating light intensity.

Before we examine some scaling techniques, we should note that less precise theories result from assessment rather than from production. Thus, many scientific psychologists try to specify the independent variables that produce psychometrically determined constructs. Substantial progress has been made in doing this for some constructs (for example, *learning, memory,* and *social loafing*), and less progress has been made on others (including concepts such as *depression, schizophrenia,* and *intelligence*).

CONCEPT SUMMARY

- Theoretical constructs are intervening variables. Several independent and dependent variables define the construct.
- Psychophysical scaling measures constructs that have well-specified inputs and outputs.
- Psychometric scaling measures assessed constructs, which means that the independent variables usually are not well specified.

Psychophysics

Psychophysics involves determining psychophysical scales—the psychological reactions to physical events having a known dimension. Boring (1950) claims that scientific psychology began with the development of procedures to measure the relation between internal impressions, such as brightness judgments, and the external world, such as light intensity. The early scientists, led by Gustav Fechner (1860, republished in 1966), who was the primary developer of psychophysical scaling methods, formulated the first mathematical laws of psychological phenomena. Fechner and other early psychophysicists concluded that private, internal judgments could be measured accurately. Just as physicists could measure light intensity, sound intensity, and weight, so too could psychophysicists measure the corresponding psychological attributes of brightness, loudness, and heaviness.

Determining how loud a sound seems or how painful a shock feels is difficult, because there is rarely a one-to-one relation between physical values and psychological values. If a rock band turned up its amplifiers to produce twice the energy, this twofold increase would not result in listeners hearing music twice as loud. To double the loudness requires nearly a 10-fold increase in energy, which means that radios, telephones, and other devices that convey sound must be calibrated so that manipulating their energy output is done proportionately to increments in perceived loudness.

E. H. Weber (1846/1948) did pioneering work in psychophysics about 20 years before Fechner. Weber wanted to determine how different two stimuli must be before they can be reliably distinguished. He had people compare heavier and lighter lifted weights to a standard weight of 300 grams. The observer said "heavier" or "lighter" as appropriate. Detecting differences became more difficult as the comparison stimuli approached the weight of the standard, and observers switched from saying "heavier" or "lighter" to "equal." This procedure permits a determination of the **difference threshold,** which is half the average difference in weight between stimuli that the observer can distinguish as heavier or lighter than the standard. For example, say an observer has to judge whether lifted weights differ from a 300-gram standard. On average, the observer might switch from saying "heavier" to "equal" at 310 grams and from "lighter" to "equal" at 290 grams. Half this 20-gram difference defines the difference threshold.

Weber found that the difference threshold increases with increases in the magnitude of the standard stimulus. In particular, **Weber's law** (as Fechner called it) states: *For a particular sensory modality, the size of the difference threshold relative to the standard stimulus is a constant.* If 10 grams is the difference threshold for a 300-gram standard and 20 grams is the difference threshold for a 600-gram standard, then Weber would predict that the difference threshold for a 900-gram weight would be 30 grams. Note that in all three cases, there is a constant fraction relation of $\frac{1}{30}$ between the threshold and the standard. Weber's law is often written as

$$\Delta I \, / \, I = K$$

where I refers to the magnitude of the standard, ΔI is the difference threshold, and K is the symbol for constancy. This law allows us to calibrate the relation between, for instance, the energy output of a guitar amplifier and the increments in perceived loudness.

Fechner was interested in other aspects of psychophysics as well, and he performed laborious experiments in which he determined the minimal energy needed to detect the presence of a stimulus, which he called the **absolute threshold.** In a typical experiment, the observer might hear (or see or weigh or smell) sequences of stimuli of increasing or decreasing intensity, to which the observer says "yes" when the stimulus is detected and "no" when it is not. Fechner operationally defined the absolute threshold as the mean of the intensities at which the observer switches from yes to no or from no to yes.

Psychophysical threshold measures are useful in businesses producing goods that involve the sensory capacities of consumers. The measures help to determine people's preferences. This is especially true of tastes, smells, and colors. Recently, threshold measures have illuminated important sensory functions. Dalton, Doolittle, Nagata, and Breslin (2000) were interested in flavor perception, which is how tastes and smells interact. You are probably aware that things taste differently—or not at all—when you have a stuffy nose from a cold. Dalton and her colleagues put this sensory combination to the test in the laboratory by first determining the absolute thresholds for a sweet taste (saccharin) and a cherry/almond smell (benzaldehyde). Then, to see whether the presence of one determined the perception of the other, they presented below-threshold concentrations of the two stimuli while they were presented simultaneously (saccharin solutions were held in the mouth as the smell was presented). They found detection of subthreshold intensities of the two stimuli presented simultaneously, because on average, the absolute threshold was now 28% lower. This integration of sensory experience was limited to "congruent" stimuli (saccharin will enhance a cherry smell but neither water nor a "meaty" taste will). These interesting findings seem to have both practical and theoretical importance, and Dalton (2002) provides additional findings.

CONCEPT SUMMARY

- Psychometrics determines difference and absolute thresholds.
- Weber's law is $\Delta I \, / \, I = K$.

Psychometrics

A popular way of assessing psychological traits that do not seem to lie on a known physical scale is the **summated rating scale**. A summated rating scale provides a score for a psychometric property of a person that derives from how that person responds to several statements about a topic that clearly are favorable or unfavorable. This abstract definition is illustrated by the Positive Affect Negative Affect Schedule (PANAS) developed by Watson, Clark, and Tellegren (1988). This scale has people rate how their present mood matches with 10 high-arousal positive mood words (for example, *interested, enthusiastic,* and *proud*) and with 10 high-arousal negative mood words (for example, *distressed, guilty,* and *scared*), rated on a scale from 1 to 5: 1 = *very slightly or not at all;* 2 = *a little;* 3 = *moderately;* 4 = *quite a bit;* and 5 = *extremely.* Summing the points awarded to positive items results in a summated rating score of positive affect. A similar procedure for the negative item yields a summated rating score of negative affect. Scales such as the PANAS are often called a **Likert scale** after the person who developed this kind of rating procedure (Likert, 1932).

Woodzicka and LaFrance (2001) used the PANAS in an experiment that asked women to imagine being sexually harassed in an interview situation. They compared the reported moods of these women with those of others who were subjected to real harassment in a contrived interview. Very few of the respondents in the imaginary harassing condition reported being scared; rather, they were angry. On the other hand, the feelings of the women who underwent the actual harassment were the reverse: 40% of the actual targets reported being scared, but far fewer said they were outraged. Thus, actually undergoing sexual harassment produces feelings that differ from those that arise when imagining such harassment. You should note that the summated score from a Likert scale involves summing *ratings.* The summation procedure assumes that, for example, an average score of 4 *(quite a bit)* on the negative affect portion of the PANAS is not only more negative than an average score of 2 *(a little),* it is two units greater. Furthermore, it assumes that a score of 5 *(extremely)* is the same distance from a score of 3 *(moderately),* as a score of 4 is from 2. The Application section of this chapter includes a discussion of this questionable assumption.

> ### CONCEPT SUMMARY
>
> - A summated rating scale is the sum of the ratings that people give to attitude statements.
> - Typically, people respond to negatively and positively oriented words or phrases on 5-point scales, which are often called Likert scales.

Self-Report Methods   Most psychometric scales and many psychophysical ones represent **self-report methods,** because the psychological data come from a personal report by the respondent and not from behavior observed and measured more directly by the researcher. Self-report methods usually yield data that are difficult for the observer to corroborate immediately and directly.

This lack of corroboration means that it can be difficult to determine the validity of the self-report. Suppose you have administered the PANAS to someone, and the person responds that her current mood is extremely proud and quite a bit determined. How do you know whether these are true reflections of her emotional state? Do these responses represent how she actually feels, or do they reveal what she believes a typical person would say in response to such a scale item? Furthermore, answers to all questions may not have easy methods of verification, so how do you determine the veracity of the total score? These threats to validity can be difficult to overcome. One way to minimize the verification problem is to ensure construct validity and to provide some sort of predictive validity. If different groups of people respond differently, yet in a theoretically predictable way, as they did in Woodzicka and LaFrance (2001), then we can be confident that something has differentially altered the mood of those people—their scale responses reflect those changes.

Self-report methods such as the Likert scales have other validity problems (Schwarz, 1999). What people report is sensitive to a number of variables, including whether these reports are open-ended or constrained by a scale, the numerical values of the scale alternatives, and the order and context of the questions. Consider just the effects of the rating scale employed. Schwarz, Knäuper, Hippler, Noelle-Neumann, and Clark (1991) asked people how successful in life they thought they were. With a rating scale ranging from 1 (*not at all successful*) to 5 (*highly successful*), Schwarz and associates found that more people reported high success than when *not at all successful* was given the numeric value of 1 on a 10-point scale. This sort of discrepancy seems easy to demonstrate (Schwarz, 1999), which indicates that the validity of a person's self-report may be extremely difficult to determine.

> ### CONCEPT SUMMARY
>
> Self-report methods can be invalid, because they often lack corroboration and are sensitive to the nature of the wording of the measuring scale.

Summary

1. The validity of observations refers to their approximate truth or falsity.

2. A criterion is an additional measure of behavior that serves as a standard for the measurement in question.

3. How well a measure predicts a criterion behavior determines the predictive validity of that measure.

4. Construct validity concerns the extent to which the dependent and independent variables reflect and measure the behavior of interest. Operational definitions and strict adherence to protocols help to minimize construct invalidity resulting from error.

5. External validity refers to whether the results of observations can be generalized to other settings and subject populations. Replicating research procedures helps to assess the generality of the observations.

6. Internal validity deals with the possibility of determining whether one variable causes changes in another. Confounding is a major threat to internal validity.

7. Reliability refers to the consistency of behavioral measures. The reliability of test results can be shown by test-retest reliability, by split-half reliability, or by using parallel forms of the test.

8. Inferential statistics permit an assessment of statistical reliability by showing whether findings result from chance factors.

9. The larger the sample size from a population, the greater the reliability and power of the statistical tests.

10. Random samples and stratified samples help to increase the external validity of the sample.

11. Meta-analysis determines whether a topic is reliable and valid by examining consistent results across many studies and by looking at effect sizes.

12. Measurement is a systematic way of assigning numbers or names to objects and their attributes.

13. Intervening variables and theoretical constructs are sometimes synonymous.

14. Theoretical constructs have well-specified inputs and outputs and are often measured psychophysically. Theoretical constructs with imprecise knowledge of inputs are usually assessed and scaled psychometrically.

15. Fechner, the founder of psychophysics, devised ways to measure both absolute and difference thresholds.

16. According to Weber's law, the size of the difference threshold relative to the standard stimulus is a constant for a particular sensory modality.

17. A summated rating scale, also called a Likert scale, is the sum of the ratings that people give to attitude statements. Typically, people respond to positively and negatively oriented statements on 5-point scales.

18. Many psychometric and psychophysical measures are self-report methods, which yield psychological data from a personal report rather than from direct observation and measurement.

19. The validity of self-reports is often difficult to determine, because the data cannot be corroborated immediately and directly by the observer.

Key Concepts

absolute threshold (181)
construct validity (165)
criterion (164)
difference (178)
difference threshold (180)
equal intervals (178)
external validity (167)
internal validity (168)
interval scale (178)
Likert scale (182)
magnitude (178)
measurement (176)
meta-analysis (174)
nominal scale (178)

ordinal scale (178)
parallel forms (171)
population (172)
power (173)
predictive validity (184)
psychometric scaling (177)
psychophysical scaling (177)
psychophysics (180)
ratio scale (178)
reliability (169)
replication (168)
sample (172)
self-report methods (183)

split-half reliability (171)
statistical reliability (171)
stratified sample (173)
summated rating scale (182)
test-retest reliability (171)
theoretical constructs (177)
true zero (178)
validity (164)
Weber's law
($\Delta I / I = K$) (180)

Exercises

1. Discuss why a test cannot be valid if it is not reliable.

2. [*Special Exercise.*] Consider each of the following measures, and indicate the type of measurement scale: October 22, 1850; the number of alarm calls by a chickadee in 1 hour; third place in a beauty contest; the fifth-highest grades in a class; and being a sophomore in college.

3. Devise a way of using Likert techniques for assessing students' attitudes toward the presence of fraternities and sororities on campus.

4. Discuss the differences between the various types of measurement scales. Indicate the scale properties of each.

Suggested Resources

Measurement theory is a complex topic. A good introduction can be found in McCall, R. B. (1990). Fundamental statistics for the behavioral sciences (5th ed.). San Diego: Harcourt Brace.

Numerous textbooks emphasize psychometrics. Any current textbook concerned with psychological testing will be helpful. The specifics of scaling can be found in Goldstein, G., & Herson, M. (Eds.) (1990). *Handbook of psychological assessment* (2nd ed.). New York: Pergamon.

 ## Web Resources

Several interesting links to many of the issues discussed in this chapter can be found at: http://www.ruf.rice.edu/~lane/hyperstat/contents.html

An interesting article on how to detect bogus theories is at: http://quasar.as.utexas.edu/BillInfo/Quack.html

The Wadsworth workshops on Research Methods include one on "Confounds: Threats to Validity" and another on "Sampling Methods," at: http://www.wadsworth.com/psychology_d/templates/student_resources/workshops/resch_wrk.html

PSYCHOLOGY IN ACTION

Validity

The validity of self-report methods is usually much more difficult to determine than it is for observational scales. Both observational and self-report methods often have strong face validity, which simply means that the questions appear to be asking about the concept under study. At face value, then, we might think that a person who claims to cry frequently would be more unhappy than someone who denies that he or she cries frequently. The face validity of a test or its components, however, may not be a good guide to its ability to measure behavior. For example, do you think a depressed person would sleep more or less than a nondepressed person? One possibility might be that someone suffering from depression would sleep constantly to escape from depressing thoughts. On the other hand, a depressed person might have difficulty in sleeping because he or she is constantly thinking about unhappy things.

Which of these two reasonable expectations best describes a depressed person? More to the point of this chapter, what kind of questions should we ask on a self-report scale of depression? We are not going to tell you about the sleeping behavior of depressed people, because the issue here goes beyond the particulars of depression. This point is that face validity rarely captures the subtleties of a problem. Rather, a substantial amount of data will permit a sensible way of validating a particular construct. The typical course of scale development has a criterion in mind as well as a background of knowledge regarding the target concept. These two sources of information guide development of the scale.

One way to understand this process is to examine the *Mental Measurements Yearbook*. This publication summarizes the characteristics of various kinds of psychometric instruments, including personality tests, intelligence scales, and aptitude tests. The publication includes information regarding a scale's reliability and validity, and the typical review of a scale includes summaries of how the test was developed and standardized. You will find that perusing this book will be very informative. As an exercise for this chapter, you might try examining how the validity for several self-report scales has been determined. You also might want to contrast those with the validity criteria used for psychometric scales that rely on more direct observations.

PART

III

Advanced Research Topics

Chapter 8
Experimental Design

Chapter 9
Complex Design

Chapter 10
Small-n Experimentation

Chapter 11
Quasi-Experimentation

In Part III, we first examine the pros and cons of using a within-subjects design, in which each participant is tested under every level of the independent variable, or a between-subjects design, in which different participants are tested under each level of the independent variable. Chapter 9 considers research designs that have more than one independent variable. These complex designs are important because they permit the analysis of both main effects of the independent variables and the interactions among them. Small-n experimentation focuses on research using a small number of subjects, which often must be used when special populations, such as schizophrenic people, are examined. The final chapter in Part III concerns quasi-experiments, which are experiments that have independent variables that are not directly varied by the researcher.

CHAPTER 8

Experimental Design

Variables should be arranged to maximize internal validity

Between-Subjects Design

- In this simplest case, the experimental group receives the independent variable, and the control group does not.
- To minimize the confounding of participant characteristics with group membership, randomly assign participants to conditions or match their characteristics between groups.

Within-Subjects Design

- Each participant receives all levels of the independent variable.
- To minimize confounding caused by carryover effects, the order of testing each level of the independent variable must be counterbalanced or randomized.

A carefully designed experiment will permit valid conclusions to be drawn about the effects of the independent variable on the dependent variable. This chapter considers how to design experiments with a between-subjects configuration, in which independent groups of subjects receive the different levels of the independent variable. It also considers a within-subjects configuration, in which all subjects receive all levels of the independent variable. A threat to validity for the between-subjects case has to do with the initial equality of the subjects in the different groups. In within-subjects experiments, the effects of one treatment may carry over to another, which could confound the effect of the independent variable.

▶ Internal Validity in Experiments

In a properly conducted experiment, the situation is controlled so that changes in dependent variables result solely from changes in independent variables. In a good experiment, we can make valid causal statements about the results. A valid observation, as noted in Chapter 7, is one that is sound or genuine because it reveals a true effect. A properly designed experiment can have valid results, and experiments that lead to valid results are said to be **internally valid** (see Cook & Campbell, 1979). By means of control (such as the joint method of agreement and disagreement), the researcher rules out inadvertent confounding, and the results reflect the effects of the intended variables. As discussed in Chapter 6, Brennen, Baguley, Bright, and Bruce (1990) were able to assert that presenting letter initials was more effective in resolving tip-of-the-tongue states than was presenting pictures. Their experiment was designed to maximize the effects of presenting pictures and to minimize the effects of extraneous variables, which means their work was internally valid.

Experiments are internally valid in principle. Internal validity does not occur automatically but, rather, through a careful selection of variables and an adequate experimental design. Underwood has noted that there is one basic principle of research design: "Design the experiment so that the effects of the independent variables can be evaluated unambiguously" (1957, p. 86). In this chapter, we will discuss features of experimental design that help to provide internal validity. In particular, we will discuss advantages and disadvantages of two types of design: between-subjects and within-subjects. A **between-subjects design** is one in which independent groups of subjects receive the different levels of the independent variable. In a **within-subjects design**, all subjects receive all levels of the independent variable. To illustrate how experimental design is related to validity, we will first consider two situations in which design flaws could prevent valid causal statements.

Executive Monkeys

The topic of stress-induced ulcers, especially among high-powered executives, is a common one in the popular press. Early laboratory experiments by Brady (1958) and his colleagues (Brady, Porter, Conrad, & Mason, 1958) demonstrated the development of stress ulcers in "executive" monkeys. Brady initially tested monkeys to see whether they could learn to respond quickly by pressing a button to avoid electric shock. Monkeys that responded at a high rate during this test were allowed to be executives in a second phase of the experiment. In the second part of the experiment, an executive monkey and a "coworker" received strong electric shocks periodically over long periods of time (usually a 4-hour session). This was considered to be a highly stressful work situation for the monkeys. The executive monkeys could press a button that would postpone the shock. In this avoidance task, the coworker of the executive received a shock every time the executive received one, but the coworker did not have any control over the occurrence of the shocks. The executive had control over the presentation of the shocks by being able to avoid them. If the executive did not press the button often enough, both he and his helpless coworker would get shocked. Brady found that the executives developed severe gastrointestinal ulcers and died, whereas the helpless coworkers did not develop any obvious disorders. This finding led Brady, along with many other psychologists, to conclude that the stress of management could produce ulcers under controlled conditions.

Brady's conclusion was considered to be a valid one for quite some time. But then a number of laboratory reports began to appear that seemed to indicate greater production of stress ulcers in helpless animals than in those who had control over electric shock (for example, Weiss, 1968). Were the earlier findings the result of poor design, or were the later results a fluke? Subsequent work by Weiss (1971) confirmed the fact that helpless animals were indeed more affected than those who had control, and his work suggested why the original studies about executive monkeys were flawed and therefore invalid. Weiss noted that Brady's executives responded at a high rate at the beginning of the experiment. Then Weiss demonstrated that animals that respond at high rates in a stressful avoidance task are likely to get ulcers, regardless of whether they are helpless or in control. Because the tendency to respond at high rates was confounded with the independent variable (helplessness or executive control) in Brady's work, some psychologists made the invalid conclusion that control under stressful situations leads to ulcers. The critical design flaw underlying the invalid conclusion was assignment of the highly responsive monkeys to the executive condition. Later we will consider some general rules for ensuring that the characteristics of the subjects do not have a confounding influence on the effects of the independent variable. Without such rules it would be difficult, if not impossible, to have an internally valid experiment.

While studies using animal subjects are common when investigating stress, it is possible to perform stress experiments on human participants in an ethical manner (see Chapter 12). Many readers of this book, not being monkeys themselves, may find such results to be more salient and easier to generalize. In these human stress experiments, the noxious stimulus is more likely to be loud noise than electric shock (e.g., Baker & Stephenson, 2000). Instead of probing for ulcers, the dependent variable in these studies is often the amount of cortisol generated. Cortisol is an important hormone related to stress and can be measured by taking saliva samples.

Meta-analysis is a statistical method for comparing results across sets of experiments and has been discussed in Chapter 7 as a useful tool for evaluating external validity in observational research. Meta-analysis is equally useful for comparing results of controlled experiments. Dickerson and Kemeny (2004) performed a meta-analysis of 208 laboratory studies of human cortisol response to acute stressors. While animal research strongly supports the hypothesis that psychological stressors can mediate cortisol responses, the goal of the meta-analysis was to determine more precisely what kinds of stressors influenced cortisol. For example, is it sufficient to create a negative affective

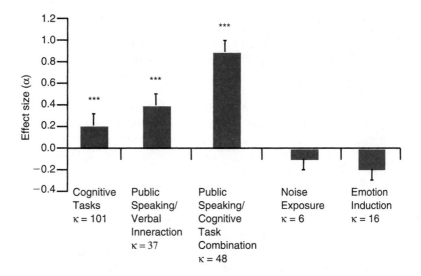

Figure 8–1 Cortisol effect size for different kinds of tasks. Higher values indicate greater effect size. $***p < .001$. From Dickerson and Kemeny (2004) with permission. Copyright American Psychological Association.

state due to any unpleasant stimulus or is there a more specific relationship between psychological stressors and cortisol in humans?

Figure 8–1 answers this question. Cognitive tasks, such as mental arithmetic, produce a statistically significant cortisol effect and so does public speaking. But noise exposure and emotion induction (e.g., from watching films) do not. Thus, distress by itself is not sufficient to produce a cortisol response. Only certain kinds of stressors are related to the human cortisol response.

Experiments with LSD

Lysergic acid diethylamide (LSD) is a hallucinogenic substance that was a popular and dangerous drug used to induce a "high" in the drug culture of the late 1960s and early 1970s. Because LSD was so popular and also seemed to produce some of the symptoms associated with schizophrenia, a severe mental disorder, psychologists tried to determine the effects of LSD on behavior in the controlled environment of the laboratory.

Laboratory research on the effects of LSD began in the early 1960s, and some of those studies provide useful lessons in designing internally valid experiments. We shall examine an early study by Jarrard (1963) that illustrates an experimental design in which each subject receives all levels of the independent variables (several different-sized doses of LSD, in this case). This type of design is called a within-subjects design, and differs from the between-subjects design used by Weiss, in which different subjects received the various levels of the independent variable (the animals were either helpless or executives, but not both).

Jarrard wanted to determine the effects of several different doses of LSD on well-established behavior. Initially, he trained rats to press a lever to obtain a food reward. When the behavior of the rats stabilized and they were performing well, Jarrard began testing the effects of LSD on the rate of lever pressing. His experiment involved six levels of the independent variable. The baseline, or control, amount of LSD was zero—the rats were injected with a saltwater solution that matched the salinity of their body fluids. The remaining five doses of LSD represented a proportion of each rat's body weight and were .05, .10, .20, .40, and .80 milligram of LSD per kilogram of body weight. The general procedure involved placing the rats in the lever box immediately after injection for a 2-hour test period. Several days separated each test of the injections.

At this point, we need to consider several problems that could prevent Jarrard from having an internally valid experiment. Suppose Jarrard tested all his animals in the same order, going from the control dose to the largest dose. Such a design could lead to problems, because the susceptibility to LSD could change across successive administrations. The rats could become more tolerant of LSD (less affected by it), or they could become sensitized (more affected by it). In either case, tolerance or sensitization, the effects of later doses of LSD would be influenced by the rats having received the earlier doses. This confounding effect also could occur if testing began with the largest dose and ended with the smallest.

Because Jarrard did not know whether LSD had long-term carryover effects, such as tolerance and sensitization, he needed to find a way to administer doses so he could determine the effects of a particular dose independently of the other doses. He chose to counterbalance the order of doses across subjects. **Counterbalancing** refers to the systematic variation of the order of conditions in an experiment. The possible confounding effect of carryover from one dose to another was counterbalanced by having each dose appear equally often at each ordinal position in the test sequence. For example, one subject might have received the following sequence: control, .05, .40, .10, .80, and .20. Another subject might have received .40, control, .10, .20, .05, and .80. The remaining four rats would then receive different orders of treatments so that for all six rats, each dose was tested first, second, third, fourth, fifth, and sixth. This procedure should balance across doses any tolerance or sensitization that could occur as a result of repeated administration of LSD. On the average, each condition occurs at each ordinal position.

Jarrard found that the pressing of a lever for food was slightly enhanced by the two smallest doses of LSD and severely impaired by the two largest doses compared with the effects of the saltwater injection (the control condition). These are internally valid results, because they are not confounded by carryover effects caused by repeated testing of the independent variable. A major topic of this chapter is prevention of carryover effects in within-subjects designs.

▶ Experimental Design

The work of Weiss and Jarrard that we have just discussed illustrates the goal of good experimental design: to minimize extraneous or uncontrolled variation to increase the likelihood that an experiment will produce internally valid results. Here we will cover some common techniques used to improve the design of experiments. This discussion should provide you with an understanding of the aims of the psychologist designing a particular experiment.

The first design decision an experimenter must make is how to assign subjects to the various levels of independent variables. The two main possibilities are to assign only some subjects to each level, as Weiss did, or to assign each subject to every level, as Jarrard did. As mentioned earlier, the first possibility is called a between-subjects design and the second a within-subjects design. Let us reconsider Weiss' study from the standpoint of the two types of design and pretend that we are going to repeat his work. The two main conditions in that experiment were the executive condition, in which the animals had control over the shocks, and the helpless condition, in which the animals received shocks regardless of what they did. Let us assume that we have 10 rats available for our study. A between-subjects design and a within-subjects design for the experiment are illustrated in Table 8–1. The between-subjects

Table 8–1 Between-subjects and within-subjects designs for Weiss' experiment with 10 rats as the subjects (numbered 1 to 10)

Between-Subjects Design

	Independent variable		
	Executive group	Helpless group	
Individual subjects	1	6	Half the subjects
	2	7	are in the executive
	3	8	group, and half are
	4	9	in the helpless group.
	5	10	

Within-Subjects Design

	Independent variable		
	Executive condition	Helpless condition	
Individual subjects	1	1	All subjects receive
	2	2	both the executive
	3	3	and the helpless
	4	4	treatments.
	5	5	
	•	•	
	•	•	
	•	•	
	10	10	

design calls for you to divide your subjects in half (into two groups of 5 rats each), with one group receiving the executive treatment and the other the helpless treatment. (The proper method for assigning subjects to each group will be discussed shortly.) The within-subjects design has all 10 rats tested with both levels of the independent variable; that is, each rat is tested in the executive condition and in the helpless condition. (The proper method to determine the order in which each subject gets these two treatments will also be discussed later.) Before reading on, consider which design you would use, and provide reasons. The factors involved in this sort of decision are considered below.

Between-Subjects Designs

The between-subjects design is conservative (safe), because there is no chance of one treatment contaminating the other—the same subject never receives both treatments. However, the between-subjects design must contend with the possibility that the subjects in the two groups are different enough to influence the effects of the treatments. Any between-subjects experiment has the potential for being confounded because of differences among the subjects in the two groups. For example, the results of Brady's experiment were confounded by putting the highly responsive animals in the executive condition.

Matching and Randomization   In any between-subjects experiment, the researcher must somehow guarantee that as few differences as possible exist among the subjects in the various treatment groups. Clearly, if we took the five animals most susceptible to stomach ulcers and put them into the executive group and the five least susceptible into the helpless condition, we might arrive at results that mask the true effects; we would have an internally *in*valid experiment. This is exactly what happened in the original executive-monkey experiment, because we now know that highly responsive animals are likely to ulcerate under stress. To prevent this kind of outcome, the experimenter tries to have groups that are equivalent at the beginning of the experiment.

One possible technique to use is called **matching,** in which important subject characteristics are matched in the various treatment conditions. In this experiment, one way to match subjects would be to administer a pretest to the animals to determine their response rates. Then subjects that had equal or very similar rates of response could be paired up. Unlike the procedure Brady used to assign subjects, this procedure calls for one member of each pair to be randomly assigned to one group and the other member to be assigned to the second group. One difficulty with matching is that an experimenter cannot match for everything. Indeed, the experimenter may not know what characteristics should be matched. Even though matched on some characteristics, the groups may differ on some other potentially relevant dimension. Thus, matching is done on the basis of the most likely confounding variables. Even so, matching on one variable could cause a mismatch on another.

In addition to the problems mentioned, another difficulty—**subject attrition**—can make matching an ineffective way to try to equate groups. Subject attrition means that one or more of the subjects in an experiment do not complete participation or their behavior changes for reasons other than the independent variable. Attrition can occur for any number of reasons. For example, a subject might get sick and fail to continue. An animal subject might die or perform so poorly that the data are uninterpretable. A human subject in the experiment might refuse to continue to participate. In a long-term experiment, the participants might mature, which means that their characteristics change during the course of the experiment. If we carefully match our subjects across conditions to equate our groups, then subject attrition in one group will make our groups unequal, and our matching will have been in vain. This may be true even if just one subject is lost from a particular group.

If group characteristics are determined by an unbiased procedure (random assignment), attrition will have a less detrimental effect. However, attrition can still pose problems with both the reliability and the validity of our observations. If some form of attrition is likely, matching should not be used.

Randomization is a more common technique to ensure the formation of equivalent groups of participants (see Chapters 4 and 7). One way to form two groups by randomization would be to assign arbitrary numbers to the participants and then pull numbered slips of paper out of a hat or some other container. Similarly, when we are ready to assign a particular participant to a condition, we could throw a die, with even throws being assigned to one group and odd throws to the other. If we do not have any dice, a table of random numbers could be used to generate odd and even digits.

A table of random numbers is provided in Table C–8 in Appendix C. Random-number tables are very easy to use. To generate odd and even numbers, select a row of numbers in the table. Proceed across the row, noting whether each number is odd or even. If you reach the end of a row, simply select a different row of numbers and continue the procedure.

Each of these methods of randomization ignores the characteristics of the participants and leads to a random, unbiased assignment to conditions. Randomization means that each participant has an equal and unbiased opportunity to be in any of the conditions of the experiment. Randomization is how Weiss improved the design of the executive-monkey experiment. However, randomization does not guarantee that groups will always be equal. By chance, more of the highly responsive animals might be assigned to one of the groups. The odds of this rare occurrence can be calculated by the methods of statistics. This is one reason experimental design and statistics are often treated as the same topic. However, experimental design has to do with the logic of arranging experiments, whereas statistics deal with calculating odds, probabilities, and other mathematical quantities. Although perfect matching may be preferable to randomization, in some cases we may not be sure about the basis of matching; when this happens, randomization is the preferred assignment procedure.

> ## CONCEPT SUMMARY
>
> ### Between-Subjects Design
>
> Separate groups of subjects receive different levels of the independent variable. To control for individual differences
>
> - randomly assign subjects to groups, or
> - match subject characteristics in each group

Within-Subjects Designs

Many experimental psychologists prefer the within-subjects design to the between-subjects design. The within-subjects design is generally more efficient, because the performance of each subject is compared across the different experimental conditions. In our experiment, this means that any differences resulting from the executive and helpless treatments would not be caused by differences between the animals in the two conditions (as could be true of the between-subjects design), because all subjects receive all treatments. One implication of this feature is that fewer subjects are required.

As indicated in the earlier discussion of Jarrard's LSD experiment, the efficient within-subjects design brings with it the serious risk of **carryover effects** from one treatment to the next, which could result in an invalid experiment. That is, the effects of one treatment may carry over to another condition. Carryover effects are particularly serious if the conditions affect each other (or carry over) in different ways (for example, the experimental condition affects the control differently than the control condition affects the experimental condition). Imagine that 10 rats first underwent the helpless condition and then were placed in the executive condition in Brady's experiment with executive monkeys. As a result of their earlier experience with being helpless, the animals may react poorly to the executive condition, in which they now have control over the shocks. This would mask any true differences between the two levels of the independent variable. Any within-subjects experiment has the danger that experience in an early part of the experiment might change behavior in a later part of the experiment, because the effects of one treatment might carry over to the other treatment. This can be caused even by routine factors, such as practice or fatigue. How do we reduce this source of invalidity?

Randomization One way to minimize carryover among treatments is to randomly determine the order of their application. A random order can be established by using a table of random numbers or by writing the treatments on slips of paper and drawing them out of a hat. The logic is the same as that just described for assigning participants to conditions in between-participants designs. However, although randomization produces equivalent treatment orders in the long run, it is less likely to be suitable when there is only a small number of treatments. In most experiments, the number of participants exceeds the

APPLICATION

Counterbalancing in the Wild

Saari and Latham (1982) wanted to determine the effect of payment schedule on the performance and attitudes of beaver trappers in southwestern Washington. The trappers worked for a forest-products company and were paid an hourly wage during the course of the following experiment.

After a baseline measure of trapping performance under the hourly payment scheme, two incentive conditions were introduced in a within-subjects design. When trappers were under a continuous reinforcement schedule, they received an additional dollar for each beaver that was trapped. When the trappers were under a variable ratio schedule of four, they received four dollars when they brought in a beaver, if they correctly predicted twice whether the roll of a die would yield an odd or an even number (by chance alone, the trapper could pick the correct solution one out of four times). Thus, in one condition there was always a one-dollar payment, whereas in the other

the payment was, on average, given once every four times. Counterbalancing of the order of treatments was accomplished in the following way. The trappers were randomly split into two groups, and then the groups alternated weekly stints under either the continuous or the variable payment schedule. The alternating schedule continued for the entire trapping season.

Saari and Latham found that the number of beavers trapped increased under both payment schedules, but the increase was much larger under the variable ratio schedule than under the continuous one. Furthermore, they found that the trappers preferred the ratio schedule to the continuous schedule.

These results are very similar to those found when rats or pigeons are put under variable ratio schedules of reinforcement. Generally, behavior is more persistent under variable schedules of reinforcement than under continuous ones.

SOURCE: Saari, L. M., & Latham, G. P. (1982). Employee reactions to continuous and variable ratio reinforcement schedules involving a monetary incentive. *Journal of Applied Psychology, 67*, 506–508.

number of treatments, so randomization is a good technique for assigning participants to conditions but not for determining the order of treatments.

Counterbalancing As mentioned earlier, Jarrard used a technique called counterbalancing to balance the order of treatments across stages of his experiment. By balancing the effects of order of treatments across subjects, Jarrard was able to minimize carryover effects. In counterbalancing, each treatment occurs in each time period of the experiment. This means that every treatment has the same chance of being influenced by confounding variables. In other words, we *counter* the effects of potential confounding variables by *balancing* them over the periods when the treatments are administered.

Complete counterbalancing requires that all possible treatment orders are used. In the executive-monkey experiment, this is easy, because there are only two orders of treatments: helpless then executive, and executive then helpless. An example of such counterbalancing is presented in the Application section.

As the numbers of conditions increase, the numbers of possible orders get larger. Three treatments have 6 different orders, four treatments have 24 different orders, five conditions have 120 different orders, and so on. So, as the number of levels of the independent variable increases, complete counterbalancing soon becomes impractical. Instead, experimenters must settle for incomplete counterbalancing, in which each treatment occurs equally often in each portion of the experiment. In other words, condition A occurs first, second, and third equally often, as do conditions B and C. This arrangement is called a **Latin-square design.**

Table 8–2 shows a 4 × 4 Latin square, which contains four treatments (1, 2, 3, and 4). The columns of the square represent the sequence of these treatments, and the rows represent participants being tested in the experiment. For example, participant 1 receives treatment 1 first, then treatment 2, followed by treatments 3 and 4. Other participants receive these four treatments in a different sequence, or order, as we usually name this independent variable. Because a Latin square must always have equal numbers of rows and columns, the experimenter must use at least the same number of participants as there are treatments. So Table 8–2 requires at least four participants for the experiment. However, it is usually desirable to have more participants than treatments, for statistical reasons. This means that in practice the experimenter must obtain a number of participants that is some multiple of the number of treatments in the Latin square. For the square shown in Table 8–2, an experimenter could use 8, 12, or 16 participants, because these numbers can be divided by 4 leaving no remainder.

What sequence of treatments should be used for these additional participants? The experimenter has two choices. First, the same Latin square can be used over and over again. For example, using the square from Table 8–2, participant 5 would receive the same order as participant 1, participant 6 the same as participant 2, participant 7 the same as participant 3, and participant 8 the same as participant 4. When this procedure is used, good statistical practice requires the experimenter to compute a test for square uniqueness. If this test turns out to be statistically significant, it means that the partial counterbalancing of treatments was not successful and the results of the experiment

Table 8–2 A Latin square for counterbalancing the order of four treatments

		Order		
	1st	2nd	3rd	4th
1	1	2	3	4
2	2	3	4	1
Participant number 3	3	4	1	2
4	4	1	2	3

are in question. This is the danger of using a Latin square as opposed to complete counterbalancing. If the experimenter is unfortunate enough to select a particular Latin square that contains treatment sequences that somehow are related to effects of the treatments, the assumption that incomplete counterbalancing is sufficient fails. Fortunately, the statistical test for square uniqueness allows the experimenter to determine the success of this assumption. If the test is not significant, then the partial counterbalancing was successful, allowing the experimenter to avoid the expense of complete counterbalancing.

The second choice for testing additional participants uses different Latin squares for each successive group of participants. So, referring again to a 4 × 4 design, participants 5 through 8 would get their own Latin square, which would have a different arrangement than Table 8–2. The advantage of this procedure is that as more Latin squares are used within an experiment, the chances of partial counterbalancing failing are decreased. So, this is a reasonable choice when enough participants are tested to allow using several different Latin squares. However, the disadvantage of this procedure is that it is not possible to calculate a statistic for square uniqueness. If the assumption of partial counterbalancing being adequate is wrong, the experimenter will never know because there is no appropriate statistical test.

Table 8–3 shows a special kind of Latin square in which each treatment precedes and follows every other treatment equally often. This is called a **balanced Latin square**. Although many experimenters believe it offers better opportunities for successful partial counterbalancing than do normal Latin squares, there is no statistical test to prove this. Even so, when it costs nothing extra to use a balanced Latin square, this should be done, because it cannot hurt the experiment—and might even help.

If the number of conditions in an experiment is even, the formula for obtaining the first row of a balanced Latin square is 1, 2, n, 3, $n - 1$, 4, $n - 2$, and so on. Here n = the number of conditions. Therefore, as shown in Table 8–3, for an experiment with four conditions, the first row of a balanced Latin square would be 1, 2, 4, 3. The remaining rows of the square are obtained by simply adding 1 to each number in the corresponding column in the previous row, with the stipulation that if the resulting number is greater than n, then n should be subtracted.

Table 8–3 Balanced Latin square for an even number of treatment conditions

		1st	2nd	3rd	4th
	1	1	2	4	3
Participant number	2	2	3	1	4
	3	3	4	2	1
	4	4	1	3	2

If the number of conditions in an experiment is odd, then two squares are needed to have every condition follow every other condition an equal number of times. The first square is obtained in exactly the same manner as described in the previous paragraph for an even number of treatment conditions. Thus, as illustrated in Table 8–4, for an experiment with five treatment conditions, the sequence for the first row would be 1, 2, 5, 3, 4. The remaining rows are obtained as described previously. The second square is simply a reversal of the sequences of the first square. Thus, the sequence of the first row of the second square in a five-condition experiment would be 4, 3, 5, 2, 1.

Counterbalancing is useful not only for assigning treatment orders but also for determining the order of testing when there is more than one dependent variable. The primary concern is to balance any potential carryover effects for any given participant. To illustrate, let us reconsider the decompression study described in Chapter 6. In that study, baby rats received several tests so that the experimenter could determine whether prenatal decompression had affected them. Suppose there is reason to believe that the infant rats' performance on one test, such as climbing, could influence their behavior on another test, such as grasping. So, even though the different measures are not independent variables in the usual sense, the order in which they are administered may affect what is measured. One test might make the infant rats tired or could, conceivably, enhance their muscle tone. If we have two measures, *A* and *B*, we can completely counterbalance the order of assessment across subjects so that the average effect might be balanced.

Table 8–4   Balanced Latin squares for an odd number of treatment conditions

		Square 1 order				
		1st	2nd	3rd	4th	5th
	1	1	2	5	3	4
Participant number	2	2	3	1	4	5
	3	3	4	2	5	1
	4	4	5	3	1	2
	5	5	1	4	2	3

		Square 2 order				
		1st	2nd	3rd	4th	5th
	6	4	3	5	2	1
	7	5	4	1	3	2
Participant number	8	1	5	2	4	3
	9	2	1	3	5	4
	10	3	2	4	1	5

In conclusion, complete counterbalancing is the safest technique for within-subjects experimental designs. When the number of treatments is small, complete counterbalancing is always preferred to Latin squares. However, with larger numbers of treatments, complete counterbalancing is often not practical. Then the experimenter must assume the risk of using partial or incomplete counterbalancing with a Latin square. A statistical test for square uniqueness (beyond the scope of this textbook, but see Kirk, 1982, or other advanced statistics texts) is available to determine whether incomplete counterbalancing was successful. If it was not, the experiment must be repeated using a different Latin square or, perhaps, by avoiding a within-subjects design entirely. Although Latin squares and within-subjects designs are very efficient, they are not appropriate for all experiments.

CONCEPT SUMMARY

Within-Subjects Design

All subjects receive all levels of the independent variable. To try to minimize carryover effects

- randomize the order of treatments, or
- counterbalance the order of treatments

▶ Control Conditions

Most experiments contain some control group (between-subjects design) or **control condition** (within-subjects design). In its simplest form, the control group is the group that does not receive the levels of interest of the independent variable. It is misleading to say that the control group does not receive the independent variable, because independent variables must, by definition, have at least two levels, one of which may be the control level. For example, say we are interested in analyzing the effect of noise on studying. Using a between-subjects design, we would expose one group of subjects to loud noise for half an hour while they were studying; this is the level of interest of the independent variable. A control group would study the same material for half an hour, but in a quiet setting. Then we would test both groups on the material. Any difference in test performance between the two groups would be attributed to the effect of noise.

In the experiment just described, the control group did not receive any treatment (no noise was introduced). This is not always the case. As you will recall from Chapter 6, we described a study on decompression in which the control condition was ground-level pressure at 728 feet. Another control condition could have been sea level (zero altitude). In another part of the country,

1,000 feet might have been the appropriate control altitude. The important characteristic of a control condition is that it provides a **baseline** against which some variable of the experiment can be compared. Sometimes the best baseline is no particular treatment, but many times the best baseline requires some activity. This problem occurs sometimes in memory research.

Let us say that a group of participants is required to learn two different lists of words (Table 8–5); the experimenter is interested in how learning one list interferes with learning the other. The experimental group (receiving the level of interest of the independent variable) first learns list A, then learns list B, and then is tested again on list A. The experimenter would like to show that learning list B interferes with remembering list A, but before any conclusion of this sort can be reached, a comparison control condition is required. Merely comparing the results of the final test of list A with the results of the first test is insufficient, because participants might do less well on the second list-A test simply because they are tired, or do better because of extra practice. If a control condition with no treatment were used, a control group would learn list A, then would sit around for the time it takes the experimental group to learn list B, and then would be tested again on list A. This would be a poor control condition, however, because participants might practice or rehearse list A while they are sitting around. Practicing would improve their final performance on the last list-A test and incorrectly make the experimental group look as if learning list B interfered with learning list A more than it really did. A proper baseline condition would occupy the control group during the time the experimental group was learning list B. Perhaps these participants would be instructed to do arithmetic or some other busywork that would prevent rehearsal. An example of such an experimental design is shown in Table 8–5. Another example is the baseline condition used by Jarrard in the LSD study. He used a placebo injection of saline instead of no injection at all. The reason for this injection baseline is that the injection itself could have disrupted the behavior of the rats. Without this comparison, there may have been an inappropriate assessment of the effects of LSD.

Sometimes the control condition is contained implicitly within the experiment. Suppose we want to study learning in rats and our independent variable is the number of food pellets (one or five) we give the rats when they make the correct response. No experimenter would bother to include a control group or condition with zero pellets, because no learning could occur under this odd circumstance. The control condition is implicit, in that five pellets can be compared with one, and vice versa. The experimenter might well be as interested

Table 8–5 Examples of experimental and control groups for list learning

	First period	Second period	Third period
Experimental group	Learn list A	Learn list B	Test list A
Control group	Learn list A	Do arithmetic	Test list A

in the effects of a single pellet as in five, so we probably would not explicitly call the one-pellet level a control condition. However, it does provide a baseline for comparison—and so, for that matter, does the five-pellet condition, because the one-pellet results can be compared with it.

Mixed Designs

Experiments need not be exclusively of within-subjects design or between-subjects design. It is often convenient and prudent to have some independent variables treated as between-subjects and others as within-subjects in the same experiment (assuming the experiment has more than one independent variable, of course). If one variable seems likely to cause transfer or carryover effects (for example, administering a drug), it can be made a between-subjects variable and the rest of the variables within-subjects. This compromise design is not as efficient as a pure within-subjects design, but it often is safer. Mixed designs are described in more detail in the next chapter.

▶ Choosing an Experimental Design

We have noted that the between-subjects design precludes carryover effects from one treatment to another, and that the within-subjects design does not confound subjects with conditions. Furthermore, we have suggested that the within-subjects design is usually more efficient than the between-subjects design, so obtaining repeated observations from the same subjects may be preferable to using independent groups. In this section, we will consider some rules of thumb for selecting an experimental design, regardless of the particular research topic. At the end of this section are several experimental problems for which you are to choose a design.

Carryover Effects

If your independent variable is likely to have a permanent effect on the participant and would prevent subsequent unconfounded testing, then a between-subjects design should be used. What sorts of independent variables would operate in this way? Independent variables that permanently alter the state or development of the participant would certainly have carryover effects. These might include effects of prenatal compression, prenatal nutrition, nearly all kinds of physiological damage (brain lesions, some drugs, toxic chemicals, and so on), most time-dependent variables (the effect of persuasion on later consumer behavior, or the effects of a particular reading technique on second-grade achievement), and any other variable whose effects are likely to be irreversible. Most participant variables (sex, age, ethnic group, and so on) require a between-subjects design, but these are not true independent variables. The special problems associated with research involving subject variables is examined in Chapter 11.

If you are interested in changes of behavior over time, such as improvements in learning, changes of strategy in a particular task, or optimal performance on a task, then you will want to use some variant of a within-subjects design. You will need to either expose your subjects to repeated measures (for example, you might place rats in a maze twice each day for a month) or give each subject several treatments over time. In effect, you are looking for a carry-over effect, which is really what a great deal of learning research is all about.

Individual Differences

You might think it trivial of us to say that people differ from each other. However, **individual differences** among participants are not a trivial problem when it comes to designing a good experiment. If your participant pool contains individuals who are markedly different from each other, or if you expect that large individual differences in behavior are likely to show up in your experiment, you may be better off using a within-subjects design rather than a between-subjects design. The within-subjects design automatically takes care of differences among your subjects. As long as you counterbalance appropriately (and carryover effects are not a problem), you can control for these individual differences in a within-subjects design.

A case in point is testing the effectiveness of drugs. Drug manufacturers know that people and animals differ in their sensitivity to drugs, which is one of the reasons Jarrard used a within-subjects design to test the effects of LSD. Once the drug is marketed, many different types of people will be taking the drugs. Therefore, it is imperative both that many different types of people be tested and that several drugs be tested on the same person. Within-subjects administration of several levels of a drug compared with a placebo will also control for individual differences that may appear on the behavioral or attitudinal task used to assess drug effects. For example, a within-subjects design is important when studying the effects of a drug on pain tolerance, because we know ahead of time that there are tremendous individual differences in reaction to pain in the absence of any externally administered substance.

Obviously, if a drug is likely to have long-term effects, a between-subjects design must be used. Another reason that many clinical tests of drug effectiveness use between-subjects designs is that participants with certain diseases are selected. The experimental group of participants is given the drug, and a control group with the same disease is given a placebo or another drug. If one of the drugs is effective, then for humanitarian reasons, all patients in the study receive it after the experimental comparison is completed.

Contrasting Between- and Within-Subjects Designs

Many research problems pose a particular dilemma: You must balance carry-over effects against the possible contaminating effect of large individual differences. There is no easy solution to this problem. One possible solution is to do the experiment one way (for example, within subjects) and then do it the other way (between subjects). Although such a tactic may seem inefficient, in the long run it might add to the generality of the results. However, when researchers have directly contrasted the two designs using the same independent variables, different results have been obtained for the two designs (Greene, 1996; Kawai & Imada, 1996).

Greene (1996) looked at the effects of the length of the retention interval in a short-term memory task. In his task, participants briefly saw a consonant trigram (for example, TSL), counted digits rapidly for 5 or 25 seconds, then attempted to recall the three consonants in the order in which they were presented. The length of time counting defines the retention interval. Using within-subjects designs, a substantial amount of earlier research showed rapid memory loss as a direct function of the length of the retention interval. Greene did the experiment both ways: one group of participants was tested at the 5-second retention interval and another at the 25-second interval (between-subjects design). One within-subjects group alternated the 5 and 25 seconds, which makes the length of the retention interval perfectly predictable as in the between-subjects case, and the other within-subjects group was tested at both of the retention intervals, which were randomly intermixed. Greene found the usual effect of poorer retention with longer retention intervals in both of the within-subjects cases, but not when he used a between-subjects manipulation.

Although Greene offers no complete explanation for the results he obtained, it is at least consistent with the idea that within-subjects designs tend to be more sensitive than between-subjects designs to the effects of independent variables. Similar superior sensitivity has been reported in the literature of human and animal learning (Grice & Hunter, 1964; Kawai & Imada, 1996).

Design Problems

For each of the following problems, decide on a within- or between-subjects design. If you think the situation warrants it, set up your experiment with both types of design. For practice, you should indicate the independent, dependent, and control variables. If you choose a within-subjects design, specify the counterbalancing procedures, and if you use a between-subjects design, indicate how subjects will be assigned to conditions. Regardless of your design, indicate your reasons for selecting either the within- or the between-subjects configuration.

1. A researcher wants to see which is easier to learn: hard-to-pronounce syllables (such as WMH, JBT, SJK), or easy-to-pronounce syllables (such as LEJ, NAM, TAL). Two lists, containing either 20 pronounceable syllables or 20 hard-to-pronounce syllables, will be prepared. Each element in a list will be shown for 2 seconds. At the end of the series, the participants will try to write down the syllables from memory. Specify the design configurations, counterbalancing or participant assignment scheme, reasons for your design selection, and the variables.

> ◣ **CONCEPT SUMMARY**

Summary of Control Techniques for Between- and Within-Subjects Designs

To Control for	Between-Subjects Design	Within-Subjects Design
Individual differences (sex, age, I.Q.)	Randomized assignment—unbiased assignment of participants to groups. Matched assignment—hold variable constant across groups (for example, test only females). Equate variables across groups (for example, use equal numbers of right-handed and left-handed participants).	Individual differences automatically controlled
Situational differences (time of day the data are collected; room temperature)	Randomize the effects of these variables. Hold constant or equate variables.	Same as between-subjects
Carryover effects (order of testing, assignment of materials)	Usually carryover effects do not occur; if they do, use same technique as in within-subjects.	Randomized order. Complete counterbalancing. Incomplete counterbalancing (Latin-square designs)

2. A cleanser manufacturer is interested in the effects of package color on the sales of Scrubbo super cleanser. Cartons of Scrubbo that are identical except for the background color of the label (maroon, pink, or aqua) will be prepared. Sales will be monitored for the next 4 months. Specify the design configurations, counterbalancing or participant assignment scheme, reasons for your design selection, and the variables.

3. A child psychologist wants to determine the effects of cloth versus paper diapers on toilet training. Day-old infants will be used to begin the project. The age at which diapers are no longer needed (to the nearest week) will be determined. Specify the design configurations, counter-

balancing or participant assignment scheme, reasons for your design selection, and the variables.

4. A researcher wants to determine whether rats learn a complex maze more quickly when practice is spaced (spread out in time) rather than massed. The effects of massing practice trials (one trial every 10 seconds) will be compared with the effects of distributing practice trials (one every 10 minutes). The number of trials the rats need to learn the maze perfectly will be counted. Specify the design configurations, counterbalancing or subject assignment scheme, reasons for your design selection, and the variables.

5. The Burpo beer company is test-marketing flavored light beers. It wants to see whether consumers prefer strawberry-, licorice-, or avocado-flavored Burpo. Several bottles of each flavor will be made. Consumers will fill out a questionnaire on how much they like the flavor, body, and aroma of the various flavors. Specify the design configurations, counterbalancing or participant assignment scheme, reasons for your design selection, and the variables.

Summary

1. Experiments with well-chosen variables and clean designs permit accurate conclusions to be drawn from the results. Such experiments are said to have internal validity.

2. In a between-subjects design, different subjects are assigned to the different levels of the independent variable.

3. In a within-subjects design, each subject receives all levels of the independent variable.

4. With a between-subjects design, there is no chance for the effects of one treatment to contaminate the effects of another. However, the differences between the people in the different groups may confound the effects of the independent variable.

5. The within-subjects design is more efficient than the between-subjects design, and we do not have to be concerned about differences between subjects contaminating the results. However, we do have to worry about the carryover of one treatment to another.

6. To ensure that the individual differences between participants in various groups are not confounding a between-subjects experiment, we should assign the participant to conditions on a random basis. Alternatively, the participants' characteristics can be matched across groups.

7. By varying the order of presenting the treatments, we can minimize the carryover effects in the within-subjects design. The order can be randomized or completely counterbalanced. When there is a large number of treatments or levels of the independent variable, we can achieve incomplete counterbalancing by using a balanced Latin square.

8. A control group or control condition provides a baseline against which some variable of an experiment can be compared.

9. If the independent variable is likely to have a permanent effect on the subject and would prevent subsequent unconfounded testing, then a between-subjects design should be used.

10. If large individual differences in thought or behavior are likely to occur, a within-subjects design may be preferable to a between-subjects design.

11. When the same experiment is conducted both between and within subjects, an independent variable is more likely to have an effect on behavior in the within-subjects case.

Key Concepts

balanced Latin square (199)
baseline (202)
between-subjects design (189)
carryover effects (196)
control condition (201)

counterbalancing (192)
individual differences (204)
internal validity (189)
Latin-square design (198)
matching (194)

randomization (195)
subject attrition (195)
within-subjects design (189)

Exercises

1. [*Special Exercise.*] What is wrong with the following experimental design? To study how the creation of mental images affects retention, an experimenter used a within-subjects design. A long list of unrelated words was presented to the participants, with each word being presented one at a time. Half the words were printed in black ink and the other half in red ink. The participants were told to create a vivid mental image of the red words and to simply say the black words over and over to themselves until the next word was shown. After all the words were presented, the participants had to write down as many of the words as they could, in any order they wished.

2. [*Special Exercise.*] Find the problem in this between-subjects experiment. An experimenter wanted to determine how a monetary payment affected attitude change. The first 22 participants to appear at the laboratory were offered 15 dollars if they agreed to publicly endorse an unpopular candidate. The next 22 participants to appear at the laboratory were offered 1 dollar if they agreed to endorse the same candidate. The percentage of people who agreed to the request in each group was the dependent variable.

Suggested Resources

A complete discussion of the advantages and disadvantages of between- and within-subjects designs can be found in Kerlinger, F. N., and Lee, H. B. (2000). *Foundations of behavioral research*. New York: Holt, Rinehart & Winston.

For a discussion of subtle biases that can occur with the use of within-subjects designs, see the following article: Poulton, E. C. (1982). Influential companions: Effects of one strategy on another in the within-subjects designs of cognitive psychology. *Psychological Bulletin, 91,* 673–690.

An interesting historical perspective of the use of control conditions in the design of experiments can be found in Boring, E. (1954). The nature and history of experimental control. *American Journal of Psychology, 67,* 573–589.

Web Resources

Additional information about internal validity can be found at: http://psych.athabascau.ca/html/Validity/index.shtml

The Wadsworth workshops considers between and within designs at: http://www.wadsworth.com/psychology_d/templates/student_resources/workshops/res_methd/btwn_wthn/btwn_wthn_01.html

Laboratory Resources

Experiments with more than two conditions, but with just one independent variable, are examined in Chapters 5 and 6 of Langston (2005). The experimental topics are how making hand gestures influence how you think and how room color influences mood. Langston, W. (2002). *Research methods laboratory manual for psychology* (2nd ed.). Pacific Grove, CA: Wadsworth Group.

The Stroop Effect

An interesting within-subjects experiment is a follow-up to the one in which you participated in Chapter 1. That experiment used a within-subjects design, and the three conditions were reading digits, naming the number of pluses, and naming the number of digits, where the name of the digits was incongruent with the number of digits (for example, you read "3 3," and you were to say "2"). Your follow-up could include a fourth condition in which the name of a digit and its quantity were congruent (for example, 4 4 4 4). You could use the three series from the original experiment and devise your own congruent fourth series. There are 32 items in a series, and the numbers (or quantities) 1 through 4 are counterbalanced in the sequence via a Latin square. You will need a stopwatch or clock to determine the time it takes to read through each series.

To design this experiment appropriately, set up a counterbalancing scheme to determine the order in which a participant receives each condition. A balanced Latin square is the best way to do this, so that across participants, each condition occurs first, second, third, and fourth equally often, and each treatment precedes and follows every other treatment equally often (see Table 8–3).

Additional information on reading and naming can be found in Chapters 1 and 13 under the heading "Stroop Effect." This effect is named after a scientist named Stroop, who first used conflicting reading and naming stimuli to study these processes (Stroop, 1935). In its use of conflicting and congruent quantities of digits, your follow-up experiment is similar to one done by Windes (1968), who used a between-subjects design. Your experiment is also similar to one done by Hintzman and associates (1972), who, using a within-subjects design, printed names of colors in congruent or incongruent ink colors and then asked the participants to name the ink color.

You might want to combine your results with those of your classmates. Each member of the class could test four participants. Each set of four participants would complete a single balanced Latin square used to determine the order of conditions. Your interest should focus on the differences among the three naming conditions: neutral (+ +), incongruent (3 3), and congruent (2 2). If your results follow those of Hintzman and coworkers, you should find that the congruent is faster than the neutral, which serves as the control condition, and the incongruent is slower than the neutral.

Hintzman, D. L., Carre, F. A., Eskridge, V. L., Owens, A. M., Shaff, S. S., & Sparks, M. E. (1972). "Stroop" effect: Input or output phenomenon? *Journal of Experimental Psychology, 95,* 458–459.

Windes, J. D. (1968). Reaction time for numerical coding and naming of numerals. *Journal of Experimental Psychology, 78,* 318–322.

CHAPTER 9

Complex Design

Between-Subjects Experiments

Description	Features	Problems
2 × 2 factorial design: two independent variables, each with two levels	Two main effects and an interaction of the two variables	Confounding of subjects with groups—assign randomly

Within-Subjects Experiments

Description	Features	Problems
2 × 2 within factorial design (treatments × treatments × subjects): each subject receives each level of 2 independent variables	More efficient than between designs; each subject is its own control; main effects and interaction	Confounding via carryover effects must be minimized—counterbalance or randomize

Mixed Designs

Description	Features	Problems
A combination of independent variables manipulated both between and within subjects	Good for looking at interaction of practice (trials) with another independent variable	Controls above must be considered; carryover is often a variable, so its effects are measured

This chapter discusses the design and interpretation of experiments that have more than one independent variable. Such multifactor experiments emphasize the interaction between independent variables. Multifactor experiments can be viewed as extensions of one-variable experiments. Some designs vary the independent variables between subjects, and others vary them within subjects. It is also possible to have a mixture of a between-subjects and within-subjects manipulation of the independent variables. We will consider all three of these possibilities here.

▶ Factorial Designs

Why perform complex experiments? Later, we will see that increased control in quasi-experiments comes about by including both subject variables and true (externally manipulated) independent variables in the study. However, increased control is not the primary reason for conducting laboratory experiments with more than one independent variable. Rather, the major reason has to do with the complexity of thought and behavior. Limiting experimental analysis to a one-at-a-time variable manipulation cannot mirror the numerous, intertwined forces that influence people outside the laboratory. Therefore, multifactor experiments are likely to have better ecological validity than single-factor experiments. The topic of ecological validity—whether an experiment has external as opposed to internal validity—was discussed earlier. We can increase the generality of our results by doing experiments that attempt to match the complexity of forces that combine to influence our thought and behavior. In addition, complex causal statements can be made, which should increase internal validity.

Does this mean that what we have said before about analysis is invalid? No. In any research problem, the basic factors need to be determined before we can make more complex observations. In much the same way that naturalistic observation and correlational studies often precede basic experimentation, simple experiments often provide the groundwork for more complex ones. Scientific maturity occurs gradually. The database grows slowly, and the theories gradually develop. We begin with description and prediction, and we end with explanation. Explanation itself goes through a developmental process—from simple experiments to complex ones.

A 2 × 2 Experiment in Social Psychology: The Sleeper Effect

An extremely common finding in memory research is that information fades over time. When new information is presented, you can easily remember it immediately, but as time passes, your ability to recall this information decreases. However, there is an interesting finding in social psychology in which the passage of time improves the effect of a persuasive message. This interesting quirk is called the **sleeper effect.** Imagine that you have just watched a television commercial for a new food product: low-fat diet pizza. You can indicate how persuasive this message was by rating how likely you are to run to your local grocery store and purchase this new food. Let us pretend that on a scale of 1 to 10, your rating was 5. If you are asked to rate this food again at a later time and you give a rating that is higher than 5, you have just demonstrated the sleeper effect: The impact of the persuasive message has increased over time.

To obtain the sleeper effect, the persuasive message must be accompanied by a **discounting cue.** This is a message that causes you to distrust the accuracy or credibility of a persuasive message. For example, imagine that you have just read a one-page rave review of a new sports car manufactured by General Motors. If you were then told that the review came from the pages of *Car and Driver* magazine, your reaction would be different than if you were told that the review was written by the General Motors press department. *Car and Driver* would be a confirming cue that improves your belief in the message, whereas the General Motors press department would be regarded as a biased source of information. The sleeper effect is most likely to be obtained when the cue—a discounting cue—casts a doubt on the source of the message.

Although many explanations of the sleeper effect have been offered, those that focus on the role of memory have been the most popular (Pratkanis, Greenwald, Leippe, & Baumgardner, 1988). One such explanation is called the *dissociation hypothesis*. At the time of presentation, the persuasive message and the discounting cue are strongly attached. Thus, they tend to cancel one another out, and little opinion change occurs. After time has passed, the link between the message and the cue gets weaker. In particular, while the message is remembered, the discounting cue is forgotten. The discounting cue is not retrieved, because the link between message and cue has weakened over time. This causes a net positive change in opinion, resulting in the sleeper effect.

To explain the logic behind a 2 × 2 experimental design, we shall consider a portion of results on the sleeper effect reported by Pratkanis and coworkers (1988). In a **2 × 2 factorial design,** there are two independent variables, each with two levels, or values. The word *factorial* indicates that all possible combinations of all levels of each independent variable are examined. Thus, as shown in Figure 9–1(a), a 2 × 2 factorial design contains four combinations

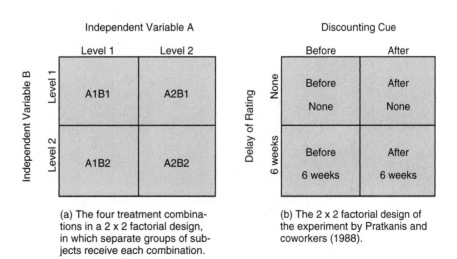

(a) The four treatment combinations in a 2 x 2 factorial design, in which separate groups of subjects receive each combination.

(b) The 2 x 2 factorial design of the experiment by Pratkanis and coworkers (1988).

Figure 9–1 (a) The four treatment combinations in a 2 × 2 factorial design, in which separate groups of subjects receive each combination. (b) The 2 × 2 factorial design of the experiment by Pratkanis and coworkers (1988).

of conditions: {A1B1}, {A2B2}, {A1B2}, {A2B1}. In the Pratkanis experiment, two independent variables were whether the discounting cue was presented before or after the persuasive message and the length of the delay (either 0 or 6 weeks) between the message and the opinion rating. Thus, there were four combinations of interest: {before-none}, {after-none}, {before-6 weeks}, and {after-6 weeks}. The design of the experiment is shown in Figure 9–1(b).

Figure 9–2 shows the effects of cue presentation on the opinion rating. The line is almost flat, indicating little effect. On the basis of Figure 9–2, we would conclude that cue presentation does not alter the sleeper effect. The effect of a single independent variable in a factorial experiment is called a **main effect**. Figure 9–2 shows that the main effect of cue presentation is almost zero, because there is almost no difference between the ratings for level 1 (before) and for level 2 (after) for cue presentation.

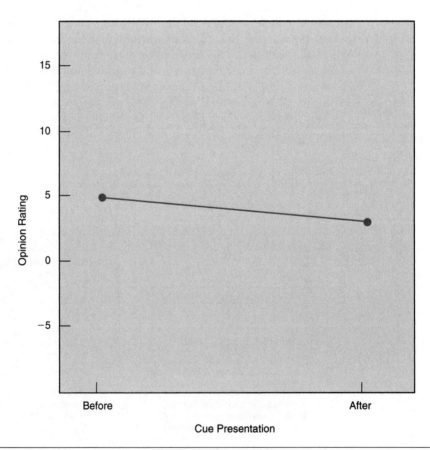

Figure 9–2 Effects of cue presentation on the sleeper effect. (Adapted from Pratkanis and coworkers, 1988.)

Now look at Figure 9–3, which shows the effects of delay on the opinion rating. Here there is a main effect. The rating is higher, indicating greater persuasion, at the 6-week delay. This result is, of course, the sleeper effect. However, based only on Figures 9–2 and 9–3, which show only main effects, we would conclude that the sleeper effect and effects of cue presentation are unrelated. Although the experiment reveals a sleeper effect, it appears that the effect has nothing to do with whether the discounting cue comes before or after the persuasive message.

However, this conclusion is wrong. Figure 9–4 shows results for all four combinations in the 2 × 2 factorial design. The interpretation of results here is quite different. When the cue comes before the message, there is no sleeper effect. When the cue comes after the message, there is a large sleeper effect. So, contrary to the wrong conclusion drawn from Figures 9–2 and 9–3, the

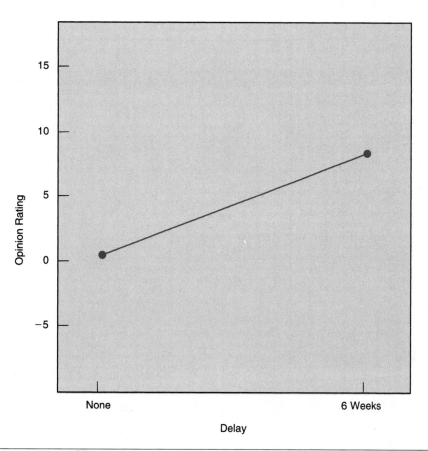

Figure 9–3 Effects of delay on the sleeper effect. (Adapted from Pratkanis and coworkers, 1988.)

timing of the discounting cue is absolutely crucial. An accurate interpretation of these results requires knowledge of all four combinations of independent variables. This outcome is called an **interaction.** An interaction occurs when the effects of one independent variable depend on the level of another independent variable. In Figure 9–4, the effects of delay depend on the presentation of the discounting cue. Thus, there is an interaction between delay and presentation.

According to Pratkanis and colleagues, the results of Figure 9–4 cast doubt on the dissociation explanation of the sleeper effect, because the dissociation explanation predicts a sleeper effect regardless of when the cue is presented. A better explanation is called *differential decay*. It states that the impact of the cue decays more rapidly than that of the message (Pratkanis et al., 1988). Presenting the cue before the message eliminates the sleeper effect by weakening the persuasive impact of the message. However, as is the case with most criti-

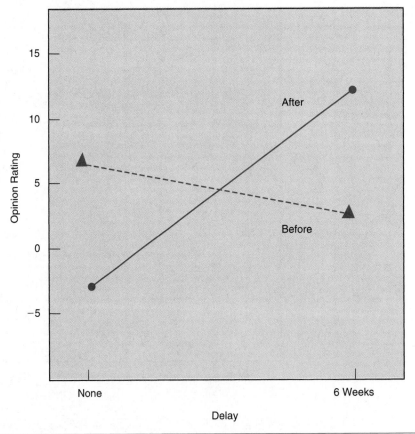

Figure 9–4 The interaction of delay and cue presentation and their influence on the sleeper effect. (Adapted from Pratkanis et al., 1988.)

cal experiments, a firm believer in the dissociation explanation might also adopt this latter explanation and argue that postulating a second factor—persuasive impact to explain the lack of a sleeper effect—applies equally to the dissociation hypothesis. Although Pratkanis and coworkers offer other arguments for differential decay, especially those that relate the sleeper effect to other findings in memory research, more research clearly is required to pin down this interesting quirk. Recent work has also related the sleeper effect to familiarity and to stimulus characteristics. Begg, Anas, and Farinacci (1992) argued that influences of both familiarity (which is not under intentional control of subjects) and recollection (which can be controlled) are relevant to the sleeper effect. Riccio, Ackil, and Burch-Vernon (1992) relate the sleeper effect to the concept of stimulus generalization, a concept that goes back to early work on classical conditioning: As a stimulus is changed from the original conditioned stimulus, its ability to evoke a response decreases systematically. In the words of Pratkanis and colleagues: "Long live the sleeper effect."

CONCEPT SUMMARY

Interactions

In multifactor experiments, an interaction occurs when the effects of one independent variable depend on the level of other independent variables.

Patterns of Interaction

Main effects are statistically independent of interaction effects. This means that knowing the amount and direction of main effects provides no information about possible interaction effects. In this section, we discuss three sets of artificial data that all have identical main effects. However, the patterns of interaction are quite different.

Figure 9–5 shows results for an experiment with two independent variables. Variable A has levels 1 and 2 with scores of 50 and 70, respectively. The difference between these two scores is the main effect of variable A, which is 20 units. (These units are whatever the dependent variable measures.

Independent Variable A			Independent Variable B		
1	2	2 – 1	1	2	2 – 1
50	70	20	30	90	60

Figure 9–5   Main effects

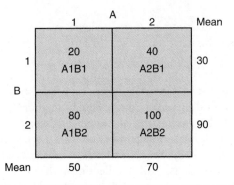

Figure 9–6   Additivity (no interaction)

For example, if the dependent variable is time, the units could be seconds. If the dependent variable is percent correct, the units would be percentage points.) Variable B has levels 1 and 2. It has a main effect of 60 units. These two main effects remain constant for all the examples in this section.

Figure 9–6 shows a 2 × 2 factorial combination with no interaction between independent variables 1 and 2. Once a value has been selected for one particular cell of the 2 × 2 matrix, all of the other cell values are determined by the main effects. Let us take cell A1B1 to illustrate this point. It has an arbitrary value of 20 units. To find the value for cell A2B1, we add the main effect of independent variable A: 20 + 20 = 40, the value for cell A2B1. To find the value for cell A1B2, we add the main effect of independent variable 2: 20 + 60 = 80. We now have three of the four cells filled in. There are two possible ways to calculate the value for cell A2B2. First, one could add the main effect of independent variable A, to cell A1B2: 20 (main effect) + 80 (value in cell A2B1) = 100. Second, we could add the main effect of independent variable B to cell A2B1: 60 (main effect) + 40 (value in cell A2B1) = 100. We get the same result (100) either way. Thus, results are additive, and additivity is another term that means no interaction has occurred between independent variables.

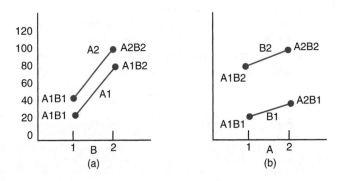

Figure 9–7   Additivity

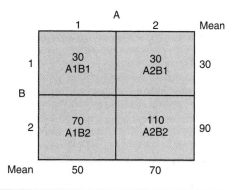

Figure 9–8 Interaction

These results are plotted in Figure 9–7. In Figure 9–7(a), independent variable B is plotted on the X-axis, and two different lines are drawn for the two levels of independent variable A. In Figure 9–7(b), independent variable A has been plotted on the X-axis. Both ways of drawing Figure 9–7 are correct. In both graphs, the two lines are parallel. This is a clear visual indication of additivity. When there is no interaction between two variables, they appear as parallel lines when graphed.

Figure 9–8 contains a 2 × 2 matrix with an interaction between independent variables A and B. If we tried to construct the cell values by adding the main effects as we did in Figure 9–6, the answer we would get would be wrong. (Try this for yourself.) When an interaction is plotted (Figure 9–9), lines do not appear parallel. Although Figure 9–7 and 9–9 represent identical main effects, the two graphs look quite different.

Figure 9–10 represents a very important kind of interaction, called a **crossover interaction.** When it is plotted (Figure 9–11), the two lines actually cross over one another. Crossover interactions are the most convincing form

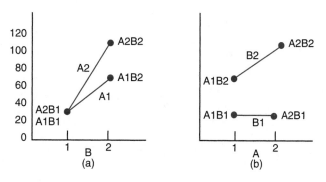

Figure 9–9 Interaction

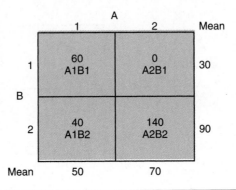

Figure 9–10 Crossover interaction

of interaction, because they cannot be explained by problems in measuring and scaling the dependent variable (see Chapter 7 for mathematical properties of different kinds of measurement scales). Again, Figure 9–10 has exactly the same main effects as Figures 9–6 and 9–8, but Figure 9–11 looks quite different from Figures 9–7 and 9–9.

The moral of this section should be very clear. Patterns of interaction must be carefully considered before one tries to interpret any main effects in an experiment that has more than one independent variable.

Control in Between-Subjects Factorial Designs

In a between-subjects design, each combination of independent variables is administered to a separate group of subjects. We want to make sure that the characteristics of the subjects are not confounded with group membership. In the ideal case, we would randomly select our subjects and then randomly as-

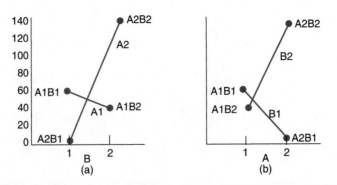

Figure 9–11 Crossover interaction

sign them to our conditions. We are usually unable to have total random selection of our subjects, because we do not have the procedures available to select, in an unbiased fashion, from *all* rats or *all* college students. It is therefore essential that we assign our subjects to conditions in a way that minimizes the possibility of confounding subject traits with our manipulations. When there are many groups in a factorial design, unbiased assignment is crucial. (Recall that Chapter 8 outlines ways to randomly assign subjects.)

Another way to make unbiased assignments of participants to groups is to use a balanced Latin square to determine group membership. The way to use this counterbalancing technique for participant assignment in a 2 × 2 design is as follows: Label the four groups (for example, A, B, C, and D) and then make a balanced square for those symbols. Use the order of conditions in the rows of the resulting Latin square to determine assignment. The first participant to appear in the laboratory is assigned to condition A, the second to B, the third to D, and the fourth to C. Then use the next row to assign the next four participants, and so on, until all participants are tested. You may have to construct many squares or use the same square repeatedly if you have more participants than cells in your square. The purpose of this procedure is the same as random assignment to conditions: to make sure there is little relation between the participant's characteristics and assignment to a particular group. One advantage of the Latin-square technique is that in a large experiment that takes a long time to conduct, the order in which the treatments are conducted is known well in advance and is also balanced across time. Thus, any historical factors that might be confounded here are balanced across groups.

In general, randomization, counterbalancing, and other control techniques help to prevent potential confounding variables from interacting with the independent variables. In your design, you should try to reduce the possibility of such unwanted interactions. There are no hard-and-fast rules for choosing a control technique. The ones used are often chosen pragmatically. The particular control procedure you use is up to you: Make sure that you minimize confoundings and that you use controls that are easy to implement.

We limited the discussion of between-subjects designs to what is often called a **random-groups design,** which refers to unbiased assignment of subjects to conditions. An alternative method of assignment is matching (see Chapter 8). In a **matched-groups design,** the experimenter tries to reduce the variability of observations between groups resulting from participant differences by matching the participants on other variables. Thus, in the sleeper effect experiment we just described, participants could be matched on the basis of IQ before randomly assigning them to conditions. (Each subgroup of matched participants is randomly assigned to the groups.) In our earlier discussions, we pointed out the difficulty of matching on relevant variables. Some subject variables, such as sex and age, can be matched across groups, or they can serve as quasi-independent variables. If matching is going to be difficult, you might want to use a complex within-subjects design, which we will discuss next.

> ## CONCEPT SUMMARY
>
> ### Factorial Designs
>
> All possible combinations of each level of each independent variable
> are examined. For example, a 3 × 3 case having independent variable
> A with levels A1, A2, and A3 and independent variable B with levels
> B1, B2, and B3 yields nine groups:
>
> - A1B1   • A1B2   • A1B3
> - A2B1   • A2B2   • A2B3
> - A3B1   • A3B2   • A3B3

▶ Complex Within-Subjects Designs

The within-subjects design is often used instead of a between-subjects design
because within-subjects manipulation is more economical (requires fewer subjects) and automatically controls for individual differences. Of course, if permanent carryover effects are likely, a within-subjects design may be inappropriate.

Using a within-subjects design can result in a substantial reduction in the
number of subjects needed for testing. However, the reduced number of subjects may require that you increase the number of observations per subject in
each condition to ensure that your data are reliable. We should obtain numerous samples of a subject's behavior (just as is done in small-*n* experiments;
see Chapter 10). By doing so, we reduce the likelihood that some extraneous
factor has influenced the results. For instance, in many learning, memory, perception, and reaction-time experiments, events occur rapidly, placing great demands on the participant. If the participant coughs or blinks at an inappropriate time, we may incorrectly underestimate performance on that trial.

Thus, whereas in a between-subjects design we test a large number of subjects, in a within-subjects design we obtain several observations on a small
number of subjects. Even with numerous observations per subject, the within-
subjects design is usually more efficient than the between-subjects one.

A Complex Within-Subjects Experiment

Switching from one mental task to another is a common activity. For example,
while driving you might switch attention from tuning the radio to looking for
a street sign. Since people are seldom able to perform several difficult mental
tasks simultaneously, understanding how you can switch among tasks is of
considerable practical and theoretical interest. One general model of switching
uses an analogy with changing gears (Monsell, 2003) in a machine. Switching

takes time and effort. Thus, several researchers have studied the costs associated with switching from one task to another.

Laboratory experiments try to simplify the switching task so that results can be interpreted with a minimum of confounding variables. So a simple switching task would be to identify either the height (tall or short) or the width (thin or thick) of a rectangle presented on a screen. When people know in advance which question will be asked, height or width, they do better and respond more quickly. However, if the questions are randomized the task is more difficult, since you cannot prepare in advance. A common way to study preparation for task switching involves presenting a cue that tells the viewer whether to process height or width. For example, the cue could be the letter *h* for height and the letter *w* for width. If there are several seconds elapsing between the cue and the rectangle stimulus, the task becomes identical to knowing in advance. But what if the time between the cue and the stimulus, called the cue-stimulus interval, is very short? According to the gear-changing model, the more time you have to prepare, the more you can jump-start the gear-changing process. So performance should be better for a long cue-stimulus interval than for a short interval.

Altman (2004) tested this hypothesis using a within-subjects experimental design. Cue-stimulus interval was one independent variable and could be either short (100 ms) or long (900 ms). Task (height versus width) was a second independent variable. Continuity, whether the task switched or repeated compared with the previous trial, was the third independent variable. Since this was a within-subjects design, all subjects experienced all conditions and their combinations.

Response time to the height task (676 ms) was slower than response time to the width task (636 ms), but this main effect did not interact with any other independent variables. This result is less interesting than the interaction between cue-stimulus interval and continuity shown in the left panels of Figure 9–12 labeled Experiment 1 and Experiment 3. First examine the open circles that represent the Repeat condition. If the same task is repeated, there is no need to switch tasks. Thus, there should be little benefit of a longer cue-stimulus interval. Now look at the filled circles that represent the Switch condition, where the task changed on successive trials. Here we would expect a substantial benefit from a longer cue-stimulus interval, since there is more time to change gears. Results show an interaction: the lines are not parallel. The benefit for the longer cue-stimulus interval is greater for the Switch condition than for the Repeat condition. Hence these results support the gear-changing model of task switching.

If Altman (2004) had only used a within-subjects design, as was the case for most studies of task switching, this would be the end of the story. However, he replicated his within-subjects experiments with two more experiments in which cue-stimulus interval was a between-subjects variable. Why would anyone do the same experiment twice? Recall our warning at the start of this section about the danger of carryover effects in within-subjects designs. Altman (2004) was not a supporter of the gear-switching model and believed that

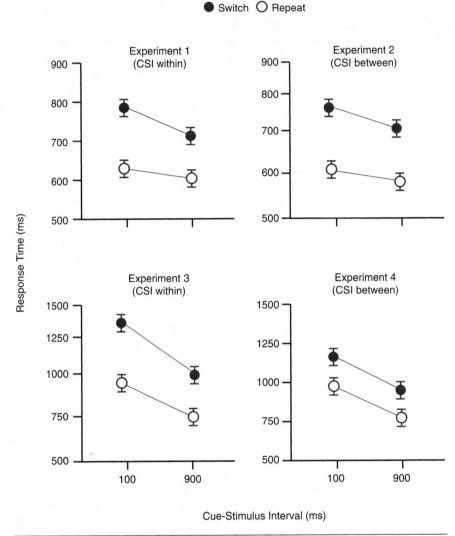

Figure 9–12 Response time as a function of cue-stimulus interval and continuity. Note that Experiments 1 and 3 are similar, as are Experiments 2 and 4. Odd-numbered experiments used a within-subjects design and even-numbered experiments used a between-subjects design. (From Altman [2004]. Copyright 2004, American Psychological Society.)

methodological carryover artifacts (Poulton, 1982) could have induced strategies that would yield incorrect results supporting the gear-changing model. Now examine the right panels of Figure 9–12 labeled Experiments 2 and 4. The interaction between cue-stimulus interval and continuity has disappeared! The lines are parallel. There is no relative benefit of a longer cue-stimulus interval for Switch trials. This raises serious questions about the interpretation

Improving the Learning of Foreign-Language Vocabulary

Many laboratory experiments indicate that imagery and the type of rehearsal can improve retention. Do these kinds of results also occur in more practical situations?

Atkinson (1975) indicates that certain kinds of rehearsal techniques can dramatically improve the learning and retention of foreign-language vocabulary. One procedure that has been successful is called the *keyword method*. We will outline how this method is appropriate for learning Russian vocabulary, although it has worked in the learning of other languages as well. The keyword method splits vocabulary learning into two parts. In the first part, the participant associates a spoken foreign word with the keyword. This is easily done, because the keyword sounds very much like the foreign word. In the second part, the participant tries to form a mental image of the keyword and the English translation interacting in some way. So, first the foreign word is connected to the keyword, and then the keyword is connected to the English translation.

In Russian, the word *dym* (as spelled in our alphabet) sounds similar to the English word *dim* and means smoke. If we use the English word *dim* as the keyword, *dim* and *dym* are first linked together. Then we might form a mental image of a dim picture that has been clouded by smoke. In Atkinson's experiments, participants hear the foreign words and are given the keyword and the English translation. The participants provide their own mental image linking the keyword to the translation.

Learning is much faster with the keyword technique than without it—control participants take about one-third longer to learn the same number of translations as do similar participants who use keywords. Tests of retention up to about 6 weeks later indicate that the participants using keywords recall about 65% more than the controls. Use of memory techniques in many situations can lead to superior retention.

SOURCE: Atkinson, R. C. (1975). Mnemotechnics and second-language learning. *American Psychologist, 30,* 821–828.

of earlier experiments that supported the gear-changing model but used only a within-subjects design. It is now necessary for those researchers who favor gear-changing to explain why no interaction occurred when cue-stimulus interval was a between-subjects variable.

Within-subjects experimental designs are widely used because of their greater efficiency compared with between-subjects designs. Usually, this is a useful and acceptable procedure. But if there is any reason to suspect carry-over effects, then a between-subjects design is the better choice. Experimenters who would like to use within-subject designs in cognitive tasks should consider a between-subjects replication of their experiments, just to ensure that the assumptions of the within-subjects design are satisfied.

> ## CONCEPT SUMMARY

Complex Within-Subjects Designs

Every participant receives all combinations of each level of the independent variables. For example, Altman's (2004) experiment had the following conditions: two cue-stimulus intervals (short, long), two rectangle decisions (height, width), and two values of continuity (switch, repeat). Thus, in the within-subjects manipulation, all subjects experienced the following eight combinations: {short height switch}, {long height switch}, {short width switch}, {long width switch}, {short height repeat}, {long height repeat}, {short width repeat}, {long width repeat}.

▶ Mixed Designs

There are advantages and disadvantages to both pure within-subjects designs and pure between-subjects designs. Many experimenters used **mixed designs** to get the best of both worlds while minimizing possible disadvantages. A mixed design has one or more between-subjects independent variables and also one or more within-subjects independent variables.

To illustrate mixed designs, we will consider two experiments dealing with driving a car. These experiments also illustrate using modern personal computers to control experiments. The desktop computer based on an Intel Pentium processor is powerful enough to control very complex professional experiments, even those using **simulators**. There are many kinds of simulators, ranging from simpler (but still quite powerful) simulators using desktop personal computers to those using rack-mounted graphic workstations costing more than 1 million dollars. A **part-task simulator** deals with only a portion of the real-world task: For example, a full-mission simulator for a Boeing 747 aircraft costs millions of dollars, whereas an effective part-task simulator costing a few thousand dollars might handle only a small set of cockpit displays. The part-task simulator would allow pilots to be trained to use the displays but not other airplane systems. This is far more cost-effective than using an expensive, full-mission simulator for learning displays.

A Route Guidance Experiment

Many new intelligent devices, especially navigation systems, are being developed for passenger vehicles. You can now rent a car so equipped, purchase an add-on system to install in your own car, or buy a new car with its own navigation device. These new Advanced Traveler Information Systems

(ATIS) can present traffic congestion and route drivers around accidents to avoid delays. However, even the best ATIS is only as good as the traffic information it obtains from the local traffic information center. Although traffic engineers would like to present information that is timely and 100% accurate, often by the time the information reaches the driver, it is no longer reliable. While making information more reliable is possible, the cost of very high levels of reliability can be extreme. So, traffic engineers need advice (from human-factors psychologists) on how reliable to make their systems. If the system is extremely reliable, it may cost too much to implement, but if the system is not reliable enough, drivers won't use it. How reliable does an ATIS have to be?

A mixed design was used to obtain data to answer this question (Kantowitz, Hanowski, & Kantowitz, 1997). The between-subjects independent variable was accuracy of traffic information: either 71% or 43% accurate. Accuracy was implemented as a between-subjects variable to avoid possible transfer effects between different accuracy conditions—for example, once a driver experienced 43% accurate traffic data, he or she might not believe subsequent data, even if it were more accurate. The within-subjects independent variable was location: either a familiar city (Seattle) or a fictitious, unfamiliar city (New City) that was topographically matched to Seattle.

Figure 9–13 shows the part-task simulator used in the experiment. The screen on the right shows a map that drivers can touch to obtain traffic information. The screen on the left shows a real-time video of traffic on the selected route. Drivers began each trial with a potential $15 bonus if they selected the fastest route. They were penalized for encountering heavy traffic by having

Figure 9–13   Battelle route guidance simulator

their bonus cut in half. This effectively simulated the frustration drivers feel on the road when they are delayed. Indeed, many drivers in the experiment exhibited emotional behaviors when they got stuck in traffic.

Results of this experiment (Figure 9–14) showed an interaction between the two independent variables. When drivers received inaccurate information, their penalty cost was high regardless of the location. When drivers received accurate information, they did worse in their home city. Drivers in an unfamiliar setting tend to follow the advice of their ATIS, but at home, they trust their own judgment and knowledge of the city more than they trust their in-vehicle ATIS. Thus, in the Seattle setting, they ignored traffic advice more than they would in a strange city and so obtained higher penalties. This result (plus other results not discussed here) implies that manufacturers of ATIS devices may have greater commercial success selling to rental car companies and to drivers who must travel in unfamiliar settings.

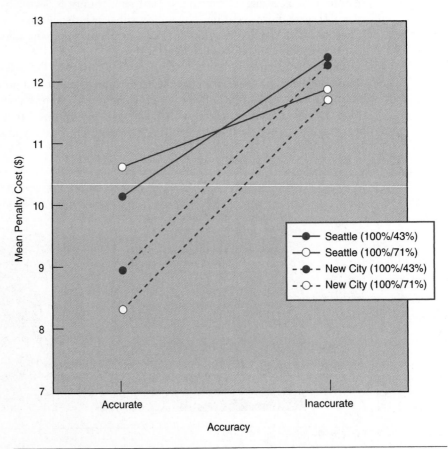

Figure 9–14 Mean penalty costs as a function of accuracy

Memory for ATIS Messages

ATIS displays communicate with the driver by presenting messages. What kind of icons (pictures) would be best for in-vehicle displays? Some icons might duplicate familiar road signs, whereas other new icons are required for special in-vehicle messages such as "low tire pressure." Would it be better to use text or icons for ATIS messages? Are messages equally effective for younger and older drivers? ATIS designers must find the answers to many questions to build effective in-vehicle systems.

A medium-fidelity driving simulator (Figure 9–15) was used to answer questions like this. Drivers sit in a chopped-down real car (called a test buck) and see a computer image as they drive down the road. A desktop personal computer is used to control the driving simulator. Although it is safer and more efficient to test drivers in a simulator, it is always prudent to validate simulator results by on-the-road testing.

A mixed design was chosen (Hanowski & Kantowitz, 1997) with age as the between-subjects variable: Both younger (<30 years of age) and older (>64 years) drivers were tested. Age was implemented as a between-subjects, quasi-independent variable so that the experimenters would not have to wait 30 years for the younger drivers to become older drivers. Message recognition interval (0 to 50 seconds) was a within-subjects variable; after a message was presented, drivers had to answer a two-choice question either immediately or after a delay. It is important for ATIS designers to know when to present messages. If a message is presented too late, drivers may not react in time, but if a message is presented too early, drivers may forget it. This issue is especially important for older drivers whose cognitive skills may not be as good as those of younger drivers.

Results (Figure 9–16) showed that younger drivers could remember in-vehicle messages equally well for both delays, but older drivers did worse when recognition was delayed 50 seconds. Although the difference for older

Figure 9–15 Battelle automobile simulator

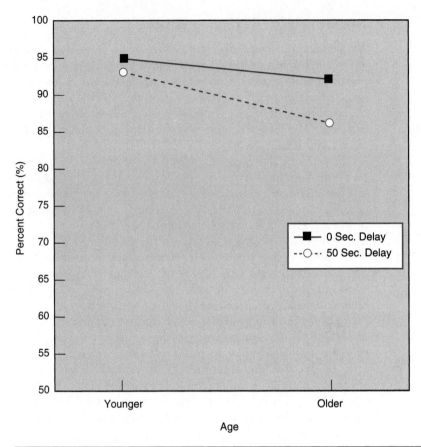

Figure 9–16 Percent correct as a function of driver age and question delay

drivers was small, in this experiment the car was set on cruise control so that drivers only had to steer the vehicle on a rural road. Larger differences would be expected under full manual control and in city driving. Research on this topic continues in many laboratories and test tracks. It seems likely that special considerations must be paid to the needs of older drivers when designing in-vehicle systems.

Summary

1. Multifactor experiments have more than one independent variable, and these variables may have more than two levels.

2. When more than two independent variables are varied, we have a factorial design in which all possible combinations of the levels of the indepen-

dent variables are examined. In a 2 × 2 factorial design, there are four combinations of levels of independent variables.

3. The primary reason for using multifactor designs is to look for interactions. An interaction is when the effects of one independent variable depend on the level of other independent variables.

4. When there are two independent variables, there are two main effects (one associated with each variable), and there can be an interaction.

5. Treatments × treatments × subjects is the designation usually given to factorial designs in which the variables are manipulated within subjects.

6. The control procedures used in multifactor experiments can be complicated, but they are similar in principle to the procedures (randomization, counterbalancing, and so on) used in experiments that have just one independent variable.

7. In a mixed design, one or more variables are varied between subjects, and one or more variables are varied within subjects.

Key Concepts

crossover interaction (219)
discounting cue (212)
interaction (216)
main effect (214)

matched-groups design (221)
mixed designs (226)
part-task simulator (226)

random-groups design (221)
simulators (226)
sleeper effect (212)
2 × 2 factorial design (213)

Exercises

1. Discuss the advantages of using complex within-subjects designs as opposed to complex between-subjects designs.

2. [*Special Exercise.*] A researcher varied the size (large or small) of the food reinforcement that was given to rats in a straight-alley maze. The time it took the rats to run down the alley was the dependent variable, and the mean time in seconds for each block of 10 trials was as follows:

	Block 1	Block 2	Block 3	Block 4
Large reward	38	30	20	15
Small reward	52	32	16	12

The experimenter concluded that because the overall time was slower in the small-reward group, large rewards lead to more rapid learning. What other conclusions can be drawn from the data in the table? Draw a figure showing these results.

3. [*Special Exercise.*] An experimenter is interested in studying the effects of practice on retention. If a within-subjects design is used and the

independent variables are types of rehearsal (rote and elaborative) and number of presentations (1, 2, 3, and 4), indicate how the words to be remembered could be counterbalanced over the four different numbers of presentations. What are some additional confoundings that must be eliminated?

Suggested Resource

Several complex experiments are reprinted in Elmes, D. G. (1978), *Readings in experimental psychology.* Chicago: Rand McNally. See especially articles 14 and 25.

Web Resource

Information concerning the Battelle Memorial Institute's research on transportation can be found at: http://www.battelle.org

Laboratory Resources

Experiments with more than one independent variable are considered in Chapters 6, 7, and 8 in Langston (2005). The research topics include mood and perception, gender-neutral pronouns, and refusal to comply with requests. Langston, W. (2005). *Research methods laboratory manual for psychology* (2nd ed.). Belmont, CA: Wadsworth.

Difficulty in Letter Detection

Detection of various kinds of targets (e.g., planes on a radar screen) usually deteriorates when the observer is distracted or is under stress of some sort (Broadbent, 1971). This experiment determines whether distraction interacts with the difficulty of the detection task.

The participant's task will be to read a newspaper article at a rapid rate, crossing out certain letters as he or she is reading. Half the detection periods will occur in a quiet setting, and the other half will take place where moderately loud music is playing. Thus, you will need a newspaper and a radio (or some other source of music).

The difficulty of the task will be determined by the particular letters that the participants are to cross out. Half the time the participants should cancel out all the *u*s they can find, and on the rest of the trials, they should cancel out all the *f*s. The letter *f* was chosen because people generally make a substantial number of errors when they try to detect *f* (Read, 1983). This occurs because the letter *f* is often pronounced as a *v* (as in the word *of*), and people usually do not cancel out those *f*s. The letter *u* was chosen because it occurs with about the same frequency as the letter *f*, and only occasionally is it pronounced in an unusual fashion (as a *w* in words beginning with a *q*, which means you might want to select newspaper passages that do not contain the letter *q*). Use a within-subjects design in this experiment. You will have to figure out some sort of counterbalancing scheme for the four conditions.

Participants should be tested in each condition once. Allow each participant to read for 30 seconds. After testing, you can calculate the error rate by dividing the number of correct detections (*f* or *u*) by the total number of *f*s or *u*s in the passage. (Be sure that you detect all the *f*s when you are scoring the data.) You should combine your results with those of other students to increase the stability of your data.

Look for an interaction in your results. Usually, the most difficult detection task is the one most affected by the distraction.

Broadbent, D. E. (1971). *Decision and stress.* New York: Academic Press.

Read J. D. (1983). Detection of F's in a single statement: The role of phonetic recoding. *Memory & Cognition, 11,* 390–399.

CHAPTER 10

*Small-*n *Experimentation*

Numerous observations on small numbers of subjects/participants

Small-*n* Designs

- Reversal design (*ABA*)
- Alternating-treatments design
- Multiple-baseline design
- Changing-criterion design

Clinical Psychology

- A case study

This chapter examines alternatives to the typical experiment in which a researcher manipulates one or more independent variables and tests one or more groups containing a large number of participants. We consider small-n designs, which exert experimental control by the careful manipulation of an independent variable on a small number of participants. These designs, which require special control procedures, are the hallmark of the behavioral approach of operant conditioning. We also examine an experiment done on a single person who apparently had multiple personalities.

In the simplest case, an experiment involves the production of a comparison between experimental and control conditions. Both between- and within-subjects designs usually include a large number of subjects, although the number is often less in the within-subjects case. Large numbers of subjects are required so that an unusual participant does not skew the results. Such designs are called **large-*n* designs** and have become the norm in psychological research; powerful statistical techniques (see Appendix B) allow the researcher to determine whether differences between the conditions are worth worrying about. An alternative approach to such designs is the **small-*n* design,** in which a very few subjects are intensely analyzed.

▶ Small-*n* Designs

Two areas within experimental psychology have resisted the use of large-*n* designs. One is psychophysics (see Chapter 7). A researcher doing psychophysical research worries less about individual differences among participants than do researchers in other areas, such as memory, because the behaviors that are measured in psychophysics are less complex, and greater control over conditions usually is possible than in memory research. The emphasis on experimental control is the hallmark of the second research area that uses small-*n* designs—the experimental analysis of behavior in terms of operant conditioning. Skinner (1963) urged using small-*n* designs in operant research because he wanted to emphasize the importance of experimental control over behavior and de-emphasize the importance of statistical analysis. Skinner believed that statistical analysis often became an end in itself, rather than a tool to help the researcher make decisions about the experimental results. The logic of the small-*n* design in operant-conditioning research appears in Sidman's (1960) book, *Tactics of Scientific Research.*

The experimental control usually achieved in traditional research with large numbers of participants and statistical inference is strived for in small-*n* research by very carefully controlling the experimental setting and by taking numerous and continuous measures of the dependent variable. Small-*n* methodology is especially appropriate to the clinical application of operant techniques to modify behavior. Typically, a therapist deals with a single client at a time, which is the limiting case of a small-*n* design. Although a therapist may treat more than one client at a time with similar methods, the numbers are very small relative to those seen in most large-*n* research. We examine small-*n* design in the context of behavior problems in children and then in a variant of case study research.

Consider the following scenario. Concerned parents seek psychological help for their child, who has temper tantrums several times a day. These tantrums are noisy, with a lot of yelling and crying, and they are violent—she often kicks things and bangs her head on the floor. When the therapist, who is a specialist in behavior modification using operant-conditioning techniques, first sees the child, what conclusions is he or she to draw? What causes this behavior? What can the therapist do to remove it and return the child to a more normal existence?

A behavior therapist would seek to discover what in the learning history of the child has produced such troublesome behavior. The focus would be on the contingencies of reinforcement that produce and maintain the child's crying, kicking, and head banging. The proposed therapy could try to change the contingencies of reinforcement, so that the child receives reward for appropriate and not maladaptive behavior. An interpretation of the plight of our fictional child might go something like the following.

One potent source of reinforcement for children is parental attention, and young children will go to great lengths to attract their parents' attention. Once, when the child was feeling alone and neglected, she began to whine and cry. The parents attended to her and thus reinforced the behavior. The next time the child felt lonely, she again tried the crying gambit—and again received reinforcement. Before long, the child found that she had to cry more loudly for attention, because her parents were both becoming used to it and trying to ignore it in hopes that she would stop. Every time the child increased the extremity of the behavior, the parents would once again start paying attention, at least for a while. So, the problem behavior increased in intensity and frequency, which resulted in the parents seeking the help of the therapist. The parents unwittingly shaped the child's behavior by reinforcing increases in extreme behavior. Just as a pigeon can be trained to walk around in figure eights by first being rewarded for making movements that approximate a figure eight, so can a child be reinforced for head banging and temper tantrums by being rewarded for successive steps along the way.

The therapist's interpretation of the child's behavior is that an unfortunate set of reinforcement contingencies sustains it. Therapy involves changing the contingencies so that positive behavior receives reward and negative behavior does not. The therapist's job, in large part, is to help the parents become effective behavior therapists themselves. The parents should start paying attention to the child when she is behaving normally. If the tantrums persist, they should try to reinforce her for lessening their intensity. If the child throws a violent tantrum to which the parents must pay attention, they should wait for a momentary lull before attending, which would reward lessening the intensity and gradually shape the tantrums to be less severe. Best of all would be to ignore the tantrums completely, if possible, which should extinguish them, because they are no longer followed by reinforcement.

The *AB* Design

Before examining solid small-*n* designs, we take a look at a common but invalid way to evaluate the effectiveness of a therapy. Research concerning the effectiveness of a therapy should be incorporated into the treatment whenever possible. This seems a fairly simple matter: Measure the frequency of the behavior that needs to be changed, then institute the therapy and see if the behavior changes. We can call this an **AB design,** where *A* represents the baseline condition before therapy and *B* represents the condition after introduction of the therapy (the independent variable). This design is used in much medical, educational, and other applied research, where a therapy or training procedure is instituted to determine its effects on the problem of interest. However, the *AB* design (Campbell & Stanley, 1966) is poor, and the careful researcher avoids using it if possible. It is an inadequate design, because changes occurring during treatment in the *B* phase may be caused by other factors that are confounded with the factor of interest. The treatment might produce the change in behavior, but so could other sources that the researcher is not aware of or has failed to control. We cannot conclusively establish that change was caused by the therapy because of a lack of control comparisons. A confounding variable might have produced the change in the absence of an independent variable. Remember, confounding occurs when other variables inadvertently vary with the primary factor of interest—in the case of the little girl, the therapy. It is crucial to control carefully the potential confounding variables so that the primary one is producing the effect. This is impossible in the *AB* design, because the therapist/researcher may not even be aware of the other variables.

A standard solution to the problem involves a large-*n* design. We randomly assign people to one of two groups. One group, the experimental one, receives the treatment; the other, the control group, does not. If the experimental condition improves with the therapy and the control does not, we may conclude that the treatment and not some extraneous factors has produced the result. In the case of therapy on an individual, such as the case of the tantrum-throwing girl, there usually is no potential control group and only one subject in the experimental "group." Because a large-*n* design depends on having a substantial number of subjects in the experimental and control conditions, it is inappropriate for use in evaluating many therapeutic situations.

The *ABA* or Reversal Design

As an alternative to the *AB* design, which is flawed, the experimenter may reverse the conditions after the *B* phase to yield an **ABA design,** which is also called a **reversal design.** The second *A* phase in the *ABA* design serves to rule out the possibility that some confounding factor influenced the behavior observed in the *B* phase. Returning the conditions of the experiment to their original baseline level, with the independent variable no longer applied, allows the experimenter to determine whether behavior returns to baseline level during the second *A* phase. If it does, then the researcher can conclude that it was the independent variable that effected change during the *B* phase. This generalization would not apply if a confounding variable happened to correlate perfectly with the independent variable, but such a situation is unlikely.

In our example of the child throwing tantrums, the therapist would instruct the parents to get baseline measures on the number of crying episodes, tantrums, and head banging when they reacted just as they normally would. Then the therapist would instruct them to alter their behavior by rewarding the child with attention when the child engaged in good behavior and by trying to extinguish the tantrums and other behavior by ignoring them altogether. If this produced a change in the frequency of the tantrums over a period of several weeks, then the therapist might ask the parents to reinstitute their old pattern of behavior to ensure that it was their attention to the child at inappropriate moments that was really controlling the child's behavior and not something else. (If the therapist were not interested in research, of course, he or she might just leave well enough alone after the successful *B* phase.) If the original treatment produced no effect on the dependent variable, the frequency of tantrums, it would be necessary to try something else. The techniques of behavior modification based on operant analysis have met with great success in the treatment of certain sorts of psychological problems. Here we consider an example.

Hart, Allen, Buell, Harris, and Wolf (1964) investigated the excessive crying of a 4-year-old nursery-school pupil, Bill, who otherwise seemed quite healthy and normal. The crying often came in response to mild frustrations that other children dealt with in more effective ways. Rather than attribute his crying to internal variables, such as fear, lack of confidence, or regression to behavior of an earlier age, the investigators looked to the social learning environment to see what reinforcement contingencies might be producing such behavior. They decided, with reasoning similar to that already discussed in the case of our hypothetical little girl, that adult attention reinforced Bill's crying behavior. Hart and colleagues set about testing this supposition with an *ABA* (actually, an *ABAB*) design.

First, it was necessary to gain a good measure of the dependent variable, crying. The teacher carried a pocket counter and depressed the lever every time there was a crying episode. "A crying episode was defined as a cry (a) loud enough to be heard at least 50 feet away and (b) of 5 seconds or more duration." At the end of each nursery school day, the total number of crying episodes was recorded. We could, perhaps, quibble some with this operational definition of a crying episode (did the teacher go 50 feet away each time to listen?), but let us assume that it is valid and reliable.

During the initial baseline of phase *A*, Bill received ordinary treatment, which involved the teacher giving attention to his crying. During the 10 days of the first baseline period, the number of crying episodes was between 5 and 10 a day, as shown in the leftmost panel of Figure 10–1, where the frequency of crying episodes is on the ordinate and days on the abscissa. For the next 10 days (the first *B* phase), the teacher attempted to extinguish the crying episodes by ignoring them while rewarding Bill with attention every time he responded to minor calamities (such as falls or pushes) in a more appropriate way. As can be seen in Figure 10–1, the number of crying episodes dropped precipitously, so that there were between 0 and 2 during the last 6 days of the first *B* phase.

This completes the *AB* phase of the design; once again, however, we cannot be certain that the reinforcement contingencies were responsible for Bill's improved behavior. Perhaps he was getting along better with his classmates, or his parents were treating him better at home. Either of these things (or others) could have improved his disposition. To gain better evidence that it was actually the reinforcement contingencies that changed Bill's behavior, the investigators returned to the baseline: Again Bill received reinforcement for crying. At first, reward of attention occurred for approximations to crying (whimpering and sulking); after the reestablishment of crying, the researchers maintained it with attention to each crying episode. As the third panel in Figure 10–1 shows, it took only 4 days to reestablish crying. This led to the conclusion that the reinforcement contingencies and not any number of other factors were responsible for the termination of crying in the first *B* phase. Finally, because this was a therapeutic situation, the investigators instituted a second *B* phase similar to the first, in which they extinguished Bill's crying once again.

In this investigation, the researchers did not use inferential statistics to justify the conclusions drawn. Rather, with good control of the independent variable and repeated measures on the dependent variable, the differences between conditions in this experiment were striking enough to decrease the need for inferential statistics. Use of *ABA* small-*n* designs can allow powerful experimental inferences. Before small-*n* designs are used, the researcher typically undertakes a functional analysis of the problem. We describe this kind of analysis in the Application section.

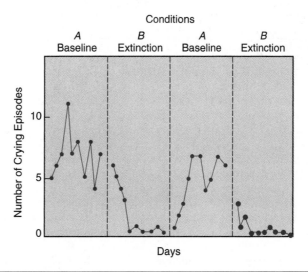

Figure 10–1 The number of crying episodes exhibited by Bill, a nursery-school student, during the four phases of an *ABAB* design initiated to control his problem crying (from Wolf & Risley, 1971, p. 316).

APPLICATION

Functional Analysis of Behavior

Most small-*n* designs are used by behaviorally oriented psychologists who believe that the control in these designs provides a powerful way to understand psychological phenomena. You will notice that most of our examples of small-*n* designs come from research concerned with applied problems, such as hyperactivity and excessive crying. Before implementing a treatment procedure on an applied problem, behavioral psychologists undertake detailed observations to determine the factors that cause the problem behavior. These systematic observations result in a **functional analysis,** and in general, they try to determine the antecedents and consequences of the behavior question (Baldwin & Baldwin, 1988; Malott, Whaley, & Malott, 1997). The term *functional* refers to the functional relation between what leads to the target behavior and the consequences that it produces. By identifying the functional relations through systematic observation, the behavioral psychologist markedly increases the chances of developing an appropriate and effective intervention procedure.

What sorts of things should be determined? Malott and associates (1997) provide a checklist of the steps in a functional analysis, which we summarize here. First, it is necessary to specify clearly the behavior of interest, including specific examples of it, as well as its frequency. Then the analysis tries to specify the outcome that the behavior produces: Is it positive or negative? Does it always occur? Does it occur immediately or after some delay? After these two things have been determined, the psychologist then tries to determine the relationship between the behavior and the outcome. For example, the analysis should show whether the behavior produces or removes the outcome. This part of the analysis hopes to determine what behavioral psychologists call the *contingency,* which includes reinforcement, punishment, escape, and avoidance.

The behavioral relationship does not occur in a vacuum, so aspects of the person and environment that may antedate the contingency need to be noted. These factors include any motivating condition and the factors that establish the motivating condition, as well as the environmental stimuli that may be associated with the response. A functional analysis of Bill's crying behavior would first determine the baseline frequency of crying and also try to define the crying (how it differs from whining, for example). Then the outcome of crying is noted and its characteristics are also recorded (how quickly the teacher pays attention to Bill when he cries, whether she is pleasant or angry, whether the attention involves both words and touch or just one or the other, etc.). Does the contingency lead to reinforcement? In this case it appears to. The behavior (crying) that produces attention increases in frequency. Why does Bill cry? Maybe he is worried when his parents are not around to help him with minor setbacks; and going to school, where his parents are missing, could help to establish that worry. Particular controlling stimuli (the *discriminative stimuli*) could be one of several: failure at a task, presence of the teacher, success by other pupils, and so on. Once these details are considered, then the behavioral psychologist can plan an intervention program that will reduce the unwanted crying. Note that a successful therapy program involves observation (the functional analysis) and experimentation— the application of a small-*n* design to ameliorate the problem.

> ## CONCEPT SUMMARY
>
> ## Reversal Design (*ABA* or *ABAB*)
>
> Interspersed between baseline periods (*A*) are independent-variable phases (*B*). If the behavior reverses to baseline levels, we assume that the independent variable caused the changes that occurred during the *B* periods.

Alternating-Treatments Design

As in the standard within-subjects experiments, small-*n* experiments often include carryover effects that prohibit using the reversal design. If the treatment introduced in the *B* phase has long-term effects on the dependent variable, then reversal is impractical. Furthermore, the experimenter may want to obtain several samples of the participants' behavior under the same independent variable or under several independent variables. There are a number of ways to solve these problems, but we will consider just two.

Rose (1978) used what could be called an *ACABCBCB* design, where *A* phases refer to baseline conditions and *B* and *C* phases include different independent variables. When presentation of different independent variables alternate, we have an **alternating-treatments design**. Rose was interested in the effects of artificial food coloring on hyperactivity in children. Two hyperactive 8-year-old girls were participants. They had been on a strict diet, the Kaiser-Permanente (K-P) diet (Feingold, 1975), which does not allow foods containing artificial flavors and colors and natural salicylates (many fruits and meats). Based on uncontrolled case studies (*AB* designs), Feingold reported that the K-P diet reduced hyperactivity.

Rose's *A* phase was the behavior of the two girls under the ordinary K-P diet. The *B* phase was another type of baseline. It involved the introduction of an oatmeal cookie that contained no artificial coloring. The *C* phase included the independent variable of interest: oatmeal cookies containing an artificial yellow dye. Rose chose this artificial color because manufactured foods commonly contain it and it had the additional benefit of not changing the taste or appearance of the cookies. (When asked to sort the cookies based on color, judges were unable to do so systematically with regard to the presence of the dye.) The participants, their parents, and the observers were blind to when the children ate the dye-laced cookie.

Various aspects of the two girls' behavior were recorded during school by several different observers. One dependent variable that Rose measured was the percentage of time that the girls were out of their seats during school. Rose found that the girls were most active during the *C* phases, when they had ingested a cookie with artificial coloring in it. Rose also noticed that there was no placebo effect. That is, the percentage of time out of their seats was essentially the same during the *A* phases (no cookie) and the *B* phases, in which the girls ate cookies without artificial coloring. So, Rose concluded that artificial colors can lead to hyperactivity in some children. Rose's cautious conclusion is supported by meta-analyses (see Chapter 7) showing small overall effect sizes for attenuating hyperactivity with the K-P diet (Hallahan, Kauffman, & Lloyd, 1999). Furthermore, Kinsbourne (1984) in a large-*n* experiment found that just 20 of 40 hyperactive children suffered negative effects from ingesting food laced with the yellow dye.

> ▶ **CONCEPT SUMMARY**
>
> ### Alternating-Treatments Design
>
> More than one independent variable is used, and there may be numerous baseline periods.

Multiple-Baseline Design

Rose's extension of the reversal design allows an experimenter to examine the effects of more than two levels of the independent variable. However, the extension does not permit experiments involving independent variables that are likely to have strong carryover effects. The **multiple-baseline design,** illus-

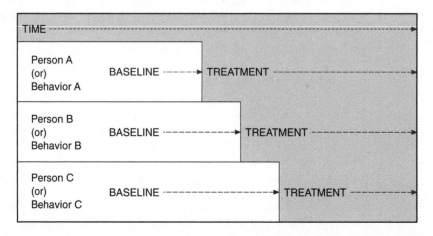

Figure 10–2   An outline of the multiple-baseline design. Different people (between subjects) or different behaviors (within subjects) have baseline periods of different lengths. The vertical lines indicate presentation of the independent variable (the treatment).

trated in Figure 10–2, is suitable for situations in which the behavior of interest may not reverse to baseline levels (that is, when there are permanent carryover effects).

Two features of the multiple-baseline design are noteworthy. First, notice that different behaviors (or different participants) have baseline periods of different lengths before the introduction of the independent variable. The baseline periods are to the left of the vertical lines, and the treatment periods, in which the independent variable has been introduced, are to the right of the vertical lines. Using such a design in the case of Bill (described earlier) might involve a continual baseline monitoring of some other unwanted behavior (say, picking fights) upon introducing the extinction period for crying. After several days perhaps, the researchers could apply the extinction procedure to the fighting behavior.

Figure 10–3 shows design and results of this hypothetical experiment. Notice that in general, one behavior occurs under baseline conditions during treatment of the other behavior. If the untreated behavior holds steady before the introduction of the independent variable and then changes afterward, the assumption is that it is the independent variable that alters the behavior and not some other change taking place over time. However, if the target behaviors are not independent—that is, if the treatment of one influences the

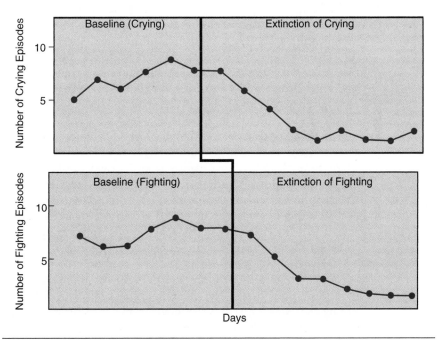

Figure 10–3   Hypothetical results of a multiple-baseline experiment on Bill. Two behaviors, crying and fighting, are extinguished after different baseline periods.

occurrence of the other (Bill's fighting decreases when crying is extinguished)—then the changes in behavior cannot be attributed to the independent variable. This problem leads us to the second important feature of the multiple-baseline design illustrated in Figure 10–2. You can use the multiple-baseline design as a small-*n* equivalent of the between-subjects design. As shown in Figure 10–2, instead of several behaviors being monitored, as in a within-subjects design, different people can be monitored for different periods before the introduction of the independent variable. This type of multiple-baseline design, as is true of the ordinary between-subjects design, should be appropriate for situations in which the independent variable will have strong carryover effects. The between-subjects multiple-baseline procedure is also appropriate for cases in which target behaviors may influence each other, such as could have occurred in our hypothetical experiment concerning Bill.

An experiment by Schreibman, O'Neill, and Koegel (1983) nicely illustrates the between-subjects form of the multiple-baseline design. Schreibman and her coworkers were interested in teaching behavior-modification procedures to the normal siblings of autistic children so that they could become effective teachers of their autistic siblings. Autism is a behavior disorder of unknown origin. It is characterized by impoverished social behavior, minimal language use, and self-stimulation of various kinds. For each of three pairs of siblings—one normal (mean age was 10 years) and one autistic (mean age was 7 years)—several target behaviors, such as counting, identification of letters, and learning about money, were chosen for the normal sibling to teach the autistic sibling. Because the normal siblings had to learn correct behavior-modification techniques, such as reinforcement for appropriate responding, the experimenters first recorded baseline measures of the normal siblings' use of correct behavior-modification techniques and the correct performance of the target behaviors by the autistic children. The baseline data for each pair of children appear to the left of the vertical lines in Figure 10–4. Learning behavior-modification techniques is likely to influence a wide variety of behaviors of both the teacher and the pupil (the normal and autistic, respectively), so the researchers used a multiple-baseline design across pairs of children. Changes in the behavior of normal and autistic children following training the normal siblings to use behavior-modification procedures appear to the right of the vertical lines in Figure 10–4. Note that correct performance by both children in each pair increased after the beginning of training. Schreibman and associates concluded that the training and not some other confounding factor (such as changes resulting from being observed) altered the behavior.

Another interesting feature in Figure 10–4 are the data points represented by plus signs and bull's-eyes. These symbols show the children's behavior in a setting that was entirely different from the training room, one in which the children did not know they were being monitored by the experimenters. Behavior in this generalization setting was very similar to the behavior in the training room, so the treatment program was effective in making general changes in the children's behavior.

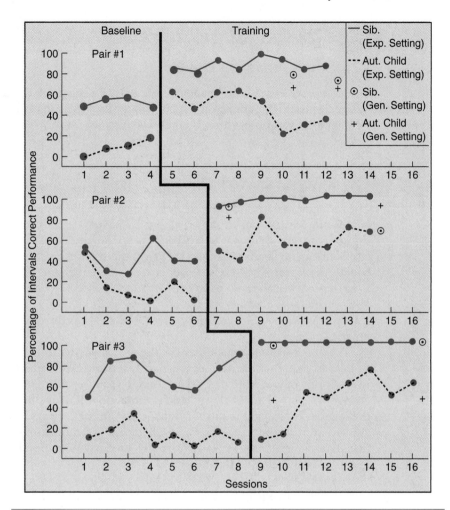

Figure 10–4 The normal siblings' use of correct behavior-modification procedures and the autistic children's appropriate responses. The baseline period is to the left of the vertical line for each pair of children. The pluses and bull's-eyes show behavior in a generalization setting (from Schreibman et al., 1983, p. 135. Copyright 1983 by the Society for the Experimental Analysis of Behavior, Inc. Reprinted by permission of the publisher and the author).

Because the sequential and gradual application allows the investigator the opportunity to alter the program if necessary, Kazdin (2001) has described the multiple-baseline design as "user friendly" (p. 139). For example, a researcher could see whether a program is working effectively. If it is, then he or she could apply it to a number of other clients. Likewise, if a treatment regimen is ineffective or otherwise unsatisfactory, a researcher could change it prior to extending it to others. These features illustrate the versatility and efficiency of a potent intervention design.

> ## CONCEPT SUMMARY
>
> ### Multiple-Baseline Design
>
> Several behaviors (within subjects) or several people (between subjects) receive baseline periods of varying length. Presentation of the independent variables occurs after the baseline periods.

Changing-Criterion Design

The **changing-criterion design** involves changing the behavior necessary to obtain reinforcement. For example, a rat may have to press a lever for food reinforcement five times for several minutes, and then the criterion behavior could change to seven lever presses to get the reinforcement. This procedure could then repeat with several other criteria. Here the independent variable is the criterion behavior necessary to obtain the outcome, and the underlying logic is similar to that of other small-*n* designs. If behavior changes systematically with the changing criteria, then we assume that the criteria are producing the change.

Therapists use changing-criterion design in a variety of behavioral therapy situations. Suppose that you see a behavioral therapist to increase the amount of studying you do. You might then contract with the therapist to give $10 to charity if you fail to study at least 1 hour on Monday through Thursday evenings. After staying with the 1-hour criterion for 2 weeks, the criterion increases so that you must study for 1 hour and 15 minutes to avoid the $10 fine. The change could increase gradually so that you eventually are studying at least 2 hours each evening.

DeLuca and Holborn (1992) used the changing-criterion design to try to increase the amount of exercise engaged in by 11-year-old boys. Initially, the baseline rate of revolutions per minute while riding a stationary bicycle was determined for each of several boys, then each boy could earn points by increasing the average number of revolutions per minute. The points could be traded for a variety of desirable objects, such as electronic games, books, and model cars. First, the boys had to increase their revolutions by 15% over the baseline to obtain points. When the boys reached criterion, it increased to 30%, and then to 45% when they attained the 30% criterion. After the boys attained the 45% criterion, DeLuca and Holborn awarded no points for 3 days. This was the return-to-baseline phase of the experiment, exactly as is done in the reversal design. The researchers wanted to ensure that the criterion for points was governing behavior. This seems to have been the case too, because each boy's revolutions per minute dropped dramatically. After 3 days of baseline, the boys returned to a 45%-over-baseline criterion, which they reattained rather quickly. This powerful treatment design was able to increase exercise levels in the boys.

> ### CONCEPT SUMMARY
>
> ## Changing-Criterion Design
>
> The criterion to obtain an outcome changes over time.

The operant-conditioning research designs described in the preceding sections are representative of the powerful research techniques developed by Skinner and his followers. Careful control has provided an enormously valuable database for psychology. Furthermore, as we have seen, the procedures used in applied settings have had substantial success. The small-*n* procedures of operant analysis are important tools for psychologists who wish to understand behavior.

▶ Clinical Psychology

A Case Study on Dissociative Identity Disorder

According to the American Psychiatric Association ([APA] 2000), a person suffering from dissociative identity disorder (DID, which was once called multiple personality disorder) has two or more personalities. These personalities recur and take charge, and the person forgets important personal information (Dorahy, 2001). The APA (2000) also states that each of various personalities "may be experienced as if it has a distinct personal history, self-image, and identity, including a separate name" (p. 526). Thus, memory dysfunction seems to be a crucial part of the DID syndrome.

Nissen, Ross, Willingham, MacKenzie, and Schacter (1988) studied a patient with DID. Their research strategy focused on a variety of memory tests that would allow them to determine to what extent one personality had access to the knowledge of other personalities. Because this research is based on a single subject ($n = 1$), it is an example of the case study, which always is classified as a small-*n* experiment, even though a survey of patients with DID found a mean of 13 different personalities per patient (Putnam, Guroff, Silberman, Barban, & Post, 1986).

The patient they studied was a 45-year-old, right-handed white woman who had been divorced five times. She has shown 22 different personalities, ranging in age from 5 to 45 years. Three personalities are male, and three are left-handed. Testing focused on eight personalities.

The general experimental procedure was to present information to one personality and, after a retention interval of 5 to 10 minutes, have the patient's psychiatrist request a change of personality. The new personality would be given a task that ordinarily would be sensitive to the prior information.

Results showed that there were some tasks in which one personality was influenced by knowledge presented to another personality and other tasks in which it was not. Simple and clear tasks did show influence. For example, one such task used four-alternative forced-choice recognition. Alice was shown 54 photographs from old high-school yearbooks and asked to rate them as sad, happy, or neutral. Bonnie was then shown a different set of 54 photographs and also asked to rate them. Bonnie then received the four-alternative forced-choice recognition test, in which four faces were presented, and Bonnie had to indicate or guess which face seemed most familiar. When the alternatives included one face previously shown to Bonnie, she selected that face 52% of the time. When the alternatives included a face that Alice, but not Bonnie, had seen before, Bonnie selected that face 42% of the time. This is higher than the 25% that could be expected by chance if Bonnie had been uninfluenced by what Alice saw. When the alternatives included one face that Alice had seen and also one that Bonnie had seen, Bonnie selected the face she had seen 33% of the time. On the remaining trials, given that Bonnie did not select the face she had seen, she selected the face that Alice had seen 63% of the time, again indicating that what Alice saw influenced Bonnie's recognition. Thus, one personality tended to remember what another personality had experienced.

A more ambiguous task, repetition priming of stem completion, did not show such influence. Alice saw words and judged how pleasant each one was. Bonnie then received a list of 24 words and judged how pleasant each one was. She next received a list of 48 three-letter word stems and had to complete them. Each stem had 10 possible correct answers. Half the word stems could make a word Alice had seen. Bonnie did not exceed the level of chance (10%) in creating such words. Thus, there was no influence from words seen by Alice. When repeating this procedure with Bonnie 5 days later, there was an influence from words that Bonnie had seen earlier, so this ruled out the possibility that Bonnie by herself would not show the repetition effect. The authors interpreted this finding to imply that ambiguous stimuli are more likely to have personality-specific interpretations and would not show influence from one personality to another. DID patients often claim to have this inter-identity amnesia for the experiences not shared by another identity, but a recent experiment involving 21 patients claiming amnesia indicates little objective evidence for this amnesia (Huntjens, Postma, Peters, Woertman, & van der Hart, 2003).

You should note that the concept of DID is controversial, because it is not clear what causes the symptoms. Some have argued that it is not really a psychiatric disorder but, rather, a construction by the patient, often during therapy (McHugh, 1992; Spanos, 1996), in response to the cultural, horror-movie view of multiple personalities. Regardless, the work by Nissen and her colleagues is an interesting study, because it combined two different methodologies not often used together in psychology. The case study appears most often in clinical psychology, whereas studies of memory most often involve many subjects. This experiment reminds us that it is possible to be creative by combining different techniques within a single experiment.

> ## CONCEPT SUMMARY

Small-*n* Designs in Clinical Psychology

The case study is a small-*n* design often used in clinical psychology. Many case studies have *n* = 1.

Summary

1. The use of small-*n* designs usually assumes that valid conclusions can be reached by making large numbers of observations on a few subjects in a carefully controlled situation.

2. The reversal design (*ABA*) is a common within-subjects design that involves independent-variable periods (*B* phases) interspersed among baseline periods (*A* phases).

3. One extension of the reversal design involves numerous baseline periods and more than two levels of the independent variable. This design is called the alternating-treatments design.

4. The multiple-baseline design involves assessing different behaviors (within-subjects) or different people (between-subjects) for baseline periods of different length before introducing the independent variable.

5. The multiple-baseline design is useful when the independent variable has strong carryover effects or the behaviors to be altered are not independent of each other.

6. The changing-criterion design involves changing the criterion behavior that produces the desired outcome.

7. The case study is a common small-*n* design used in clinical psychology.

Key Concepts

AB design (237)	changing-criterion	multiple-baseline design
ABA design (237)	design (246)	(242)
alternating-treatments	functional analysis (240)	reversal design (237)
design (241)	large-*n* designs (235)	small-*n* design (235)

Exercises

1. Discuss the logic underlying the use of the reversal design and the alternating-treatments design. How do these relate to Mill's joint method of agreement and difference?

2. Is the clinical case study described in this chapter a valid experimental design? Why, or why not?

Suggested Resource

The standard work on the applications of learning principles to behavior problems is Kazdin, A. E. (2001). *Behavior modification in applied settings* (6th ed.). Belmont, CA: Wadsworth/ThomsonLearning.

Web Resources

Many applications of small-*n* designs are on the web. Their use in zoos can be found at: http://www.memphiszoo.org/vet/opcond.htm

The Wadsworth Research Methods workshops discuss single subject designs at: http://www.wadsworth.com/psychology_d/templates/student_resources/workshops/res_methd/non_exper/non_exper_08.html

Laboratory Resource

An interesting treatment of the small-*n* approach is found in Chance, P. (1998). *First course in applied behavior analysis*. Pacific Grove, CA: Brooks/Cole.

Can You Put Yourself on a Better Schedule of Reinforcement?

All of us have habits we would like to break and others we would like to develop. Smoking, drinking, nail-biting, watching too much television, and not studying enough are some of the bad habits that college students often say they would like to alter. Failure to control these behaviors is often blamed on laziness or a defective personality. However, a behavioral analysis of such problems suggests a simple alternative to these interpretations: Bad habits are being reinforced, and to change them, we must alter the schedule of reinforcement by which we live. If all these bad habits are learned, then they can be altered by learning too. The general aim is to alter the reinforcements in our lives so that they occur after desirable behavior and not after undesirable behavior.

Suppose you are in danger of flunking out of school because you study too little and, being addicted to the movies, you attend them too often. You know you have a problem, but you are in a rut and do not know how to get out. What can you do to modify your behavior?

The first step is to set a goal for yourself. It is not enough to say that you want to study more; you must have a concrete, measurable goal. Say you decide to study 6 hours a day outside of class. Your second step would be to institute some means of carefully monitoring your study behavior. How much do you already study, on the average? You should carry a notebook, record every studying episode as it occurs each day, and then total these episodes at the end of the day. You can also get a weekly average.

Say you discover at the end of a week that you are averaging 59 minutes of studying per day; obviously, you are a long way from your target of 6 hours a day. The next step is to set yourself a realistic goal in your first attempt. It might be too much of a shock to your system to go directly from 1 to 6 hours of studying per day; worse, you might give up early on, deciding it is impossible. So, let us assume that you plan to increase your studying to 2 hours a day at first. But how? You should analyze the situation and see what activities prevent you from studying. The main deterrent is your going to the movies, but surely other activities also intrude. You might set up an activity schedule to monitor your behavior, as shown in the table on page 252.

You should then try to change your environment so that it is more conducive to study. Try to avoid those friends who might encourage you to go to the movies. Do not avoid them entirely, of course, but plan to spend more time at the place where you study. Analyze your study area—are there many distractions? (These might include roommates, magazines, radios, and televisions.) If there are many distractions, abandon your room as a place of study, and find a quiet hideaway where only you and your books will be present. Studies have shown that if you can associate a particular place exclusively with study behavior and then force yourself to go to this place, you can increase studying dramatically. Finally—and this is one of the most important steps—you must figure out a reward for yourself for successfully studying the allotted amount of time. For example, you could promise yourself that if you have studied 2 hours each day during the first week, you can go to the movies with your friends. Thus, one of the main reinforcers in your life—going to the movies—is made contingent on other behavior. In essence, you are reinforcing yourself for studying.

During the next week, try studying 3 hours a day, continuing to carefully monitor your time and study habits. In each successive week, increase your amount of study per day until you reach your goal in a few weeks. Technically, you are *shaping* study behavior in yourself by reinforcing successive approximations to the target behavior, just as animals are taught complicated tricks by being reinforced for gradual approximations to them. If you can keep the reinforcement contingencies in place, you will have dramatically changed your behavior.

The case we have used here may not apply directly to your situation, but in all likelihood, you have habits you would like to break or change.

You can do so by applying the rules specified here: Set a concrete target goal, and by reinforcing yourself for each step taken, gradually alter your behavior to approximate that goal. Martin and Pear (1999) have outlined a number of ways to use behavior modification procedures to develop self-control in a variety of situations. Their interesting book, *Behavior Modification: What It Is and How to Do It,* also provides a solid background on the principles of learning that underlie the procedures of behavior modification.

Time	Monday	Tuesday	Wednesday	Thursday	Friday	Saturday	Sunday
7:00							
8:00							
9:00							
10:00							
11:00							
12:00							
1:00							
2:00							
3:00							
4:00							
5:00							
6:00							
7:00							
8:00							
9:00							
10:00							
11:00							

CHAPTER **11**

Quasi-Experimentation

Increasing internal validity when the variables are selected, not manipulated

Sources of Invalidity in Quasi-Experiments

- artifacts
- history
- delayed effects
- maturation
- regression
- selection bias mortality

How One Makes Valid Causal Statements in:

Case Studies

- Use *deviant-case analysis* (a nonequivalent control group); examine several dependent variables

Interrupted Time Series

- Use *nonequivalent control group*; study several dependent variables; search for additional natural treatments

Subject-Variable Research

- Use *matching* on potentially relevant characteristics; beware of regression artifacts

Developmental Research (Age)

- Use *cross-sequential design* to minimize generation and time-of-test confoundings; include *true independent variable*, and look for interactions

This chapter considers research that includes independent variables that are selected rather than directly manipulated by the experimenter. Most experiments done in the field and many in the laboratory have subject variables as the independent variables. Subject variables, such as age and intelligence, occur naturally and are selected by the researcher for subsequent observation and analysis. These naturally occurring treatments represent a form of correlation—they are, in essence, dependent variables. Selecting rather than manipulating independent variables poses many difficult control and interpretive problems.

▶ Internal Validity in Quasi-Experiments

Quasi-experiments refer to experimental situations in which the experimenter does not directly manipulate variables as in a typical laboratory experiment (Reichardt and Mark, 1998). In a quasi-experiment, some or all of the variables are selected, which means that they are not under direct control of the experimenter. Either the effects of natural "treatments" (such as disasters) are observed, or particular subject variables (such as age, sex, and weight) are of interest. In either case, we must be wary of internal validity, because, as mentioned, the experimenter does not manipulate the variables. In other words, the joint method of agreement and difference is not under direct control. Quasi-experiments have the advantage of being intrinsically interesting, and they also allow researchers to examine variables that would be unethical to manipulate directly. In this chapter, we consider the pitfalls of quasi-experiments and how to minimize those problems.

Natural Treatments

Ex post facto analyses of the effects of some naturally occurring event, such as a disaster or a change in school curricula, are usually interesting and important, but they are often difficult to interpret in a causal fashion. Most quasi-experiments involving naturally occurring treatments have a structure that is similar to some of the small-n experiments (ABA) discussed earlier. We might, for example, have records of third-grade achievement before and after (the A phases) the introduction of a new method for teaching reading (the B phase). Note carefully: This example does not represent a true reversal design, because there is not a removal of the treatment to allow a return to the original baseline. In fact, most quasi-experiments of the general form **observation-treatment-observation** cannot be true reversal designs for two reasons: (1) The treatment is not under the experimenter's control and (2) most natural treatments, such as curriculum revision, are likely to have long-term carryover effects. We must be concerned not only with carryover effects but also with the changes in the participants themselves. If we examine the effects of a new reading program on third-grade achievement, one thing that is confounded with the introduction of our treatment is a change in the age of our participants. Although age itself does not cause anything, many important changes correlate with age: more experience in school, better test taking, improved linguistic skills, better social adjustment, biological maturation, and the like. These changes, which are called **maturation**, nearly always can confound the results of research concerned with natural treatments. Furthermore, in a classroom setting, numerous outside influences could affect the results. Because the researcher does not have direct control over the setting, the participants are not insulated from numerous possible distractions, as they are in a true experiment. This source of confounding is called **history** by Cook and Campbell (1979).

Thus, two particular threats to internal validity with naturally occurring treatments are the history of the participant and any changes in the participant that occur over time. Either or both of these factors could vary directly, inversely, or not at all with the intended treatment. In addition, the effects of history and change could interact in several different ways. Ways to minimize these difficulties (for example, matching) generally involve more active participation on the part of the experimenter. One thing that could be done in ex post facto analysis of the effects of reading techniques is to find a control-group third-grade class that did not have this new technique imposed on it, which would result in a quasi-experimental design similar to the one shown in Table 11–1. This looks like an ordinary experimental design, but remember—we have no direct control over the situation, and as we shall soon see, by adding a matched control group, we have incurred additional threats to internal validity. This type of design is sometimes called a **nonequivalent control group** design, because random assignment to conditions is not used and matching is attempted after the fact. Because the participants are not randomly assigned to groups, we have the possible problem of **selection bias.** As discussed in Chapter 6, random assignment to conditions generally equates the participant characteristics in the various conditions of the experiment. With natural treatments, on the other hand, we select our participants, not assign them, and we have no guarantee that our selection will be as unbiased as randomization in a true experiment.

We will now consider two quasi-experimental designs that appear in the psychological literature: the one-shot case study, and the interrupted-time-series design.

One-Shot Case Studies

We can view the **one-shot case study** in the following way: We have a long-term treatment on an individual, and after the fact, we obtain some measurements of that individual's thought and action. If we use the same notation that we used for the reversal design, we can call this an *AB* design (where *A* is the

Table 11–1 A hypothetical quasi-experimental design for examining curricula changes on third-grade achievement scores

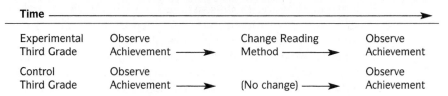

NOTE: The third-grade classes are assumed to be very similar, differing only in terms of the imposed curriculum change. There was not random assignment to the two groups, and the control group usually is determined ex post facto. Thus, this design includes a nonequivalent control group.

history and *B* is the current behavior). Treatments occur, and then we observe their effects. Note that the treatments do not allow baseline observations. Viewing the one-shot case study as an *AB* design immediately points to the threat to internal validity: There is no baseline or control condition.

If a small-*n* design cannot be used, then deviant-case analysis is one way to obtain a control group in case-study research. In deviant-case analysis (see Chapter 4), we take an individual as similar as possible to our case except for a crucial missing treatment (a drunkard for a father, a disabling illness, and so forth) and then determine how the individuals are different from each other. The similar individual is a nonequivalent control, not a true control. Reconsider the case of P. Z. that was discussed in Chapter 4. P. Z. was an elderly, world-famous scientist who suffered from a severe memory loss and had a history of alcohol abuse (Butters & Cermak, 1986). Deviant-case analysis was used to determine whether the memory deficit could be attributed to the alcohol abuse. A similar-aged colleague of P. Z. was tested for the retention of facts and names that should have been familiar to him and to P. Z. The colleague is the companion person for the deviant-case analysis. Whereas P. Z. showed a severe retention loss, the colleague did not. Because the comparison case had not abused alcohol, Butters and Cermak concluded that alcohol was the causal factor in the memory loss.

In this deviant-case analysis, the quasi-independent variable—alcohol abuse—was selected, not manipulated. Furthermore, the comparison case is a nonequivalent control, because the case also was selected and not randomly assigned to the "control" condition. These threats to internal validity make it difficult to make firm causal conclusions. The best that the researcher can hope for is to probe for suspected causal factors as carefully as possible. The comparison case permits the tentative conclusion that simply being old or being a scientist does not by itself result in severe memory deficits. Additional comparisons showed that P. Z.'s inability to remember new information was similar to that exhibited by other alcoholics (also a nonequivalent control group). Alcohol abuse is the prime suspect remaining.

In a sense, therefore, interpreting a case history is similar to doing detective work. The typical case study involves a large number of dependent variables. Thus, the researcher who wishes to make causal statements on the basis of a case study has to look for important clues and then interpret the meaning of those clues in the context of all the other observations. Be careful how you interpret this discussion. As a laboratory research design, the one-shot case study with only one or two dependent variables would be sloppy and internally invalid. It is simply a terrible experimental design. However, in the typical case study, in which a great deal of information is available, causal "detective" work is often more reasonable and more likely to lead to internally valid conclusions. The researcher gains control by increasing the number and complexity of the observations. Remember too that case studies often involve retrospective reports, which means that the life-history "facts" may be forgotten or distorted. A cautious investigator might tentatively accept the reports as internally valid.

Case studies are a major source of descriptive data for clinical psychology. As we have just seen, deriving causal conclusions from them is very difficult. Can case studies be used for prediction? This issue is addressed in the Application section.

A European study (Hygge, Evans, & Bullinger, 2002) took advantage of the simultaneous opening and closing of the Munich airport to create a one-shot quasi-experiment. Two experimental groups consisted of children who either were exposed to aircraft noise at the old airport or would be exposed at the new airport. Two control groups, matched on sociodemographic variables, were not exposed to aircraft noise. Data were collected in three waves: Wave 1 was 6 months prior to the opening of the new airport, Wave 2 was one year later, and Wave 3 was 2 years later. Testing was conducted in a sound-isolated mobile van so that there was no confounding with immediate noise effects.

Figure 11–1 shows results for a long-term memory test in which children recalled information a day after reading it. At the old airport, memory with aircraft noise was worse before the airport closed (Wave 1). But once the airport closed, the effects of noise disappeared. We would expect the opposite findings at the new airport. At Wave 1 there was no statistically significant effect of noise. However, at Wave 3 performance was better without noise. These results show that noise influences memory but that this effect is reversible when the noise source is removed.

It is interesting to compare this quasi-experiment with an ex post facto (after the fact) study of aircraft noise around Heathrow Airport in London. Haines, Stansfeld, Head, and Job (2002) correlated standardized tests in mathematics, science, and English with aircraft noise exposure; exposure varied according to distance from the airport. Exposure was statistically related to poorer reading and mathematics test scores. However, when other socioeconomic variables were statistically controlled, this correlational association disappeared. In general, results from quasi-experiments are more robust than results from ex post facto studies because scientists prefer statements about causation to statements about correlation.

Another quasi-experiment studied effects of construction noise on residents of college dorms (Ng, 2000). The noise level from outside building construction varied in three dorm wings (near, central, far). Four kinds of measures were taken: a questionnaire survey, self-completed activity logs, resident turnover record, and external observation of windows open or closed. Higher percentages of residents in the noisier wings reported interference with activities such as telephone conversations. Near-wing residents reported keeping their windows closed more often than residents of quieter wings. However, while the objective external observation of windows found more open windows in the quieter wings, there was no reliable effect or interaction of whether or not construction was going on. The most important correlate of number of open windows was outside temperature.

All quasi-experiments are not automatically equally useful just because they are quasi-experiments. Comparing the two quasi-experiments discussed in this section reveals that the European study was more sophisticated and

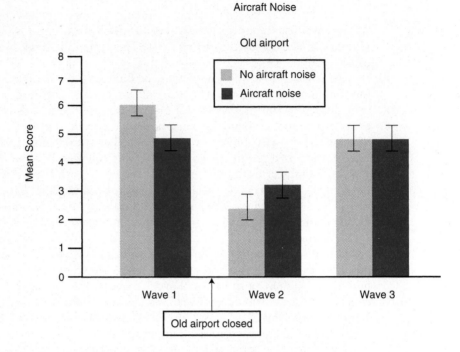

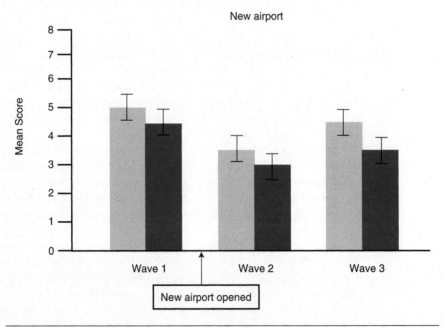

Figure 11–1 Mean score on the long-term memory task as a function of airport, noise group, and measurement wave. Error bars show standard errors of the means. (From Hygge et al., 2002, with permission.)

APPLICATION

Predicting Behavior From Case Studies

Case studies provide substantial information about an individual, and clinical psychologists often rely on them to determine the causes of current behavior. However, such an endeavor may be difficult, and making valid causal statements based on case studies may be impossible. Are case studies good for predicting future behavior? You know that prediction on the basis of correlations can be successful. Can the information from a case study be used in the same way?

Given that you are a psychology major taking a college-level course in research methods, can we predict that you will be a research psychologist? Based just on your case, our prediction is likely to be inaccurate. If we examine the case histories of some psychologists, it is easy for us to see that prediction can be poor.

John B. Watson (1878–1958), founder of the school of behaviorism in psychology and pioneer in the field of learning, was a philosophy major as an undergraduate. After he was forced out of academic psychology because of an adulterous affair with a graduate student, he became an executive in a large advertising agency.

Probably none of his classmates or teachers would have predicted that B. F. Skinner would become an influential and famous psychologist. Skinner was an English major as an undergraduate, and after graduation he spent some time leading a bohemian life as an aspiring writer of fiction.

As a more contemporary example, consider Gordon H. Bower, the distinguished investigator of learning and memory. Bower, who wanted to be a psychiatrist, attended college on a baseball scholarship. He had received offers of professional baseball contracts, but a fortunate experience in an experimental psychology course and a desire to avoid the military draft led him to choose experimental psychology over baseball.

Each of these vignettes indicates that accurate predictions from case studies can be difficult. This difficulty is very obvious in the field of criminal law, where it is often necessary to predict whether convicted felons will continue their criminal behavior or be law-abiding citizens following their release. There is considerable controversy in psychology and psychiatry concerning attempts to predict the future actions of a dangerous criminal, such as a murderer or a rapist. Accurate predictions about rapists and murderers are crucial, but difficult. Usually, only a weak probabilistic statement can be made: "The chances are that this criminal will not rape again." Most people do not consider this a strong enough prediction. To generate more accurate predictions, we need more detailed information than a simple case study can provide. At the very least, a substantial number of correlations among various kinds of behavior patterns must be made before reasonable predictions are possible. An important area of research awaits you.

more elegantly designed. Many of the measures taken in the college dorm study did not discriminate between construction noise being present or absent. This is a weakness shared with ex post facto studies of noise. In contrast, the Munich study controlled several variables, such as the presence of noise during data collection.

Interrupted-Time-Series Design

The **interrupted-time-series design** is often encountered in quasi-experimental research, and it represents the logical extension of the general observation-treatment-observation design (see Table 11–1). In the simplest time-series design, we have a single experimental group for which we have multiple observations before and after a naturally occurring treatment. Instead of examining just one or two third-grade classes, we could observe third-grade classes over several years, or we could follow the achievement of the pupils across their entire school career. We need to know when the time series is interrupted by some treatment. Then we compare observations before and after the treatment to see whether it had any effect. Suppose we had records of public-school achievement for a city that added fluoride to its water one year. We would plot achievement against time and look for changes in achievement subsequent to fluoridation.

Such a hypothetical time-series analysis is shown in Figure 11–2. What we look for in a time-series analysis are changes following interruption by the treatment. Note the rather dramatic increase in achievement following the introduction of fluoride. Can we assert that fluoride causes better achievement? No—for the same reason that we have difficulty interpreting a single correlation coefficient. Possibly fluoride had an indirect effect, which means that

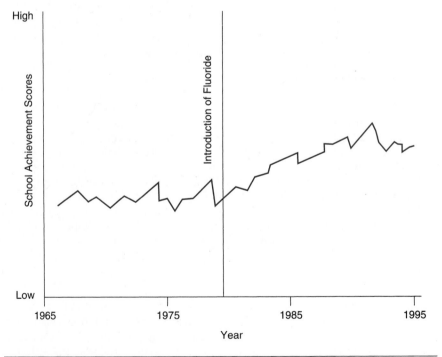

Figure 11–2 A hypothetical time-series analysis of the effects of fluoride on school achievement scores.

some confounding factor is the principal cause. Perhaps fluoride reduced absenteeism resulting from dental appointments, and it was the reduced absences that permitted higher achievement. The possibility of such indirect effects makes it difficult for researchers to arrive at internally valid conclusions.

In our example, we could examine the absence rate before and after the introduction of fluoride. This could be done by plotting absence rate as well as achievement over time, or we could try to find a control group that was similar to our experimental group but was untreated with fluoride. Finding a satisfactory control group might be difficult (imagine trying to find a town that differed from yours on only one dimension). Furthermore, such a control group would be nonequivalent and leave us open to the problems of matching. Of course, our control group would have to have an absence rate similar to that of the experimental group, but it would still be nonequivalent (because random assignment was not used).

Although a no-treatment control is often desirable, there are other things to look for in a time-series analysis that may be helpful (back to the detective's clues). We can use several dependent variables, such as absenteeism and the number of extracurricular activities, but we also can examine other treatments in much the same way that a case study is combed for additional hints. Time series often involve a long time period, so the researcher has to rely on the availability of complete and accurate records. In our example, we would need to have detailed records of every student, the administration, and the faculty to make internally valid statements. Without these records, we could not rule out plausible alternative explanations.

Even with the records, there may be difficulties. The innumerable other changes that can take place mean confounding is always a threat to internal validity. Over a 30-year period, performance in school could change for several reasons, and these natural treatments could operate independently or could interact. Changes in teachers and administrators, curricula, and economics occur, which could all lead to internal invalidity. A major source of confounding in a long-term time series is what is called **mortality**. Pupils graduate and move away, or they may die. Such changes in the group of participants would lead to a special form of selection bias (Cook & Campbell, 1979), because the same participants would not be studied before and after the introduction of the treatment.

The difficulties of the interrupted-time-series design are magnified when the effect of the treatment is delayed or masked by other variables (Cook & Campbell, 1979). The effects of fluoride are unlikely to be immediate. Fluoride reduces dental problems, such as cavities. If absenteeism changes because of a reduction in cavities, then we might have additional interpretive problems. Cavities take time to develop, and fluoride does not eliminate cavities once they have taken hold. Thus, the effects of fluoride might be delayed, and we would not be in a position to interpret what caused the changes in achievement. Furthermore, the effects of fluoride could be masked by the intrusion of some variable that counteracts its effects, such as a bubblegum factory moving to town.

These cautions notwithstanding, the interrupted-time-series design is very useful, especially in applied research. A good example of a time-series analysis is a study by McSweeny (1978), who showed that the introduction of a small fee for directory assistance (the "Information" operator) dramatically reduced the number of directory-assistance calls. Because most such calls were for numbers and addresses that were published, the telephone company wanted to eliminate these nonessential calls to keep the lines open for essential assistance. The number of daily calls in Cincinnati dropped by about 70,000 following the introduction of the 20-cent fee, showing that the strategy was an effective one.

Phillips used time-series analyses to investigate some of the psychological reasons leading to death. In an extensive and interesting series of papers, Phillips examined some of the causes of natural death (1972), the precipitants of suicide (1977, 1978), and the causes of homicides (1983). His general strategy involved determining the number of deaths before and after a particular event. Thus, death rate was the dependent variable, and the quasi-independent variable was the event that interrupted the time span over which Phillips made his observations. Let us examine how he used an interrupted-time-series analysis to investigate the effects of mass-media violence on homicide rates in the United States.

Phillips began his study of the effects of media violence on homicides by carefully examining the literature on television violence and aggression (see the discussion in Chapter 5 about the work by Eron and associates). From this literature, he concluded that aggression was most likely to occur following a story in which violence appeared to be (a) justified, (b) exciting, (c) real, and (d) rewarded. A natural violent event that fits these characteristics is a heavyweight boxing match. Using an interrupted-time-series analysis, Phillips determined the number of homicides that occurred before and after boxing matches that received wide media presentation over the period 1973 to 1978.

Phillips found a remarkable 12.4% increase in homicide rates following the publicized boxing matches. He also found that this increase could not be attributed to extraneous variables, such as the season of the year or the day of the week. If there is a causal relationship here, how did Phillips determine the aspects of prizefighting that led to increase in homicides? Phillips became a detective. First, he determined that boxing matches do not simply precipitate a homicide that would have occurred in the absence of the match. He arrived at this conclusion by showing that the number of homicides did not go down before boxing matches, which they would have to do if the homicide rate were roughly constant over time and were merely pushed into reality by the match. Second, Phillips ruled out the possibility that the homicide rate increased because boxing matches were associated with gambling. He found that other major sporting events usually associated with gambling, such as the Super Bowl and the World Series, did not lead to an increase in the homicide rate.

Phillips concluded that the relationship between boxing and homicide rate was probably a result of modeling; that is, social learning processes that induced people to model or imitate others seemed to account for the increase in homicides following the major prizefights. Phillips' reasoning went like this: If imitation or modeling is important, then the victims of homicides should be similar to the losers of boxing matches. This means that, for example, if a young white male loses a boxing match, then the murders of young white males should increase, but the murders of young black males should not. Phillips found substantial evidence to support his modeling idea: The increase in homicide rate following a boxing match mostly included murders of people who were very similar to the losers of the match.

Phillips' use of the interrupted-time-series analysis has been a valuable way to determine the effects of media violence on homicide rate. His use of detective work in trying to arrive at a causal analysis of his findings is a good lesson in probing for answers and rejecting alternative explanations.

The most effective interrupted-time-series design has one or more control time series. The control groups are not given the treatment. Thus, control data provide information about how the experimental series might behave in the absence of treatment. Of course, because we are discussing quasi-experiments, the control group is not selected randomly.

In Michigan, the drinking age was increased from 18 to 21 years in 1979. How did this affect traffic accidents? Figure 11–3 answers the question with a

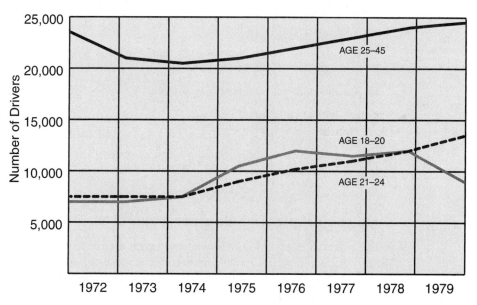

Figure 11–3 Crash-involved drivers in Michigan reported as having been drinking alcoholic beverages. This graph was copied, with permission, from the original source. Technically, it should be a bar graph, because data occur only once per year. However, we have not redrawn this figure, because three bars for each year might be difficult to read. Note that the decline from 1978 to 1979 is discrete rather than continuous. (From Wagenaar, 1981.)

quasi-experiment conducted at the University of Michigan Transportation Research Institute (Wagenaar, 1981). It shows one experimental time series for drivers 18 to 20 years old who were involved in crashes while drinking. This graph shows a decrease in traffic accidents in 1979. However, there might be alternate explanations for this result that are not connected to decreased alcohol consumption. For example, if the price of gasoline had increased that year, or more snow had fallen than usual, the amount of driving could have decreased, leading to fewer traffic accidents. The two control series for drivers aged 21 to 24 years and 25 to 45 years rule out this alternate explanation, because accidents did not decrease for these two groups. Thus, when the control series are also considered, our confidence in the explanation that decreased alcohol consumption accounted for the drop in accidents is bolstered. Adding one or more control series substantially improves interrupted-time-series quasi-experiments.

CONCEPT SUMMARY

Increasing Internal Validity

In case studies, use

- deviant-case analysis
- nonequivalent control
- multiple dependent variables

In interrupted-time-series studies, use

- nonequivalent control
- multiple dependent variables

(Beware of confounding caused by lack of control.)

Designs Employing Subject Variables

Much research in psychology is concerned with differences in the way various groups of people behave. A **subject variable** is some measurable characteristic of people. Examples are numerous and include intelligence (IQ), weight, anxiety, sex, age, need for achievement, attractiveness, race, and ability to recall dreams, as well as many types of pathological conditions (schizophrenia, alcoholism, brain damage, and so on). Subject variables are often used in psychological research. However, their use demands special consideration, because investigation or selection of them is made after the fact. Thus, because the subject variables are not manipulated directly, designs using subject variables represent one more type of quasi-experimental research.

In experiments, an investigator has control over manipulation of the independent variable; it can be manipulated while all else is held constant. If we are interested in the effect of pornographic movies on physiological arousal and later sexual excitement, we can take two statistically equivalent groups of people (or the same people at different times), show them a movie with pornographic scenes included or omitted (while we hold other variables constant), and measure their responses. We can then be confident (but never certain) about whether the difference between the movies produced any observed differential effect in arousal. The case is very different with subject variables, though. An experimenter cannot manipulate a subject variable while holding other factors constant. He or she can only select participants who already have the characteristic to some degree and then compare them on the behavior of interest. If the participants in the different groups (say, high, medium, and low IQ) differ on the behavior, we cannot conclude that the subject-variable difference produced or is responsible for the difference in behavior. The reason is that other factors may vary with the subject variable and thus be confounded with it. So, if high-IQ participants perform some task better than low-IQ participants, we cannot say that IQ produced or caused the difference, because the different groups of participants are likely to vary on other relevant dimensions, such as motivation, education, and the like. When subject variables are investigated, we cannot safely attribute differences in behavior to them, as we can with true experimental variables. Such designs, then, essentially produce correlations between variables, and we should be wary of the same types of confounding that occur in correlational research. We can say that the variables are related, but we cannot say that one variable produced or caused the effect in the other variable.

This is a very important point, so let us consider an example. Suppose an investigator is interested in the intellectual functioning of people suffering from schizophrenia. People diagnosed as belonging to this group are given numerous tests meant to measure various mental abilities. The researcher also gives these tests to another group of people, so-called normals, as a control measure. He or she discovers that schizophrenics do especially poorly (relative to normals) in tests involving semantic aspects of language, such as understanding the meaning of words or comprehending prose passages. The investigator concludes that the schizophrenics perform these tests more poorly *because* they are schizophrenics and that their inability to use language well in communication is a likely contributing cause of schizophrenia.

Studies like this are common in some areas of psychology. Conclusions similar to those just mentioned are often drawn, but they are completely unjustifiable. Both conclusions are based on correlations, and other factors could well be the critical ones. For any number of reasons, people with schizophrenia may do more poorly than people who do not have schizophrenia. They may not be as intelligent, as motivated, as educated, or as wise at taking tests. Possibly the fact that they have been institutionalized for a long time, with resulting poverty of social and intellectual intercourse, accounts for the differences. We cannot conclude that the reason the two groups differ on verbal tests is schizophrenia or its absence in the two groups. Even if we could, it would certainly not imply the other conclusion: that language problems are involved in causing schizophrenia. Again, all we would have is a correlation between these two variables, with no idea of whether or how the two are causally related.

Use of subject variables is very common in all psychological research, but it is absolutely crucial in areas such as clinical and developmental psychology. Thus, the problems with making inferences from such research should be carefully considered. A primary variable in developmental psychology is age, a subject variable, which means that much research in this field is correlational in nature. In general, the problem of individual differences among participants in psychology is often ignored, though there are often appeals to consider the problem as crucial (for example, Underwood, 1975). Let us look at some ways to make more sound inferences from experiments that use subject variables.

Matching

The basic problem in the investigation of subject variables, and in other quasi-experimental research, is that whatever differences are observed in behavior may be caused by other confounded variables. One way to try to avoid this problem is by **matching** participants on the other relevant variables. In the comparison of schizophrenics and normals, we noted that the two groups were also likely to differ on other characteristics, such as IQ, education, motivation, institutionalization, medication, and perhaps even age. Rather than simply comparing the schizophrenics with normals, we might try to compare them with another group more closely matched on these other dimensions so that the main difference between the groups is in the presence or absence of schizophrenia. For example, we might use a group of neurotics who, on the average, are similar to the schizophrenics in terms of age, IQ, length of time institutionalized, sex, and some measure of motivation. When the two groups have been matched on all these characteristics, we can more confidently attribute any difference in performance between them to the factor of interest, namely, schizophrenia. By matching, we attempt to introduce the crucial characteristic of experimentation—being able to hold extraneous factors constant to avoid confoundings—into what is essentially a correlational observation. Our goal is to be able to infer that the variable of interest (schizophrenia) produced the observed effect.

There are several rather serious problems associated with matching. For one thing, matching often requires a great deal of effort, because some of the relevant variables may be difficult to measure. Even when we go to the trouble of taking the needed additional measures, we may still be unable to match the groups, especially if few participants are involved before matching is attempted (for example, research on an unusual type of brain damage or other medical disorder). Even when matching is successful, it often greatly reduces the size of the sample on which the observations are made. Thus, we then are less confident that our observations are reliable (stable and repeatable).

Matching is often difficult, because crucial differences among participants may have subtle effects. In addition, the effects of one difference may interact with another. Thus, *interactions* among matched variables may confound the results. To illustrate these difficulties, let us reconsider some of the work done by Brazelton and associates on neonatal behavior mentioned in Chapter 4 (Lester & Brazelton, 1982).

Brazelton's primary interest was in cultural differences in neonatal behavior, as measured by the Brazelton Neonatal Behavioral Assessment Scale. The general strategy was to compare neonates from various cultures and ethnic groups with neonates from the United States. In these quasi-experiments, culture or ethnic group, which was a subject variable, was the quasi-independent variable. Attempts were usually made to match the neonates from different cultures along various dimensions, such as birth weight, birth length, and obstetrical risk (including whether the mother received medication during birth, whether the baby was premature, and so on). Lester and Brazelton showed that there was a synergistic relationship among these factors. **Synergism** in a medical context means that the combined effects of two or more variables are not additive—the combined effect is greater than the sum of the individual components—which means that the variables interact. The way in which neonatal characteristics and obstetrical risk interact is as follows: Studies have shown that the behavior (as measured by the Brazelton scale) of slightly underweight infants is more strongly influenced (negatively) by small amounts of medication taken by the mother than is the behavior of neonates who are closer to the average in weight. So, it is very difficult to match participants appropriately, because low birth weight interacts with medication, which has effects on the behavior of the children. Even though the neonates are carefully selected, the synergistic relation between the matched variables can influence the results. This is an especially difficult problem in Brazelton's work, because much of his research examined neonates from impoverished cultures, where birth weight is low and obstetrical risk is very high. Generally, you should remember that matched variables are rarely under direct control, which means that the possibility of confounding is always present.

Another problem with matching involves the introduction of the dreaded **regression artifact.** Under certain conditions in many types of measurements, a statistical phenomenon known as **regression to the mean** occurs. The mean of a group of scores is what most people think of as the average—the total of all observations divided by the number of observations. For example, mean intelligence in a sample of 60 people is the sum of all their intelligence-test scores divided by 60 (see Appendix A). Generally, if people who received extreme scores (that is, very high or very low) on some characteristic are retested, their second scores will be closer to the mean of the entire group than were their original scores.

Extreme scores are likely owing to measurement error. If the error is random and normally distributed (see Appendix A), then subsequent measures will have smaller errors—they will be less extreme. Consider an example. We give 200 people a standard test of mathematical reasoning for which there are two equivalent forms, or two versions of the test that are equivalent. The average (mean) score on the test is 60 of 100 possible points. We take the 15 people who score highest and the 15 who score lowest. The means of these groups are 95 and 30, respectively. Then we test them again on the other form of the test. We might find that the means of the two groups are 87 and 35. On the second test, the scores of the two extreme groups regress toward the mean; the high-scoring group scores more poorly, whereas the low-scoring group has somewhat better scores. This sequence of events is illustrated in Figure 11–4. In the high-scoring group, some people whose true scores were somewhat lower than the scores they received were simply lucky on the first test and scored higher than they should have. When retested, these participants tend to score lower—nearer their true score. The situation is reversed for the low-scoring group.

This regression toward the mean is always observed when there is a less-than-perfect correlation between the two measures. The more extreme the selection of scores, the greater the regression toward the mean. It also occurs in all types of measurement situations. If abnormally tall or short parents have a child, the child's adult height will probably be closer to the population mean than to the height of the parents. As with most statistical phenomena, regression to the mean is true of groups of observations and is probabilistic (that is, it may not occur every time). For example, in the second test of mathematical reasoning, a few individual participants may score higher or lower than before, but the group tendency will be toward the mean. In any event, if we had selected participants on the basis of their reasoning scores and then matched them in two groups, subsequent differences may have been caused by some treatment or may have been the result of regression to the mean. If we do not have the true scores and we do not use random assignment, then regression to the mean may be a confounding factor leading to changes in behavior.

Ex post facto research and quasi-experiments with subject variables are conducted often to evaluate educational programs, so those who practice such research need to be aware of the many thorny problems associated with it.

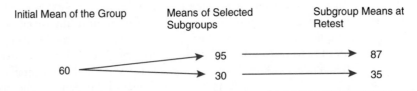

Initial Mean of the Group   Means of Selected Subgroups   Subgroup Means at Retest

60 → 95 → 87
60 → 30 → 35

Figure 11–4 Hypothetical changes in IQ scores resulting from regression to the mean. The high-scoring and low-scoring subgroups regressed toward the mean of the entire group when they were retested.

Without matching, an investigator may not be able to say much about the results. Matching helps to alleviate the problem of confoundings in some cases, but then the possibility of regression artifacts arises—and many researchers seem unaware of this problem.

An excellent example of how conclusions should not be formed when matching is omitted is provided by a study of coaching on the SAT (Powers & Rock, 1998). Companies that sell coaching services claim that students will improve their SAT scores substantially by taking these courses. The basis for this claim is a comparison of test scores for coached students before (pretest) and after (posttest) coaching. However, this conclusion can and should be questioned, because examining only coached students is an inadequate quasi-experimental design. Biased estimates for the effects of coaching are likely, because coached and uncoached students may differ on many factors, which may account for results. For example, coached students may have parents with higher income and education, so a much better quasi-experimental design would be to compare coached and uncoached students who are matched on at least some of these potentially confounding variables.

Figure 11–5 shows pre- and posttest scores for coached and uncoached students (Powers & Rock, 1998). There is an improvement in test scores for coached students, but there is also an improvement for uncoached students. The net gain (coached gain minus uncoached gain) for coached students was only 8 points for verbal scores and 22 points for math scores. This gain is much lower than what has been claimed by coaching companies. However,

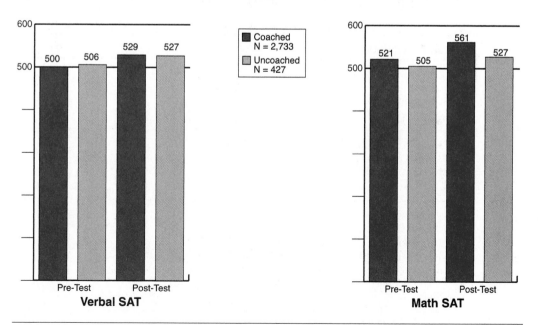

Figure 11–5   Pre- and posttest SAT scores. (Data from Powers & Rock 1998.)

even this modest gain does not tell the whole story, because the coached and uncoached students are unmatched.

Table 11–2 shows some ways in which coached and uncoached students differ. Any of these differences might bias estimates of coaching effectiveness. When appropriate statistical analyses are performed using matching data, the effect of coaching is small (Powers & Rock, 1998): about 7 points for verbal scores, and about 16 points for math scores. So, beware of results from observational studies comparing pre- and posttest results for an unmatched single group. For SAT scores, the claim that large improvements arise for a coached group of students is dubious.

When matching is a practical possibility, and when regression artifacts are evaluated, we can be somewhat more confident of conclusions from our results. However, we still have only a correlation, albeit a very carefully controlled one. Matching is useful, but it is not a cure-all. In our example involving schizophrenics, if the schizophrenics perform worse than the new matched control group of neurotics, can we then conclude that schizophrenia *produces* inferiority in language usage? No, we cannot. There could be something else, some other difference between the two groups. We can never be sure that we matched on the relevant variables. (Perhaps neurotics are superior in their use of language!)

Table 11–2 Some characteristics of coached and uncoached examinees

	Coached (%)	Uncoached (%)
Father's education		
High school or less	13	26
Some college	40	49
Some graduate school	47	25
Parent's income		
Less than $40,000	23	39
$40,000 to $80,000	34	43
More than $80,000	43	18
Ethnicity		
Asian American	21	8
White	58	72
African American	11	9
Mexican American	3	4
Other Hispanic	3	3
American Indian	1	1
Other	4	3

SOURCE: Powers and Rock (1998).

> ### CONCEPT SUMMARY
>
> ## Matching
>
> Be alert for
>
> - synergism
> - regression artifacts

Age as a Variable

One subject variable, age, deserves its own discussion for two reasons. First, developmental psychology is a popular and important part of scientific psychology. Second, age as a variable poses very difficult confoundings that have generated some interesting and powerful research designs.

Suppose we are interested in determining the effects of age on the ability to use two types of learning strategies. One strategy might improve recall (Tversky & Teiffer, 1976), because when our participants use this strategy correctly, they will be able to associate one thing with another. In remembering the names of simple objects (for example, *knife, tree,* and *cat*), participants recall one object that helps them recall another object (for example, recalling *cat* reminds them of *tree,* because cats climb trees, and trees make them think of *knife,* because they carve their initials in a tree with a knife). We will call this the *recall strategy.* The other strategy might help your participants to recognize things (as in a multiple-choice test). In this *recognize strategy,* participants look for minute differences among objects so that they can later specify which of several similar objects was actually shown to them.

Suppose we decide to see how children of different ages use these two strategies. How are we going to design our project? The most straightforward (and most likely) design is the **cross-sectional method.** Using this method, we would select children of different ages (for example, 5, 8, and 12 years) and then randomly assign half of each age group to one of the strategy conditions. Or, we could use the more time-consuming **longitudinal method.** Hence, we would test a participant when he or she was 5, then at 8, and then again at age 12. In the cross-sectional method, we figuratively cut through the age dimension, and in the longitudinal method, we follow a particular individual along the age dimension. These two developmental methods are quite often used in studies in which age is a variable, yet they both contain serious confoundings that could make the internal validity of the research highly suspect.

What are some of these serious confoundings? Before we can discuss them, we need to discuss age itself. Age is a subject variable, so it cannot be considered a true independent variable. Age is a dimension; in particular, it is a time dimension along which we can study behavior. Some developmental psychologists have suggested that we consider age as a dependent variable, because it is a variable that varies with other participant characteristics from birth to death (Wohwill, 1970).

In any event, we cannot directly vary age, so we must be wary of any concomitant variables associated with it. Different research designs have different confoundings. In the cross-sectional method, age is confounded with the generation of birth. Not only is one of the authors of this textbook 22 years older than his son, he and his son also differ in terms of the generations in which they were born, and generation itself is a complex variable. In this sense, the generation gap is real—someone born in 1942 is not just 22 years older than someone born in 1964. The older person was born into a different world populated by different people who had different attitudes and education than the counterparts (what the developmental psychologists call *cohorts*) of the younger person.

When we use the longitudinal method, we follow a particular individual who will maintain the same cohorts. With this method, therefore, we do not have to worry about the generation/age confounding. However, the longitudinal method confounds age with time of treatment or testing. If you test the memory of a child at age 5 and then at age 12, not only is the person seven years older on the second test, the world has changed in the interim. Using the longitudinal method, we might find that college students' attitudes about energy conservation in 2006 have changed since the subjects were 5 years old in 1992. Is the change in attitude owing to a change in age or to a change in the world?

Figure 11–6 shows some research designs that can be used when age is a variable. The **time-lag design** (the design indicated along the diagonal) aims at determining the effects of time of testing while holding age constant (only 19-year-olds are tested in this example). As is true of the cross-sectional design, the time-lag design confounds cohorts of the participants with the target variable.

Schaie (1977) has outlined many sophisticated designs to overcome the confoundings we have just described. One of these designs is illustrated in Fig-

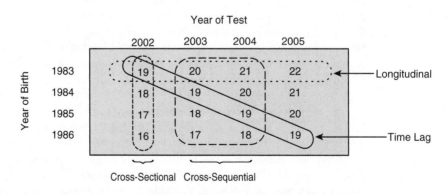

Figure 11–6   Some quasi-experimental designs used when age is a variable at the time of testing.

ure 11–6. The **cross-sequential design,** indicated by the central box, involves testing two or more age groups at two or more time periods. This design includes features of the other three designs we have mentioned. Participants of different ages are tested at the same time, as in the cross-sectional method; an individual is tested successively, as in the longitudinal method; and different participants of the same age are tested at different times, as in the time-lag design. In the cross-sequential design, therefore, the researcher can determine the effects of most of the potential confoundings. Consider just one example from Figure 11–6: the 20-year-old who was born in 1987. The effects of age are tested both longitudinally and sectionally (a 20-year-old is compared with participants of different ages in 2007 and is tested again in 2008). If the effects of age are the same in both of these comparisons, then we can rule out cohorts and time of testing as important confoundings.

The cross-sequential design is cumbersome. Many participants have to be tested over a period of time, which may make a research project impractical. Therefore, this design is not used as often as it probably should be. Most developmental researchers use the more manageable cross-sectional design.

A typical cross-sectional experiment has age as a quasi-independent variable, as well as another true independent variable. In the Tversky and Teiffer (1976) study outlined earlier, three age groups were tested on their ability to use the recall strategy and the recognize strategy. The recall strategy improved retention at all ages (5, 8, and 12), but the recognize strategy proved beneficial only to the oldest children. Such results are an example of an **interaction** (see Chapter 9), which means that the effects of one variable are dependent on the level of the other variable—the effects of type of strategy depended on the age of the participants.

The tactic of using age and a true independent variable in developmental research means that the researcher expects an interaction. Whatever variables are confounded with age might be differentially affected by a true independent variable (in the Tversky and Teiffer study, age was confounded with grade in school in addition to the usual confoundings associated with a cross-sectional design). The clever psychologist tries to pinpoint what components of age determine thought and behavior, and the search for particular interactions may help. The purpose of both the cross-sequential design and the search for interactions is to enhance the internal validity of developmental research. Age is a complex variable, and we must simplify it to have a valid analysis.

A final way that the internal validity of research with subject variables can be enhanced is to use construct validity as a mode of converging operation (see Chapter 13). Instead of searching for interactions to try to tease apart the true effects of a subject variable from those effects owing to variables that are correlated with it, we could coordinate the results with a particular theory. Highly refined theories of personality and child development use this technique. For example, Piaget developed a comprehensive theory of child development that makes particular predictions about the kinds of behavior exhibited by children at different stages of cognitive development (Piaget & Inhelder, 1969). Although these stages are partially associated with chronological age, they are presumed to be a function of maturation and experience. Thus, the stage of development, as shown in certain kinds of behaviors, and not age, is viewed as the causal factor. Piaget's theory specifies how and when these stages will occur, so that age-related behavioral differences should fit into the network of the theory. When the predicted changes do occur (that is, when they agree with Piaget's theory), we say that there is construct validity for the theory. The theory permits one to rule out the effects of a correlated variable (age, in this case) and converge on an explanation of why certain behaviors are observed.

CONCEPT SUMMARY

Threats to Internal Validity in Quasi-Experimental Research with Some Solutions

Research Procedure	Threat to Internal Validity	Ways to Enhance Internal Validity
Case studies	Source of causation; baseline "condition" maturation; history; selection bias	Deviant-case analysis (a nonequivalent control); detective work
Interrupted time series	Changes in participants and environment; delayed effects	Nonequivalent control group; detective work
Subject variables	Dimensions on which to match; regression artifacts	Matching; include true independent variable, and seek interactions
Age as a variable	Confoundings with time of testing; generation of birth	Cross-sequential design; include a true independent variable and seek an interaction; converging operations

Summary

1. In research that is internally valid, straightforward statements can be made about cause and effect. In quasi-experimental research, in which there is no direct control over the independent variables (they are examined after the fact), causal statements may not be possible because of confoundings.

2. Quasi-experiments have one or more ex post facto components: naturally occurring variables, subject variables, or both.

3. When there are natural treatments, problems such as history, maturation, selection bias, and nonequivalent control groups may confound the results.

4. One-shot case studies and the interrupted-time-series design are two quasi-experimental procedures with low internal validity. The researcher must be a good detective to determine the causal agents in these procedures, because mortality and delayed effects are threats to internal validity.

5. The researcher also needs to be a good detective when he or she tries to handle subject variables by matching participants on the basis of particular characteristics. Just what characteristics are to be matched often poses a difficult problem. Those characteristics also may regress toward the mean in many instances, and interactions among the matched variables may occur.

6. Age as a subject variable provides many real threats to internal validity, because it is confounded with numerous other factors.

7. Using the cross-sequential design and looking for interactions of age with true independent variables are two ways to enhance the internal validity of developmental research.

Key Concepts

cross-sectional method (271)
cross-sequential design (273)
history (254)
interaction (273)
interrupted-time-series design (260)
longitudinal method (271)

matching (266)
maturation (254)
mortality (261)
nonequivalent control group (255)
observation-treatment-observation (254)
one-shot case study (255)

quasi-experiment (254)
regression artifact (267)
regression to the mean (267)
selection bias (255)
subject variable (264)
synergism (267)
time-lag design (272)

Exercises

1. [*Special Exercise.*] A considerable amount of evidence indicates there is an inverse relationship between birth order and intelligence (Zajonc & Marcus, 1975). Birth order refers to the order in which children enter the family unit (first-born, second-born, and so on). Intelligence tends to be lower for later-born children than for the earlier ones. List as many factors as you can that might be confounded with birth order. How might you determine which of these factors is important in influencing intelligence? In other words, how do we enhance internal validity when birth order is the variable? What quasi-experiments can be done?

2. The *Journal of Applied Psychology* often reports studies that used an interrupted-time-series design. Examine several recent issues, and note, in particular, any control conditions that are included.

3. Age as a variable in geriatric research (the study of old age) is often more difficult to analyze than in child development studies. Why?

4. Discuss the ways in which mortality, selection bias, history, and maturation can threaten the internal validity of quasi-experiments.

Suggested Resources

Donald T. Campbell has written a great deal about quasi-experimental research. The best place to begin is with the first book listed here. More detail is presented in the second. Campbell, D. T., & Stanley, J. C. (1966). *Experimental and quasi-experimental designs for research.* Chicago: Rand McNally. Cook, T. D., & Campbell, D. T. (1979). *Quasi-experimentation: Design and analysis issues for field settings.* Chicago: Rand McNally.

A more current book is Rosenbaum, P. R. (1995). *Observational studies.* New York: Springer Verlag. This is an advanced statistical text that presents considerable detail about quasi-experiments.

Web Resources

An application of quasi-experimental design to field studies involving the capture and recapture of animals can be found at: www.stat.sfu.ca/~cschwarz/ papers/2000/euring/quasi.experiment.pdf

The Wadsworth Workshops consider nonexperiment research here: http://www.wadsworth.com/ psychology_d/templates/student_resources/workshops/res_methd/non_exper/non_exper_01.html

A Quasi-Experiment

Try these quasi-experiments as a follow-up to the correlational research described in the Psychology in Action section for Chapter 5. The project there dealt with the relationship between amount of sleep and tension or migraine headaches.

If you recorded demographic data (age, sex, year in school) for each of your participants in the sleep/headache research, you can do a quasi-experiment using one of your demographic variables to define your independent variable. For example, you could compare the number of headaches reported by men and women. Another quasi-experiment could examine the amount of sleep obtained by freshmen, sophomores, juniors, and seniors. There are other possibilities, which we will allow you to figure out.

Although these quasi-experiments may look like ordinary between-subjects experiments, do not forget that you have not manipulated an independent variable—your groups here are determined by selection, not manipulation. Thus, you need to be cautious about making causal statements.

The Practice of Scientific Psychology

This section contains crucial material on the initial and final aspects of practicing psychological science. The information has been presented so that these chapters can be read in any order and at almost any time during the course. The purpose of this flexibility is to allow you and your instructor to use this information whenever needed to meet the goals of your course. Chapter 12 (on ethics) contains important information that should be considered before undertaking a research project. The final two chapters concern interpreting and then presenting the data in written or oral form, which will allow you to complete a research project.

CHAPTER 12

Conducting Ethical Research

Follow the American Psychological Association's guidelines for research with humans and animals.

Ethical Considerations in Research

- Is my project designed in accordance with contemporary ethical standards?
- Will my human participants be treated in a dignified fashion without having their personal freedom violated or their physical or emotional health damaged?
- Will I treat my animal subjects in a humane fashion?
- Do I understand the ethical principles behind drug research?
- Have I read and understood the ethical principles espoused by the American Psychological Association?
- Am I an honest scientist?

The scientific enterprise creates ethical dilemmas. Scientific knowledge and techniques that can be used for human betterment can be turned to manipulative and exploitative purposes as well. Just as results of research in atomic physics can be used for the treatment of cancer as well as for destructive weapons, so methods discovered to reduce prejudice toward minority groups, to eliminate troublesome behavior problems, or to facilitate learning in school may also be used to manipulate political allegiance, to create artificial wants, or to reconcile the victims of social injustice to their fate. The double-edged potential of scientific knowledge poses ethical problems for all scientists. To the extent that psychological research deals with important problems and potent methods, psychologists must recognize and alert others to the fact that the potential for misuse of research increases its potential for constructive application (American Psychological Association [APA], 1982, p. 16).

▶ Research with Human Participants

The quotation introducing this chapter is from a publication of the APA. It comes from a preamble to a lengthy discussion of ethical principles covering all aspects of psychology and is presented in abbreviated form here to emphasize the ethical obligations of researchers in all areas of science. These obligations are straightforward in principle but difficult to implement. We examine both the ethical principles and the problems associated with putting them into practice in psychology. Psychologists worry about the ethics of research involving both human participants and animals. Although some of this concern is selfish, owing to fear of restriction of research funds and loss of access to subject populations, most psychologists are ethical persons who have no desire to inflict harm on anyone. The mad researcher, who will do anything to obtain data, is largely fictional.

An experimenter cannot be completely impartial and objective in judging the ethical issues concerning his or her own work, so most universities and research institutions have peer committees that judge the ethicality of proposed research. Indeed, any federally funded research must be approved by such a committee before any funding is granted.

Various ethical issues become obvious in the context of an actual research project. Imagine you are a psychologist interested in determining to what extent depressive feelings influence how well people remember. One very important reason why you want to study this topic is that depression is a fairly common emotional problem among college students, and you would like to determine how this problem could affect academic performance. You decide to do a tightly controlled laboratory experiment to determine the effects of depression on memory. You want to induce depression in some of your participants and then compare their memory to that of other participants who were not induced to be depressed. You induce depression in your subjects by a procedure devised by Velten (1968). In this procedure, participants read aloud 60 self-referent statements associated with the mood in question. In this case, the participant reads statements that are supposed to induce depression, beginning with relatively mild ones, such as "Today is neither better nor worse than any other day," and progressing to more extreme ones, such as "I feel so bad that I would like to go to sleep and never wake up." Velten's procedure induces a mild, temporary depression. Participants report feeling depressed, and their behavior suffers on a variety of tasks.

Many details of this experiment have not been specified, but it should be obvious that the welfare of the research participants in this study could be jeopardized (for complete details of this experiment, see Elmes, Chapman, & Selig, 1984). Inducing a negative mood (such as depression) in college students could have disastrous effects on their social and intellectual functioning. How can you, as an ethical researcher, try to preserve and protect the fundamental human rights of your participants? What would you do to protect their welfare and at the same time conduct an internally valid experiment?

In a review of research on mood and memory, Bower and Forgas (2000) listed a number of studies in which depression was induced in college students. In some experiments, a happy mood was induced in participants. Do the ethical considerations depend on the kind of mood—happy or sad—that is induced in a participant? Also, researchers have used several different mood-induction procedures in their experiments. Besides the Velten (1968) procedure just described, hypnosis and music have been used to induce a depressed or happy mood. Do ethical considerations depend on the mood-induction technique? These questions concerning mood-induction research illustrate how ethical issues associated with psychological research may vary according to the specific circumstances in the experiment.

The APA (2002) has provided ethical guidelines for researchers. The association has outlined 10 general principles governing the conduct of research with human participants. To consider how the welfare of the students was protected in those studies, we examine the principles that guide research involving human participants (the welfare of animals in research will be examined later in this chapter). *You should read and understand these ethical principles before you conduct a research project with human participants.*

8.01 Institutional Approval
When institutional approval is required, psychologists provide accurate information about their research proposals and obtain approval prior to conducting the research. They conduct the research in accordance with the approved research protocol.

8.02 Informed Consent to Research
(a) When obtaining informed consent as required in Standard 3.10, Informed Consent, psychologists inform participants about (1) the purpose of the research, expected duration, and procedures; (2) their right to decline to participate and to withdraw from the research once participation has begun; (3) the foreseeable consequences of declining or withdrawing; (4) reasonably foreseeable factors that may be expected to influence their willingness to participate such as potential risks, discomfort, or adverse effects; (5) any prospective research benefits; (6) limits of confidentiality; (7) incentives for participation; and (8) whom to contact for questions about the research and research participants' rights. They provide opportunity for the prospective participants to ask questions and receive answers. (See also Standards 8.03, Informed Consent for Recording Voices and Images in Research; 8.05, Dispensing With Informed Consent for Research; and 8.07, Deception in Research.)

(b) Psychologists conducting intervention research involving the use of experimental treatments clarify to participants at the outset of the research (1) the experimental nature of the treatment; (2) the services that will or will not be available to the control group(s) if appropriate; (3) the means by which assignment to treatment and control groups will be made; (4) available treatment alternatives if an individual does not wish to participate in the research or wishes to withdraw once a study has begun; and (5) compensation for or monetary costs of participating including, if appropriate, whether reimbursement from the

participant or a third-party payor will be sought. (See also Standard 8.02a, Informed Consent to Research.)

8.03 Informed Consent for Recording Voices and Images in Research
Psychologists obtain informed consent from research participants prior to recording their voices or images for data collection unless (1) the research consists solely of naturalistic observations in public places, and it is not anticipated that the recording will be used in a manner that could cause personal identification or harm, or (2) the research design includes deception, and consent for the use of recording is obtained during debriefing. (See also Standard 8.07, Deception in Research.)

8.04 Client/Patient, Student, and Subordinate Research Participants
(a) When psychologists conduct research with clients/patients, students, or subordinates as participants, psychologists take steps to protect the prospective participants from adverse consequences of declining or withdrawing from participation.

(b) When research participation is a course requirement or an opportunity for extra credit, the prospective participant is given the choice of equitable alternative activities.

8.05 Dispensing With Informed Consent for Research
Psychologists may dispense with informed consent only (1) where research would not reasonably be assumed to create distress or harm and involves (a) the study of normal educational practices, curricula, or classroom management methods conducted in educational settings; (b) only anonymous questionnaires, naturalistic observations, or archival research for which disclosure of responses would not place participants at risk of criminal or civil liability or damage their financial standing, employability, or reputation, and confidentiality is protected; or (c) the study of factors related to job or organization effectiveness con-

ducted in organizational settings for which there is no risk to participants' employability, and confidentiality is protected or (2) where otherwise permitted by law or federal or institutional regulations.

8.06 Offering Inducements for Research Participation
(a) Psychologists make reasonable efforts to avoid offering excessive or inappropriate financial or other inducements for research participation when such inducements are likely to coerce participation.

(b) When offering professional services as an inducement for research participation, psychologists clarify the nature of the services, as well as the risks, obligations, and limitations. (See also Standard 6.05, Barter With Clients/Patients.)

8.07 Deception in Research
(a) Psychologists do not conduct a study involving deception unless they have determined that the use of deceptive techniques is justified by the study's significant prospective scientific, educational, or applied value and that effective nondeceptive alternative procedures are not feasible.

(b) Psychologists do not deceive prospective participants about research that is reasonably expected to cause physical pain or severe emotional distress.

(c) Psychologists explain any deception that is an integral feature of the design and conduct of an experiment to participants as early as is feasible, preferably at the conclusion of their participation, but no later than at the conclusion of the data collection, and permit participants to withdraw their data. (See also Standard 8.08, Debriefing.)

8.08 Debriefing
(a) Psychologists provide a prompt opportunity for participants to obtain appropriate information about the nature, results, and conclusions of the research, and they take reasonable steps to correct any misconceptions that participants may have of which the psychologists are aware.

(b) If scientific or humane values justify delaying or withholding this information, psychologists take reasonable measures to reduce the risk of harm.

(c) When psychologists become aware that research procedures have harmed a participant, they take reasonable steps to minimize the harm.

8.09 Humane Care and Use of Animals in Research
(a) Psychologists acquire, care for, use, and dispose of animals in compliance with current federal, state, and local laws and regulations, and with professional standards.

(b) Psychologists trained in research methods and experienced in the care of laboratory animals supervise all procedures involving animals and are responsible for ensuring appropriate consideration of their comfort, health, and humane treatment.

(c) Psychologists ensure that all individuals under their supervision who are using animals have received instruction in research methods and in the care, maintenance, and handling of the species being used, to the extent appropriate to their role. (See also Standard 2.05, Delegation of Work to Others.)

(d) Psychologists make reasonable efforts to minimize the discomfort, infection, illness, and pain of animal subjects.

(e) Psychologists use a procedure subjecting animals to pain, stress, or privation only when an alternative procedure is unavailable and the goal is justified by its prospective scientific, educational, or applied value.

(f) Psychologists perform surgical procedures under appropriate anesthesia and follow techniques to avoid infection and minimize pain during and after surgery.

(g) When it is appropriate that an animal's life be terminated, psychologists proceed rapidly, with an effort to minimize pain and in accordance with accepted procedures.

SOURCE: American Psychological Association. (2002). *Ethical principles of psychologists and code of conduct.* Copyright © 2002 by the American Psychological Association. Adapted with permission.

These principles are intended to protect the welfare of research participants, and they can be summarized by noting that the experimenter has an obligation to minimize harm to the participant. The participant should be warned ahead of time if there is potential harm; the participant should be able to withdraw if he or she chooses; and deception should be used carefully. The experimenter is obligated to undo any harm, and the results should remain confidential with regard to a particular participant unless agreed with the participant otherwise. These principles need to be reckoned with in any research project.

Informed Consent and Deception

The ethical researcher informs participants beforehand of all aspects of the research that might reasonably be expected to influence willingness to participate and explains all other aspects of the research about which participants inquire. This means that the participants must be forewarned about those aspects of the research that may have detrimental effects. In most psychological research, participants receive complete information about what they will be asked to do during the research project, so that they can give **informed consent** about their understanding of the possible problems associated with participation. Participants are rarely misled as to the nature of the experiences they will have during the experiment. Furthermore, an experimenter usually states the purpose of the experimental procedure truthfully. Nonetheless, experimenters sometimes mislead participants about the true purpose of an experiment. This false description is often referred to as a "cover story." This kind of **deception** is usually done to control participant reactivity. For instance, a researcher interested in whether people behave more assertively in same-gender groups than in mixed-gender groups tells people that they will be working on problems that require group cooperation. They are also told that the purpose of the experiment is to evaluate the difficulty of these tasks. The researcher is concerned that participants' behavior might change if they know the real purpose of the experiment. In this case, information regarding the hypothesis under test probably will not change anyone's decision to participate, but this information might change performance on the task. Deception of this sort, although usually harmless, must be considered carefully, because the participant's consent is not fully informed. A person might choose not to participate in a particular experiment because he or she does not approve of the purpose of the experiment.

Even more rare than deception concerning the purpose of an experiment is deception concerning the experiences that the participant will have during the experiment. Such deception is, unfortunately, necessary to answer some research questions. For example, if an investigator wants to see how well people recall information that they are not actively trying to remember, he or she might not inform participants that the experiment requires a memory test. Obviously, the omission of information prevents participants from giving fully informed consent.

Thus, whenever a research question requires deception, the ethical researcher faces a dilemma. Obviously, people must be warned if the procedure will place them in serious danger of physical or psychological harm. Deception in such cases is clearly unethical. When a procedure involves only minor risks, on the other hand, the decision regarding full disclosure to participants is more difficult. In all cases, the potential benefits of the research must be weighed against the actual and potential costs to the participant. Only when the potential benefits of the experiment far exceed any risks to the participant can deception be justified. Even then, participants should always receive as much information as possible, and they should know that they can end their participation at any time without negative consequences.

Let us reexamine the depression and memory experiment we discussed earlier, focusing on the question of informed consent. The people who signed up to participate were told that some of the things they were going to do in the experiment might make them feel unhappy, and they were given the opportunity to refuse to participate. The specific nature of the manipulation, such as the Velten technique and who was going to serve in the experimental group, was not disclosed ahead of time. People may have reacted unusually if they knew all the details. Because the effects of the mood induction were known to be temporary, the researchers believed that partial information was enough to permit informed consent. Here, although some information was omitted, participants were not misled about what to expect in the experiment.

The issues surrounding informed consent and deception often require considerable thought and deliberation to arrive at ethical solutions. Indeed, researchers continue to debate the appropriateness of deception in psychological experiments (for example, see Bröder, 1998; Kimmel, 1998; Korn, 1998; Ortmann & Hertwig, 1997, 1998; and Pittenger, 2002). Individual researchers are seldom left to their own devices to make these decisions. Supposedly, every research institution in this country has a standing committee that must approve any experimental procedure involving human beings. These committees try to ensure the ethical treatment of experimental participants. We discuss these boards in more detail later.

In sum, fully informed consent is the norm in most areas of psychology. Occasionally, some information is withheld or participants are misled to prevent subject reactivity. In such cases, the experimenter, as well as members of institutional review boards (discussed in detail later), take great care in deciding whether the benefits of the procedure outweigh the risks to the participants.

Freedom to Withdraw

As mentioned briefly in the previous section, participants should be allowed to decline to participate or to withdraw at any time. Everyone would agree that the mad scientist who straps participants to the chair is unethical. Moreover, few people would deny that people who are unhappy about participating should have the **freedom to withdraw**. Where, then, is the ethical dilemma? The major problem revolves around the definition of a willing volunteer participant. Consider the participant pool for the depression and memory experiment: undergraduate students (mostly freshmen and sophomores) taking introductory psychology. They sign up to participate in experiments, and they usually receive some sort of course credit for their service. Are they volunteering when they sign up, or are they under some sort of coercion that they have inferred from the situation? If the students actually receive extra credit, they are likely to be acting on their own volition. If they must participate as part of a course requirement, then the freedom to participate or not is less obvious. When students are required to participate, they should have some optional way of fulfilling the requirement, such as writing a paper or attending a special lecture. The point, then, is to provide freedom to participate or not as they choose.

Generally, when the pool of potential participants is a captive audience, such as students, prisoners, military recruits, and employees of the experimenter, the ethical researcher considers the individual's freedom to withdraw or to participate. In the depression and memory experiment, volunteer students were recruited with the lure of extra credit (participation was not mandatory). When they signed up, they were forewarned about the possibility of unhappiness (they could agree to participate or not). The instructions at the beginning of the experiment informed them that they had the option of quitting at any time and still receiving full extra credit (they were free to withdraw).

Protection from Harm and Debriefing

The APA suggests an additional safeguard to provide research participants with **protection from harm.** Participants should have a way to contact the investigator following participation in the research. Even the most scrupulously ethical project of the minimal-risk sort may have unintended aftereffects. Thus, the participant should be able to receive help or advice from the researcher if problems should arise. We have had participants cry (out of frustration and embarrassment) during what was supposed to be a standard, innocuous memory experiment. Those participants may have carried away from the experiment a negative self-image or strong feelings of resentment toward the experimenter in particular or research in general.

Because of such unintended effects, the prudent researcher provides detailed **debriefing,** which means that the investigator explains the general purposes of the research. This is particularly important when students have participated as part of a course requirement; we believe it is the experimenter's responsibility to make the experiment an educational experience for students of psychology. Regardless, the researcher should always describe the manipulations so that any questions or misunderstandings may be removed.

Let us apply the principles of debriefing and protection from harm to the depression and memory experiment. At the end of that project, the participants were given a list of phone numbers of people who could be contacted in the unlikely event that the participants felt depressed following the experiment. The list of contacts included the principal investigator, a counselor, and the dean of student affairs and his assistant. Also, the day after participation, each participant who had read the depression-inducing statements was phoned by one of the experimenters, who tried to determine whether the participant was having any negative aftereffects.

The participants received thorough debriefing. They were told about the mood-induction procedure and how its effects were temporary. In addition, other details of the experimental design and rationale were outlined, and any questions the participants had were answered.

Removing Harmful Consequences

Debriefing participants and giving them contact numbers may not be sufficient in a risky project. If a participant could suffer long-term consequences as a result of serving in a research project, the investigator has the responsibility for **removing harmful consequences**. The feelings of resentful participants may be difficult to reverse, because the resentment may be unintended and undetected. However, where the risks are known, the ethical investigator must take steps to minimize them.

Before the debriefing in the depression and memory experiment, the participants read a series of self-referent statements designed to induce elation. This exercise was supposed to counteract the effects of the negative mood induced earlier. Then the participants were questioned about their current feelings, and they were also asked to sign a statement that said they left the experiment feeling no worse than when they began it. All participants signed the statement, but had they not, a contingent plan was to keep them in the laboratory under the supervision of one of the experimenters until they felt better.

Confidentiality

What a participant does in an experiment should be confidential unless otherwise agreed with the participant. An ethical researcher does not run around saying things like: "Bobby Freshman is stupid; he did more poorly than anyone else in my experiment." Also, personal information about particular participants, such as their attitudes toward premarital sex or their family income, should not be revealed without their permission. The principle of **confidentiality** seems straightforward, but a researcher can be faced with an ethical dilemma when trying to uphold it.

This dilemma arose in the depression and memory experiment. The experimenter was confronted with an ethical problem, because he believed it was necessary to violate the principle of confidentiality to uphold the principle of protection from harm. How did this dilemma develop? One of the first tasks of the participants was to answer some questions concerning their mental health. They indicated whether they were currently seeking professional help for a personal problem. If they were, they provided some details about the problem and the therapeutic procedure. The participants were assured that their answers were confidential. Then the students completed a clinical test that assessed their current level of depression. If a participant indicated that he or she was being treated for depression and scored high on the test, the experiment was discontinued at that point. The researchers wanted to minimize harm and maximize frank, open responding by assuring the students of the confidential nature of their responses and by using the depression test to prevent a depressed person from becoming even more depressed by the mood-induction procedure. Nevertheless, an ethical dilemma arose. In the course of the experiment, two students scored very high on the depression test, and one of them was not undergoing therapy. Because the test was known to be a reliable and valid predictor of clinically serious depression, the principal investigator believed that it was necessary to warn one of the college's counselors about the two students who appeared to have very high levels of depression. Then, under the guise of a routine interview, the counselor talked to these students.

This type of dilemma occurs frequently in research. To adhere to one ethical principle may necessitate violating another. Easy choices vanish when this happens. In the case we mentioned, if the highly depressed students had suspected that the investigator had betrayed their confidence, permanent resentment and mistrust could have resulted. On the other hand, the investigator could not ignore that these students, particularly the one not undergoing therapy, were in severe distress. At the time, ensuring that the students received help seemed much more important than upholding their right to confidentiality.

As our example illustrates, ethical decisions must sometimes be made on the basis of pragmatic concerns. In other words, people involved in making decisions about a research project must focus on how best to protect the participants and, at the same time, conduct a meaningful, valid project. To see how difficult some ethical decisions can be, examine the Application.

The responsibility for ethical practice rests on the researcher, review boards, and journal editors who review research for publication. In limited instances, a researcher might justify deception, concealment, and breaches of confidentiality. However, such questionable ethical practices must be avoided if possible. Ethical violations are not prerequisites of good research.

CONCEPT SUMMARY

When conducting research with human participants, an ethical researcher

- ensures that participants are fully informed as to the experimental procedure and give their consent before beginning the experiment.
- uses deception only when there is no other way to answer the research question and only when the potential benefit of the experiment far exceeds any risk to the participants.
- ensures that participants feel free to withdraw from the experiment at any time without fear of penalty.
- removes any harmful consequences resulting from the experiment, including long-term consequences.
- maintains confidentiality regarding information about participants acquired during the course of the experiment.

APPLICATION

Ethical Research Projects

Imagine you direct an ethics review board and must decide whether to allow the following examples of proposed research:

1. An environmental psychologist sits in a crowded library and keeps detailed records of seating patterns.

2. An environmental psychologist makes videotapes of seating patterns in a library. These tapes are maintained indefinitely, and library patrons do not know they have been filmed.

3. An experimental psychologist tells students that she is interested in their reading comprehension when, in reality, she is recording the speed of their responses rather than their comprehension.

4. A social psychologist is studying bystander intervention in a liquor store. Permission has been obtained from the store manager. In clear view of a patron, an experimenter "steals" a bottle of liquor. A second experimenter approaches the patron and asks, "Did you see him steal that bottle?"

5. A social psychologist connects surface electrodes to male participants, with their prior approval. These participants are told that the electrodes are connected to a meter in front of them that measures sexual arousal. In reality, the meter is controlled by the experimenter. Participants are then shown slides of nude males and females. The meter gives high readings for pictures of males,

leading the participants to believe they have latent homosexual tendencies.

People do not agree about which of these examples constitute(s) ethical or unethical research, and we will not presume to give you definitive answers. Informal discussion with our colleagues reveals that only the first example received unequivocal clearance as an ethical project. Because the psychologist merely observed strangers, informed consent did not seem necessary. Any individual, psychologist or not, could easily observe these same people in the library. Our colleagues rated the potential harm as extremely small.

Some people raised objections to every other example. Number 2 invaded personal privacy, because the tapes were not erased after data analysis. Most colleagues accepted number 3 only if the experimenter carefully debriefed participants by explaining the nature and reasons for the deception. Example number 4 describes an actual project in which a patron denied seeing the theft and then called the police as soon as she left the store. The investigator had to go to the police station and bail out the experimenters. Number 5 describes another real experiment, and our colleagues did not think it was ethical, even with debriefing. Even immediate, extensive debriefing probably could not remove the potential psychological harm of making a participant believe that he had hidden homosexual tendencies. Devising an ethical research project can be difficult.

▶ Ethics in Research with Animals

Although the majority of research in contemporary psychology focuses on humans, an appreciable number of studies focus on animals (Miller, 1985). Animals are often used to answer questions that would be impossible or impractical to answer using human beings. Some people believe, however, that animals should not be used in various kinds of research (Bowd, 1980; Bowd & Shapiro, 1993). For example, Rollin (1985) argued that if the concept of legal and moral rights can be applied to human research, it can also be applied in the same way to animal research. He suggested that the status of research with animals needs elevation to that of human participants, with many of the same rules that govern human research being applied to animals. Recently, reports in the media have discussed the purported mistreatment of laboratory animals and the attempts of animal-rights advocates to limit the use of animals in research. Therefore, a consideration of why animals are used in research is important, and an understanding of the ethical safeguards for animals is necessary.

Animals are also the subjects of research because they are interesting and because they form an important part of the natural world. The number of bird-watchers, amateur naturalists, and comparative psychologists and ethologists readily attest to the interest. More important in terms of ethical concerns, however, is that animals serve as convenient, highly controlled models for humans *and* other animals. The APA (2003) provides additional information regarding the use of animals in psychological research.

Arguments against Research with Animals

Ethics prohibit experimentally induced brain damage in human beings, preclude deliberate separation of a human infant from its parents, forbid testing of unknown drugs on human beings, and generally exclude dangerous and irreversible manipulations on human beings. Animal-rights advocates believe that research on animals should have the same prohibitions. According to these advocates, researchers need to uphold the rights of both human beings and animals; they believe, for example, that experimental destruction of a monkey's brain is as ethically reprehensible as the destruction of the brain of a human being. Three points summarize the animal-rights advocates' position: (a) Animals feel pain, and their lives can be destroyed, as is true of humans (Roberts, 1971); (b) destroying or harming any living thing is dehumanizing to the human scientist (Roberts, 1971); and (c) claims about scientific progress being helped by animal research are a form of racism and, like interracial bigotry, are completely unwarranted and unethical. Neglecting the rights and interests of other species has been called **speciesism** by Singer (1978). Most experimental psychologists, especially psychobiologists, have strong reservations about the validity of these points. Let us consider each in turn.

Arguments for Research with Animals

The first point is that animals feel pain and suffering. Certainly, this is true, but ethical standards exist in all scientific disciplines that use animals as research subjects. A major portion of these principles concerns the proscription of undue pain and inhumane treatment. No ethical psychologist would deliberately mistreat research animals, nor would an ethical psychologist deliberately inflict undue harm on an animal. When pain and suffering are inflicted on an animal, it is only after considerable deliberation by the scientist and the appropriate ethics review boards. Such deliberations weigh the suffering of the animal against the potential benefits of the experiment. Only when the benefits far exceed the harm is the experiment approved and conducted. Finally, an important point to make about behavioral research on animals is that much of it does not involve pain or physical harm to the animals being studied.

The second plank of the animal-rights platform is that the destruction of any living thing is dehumanizing to the human scientist. Presumably, plants are not meant to be included here, for as human beings, we must destroy plants, if not animals, to survive. Even if this proscription against killing living things is limited to animals, it has a number of serious implications beyond eliminating animal research. If one uses this argument against animal research, then one should not eat meat of any kind. Likewise, one should not use any products derived from the destruction of animals (for example, leather). Finally, if the destruction of animals is dehumanizing, then is it not also dehumanizing to benefit from the destruction of animals? If so, then a true believer in animal rights should forsake most of the wonders of modern medicine, because virtually all of it has benefited from animal research. However, consistent adherence to a belief in animal rights is often difficult. The difficulty is illustrated in a survey of activists who attended a large rally in support of animal rights (Plous, 1991). Plous reported that a substantially higher percentage of activists claimed to be vegetarians or vegans (people who eat no animal products, including milk and eggs) than did people in general. Many activists said they did not use leather goods. Nevertheless, a majority of animal-rights activists (53%) reported that they bought leather goods, ingested animal flesh, or both.

Finally, there is the charge that scientific progress at the expense of animals is simply speciesism, the belief that the sacrifice of members of other species is justified if our species benefits. As a criticism against animal research, this argument ignores the fact that a significant amount of animal research benefits the welfare of animals. For example, Miller (1985) points out that research on learned taste aversion in rats has led to new, nonlethal means of keeping coyotes away from sheep and crows away from crops. Similarly, research on how hatchling ducks imprint on human caretakers has been used to better prepare artificially incubated condor chicks for the wild.

In any case, even if using animals for the benefit of human beings is a form of speciesism, it is doubtful that many people would give up the benefits already achieved or the possible future benefits to be derived from animal research. Consider this quote from Robert J. White, an eminent neuroscientist and neurosurgeon, who conducted research on monkeys that involved removing the brain of the animal: "As I write this article, I relive my vivid experiences yesterday when I removed at operation a large tumor from the cerebellum and brain stem of a small child. This was a surgical undertaking that would have been impossible a few decades ago, highly dangerous a few years ago, but is today thanks to extensive experimentation on the brains of lower animals, routinely accomplished with a high degree of safety" (White, 1971, p. 504).

In addition to the benefits of experimental neurosurgery, numerous benefits are derived from behavioral research with animals. Overmier and Carroll (2001) note that psychological experiments with animals have led directly to benefits in the treatment of such diverse psychological problems as phobias, anxiety disorders, depression, eating disorders, alcoholism and drug addiction, and sleep disorders. Moreover, animal experiments have given rise to behavioral technologies, such as biofeedback, that have been used to help individuals with neuromuscular disorders regain control over their bodies. Psychological research with animals has also demonstrated experimentally the link between psychological stress and physical health. Other studies have demonstrated that the detrimental effects of physically separating an infant from its parents—as is necessary when a newborn must be placed in an incubator to sustain its life—can be largely reversed simply by stroking the infant during three 15-minute periods during the day. Miller describes a variety of other benefits that have arisen from behavioral research on animals, his point being that the benefits of psychological experimentation on animals are substantial, contrary to the claims made by some animal-rights activists (Plous, 1991).

Gallup and Suarez (1985) reviewed the rationale, extent, and use of animals in psychological research. They considered the possible alternatives and concluded that in many cases there is no viable alternative to the use of animals in psychological research. Professional support for the use of animals in both research and teaching has remained high even as the use of animals in research has declined over time (Rowan & Loew, 1995). Eighty percent of respondents in a recent survey of APA members indicated general support for animal research (Plous, 1996a). Similar results were obtained from a sample of undergraduate psychology majors (Plous, 1996b). It should be noted, however, that the psychologists did not uniformly support all animal research. Many disapproved of studies involving pain or death, and the majority supported federal protection for rats, mice, and birds equivalent to that provided for primates (Plous, 1996a).

Guidelines for Use of Animals in Research

Psychologists have focused on the humane and ethical treatment of animals used in research for a long time (Greenough, 1992). For example, one early statement of humane treatment (Young, 1928) asserted that animals used as research subjects "shall be kindly treated, properly fed, and their surroundings kept in the best possible sanitary condition" (p. 487). This concern is echoed in the modern guidelines of the APA (2003) governing research with animals, which state as a general principle:

Psychology encompasses a broad range of areas of research and applied endeavors. Important parts of these endeavors are teaching and research on the behavior of nonhuman animals, which contribute to the understanding of basic principles underlying behavior and to advancing the welfare of both human and nonhuman animals. Clearly, psychologists should conduct their teaching and research in a manner consonant with relevant laws and regulations. In addition, ethical concerns mandate that psychologists should consider the costs and benefits of procedures involving animals before proceeding with the research. (p. 1)

As in virtually any human enterprise, abuses of humane treatment sometimes occur in the use of animals in research. However, these abuses go against the standard practice of animal researchers. Ethical researchers treat animals humanely. When people uncover unethical treatment of animals, they should seek to punish the researchers in question. Just because some abuses occur, it does not follow that all animal research should be prohibited. The typical view of animal-rights activists (Plous, 1991) derives from a philosophical position that prohibits the use of animals for human benefit as a general rule, not just for research. You must decide for yourself what attitude to take toward animal research, but the importance of the issue necessitates that you critically consider each side of the debate and its implications.

The following principle outlines the primary considerations for researchers using animal subjects as specified in the APA (2002) ethics code. A more detailed specification of principles such as this is found in the APA's (2003) *Guidelines for Ethical Conduct in the Care and Use of Animals.*

8.09 Humane Care and Use of Animals in Research

APA recommends that seven factors be considered for ethical and humane treatment of animals. Psychologists comply with all legal strictures and professional codes. All use of animals is supervised by researchers experienced in testing and maintaining laboratory animals. All people using animals in research have appropriate training for the animals' care, use, and maintenance. Psychologists make efforts to maintain comfort and health and to minimize pain of animals. In addition, pain and discomfort should only be imposed on animals if no alternative is available and "the goal is justified by its prospective scientific, educational, or applied value" (APA, 2002; p. 12). If surgery is used, then care is taken to maintain health and minimize pain. "When it is appropriate that an animals life be terminated, psychologists proceed rapidly, with an effort to minimize pain and in accordance with accepted procedures" (p. 12).

> ► **CONCEPT SUMMARY**
>
> When deciding whether to engage in research with animals, you should consider
>
> - whether you accept the proposal that animals deserve to be treated as equivalent to humans and the full implications of this philosophical position
>
> When conducting research with animal subjects, an ethical researcher
>
> - ensures that the research is supervised by a trained psychologist
> - subjects animals to pain or discomfort only when no alternative procedure is available and the knowledge to be gained justifies the suffering of the animal
> - makes every effort to minimize any pain or discomfort associated with the experiment

► Scientific Fraud

In Chapter 1, we discussed inadvertent researcher bias. Here, in the context of ethics, we consider deliberate bias by scientists—**fraud**. When scientists engage in research, they expend substantial time and effort, and their prestige and career advancement often depend on its success. Under these pressures, some scientists are not completely honest in their treatment of their experiments and their data. Instances of deliberate fraud take many forms (Responsible Science, 1992) and include sloppy research practices such as not keeping adequate records, "fudging" or "cooking" data to make results look better, and fabrication of data, which includes reporting observations that were never made (also see Kohn, 1986). A survey of science doctoral candidates and science faculty indicates that these kinds of fraudulent practices occur with enough frequency to merit some concern about the ethical status of science (Swazey, Anderson, & Lewis, 1993).

A frequently cited example of fudging is the case of Sir Cyril Burt. He was a well-respected psychologist who studied the role of heredity in intelligence. He published several papers reporting data collected on identical twins, some reared together and others reared apart. The data were collected in the period 1913–1932. In three papers, he reported a correlation in IQ scores of .944 for twins reared together and of .771 for twins reared apart. Although the correlations were identical for the three papers, each reported an appreciably different number of participants. That the correlations remained unchanged despite the addition of new participants is extremely improbable. This evidence, along with other suspicious facts, led some scientists and historians to conclude that Burt's data were not completely honest (Kohn, 1986; Broad & Wade, 1982).

There are a number of examples of forging data. A famous case is that of the "Piltdown Man" discovered in England in 1912. The Piltdown Man consisted of a skull of humanoid appearance and an apelike jawbone. The bones supposedly represented the "missing link" between apes and humans. The finding was widely, although not universally, accepted for 57 years, until suspicious scientists used a variety of dating methods to show that the jaw was of modern origin, whereas the skull was substantially older. The scientists discovered that the jaw was identical to that of an orangutan. Piltdown Man was a hoax, and although there are a number of theories as to who perpetrated the fraud, the evidence is inconclusive.

Deliberate researcher bias can be more subtle than forging or even fudging data. A researcher can choose not to report results that are incompatible with a personal theory or even with his or her political or social beliefs. Similarly, a biased scientist may design projects such that negative or ideologically bad results are unlikely.

How do we detect fraud? Science is self-correcting. The truth will win out. When an important finding is published, the scientific community takes it seriously and pursues the implications of the reported data. When other scientists try to repeat the fraudulent experiment, they will fail to get the reported results, and such failures will eventually lead scientists to conclude that the findings were not real. Thus, the repetition of experiments is important to detecting scientific fraud (Barber, 1976). Direct, specific repetitions are called **replications.** It may take many failed replications and years of effort, however, before the entire scientific community agrees that the fraudulent results should be discarded, a fact that illustrates the serious consequences of scientific fraud.

A related problem is **plagiarism,** or taking credit for someone else's ideas, data, or words. While it may be obvious to you that you should not use someone else's data as your own, plagiarism may be much less obvious in other cases. If you are using someone else's words, you should use quotation marks with an appropriate citation. While it may seem natural and unavoidable, slightly rewording someone else's writing is also inappropriate. To avoid this, write without looking directly at the source you are describing. The trickiest case may be that of *idea plagiarism* (Marsh, Landau, & Hicks, 1997). If the idea came from someone else, you should give that person credit even if you are not quoting him or her directly. One potential problem is that people may accidentally lose track of who generated which ideas, especially since ideas are often generated in on-the-fly verbal discussions. To avoid this problem, it is best to agree on authorship at the beginning of a project, contingent on work progressing as allocated.

Most ethical review boards, which are discussed in the next section, monitor the scientific practices that could lead to scientific fraud. Moreover, individuals guarantee federal granting agencies that they have not engaged in fraudulent practices. On discovering fraud, the granting agencies suspend the grant and may attempt to recover funds that have been expended. Researchers who are guilty of fraud will not receive additional grants. Thus, institutions and granting agencies also play a role in containing fraud.

> ### CONCEPT SUMMARY
>
> Fraud is discovered by
>
> - replication of research
>
> Fraud is contained by
>
> - institutional boards
> - granting agencies

▶ Monitoring Ethical Practices

The APA provides ethical guidelines for psychological research. Acceptance of membership in the association commits the member to adherence to these principles. The principles are also intended for nonmembers, including students of psychology and others who work on psychological research under the supervision of a psychologist.

The APA established an Ethics Committee that fulfills a number of purposes. Through publications, educational meetings, and convention activities, the Ethics Committee educates psychologists and the public about ethical issues related to psychological research. The committee also investigates and adjudicates complaints concerning unethical research practices. Examples of these cases can be found in an APA (2005) publication titled *Ethics in Plain English: An Illustrative Casebook for Psychologists*, second edition. The Ethics Committee also publishes an annual report in *American Psychologist* (for example, APA, 2004). The APA ethical principles we describe in this chapter were approved in 2002 and went into effect in June 2003.

A substantial amount of psychological research is funded by one of the arms of the Public Health Service (PHS), which is part of the United States Department of Health and Human Services. The PHS has a division called the Office of Research Integrity, which has as its duty the protection of the integrity of PHS research programs. This is a major effort. Each year the PHS provides several billion dollars to support over 30,000 research grants in a number of disciplines, including psychology. The Office of Research Integrity and the APA combine to consider the prevention of fraud and the protection of research participants. Furthermore, any institution that receives money from the federal government—which means virtually every U.S. institution that engages in research—must have an **institutional review board** (IRB) that oversees the protection of human participants and an institutional animal care and use committee that oversees the protection of animal subjects. All experiments must be approved by the members of these committees. Federal regulations require that each IRB have at least five members who are qualified to review the kind of research typically conducted within the institution. Furthermore, if an IRB regularly reviews research involving vulnerable individuals (for example, children, prisoners, the mentally disabled), the committee should include at least one member whose area of expertise deals with such individuals. There must be at least one member whose primary concern is in a scientific area and one member whose primary concern is in a nonscientific area. There must also be someone on the committee, usually an attorney, who can ascertain whether proposed research violates any laws or federal regulations. Finally, regulations require that at least one member of the committee be otherwise free from affiliation with the institution. This diversity in membership helps to ensure that the rights of individuals participating in research are protected.

How does an IRB make its decision regarding the ethicality of a particular research project? First, it assesses the level of risk involved in the procedure. Many psychological experiments are classified as involving only "minimal risk." Minimal risk means that the experimental procedures involve no greater risk than is associated with daily activities. If greater than minimal risk is deemed necessary for research purposes, then the IRB must decide whether these risks are reasonable in relation to the benefits that would be gained from the research. The IRB also ensures that participants are fully informed before the experiment and that their safety and confidentiality are safeguarded.

Becoming acquainted with the institutional review process should help to reassure you that ethical research in psychology, and in other sciences, is the rule and not the exception. Because of safeguards built into the structure of research institutions, scientists cannot simply rely solely on their own judgment to protect the animals and humans participating in their experiments. Furthermore, the boards help to emphasize honesty in research, which helps to reduce fraudulent practices.

Summary

1. An ethical investigator protects the welfare of research participants by following the ethical standards of the American Psychological Association.

2. Informing the participant about the experiment before participation and minimal use of deception on the part of the investigator allow the participant to make a reasoned judgment about whether to participate.

3. The participant has the right to decline to serve in an experiment or to withdraw from an experiment at any time.

4. In an ethical investigation, the participant is protected from physical and mental harm.

5. After the data have been collected, participants should be carefully debriefed to remove any misconceptions that may have arisen.

6. Any harmful consequences resulting from an experiment should be removed by the investigator.

7. Unless the participant otherwise agrees, information relating to his or her participation is confidential.

8. Attempts to uphold ethical principles sometimes lead to a dilemma in that adherence to one principle may violate another.

9. When animal subjects are used, care should be taken to minimize their pain and discomfort.

10. Ethical scientists are honest. They do not engage in activities that misrepresent the conduct and outcome of research.

11. Scientific fraud can be detected by replications of research, and it is monitored by institutional boards and granting agencies.

12. Institutional review boards help monitor ethical practices in research and ensure the ethical treatment of participants.

Key Concepts

confidentiality (285)
debriefing (284)
deception (282)
fraud (292)
freedom to withdraw
  (283)

informed consent (282)
institutional review
  board (294)
plagiarism (293)
protection from harm
  (284)

removing harmful
  consequences (285)
replication (293)
speciesism (288)

Exercises

Reconsider the ethical principles presented in this chapter, and read the list of ethical principles published by American Psychological Association (2002).

1. Read selections from the *Ethics in Plain English: An Illustrative Casebook for Psychologists,* second edition, published by the American Psychological Association (2005), which is probably available in your library. This book describes different ethical issues facing psychologists. Select two cases and consider the ethical principle(s) involved in each. Describe why you agree or disagree with the adjudication of the ethics committee.

2. This exercise involves researching and thinking critically about the ethics of two famous controversial experiments: Milgram's study of obedience, and the Stanford Prison Experiment. We provide some background here, but if you are unfamiliar with the studies, we recommend you watch Zimbardo's (2001) *Discovering Psychology* video on the power of the situation (tape 19). This video contains actual footage from both of these studies. Seeing what the subjects experienced will help you to understand the issues far more than any verbal description we could provide.

   A. In Stanley Milgram's study of obedience, subjects were instructed to continue shocking a disobedient learner even though the victim clearly was experiencing pain and, potentially, a medical emergency.

Milgram's subjects did not know that the victim was actually a confederate who received no shocks at all. Milgram's major finding was that a large proportion of subjects willingly administered high levels of electric shock to the victim; such levels of obedience had not been predicted by major researchers in the field. Are such important and surprising research findings "worth" the psychological suffering experienced by the subjects? Research the Milgram study, and read commentaries on both sides of the issue. Do you think the Milgram study was unethical? Why, or why not? When are these levels of deception and psychological suffering acceptable? To get started, you might look at the following references:

Baumrind, D. (1964). Some thoughts on ethics on research: After reading Milgram's 'Behavioral study of obedience.' *American Psychologist, 19,* 421–423.

Milgram, S. (1963). Behavioral study of obedience. *Journal of Abnormal and Social Psychology, 67,* 371–378.

Milgram, S. (1964). Issues in the study of obedience: A reply to Baumrind. *American Psychologist, 19,* 848–852.

Milgram, S. (1977). Ethical issues in the study of obedience. In S. Milgram (Ed.), *The individual in a social world* (pp. 188–199). Reading, MA: Addison-Wesley.

B. In the Stanford Prison Experiment, subjects were randomly assigned to the roles of guard or prisoner and then enacted these roles in a simulated prison in the basement of the Stanford Psychology building. The experiment became too real—the guards began mistreating the prisoners, and some of the prisoners suffered psychological breakdowns. The experiment was terminated after only 6 days instead of the planned 2 weeks. Research this study, and think about the ethical issues involved. To get started, you might look at the following references:

Haney, C., Banks, W., & Zimbardo, P. Z. (1973). Interpersonal dynamics in simulated prison. *International Journal of Criminology and Penology, 1,* 69–97.

Haney, C. & Zimbardo, P. Z. (1998). The past and future of U.S. prison policy: Twenty-five years after the Stanford Prison Experiment. *American Psychologist, 53,* 709–727.

Zimbardo, P. Z. (1973). On the ethics of intervention in human psychological research: With special reference to the Stanford Prison Experiment. *Cognition, 2,* 243–256.

3. Although there are federal guidelines for conducting human and animal research, much is regulated at the university level. Discover what procedures your university has enacted to protect the welfare of research subjects, both human and animal. Most notably, any project will need to be approved by your institutional review board; obtain and read the application form. Researchers may also be required to take an ethics class.

Check to see if your university has an online ethics class; if so, check it out. You can also look at the website of the National Institute of Health's Office of Human Subjects to see details of federal regulations; its web-page is http://ohsr.od.nih.gov and contains links to online ethics classes.

Suggested Resources

A wide range of ethical issues and perspectives are covered in Bursoff, D. N. (1999). *Ethical con-flicts in psychology* (3rd ed.). Washington, DC: American Psychological Association.

You can read about the place of deception in social psychology research in Korn, J. H. (1997). *Illusions of reality: A history of deception in social psychology*. Albany, NY: State University of New York Press. Besides those cited in the text, additional articles on animal research include: Bowd, A. D. (1980). Ethical reservations about psychological research with animals. *Psychological Record, 30*, 201–210. Devenport, L. D., & Devenport, J. A. (1990). The laboratory animal dilemma: A solution in our backyards. *Psychological Science, 1*, 215–216. Hoff, C. (1980). Immoral and moral uses of animals. *New England Journal of Medicine, 302*, 115–118. Miller, N. E. (1985). The value of behavioral research on animals. *American Psychologist, 40*, 423–440.

Articles on ethical issues for clinical research include: Imber, S., Glanz, L. M., Elkin, I., Sotsky, S. M., Boyer, J. L., & Leber, W. R. (1986). Ethical issues in psychotherapy research: Problems in a collaborative clinical study. *American Psychologist, 41*, 137–146. Melton, G., & Gray, J. (1988). Ethical dilemmas in AIDS research: Individual privacy and public health. *American Psychologist, 43*, 60–64.

Articles on the ethics involved in socially sensitive research include: Scarr, S. (1988). Race and gender as psychological variables: Social and ethical issues. *American Psychologist, 43*, 56–59. Sieber, J. E., & Stanley, B. (1988). Ethical and professional dimensions of socially sensitive research. *American Psychologist, 43*, 49–55.

 ## Web Resource

Several interesting websites are devoted to ethical issues in research. Two that we liked are: http://www.apa.org/ethics and http://www.nap.edu/readingroom/books/obas

 ## Laboratory Resource

Langston gives an example of an IRB proposal in Appendix B of Langston, W. (2005). *Research methods laboratory manual for psychology* (2nd ed.). Belmont, CA: Wadsworth.

Understanding and Remembering Consent Forms

According to the American Psychological Association (2002), all psychological experiments require a subject's informed consent before his or her participation. How meaningful is a subject's signature on a consent form, however, if he or she did not understand and does not remember the information from the consent form?

Mann (1994) had subjects read either a consent form or an information sheet about a hypothetical functional magnetic resonance imaging brain scanning experiment. The information sheet was the same as the consent form, except that it did not require a signature. Subjects then answered questions about the allegedly upcoming procedure. Even though they had just read the consent form/information sheet, only a minority of Mann's subjects were able to correctly answer the following questions:

- What type of device will we use to study your brain? (38% correct)

- How does this device work? (47%)

- Are there risks to this procedure? (48%)

- What can you do if the sound of the machine bothers you? (45%)

- What can you do if you have a complaint about the study? (39%)

- What will the researchers do for you if you get hurt? (47%)

- Name two of the four things your signature on the consent form means. (20%)

In addition, 62% of subjects who had signed the consent form thought they had lost their right to sue the experimenter, compared with only 16% of those who had merely read the information sheet.

If you are planning a study of your own, you will have created a consent form that you can use in this demonstration. If not, ask your teacher for one. Design a series of questions that will test people's comprehension and memory for the consent form. Have your friends read the consent form, and then ask them to answer (from memory) your questions. How much do your friends remember about what they have just read? Do they know the risks and benefits associated with the study? If not, have they really given their informed consent, even though they signed the forms?

Mann, T. (1994). Informed consent for psychological research: Do subjects comprehend consent forms and understand their legal rights? *Psychological Science, 5,* 140–143.

CHAPTER 13

Interpreting the Results of Research

How to assess whether the research is both reliable and valid

Questions to Answer

- *Is there a scale-attenuation problem?* Are there ceiling or floor effects?

- *Is a regression artifact present?* Do the data provide a "true" measure of the behavior?

- *Are the experimental results reliable?* Has the experiment been replicated directly? Have conceptual or systematic replications been undertaken?

- *Have the results and concepts been validated by converging operations?* Do the results of several converging operations eliminate alternative explanations of the results?

After you have collected and analyzed your data, you are in a position to interpret them. This chapter will help you to understand some of the pitfalls that impede correct interpretation of your data. We will consider problems associated with the interpretation of both specific results and results from a connected series of studies. Your data, even if collected and statistically analyzed correctly, may be difficult to interpret if performance is extremely good or extremely bad (the scale-attenuation problem). Often your participant's true score or performance differs from the data you have collected, which means that a regression artifact has occurred. Have you obtained reliable results—would you find the same effect if the research were replicated? Are your data valid—do several results converge on an understanding of a concept? Solutions to these problems are suggested.

▶ Interpreting Specific Results

The Problem of Scale Attenuation

The first topic we consider here is important but often overlooked in psychological research. The general problem is how to interpret performance on some dependent variable in an experiment when performance exceeds the limitations of the measurement scale. When performance is at the upper limit of the scale, we say we have a **ceiling effect.** An example of a ceiling effect might be a math test that is so easy that nearly everyone in the class gets all the problems correct. When performance is at the bottom of the scale, we say we have a **floor effect.** An example of a floor effect might be another math test that is so difficult that no one in the class gets any of the problems correct. Collectively, ceiling and floor effects are known as **scale-attenuation effects.**

To best illustrate scale-attenuation effects, we will use an example of a physical rather than a psychological scale. The advantage of a physical scale is that its accuracy can be objectively determined. We will therefore look at how ceiling effects can make the measurement of a physical characteristic, namely weight, problematic. We will then show how scale attenuation can hinder the interpretation of psychological measures.

Suppose two obese men decided to make a bet as to who could lose the greatest amount of weight in a certain amount of time. One man looked much heavier than the other, but neither was sure what he actually weighed, because they both made a point of avoiding scales. The scale they decided to use for the bet was a common bathroom scale that ran from 0 to 300 pounds. On the day they were to begin their weight-loss programs, each man weighed himself while the other watched, and to their great surprise, both men weighed in at exactly the same value, 300 pounds. So, despite their different sizes, the men decided that they were beginning their bet at equal weights.

The problem here is one of ceiling effects in the scale of measurement. The weight range of the bathroom scale did not go high enough to record the actual weight of these men. Suppose that one really weighed 300 and the other 350 if their weights had been measured on a scale that had a greater range. After 6 months on the weight-loss program, let us further suppose, each man actually lost 100 pounds. They reweighed themselves at this point and discovered that one now weighed 200 pounds and the other 250. Because they thought they had both started at the same weight (300), they reached the erroneous conclusion that the person who presently weighed 200 pounds had won the bet (see Figure 13–1).

Unfortunately, scale-attenuation effects in research may not be as obvious as the ceiling effect in our contrived example. However, scale attenuation can lead to highly erroneous conclusions, so it is important that you know what to look for in your own research and in the work of others. You should not only be wary of the scale used to measure behavior but also consider the task imposed on the persons participating in the project. For example, suppose you devised a memory experiment that involved recalling phone numbers. The

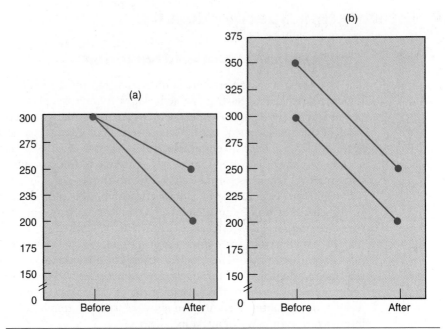

Figure 13–1 The left panel (a) illustrates the situation as the obese men be-lieved it to be—they started at the same weight, and one lost twice as much as the other. The right panel (b) reveals the actual case, with the ceiling effect in the scale of measurement removed. In fact, both men lost 100 pounds. Scale attenuation (ceiling and floor effects) can hide actual differences that may exist between con-ditions in an experiment.

people in your experiment had to study a typical seven-digit phone number for 1 minute and then had to dial that number on a telephone. You would prob-ably discover that all of your participants did fine; in fact, they all remembered the numbers perfectly. What does that tell you? If a task is too easy (or too dif-ficult), differences in behavior will not appear. Whenever you examine re-search results, you should ask yourself: Are the limits on performance I ob-serve legitimate ones, or are they imposed by the measurement scale or the task used to assess behavior?

The Effect of Temporal Lobe Damage on Memory Let us consider the results of an experiment that contains a scale-attenuation problem. Yonelinas and colleagues (2002) recently published an experiment in which they com-pared the performance of people who had sustained damage to the medial tem-poral lobes of the brain due to prolonged hypoxia (oxygen deprivation) with that of age-matched controls. Damage to the medial temporal lobes has long been known to result in deficits in the ability to recollect past events. The ques-tion examined by Yonelinas et al. was whether certain types of memory tests were more adversely affected by medial temporal lobe damage than others.

The medial temporal lobes are believed to be important for the conscious retrieval of past events. Some memory tests rely more on conscious retrieval than do others, so a comparison of different types of memory tests could be informative with regard to whether medial temporal lobe damage affects conscious retrieval of past events. To examine this, they compared performance on a recognition test with performance on a recall test. On the recognition test, people were first exposed to 15 unrelated words, and 15 minutes later were asked to differentiate between the words they had encountered earlier and items that were new to the experiment. By contrast, the recall test included the same initial exposure to 15 words, and the same 15-minute delay, but the participants were asked to simply recall the names of the objects or words they encountered earlier. Many researchers have argued that the recognition test relies less on the ability to consciously recollect past events, because the information to be remembered is provided to participants, and they simply have to discriminate among old and new items. By contrast, the recall test puts paramount importance on the ability to recollect past events, because one has to search memory to retrieve past events without any external support. Thus, if medial temporal lobe damage disrupts conscious retrieval, recall should be more impaired in this group relative to control subjects than recognition performance.

In fact, Yonelinas et al. (2002) found that people with damage to medial temporal lobes performed more poorly than control participants, and these deficits were greater for recall than recognition. The results are presented in Figure 13–2. The difference in recall between the two groups was 15%, but the difference in recognition was only 7%. This is consistent with the notion that medial temporal lobe damage disrupts conscious retrieval of past events. However, as you can see in Figure 13–2, recognition performance was considerably higher than recall, which suggests that scale attenuation, in this case ceiling effects, might be influencing the data. In fact, an examination of the raw data (found in Wixted & Squire, 2004) reveals that nearly half of the control participants in this study had perfect recognition performance, as did many of the brain damage patients. Thus, the recognition test that was used was not sensitive to high levels of performance, much like the scale for the obese men in the earlier example. This ceiling effect in the brain damage study makes it impossible to conclude whether measures of recall and recognition were differentially affected by medial temporal lobe damage.

Solutions to Scale Attenuation   When ceiling or floor effects do exist, it is important not to draw any strong conclusions about the data. A prudent investigator would hesitate to draw any conclusion from the data in Figure 13–2 about differential effects of brain damage on recall and recognition.

Unfortunately, there are no hard-and-fast rules for avoiding scale attenuation problems. Researchers usually try to design their experiments to avoid extremes in performance, and they often test small groups of pilot participants (see Chapter 1 for a discussion of pilot work). If these participants perform

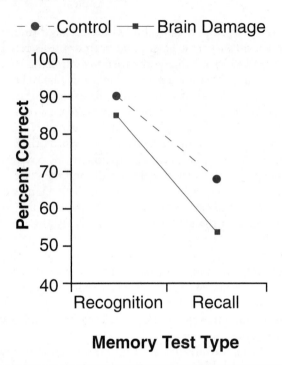

Figure 13–2 The probability of correctly remembering a word on a recognition or recall test for control subjects and for those with brain damage to the medial temporal lobes. Notice that the difference between the two groups is smaller for recognition than recall. Also note that the recognition results are much closer to perfect performance (100%) than the recall results. (Created from the data collected by Yonelinas et al., 2002, which was included in Wixted & Squire, 2004.)

near the ceiling or floor of the scale, then revision of the experimental task often will be necessary. For example, if performance in a memory experiment is too good, as in the Yonelinas study, the amount of material being presented can be increased so as to lower performance. Similarly, if the task is so hard that people barely remember anything, the task can be made easier by reducing the amount of material, presenting it more slowly, and so on. The careful investigator will usually make the effort to test pilot participants before launching into an experiment that may turn out later to have been flawed by ceiling or floor effects. As noted in Chapter 1, the testing of pilot participants also permits the researcher to learn about other problems in the design or procedure of the experiment.

Pilot work is particularly important when there is a change in the subject population. For example, the researcher who perfects his or her paradigm with college students may have difficulties when trying to compare their performance with that of older adults. If older adult performance is much lower to begin with, it may be very difficult to see the effects of a manipulation aimed at decreasing performance (due to a floor effect). To deal with this problem, sometimes researchers change the experimental conditions for older adults to bring their performance up to the level of younger adults and then examine the effect of a manipulation on that corrected performance level (for example, Jacoby, Bishara, Toth, & Hessels, 2005).

CONCEPT SUMMARY

Beware of Ceiling and Floor Effects

Conduct pilot work to determine scale sensitivity and task difficulty.

Regression Artifacts

A serious problem in many areas of research is known as statistical **regression to the mean,** or the **regression artifact.** The word *artifact* in this context refers to an unwanted effect that occurs during an investigation (thus, it is a synonym for *confounding factor*), and *regression* means to go back to the mean or true score (this problem was outlined in Chapter 11, but we now consider it in detail).

You can best appreciate this unwanted phenomenon by allowing yourself to become a victim of it. Try the following exercise, proceeding through the steps as given:

1. Roll six dice on a table in front of you.
2. Place the three dice showing the lowest numbers on the left and the three dice showing the highest numbers on the right. In case of ties, randomly assign the dice to the two groups.
3. Compute and record the mean number per die for each group of three dice.
4. Raise both hands over your head and loudly proclaim, "Improve, in the name of science!"
5. Roll the three low-scoring dice and compute a new mean number per die for the low group.
6. Roll the three high-scoring dice and compute a new mean number per die for the high group.
7. Compare the pre- and posttreatment scores for both groups of dice. Combine your data with that of your classmates, if possible.

On the average, this experiment will produce an increase in the performance of the low group and a decrease in the performance of the high group.

You might be tempted to conclude not only that invoking the name of science has a beneficial effect on underachieving dice, but that overachieving dice require more individual attention to maintain their outstanding performance. Such conclusions, however, fail to consider the effects of regression to the mean. This regression artifact reflects the tendency of many types of measures to yield values close to their mean. You know that the role of a fair die can yield values from 1 to 6 but that the average value from many rolls will be about 3.5. The likelihood of the average of three dice being close to 3.5 is higher than the likelihood of this average being close to 1 or 6. Thus, when you select three dice that give you a low average and then you roll them again, they will tend to yield a higher average value (a value closer to the mean of 3.5). In the same way, the three dice in the high group should yield a lower value when rolled again.

What does all this have to do with psychological research? By now you are well aware that accurate measurement lies at the heart of assessing the effects of a variable. Whenever there is a measurement error, such as the regression artifact, there is also the possibility of wrongly concluding that some sort of change has occurred or has failed to occur. Although this statement may appear less than profound to you, a number of psychological studies have been faulted for failing to take adequate account of its truth.

Quasi-experimental designs (see Chapter 11), such as the dice exercise, are particularly susceptible to bias because of the regression artifact. In such studies, you will remember, participants are not assigned to treatment and control groups on a random basis but on the basis of some factor or factors not under experimental control, such as IQ or SAT scores. Whenever participants are assigned to groups because of particularly high or particularly low test scores, regression artifacts are a danger. In a group chosen for low values on some measure, regression to the mean might inflate the apparent effect of some treatment (for example, "Improve, in the name of science!"). Conversely, when a group is chosen for high values on some measure, the effects of a treatment might be masked by the group's tendency to score closer to the mean (and hence lower) on a second test.

The reason regression to the mean often occurs is that all psychological measures are subject to a certain amount of unreliability, or measurement error. Without measurement error, no regression artifact is possible. For instance, if you were to measure the height of each of your classmates to the nearest foot and then measure the shortest and tallest of them again, you would be unlikely to observe any regression to the mean, because such gross physical measurements are nearly perfect. With any measure that is not perfectly reliable, however, the group of participants obtaining the highest scores contains not only those who really belong in the highest category but also others who are placed in this category owing to chance errors of measurement. On a retest, the chance measurement errors that inflated some of the scores are unlikely to be as large; therefore, the observed score will not be as high. The regression artifact does not imply that the true score of the participant has changed. Regression to the mean merely implies that the initial measurement contained error. To illustrate this point more clearly, an example of regression to the mean with a physical scale might be useful. Imagine that you measured the weight of each of your classmates on an unreliable bathroom scale: On any given weighing, it could err by as much as 25 pounds in either direction. As a consequence, some people of average weight were recorded as being very heavy and others as being very light. If you were to weigh everyone again on the same scale, it is unlikely that the average people who weighed in at the extreme ends of the scale would get the same erroneous readings a second time. The second weighing of the high- and low-weight people would therefore show regression to the mean; however, no one would claim that there was any actual change in weight.

Regression in Compensatory Education The importance of regression artifacts in quasi-experimental studies of education has been the subject of much debate. One influential study of the effects of the Head Start program of the 1960s (Cicirelli & Granger, 1969) received particular attention. In this study, called the Westinghouse-Ohio study, children completing their Head Start experience were randomly selected for evaluation. A control population of children from the same area who had been eligible for the program but had not attended was then defined. Control children were selected at random to be matched with experimental children on the basis of sex, racial or ethnic-group membership, and kindergarten attendance. After the final selection of experimental and control participants was made, additional measures of socioeconomic status, demographic status, and attitude were compiled and compared in the two groups. Differences were reported to be slight. Measures of experimental (Head Start) and control (no Head Start) children's academic achievement and potential were then computed and compared. The general conclusion from this large study was that Head Start was not effective in removing the effects of poverty and social disadvantage.

Other psychologists (Campbell & Erlebacher, 1970a) were quick to criticize this study on several grounds. First, they pointed out that the results of the study were undoubtedly caused partially by regression artifacts. Worse, the magnitude of the artifacts could not be estimated, casting doubt over the entire set of findings.

What is the basic problem? Can you see why the matching of participants may not have been effective? Cicirelli and Granger laudably tried to match the sample of disadvantaged children who had been in the Head Start program with others from the same area who had not been in the program. Differences that show up later between the two groups should result from the program. Right? Not necessarily. That conclusion is correct only if the two samples came from the same underlying population distributions, which is unlikely.

What is more likely is that the two populations differed, with the disadvantaged treatment (Head Start) children coming from a population that was poorer in ability than the control (no Head Start) children. The treatment children were usually preselected to be from a disadvantaged background: That is why they were included in the program. The control participants, on the other hand, who were not in the program, were likely to be from a different population that was greater in ability (a nonequivalent control group). The basic problem was that participants were not randomly assigned to conditions, so the researchers tried to match control participants with experimental participants. To match samples from these different populations, the experimenters had to select children *above* the population mean for the disadvantaged treatment group and *below* the population mean for the control group. When this was done, the regression artifact was introduced. When each group was retested, the participants' performance tended to regress to the mean of the group. In other words, the disadvantaged group tended to perform worse on the retest, and the control group tended to perform better.

Regression to the mean can occur in the absence of any treatment being given and despite matching. Because in the Head Start study we already expected a difference between groups (favoring the control), regression to the mean makes it difficult to evaluate the outcome of the study. Cicirelli and Granger found no difference between the groups. Given that the treatment (Head Start) group was probably worse to begin with, does this mean the group actually improved because of Head Start?

It is impossible to answer this question, because in the Westinghouse-Ohio evaluation of Head Start, the direction or magnitude of regression artifacts could not be assessed. In the preceding paragraph, we made reasonable assumptions concerning regression artifacts in this type of study. Strictly speaking, however, we cannot conclude that Head Start had no effect. In fact, we cannot draw any conclusion based on that study, because we do not know how regression artifacts affected the results.

In general, then, regression artifacts of a difficult-to-estimate magnitude are highly probable in this type of study, a fact acknowledged by most researchers. Why, then, would such studies be conducted, particularly when important political, economic, and social decisions will be based on their results? This question was raised both by Campbell and Erlebacher (1970a, 1970b) and by Cicirelli and his supporters (Cicirelli, 1970; Evans & Schiller, 1970). Their answers were quite different, and they represent the type of issue that frequently confronts scientists but which science can never resolve. Campbell and Erlebacher (1970a) proposed that bad information was worse than no information at all—that if properly controlled experiments could not be performed, then no data should be gathered. On the other side of the issue, Evans and Schiller replied, "This position fails to understand that every program *will* be evaluated by the most arbitrary, anecdotal, partisan, and subjective means" (p. 220). Campbell and Erlebacher concurred but stated that "we judge it fundamentally misleading to lend the prestige of science to any report in a situation where no scientific evaluation is possible" (1970b, p. 224). As a final solution, they proposed that a commission "composed of experts who are not yet partisans in this controversy" be convened to decide the matter.

Possible Solutions We may not be able to decide this issue on strictly rational grounds, but we can all agree that a research study should be conducted according to the best scientific procedures available. After the fact, of course, we are not able to interpret the results of a quasi-experimental study in which there are substantial and unknown regression artifacts. So, the question becomes: How could the Westinghouse-Ohio study have been properly conducted? The best way would have been to randomly assign participants to either the no-treatment or the treatment condition. There is no substitute for random assignment in eliminating confounding factors (that is, there is no substitute for doing a true experiment). However, it seems unfair to give half the children who seek the help of a remedial program no training whatsoever. Of course, there is no guarantee at the outset that the program will be beneficial to them; that is what the study is designed to discover. The same issue arises in medical research when a control group with a disease is given a placebo rather than a treatment drug. The argument could be made in both cases that in the long run, more people will be aided by careful research into the effectiveness of treatments than may be harmed because treatment is withheld. Unfortunately, the issue is not quite that simple. In the case of medical research, for example, preliminary testing of an anti-encephalitis drug showed that 72% of the patients receiving the drug survived the disease and led normal lives but that only 30% of the control group, which received placebos, survived (Katz, 1979). Is such a toll necessary for effective research design in drug development? Again, the issue is difficult to resolve solely on rational or scientific grounds.

There are other solutions to the regression problem (in the Westinghouse-Ohio study) besides random assignment. One is to randomly assign all the children to different groups and put them in different programs to pit the effectiveness of the programs against one another. The difficulty here is that we do not have a no-treatment baseline, and if the programs turn out to be equally effective, we would not know whether any of them were better than no program at all.

CONCEPT SUMMARY

- Regression artifacts mask true behavior in quasi-experiments and matching studies.
- Use random assignment to treatments whenever possible.

▶ Interpreting Patterns of Research

The problems of scale attenuation and regression artifacts focus on the results of a particular piece of research. The topics we want to examine now are concerned with interpreting patterns of research. No single observation can stand alone for long. When we are confronted with the results of psychological research, we must always ask whether they are reliable and valid. In Chapter 7, we discussed the reliability and validity of data. Here we will expand on some of that discussion so you can grasp the importance of determining whether a particular result displays regularity and whether a particular datum fits with other, related observations.

Reliability and Replication

Suppose we have been hired to assess presidential preferences in the United States. Our job is to find out who the people seem to prefer for president in the upcoming election. After we develop a survey, we take a random sample of the people in the United States. What sorts of things will make us confident of our results? First, we can be more confident that the results accurately reflect the attitudes of the population if our sample consists of 100,000 people rather than only 100. Second, we should expect a second random sample to yield a similar result (assuming that one of the major candidates has not committed a gross moral or legal transgression during the time between the two surveys). Large numbers of observations and a repeatable result are two key factors to ensure reliability. We should always try to maximize the number of observations and devise our research in a way that allows us to determine whether our results are consistent over time.

Test Reliability   In Chapter 7, we discussed the ways in which **test reliability** is assessed. Remember that a reliable test is one that yields consistent results. It is a good rule of thumb to have as many observations as possible for each participant in an experiment, to ensure reliable measurement. If a test is inconsistent because it is poorly designed (and not because of changes in the person taking the test), we will be unable to determine whether the test is measuring what it is supposed to measure. Thus, an unreliable test is also one that is invalid. The same is true of experiments, which we will discuss next.

Experimental Reliability: Replication   The basic issue regarding reliability of experimental results is simply this: If an experiment were repeated, would the results be the same as those found the first time? Obviously, repeatability is a crucial topic in psychological research, for an experimental outcome may be worthless if we cannot have reasonable certainty that the results are reliable. Because we usually are unable to conduct the same study twice using the same participants (with the possible exception of some small-*n* work), we usually repeat an experiment with a different sample of participants. If the results of the two experiments are similar, we can be confident that we have demonstrated reliability.

Many psychologists find **experimental reliability** more convincing than statistical reliability, because a statistically reliable finding in a single experiment may be the result of a set of accidental circumstances that favor one condition over another. We emphasize that the results of any particular experiment are to be viewed against the background of others on the same issue. (See Chapter 7 for an overview of meta-analysis, a useful statistical method for summarizing across many studies investigating a single issue.) If a phenomenon is not repeatable, we are likely to find out rather quickly. **Replication,** a synonym for *copy* or *reproduction,* is the term usually used to describe experimental reliability.

Even though replication is very important, however, you may find it tough to find an exact replication published in a separate paper (see exercise 4 at the end of this chapter). We describe here one extreme example of this. One of the most famous studies in psychology is Bartlett's (1932) demonstration of how culturally based schemas guide people's reconstruction of a story. Subjects who read an Indian tale misremembered objects (for example, "dugout") to be ones that were familiar to them (for example, "canoe"). We bet that your introductory textbook cites this study, and yet the only results presented were anecdotal. A direct replication of this classic and much-cited study was not published until more than 70 years after the original (Bergman & Roediger, 1999).

We will now consider an example of replication in the context of a series of famous experiments conducted by Luchins (1942).

Luchins' Einstellung (Set) Experiments   Abraham S. Luchins (1942) was interested in the following: "Several problems, all solvable by one somewhat complex procedure, are presented in succession. If afterward a similar task is given which can be solved by a more direct and simpler method, will the individual be blinded to this more direct possibility?" Participants may develop a particular approach to a class of similar problems. After the problems are changed so that this set (as in mind set) is no longer the most efficient method of solution, will people hang on to the set, or will they recognize the more direct method? The German word for *set* is **Einstellung;** our everyday problem solving frequently involves an Einstellung: We try our habitual ways of attacking a particular problem even though we may have more efficient procedures readily available to us.

Luchins usually used the water-jar problem in his experiments. People were given two or three jars of water of varying capacity and were supposed to figure out how to obtain a required amount of water by performing arithmetic operations on the volumes the jars would hold. For example, if jar A holds 6 gallons, jar B holds 15 gallons, and jar C holds 2 gallons, how can you obtain exactly 7 gallons? In this example, you could fill jar B (15), then fill jars A (6) and C (2) from the contents of B, leaving 7 gallons in B. The basic 11 problems appear in Table 13–1. To become familiar with the Einstellung effect, solve all 11 problems in order before you continue reading.

In Luchins' first study, the first problem served as an illustration of the task. The appropriate solution is to take the larger jar (29) and subtract the smaller jar (3) three times to get the desired amount (20). Participants next solved problems 2 through 6, which may be considered set-establishing problems, because they all are most easily solved by the same method of solution. In each case, the solution is to take the largest jar (always the middle one), subtract the first jar once, and finally subtract the last jar twice. If we label the jars *A, B,*

Table 13–1   Water-jar problems Luchins used in his Einstellung experiments

| Problem | Given the following empty jars as measures | | | Obtain the required amount of water |
	A	B	C	
1	29	3		20
2	21	127	3	100
3	14	163	25	99
4	18	43	10	5
5	9	42	6	21
6	20	59	4	31
7	23	49	3	20
8	15	39	3	18
9	28	76	3	25
10	18	48	4	22
11	14	36	8	6

and C from left to right, then the set the subjects developed for problems 2 through 6 can be represented as $B - A - 2C$.

Besides the experimental or Einstellung group, there were two others. One group, a control of sorts, began with problems 7 and 8 so that the experimenter could see how the group would solve them with no induced set solution. Another group was treated in the same manner as the Einstellung group, except that before problem 7, each participant wrote "Don't be blind" on the response sheet. Luchins had the participants write this phrase so that they would be cautious and not be foolish when they solved subsequent problems. Thus, the primary dependent variable was the number of participants using the Einstellung solution $(B - A - 2C)$ on problems 7 and 8, even though problems 7 and 8 had much more efficient and direct solutions ($A - C$ for problem 7, and $A + C$ for problem 8). The results were that none of the control participants used the inefficient solution in solving problems 7 and 8, 81% of the Einstellung participants used the inefficient solution on 7 and 8, and the "Don't be blind" warning reduced the use of the Einstellung solution to about 55%. Furthermore, after doing problem 9, which cannot be solved via the set-inducing method, 63% of the Einstellung participants continued with the old solution on problems 10 and 11, whereas only 30% of the "Don't be blind" participants reverted to the set solution.

How reliable are the results from this experiment? Luchins' work was published before the use of statistical tests was common in psychological research, so statistical tests to establish reliability were not performed. However, such tests were largely unnecessary in this case, because Luchins provided us with evidence that his results could be replicated in other experiments. Many experiments are included in the original report, and the results are in general agreement with the Einstellung results just outlined. Altogether, Luchins tested more than 9,000 participants in his original studies. As noted previously, experimental reliability or replication is an exceptionally convincing way to demonstrate the reliability of a phenomenon—the Einstellung effect is a reliable one.

There are three types of replications: (a) direct, (b) systematic, and (c) conceptual. **Direct replication** is simply repeating an experiment as closely as possible with as few changes as possible in the method. Luchins replicated his original experiment several times with only slight changes in the participant population tested; such experiments constitute cases of direct replication.

In a **systematic replication,** all sorts of factors are changed that the investigator considers irrelevant to the phenomenon of interest. If the phenomenon is not illusory, it will survive these changes. So, for example, in a systematic replication of Luchins' experiments, we might vary the nature of the problems so that the set involves a different rule (or several different rules), vary the instructions, vary the type of participants used, and so on. The Einstellung effect should be robust across all of these manipulations. If it is not, then we have found that variables previously thought to be irrelevant are actually important, and this is crucial knowledge.

In a **conceptual replication,** we attempt to replicate a phenomenon or concept in an entirely different way. In the language of Chapter 1, we simply use a different operational definition of the concept. Luchins examined other tasks besides the water-jar problem to establish the Einstellung phenomenon in diverse situations. He used series of geometry problems, words hidden in letters, and paper mazes. Although the operational definitions of a problem and of a solution changed from experiment to experiment, in each case participants solved several problems that had a unique solution before they came to the critical problems that could be solved either by the Einstellung solution or by a much more simple and direct solution. Just as in the water-jar experiments, participants usually used the old, circuitous solution and ignored the more efficient solution. These experiments constitute conceptual replications of the concept of Einstellung. Although Luchins' classic experiment is more than a half-century old, it is still being replicated in modern times (Schooler, Ohlsson, & Brooks, 1993) and cited in current literature (Chen & Mo, 2004).

You should note the following carefully: The problem of reliability of results is interwoven with the problem of generality and validity (see Application section). In general, researchers need to be careful about assuming that results will generalize to other subject populations. Most psychology experiments are conducted using white, middle-class college students as the subjects—hardly a representative group! College students are often the subjects of choice due to the ease with which they can be recruited for experiments (perhaps you yourself are required to participate in experiments as part of your course requirements). While much research using college students does indeed replicate, we should be careful about assuming replication. For example, psychologists have begun to study how non-Western cultures are different from that traditionally studied in psychology. Not only does self-concept vary in Eastern cultures (for example, Markus & Kitayama, 1991), so does the way people typically approach and solve problems (for example, Nisbett, Peng, Choi, & Norenzayan,

2001). Differences occur not only across cultures but also across ages. For example, older adults' performance often varies depending on the type of material used in the study. One study of off-topic speech found differences between older and younger adults only when the older adults were discussing their own lives and not when they were describing pictures (James, Burke, Austin, & Hulme, 1998). Similarly, results on older adult conformity depend on whether the stimuli are emotionally meaningful (Pasupathi, 1999). Psychologists are often eager to design interventions aimed at reducing the effects of aging; before doing so, however, they should be careful that their failure to obtain similar results with older adults is not simply due to the materials used in the experiment. As we progress from direct to systematic to conceptual replication, we show not only reliability but also increasing validity. Are we studying something that ties in with or is related to our knowledge of other psychological phenomena in a reasonable way? A conceptual replication is closely related to converging operations, which are procedures that validate a hypothetical construct used to explain behavior by eliminating alternative explanations.

CONCEPT SUMMARY

To ensure experimental reliability, conduct

- direct replications, in which as little as possible is changed
- systematic replications, in which many things are varied to determine which variables are truly relevant
- conceptual replications, in which the same question is asked using different variables to demonstrate generality

Converging Operations

Suppose that Luchins had conducted just the one experiment outlined in Table 13–1. What sorts of conclusions could he have drawn from his results (assume also that he directly replicated the study so that he knew his results were reliable)? Can he legitimately conclude that Einstellung caused the results? Without additional independent evidence, he could have said that the results were owing to a "water-jar effect" or "B A 2C effect" rather than to an Einstellung effect. This is because each of these concepts was part of the one experiment, and each is a reasonable cause of the results. By doing systematic and conceptual replications, Luchins ruled out the alternative hypotheses of effects limited to particular variables and made the concept of Einstellung a reasonable explanation of the rigidity seen in many problem-solving situations.

In other words, the results of experiments that had different rules and different problems converged on the Einstellung hypothesis by systematically

APPLICATION

A Failure to Replicate

A variety of behavior-modification techniques (see Chapter 9) have been very successful in treating certain kinds of psychological disorders, including phobias and anxiety, among others. However, these techniques have been spectacularly unsuccessful in treating smoking and overeating behaviors. Current estimates indicate that only 10% to 20% of the people treated for smoking or obesity maintain the benefits of behavior therapy (Schachter, 1982). In other words, about 80% to 90% of the smokers return to smoking after the therapy, and about the same percentage of obese people gain weight after therapy.

Why is there such a dramatic failure to replicate the success seen with other disorders? The standard interpretation is that smoking and overeating are addictions, which means that these habits are more difficult to break than other unfortunate habits, such as snake phobias. Recently, Schachter has argued that this interpretation is misleading. Schachter interviewed a substantial number of people in two areas of New York State. These people, who represented a broad cross-section of the population, were asked a number of health-related questions. What Schachter found was surprising. The success rate for smokers who had tried to quit was nearly 64%, and the average length of time they had refrained from smoking was about 7 years. The corresponding figures for the obese people who had tried to lose weight were 63% and more than 11 years of successful weight reduction. These results are markedly different from the low success rates observed for smokers and overeaters after they had completed formal therapy. Why?

There are at least two reasons that Schachter found higher success rates. First, people in the general population are likely to have tried to quit smoking or lose weight several times; in contrast, the therapy results generally refer to one stint in therapy. Thus, the repeated attempts at self-therapy may have increased the number of successful outcomes. Second, those who seek professional help might do so because they have been very unsuccessful in treating themselves. For whatever reason, those who undergo therapy may have a particularly tenacious problem, which would bias against successful results.

Schachter offers his findings as encouragement to those who have tried to lose weight or quit smoking and have failed. "If at first you don't succeed, try, try again."

Schachter, S. (1982). Don't sell habit-breakers short. *Psychology Today, 16,* 27–33.

eliminating alternative hypotheses. **Converging operations,** then, are a set of two or more operations that eliminate alternative concepts that might explain a set of experimental results. The importance of converging operations in psychological research was initially emphasized in a landmark paper by Garner, Hake, and Eriksen (1956). They noted that converging operations are necessary to validate operationally defined concepts (see Chapter 1) as well as experimental results. When an abstract concept—Einstellung, for example—is limited to one operational definition, the meaning of the concept is effectively limited to a description of the operations involved. When the concept can be operationally defined in several different ways, however, it can have meaning beyond its operations. Thus, Einstellung refers to a blindness to an easy solution to a problem as a result of prior experience with similar problems having more difficult solutions. The meaning of the term transcends its operational definitions and has construct validity (see Chapter 3). Because converging operations are crucial to an understanding of psychological research and psychological theorizing, we will consider two more examples of converging operations at work.

Memory Search: Motivation or Priming?   Before the discussion continues, we want you to think about the following statement: Extroverts are more likely than introverts to succeed academically and professionally. Why do you think this might be the case? Write down a list of possible reasons, and put your list aside.

Now think about your own life. For each of a series of personality dimensions, think of and write down past behaviors of your own that you think reflect your standing on that dimension. The personality dimensions are: (a) lazy–industrious, (b) calm–anxious, (c) patient–impatient, and (d) shy–outgoing. Record as many memories as come to mind for each dimension.

Of interest is what you recorded for the shy–outgoing dimension. While the connection between the two parts of the demonstration may have been obvious to you, in the real study (Sanitioso, Kunda, & Fong, 1990) subjects were convinced that these were really two different experiments. In the first phase, half the subjects thought of reasons why extroversion led to success, whereas the other half thought of reasons why introversion led to success. Then all subjects retrieved autobiographical memories for each of a series of personality dimensions. The critical finding was that subjects' first memory tended to be consistent with the trait associated with success. The experimenters wanted to claim that subjects were motivated to search through memory to find evidence consistent with the desired trait. What do you think of this explanation? Can you think of other possible explanations for the results?

One possibility we have already suggested is that subjects somehow saw through the experimenters' premise and realized the connection between the phases of the experiment. Thus, they may have realized that they should try and remember events that matched the trait presented in phase I. This would be an example of a demand characteristic (see Chapter 4). In a follow-up study, Sanitioso and colleagues chose to use a converging method that they thought would be less susceptible to demand characteristics: reaction time. They ran the same experiment, but with one critical twist: Of interest was how long it took people to come up with a memory in each condition. When subjects were in the extrovert-success condition, they were much faster to come up with an extroverted memory than an introverted memory. The reverse pattern held in the introvert-success condition.

A crucial question remained: How critical was motivation to the results? That is, while the results might have been due to a motivated search through memory, another explanation was also possible: priming. Subjects are often faster to respond in a domain they have just encountered, regardless of any motivational factors. So Sanitioso and colleagues (1990) did another experiment to tease apart priming and motivation. They did the same sort of experiment, but with subjects generating reasons for success in phase I and autobiographical memories in phase II. Critically, however, they changed the success domain in phase I from academic and professional success to success as a police officer. The subjects were Princeton undergraduates who were unlikely to become police officers. If priming accounts for the effect, then the priming effect should occur regardless of the self-relevance of the success. If motivation is key, however, the effect should occur only in success domains in which subjects are motivated to see the desired trait in themselves. This latter possibility was supported; the Princeton undergrads were affected by the success manipulation in only the academic domain and not the police officer domain.

Sanitioso and associates (1990) concluded that subjects did, indeed, conduct motivated searches through memory to find evidence (memories) to support a desired self-perception. They used converging operations to eliminate the alternate explanations of demand characteristics and priming. (See Klein & Kunda, 1993; Kunda, 1990; and Kunda & Sanitioso, 1989, for related work and theoretical background.)

Personal Space   The concept of **personal space** implies that people are surrounded by invisible bubbles designed to protect them from a wide variety of social encroachments. How do psychologists know that such bubbles exist? They cannot be sensed directly by vision, smell, touch, and the other senses, so the concept must be evaluated indirectly. The next two experiments demonstrate that there is a personal-space bubble; they use two different kinds of spatial invasion and yield similar results.

Ironically, the personal-space bubble that helps a person to maintain privacy is best studied by invasions that violate the privacy it affords. A simple experiment conducted by Kinzel (1970) shows one operation that defines personal space. Kinzel was interested in the personal-space bubbles surrounding violent and nonviolent prisoners. One independent variable was a subject variable (see Chapter 10), which was classification of prisoners as violent (having inflicted physical injury on another person) or nonviolent. Each prisoner stood in the center of an empty room 20 feet wide and 20 feet long. The experimenter then approached from one of eight directions (the second independent variable) until the prisoner said "Stop" because the experimenter was too close. The dependent variable was the distance between prisoner and experimenter when the prisoner said "Stop." If there is no personal-space bubble, the experimenter should be able to walk right up to the prisoner (distance = 0 feet). Control variables were the room and the experimenter, which were the same throughout the experiment. Results of this experiment are shown in Figure 13–3. It is clear that violent prisoners have larger personal-space bubbles than do nonviolent prisoners.

This experiment may not have entirely convinced you that personal-space bubbles exist. In Kinzel's experiment, the personal-space bubble was operationally defined as the point at which the participant said "Stop." A concept based on only one experiment is just a restatement of that particular experimental finding. You may think that there is something strange about a person walking right up to another person without saying anything. Certainly, if this happened to you on the street, you would think it unusual, to say the least. The next experiment avoids this potential difficulty.

To avoid actively invading someone's personal-space bubble, Barefoot, Hoople, and McClay (1972) gave subjects the opportunity to invade the experimenter's bubble. The experimenter sat near a water fountain and pretended to read a book. Anyone getting a drink of water had to invade the experimenter's personal space. The independent variable was the distance between the experimenter and the water fountain. This could be either 1 foot, 5 feet, or 10 feet. This last distance was large enough so that it exceeded the bounds of the experimenter's personal space, and thus was a control condition. A confederate kept track of the number of persons passing by the fountain in each of the three experimental conditions. The dependent variable was the percentage of passersby who drank from the fountain. When the experimenter was 1

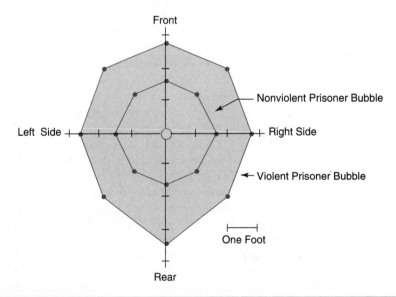

Figure 13–3 Looking down on the personal-space bubble of violent and nonviolent prisoners. (From A. F. Kinzel, "Body-buffer zone in violent prisoners," *The American Journal of Psychiatry, 127,* 1970, 59–64. Copyright © 1970 American Psychiatric Association.)

foot away, only 10% drank; when 5 feet away, 18% drank. Finally, at a distance of 10 feet, 22% drank from the fountain. More recently, Ruback and Snow (1993) found that territorial behavior at water fountains was also influenced by race, with white and black participants reacting differently to intrusions.

Using a very different operational definition of personal space, these results agree with those of the active-invasion paradigm used by Kinzel. The single concept of a personal-space bubble explains findings of both experiments. Hence, the experiments provide converging operations supporting the personal-space concept.

The examples of converging operations we have just detailed are actually rather simple, because only a small number of experiments or conditions were needed to provide validity and generality. In actual practice, many concepts and phenomena require a considerable amount of independent evidence before they can be considered valid.

Concepts defined in terms of converging operations are not static. They are modified as we gather additional evidence relevant to the concept. For example, the concept of a motivated memory search remains to be generalized to other personality domains than extroversion-introversion. In a similar fashion, recent research indicates that the size of the personal-space bubble differs for different cultures: The bubble appears to be larger for white than Hispanic individuals (Beaulieu, 2004). Because our knowledge is never complete, the meaning of a concept is always open to revision. As we interpret the results of our research, we should therefore keep in mind that our interpretation and conclusions are always tentative: Our words on any issue are unlikely to be the last (see Chapter 2).

We leave you with one recent example of this: Schmolck, Buffalo, and Squire (2000) published a study of college students' memories of hearing the verdict in O. J. Simpson's *murder* (as distinct from civil) trial. Subjects' accounts at 15 and 32 months after the verdict were often different from their own accounts acquired just 3 days after the trial's conclusion. Many more errors occurred following 32 months than following 15; the authors concluded that this was due to the passage of more time. However, Horn (2001) published an alternative explanation—namely, that interference (and not the passage of time) led to the increase in errors in the 32-month group. This argument hinges on the fact that the verdict in Simpson's *civil* trial occurred before the 32-month test but after the 15-month test. Thus, subjects in the 32-month condition were not only tested after a longer delay but after a potentially interfering event: the civil trial verdict. The original researchers responded with new arguments against the interference explanation, such as the extreme differences in media coverage of the two trials and the specificity of the memories collected (Squire, Schmolck, & Buffalo, 2001). Our point is not to tell you which answer is the correct one but to illustrate that others may disagree with our interpretations and conclusions, and that such disagreement often sparks new research and theorizing.

> ◢ **CONCEPT SUMMARY**
>
> **Converging Operations**
> - provide validity for concepts and hypotheses.
> - eliminate alternative explanations by two or more operations.

Summary

1. Several pitfalls may make it difficult for experimenters to interpret the results of their research.

2. Some of these pitfalls pose problems in particular research projects, and others make it difficult to interpret patterns of research. Scale attenuation and regression artifacts can lead to the misinterpretation of the results of a specific project; replications (reliability) and converging operations (validity) are important for interpreting patterns of research.

3. Scale attenuation refers to an inability to observe differences in thought and behavior because performance is either too good (a ceiling effect) or too poor (a floor effect).

4. The scale must be spread out or the task modified to handle the attenuation problem.

5. Regression to the mean is likely to occur whenever participants are selected on the basis of high or low scores on some dependent measure. The regression artifact refers to the tendency of participants with extreme scores on a first test to have scores closer to the mean on a second test.

6. Random assignment is the best way to guard against regression artifacts.

7. An experiment that can be replicated is a reliable one, as is a test whose results are consistent.

8. The three types of replications are direct, systematic, and conceptual.

9. Converging operations are several independent procedures that support the meaning of an abstract concept.

10. The need for converging operations demands that scientific research on a problem be varied and extensive.

Key Concepts

ceiling effect (301)
conceptual replication (313)
converging operations (315)
direct replication (313)
Einstellung (311)

experimental reliability (310)
floor effect (301)
personal space (317)
regression artifact (305)
regression to the mean (305)

replication (311)
scale-attenuation effects (301)
systematic replication (313)
test reliability (310)

Exercises

1. [*Special Exercise.*] Here is another design problem for you. Reread the description of Luchins' experiment outlined in Table 13–1. There seem to be several problems with that study; see whether you can pinpoint two or three of them. As a hint, consider the following questions: Did Luchins use an appropriate control group? If not, what should be the control condition? Are there points in the study that require counterbalancing? What additional dependent variables might have been informative?

2. Examine figures and tables in several recent journal articles. See whether you can discover any ceiling or floor effects. If you find any—and it may take a while—read the article to determine whether the investigator was aware of the scale-attenuation problem. Can the problem be rectified?

3. Pinpointing regression artifacts may be difficult. However, in an attempt to discover a regression problem, you might find it worthwhile to examine several assessment studies that use subject variables. If you find evidence for a regression artifact, try to determine why the study was published. Remember our discussion of medical research and the difficulty of random assignment. Try these two journals: the *Journal of Educational Psychology* and the *Journal of Applied Psychology*.

4. Try to find an example of each type of replication in recent journals. You may not find any examples of direct replication, and yet Barber (1976) has asserted that direct replications are crucial to the advancement of psychology. Why do direct replications seldom appear in the literature? Similarly, failures to replicate often do not make it into the literature. Why do you think this is the case? Try and locate an example in the literature.

5. More often than not, good examples of converging operations can be found in a single journal article. Papers by Mayer, Paivio, and Thios and D'Agostino, listed in the Suggested Resources, offer evidence of converging operations at work. You might take a look at these articles.

6. Revisit the Mozart effect described in the sample paper in Chapter 3. Remember that Nantais and Schellenberg (1999) replicated the effect using the exact same procedures as in the original papers (Rauscher, Shaw, & Ky, 1993, 1995); they found improvement in the ability to predict the appearance of a folded and cut piece of paper (see Figure 3–4) after subjects listened to Mozart. Others who have not used this exact spatial-temporal task have failed to replicate the effect (for example, Steele, Bass, & Crook, 1999). First, comment generally on what it means for an effect to be so tightly constrained; that is, how interesting is an effect that requires very specific circumstances to occur? Second, suppose you wanted to replicate the Mozart effect beyond the paper folding task. What progression of spatial tasks might you suggest?

7. Imagining childhood events increases subjects' self-rated beliefs that the events actually occurred; this is termed the *imagination inflation effect*. These studies generally have three phases: a first phase, during which all

events are rated for likelihood of occurrence; a second phase, in which a subset of events are imagined; and a third phase, in which likelihood is rated again. For details, see Garry, M., Manning, C. G., Loftus, E. F., & Sherman, S. J. (1996). Imagination inflation: Imagining a childhood event inflates confidence that it occurred. *Psychonomic Bulletin & Review, 3,* 208–214. Heaps, C., & Nash, M. (1999). Individual differences in imagination inflation. *Psychonomic Bulletin & Review, 6,* 313–318. Some researchers have argued that a regression artifact drives this effect. Research the effect, explain the regression argument, and evaluate it. *Hint:* consider the fact that events are not randomly assigned to the low versus high prior likelihood conditions.

Suggested Resources

The following three articles illustrate both reliability and converging operations. Read them carefully. They are also available in the book *Readings in Experimental Psychology* by Elmes (Chicago: Rand McNally, 1978): Mayer, R. E. (1977). Problem-solving performance with task overload: Effects of self-pacing and trait anxiety. *Bulletin of the Psychonomic Society, 9,* 283–286; Paivio, A. (1975). Perceptual comparisons through the mind's eye. *Memory and Cognition, 3,* 635–647; Thios, S. J., & D'Agostino, P. R. (1976). Effects of repetition as a function of study-phase retrieval. *Journal of Verbal Learning and Verbal Behavior, 15,* 529–536.

Web Resource

Several excellent general-purpose websites that contain a variety of information about the research process can be found at: http://www.socialpsychology.org and http://psych.hanover.edu/research/exponnet.html

Laboratory Resource

Using converging operations is an example of strong inference (see Chapter 2). In his laboratory manual, Langston (2005) considers experiments exemplifying strong inference in Chapter 10. The topic is a fascinating one concerning obstacle detection by the blind. Langston, W. (2005). *Research methods laboratory manual for psychololgy* (2nd ed.). Pacific Grove, CA: Wadsworth Group.

Studying Mental Blocks

- *Folk* is pronounced *foke,* with the *l* being silent.
- *Polk* is pronounced *poke,* again with the *l* being silent.
- How is the name of the white of an egg pronounced?

If you just pronounced *yolk* in answering the question, this section is for you. *Yolk* is an erroneous answer; the white part of an egg is the *albumen*. The *yolk*, as you probably know, is the yellow part. The sentences preceding the question featured words that rhyme with *yolk* and, therefore, primed you for the word *yolk*. When you were asked the question about eggs, *yolk* readily came to you as the answer. If you had not been primed with the two sentences, you probably would not have responded *yolk*. The recent experience of reading the sentences blocked you from giving the correct answer. Here are two more examples, although you may be more wary now: Pronounce the word produced by the letters T-O-P-S. What does a car do at a green light?

Say *tin* out loud ten times. What is an aluminum can made of? Although you may have answered these questions correctly, if you try them on a friend we think you will find them effective in producing the erroneous answers *stop* and *tin*. You should probably ask the questions aloud, rather than tell your friend to read them.

Such blocks in memory retrieval may play a part in limiting creative thinking (Roediger & Neely, 1982). When people try to solve a problem and fail, they often say that their minds are "in a rut." Usually, they mean that when they attempt to solve the problem, they are blocked from retrieving a new solution by repeatedly thinking of all the erroneous solutions that previously have been tried. This is the same as the Einstellung effect shown by Luchins' participants.

You can study the same effect by having some friends read through the priming sentences before the target ones. Compare their behavior with others who do not read the priming sentences. You should consider having the latter group read (or hear) some nonpriming sentences to control for the amount of mental work you have your participants do.

If you are interested in additional ways of studying mental blocks, the following references may be of interest.

Marsh, R. L., Landau, J. D., & Hicks, J. L. (1996). How examples may (and may not) constrain creativity. *Memory & Cognition, 24,* 669–680.

Marsh, R. L., Ward, T. B., & Landau, J. P. (1999). The inadvertent use of prior knowledge in a generative cognition test. *Memory & Cognition, 27,* 94–105.

Roediger, H. L., & Neely, J. H. (1982). Retrieval blocks in episodic and semantic memory. *Canadian Journal of Psychology, 36,* 213–242.

Smith, S. M. (1995). Getting into and out of mental ruts: A theory of fixation, incubation, and insight. In R. J. Sternberg & J. E. Davidson (Eds.), *The nature of insight* (pp. 229-251). Cambridge, MA: MIT Press.

CHAPTER 14

Presenting Research Results

Writing Research Reports

What to Include in the . . .

- *Abstract:* What you did to whom, and what you found
- *Introduction:* Why you are doing this research; the hypothesis you are testing
- *Method:* A description of all variables; enough detail so that someone else can repeat your project
- *Results:* Tables and/or figures that summarize your results and point the reader to the most pertinent data
- *Discussion:* State how your results relate to the hypotheses tested; include relevant inferences and conclusions
- *References:* All references cited in your paper belong here.

Presentation of results is an important step in research. This chapter guides you through the process of writing research reports, explains the process of submitting articles for publication, and offers advice for giving oral presentations to explain your research.

▶ How to Write a Research Report

You have now learned how to formulate an idea for an experiment, review the literature, design a procedure, collect your data, and analyze your results. If your project was carefully done and you obtained interesting data, you are now obligated to publicize your results. We believe that to maintain the self-correcting nature of science, it is important to publish good data. However, this does not mean that journals should be cluttered with information derived from every undergraduate project. If your research is promising, you will receive encouragement from your instructor. Regardless of whether you will try to publish the results of your experiment, it is likely that your course requires a written report of your results.

In the following section, we will review the format of a typical report and discuss some of the stylistic considerations that make up a comprehensible paper. If you follow our suggestions for reading articles (see Chapter 3), you will probably have a pretty good idea about the format of a research report, and you will probably have a good feel for technical writing style. Some aspects of technical writing are not too obvious, so we will discuss them here. What we present are general guidelines. If you need additional information, examine R. J. Sternberg's (1993) book *The Psychologist's Companion* and (1992) article "How to Win Acceptances by Psychology Journals: 21 Tips for Better Writing," as well as D. J. Bem's (1987) chapter, "Writing the Empirical Journal Article." The 2001 revision of the *Publication Manual of the American Psychological Association* (APA, 2001b) will also help, because it is the official arbiter of style for almost all of the journals in psychology and education. The sample article in Chapter 3 is also a useful source of information.

Format

The outline of a typical report in Figure 14–1 emphasizes the sequence and format of pages you will have to put together in your APA-style manuscript. This version of the article is known as the **copy manuscript** and is assembled in a particular manner to facilitate the editorial and publication process. A run-through of that sequence will give you an idea of what you are supposed to include.

Your cover page contains the **title** of your project, your name, your affiliation (your institution or place of business), and your **running head.** The running head is the heading that will appear at the top of the published article, and it is typed in capital letters near the top of the cover page of the copy manuscript. The **short title,** which appears at the top of each page of the copy manuscript, consists of the first few words of the title and is used to identify the manuscript during the editorial process only. The short title and running head should not be confused. You should double-space the lines on the cover page and every other page of the copy manuscript.

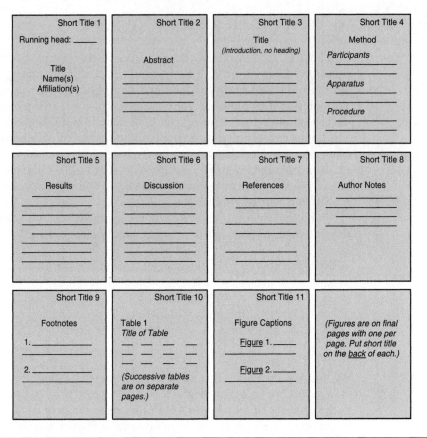

Figure 14–1   Page sequence for a one-experiment report in APA format.

The next page, page 2, contains the heading "Abstract" and the **abstract** itself. Do not indent the first line of the abstract. On this page and on all subsequent ones (except the figures), you should have an abbreviated title and the page number in the top right-hand corner of the page.

At the top of page 3 is the full title, followed by the **introduction.** Ordinarily, you do not have a heading for the introduction. After your introduction is finished, the **Method** section begins. Generally, for a write-up of one experiment, you will type the word "Method" in the center of a line to begin the section. You should begin the Method section immediately after the introduction; a page break is not used here. Note the format shown for the headings on page 4 in Figure 14–1. The headings differ somewhat for multiexperiment papers; these details are covered in the APA (2001b) manual. The side headings, such as "Participants," "Apparatus," and "Procedure," help to guide the reader by breaking down the method section into three subsections.

The **Results** section immediately follows the Method section. Do not include **figures** and **tables** in the body of this section; they come at the end of the report. Next comes the **Discussion,** which ends the major textual portion of your report.

The **references** begin on a separate page. The format for presenting references is complex, and you should use care in preparing them. The article in Chapter 3 contains many of the different styles of references that you will have to document. Look them over carefully, and if you have any questions, ask your instructor. You might also study the APA *Publication Manual* and recent journal articles. (See Table 14–1 for a summary of the general formats for common references.) Any author notes and footnotes appear on separate pages after the references. For most college laboratory reports, footnotes are not necessary. When you prepare something for publication, you may acknowledge financial aid and intellectual support, which should appear on the author-notes page. General acknowledgments are not numbered. Other, perhaps peripheral, information should appear as numbered footnotes on a separate footnote page, but such footnotes are generally discouraged.

Following the footnotes are your data tables mentioned in the Results section. Each table should be on a separate page and numbered consecutively, according to its appearance in the Results section. Make the titles of your tables short but communicative. **Figure captions** are numbered consecutively and appear on a separate page following the data tables. Finally, you have your figures, each on a separate piece of paper. Put your name (or the short title) and the number of the figure on the back. Tables and figures are separated from the text, one per page, to facilitate the typesetting process.

As mentioned before, copy manuscripts are organized in this fashion to accommodate the publisher. However, you should note that there is a special section in the APA *Publication Manual* about the accepted format for student papers submitted for a course requirement but not for publication. For example, in student papers, tables and figures may be interspersed in the text. You

Table 14–1 General forms for the reference list	
Type of Source	**Format**
Periodical (for example, journal)	Author, A. A., Author, B. B., & Author, C. C. (1999). Title of article. *Title of Periodical, xx,* xxx–xxx.
Nonperiodical (for example, book)	Author, A. A., Author, B. B., & Author, C. C. (2000). *Title of work.* Location: Publisher.
Part of a nonperiodical (for example, book chapter)	Author, A. A., Author, B. B., & Author, C. C. (2001). Title of chapter. In A. Editor, B. Editor, & C. Editor (Eds.), *Title of book* (pp. xxx–xxx). Location: Publisher.
Online document	Author, A. A. (2001). *Title of work.* Retrieved month, day, year, from source.

should check with your professor or department regarding the preferred format for class projects. However, we recommend learning the APA publication format, because it provides good practice for preparing your future publications.

Sample Manuscript

A sample manuscript appears on the following pages. The research that led to this manuscript was performed by the first author (David Gallo) and the second author (Meredith Roberts) while they were undergraduates at Wesleyan University working with the third author (Dr. John Seamon). The research began as a project in a methodology course in which David Gallo was enrolled, one like the course in which most students reading this text are enrolled. These Wesleyan students, with the help of their professor, converted a student project into a publishable article contributing to the psychological literature on human memory. You should note the sequence of pages, where typing begins on a new page, and what information is provided in each section. An aspect missing from this manuscript that may appear in one of yours is a separate footnote page. Also, you may choose to include figures that depict data in a graphical form in addition to (or in place of) tables. Note carefully how the references are cited in the reference section. One aspect of this manuscript that is different from the standard **APA format** is the use of the term *subjects* instead of *participants*. Although the current APA format requires the use of the term *participants* for humans participating in research, some journals not affiliated with the American Psychological Association (like the one that published the following research paper) permit the use of either *participants* or *subjects*. Hence the term *subjects* was used in this paper at the discretion of the authors.

The following paper is taken from Gallo, D. A., Roberts, M. J., & Seamon, J. G. (1997). Remembering words not presented in lists: Can we avoid creating false memories? *Psychonomic Bulletin & Review, 4,* 271–276. (Copyright 1997 by the Psychonomic Society Inc. Reprinted by permission of the authors and the publisher.)

Running Head: FALSE RECOGNITION

Remembering Words Not Presented in Lists: Can We Avoid Creating False Memories?

David A. Gallo, Meredith J. Roberts, and John G. Seamon

Wesleyan University

Abstract

Can subject avoid creating false memories in Roediger and McDermott's (1995) false recognition paradigm if they are forewarned about this memory illusion? We presented subjects with semantically related word lists, followed by a recognition test. The test was composed of studied words, semantically related nonstudied words (critical lures), and unrelated nonstudied words. One group of subjects was uninformed about the false recognition effect, a second group was urged to minimize all false alarms, and a third group was forewarned about falsely recognizing critical lures. Compared to the uninformed and cautious subjects, the forewarned subjects reduced their false alarm rate for critical lures, and they made remember and know judgments equally often for recognized studied words and critical lures. But forewarning did not eliminate the false recognition effect, as these subjects and those in the other groups made numerous false recognitions in this task.

Remembering Words Not Presented in Lists: Can We Avoid Creating False Memories?

In a special issue of the *Journal of Memory and Language* devoted to research on memory illusions, Roediger (1996) provided an historical overview of errors in perception and memory. He defined a *memory illusion* as an instance in which a person's report of a past event seriously deviates from the actual event. One striking example offered as evidence of a memory illusion was Deese's (1959) finding of false recall in a list learning paradigm. Deese presented subjects with lists of semantic associates to nonpresented critical words. For example, for the critical word *needle,* the presented list consisted of *thread, pin, eye, sewing, sharp, point, pricked, thimble, haystack, pain, hurt,* and *injection.* When the subjects were given a free recall test after each list's presentation, the nonpresented critical word was often erroneously recalled more frequently than nonpresented but unrelated words. This procedure induced subjects to recall specific words that were never presented in the lists. Beginning with Roediger and McDermott (1995), there has been a revival of interest in this paradigm for studying this false memory effect (e.g., McDermott, 1996; Payne, Eli, Blackwell, & Newschatz, 1996; Read, 1996; Schacter, Verfaellie, & Pradere, 1996).

Roediger and McDermott (1995) reported two experiments that replicated and extended Deese's result. In their first experiment, the subjects were read six of Deese's lists that elicited the highest frequency of false recall. After each list was presented, the subjects were given a free recall test, followed by a recognition test after all of the lists were recalled. The recognition test was composed of studied words, nonstudied critical words (hereafter referred to as critical lures), and nonstudied unrelated words. Roediger and McDermott found that the critical lures were falsely recalled and recognized more frequently than other nonstudied words.

In their second experiment, Roediger and McDermott modified their procedure. Half of the subjects received a free recall test after each study list presentation, and half performed unrelated math problems instead. On the subsequent recognition test, the researchers made use of Tulving's (1985) remember vs. know judgment task. For any recognized word, the subjects had to indicate whether they specifically remembered the word's occurrence at study (a remember judgment) or they merely knew the word had been presented in the absence of any specific recollection (a know judgment). Roediger and McDermott found that the study and recall condition led to more false recognitions of critical lures than did the study and math condition. However, the subjects in both conditions produced false alarms to the critical lures at rates that were comparable to the corresponding hit rates for studied words. Moreover, the results showed that recognized critical lures were often characterized as remembered in the remember vs. know judgment task, especially in the study and recall condition. These observations led Roediger and McDermott to describe the false recognition effect as a "powerful illusion of memory" (p. 803). An illusion that is all the more surprising, they said, because it was observed under intentional learning conditions, with short retention intervals, in a list-learning laboratory procedure that normally produces few errors, and with professional memorizers (college students) as subjects.

The primary purpose of the present research was to determine whether subjects could avoid creating false memories in Roediger and McDermott's false recognition paradigm if they were forewarned about this memory illusion. To our knowledge, no one has specifically determined if this false memory effect could be diminished or eliminated by the subjects' knowledge, but prior research has asked whether different experimental conditions could influence this effect. For example, McDermott (1996, Experiment 2) gave subjects multiple study and recall tests with the same word lists presented in either a blocked or random manner. She found that random presentation produced less false recall than blocked presentation, but both forms of presentation still yielded false recalls after multiple study-test trials or a final recall test given 24 h later. Payne et al. (1996) observed a similar effect in showing that recognition of critical lures did not decrease over a 24 h retention interval. Finally, Read (1996) manipulated encoding instructions by having subjects memorize word order or engage in elaborative or maintenance rehearsal during list presentation. He found that all three encoding conditions yielded high levels of false recall for critical words, but the false recalls were lowest for the subjects who focused on word order. These studies indicate that this false memory effect persists through multiple study and test trials (McDermott, 1996), a 24 h delay between study and test (McDermott, 1996; Payne et al., 1996), and elaborative or maintenance rehearsal during encoding (Read, 1996). But false memory for critical words is diminished when the words are randomized over lists (McDermott, 1996) or the subjects attempt to memorize word order at study (Read, 1996).

Following those studies, the present research sought to determine if the false recognition of critical lures could be attenuated or eliminated by the use of forewarning instructions. Curiously, we found no published research on the effects of foreknowledge on perceptual or memory illusions. For perceptual illusions, such research may have been unnecessary as Gregory (1987) notes that these illusions occur even when people know that they are perceiving an illusion. For example, we may know that the lines in the Muller-Lyer illusion are equal in length, yet one line still appears to be longer than the other. Perceptual illusions fool us because perceptual processes work extremely rapidly and do not take everything that we know into account in the process of forming a percept (Gregory, 1987). Memory illusions also fool us, but they do so over a more extended time frame that includes study and test conditions. Memory illusions may thus provide greater opportunity than perceptual illusions to be influenced by the subject's knowledge. To the extent that foreknowledge can be used during encoding or retrieval to devise compensatory cognitive strategies, an illusion may be diminished or eliminated.

The only statements we found about the effects of foreknowledge on false memory are located in two places in Roediger and McDermott's (1995) research. One statement suggests that forewarning might be effective in minimizing the false recognition of critical lures, whereas the other statement suggests little effect of forewarning. For example, the authors noted that they dropped the only subject from their analysis who had no false recalls of the critical words because at the end of Experiment 2 when the subjects were asked if they "knew what the experiment was about," this subject reported that "she noticed that the lists seemed designed to make her think of a nonpresented word" (p. 808). This subject may have adopted a strategy that permitted her to overcome the memory illusion. However, Roediger and McDermott also reported that "informal demonstration experiments with groups of sophisticated subjects, such as wily graduate students who knew we were trying to induce false memories" still produced a strong false memory effect (p. 812). To the extent that these subjects were fully informed about this memory illusion before study, this observation suggests that forewarning will have a minimal effect on the false recognition of critical words.

The present research tested these foreknowledge alternatives systematically by comparing groups of subjects with different instructional sets in a modified version of the Roediger and McDermott (1996, Experiment 2) paradigm. To the extent that this false memory effect is a memory illusion that functions like a perceptual illusion, foreknowledge of the effect may have little or no effect on the recognition of critical lures. But if this memory illusion differs from perceptual illusions in that it allows greater opportunity for performance to be influenced by encoding or retrieval strategies, foreknowledge of the illusion should attenuate the effect to the extent that people can devise effective compensatory strategies. We presented subjects with blocked lists of semantically related words for study, followed by a recognition test after all lists were presented. One group of subjects was uninformed about the false recognition effect, a second group was urged to be cautious at the time of the recognition test to minimize all false alarms, and a third group was forewarned of the specific illusion by a demonstration and instructions before study. Based on Roediger and McDermott's findings, we hypothesized that the subjects in the uninformed condition would produce a strong false recognition effect. Subjects in the cautious and forewarned groups provide novel test conditions and, compared to the uninformed condition, they should produce either a comparable or diminished effect.

Method

Subjects

The subjects were 48 Wesleyan University undergraduates who served as paid volunteers. None had participated in any related memory search.

Materials

We used 16 of Roediger and McDermott's 24 word lists for study and test words (see their appendix). Each list was composed of 15 associates to a nonpresented critical word (i.e., a critical lure). Within a list, the order of the word was constant and the strongest associates to the critical lure normally occurred first. For example, the list associated with the critical lure *sleep* consisted of the following words: *bed, rest, awake, tired, dream, wake, snooze, blanket,*

Remembering Words 7

doze, slumber, snore, nap, peace, yawn, and *drowsy.* For counterbalancing purposes, the 16 lists were divided into two sets of eight lists, labeled A and B. Half of the subjects in each condition received Set A for study and half received Set B. The set not used during study provided distracters for the recognition test.

Procedure

During study, the subjects were presented with an auditory tape containing eight lists of 15 words presented in blocked fashion. The words were spoken by a male voice at a rate of 1.5 s per word, and a tone separated each list. The subjects, who were tested in groups of up to six, were told to remember the words for a recognition memory test that would follow.

After all 120 study words were heard, the subjects were given a visual recognition memory test consisting of 64 words. Following Roediger and McDermott's test procedure, this test contained three items from each studied list (serial positions 1, 8, and 10), the nonpresented critical lure from each studied list, three items from each nonstudied list (serial positions 1, 8, and 10), and the critical lure from each nonstudied list, all listed in a random order. Each word was accompanied by a plus (+) and minus (−) sign and the letters R and K (for Remember and Know).

The subjects were instructed to examine the words in sequential order at a self-paced rate and make a decision for each word on the list. They were told to circle the plus sign for any word that they recognized from the study tape or the minus sign for any word they failed to recognize. In addition, following Tulving (1985), the subjects were instructed to make a *remember* or *know* judgment for each recognized word by circling R or K on their answer sheets. The subjects were told to circle R if they had a conscious recollection of the word from the study lists, such as the way the word was presented or what they were thinking about at the time, or K if they were sure the word was presented but they could not recollect its actual occurrence or any related details. These instructions for remember and know judgments were similar to those used by Rajaram (1993) and Roediger and McDermott (1995). After the recognition test, the subjects completed a questionnaire that assessed their awareness of the organization of the word list at study and asked for a description of any strategies that were used to reduce false recognitions.

Remembering Words 8

The variable of primary interest in this experiment was the effect of foreknowledge on the false memory effect. Accordingly, three groups of 16 subjects received different instructions at study or test. In the uninformed condition, the subjects were not told about the false recognition effect. Instead, they were given standard instructions to try to remember as many words as possible for a subsequent recognition test. This condition is similar to the general procedure used by Roediger and McDermott (1995, Experiment 2).

In the cautious condition, the subjects were also uninformed about the false recognition effect during study, but they were asked to be careful on the recognition test in order to minimize their false recognitions to all words. This condition was designed to determine if merely asking subjects to be cautious was sufficient to minimize the false recognition effect for critical lures. Unlike the subjects in the uninformed condition who received no information about the words used in the recognition test, these subjects were told that some words on the test were similar to words heard at study but were not actually presented. No other information was provided.

In the forewarned condition, the subjects were provided with detailed information and examples of the false recognition effect prior to the presentation of the study lists. Because the subjects were specifically told that the study lists were designed to try to make them falsely recognize related but nonpresented words, this condition allowed subjects the chance to devise strategies to reduce or eliminate the false recognition effect. As part of the forewarning procedure, the subjects participated in a false recognition demonstration before instructions for the actual experiment were given. The subjects were read a sample list of words and told that they would be given a practice recognition test to familiarize themselves with the procedure. The list was obtained from Roediger and McDermott and not used elsewhere in this experiment. Following the presentation of the sample list, subjects were given an eight-word recognition test, constructed in the same manner as our actual test. Three of the words were from the sample list (serial positions 1, 8, and 10), one word was the nonpresented critical lure, and four words were unrelated distracters taken from another Roediger and McDermott list not used again in this experiment.

Remembering Words 9

After the subjects completed the sample recognition test, the critical lure was identified, and the false recognition effect was described.

These subjects were further informed that prior research had demonstrated that presenting lists of words that were semantically associated to nonpresented words led to high levels of false recognition of the critical lures. This discussion was followed by a reading of another sample list of 15 related words, along with its critical lure from another Roediger and McDermott list that was not used again in this experiment. The subjects were told that the lists that they would hear at study were constructed in the same fashion as the sample lists. Their task was to minimize the false recognition of critical lures without sacrificing their recognition of words presented at study. Care was taken to ensure that the subjects understood the manner in which the study lists were constructed, the nature of the false recognition effect, and the goal of minimizing the false recognition of critical lures. Prior to the recognition test, the subjects were reminded of their task. Together, these procedures provide a strong test of any possible effect of forewarning.

Results

The primary data consisted of the responses to the recognition test for subjects in the uninformed, cautious, and forewarned conditions and the remember vs. know judgments for all of the words that were recognized. These results are shown in Table 1 for each condition and response measure.

Table 1 indicates that the hit rate for studied words varied across groups, and this observation was supported by the results of an analysis of variance, $F(2, 42) = 4.62$, $MSe = .02$, $p < .02$. The hit rate for the uninformed group (.76) was greater than that for the cautious group (.65), $t(30) = 2.33$, $SEM = .05$, $p < .05$, and the forewarned group (.63) $t(30) = 3.01$, $SEM = .04$, $p < .01$, whereas the hit rates for the cautious and forewarned groups did not vary, $t < 1$. There was also an effect of groups on the false recognition rate for critical lures, $F(2, 42) = 11.05$, $MSe = .05$, $p < .001$, as the rate for the forewarned group (.46) was less than that for the uninformed group (.81), $t(30) = 4.84$, $SEM = .07$, $p < .001$, and the cautious group (.74), $t(30) = 3.36$, $SEM = .08$, $p < .01$. The false alarm rates for critical lures for the uninformed and cautious group did not vary, $t < 1$, and there were no overall effect of groups on the false alarm rates for nonstudied words or unrelated critical lures, both F's < 1.

In addition to producing the highest hit rate, the uninformed group also produced a strong false memory effect by falsely recognizing the nonpresented critical lures (.81) at least as frequently as the studied words (.76), $t(15) = 1.25$, $SEM = .04$, $p > .10$. On the remember vs. know judgment task, these subjects selected remember responses more frequently than know responses for recognized studied words, $t(15) = 4.43$, $SEM = .06$, $p < .001$, and falsely recognized critical lures, $t(15) = 2.40$, $SEM = .11$, $p < .05$. Their false alarm rates for nonstudied words and unrelated critical lures were the same (.15), and most of these false alarms were judged as know responses. These results closely replicate Roediger and McDermott's (Experiment 2, Table 2) results and indicate that when subjects are uninformed about this memory illusion, they cannot differentiate list items from semantically related but nonpresented items.

The finding that subjects in the cautious group had a significantly lower overall hit rate and nonsignificantly lower false alarm rates than subjects in the uninformed group suggests that the instructions to be cautious influenced recognition performance. But even though these subjects exercised caution, they still demonstrated a false memory effect by recognizing critical lures (.74) at least as often as studied words (.65), $t(15) = 1.8$, $SEM = .05$, $p > .05$. However, these subjects, who selected remember responses over know responses for recognized studied words, $t(15) = 2.67$, $SEM = .06$, $p < .05$, did not differentiate these responses for falsely recognized critical lures $t < -1$. Their false alarm rates were the same for nonstudied words and unrelated critical lures (.12), and most of these false alarms were judged as know responses. These results indicate that instructing subjects to be cautious can lower the hit rate for studied words and reduce the likelihood that falsely recognized critical lures will be judged as remembered from the prior lists. But such instructions do not diminish the false recognition effect. Merely asking people to be cautious about their false alarms has little effect on this memory illusion.

Most important, the subjects in the forewarned group had a lower overall hit rate and a lower false alarm rate for critical lures than subjects in the uninformed group. At the same time, they had a comparable hit rate and a lower critical lure false alarm rate than subjects in the cautious

group. These subjects still made more false recognitions of critical lures (.46) than unrelated

critical lures (.14), $t(15) = 5.39$, $SEM = .06$, $p < .001$, demonstrating the persistence of the

false memory effect. But their lower rate of false recognition of critical lures, relative to that rate

for either the uninformed (.81) or cautious (.74) groups, and their lower rate of false recognition

of critical lures relative to their hit rate, $t(15) = 3.2$, $SEM = .05$, $p < .01$, indicates that fore-

warning instructions diminished the false recognition effect. Moreover, unlike the uninformed

subjects, these subjects did not differentiate between remember and know judgments for either

recognized studied words, $t(15) = 1.0$, $SEM = .05$, $p > .10$, or critical lures, $t(15) = -1.3$,

$SEM = .08$, $p > .10$. As in the previous conditions, the false alarm rates for nonstudied words

and unrelated critical lures were the same (.14), with the majority of these false alarms judged as

know responses. These results demonstrate that forewarning instructions can reduce the magni-

tude of the false recognition effect by reducing the proportion of falsely recognized critical lures

and the proportion of those false recognitions judged to be remembered from study.

The Postexperiment Questionnaire

An open-ended questionnaire was given to all subjects at the end of the experiment. It was

designed to provide information about subject awareness of study list organization and the types

of strategies that were used to maximize performance on the recognition test. For subjects in the

cautious group, we were interested in determining how they might reduce their false alarms to all

nonstudied words, whereas for subjects in the forewarned group, we wanted to know how they

attempted to minimize their susceptibility to recognizing critical lures. Each subject's written

statement was sorted into one of four categories based on the specific strategy that was described.

Those categories consisted of the following: no strategy indicated (these subjects made no report

of any strategy), maintenance rehearsal (these subjects focused on the sound of each list word or

repeated them silently during study), elaborative rehearsal (these subjects focused on list themes

by linking study words by semantic associations or forming visual images of the words), and

determine critical lures (in addition to focusing on each list's theme, these subjects tried to determine and remember each list's critical lure). Table 2 shows the number of subjects in each category from each group, along with the corresponding average hit rate for studied words and false alarm rate for critical lures. False alarm rates for nonstudied words and unrelated critical lures were not included because these rates were low in each condition and did not differ across groups.

The results shown in Table 2 indicate that subjects in the uninformed and cautious groups produced a similar pattern of results. These subjects were more apt to report that they used elaborative rehearsal as their primary means of remembering list words (17 of 32, or .53) than either maintenance rehearsal (3 of 32, or .09) or a strategy aimed at determining the critical lures (5 of 32, or .16). Although these subjects spontaneously used elaborative processes which are typically more effective than maintenance processes to remember the study words (e.g., Craik & Watkins, 1973), most of them were not aware of the nature of this experiment and they did not try to determine the critical lures on their own. This was true even after subjects in the cautious group were told that some nonpresented test words would be similar to study words. A far different pattern of results is seen in Table 2 for the subjects in the forewarned group. The most commonly reported strategy for these subjects was to determine the critical lures. Elaborative or maintenance rehearsal was infrequently reported, and the number of subjects who reported no strategy was comparable to other groups.

The results of Table 2 make two important points. The first point is that the instructions given to the subjects in this task influenced the type of strategy that was used. When subjects were merely told that they would be tested on lists of words (uninformed group) or urged to be cautious for a test (cautious group), the majority of them wisely adopted elaborative rehearsal processes to maximize their memory performance. However, when they were told in advance about the memory illusion (forewarned group), many of these subjects tried to determine the specific critical lures that might appear on the recognition test. The second and more important point is that subjects in all conditions were susceptible to the false recognition effect, regardless of self-reported strategy. If we examine only those categories in Table 2 with the most subjects, the false recognition of critical lures was greater for subjects in the uninformed (.89) and cautious (.82)

groups who used elaborative rehearsal than subjects in the forewarned (.45) group who tried to

determine critical lures. But note that even those subjects in the forewarned group who tried to

find critical lures falsely recognized nearly half of them. Those subjects understood the fore-

warning instructions and tried to minimize the false recognition effect, yet they were still influ-

enced by the memory illusion they were actively trying to resist. Clearly, forewarning

instructions diminished but did not eliminate the false recognition effect.

An In-Class Demonstration

As part of a regular meeting of the third author's class, Psychology 221, Human Memory, 25

Wesleyan University students participated in an in-class demonstration on the effect of forewarn-

ing. Prior to the demonstration, the students were given a detailed description of Roediger and

McDermott's experiment, along with a sample list and critical lure. The instructor then informed

them that they would be read eight lists of words, and their job was to devise a strategy to mini-

mize the false recognition of critical lures. The study lists and recognition test were constructed in

the same fashion as the present experiment. The lists were read at a rate of approximately 1.5 s

per word, and remember and know judgments were not made at test. The results closely paral-

leled those from the forewarned group in the present experiment for hit rate (.67), false alarms for

critical lures (.49), and false alarms for nonstudied words (.19) and unrelated critical lures (.22).

Even though the memory students still falsely recognized critical lures greater than unrelated crit-

ical lures, $t(24) = 7.57$, $SEM = .04$, $p < .001$, their level of false recognition for critical lures

was lower than their hit rate for studied words, $t(24) = 3.40$, $SEM = .05$, $p < .01$. These findings

indicate that the memory students were susceptible to this memory illusion, albeit at an attenu-

ated level. Thus, in both a formal laboratory setting and a less formal classroom setting, forewarn-

ing instructions served to diminish but not eliminate the effect of this memory illusion.

Discussion

The study demonstrated several important points. First, when subjects were uninformed about

the memory illusion, they demonstrated a strong false recognition effect. These subjects falsely recognized critical lures at a rate that was comparable to their hit rate for studied words, and they were more likely to indicate that they specifically remembered those words from study than simply knew that they were presented. Second, when subjects were urged to be cautious about false alarms to all words, they still demonstrated a strong false recognition effect as their false alarm rate for critical lures was comparable to their hit rate for studied words. However, instructions to be cautious decreased the likelihood that falsely recognized critical lures would be remembered from study. Third, when subjects were forewarned about the memory illusion, they demonstrated a diminished false recognition effect. These subjects reduced their false alarm rate for critical lures, and they made remember and know judgments equally often for recognized studied words and critical lures. Fourth, a postexperiment questionnaire indicated that the majority of the subjects in the uninformed and cautious groups used elaborative rehearsal to try to remember the study words, whereas many subjects in the forewarned group tried to determine the critical lures. The subjects in the forewarned group who sought the critical lures were still susceptible to the memory illusion. Finally, the effects of forewarning on false recognition were shown to be reliable by the results of an in-class demonstration.

Our finding that forewarning instructions diminished but did not eliminate the false recognition effect provides an empirical link between perceptual and memory illusions. Earlier, Roediger and McDermott (1995) suggested that the false memory effect functions as a perceptual illusion when they stated that "Just as perceptual illusions can be compelling even when people are aware of the factors giving rise to the illusion, we suspect that the same is true in our case of remembering events that never happened." (p. 812). Our results do not disagree; both knowledgeable and uninformed subjects falsely recognized critical lures. The present procedures allowed forewarned subjects the opportunity to devise strategies to reduce their susceptibility to critical lures. Yet even though many subjects in their group sought to determine those critical lures, they still falsely recognized almost half of them. This memory illusion can be influenced by a subject's knowledge because the procedures used in this task allow time for that knowledge to be used. But even when the subjects were armed with this knowledge, false recognitions still occurred. Given the extensive

Remembering Words 15

training procedures used in the forewarned condition, it is not obvious how we might have better informed our subjects about this illusion, nor is it clear that a better strategy exists to ward off its effect than trying to determine the critical lures. This strategy was not wholly effective, and its effectiveness would be expected to diminish as the number of study lists grows larger than the memory span. Clearly, even knowledgeable subjects make memory errors in this task.

To explain this memory illusion, some researchers have adopted Underwood's (1965) *implicit activation response hypothesis* that suggests that when subjects encode words, they think of semantic associates to those words at study (e.g., Roediger & McDermott, 1995; Schacter et al., 1996). In the present experiment, listening to lists of semantically related words may activate representations for critical lure because they are the highest semantic associates of the list items. On the subsequent recognition test, subjects may falsely recognize those words on the basis of implicit stimulus familiarity or explicit retrieval of the study context. If the representations for the critical lures are not consciously activated at study, subjects may falsely recognize those words at test, but they may be more apt to say that they know that those items were presented than to say that they specifically remember their presentation. If those representations were consciously activated at study, subjects may not only falsely recognize those items, they may also say that they remember their presentation. In both instances, subjects would be making a source monitoring error about the critical lures. Forewarned subjects in the present experiment may have reduced both their false alarm rate and their frequency of remember judgments to critical lures by rejecting any lures at test that were consciously activated at study and identified as related but nonstudied words. However, these subjects would still be prone to false recognitions, albeit at a lower rate and with a lower frequency of remember judgments than the other conditions, because they could still be fooled by critical lures that were nonconsciously activated at study or were consciously activated but not identified as nonstudied words.

Finally, psychologists have long known that memory errors occur in nonlaboratory settings (e.g., Bartlett, 1932; Munsterberg, 1908), and there is currently great controversy over the possibility of recovered/false memories of childhood abuse (Loftus, 1993). We do not claim that the present paradigm offers a general method for studying false memory or that the present findings can generalize to memories of child abuse (see Freyd & Gleaves, 1996, and Roediger & McDermott, 1996, for comments on these issues). Rather, we think that the present false recognition research has practical value in understanding the degree to which knowledge can be used to inoculate a person against a false memory effect. Are memory errors always likely to plague us because remembering is fundamentally constructive in nature, as Roediger and McDermott (1995) assert, or might we overcome these errors by understanding the conditions under which they are likely to occur? Our findings suggest that inoculation by knowledge may achieve only limited success as knowledgeable people could only partially control their susceptibility to remembering events that never occurred.

Remembering Words 17

References

Bartlett, F. C. (1932). *Remembering: A study in experimental and social psychology.*
   Cambridge: Cambridge University Press.

Craik, F. I. M., & Watkins, M. J. (1973). The role of rehearsal in short-term memory.
   Journal of Verbal Learning and Verbal Behavior, 12, 599–607.

Deese, J. (1959). On the prediction of occurrence of particular verbal intrusions in immediate
   recall. *Journal of Experimental Psychology, 58,* 17–22.

Freyd, J. J., & Gleaves, D. H. (1996). "Remembering" words not presented in lists:
   Relevance to the current recovered/false memory controversy. *Journal of Experimental
   Psychology: Learning, Memory, and Cognition, 22,* 811–813.

Gregory, R. L. (1987). Illusions. In R. L. Gregory (Ed.), *The Oxford companion to the mind.*
   New York: Oxford University Press.

Loftus, E. F. (1993). The reality of repressed memories. *American Psychologist, 48,*
   518–537.

McDermott, K. B. (1996). The persistence of false memories in list recall. *Journal of
   Memory and Language, 35,* 212–230.

Munsterberg, H. (1908). *On the witness stand: Essays on psychology and crime.* New York:
   Clark, Boardman, Doubleday.

Payne, D. G., Elie, C. J., Blackwell, J. M., & Neuschatz, J. S. (1996). Memory illusions: Recalling, recognizing, and recollecting events that never occurred. *Journal of Memory and
   Language, 35,* 261–285.

Rajaram, S. (1993). Remembering and knowing: Two means of access to the personal past.
   Memory & Cognition, 21, 89–102.

Read, J. D. (1996). From a passing thought to a false memory in 2 minutes: Confusing real and
   illusory events. *Psychonomic Bulletin & Review, 3,* 105–111.

Roediger, H. L. III. (1996). Memory illusions. *Journal of Memory and Language, 35,*
   76–100.

Remembering Words 18

Roediger, H. L. III, & McDermott, K. B. (1995). Creating false memories: Remembering
words not presented in lists. *Journal of Experimental Psychology: Learning, Memory, and
Cognition, 21,* 803–814.

Roediger, H. L. III, & McDermott, K. B. (1996). False perceptions of false memories.
Journal of Experimental Psychology: Learning, Memory, and Cognition, 22, 814–816.

Schacter, D. L., Verfaellie, M., & Pradere, D. (1996). The neuropsychology of memory illusions: False recall and recognition in amnesic patients. *Journal of Memory and Language,
35,* 319–334.

Tulving, E. (1985). Memory and consciousness. *Canadian Psychologist, 26,* 1–12.

Underwood, B. J. (1965). False recognition produced by implicit and verbal responses. *Journal
of Experimental Psychology, 70,* 122–129.

Remembering Words 19

Author Notes

Appreciation is expressed to Chun Luo for helpful comments on an earlier draft of this paper. This research was supported by a Wesleyan Grant in Support of Scholarship made to J. G. S. Correspondence should be addressed to him at the Department of Psychology, Wesleyan University, Middletown, CT 06459-0408 (e-mail: jseamon@wesleyan.edu).

Table 1

*Mean Recognition for Studied and Nonstudied Words
and Related and Unrelated Critical Lures*

	Proportion of Recognized Words		
	Overall	R	K
Uninformed Condition			
List Words			
Studied	.76	.52	.24
Nonstudied	.15	.03	.12
Critical Lures			
Related	.81	.55	.27
Unrelated	.15	.06	.10
Cautious Condition			
List Words			
Studied	.65	.41	.24
Nonstudied	.12	.03	.09
Critical Lures			
Related	.74	.37	.38
Unrelated	.12	.01	.11
Forewarned Condition			
List Words			
Studied	.63	.34	.28
Nonstudied	.14	.02	.12
Critical Lures			
Related	.46	.19	.28
Unrelated	.14	.03	.11

Note. R = Remember Judgment; K = Know Judgment. Instances where remember and know proportions do not sum to the overall proportion reflect rounding to two decimal places.

Table 2

Hits for Studied Words and False Alarms For Critical Lures

According to Self-Reported Strategies

	Self-Reported Strategy			
	None Indicated	Maintenance Rehearsal	Elaborative Rehearsal	Determine Critical Lures
Uninformed Condition				
N	3	2	8	3
Hits	.71	.71	.81	.74
FAs	.83	.81	.89	.58
Cautious Condition				
N	4	1	9	2
Hits	.56	.83	.66	.71
FAs	.59	.88	.82	.63
Forewarned Condition				
N	4	2	3	7
Hits	.49	.65	.65	.68
FAs	.28	.69	.58	.45

Note. N represents the number of subjects; hits and false alarms are proportions.

Style

Now that you have some idea of format, let us consider style. After suffering through some obscurely written article, you will no doubt recognize the advantage of clear, unambiguous writing. The APA format helps to standardize the order and general content. However, making sure that the reader understands what you are saying is up to you. We have read many research reports prepared for our classes, and we have found that the biggest problem is transition, or flow, from one section to the next. Many students write as though they were composing a surprise-ending short story, even though their report should be as straightforward as possible.

Your title should be short (10 to 12 words) and concise. The title should be meaningful in and of itself; it should be able to stand alone. It should not contain any extraneous words such as "a study of." Usually the title states the independent variables and dependent variables of the study.

Your abstract should include your variables (independent, dependent, and important control variables), number and type of participants, major results, and important conclusions. Students often include too much detail in the abstract; remember, you only have a few words (fewer than 120), so state only the most essential aspects of the project so that a potential reader will have a general, but clear, idea of what was done and what was found. The body of your report should expand on the abstract. (This is why most abstracts are written last, even though the report might be clearer if the abstract were written first, as the outline for the main part of the work.)

In the introduction, you should state why you are interested in a particular issue, what other investigators have found, and what variables you will be examining. You should begin by stating a broad perspective on the issue, then quickly narrow down to the specific question that interests you. You should lead the reader through the *relevant* research, always keeping in mind that you are setting up your own research question. Therefore, avoid discussion of tangential issues. Toward the end of the introduction, give the reader an overview of your experiment, specifying your hypotheses explicitly and outlining any predictions derived from theories you have discussed. By the end of the introduction, the reader should see your experiment as filling an important gap in our knowledge.

In the Method section, state how you examined the variables you described at the end of the introduction. Here, it is important to be clear and complete. By the time you write the Method section, you are quite familiar with the details and complexities of your experiment. This familiarity makes it difficult to realize that the reader of your report is learning of these details for the first time. As you write, try to tell the reader everything he or she would need to know to be able to repeat your experiment, but do not include any extraneous variables. Often authors divide their Method section into three subsections: participants, materials (or apparatus), and procedure. The participants subsection specifies the number of participants in the study, the population from which they were drawn (for example, the introductory psychology class at your university), and their incentive for participating (for example, course credit). If any participants were discarded for any reason, that should be mentioned in this section. The **materials** (or apparatus) subsection should describe all relevant aspects of the materials used in the experiment. The next subsection, procedure, often begins with a description of the experimental design, then states the instructions given to participants (if they are human), and generally leads the reader through the various phases of the experiment.

In the Results section, state what happened when you examined the variables. Clarity is important here. Avoid simply listing your statistical analyses with minimal comment. Instead, state each finding in plain English first, then support it with statistics. Your Results section should end with a summary of the purpose and results of your experiment.

In your discussion, state what the effects of the variables mean for the issue at hand. The biggest danger in this section of the paper is lack of organization. Before you begin writing, you should know the points you want to make. Make them concise and easy to understand. The discussion should follow up the issues pointed out in the introduction. Also, as in the introduction, avoid straying onto tangents. When the reader has completed your report, he or she should be able to state the main conclusions in a sentence or two. Be careful, however, in the conclusions you draw; avoid grandiose statements. Science advances in small steps; your experiment need not be earthshaking to be scientifically important.

Finally, the body of your report should represent a tight package, not a disjointed essay containing sections that seem independent of each other. You have to tell your readers what you were trying to do more than once. Do not be afraid to be somewhat redundant by having each section build on the previous one. If you repeat the purpose of your research often enough, every reader will have gotten something from your report by the time he or she gets to the reference list. Table 14–2 summarizes the information that should be included in each section of your report.

The APA *Publication Manual* (2001b) outlines writing style considerations as follows: orderly expression of ideas, smoothness of expression, economy of expression, precision, and clarity. It also offers strategies to improve one's writing style. These guidelines warrant some discussion, so we now consider aspects of writing style.

Scientific writing demands clarity, so each word has to be chosen carefully. Consider these sentences that regularly appear in undergraduate research reports: "I ran the subjects individually" and "The white albino rat was introduced to the Skinner box." Actually, none of the subjects in the study from which the first sentence was pulled did any running during the course of the project. What the author meant to say was, "I tested the subjects individually." From reading about rats introduced to Skinner boxes, you might conclude that the researcher had very clever rats. The rat did not shake hands with a box; all that happened was that the rat was put into the operant-conditioning chambers. Furthermore, "white albino" is redundant. All albino rats are white. The lesson

Table 14–2   Summary of the information in each section of a research report

Section	Information
Title	Experiments: State independent and dependent variables— "The effects of X and Y." Other studies: State the relationships examined— "The relation between X and Y."
Abstract	In less than 120 words, state what was done to whom, and summarize the most important results.
Introduction	State what you plan to do and why (you may have to review results from related research). Predicted results may be appropriate.
Method	Present enough information to allow someone else to repeat your study exactly the way you did it. For clarity, use subheadings (*Participants, Apparatus,* etc.), and make sure that dependent, independent, participant, and control variables are specified.
Results	Summarize important results in tables or figures. Direct the reader to data that seem most relevant to the purpose of the research.
Discussion	State how the results relate to the hypotheses or predictions stated in the introduction. Inferences and theoretical statements are appropriate.
References	In APA format, list only those references that were cited in your report.

here is that in scientific writing, you must be careful to choose the correct word or phrase and avoid ambiguity. Also, be cautious when using pronouns such as *which, this, that, these,* and *those.* Many students find it irresistible to begin a paragraph with one of these pronouns, and more often than not, the referent for the pronoun is not easy to determine. You can usually avoid any ambiguity by including the referent of the pronoun each time it is used.

After you have decided on your words and phrases, put them together carefully. A common problem among some writers is to shift verb tenses abruptly. In general, use the past tense in the review of other studies in your introduction (Smith *found*) and in your method (the subjects *were*). When you are describing and discussing your data, the present tense is usually appropriate (The data *show* that . . ., which *means* that).

Make sure that collective and plural nouns agree with their verbs and pronouns. Plural words that end in *a,* such as *data, criteria,* and *phenomena* are troublesome. Each of these nouns is plural, so they require plural verbs and pronouns. "These data *are*" is correct, but "this phenomena *is*" is not correct. The singular forms for these nouns are *datum, criterion,* and *phenomenon* (this phenomenon *is*), respectively.

Many scientific writers overuse the passive voice in their reports. Consider this statement: "It is thought that forgetting is caused by interference." Although this sentence is fairly concise (and precise), it is also stuffy and less direct than "We think that interference causes forgetting," which is really what was meant. Be careful about using either the active or the passive voice too much. If you overuse the passive voice, your report sounds stuffy. If you overuse the active voice, you may take interest away from what you did and place too much emphasis on yourself (I think, I did, and so on). If you want to emphasize what was done and not who did it and why, use the passive construction. On the other hand, if you think that the agent of the activity is also important, or if the reason for the action is important, use the active voice.

The careful writer avoids language that is sexist. The APA recommends that the use of *he* (and *his* and *him*) as a generic pronoun be avoided by changing to a plural construction or by using *he and she*. Generally, the writer should strive for accurate, unbiased communication. The APA *Publication Manual* contains a section devoted to the reduction of language bias.

Scientific writing requires the use of consistent terminology; if you assign labels to things (for example, labeling participant groups *informed* and *uninformed*), use these labels throughout the paper. You may have been taught in English classes to try to vary descriptions of repetitive things to avoid boring the reader. However, in scientific writing, changing terminology only adds confusion. It is important that the reader know that when you introduce a new term, it refers to a concept different from ones previously discussed.

Writing a cogent, well-organized research article is a skill that requires considerable effort and practice. More is involved than simply allocating information to the correct sections. There are many fine points of style, usage, and exposition that distinguish lucid, well-written articles from obscure and tortuous ones. While writing your report, you should make frequent use of standard references for points of style and grammar. In addition, consult the APA *Publication Manual* regarding aspects of technical writing that are particularly relevant to psychology journal articles, including the organization and content of each section, the economy and precision in the expression of ideas, the presentation of data and statistics, and so forth. We highly recommend the aforementioned book by Sternberg (1993), a recent article by Sternberg (1992), and a chapter by Bem (1987) for excellent advice and specific examples of good and poor style, phrasing, and organization in psychology articles. Finally, and perhaps most importantly, you should allocate time for revising and rewriting your manuscript, with the aforementioned stylistic comments in mind. No one can write a publishable manuscript on the first try; revision is a crucial part of the writing process.

▶ How to Publish an Article

Assume that your article has been written, proofread, and corrected, and the last page has just emerged from your printer. Now what? Although it is unlikely that your first student effort will produce an article of professional quality, you may nevertheless find it interesting to discover what happens when a professional psychologist submits an article to a journal.

The first step is to send copies of the manuscript (the technical term for an unpublished work) to a small number of trusted associates who can check it over to make sure that it has no obvious or elementary flaws and that it is written clearly. Once the comments come back, the indicated corrections are made and, with some trepidation, the author commits the manuscript to the mail, addressed to the editor of the most appropriate journal. After this, it is necessary to exhibit great patience for the next few months. The review process is slow. (The editor who receives the manuscript typically is extremely busy juggling many responsibilities—teaching, conducting his or her own research, supervising undergraduate and graduate students, and so on.) Two or three weeks after submitting the article, the author receives a form letter thanking him or her for interest in the journal and acknowledging receipt of the manuscript. The manuscript gets a number (such as 99–145), and if an associate editor has been assigned to handle it, the author is instructed to direct all future correspondence to that editor.

The editor sends copies of the manuscript to two or three reviewers. Some journals allow the author to have anonymous reviewing, where the author's identity is concealed. This is for those who do not believe in the impartiality of reviewers. The reviewer, who may also review for several other journals, may take a day or two to carefully read and evaluate a manuscript. Then a summary statement is sent to the editor. When the reviewers are in agreement, the editor's decision is easy. Should the reviewers disagree, the editor must carefully read the manuscript and sometimes may request a third opinion. Finally, an editorial decision is reached and the author receives a letter stating either (a) why the manuscript cannot be published, (b) what kind of revisions are needed to make the manuscript acceptable, or (c) that the journal will publish the article. Because rejection rates for manuscripts are quite high in most journals (above 70%), editors spend a great deal of time devising tactful letters of rejection.

Whether or not the article was accepted, the comments of the reviewers are most valuable. The best psychologists in the area have provided, free of charge, their careful opinions about the research. Of course, reviewers can also make mistakes. Any author who disagrees with a review has the privilege of writing to the editor. Although this action will usually not result in the article being accepted, it is important that rejected authors have the right to appeal or protest. Anyway, there are always other journals.

If the article was accepted for publication, the author is still not yet finished. Some revision of the manuscript may be required. The copyright for the article is signed over to the publisher. Some months later, the author receives galley or page proofs from the publisher. These must be carefully checked to ensure that the words and tables set in type by the printer match those in the original manuscript. After making corrections, the author returns the article to the publisher. Several months later, the article finally appears in the journal. The entire process, from submission of the manuscript until final publication, takes a year or more. Authors do not get paid for articles in journals, but on the other hand, neither are they charged for the privilege of appearing in print. Having a research report published in a journal makes the results available to any interested scientist. Moreover, it makes the results available to researchers many years in the future.

▶ How to Give an Oral Presentation

Another avenue for sharing results is psychological conventions. Although most research is eventually submitted to a scientific journal, conventions are often the first place that research is reported. Psychologists gather in groups of varying size to present the results of their most recent research. Some of these conventions are very specific in the type of research reported (for example, neuropsychological research only), whereas others are much more general, including all areas of psychology. These conferences allow scientists to meet and discuss recent and ongoing research—work that has not yet been published. The results of student research are sometimes presented at such conferences. After conducting a research project, if you think it is worth sharing with the scientific community, you might ask your professor about appropriate conventions in your area. If your professor agrees that the work is good enough to present at such a convention, he or she will explain to you how to submit your research.

Oral presentations are also important in many other settings—in class presentations, in informal research groups, or to your psychology class or Psi Chi group. The tips below should help you with these other sorts of talks, too.

Content

If your paper is accepted, you will probably be given approximately 15 minutes in which to present your research and about 2 to 3 minutes at the end to answer questions. In general, your talk will differ from a written report in that you will be able to present only a portion of what you would write. Therefore, you should not get bogged down in detail, whether it be related research, procedural details, statistics, or secondary findings. You will have time only to present the basic problem and why it is interesting, your method of attacking the problem, and what you found.

Your talk should begin like a brief introduction of a written report: State the question and why it is interesting. Knowing when to define terms and when to assume that your audience already knows the technical terms you will use can be a tricky issue. However, because your audience will likely be somewhat diverse, a good rule is to define any terms that are not generally known by all psychologists. You should briefly review the research in the literature that is most directly related to your experiment and state your research question, as well as any hypothesis you had.

After setting up the question, give a description of how you tried to answer it. Define your independent and dependent variables. Give enough detail here to be understandable, but be careful not to get bogged down in procedural detail. You should then present your results. Present the data in the clearest way possible; usually, this means using figures or tables containing means or other descriptive data. As in written reports, do not simply describe the statistical tests performed and their significance levels. Instead, tell your audience in general terms what your results were (for example, people performed better in the visual condition than in the auditory condition), and then back your statement with a significance test or just say the results are statistically significant by appropriate tests.

You should wrap up the talk with a reminder of your original hypothesis and whether (or not) it was upheld. You should then state the conclusions that you draw from your research. If you plan to continue research in this area, you might briefly describe the next questions your research will be addressing.

Style

We have several stylistic suggestions for presenting your results. First, although it is probably advisable to memorize the first and last sentences of your talk, you should not read the talk. Instead, make a brief outline of the points you wish to make and speak from the outline. This approach may seem difficult at first, but with practice, you can learn to speak from an outline. This method will allow you to make eye contact with the audience and will make your talk more interesting and easier to follow.

Whenever possible, it is advisable to use visual aids, such as overheads or slides. These help your audience to follow your logic in the Introduction and Method sections, and they are crucial in presenting results. One popular approach is to have an overhead containing a brief outline of the introduction, one with an outline of your experimental method, a figure or table with your results, an overhead with a written summary of your results, and finally, one with your conclusions. Be careful not to clutter your visual aids with too much detail, and make sure that the font is big enough that people in the back of the room will be able to see your overheads or slides clearly.

Finally, practice your talk! Practice by yourself until you feel comfortable speaking from an outline and you get the talk to last the correct amount of time. Some people find that speaking in front of a mirror helps them to notice distracting gestures that they should try to avoid. A tape recorder can be used to help you notice extraneous sounds ("um's" and "uh's"), which should be avoided. Taping yourself will also allow you to notice other unwanted habits, such as excessive use of run-on sentences. After you feel comfortable with your talk, ask your friends to listen and provide constructive criticism. Finally, you might ask your professor to listen to your talk; he or she will likely have many suggestions for making the talk more effective. Further advice on giving research talks can be found in Darley and Zanna's (1987) chapter.

The oral presentation of research is an important method used by scientists to present their research to interested parties. Due in part to the lags of at least 1 year between submission of a manuscript to a journal and actual publication of the paper, research presented at conferences is almost always more recent than that found in the journals. Thus, it is beneficial for scientists to attend conference presentations. It is also in the best interest of scientists to present their own research at conferences, because this forum allows them to receive immediate feedback on their research from experts who share their interests. Thus, the ability to give effective oral presentations is a central part of the career of a research psychologist.

▶ How to Give a Poster Presentation

Although talks are an efficient way to present research at psychological conventions, another option is to give a poster presentation. Also, if you present at a national conference, this may be the only option available to a junior investigator. Poster sessions usually involve dozens of participants in the same large room, simultaneously presenting their individual posters to small groups of people who gather around. Posters are prepared beforehand, brought to the convention, and tacked to a large poster board. You should also have miniature handouts of your poster available for audience members to take with them. If your psychology department has a poster printer, it can be prepared in PowerPoint or a similar presentation program, and printed directly to large poster paper. Alternately, if your department does not have a printer of this kind, the different sections of the poster can be printed in fragments on letter-sized paper, numbered, and posted to the poster board in the proper order. Either way, preparing the poster should involve the same principles as preparing an effective talk discussed in the previous section. However, there are a few important differences to consider.

The primary difference between a talk and a poster is that when you present a poster you will typically have much less time to explain your project to your audience. A good rule of thumb is to be prepared to explain your poster, from the initial question and rationale, through the results and conclusions, within 2 minutes. Thus, many of the peripheral details of the method or secondary hypotheses will have to be omitted. You should be prepared to talk about these issues if asked, or if an audience member seems particularly interested, but there should be a priority placed on being brief and concise. The presentation should be kept short because poster sessions usually include dozens of posters and only last 1 or 2 hours. Thus, your audience usually wants to see several other posters during a poster session and has a limited amount of time to visit each one. Avoid holding your audience captive. If your description and explanation takes 10 minutes, audience members will often feign interest out of politeness (simply walking away would be rude), but they may be annoyed, and may stop paying attention before you have finished. Many convention goers "window-shop" at poster sessions, stopping to pick up a handout, and like to listen to a brief description, but do not necessarily have time for a detailed description of your project. If an audience member is particularly interested in your research project, she will likely ask specific questions, or will share information about her own relevant research. This is one of the advantages to a poster presentation: There is an increase in the intimacy of the communication, allowing you to get feedback on your project. Thus, although a convention talk may reach more audience members, poster presentations have the advantage of being more interactive.

Summary

1. The APA format provides a framework for writing a report. Reports should be written in a clear, unambiguous style.

2. After an article has been written and reviewed by colleagues, it can be submitted to a journal for publication. The publication process can sometimes take 1 year.

3. Oral presentations of research can be presented at conventions. Research presented at these conventions is almost always more recent than that found in journals.

4. For psychological science to progress, reports must be presented and published, and knowledgeable consumers must critically evaluate them.

Key Concepts

abstract (326)	figures (326)	results (326)
APA format (328)	introduction (326)	running head (325)
copy manuscript (325)	materials (351)	short title (325)
discussion (327)	method (326)	tables (326)
figure captions (327)	references (327)	title (325)

Exercise

1. Look up the procedure for submitting a manuscript for a specific journal. Normally, these can be found inside the front cover of the journal. What special requirements does the journal have? Also note that not all journals follow exact APA style; for example, the style of journals published by the Psychonomic Society differs in minor ways from APA format. Go to the website of the Psychonomic Society (http://www.psychonomic.org) and read the submission and publication guidelines.

Web Resources

There are several outlets for publication of undergraduate research on the web. These include the *Psi Chi Journal of Undergraduate Research,* which is published by the National Honors Society in psychology, at: http://www.psichi.org/pubs/journal/submissions.asp, and the *Undergraduate Journal of Psychology,* at: http://www.psych.uncc.edu/Journal.htm

The latest information regarding the APA citation format for electronic media can be found at: http://www.apastyle.org/elecmedia.html

Statistical Appendices

Descriptive Statistics

Organizing and summarizing

Useful Computational Formulae

Measures of Central Tendency	Measures of Dispersion

Mode

The most frequent score

Median

The middle score

Mean

$$\overline{X} = \Sigma X / n$$

Variance

$$s^2 = \frac{\Sigma X^2}{n} - \overline{X}^2$$

Standard Deviation

$$s = \sqrt{\frac{\Sigma X^2}{n} - \overline{X}^2}$$

Facts about the Normal Distribution

- Of all scores, 68% are within ± 1 standard deviation of the mean.
- Of all scores, nearly 96% are within ± 2 standard deviations of the mean.
- Of all scores, 99.74% are within ± 3 standard deviations of the mean.
- Standard scores (z scores) are differences between individual scores and the mean expressed in units of standard deviations.

Explanation of Symbols

- X and Y are individual scores (data).
- X^2 is each score squared.

- n is the number of observations or subjects.
- ΣX^2 refers to adding up the scores after each has been squared.

- Σ refers to the act of adding (or summing).
- $(\Sigma X)^2$ means the square of the sum of the raw scores.

APPENDIX **A**

Descriptive Statistics

▶ Descriptive Statistics: Telling It Like It Is

We have conducted research to collect data about a psychological topic. What are we going to do with the numbers? First, we need to systematize and organize them. We do not have to look at the whole array of numbers produced by participants in the different conditions of an experiment. Instead, we can look at a briefer version. Descriptive statistics provide the summarizing and systematizing function. The two main types of descriptive statistics are *measures of central tendency* and *measures of dispersion* (variability).

Let us consider a hypothetical experiment. A drug company has sponsored a test of the effects of LSD on the behavior of rats, so we decide to see how the drug affects the rats' running speed. Forty food-deprived rats have been trained to run a straight-alley maze for a food reward. We randomly assign them to two groups. To one group we administer LSD by injection and observe the effect on the speed with which the rats run the alley for food 30 minutes after the injection. The other group is tested in a similar manner 30 minutes after receiving an injection of an inert substance. The following are the running times (in seconds) for the 20 control subjects: 13, 11, 14, 18, 12, 14, 10, 13, 13, 16, 15, 9, 12, 20, 11, 13, 12, 17, 15, and 14. The running times for the subjects receiving the LSD injections are 17, 15, 16, 20, 14, 19, 14, 13, 18, 18, 26, 17, 19, 13, 16, 22, 18, 16, 18, and 9. Now that we have the running times, what do we do with them? We might want some sort of graphical representation of the numbers. One type of graph is the **histogram** shown in the two panels of Figure A–1, where the running speeds in seconds appear along the abscissa (*X*-axis), and the frequency with which each occurred in the two conditions is displayed along the ordinate (*Y*-axis). Running times for the control subjects are given in the top histogram, and those for the experimental subjects are shown in the bottom one. Another way to represent the same information is a **frequency polygon.** Its construction is equivalent to that of the histogram; you can visualize this type of graph by connecting the midpoints of the bars in the histogram.

In both conditions in Figure A–1, the greatest number of scores occurs in the middle, and the scores tend to decrease in frequency as running times become smaller or larger. Both the histogram and frequency polygon are types of **frequency distributions.** They help to systematize the data, but there are more efficient summary descriptions.

Central Tendency

The most common summary description of data is a measure of **central tendency,** which indicates the center of the distribution of scores. By far, the most common measure of central tendency in psychological research is the **mean.** The mean ($\bar{X}$) is the sum of all the scores (ΣX) divided by the number of scores (n), or $\bar{X} = \Sigma X/n$. It is what most people think of as the average of a set of numbers, although the term *average* technically applies to any measure of central tendency. The sums of the running times for the experimental and control conditions in our hypothetical experiment were 338 and 272 seconds, respectively. Because there were 20 observations in each condition, the means are 16.9 seconds for the experimental condition and 13.6 seconds for the control group.

The mean is by far the most useful measure of central tendency, and almost all inferential statistics, which we come to later, are based on it. Therefore, this statistic is used whenever possible. However, two other measures of central tendency are sometimes employed. The second most common measure is the **median.** It is the score above which half of the distribution lies and below which the other half lies. The median, then, is the midpoint of the distribution. When there is an odd number of scores in the distribution, such as 27, the median is the 14th score from the bottom or top, because that score divides the distribu-

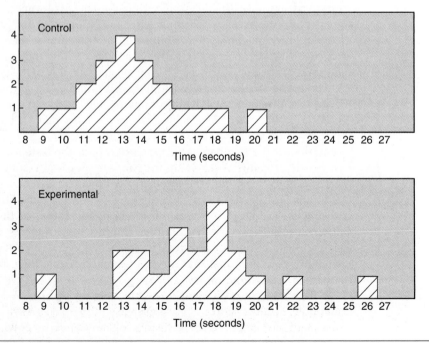

Figure A–1   Histograms representing scores for 20 subjects in the control and experimental conditions of the hypothetical LSD experiment.

tion into two groups of thirteen scores. When the number of scores (n) is an even number, the median is the arithmetic mean of the two middle scores, if the scores are not tied. So the median of the scores 66, 70, 72, 76, 80, and 96 is (72 + 76)/2, or 74. When the two middle scores are tied, as in the distribution of scores from the hypothetical LSD experiment, the convention is to designate the median as the appropriate proportion of the distance between the limits of the particular score, where the limits are a half score above and below the tied score. Consider the distributions of scores from our experiment. If we arrange the 20 control running times from lowest to highest, we discover that the 8th, 9th, 10th, and 11th scores are all 13. Under such conditions, the 10th score is considered the median, and it lies three quarters of the distance between the limits of 12.5 and 13.5. So the median would be 12.5 + .75, or 13.25, for the control subjects. By the same reasoning (and you should try it yourself), we find that the median for the experimental subjects is 17.

Why is the median used? The primary reason is that it has the desirable property of being insensitive to extreme scores. In the distribution of scores of 66, 70, 72, 76, 80, and 96, the median of the distribution would remain exactly the same if the lowest score were 1 rather than 66 or the highest score were 1,223 rather than 96. The mean, on the other hand, would differ widely with these other scores. Often this benefit can be extremely useful in summarizing data. In our LSD experiment, suppose that one of the rats given LSD had stopped halfway down the alley to examine a particularly interesting feature of the runway before continuing on its way to the goal box, and its time to complete the runway was 45 minutes or 2,700 seconds. If this score replaced the 26-second score in the original distribution, the mean would go from 16.9 seconds to 150.6, or from 3.30 seconds greater than the control mean to 137.0 seconds greater, because of only one very deviant score. In such cases, researchers often use the median score rather than the mean to represent the central tendency. Using the mean seems to give an unrepresentative estimate of central tendency because of the great influence of the one deviant score. However, using the median often severely limits any statistical tests that can be applied to the data.

The final measure of central tendency, which is almost never reported in psychological research, is the **mode,** or the most frequent score in the distribution. In the distribution of control scores in our experiment, it is 13, and in the distribution of experimental scores, it is 18.

Measures of Dispersion: Variability in Data

Measures of central tendency indicate the center of the scores, whereas measures of dispersion indicate how the scores are spread out about the center. The simplest measure of dispersion is the **range,** which is the difference between the highest and lowest scores in the distribution. For the control rats in the LSD experiment, the range is 11 (20 − 9), and for the experimental rats, it is 17 (26 − 9). The range indicates only the extreme scores, so it is rarely used.

The most useful measures of dispersion are the **standard deviation** and the **variance** of a distribution. The standard deviation is most useful as a descriptive statistic, whereas the variance of a distribution is employed in inferential statistics. As we shall see, the two are closely related.

One number that reflects the amount of spread that the scores exhibit around some central-tendency measure, usually the mean, is the *mean deviation*. This is calculated by taking the difference between the mean and every score in a distribution, summing these differences, and then dividing by the number of scores. However, we need to take the mean *absolute* difference (that is, to ignore the sign of the difference or whether the score was greater or less than the mean). The reason is that the sum of the deviations of scores about the mean is always zero, a defining characteristic of the mean (see Table A–1). Thus, the mean deviation must be the *absolute* mean deviation. The mean deviations for our hypothetical experimental conditions in the LSD experiment are calculated in Table A–1. The symbol $\|$ indicates the absolute value of a number, so $|-6| = 6$.

Table A–1   Calculation of the mean deviations and absolute mean deviations from two sets of scores. The sum of the deviations (differences) in calculating the mean deviation is zero, which is why it is necessary to use the absolute mean deviation.

Control group			Experimental group		
X	$(X - \overline{X})$	$\lvert X - \overline{X} \rvert$	X	$(X - \overline{X})$	$\lvert X - \overline{X} \rvert$
9	−4.60	4.60	9	−7.90	7.90
10	−3.60	3.60	13	−3.90	3.90
11	−2.60	2.60	13	−3.90	3.90
11	−2.60	2.60	14	−2.90	2.90
12	−1.60	1.60	14	−2.90	2.90
12	−1.60	1.60	15	−1.90	1.90
12	−1.60	1.60	16	− .90	.90
13	− .60	.60	16	− .90	.90
13	− .60	.60	16	− .90	.90
13	− .60	.60	17	+ .10	.10
13	− .60	.60	17	+ .10	.10
14	+ .40	.40	18	+1.10	.10
14	+ .40	.40	18	+1.10	1.10
14	+ .40	.40	18	+1.10	1.10
15	+1.40	1.40	18	+1.10	1.10
15	+1.40	1.40	19	+2.10	2.10
16	+2.40	2.40	19	+2.10	2.10
17	+3.40	3.40	20	+3.10	3.10
18	+4.40	4.40	22	+5.10	5.10
20	+6.40	6.40	26	+9.10	9.10

$\Sigma X = 272$ Total = 0.00   Total = 41.20 $\Sigma X = 338$ Total = 0.00   Total = 52.20

$\overline{X} = 13.60$ $\overline{X} = 16.90$

Absolute mean deviation $= \dfrac{41.20}{20} = 2.06$ Absolute mean deviation $= \dfrac{52.20}{20} = 2.62$

The absolute mean deviation of a set of scores is an adequate measure of dispersion and is based on the same logic involved in finding the mean of a distribution. However, the standard deviation and variance are preferred to the mean deviation, because they have mathematical properties that make them much more useful in advanced statistical computations. The logic behind their calculation is quite similar to that of the mean deviation, which is why we have considered the mean deviation here. In calculating the mean deviation, we had to determine the absolute value of the difference of each score from the mean so that these differences would not sum to zero. Instead of taking the absolute difference, we could have gotten rid of the troublesome negative numbers by squaring the differences. This is exactly what is done in calculating the variance and standard deviation of a distribution.

The *variance* of a distribution is defined as *the sum of the squared deviations from the mean, divided by the number of scores.* In other words, each score is subtracted from the mean and squared, then all these values are summed and divided by the number of scores. The formula for the variance is

$$s^2 = \frac{\Sigma(X - \overline{X})^2}{n} \qquad \text{(A--1)}$$

where s^2 represents the variance, X the individual scores, $\overline{X}$ the mean, and n the number of scores or observations. The *standard deviation* is simply the *square root of the variance* and is therefore represented by s. So

$$s = \sqrt{\frac{\Sigma(X - \overline{X})^2}{n}} \qquad \text{(A--2)}$$

Calculation of the standard deviations for the control and experimental conditions in the LSD experiment by the mean-deviation method is illustrated in Table A–2.

The formulas for the variance and standard deviation of a distribution shown in Equations A–1 and A–2 are rather cumbersome, and in practice, the equivalent computational formulas are used. The standard-deviation formula is

$$s = \sqrt{\frac{\Sigma X^2}{n} - \overline{X}^2} \qquad \text{(A--3)}$$

where ΣX^2 is the sum of the squares of all the scores, $\overline{X}$ is the mean of the distribution, and n is the number of scores. Similarly, the formula for variance is

$$s^2 = \frac{\Sigma X^2}{n} - \overline{X}^2 \qquad \text{(A--4)}$$

The standard deviations for the experimental and control scores are calculated by the computational formula shown in Table A–3. The value in each case is the same as when the definitional formula is used.

Table A–2 Calculation of the standard deviation, s, for the control and experimental conditions by the mean-deviation method

	Control group			Experimental group	
X	$(X - \bar{X})$	$(X - \bar{X})^2$	X	$(X - \bar{X})$	$(X - \bar{X})^2$
9	−4.60	21.16	9	−7.90	62.41
10	−3.60	12.96	13	−3.90	15.21
11	−2.60	6.76	13	−3.90	15.21
11	−2.60	6.76	14	−2.90	8.41
12	−1.60	2.56	14	−2.90	8.41
12	−1.60	2.56	15	−1.90	3.61
12	−1.60	2.56	16	− .90	.81
13	− .60	.36	16	− .90	.81
13	− .60	.36	16	− .90	.81
13	− .60	.36	17	+ .10	.01
13	− .60	.36	17	+ .10	.01
14	+ .40	.16	18	+1.10	1.21
14	+ .40	.16	18	+1.10	1.21
14	+ .40	.16	18	+1.10	1.21
15	1.40	1.96	18	+1.10	1.21
15	1.40	1.96	19	+2.10	4.41
16	2.40	5.76	19	+2.10	4.41
17	3.40	11.56	20	+3.10	9.61
18	4.40	19.36	22	+5.10	26.01
20	6.40	40.96	26	+9.10	82.81

$\Sigma X = 272$ Total $= 0.00$ $\Sigma(X-\bar{X})^2 = 138.80$ $\qquad$ $\Sigma X = 338$ Total $= 0.00$ $\Sigma(X-\bar{X})^2 = 247.80$

$\bar{X} = 13.60$ $\qquad\qquad\qquad\qquad\qquad\qquad\qquad$ $\bar{X} = 16.90$

$$s = \sqrt{\frac{\Sigma(X-\bar{X})^2}{n}} \qquad\qquad\qquad s = \sqrt{\frac{\Sigma(X-\bar{X})^2}{n}}$$

$$s = \sqrt{\frac{138.80}{20}} \qquad\qquad\qquad s = \sqrt{\frac{247.80}{20}}$$

$$s = 2.63 \qquad\qquad\qquad\qquad s = 3.52$$

To describe an array of data, psychologists usually present two descriptive statistics, the mean and the standard deviation. Although there are other measures of central tendency and dispersion, these are most useful for descriptive purposes. Variance is used extensively in inferential statistics (see Appendix B).

▶ The Normal Distribution

In the histograms in Figure A–1 representing the running times of the rats in the two conditions of our hypothetical experiment, most of the scores pile up in the center and tail off toward the ends (or tails) of the distribution, espe-

Table A–3 Calculation of the standard deviation, s, for the control and experimental conditions by using the computational formula (also called the raw-score method). The same values are obtained as when the definitional formula is used (see Table A–2), but the calculations are much easier to perform.

X	X²	X	X²
9	81	9	81
10	100	13	169
11	121	13	169
11	121	14	196
12	144	14	196
12	144	15	225
12	144	16	256
13	169	16	256
13	169	16	256
13	169	17	289
13	169	17	289
14	196	18	324
14	196	18	324
14	196	18	324
15	225	18	324
15	225	19	361
16	256	19	361
17	289	20	400
18	324	22	484
20	400	26	676

$\Sigma X = 272$ $\Sigma X^2 = 3{,}838$ $\Sigma X = 338$ $\Sigma X^2 = 5{,}960$

$\overline{X} = 13.60$ $\overline{X} = 16.90$

$\overline{X}^2 = 184.96$ $\overline{X}^2 = 285.61$

$$s = \sqrt{\frac{X^2}{n} - \overline{X}^2}$$ $$s = \sqrt{\frac{X^2}{n} - \overline{X}^2}$$

$$s = \sqrt{\frac{3{,}838}{20} - 184.96}$$ $$s = \sqrt{\frac{5{,}960}{20} - 285.6}$$

$s = 2.63$ $s = 3.52$

cially for control subjects. Most psychological data tend to look like this when represented graphically; they often approximate the **normal curve** or **standard normal distribution,** where scores are most numerous in the middle, decline in frequency with distance from the middle, and do so in a fairly symmetrical way. A score 10 points above the middle is about as common as a score 10

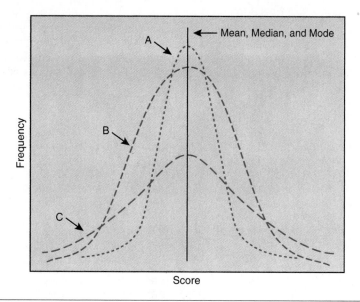

Figure A–2 Three examples of the normal curve that differ in variability. *C* has the greatest variability and *A* the least. The normal curve is a symmetrical distribution in which the mean, median, and mode all have the same value.

points below it. Several examples of normal curves are shown in Figure A–2. First, note that in all three distributions, the mean, median, and mode are the same. The main difference in the distributions is in their variability. The tall, thin curve *A* has a smaller variance (and, of course, standard deviation) than the other two, whereas the flat, broad curve *C* has a larger variance than the others. All three curves, though, are normal curves.

Each side of the normal curve has a point where the curve slightly reverses its direction; it starts bending outward more. This is called the *inflection point* and is labeled in the normal curve shown in Figure A–3. The inflection point in the curve is always one standard deviation from the mean, and the normal curve has the useful property that specific proportions of the distribution of scores it represents are contained within specific areas of the curve itself. About 68% of all scores are contained within one standard deviation of the mean (34% on each side). Similarly, almost 96% of the scores are contained within two standard deviations of the mean, and 99.74% of the scores are within three standard deviations. The percentage of each area is shown in Figure A–3. This is true of all normal curves, no matter how sharp or flat they are.

This property of normal curves is extremely useful because if we know an individual's score and the mean and standard deviation in the distribution of scores, we also know the person's relative rank. For example, most IQ tests are devised so that the population mean is 100 and the standard deviation is 15. If a person has an IQ of 115, we know that he or she scored higher than 84% of all people on the test (50% of the people below the mean and 34% above).

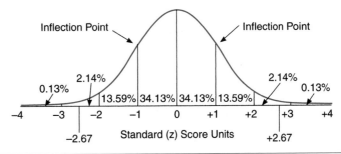

Figure A–3 Proportions of scores in specific areas under the normal curve. The inflection points are one standard deviation from the mean.

Similarly, a person with an IQ of 130 scored higher than almost 98% of all people, and a person with an IQ of 145 scored higher than 99.87% of the population. See whether you can arrive at these percentages by adding up the appropriate areas in Figure A–3.

Most distributions of scores in psychological data are, or at least are assumed to be, normal. (Often with small samples, as in our hypothetical data in Figure A–1, it is difficult to tell whether the distribution is normal.) Scores are compared across normal distributions with different means and variances in terms of **standard scores** or *z scores*. This score is simply the difference between an individual score and the mean expressed in units of standard deviations. So an IQ of 115 translates to a *z* score of 1.00, that is, $(115-100)/15$; and an IQ of 78 translates to a *z* score of -1.47, that is, $(78-100)/15$. Standard scores are useful because they allow comparison of the relative ranks of scores for a person across distributions in which the means and standard deviations vary greatly. Grades in courses should be calculated in terms of *z* scores if the means and standard deviations of the scores vary widely from one test to the next. Thus, a person's eventual rank in the class is calculated more faithfully by finding the mean of the *z* scores than by finding the mean of the raw scores of the tests.

When data in an experiment are said to be *normally distributed*, it means that if they were graphed, they would form a normal distribution, as in Figure A–3. Thus, *normal*, as it is used in psychological research, usually refers to a type of distribution (there are many other types of distributions) and is not a value judgment as to the goodness or badness of the scores.

Correlation Coefficient

In Chapter 5, correlational research is described. The purpose of correlational research is to see how two or more attributes of an organism vary together. The strength and direction of a correlation are determined by the calculation of a correlation coefficient. We will consider just one: *Pearson product-moment correlation coefficient,* or *r*. Shown in Box A–1 is the calculation formula for *r*, using the hypothetical data relating head size to memory performance discussed in Chapter 5. Box A–2 repeats this analysis, using the computerized statistical package called SPSS.

Regardless of how you calculate r, you should read the appropriate sections of Chapter 5 that discuss the use and interpretation of a correlation coefficient.

Box A–1   Computing Pearson r

Let us call one set of numbers in Table A–4 X scores and the other set Y scores. For example, head sizes might be X scores and words recalled Y scores. The formula for computing Pearson r from the raw scores in panels (a), (b), or (c) of Table 5–3 is as follows:

$$r = \frac{n \, \Sigma XY - (\Sigma X)(\Sigma Y)}{\sqrt{[n \, \Sigma X^2 - (\Sigma X)^2] \, [n \, \Sigma Y^2 - (\Sigma Y)^2]}} \tag{A–5}$$

The n refers to the number of participants on which observations are taken (here, 10); the terms ΣX and ΣY are the totals of the X and Y scores, respectively; ΣX^2 and ΣY^2 are the sum of all the X (or Y) values after each is squared; and the $(\Sigma X)^2$ and $(\Sigma Y)^2$ are the total of all the X or Y values with the entire total or sum squared. This leaves the value ΣXY, or the sum of the cross-products. This is obtained very simply by multiplying each X value by its corresponding Y and then summing these products. You may see other formulas for calculation of Pearson r besides the raw-score formula in Equation A–5, but these will be equivalent (in general) to the one presented here. An illustration of how Pearson r is calculated using this raw-score formula is presented in Table A–4 using the data from the (a) column of Table 5–3. You should try to work out the values for Pearson r for the (b) and (c) panels yourself, to make certain you understand how to calculate the values and to gain an intuitive feel for the concept of correlation. The values of r are given below the appropriate columns in Table 5–3.

Table A–4   Calculation of Pearson r for the data in the first (A) column of Table 4–3, by the raw-score formula (Equation A–5)

Subject number	X Head size (cm)	X^2	Y Words recalled	Y^2	X·Y
1	50.8	2,580.64	17	289	863.60
2	63.5	4,032.25	21	441	1,330.50
3	45.7	2,088.49	16	256	731.20
4	25.4	645.16	11	121	279.40
5	29.2	852.64	9	81	262.80
6	49.5	2,450.25	15	225	742.50
7	38.1	1,451.61	13	169	495.30
8	30.5	930.25	12	144	366.00
9	35.6	1,267.36	14	196	498.40
10	58.4	3,410.56	23	529	1,343.20

$n = 10$ $\Sigma X = 426.70$ $\Sigma X^2 = 19,709.21$ $\Sigma Y = 151$ $\Sigma Y^2 = 2451$ $\Sigma XY = 6,915.90$

Table A–4 Calculation of Pearson r for the data in the first (A) column of Table 4–3, by the raw-score formula (Equation A–5) *(Continued)*

$$r = \frac{n\Sigma XY - (\Sigma X)(\Sigma Y)}{\sqrt{[n\Sigma X^2 - (\Sigma X)^2][n\Sigma Y^2 - (\Sigma Y)^2]}}$$

$$r = \frac{10(6,915.90) - (426.70)(151)}{\sqrt{[(10)(19,709.21) - (426.70)^2][(10)(2,451) - (151)^2]}}$$

$$r = \frac{69,159.00 - 64,431.70}{\sqrt{[197,092.10 - 182,072.89][24,510 - 22,801]}}$$

$$r = \frac{4,727.30}{\sqrt{[15,019.12][1,709]}} = \frac{4,727.30}{\sqrt{25,667,829.89}}$$

$$r = \frac{4,727.30}{5,066.34}$$

$$r = +.93$$

Box A–2 Calculation of *r* by SPSS Software and Excel

The SPSS statistical package is one of many current ones available for personal computers. Other packages include MINITAB and STATISTICA. There is a program available on the Web called *Statlets* (http://www.statpoint.com), which can be used at no cost for educational purposes. SPSS is designed for quantitative data analysis in many fields, including psychology. The version of SPSS that produced the output shown on page 373 was used with Windows XP.

As follows, you can see the output from SPSS in which the head size and words-recalled data from Table A–4 were correlated. First, the data are entered into SPSS by typing it into the spreadsheet-type interface. Then, the Analyze pull-down menu was selected, followed by the Correlation function, and then bivariate (because two variables were being correlated). This resulted in a calculation of $r = .933$, which is shown under the heading *var00001* and next to *var00002,* which indicates that it was those two variables that were correlated. Note that *var00001* is Head Size and *var00002* the memory score, as indicated at the beginning of the computer session.

SPSS and the other statistical packages just noted can calculate any of the statistics covered in Appendixes A and B. Furthermore, these programs are able to perform a variety of additional analytic procedures, which are well worth learning how to use.

The popular spreadsheet program Excel, which is part of Microsoft Office, can also be used to calculate a correlation coefficient. To begin, the observations that will be correlated should be placed in separate columns. You can type in the head size and memory data from p. 373. The correlation function will be used to calculate the correlation coefficient. To use the correlation function, select an empty cell, and input an = sign, which will open the function menu in a toolbar at the top of the page. Click on the down arrow on the function toolbar to see a menu of functions (i.e., computations) available to you. If *correl* is not in the list, select the *More functions* option, and locate the *correl* function (the functions are listed alphabetically). When you select *correl,* a window appears asking you to enter two separate arrays. Select each of the arrays (i.e., columns) that you want to correlate with one another by clicking and dragging the cursor over them. That is, select the head size column as *Array 1* and the Memory column as *Array 2,* and then click *OK*. The Pearson product-moment correlation for the two columns will appear in the cell. The significance, or *p,* value is not provided in Excel, but this can be located in Table C–7 (Appendix C).

Box A–2 *(continued)*

```
Head Size (VAR00001)      Memory (VAR00002)

VAR00001                  VAR00002
 1.  50.8                 17
 2.  63.5                 21
 3.  45.7                 16
 4.  25.4                 11
 5.  29.2                  9
 6.  49.5                 15
 7.  38.1                 13
 8.  30.5                 12
 9.  35.6                 14
10.  58.4                 23

          Correlations
                                      VAR00001  VAR00002
VAR00001  Pearson Correlation         1          .933
          Sig. (2-tailed)              .         .000
          N                           10        10


VAR00002  Pearson Correlation          .933      1
          Sig. (2-tailed)              .000       .
          N                           10        10


SPSS Inc. Headquarters
233 S. Wacker Drive, 11th floor
Chicago, Illinois 60606
312.651.3000
www.spss.com
```

Additional Information on Descriptive Statistics

Explore the step-by-step presentation of central tendency, variability, *z* scores, and correlation on the Wadsworth Psychology Resource Center, Statistics and Research Methods activities at *http://psychology.wadsworth.com/workshops/workshops.html*

A complete statistics book with analysis and demonstration package can be found at *http://davidmlane.com/hyperstat/index.html*

Inferential Statistics

What statistical test should I use when . . .

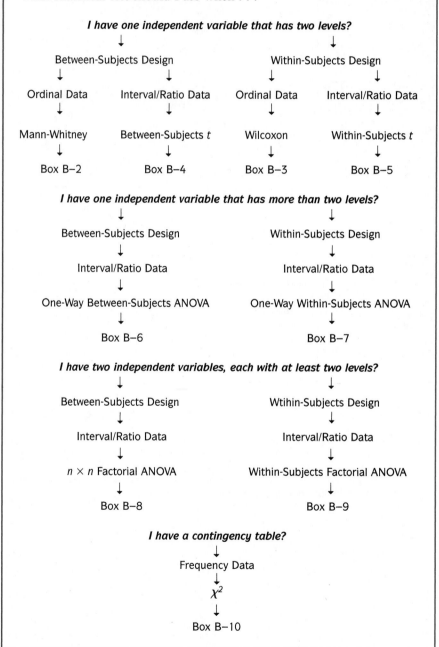

I have one independent variable that has two levels?

Between-Subjects Design		Within-Subjects Design	
Ordinal Data	Interval/Ratio Data	Ordinal Data	Interval/Ratio Data
Mann-Whitney	Between-Subjects t	Wilcoxon	Within-Subjects t
Box B–2	Box B–4	Box B–3	Box B–5

I have one independent variable that has more than two levels?

Between-Subjects Design	Within-Subjects Design
Interval/Ratio Data	Interval/Ratio Data
One-Way Between-Subjects ANOVA	One-Way Within-Subjects ANOVA
Box B–6	Box B–7

I have two independent variables, each with at least two levels?

Between-Subjects Design	Wtihin-Subjects Design
Interval/Ratio Data	Interval/Ratio Data
$n \times n$ Factorial ANOVA	Within-Subjects Factorial ANOVA
Box B–8	Box B–9

I have a contingency table?

Frequency Data

χ^2

Box B–10

Inferential Statistics

▶ Statistical Reasoning

Descriptive statistics are concerned with describing or summarizing data. The results from our LSD experiment (in Appendix A) can be summarized by saying that the control group had a mean running time of 13.60 seconds and a standard deviation of 2.63 seconds, whereas the experimental rats injected with LSD had a mean of 16.90 seconds and a standard deviation of 3.52 seconds. On average, the experimental rats ran 3.30 seconds slower than the controls, but should we take this difference seriously? Perhaps it resulted from chance factors, such as measurement error or a few rats in the control group having a particularly good day and thus feeling like running a bit faster. How can we judge whether the difference between the two conditions is real (reliable) or a fluke? Inferential statistics are used to answer this question.

In actual practice, answering this question is not too complicated. We choose an appropriate statistical test for the experimental situation, perform a few straightforward computations on a calculator (or computer), and then consult a special table. The table informs us of the probability that the difference we found between our conditions is a result of chance factors. If it is sufficiently unlikely to have occurred by chance, we conclude that the difference is statistically significant, or reliable. The computational procedures are often quite simple, but the logic behind them needs to be explained so you will understand how statistical inferences are made.

Sampling

A **population** is a complete set of measurements (or individuals or objects) having some common observable characteristic (see Box B–1). Examples of populations are all U.S. citizens of voting age, all albino rats that have had injections of LSD, and all people asked to remember a list of 50 words. Of course, it is impossible to study the entire population in any of these cases. If we could measure the entire population of rats for running speed after either an injection of LSD or an injection of a chemically inert substance, we would have a better idea of the effects of LSD. (Any difference, of course, might still be attributable to measurement error.) However, because it is almost always impractical to measure an entire population, we must sample from it. A **sample** is a subset of a population, and it is what we are usually examining when we compare experimental conditions. Thus, we make statistical inferences

Box B–1 Statistical Notation

Characteristics of a population of scores are called *parameters,* and characteristics of a sample of scores drawn from a larger population are *statistics.* The mean of an entire population of scores is a parameter, and the mean of a sample is a statistic. Different symbols are used for population parameters and sample statistics. Some of the most common are listed here. Several of the concepts have already been explained, and the others will be discussed in the next few pages.

N = number of scores in a population

n = number of scores in a sample

μ = population mean (μ is pronounced mu)

$\bar{X}$ = sample mean

σ^2 = population variance (σ is pronounced sigma)

s^2 = sample variance $\dfrac{\Sigma(X - \bar{X})^2}{n}$

$\hat{s}^2$ = unbiased estimate of population variance $\dfrac{\Sigma(X - \bar{X})^2}{n - 1}$

σ = population standard deviation

s = sample standard deviation

$\hat{s}$ = sample standard deviation based on the unbiased variance estimate

$\sigma_{\bar{x}}$ = standard error of the mean $\dfrac{\sigma}{\sqrt{N}}$

$s_{\bar{x}}$ = estimated standard error of the mean $\dfrac{s}{\sqrt{n}}$ or $\dfrac{s}{\sqrt{n - 1}}$

when we draw a conclusion about an entire population on the basis of only a sample of observations. We really want to know about the effects of LSD and the inert substance on rats in general, but we hope to draw this conclusion from a sample of, say, 20 rats in each condition.

Technically, we can only *generalize* about the population from which we have sampled, but if we took this statement literally, experimental research would hardly be worth doing. If we received 50 rats from a supply house, selected a sample of 40, and then randomly assigned them to the two conditions of our experiment, would our conclusions be true only of the population of 50 rats? Well, perhaps technically, but no one would care about the result if this were so, and we would not have wasted our time doing the experiment. We at least want to assume that the results are characteristic of that strain of rats, and, perhaps, that these results also generalize to other species, including human beings. The problem is the same in research with human beings.

Suppose you are a researcher at the University of Toronto interested in some aspect of social behavior. You prepare your experiment, which has three conditions, and you plan to use students from introductory psychology courses as participants—a common practice. You display a sign-up sheet, randomly assign the volunteers to the three experimental conditions when they show up, and collect your data. To whom do your conclusions generalize? To introductory psychology students at the University of Toronto who volunteered for your experiment? If so, who cares about what you found? In practice, psychologists assume that their results generalize more widely than to the limited population from which they sampled for their experiment.

The Distribution of Sample Means One way we could check on the reliability of our hypothetical LSD experiment would be to perform the experiment repeatedly using new groups of rats. Of course, obtaining exactly the same mean running times for the experimental and control conditions in these replications would be unlikely. The means in seconds for the experimental and control conditions in four replications might be 17.9 and 12.5, 16.0 and 13.4, 16.6 and 14.5, and 15.4 and 15.1. Because the experimental rats that receive the LSD always run slower than the control rats, we would have more confidence in our original finding, although the difference is rather small in the last replication. If we repeated the experiment like this and plotted the distribution of the sample means obtained in the two conditions, the distributions would tend to be normal, and they would have all the characteristics of a normal distribution, such as a certain proportion of the scores falling under a certain part of the curve. A plot of the difference between the sample means in each experiment would also be normally distributed.

To give you a better idea of the **distribution** of sample means concept, let us borrow an example from a class demonstration by Horowitz (1974, pp. 179–182). Horowitz manufactured a population of 1,000 normally distributed scores so that the mean and standard deviation of the entire population would be known, which is almost never the case in actual research situations. His 1,000 scores ranged from 0 to 100 and had a mean of 50 and a standard deviation of 15.8. The scores were listed on 1,000 slips of paper and placed in a container. Horowitz had 96 students take samples of 10 slips from the container and calculate the mean. On each draw from the container, the student took out a slip, noted its number, and then replaced the slip. The slips were then somewhat mixed up in the container, another slip was drawn, and so on. After each student calculated the mean of the 10 scores in his or her sample, Horowitz collected all 96 sample means and plotted their distribution, which is represented in Table B–1. The intervals between which means might fall are on the left, and the number of means falling within each interval is on the right. Notice that the distribution is almost perfectly symmetrical, with almost as many scores in any interval a certain distance below the true mean of the population (50) as above it. Also, the mean of the 96 sample means (49.99) is quite close to the actual mean of the population (50). The main thing you

Table B–1   The distribution of sample means for the 96 samples taken by students in Horowitz's class. Each sample mean was based on 10 observations.

Interval	Frequency	
62.0–63.9	1	
60.0–61.9	1	
58.0–59.9	3	
56.0–57.9	7	
54.0–55.9	9	
52.0–53.9	12	
50.0–51.9	15	Mean of sample means = 49.99
48.0–49.9	15	Standard deviation (s) of sample means = 5.01
46.0–47.9	13	
44.0–45.9	9	
42.0–43.9	6	
40.0–41.9	3	
38.0–39.9	1	
36.0–37.9	1	
	96 samples	

After Horowitz, 1974, *Elements of statistics for psychology and education,* Table 8.1. Copyright 1974 by McGraw-Hill. Reprinted with permission.

should notice in Table B–1 is the great variability among the sample means. Although each sample of 10 was presumably random, not biased in any way, and came from the same population, one sample had a mean of 37.8, whereas another had a mean of 62.3. If you did an experiment and found two very different sample means and you tried to decide whether they came from the same underlying distribution or two different distributions, you might think that such a large difference indicated that they came from different distributions. In other words, you would think that the experimental treatment produced scores reliably different (from a different distribution) than the control scores. Usually this is a good rule—the larger the difference between means in the conditions, the more likely the means are to be reliably different—but as we have seen, even random sampling from a known distribution can produce sample means that differ greatly from each other and from the true population mean, which is known in this case. While pondering small differences between means, keep this lesson in mind. Is the 3.30-second difference between experimental and control means in our hypothetical LSD experiment really reliable?

The Standard Error of the Mean   The **standard error of the mean** is the standard deviation of a distribution of sample means. In the data in Table B–1, it is 5.01. The standard error of the mean gives us some idea as to the amount of variability in the distribution of sample means, or how likely it is that the value of any particular sample mean is in error. Large standard errors indicate great variability, whereas small ones tell us that a particular sample mean is likely to be quite close to the actual population mean. Thus, the standard error of the mean is a very useful number.

You might be wondering why we bother to tell you about the standard error of the mean if to calculate it you must repeat an experiment numerous times to get the distribution of sample means and then calculate its standard deviation. Fortunately, you do not. The formula for finding the standard error of the mean (represented by $\sigma_{\bar{x}}$) is simply the standard deviation of the population (σ) divided by the square root of the number of observations ($\sqrt{n}$). Or

$$\sigma_{\bar{x}} = \frac{\sigma}{\sqrt{n}} \qquad \text{(B–1)}$$

Now, if you are still with us you might well be thinking, "Terrific. What good does this do me if the standard deviation of the population, the numerator in Equation B–1, is never known?" That question has occurred to statisticians too, so they have devised a method for estimating the standard deviation of the population from the standard deviation of a sample. If you look back at Equation A–2 in Appendix A, where the formula for the standard deviation of a sample (s) appears, and simply replace the n in the denominator by $n - 1$, you have the formula for getting an unbiased estimate of σ, the standard deviation of the population. The equation for finding the standard error of distribution of sample means (called the standard error of the mean, or $s_{\bar{x}}$) is

$$\text{Estimated } \sigma_{\bar{x}} = s_{\bar{x}} = \frac{s}{\sqrt{n-1}} \qquad \text{(B–2)}$$

Because the standard error of the mean indicates our error in assuming that our sample mean represents the population mean, we want it to be as small as possible. Equations B–1 and B–2 tell us how to do this: Increase the size of the sample, n, which increases the denominator in the equation. The greater is n, the sample size, the smaller will be the standard error of the mean, $s_{\bar{x}}$. In a population involving 1,000 scores, the sample mean should be closer to the population mean if there are 500 observations in the sample rather than only 10.

Horowitz drove this point home to the 96 students in his class by having them repeat the exercise of drawing slips from the population of 1,000 scores and calculating the mean again, but this time, he had them sample 50 slips rather than only 10. The resulting distribution of sample means is shown in Table B–2. This time, with larger samples, there is much less variability in the sample means. They are much closer to the actual population mean of 50. The standard deviation of the distribution of sample means, or the standard error of the mean, is 2.23, as opposed to 5.01 when the sample size was only 10. If $n = 100$ in a sample from the 1,000 scores, the standard error of the mean would be 1.59; with a sample of 500 it would be .71, and with 1,000 scores in a sample, it would be only .50. (These were calculated from Equation B–1, because the standard deviation, σ, is known for the entire population.) The reason we might not get the population mean even with a sample of 1,000 is that the sampling was done with *replacement*. That is, after a slip was drawn, it was returned to the container and might have been drawn again and again, but some slips were never drawn.

Table B–2   The distribution of sample means for the 96 samples taken by students when sample size (*n*) = 50. The distribution is again normal, as in Table B–1, but when each sample is based on a larger sample size, as it is here, the variability of the distribution (represented by the standard error of the mean) is much smaller.

Interval	Frequency
55.0–55.9	1
54.0–54.9	3
53.0–53.9	5
52.0–52.9	9
51.0–51.9	13
50.0–50.9	17
49.0–49.9	16
48.0–48.9	14
47.0–47.9	9
46.0–46.9	6
45.0–45.9	2
44.0–44.9	1
	96 samples

Mean of sample means = 49.95
Standard deviation (*s*) of sample means = 2.23

After Horowitz, 1974, *Elements of statistics for psychology and education,* Table 8.2. Copyright 1974 by McGraw-Hill. Reprinted with permission.

The lesson to be learned is that we should always try to maximize the number of observations—the sample size—in experimental conditions so that the statistics obtained will be as close as possible to the population parameters.

Testing Hypotheses

Scientists set up experiments to test hypotheses. The conventional statistical logic for testing hypotheses goes something like this: An experimenter arranges conditions, such as the experimental (LSD) and control (placebo) in our experiment with rats to test an **experimental hypothesis.** The experimental hypothesis in this case is that LSD will have some effect on running speed. This is tested against the **null hypothesis,** which maintains that the two conditions do not differ in their effects on running speed. In other words, the experimental hypothesis holds that the samples of running speeds come from two different underlying populations (that is, populations with different distributions), and the null hypothesis maintains that the two samples come from the same distribution. Statistical tests allow us to find the likelihood with which the null hypothesis can be rejected. How unlikely must a null hypothesis be to be rejected? If an experimental result differs from that to be expected by the null hypothesis (so much so that a difference that great would be expected on the basis of chance only 5 times in 100), we conclude that the null hypothesis can be rejected. This .05 **level of significance** is just a convention. Many psychologists prefer a more conservative .01 level for rejection, so that a null hypothesis is rejected only if the experimental result is likely to occur by chance in one case in 100. At any rate, the experimental hypothesis is tested, in a sense, indirectly. It is not affirmed, but the null hypothesis is rejected.

The logic of pitting an experimental hypothesis against the null hypothesis has come under attack in recent years for several reasons. Some argue that it gives a misleading idea about how scientists operate. For one thing, not many researchers wander about the world losing any sleep over or investing any thought into the null hypothesis. In general, experiments are set up to test our theories, and what is of primary concern is how the results can be interpreted or accounted for by our theories. Of special interest is the case in which important experimental results seem irreconcilable with the major theories of a phenomenon. Experiments are important because of what they tell us about our theories and ideas—this is why we designed them in the first place—and not about rejection of the null hypothesis. Even so, the logic of testing hypotheses against the null hypothesis is widely used as an introduction, however oversimplified to the way scientific inference proceeds. Thus, we present it here.

Testing Hypotheses: Parameters Known   The logic of testing hypotheses against the null hypothesis can be aptly illustrated in cases in which the parameters of a population are known and we wish to determine whether a particular sample comes from the population. Such cases are quite unusual in actual research, of course, because population parameters are rarely known. Suppose you were interested in whether the members of your experimental-psychology class were reliably above the national mean in intelligence as measured by IQ tests (or reliably below, as the case may be). We know the population parameters in this case: The mean is 100, and the standard deviation is 15. You could test your class easily enough by giving them the short form of some intelligence test, such as the Otis, developed for group testing.

Suppose you randomly sampled 25 people from your class of 100 and found the mean IQ of the sample to be 108 with a standard deviation of 5. How do we go about testing the experimental hypothesis that the class is reliably brighter than the population as a whole? First, let us consider the hypotheses. The experimental hypothesis is that the students are brighter than people in the nation as a whole, or that the IQ scores of the students sampled come from a different population than randomly selected people. The null hypothesis is that there is no reliable difference between our sample and the national mean, or that the students in the class are a sample from the same national population. If the null hypothesis were actually the case, the difference between the sample mean of 108 and the population parameter mean (μ) of 100 would result from random factors. Certainly this is not implausible, because we have seen from our discussion of the distribution of sample means how much a sample mean can differ from a population parameter, even when the sample is selected in an unbiased manner. Remember Horowitz's classroom demonstration, the results of which are portrayed in Tables B–1 and B–2.

The normal curve, the distribution of sample means, and z scores can help us to determine how likely it is that the null hypothesis is false. When unbiased samples are taken from a larger population, the means of these samples are normally distributed. With normal distributions, we can specify what proportion of the distribution falls under each part of the curve (as shown in Figure A–3 in Appendix A). Remember also that the z scores are the calculation of any score in a normal distribution in standard deviation units from the mean.

All this is by way of review. Now, how does this help us? What we do in testing the hypothesis that the sample is actually from a population with a mean IQ greater than the population at large is to treat the sample mean as an individual score (in terms of our earlier discussion) and calculate a z score on the basis of the deviation of the sample mean from the population mean. In our case, we know the population mean is 100 and the class mean of the randomly selected students is 108. To calculate the z score, we also need to know the standard error of the mean, the standard deviation of the distribution of sample means. The equation for the z score here is

$$z = \frac{\overline{X} - \mu}{\sigma_{\overline{x}}} \qquad (B\text{--}3)$$

The standard error of the mean $(\sigma_{\overline{x}})$ is found by dividing the standard deviation of the population (σ) by $\sqrt{n}$ (see Equation B–1), so $\sigma_{\overline{x}}$ is $15/\sqrt{25}$, or 3. Thus, z is $(108 - 100)/3$, or 2.67. This result, 2.67, allows us to reject the null hypothesis with reasonable confidence and conclude in favor of the alternative hypothesis, that the class is actually superior in IQ to the population at large. We establish this by asking the question: How likely is a z score of 2.67 when a sample mean is drawn from a larger population whose mean is actually 100? The answer is that it will occur only .0038 of the time, or 38 times in 10,000. (In the next paragraph, we will discuss how this was calculated.) The custom in rejecting the null hypothesis is that if it could only occur 1 time in 20 by chance, we would reject it, so the difference in the class sample mean is *reliably different,* or **significantly different,** from the mean of the population.

To explain how this rather remarkable conclusion is reached, we need to refer again to the special property of the normal curve, which is that a certain proportion of cases fall under each part of the curve. Looking at Figure B–1, we see that having a z score of ±2.00 is highly improbable. Greater scores in either direction occur only 2.15% of the time. In other words, the probability of such an occurrence is .0215. This is also below the 5% or .05 level of significance, so any mean score two or more standard deviations from the population mean is considered, using the logic we have outlined here, significantly different from the population mean. In fact, the critical z value for rejecting the null hypothesis at the .05 level of significance is ±1.96. Table C–1 (in Appendix C) presents (a) z scores from zero to four, with (b) the amount of area between the mean and z, and (c) most important, the amount of area beyond z. The amount of area beyond z is the probability of finding a score that distant from the mean on the basis of chance alone. Once again, when this

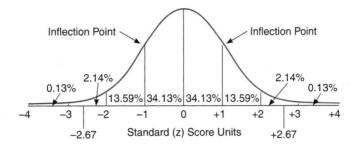

Figure B–1   Proportions of scores in specific areas under the normal curve. The inflection points are one standard deviation from the mean.

There are two sides or tails to the distribution: positive and negative. If an experimenter simply asserts that there should be a difference between an experimental and a control condition but does not specify the direction of the difference, this is called a *nondirectional hypothesis*. If a $z = 2.67$ is found, it is necessary to look up the probability that this will occur in both the positive and negative tails of the distribution and add the two, because the experimenter has not specified whether the difference should be positive or negative. When the experimenter has specified the direction of difference, one need only look up the probability in one tail. Because the distribution is symmetrical, the probability that the null hypothesis can be rejected is half as great with a one-tailed as with a two-tailed test. The less certain one is about the outcome of an experiment, the greater the difference between conditions must be for it to be decided that it is not due to chance.

probability falls below .05, as it does with z scores of ± 1.96 (or more), we reject the null hypothesis. Notice that with a z of 2.67, as in our IQ example, the probability of such a rare occurrence is only .0038 (see Figure B–1).

The statistical problem we have just considered—comparing a sample mean to a population parameter to see whether the sample came from that population—is rather artificial, because population parameters are rarely known. However, this example does exhibit characteristics of most common statistical tests. In all tests, some computations are performed on the data or raw scores, a value is found as in the z score just calculated, and then this value is compared with a distribution of values so that we can determine the likelihood that such a value could be obtained if the null hypothesis were in fact true. This distribution tells us, then, with what probability our result could be attributed to random variation. If the probability is less than 5 cases in 100 ($p < .05$), then we say the null hypothesis can be rejected. This probability is sometimes called the **alpha (α) level,** and as already mentioned, some psychologists prefer values of .01 or even smaller so that they can be more certain that the null hypothesis should be rejected.

Our z-score test can also serve to introduce you very briefly to other important statistical concepts. First, as shown in Table B–3, let us consider two types of errors that can be made by applying statistical tests to experimental data. A **type 1 error** is rejection of the null hypothesis when it is actually true, and the

Table B–3 The nature of type I and type II errors. A type I error occurs when the experimenter falsely rejects a true null hypothesis. The probability of this occurring is determined by the a level. A type II error occurs when the experimenter does not reject a false null hypothesis. When the null hypothesis is false and rejected, the experimenter has made a correct decision, which is determined by the power of the experiment.

Decision of experimenter	Actual state of affairs in the population	
	The independent variable *had no* effect; the null hypothesis is true.	The independent variable *had* an effect; the null hypothesis is false.
Reject null hypothesis	*Type I error*—a false decision that an effect exists, which occurs with probability α.	*Correct decision*—this is determined by the power of the experiment.
Do not reject null hypothesis	*Correct decision*	*Type II error*—a failure to detect that the treatment had an effect.

probability that this error will occur is indexed by the alpha level, which the experimenter selects. If the alpha level is $p = .05$, then we shall mistakenly reject the null hypothesis in 5 cases in 100. This illustrates the probabilistic nature of inferential statistics; we are not absolutely certain that a null hypothesis can be rejected, only reasonably certain. Thus, the lower α level or p level we use in determining statistical significance, the less chance we have of making a type 1 error. However, this increases the probability of a **type 2 error,** which occurs when we *fail* to reject the null hypothesis when it is actually *false*. Thus, by setting α levels at different points, we systematically decrease and increase the two types of errors.

Scientists are generally conservative in such matters, so the α level is usually kept fairly small, such as .05 or .01 (rather than, say, .10 or .15). Thus, we minimize the error of rejecting the null hypothesis when it is true, or of claiming a difference in our results when a difference is not there. As a consequence, though, we increase the probability of type 2 errors. A *conservative* statistical test minimizes type 1 errors, whereas more *liberal* statistical tests increase the probability of a type 1 error but decrease that of a type 2 error.

Unfortunately, we can never know positively in our experimental situations whether we are committing type 1 or type 2 errors. We find this out primarily by doing experimental replications of our results, but also by calculating the power of a statistical test. The *power* of a test is the probability of rejecting the null hypothesis when it is actually false; thus, we always want to maximize the power of our statistical tests. This is not the place to describe how the power of tests is calculated, but we will note the two main factors that influence power. Look back to the z-score formula in Equation B–3. Whatever would make the z score larger would increase the power of the statistical test, or the likelihood of rejecting the null hypothesis. The value μ, the population mean, is fixed. Thus, only two changes in the values of equation B–3 can affect z. One is the difference between the sample mean and the population mean $(\overline{X} - \mu)$ and the other is n, the size of the sample. If the discrepancy between μ and $\overline{X}$ is increased (or, in other cases, if the difference between sample means in an experimental comparison is increased), the probability of rejecting the null hypothesis is also increased.

However, there is nothing we can do about the size of the difference between means; it is fixed. We can increase the power of our statistical tests by increasing the sample size. The reason is that with larger samples we can be more confident that our sample means represent the mean of the populations from which they are drawn, and thus we can be more confident that any difference between a sample mean and a population mean (or between two sample means) is reliable. Sample size can have a great effect on the power of a test, as shown in Table B–4. Presented there are the z scores and p values for our difference between a sample mean of 108 IQ points and the population mean of 100 as the sample size varies. As the sample size varies, so will our conclusion as to whether the sample came from a national population or a

Table B–4 How varying sample size (n) affects the power of a statistical test, or how likely it is that the null hypothesis can be rejected when the test is used.

The example is from the z score (calculated in the text) on a mean sample IQ of 108, where

$$z = \frac{\overline{X} - \mu}{\sigma_{\overline{X}}}$$

If the mean difference remains the same but n increases, z increases because

$$\sigma_{\overline{X}} = \frac{\sigma}{\sqrt{n}}$$

n	$\overline{X} - \mu$	$\sigma_{\overline{X}}$	z	$p^{\dagger}$
2	8	13.14	.61	.2709
5	8	6.70	1.19	.1170
7	8	5.67	1.41	.0793
10	8	4.74	1.69	.0455*
12	8	4.33	1.85	.0322*
15	8	3.88	2.06	.0197*
17	8	3.64	2.20	.0139*
20	8	3.35	2.38	.0087*
25	8	3.00	2.67	.0038*
50	8	2.12	3.77	.0001*
75	8	1.73	4.62	<.00003*
100	8	1.50	5.33	<.00003*

*All these values meet the conventional level of statistical significance, $p < .05$ (one-tailed).
$^{\dagger}p$ Values are one-tailed.

more restricted, high-IQ population. If we assume that the null hypothesis is actually false here, then by increasing sample size, we decrease the probability of a type 2 error, or increase the power of the test we are using.

One final issue to consider is the *directionality* of statistical tests. According to conventional logic involved in testing an alternative hypothesis against the null hypothesis, the alternative hypothesis may be **directional** or **nondirectional.** If an experimental and a control group are in an experiment, a nondirectional alternative hypothesis would be that the two groups differ in performance on the dependent variable. A directional hypothesis would, in addition, state the predicted direction of the difference; for example, the experimental group might be predicted to do better than the control.

This distinction is important, because if the alternative hypothesis is directional, a **one-tailed** (or **one-sided**) **statistical test** is used, but if the alternative hypothesis is nondirectional, a **two-tailed** (**two-sided**) **test** is used. One versus two "tails" refers to whether we consider one or both tails of the distribution when we look up a p level associated with the result of a statistical test (say, $z = 1.69$).

Examine Figure B–1 once again. We took a sample ($n = 25$) of students, determined that the mean IQ of the sample was 108, and calculated a $z = +2.67$ in testing to see whether this was different from the mean population IQ of 100. If we had no prior expectation of how the sample IQ should deviate from the normal population—if we thought it could be either higher or lower—this would have a nondirectional hypothesis. In fact, we did expect the sample IQ to be greater than 100, so we tested a directional hypothesis and thus used a one-tailed test. This means we looked up the resulting z score in only one tail of the normal distribution, that greater than zero. A $z = +2.67$ leads to a one-tailed p value of .0038. If the hypothesis were nondirectional, then we have no a priori right to expect the resultant z score to be greater instead of less than zero. The z score could be in the positive or negative tail. Because the difference could have occurred in either direction, we use a two-tailed test. In practice, the two tails of the distribution are symmetrical, so we simply double the p level for the one-tailed test. In our example, if the hypothesis had been nondirectional, p would equal $2 \times .0038$, or .0076, which is still well below .05.

Two-tailed tests are more conservative and less powerful than one-tailed tests: It is harder to reject the null hypothesis. If we are uncertain about the outcome of an experiment, we need a greater value of the statistic to allow us to declare a difference. In practice, most investigators prefer to use the more conservative two-tailed test with sufficient power ensured by fairly large sample sizes.

In the remainder of this appendix, we show you how to calculate several statistical tests. We believe it is important for you to do some of these calculations by hand or with a calculator. When you carefully work through the calculations, you become familiar with the logic and components of the statistical test. However, as we noted in Appendix A (see Box A–2), many statistical tests can be done automatically by sophisticated calculators and computers. All you need to do is access a particular statistical program and then enter your data.

Most of the statistical tests outlined in this appendix can be done by the computer package MINITAB. We suggest you become familiar with the statistical capabilities of the computing equipment available to you. Computers can conduct statistical tests faster and more accurately than you can, and they relieve some of the tedium associated with the more complex statistical tests that require numerous complicated calculations.

Tests for Differences Between Two Groups

A variety of statistical tests exist for almost every purpose. At present, we are interested in discussing tests that assess the reliability of a difference between two groups or conditions. How do we pick an appropriate test from all those available? There is no hard-and-fast rule. Tests vary in the assumptions they make, their power, and the types of situation for which they are appropriate. Perhaps the most popular test for the difference between two means in psychological research is the *t* test. Because the *t* test provides the same estimate of reliability as does the simple analysis of variance (discussed next), we will first concentrate on two other tests, the Mann-Whitney *U* test and the Wilcoxon signed-ranks test. These tests also are useful in introducing yet another type of statistical test.

The Mann-Whitney and Wilcoxon tests are **nonparametric statistics** as opposed to **parametric statistics.** Parametric statistical tests, such as analysis of variance and *t*, are those that make assumptions about the underlying population parameters of the samples on which the tests are performed. Common assumptions of parametric tests are that the variances of the underlying populations being compared are equivalent, that the underlying distributions are normal, and that the level of measurement is at least an interval scale. If these assumptions are not met, the test may be inappropriate, but how can we ever know whether the assumptions underlying the test are met if we do not know the population parameters? Usually we cannot, except by estimating population parameters from sample statistics. However, if we turn to nonparametric statistical tests, the problem does not arise, because these tests make no assumptions about the underlying population parameters. This is why these tests are often called distribution-free statistics. Because the parameters cannot be known anyway, this provides an important reason for using nonparametric tests. Another reason is that these tests are generally very easy to calculate and can often even be done by hand. However, nonparametric tests are usually less powerful than parametric tests used in the same situation; that is, they are less likely to allow the null hypothesis to be rejected.

The **Mann-Whitney *U* test** is used when we want to compare two samples and decide whether they come from the same or different underlying populations. It is used when the two samples are composed of different subjects—between-subjects designs. The underlying rationale for the Mann-Whitney test will not be discussed here. The logic is the same as in other statistical tests in which a value is computed from the test and compared with a distribution of values to determine whether the null hypothesis should be rejected. The way in which the Mann-Whitney test is applied to data is outlined in Box B–2,

Box B–2 Calculation of a Mann-Whitney U Test

These data are from our hypothetical experiment involving the effects of LSD on the running speeds of rats. Using the Mann-Whitney U test to test the reliability of the difference between our two samples, we follow these steps:

Step 1 Rank all the numbers for *both groups* together, beginning with the smallest number. Assign it the lowest rank.

Control (placebo)		Experimental (LSD)	
Latency (sec.)	Rank	Latency (sec.)	Rank
9	1.5	9	1.5
10	3	13	11.5
11	4.5	13	11.5
11	4.5	14	17
12	7	14	17
12	7	15	21
12	7	16	24.5
13	11.5	16	24.5
13	11.5	16	24.5
13	11.5	17	28
13	11.5	17	28
14	17	18	32
14	17	18	32
14	17	18	32
15	21	18	32
15	21	19	35.5
16	24.5	19	35.5
17	28	20	37.5
18	32	22	39
20	37.5	26	40
	$\Sigma \, \text{rank}_1 \;\; 295.5$		$\Sigma \, \text{rank}_2 \;\; 524.5$

Note: When scores are tied, assign the mean value of the tied ranks to each. Thus, for both 9-second times in this example, the rank 1.5 is assigned (the mean of 1 and 2).

Step 2 The equations for finding U and U' are as follows, where n_1 is the size of the smaller sample, n_2 is the size of the larger sample, ΣR_1 is the sum of the ranks of the smaller sample, and ΣR_2 is the sum of the ranks of the larger sample. The subscripts are important only if the sample sizes are unequal, which is not the case here.

$$U = n_1 n_2 + \frac{n_1(n_1 + 1)}{2} - \Sigma R_1$$

$$U = (20)(20) + \frac{(20)(21)}{2} - 295.5$$

Box B-2 *(continued)*

$U = 400 + 210 - 295.5$

$U = 314.5$

$U' = n_1 n_2 + \dfrac{n_2(n_2 + 1)}{2} - \Sigma R_2$

$U = (20)(20) + \dfrac{(20)(21)}{2} - 524.5$

$U' = 85.5$

Actually, it is only necessary to compute U or U', because the other can be found according to the equation

$U = n_1 n_2 - U'$

    or

$U' = n_1 n_2 - U$

Step 3   Take U or U', whichever value is *smaller*, and look at Table C-2 (in Appendix C) to see whether the difference between the two groups is reliable. The values in the table are recorded by different sample sizes. In this case, both sample sizes are 20, so the critical value from the table is 88. For the difference between the two groups to be judged reliable, the U or U' from the experiment must be *less than* the appropriate value shown in Table C-2. Because 85.5 is less than 88, we can conclude that the difference between the two groups is reliable at the .001 level of significance.

Note: Table C-2 is only appropriate when the sizes of the two samples are between 8 and 21. For other cases, consult an advanced text.

where the reliability of the difference between the two samples in our hypothetical LSD experiment is tested.

The **Wilcoxon signed-ranks test** is also used in testing for the difference between two samples, but in this case the design must be a *related-measures design.* In other words, either the same subjects must serve in both the experimental and control groups (a within-subjects design), or the subjects must be matched in some way. Of course, precautions must be taken in within-subjects designs to ensure that a variable such as practice or fatigue is not confounded with the variable of interest.

Before considering the signed-ranks test, let us examine its simpler cousin, the sign test, which is appropriate in the same situations. The sign test is the essence of simplicity. Suppose we have 26 participants serving in both conditions of an experiment, and we predict that when participants are in the experimental condition, they will do better than when they are in the control condition. Now, suppose that 19 participants actually do better in the experimental condition than in the control, and that the reverse is true for the other 7. Is this difference reliable? The sign test yields an answer to this question without our needing to know what the actual scores were. Under the null hypothesis, we might expect 13 participants to perform better in the experimental condition and 13 to perform better in the control. The sign test allows us to compute the exact probability that the null hypothesis is false when there are 19 cases in the predicted direction but also 7 reversals or exceptions. The null hypothesis can be rejected in this case with a .014 significance level (one-tailed); with a nondirectional prediction, p equals .028 (two-tailed). In Table C–3 (in Appendix C) are the α levels (one-tailed) for situations with sample sizes from 3 to 42 when there are x number of exceptions to the predicted hypothesis. So, for example, when there are 16 participants in the experiment (remember, in both conditions) and 13 show the predicted pattern of results whereas 3 exhibit reversals, we can reject the null hypothesis at the .011 level of significance (one-tailed).

The sign test uses very little of the data from an experiment, just whether the participants performed better or worse in one condition than in another. For the sign test, the direction of the difference and not its magnitude is what matters. The sign test therefore wastes much of the information gathered in an experiment and is not a very powerful statistical test. The Wilcoxon signed-ranks test is used as the sign test in situations where the same (or matched) participants are in two conditions, and the direction of the difference is taken into account too. For this reason it is also called the *sized sign test*. The Wilcoxon test is more powerful than the sign test. Box B–3 shows how the Wilcoxon signed-ranks test is used.

Box B–3 Calculation of the Wilcoxon Signed-Ranks Test

Imagine an experiment designed to test whether Professor von Widget's memory course really works. A group of 30 participants is presented with 50 words to remember. Then the participants are randomly separated into two groups, and a check indicates that the groups do not differ reliably in terms of the mean number of words recalled. The experimental group is given Professor von Widget's 3-week course, and the control group is not. Then all 30 participants are tested again on another 50-word list. The controls show no improvement from one list to another. The question is whether the experimental participants' memories were reliably improved. (*Note:* We could—and should—also compare the experimental participants' performance on the second test with that of the controls. The Mann-Whitney test is appropriate for this comparison. Do you know why?) We use the Wilcoxon signed-ranks test to assess whether the experimental participants improved reliably from the first test to the second.

Box B-3 *(continued)*

Step 1 Place the data in a table (such as the one that follows) where both scores for each participant (before and after the memory course) are paired together. Find and record the difference between the pairs.

	Mean number of words recalled			
Subject	Before	After	Difference	Rank
1	11	17	+ 6	14
2	18	16	− 2	5.5
3	9	21	+12	15
4	15	16	+ 1	2.5
5	14	17	+ 3	8.5
6	12	15	+ 3	8.5
7	17	16	− 1	2.5
8	16	17	+ 1	2.5
9	15	20	+ 5	13
10	19	16	− 3	8.5
11	12	13	+ 1	2.5
12	16	14	− 2	5.5
13	10	14	+ 4	11.5
14	17	20	+ 3	8.5
15	6	10	+ 4	11.5
	$\overline{X} = 13.80$	$\overline{X} = 16.07$		

Step 2 Rank the values of the differences according to size, beginning with the smallest. *Ignore the sign.* Use the absolute values of the numbers. For tied ranks, assign each the mean value of the ranks. (See the right-hand column of the table here.)

Step 3 Add the ranks for all the difference values that are negative (5.5 + 2.5 + 8.5 + 5.5 = 22.0) and positive (14 + 15 + 2.5 + 8.5 + 8.5 + 2.5 + 13 + 2.5 + 11.5 + 8.5 + 11.5 = 98.0). These are the signed-rank values.

Step 4 Take the signed-rank value that is smallest (22), and go to Table C-4 in Appendix C. Look up the number of pairs of observations (listed as *n* on the left). There are 15 in this case. Then look at the number under the desired level of significance. The direction of the outcome was predicted (we expected the memory course to help rather than hurt recall of words), so let us choose the value under the .025 level of significance for a one-tailed test. This value is 25. If the smaller of the two values from the experiment is *below* the appropriate value in the table, then the result is reliable. Because 22 is below 25, we can conclude that Professor von Widget's course really did help participants recall words.

Note: Remember that the controls showed no improvement in performance from one test to the other. This is a crucial bit of information, for otherwise, we could not rule out two plausible competing hypotheses—one is that the improvement on the second list was simply owing to practice on the first, and the other is that the second list was easier than the first.

In Boxes B–4 and B–5, we present the corresponding t tests for the analyses presented in the previous two boxes. The t test is a parametric test, which means that we assume that the underlying distributions are roughly normal in shape. Furthermore, the t test and other parametric tests were designed to be used on data that are at least interval in nature. The U test and the sign test require only ordinal data. The t tests are essentially based on z scores having to do with the standard error of the difference between means. Thus, even if the computational formulas appear unusual at first, the underlying logic is the same as that discussed earlier in this chapter.

Magnitude of Effect   In summary, calculating a statistic such as z or t allows us to determine whether the results are owing to chance factors. Determining the α level of a difference, as in Box B–4, tells us that the difference is significant statistically, and we can reject the null hypothesis. An interesting characteristic of t (and the F test that we discuss next) is that the value of t needed to reject the null hypothesis decreases as the degrees of freedom increase. This means that the power of t increases with sample size, just as z increases (see Table B–4). It is also the case, as the formula for the independent groups t in Box B–4 indicates, that as we hold the difference between means constant, increasing the sample size (n) will increase the value of t by making the denominator smaller. This too will allow us to have more power and reject more null hypotheses. In some cases, then, it is possible that very small differences between means will be statistically significant. Usually when we do an experiment, we want substantial differences between means—a big effect of the independent variable. With a very powerful experiment, however, we can detect differences between means that are exceptionally small. In the latter instance, we may not know whether the difference is owing to a powerful independent variable or a very powerful statistical test.

How do we know when we have a powerful independent variable? To determine the **magnitude of effect,** which is often called the **effect size** of the independent variable, we need a way of showing the degree to which belonging in a particular group predicts the behavior. In the example in Box B–4, we would like to have a calculation that would allow us to have some idea as to whether a rat had received a placebo or LSD. The information we need is a correlation coefficient, because we want to predict what happened to a rat in much the same way we would want to predict a memory score based on head size as in Box A–1. After we have conducted a t test, we can then calculate a correlation to assess the effect size. The correlation coefficient that would be appropriate here is r_{pb}, which is called the **point-biserial correlation.** The formula is

$$r_{pb} = \sqrt{t^2/(t^2 + df)} \tag{B-4}$$

The value of r_{pb} can be between 0 and +1.00. By convention, values up to .3 are considered to be small, a value from .31 to .5 is moderate, and values over .5 are appreciable (Thompson & Buchanan, 1979). For the data in Box B–4, $t = 3.27$ and $df = 38$, which by Equation B–4, yields $r_{pb} = .47$. This would be deemed a moderate effect. The same formula for r_{pb} could be used for the results in Box B–5. Why don't you determine what it is?

Box B-4 Calculation of a Between-Subjects *t* Test

These are hypothetical experimental data previously discussed (see Box B-2). The calculation formula is

$$t = \frac{\overline{X}_1 - \overline{X}_2}{\sqrt{\left[\frac{\Sigma X_1^2 - \frac{(\Sigma X_1)^2}{n_1} + \Sigma X_2^2 - \frac{(\Sigma X_2)^2}{n_2}}{n_1 + n_2 - 2}\right]\left[\frac{1}{n_1} + \frac{1}{n_2}\right]}}$$

$\overline{X}_1$ = mean of group 1
$\overline{X}_2$ = mean of group 2
n_1 = number of scores in group 1
n_2 = number of scores in group 2

ΣX_1^2 = sum of squared scores in group 1
ΣX_2^2 = sum of squared scores in group 2
$(\Sigma X_1)^2$ = square of group-1 sum
$(\Sigma X_2)^2$ = square of group-2 sum

Control (placebo)				Experimental (LSD)			
X	X²	X	X²	X	X²	X	X²
9	81	13	169	9	81	17	289
10	100	14	196	13	169	18	324
11	121	14	196	13	169	18	324
11	121	14	196	14	196	18	324
12	144	15	225	14	196	18	324
12	144	15	225	15	225	19	361
12	144	16	256	16	256	19	361
13	169	17	289	16	356	20	400
13	169	18	324	16	356	22	484
13	169	20	400	17	289	26	676

$\Sigma X = 272$ $\Sigma X^2 = 3{,}838$ $\Sigma X = 338$ $\Sigma X^2 = 5{,}960$
$\overline{X} = 13.60$ $\overline{X} = 16.90$

Step 1 After calculating ΣX, ΣX^2, and $\overline{X}$ for each group (by the way, there is no need to rank order our data), we need to calculate $(\Sigma X)^2/n$ for each group: $(272)^2/20 = 3{,}699.20$ and $(338)^2/20 = 5{,}712.20$. Then we need to determine $\Sigma X^2 - (\Sigma X)^2/n$ for each group: $3{,}838 - 3{,}699.2 = 138.8$ and $5{,}960 - 5{,}712.2 = 247.8$

Step 2 Now we add the two group figures we obtained in the last step: $247.8 + 138.8$, and divide this sum by $n_1 + n_2 - 2$: $386.6/38 = 10.17$.

Step 3 The quotient obtained in Step 2 (10.17) is multiplied by

$$\left[\frac{1}{n_1} + \frac{1}{n_2}\right] \quad (10.17)(2/20) = 1.02.$$

Step 4 We now take the square root of the product obtained in Step 3: $\sqrt{1.02} = 1.01$.

Box B–4 *(continued)*

Step 5   We find the absolute difference between the mean scores of the two groups (by subtracting one from the other, and ignoring the sign): $16.90 - 13.60 = 3.30$.

Step 6 $t =$ The difference between means (Step 5) divided by the results of Step 4: $3.30/1.01 = 3.27$. So, our $t = 3.27$. To evaluate this, we look in the tabled values of t in Table C–5 in Appendix C. We enter this table with the number of degrees of freedom (df) in our experiment, which means the number of scores that are free to vary. For a between-subjects t, the degrees of freedom are $n_1 + n_2 - 2$; in this case, $df = 38$. For $p = .05$ and $df = 38$, the critical value of t is 2.04 in our table (always take the next-lowest df to calculate the critical value). Our obtained t exceeds the critical value, so we can reject the hypothesis that our two groups have the same running scores—that is, LSD had an effect on the behavior of our subjects.

Box B–5 Calculation of a Within-Subjects t Test

The hypothetical data are from Professor Widget's experiment (see Box B–3). The computational formula for the within-subjects t test is as follows:

$$t = \sqrt{\frac{n-1}{[n\Sigma D^2/(\Sigma D)^2]-1}}$$

where $n =$ number of participants and $D =$ difference in the scores of a given subject (or matched participant pair) in the two conditions.

Participant	Before	After	Difference	D^2
1	11	17	+ 6	36
2	18	16	− 2	4
3	9	21	+12	144
4	15	16	+ 1	1
5	14	17	+ 3	9
6	12	15	+ 3	9
7	17	16	− 1	1
8	16	17	+ 1	1
9	15	20	+ 5	25
10	19	16	− 3	9
11	12	13	+ 1	1
12	16	14	− 2	4
13	10	14	+ 4	16
14	17	20	+ 3	9
15	6	10	+ 4	16
	$\overline{X} = 13.80$	$\overline{X} = 16.07$	$\Sigma D = 35$	$\Sigma D^2 = 285$
			$(\Sigma D)^2 = 1{,}225$	

Mean number of words recalled

Box B–5 *(continued)*

Step 1 After you arrange the scores for each participant in pairs as shown in this table, record the difference between each pair and then square each of these difference scores.

Step 2 Add the difference scores across participants, which yields ΣD, then square this sum to get $(\Sigma D)^2$: $\Sigma D = 35$, and $(\Sigma D)^2 = 1{,}225$.

Step 3 Calculate the sum of the squared difference scores to get $\Sigma D^2 = 285$.

Step 4 Multiply ΣD^2 (Step 3) by the number of participants: $285 \times 15 = 4{,}275$.

Step 5 Divide the product found in Step 4 by $(\Sigma D)^2$: $4{,}275/1{,}225 = 3.49$, and then subtract 1 from the result: $3.49 - 1 = 2.49$.

Step 6 Divide the number of participants less 1 $(n - 1)$ by the result of Step 5: $14/2.49 = 5.62$.

Step 7 $t = \sqrt{5.62} = 2.37$.

Step 8 To evaluate t, compare it to the critical values shown in Table C–5 in Appendix C. Enter the table with $n - 1\ df$, and for this study $df = 14$. With $df = 14$, the critical value of t is 2.145 for $p = .05$. The obtained t exceeds the critical value, so we can conclude that von Widget's course really did affect word recall.

The most important additional measure of effect size that you need to know is η (eta), which is used to determine how wrong the null hypothesis is after conducting an F test. To anticipate the discussion in the next section, the F test in its simplest form is much like the t test, except that there are more than two levels of the independent variable (say, several dosages of LSD). More complicated experiments that have two or more independent variables, each with several levels, can also be analyzed with the F test. As with r_{pb}, η is a correlation between the scores on the dependent variable and group membership. The larger the value of η, the better we can predict group membership on the basis of a participant's score, which means a larger effect size.

In an analysis of variance, we calculate the ratio of two variances (this will become clear momentarily), and significance is related to two degrees of freedom: one df for the numerator (n), and one for the denominator (d) of the F ratio. So, the formula for η is:

$$\eta = \sqrt{df_n \times F/(df_n \times F) + df_d} \qquad \text{(B–5)}$$

Measures of magnitude of effect have another important use, which is also related to the fact that rejecting the null hypothesis is dependent on sample size. Suppose we conduct an experiment and discover that the value of t is not large enough to reject the null hypothesis even though the difference between means is not zero (that is, they differ). One reason that the t value is small could be that the sample size is too small to detect a statistically significant difference between the means. In this case, a prudent researcher would calculate the appropriate measure of magnitude of effect, such as r_{pb}. If the coefficient yields a moderate or appreciable value, then it might be wise to increase the sample size in the experiment to reject the null hypothesis. Getting statistically significant results is important, but it is really only "half the battle." Significant results that are very small are not particularly exciting. Appreciable effects that are not statistically significant probably mean that you are on to something, and an increase in statistical power is warranted.

The Analysis of Variance

Most psychological research has progressed beyond the stage where there are only two conditions (an experimental and a control that are compared with each other). Investigators typically have more than two conditions in psychological research. In our example of the effects of LSD on running speed of rats, it may be quite useful to vary the amount of LSD administered to the rats. Perhaps low dosages and high dosages produce different effects. We could not determine this from the two-group design where one group received LSD in some amount and the other did not. To evaluate the results of such an experiment with multiple groups, we must use the analysis of variance. A simple analysis of variance is used in situations where one factor or independent variable (such as amount of LSD) is varied systematically and, thus, is usually called a *one-factor analysis of variance*.

Often researchers are interested in varying more than one factor. They may want to vary two or more factors simultaneously. In such complex or multifactor experimental designs, the **analysis of variance** is also appropriate, but it is more complex. In this section, we introduce you to the logic of both simple and multifactor analyses of variance (abbreviated *ANOVA*).

Simple ANOVA   The heart of the ANOVA procedure is a comparison of variance estimates. We have already discussed the concept of variance and how it is estimated from one particular sample of observations. You should refer back to the section on measures of dispersion if the concept of variance is unclear. Recall that the equation for the unbiased estimate of the population variance is

$$\hat{s}^2 = \frac{\Sigma(X - \overline{X})^2}{n - 1} \tag{B-6}$$

and that when the deviation of scores from the mean is large, the variance will be great. Similarly, when the deviations from the mean are small, the variance will be small.

In the ANOVA, two independent estimates of variance are obtained. One is based on the variability between the different experimental groups—how much the means of the different groups differ from one another. Actually, the variance is computed as to how much the individual group means differ from the overall mean of all scores in the experiment. The greater the difference among the means of the groups, the greater will be the **between-groups variance.**

The other estimate of variance is the **within-groups variance.** This is the concept we discussed in considering estimates of variance from individual samples. Now we are concerned with finding an estimate of within-groups variance that is representative of all the individual groups, so we take the mean of the variances of these groups. The within-groups variance gives us an estimate of how much the participants in the groups differ from one another (or the mean of the group). Two variance estimates are obtained, one for the variance within groups and one for the variance between groups, but what good does this do?

The basic logic of testing to see whether the scores of the different groups or conditions are reliably different is as follows. The null hypothesis is that all the participants in the various conditions are drawn from the same underlying population; the experimental variable has no effect. If the null hypothesis were true and all the scores in the different groups came from the same population, then the between-groups variance should be the same as the within-groups variance. The means of the different groups should differ from one another no more and less than do the scores within the groups. For us to reject the null hypothesis, then, the means of the different groups must vary from one another more than the scores vary within the groups. The greater the variance (differences) between the groups of the experiment, the more likely the independent variable is to have had an effect, especially if the within-groups variance is low.

The person who originated this logic was the eminent British statistician R. A. Fisher, and the test is referred to as an *F* test in his honor. The *F* test is simply a ratio of the between-groups variance estimate to the within-groups variance estimate, so

$$F = \frac{\text{between-groups variance}}{\text{within-groups variance}} \qquad \text{(B–7)}$$

According to the logic just outlined, the *F* ratio under the null hypothesis should be 1.00, because the between-groups variance should be the same as the within-groups variance. The greater the between-groups variance is than the within-groups variance and, consequently, the greater the *F* ratio is than 1.00, the more confident we can be in rejecting the null hypothesis. Exactly how much greater the *F* ratio must be than 1.00 depends on the **degrees of freedom** in the experiment, or how free the measures are to vary. This depends both on the number of groups or conditions in the experiment and on the number of observations in each group. The greater the number of degrees of freedom, the smaller need be the value of the *F* ratio to be judged a reliable effect, as you can see from examining Table C–6 in Appendix C. Follow the computational example in Box B–6 carefully to get a feel for the analysis of variance for between subjects. Box B–7 illustrates an ANOVA for a within-subjects experiment.

Box B–6   Computing Simple ANOVA: One Variable Between Subjects

This ANOVA is often called a *one-way ANOVA* because there is only *one* independent variable. Imagine you have just performed an experiment testing the effects of LSD on the running speeds of rats, but that there were three levels of LSD administered rather than two as in our earlier example. Ten rats received no LSD, 10 others received a small amount, and a third group received a great amount. Thus, the experiment uses a between-subjects design where amount of LSD (none, small, large) is the independent variable and running time is the dependent variable. First, calculate the sum of the scores (ΣX) and the sum of the squared values of the scores (ΣX^2).

	Amount of LSD		
	None	**Small**	**Large**
	13	17	26
	11	15	20
	14	16	29
	18	20	31
	12	13	17
	14	19	25
	10	18	26
	13	17	23
	16	19	25
	12	21	27
ΣX =	133	175	249
$\overline{X}$ =	13.30	17.50	24.90
ΣX^2 =	1,819	3,115	6,351
$\Sigma\Sigma X$ =	557	$\Sigma\Sigma X^2 = 11,285$	

A basic quantity in calculating analysis of variance is the *sum of squares,* which is an abbreviation for the *sum of squared deviations from the mean.* If you look back to Equation A–1 (in Appendix A), which defines the variance of a sample, you will see that the sum of squares is the numerator. Three sum of squares are of interest. First, there is the total sum of squares (*SS* Total), which is the sum of the squared deviations of the individual scores from the grand mean or the mean of all scores in all groups in the experiment. Second, there is the sum of squares between groups (*SS* Between), which is the sum of the squared deviations of the group means from the grand mean. Third, the sum of squares within groups (*SS* Within) is the mean of the sum of the squared deviations of the individual scores within groups or conditions from the group means. It turns out that *SS* Total = *SS* Between + *SS* Within, so that in practice, only two sums of squares need be calculated. The third can be found by subtraction.

These sums of squares could be calculated by taking the deviations from the appropriate means, squaring them, and then finding the sum, but such a method would take much time and labor. Fortunately, there are computational formulas that allow the calculations to be done more easily, especially if the values of ΣX and ΣX^2 have been found for each group, as in the present data. The formula for finding the total sum of squares is

Box B–6 *(continued)*

$$SS\ \text{Total} = \Sigma\Sigma X^2 - \frac{T^2}{N} \tag{B–8}$$

where $\Sigma\Sigma X^2$ means that each score within each group is squared (X^2) and all these squared values are added together, so ΣX^2. There are two summation signs, one for summing the squared values within groups and one for then summing these ΣX^2 across the different groups. T is the total of all scores, and N is the total number of scores in the experiment. So, SS Total in our example is calculated in the following way:

$$SS\ \text{Total} = \Sigma\Sigma X^2 - \frac{T^2}{N}$$

$$SS\ \text{Total} = 1{,}819 + 3{,}115 + 6{,}351 - \frac{(133 + 175 + 249)^2}{30}$$

$$SS\ \text{Total} = 11{,}285 - \frac{310{,}249}{30}$$

$$SS\ \text{Total} = 11{,}285 - 10{,}341.63$$

$$SS\ \text{Total} = 943.37$$

The between-groups sum of squares is calculated with the following formula:

$$SS\ \text{Between} = \Sigma \frac{(\Sigma X)^2}{n} - \frac{T^2}{N} \tag{B–9}$$

The first part of the formula means that the sum of the values for each group is squared and then divided by the number of observations on which it is based, or $(\Sigma X)^2/n$. Then these values are summed across groups, so $\Sigma(\Sigma X)^2/n$. The second part of the formula is the same as the SS Total:

$$SS\ \text{Between} = \Sigma \frac{(\Sigma X)^2}{n} - \frac{T^2}{N}$$

$$SS\ \text{Between} = \frac{17{,}689}{10} + \frac{30{,}625}{10} + \frac{62{,}001}{10} - 10{,}341.63$$

$$SS\ \text{Between} = 11{,}031.50 - 10{,}341.63$$

$$SS\ \text{Between} = 689.87$$

The sum of squares within groups can be found by subtracting SS Between from SS Total, so SS Within $= 943.37 - 689.87 = 253.50$. As a check, we should also calculate it directly. This is done by computing an SS Total (as in Equation B–8) for each group and summing all these sums of squares for the individual groups. Unless we have made an error, this quantity should equal SS Within obtained by subtraction. Note that

$$\frac{(\Sigma\Sigma X)^2}{N} \quad \text{or} \quad \frac{T^2}{N}$$

is called the *correction term,* because it is taken out of most SS.

Box B–6 *(continued)*

After we have obtained the various sums of squares, it is convenient to construct an ANOVA table such as the one that follows. In the far left column appears the source of variance, or source. Keep in mind that there are two primary sources of variance we are interested in comparing—between groups, and within groups.

In the next column are the number of degrees of freedom (*df*). These can be thought of as the number of scores that are free to vary, given that the total is fixed. For the degrees of freedom between groups, if the overall total is fixed, all groups are free to vary except one. Thus, the between-groups *df* is the number of groups minus one. In our example, then, it is $3 - 1 = 2$. The within-groups *df* is equal to the total number of scores minus the number of groups, because there is one score in each group that cannot vary if the group total is fixed. So, the within-groups *df* is $30 - 3 = 27$. The total *df* = between-groups *df* + within-groups *df*.

The third column includes the **sum of squares** (*SS*), which have already been calculated. The fourth column represents the *mean squares* (*MS*), which are found by dividing the *SS* by the *df* for each row. Each mean square is an estimate of the population variance if the null hypothesis is true. However, if the independent variable had an effect, the between-groups mean square should be larger than the within-groups mean square.

As discussed in the text, these two values are compared by computing an *F* ratio, which is found by dividing the *MS* Between by the *MS* Within. Once the *F* value is calculated, it is necessary to determine whether the value reaches an acceptable level of statistical significance. By looking at Table C–6 in Appendix C, we can see that for 2 and 26 degrees of freedom (the closest we can get to 2 and 27), an *F* value of 9.12 is needed for the .001 level of significance. Our *F* value is greater than 9.12, so we can conclude that the groups varied reliably in running speed because of variation in the independent variable—amount of LSD injected.

Source	df	SS	MS	F	p
Between-groups	2	689.87	344.94	36.73	< .001
Within-groups	27	253.50	9.39		
Total	29	943.37			

Note: If you compute ANOVA with the aid of a calculator, watch out for errors. If you come up with a negative sum of squares within-groups (by subtracting *SS* Between from *SS* Total), you will know you made an error. You cannot have a negative sum of squares. You should compute *SS* Within both by subtraction and directly, anyway, as a check. One common error is to confuse ΣX^2 (square each number and then sum the squares) with $(\Sigma X)^2$, which is the square of the total of the scores.

Box B–7   Within-Subjects (Treatments × Subjects) ANOVA: One Variable

We could have conducted the previous three-level LSD study with a within-subjects rather than a between-subjects design. Of course, we would have counterbalanced the order of administering dosages across subjects. Let us assume

Box B–7 *(continued)*

that we used nine subjects in our within-subjects LSD study: Three subjects received the dose order None-Large-Small, three received the doses in the order Small-None-Large, and three were dosed in the order Large-Small-None. After each dose of LSD, the rat's running time in the straight alley was recorded. We could analyze the effects of order by a two-factor, within-subjects ANOVA (see Box B–9), but for the purposes of this illustration, we will ignore the effects of treatment order.

In a within-subjects ANOVA, we need to calculate the following kinds of variability:

SS Total—This is the variation about the mean of all the scores. *SS* Total is the sum of the remaining sums of squares.

SS Treatment—This is the difference among the treatment conditions and is calculated like *SS* Between in the previous ANOVA.

SS Subjects—This estimates the differences among individuals in our experiment and is used to calculate the next *SS*.

SS Error or *SS Treatment* × *Subject*—This represents the random variability that would occur in the scores of the same individuals in the same conditions. This interaction gives the ANOVA the name *Treatments* × *Subjects*. Usually, this *SS* is called *error variance,* and it is the denominator of the *F* ratio of the treatment effect.

We will use the hypothetical data from the first nine subjects of the LSD study shown in Box B–6. We will assume the ordering of treatments as mentioned earlier. You should set up your data table as follows, so that the scores for each subject are in a row. Leave room so that a given subject's total score summed across treatments can appear in the table. You might also want to leave room for the squares of the scores and the squares of the subjects' totals.

	Running times				
	Amount of LSD			Subject	Subject total
Subject	None	Small	Large	total	squared
1	13	17	26	56	3,136
2	11	15	20	46	2,116
3	14	16	29	59	3,481
4	18	20	31	69	4,761
5	12	13	17	42	1,764
6	14	19	25	58	3,364
7	10	18	26	54	2,916
8	13	17	23	53	2,809
9	16	19	25	60	3,600
ΣX =	121	154	222	497	
ΣX^2 =	1,675	2,674	5,622		27,497
	$\Sigma\Sigma X$ = 497	$\Sigma\Sigma X^2$ = 9,971 (1,675 + 2,674 + 5,622)			

Box B–7 *(continued)*

Step 1 When you calculate $\Sigma\Sigma X$ by adding the three treatment totals (121 + 154 + 222), you can check your accuracy by adding up the subject totals, the sum of which should equal $\Sigma\Sigma X$. Calculate ΣX^2 for each treatment, $\Sigma\Sigma X^2$, and the sum of the squares of the subject totals (last column).

Step 2 Calculation of the correction term, C

$C = (\Sigma\Sigma X)^2/N$, where N = the total number of scores in the table
(9 subjects $\times$ 3 scores for each subject)
$= 497^2/27$
$= 247{,}009/27$
$= 9{,}148.48$

Step 3 SS Total $= \Sigma\Sigma X^2 -$ Step 2
$= 9{,}971 - 9{,}148.48$
$= 822.52$

Step 4 SS Treatments $= SS$ Dose. SS Dose is calculated by summing the squares of the treatment totals, dividing that sum by the number of scores in each treatment, and then subtracting C (Step 2).

$$SS \text{ Dose} = \frac{121^2 + 154^2 + 222^2}{9} - \text{Step 2}$$
$= 87{,}419/9 -$ Step 2
$= 9{,}737.89 - 9{,}148.48$
$= 589.41$

Step 5 SS Subject = Sum of the squared subject totals (final column in the table) divided by the number of scores per subject (3) minus C
$= 27{,}947/3 -$ Step 2
$= 9{,}315.67 - 9{,}148.48$
$= 167.19$

Step 6 SS Error $= SS$ Total $- SS$ Dose $- SS$ Subject
$=$ Step 3 $-$ Step 4 $-$ Step 5
$= 822.52 - 589.41 - 167.19$
$= 65.92$

Step 7 Determination of df

df Total $=$ # scores $- 1 = 26$
df Dose $=$ # treatments $- 1 = 2$
df Subject $=$ # subjects $- 1 = 8$
df Error $= (df$ Dose$)(df$ Subject$) = 16$

Step 8 Determination of MS
MS Dose $= SS$ Dose/df Dose $= 589.41/2 = 294.71$
MS Error $= SS$ Error/df Error $= 65.92/16 = 4.12$

Box B–7 *(continued)*

Step 9 $F = MS\ \text{Dose}/MS\ \text{Error} = 294.71/4.12 = 71.53$

Step 10   Summary Table

Source	SS	df	MS	F
Subjects	167.19	8		
Dose	589.41	2	294.71	71.53
Error	65.92	16	4.12	
Total	822.52	26		

We determine the significance of the *F* ratio by entering Table C–6 (in Appendix C) with 2 and 16 degrees of freedom. Our obtained *F* greatly exceeds those needed for significance with 2 and 16 *df*, so we can conclude that dose level of LSD influenced the running times of our rats.

If the simple analysis of variance yields a significant *F* ratio, there is still more we would like to know—in particular, which of the individual conditions vary among themselves. This is especially important in cases where manipulation of the independent variable is qualitative in nature. *Quantitative* variation of an independent variable is when the quantity of an independent variable is manipulated (for example, amount of LSD), whereas *qualitative* variation is when conditions vary but not in some easily specified quantitative manner. An example of qualitative variation is an instructional manipulation in which the different conditions vary in terms of the instructions given at the beginning of the experiment. In such situations, it is not enough simply to say that the conditions vary reliably from one to another. It is of interest to know which particular conditions differ. To answer this question, we need to perform tests after the simple ANOVA. In these follow-up tests (generally called post hoc tests), the conditions of the experiment are taken two at a time and compared so that we can see which pairs are reliably different. There are several statistical tests for this purpose. We could perform ANOVA on groups taken as pairs, which is equivalent to performing *t* tests, but usually other tests are done. These include the Newman-Keuls test, the Scheffé test, Duncan's multiple-range test, Tukey's HSD (honestly significant differences) test, and Dunnett's test. These tests vary in their assumptions and their power. You should consult statistical texts when you need to use a follow-up test. Follow-up tests are also used when manipulation of the independent variable is quantitative in nature. These are called *trend tests* (we will not discuss them here).

Multifactor ANOVA   To discover the multiple determinants of behavior and how they interact, we must perform experiments in which more than one factor is varied simultaneously. The appropriate procedure for analyzing results of such experiments is the *multifactor ANOVA*. There may be any number of factors in the experiment, but it is rare to find more than four variables of interest manipulated simultaneously. When there are two factors, the analysis is referred to as a two-way ANOVA; when there are three factors, it is a three-way ANOVA; and so on.

The importance of such complex designs involving more than one factor is that they allow the experimenter to assess how different factors may *interact* to produce a result. Recall that an interaction occurs when the effect of one experimental variable is influenced by the level of the other experimental variable. When performing a complex analysis of variance, we find out the separate effects of each factor in the experiment (called **main effects**) and also how the variables affect one another (called **interaction effects,** or simply *interactions*).

In Boxes B–8 and B–9, we present some recipes for complex ANOVAs. Because of space limitations, we have refrained from presenting much of the logic behind these tests. However, you should find the examples useful in analyzing your own results even if you have not had a formal course in statistics.

Box B–8   Calculation of a 2 × 2 ANOVA

This is a between-subjects design. The data are from a memory experiment in which participants had to remember words of either high imagery (cigar) or low imagery (democracy). Some participants simply said the words to themselves as they were presented (rote rehearsal), and the other participants tried to get a mental image of the words (elaborative rehearsal).

High-imagery words		Low-imagery words	
Rote rehearsal	Elaborative rehearsal	Rote rehearsal	Elaborative rehearsal
5	8	4	7
7	8	1	6
6	9	5	3
4	7	6	3
4	10	4	5
9	10	3	6
7	8	4	2
5	9	4	4
5	8	5	5
6	9	3	4
ΣX = 58	86	39	45
ΣX^2 = 358	748	169	225

$\Sigma\Sigma X^2 = (358 + \ldots + 225) = 1{,}500$ $\Sigma\Sigma X = 228$

Step 1   Square the grand sum ($\Sigma\Sigma X = 228$), and divide by the total number of scores (40). $(\Sigma\Sigma X)^2/N = (228)^2/40 = 1{,}299.6$. This is the correction term.

Box B-8 *(continued)*

Step 2 SS Total $= \Sigma\Sigma X^2 - (\Sigma\Sigma X)^2/N$. Subtract the results of Step 1 from 1500. SS Total $= 200.4$.

Step 3 SS Imagery. Get the sum of all scores in each imagery condition, square each sum, then divide each sum by the number of scores yielding each sum, add the two quotients, and then subtract the results of Step 1 from the last sum.

$$SS \text{ Imagery} = (58 + 86)^2/20 + (39 + 45)^2/20 - \text{Step 1}$$
$$= \frac{144^2 + 84^2}{20} - 1{,}299.6$$
$$= 1{,}389.6 - 1{,}299.6$$
$$= 90$$

Step 4 SS Rehearsal. This is calculated in the same manner as Step 3, except that you base your calculations on the grand sum of each type of rehearsal.

$$SS \text{ Rehearsal} = \frac{(86 + 45)^2 + (58 + 39)^2}{20} - \text{Step 1}$$
$$= 1{,}328.5 - 1{,}299.6$$
$$= 28.9$$

Step 5 SS Imagery $\times$ Rehearsal. Square each group sum, and add the squares. Then divide each sum by the number of scores in each sum. From the last result, subtract the SS Imagery (SS I; Step 3), SS Rehearsal (SS R; Step 4), and Step 1.

$$SS\ I \times R = \frac{58^2 + 86^2 + 39^2 + 45^2}{10} - \text{Step 1} - \text{Step 3} - \text{Step 4}$$
$$= 14{,}306/10 - 1{,}299.6 - 90 - 28.9$$
$$= 12.1$$

Step 6 SS Error. Subtract each of your treatments SS from SS Total.

$$SS \text{ Error} = 200.4 - 90 - 28.9 - 12.1$$
$$= 69.4$$

Step 7 Determining degrees of freedom

$$df \text{ Total} = \text{the number of measures less one } (40 - 1) = 39$$
$$df \text{ Imagery} = \text{number of levels of Imagery less one } (2 - 1) = 1$$
$$df \text{ Rehearsal} = \text{number of levels of Rehearsal less one } (2 - 1) = 1$$
$$df\ I \times R = df \text{ Imagery} \times df \text{ Rehearsal } (1 \times 1) = 1$$
$$df \text{ Error} = df \text{ Total} - df \text{ Imagery} - df \text{ Rehearsal} - df\ I \times R$$
$$(39 - 1 - 1 - 1) = 36$$

Step 8 Summary table. Calculate mean squares (MS) by dividing SS by the number of df. Then calculate the F ratios by dividing the treatment MS by the MS Error.

Box B–8 *(continued)*

Source	SS	df	MS	F	p
Imagery	90.0	1	90.0	46.6	<.05
Rehearsal	28.9	1	28.9	15.0	<.05
Imagery × Rehearsal	12.1	1	12.1	6.3	<.05
Error	69.4	36	1.9		

Summary table of a 2 × 2 ANOVA

Step 9 To determine the significance of the F ratio, enter statistical Table C–6 with the *df* for the numerator (in this case it is always 1), and with the *df* for the denominator (*df* Error), which is 36, for any effect you are interested in.

We can conclude that the type of words and type of rehearsal both influenced recall, but we should note that the effects of word type were dependent on the type of rehearsal (that is, we obtained an interaction).

Box B–9 Factorial ANOVA with Repeated Measures (Within-Subjects): A Treatment × Treatment × Subjects Design

Subject	Rote rehearsal retention interval 2 sec	12 sec	Elaborate rehearsal retention interval 2 sec	12 sec	Subject total	Rehearsal total Rote	Elab.	Retention total 2 sec	12 sec
1	15	3	11	11	40	18	22	26	14
2	20	15	19	18	72	35	37	39	33
3	18	2	18	19	57	20	37	36	21
4	15	13	16	15	59	28	31	31	28
5	10	1	17	12	40	11	29	27	13
6	14	5	16	13	48	19	29	30	18
7	17	6	19	18	60	23	37	36	24
8	19	12	16	19	66	31	35	35	31
9	11	4	9	12	36	15	21	20	16
10	17	10	14	7	48	27	21	31	17
11	18	11	18	10	57	29	28	36	21
12	18	4	20	19	61	22	39	38	23
13	16	9	19	18	62	25	37	35	27
14	18	6	19	17	60	24	36	37	23
15	10	5	10	7	32	15	17	20	12
16	16	5	19	18	58	21	37	35	23

ΣX = 252 111   260 233   856   363 493   512 344
ΣX^2 = 4,114 1,033   4,408 3,669 47,776   24,820   24,910
$\Sigma\Sigma X$ = 856 $\Sigma\Sigma X^2$ = 13,224

Box B–9 *(continued)*

In a within-subjects ANOVA, we need to calculate both column (treatment) and row (subject) totals, because participants are serving as their own control condition. In fact, our error variance is estimated by the interaction of subjects within treatments (see Box B–7). Arrange your data table so that the scores of a single participant are in a row. It is usually a good idea to leave room so that treatment totals for a single participant may be placed in the table. We will analyze the data from Experiment 1 by Elmes and Bjork (1975). In their study, participants either rote or elaboratively rehearsed words, and then they performed a distracting math task for 2 or 12 seconds before attempting to recall the words. Thus, this is a 2×2 within-subjects design. The individual participants' total recall scores are shown in the table that begins this box.

Step 1 Determine the total score/participant (row) and total score/treatment combination (column). Find each participant's total score for every independent variable. The participant totals for a particular independent variable (for example, participant 1 has rehearsal totals of 18 and 22) should add up to that participant's total score (in this case, 40). Determine each treatment total by adding the appropriate column sums; check your answer by also adding the participant totals for that level of the independent variable. For example, the Rote Rehearsal total $= 252 + 111 = 363$ (sum of columns 1 and 2, which is equal to the sum of column 6).

Step 2 Determine the correction term (C). $C = (\Sigma\Sigma X)^2/N$, where $N =$ the number of measures in the table. $N = 16$ subjects $\times$ 4 scores $= 64$.

$$\begin{aligned} C &= 856^2/64 \\ &= 732,736/64 \\ &= 11,449 \end{aligned}$$

Step 3 SS Total $= \Sigma\Sigma X^2 -$ Step 2
$$\begin{aligned} &= 13,224 - 11,449 \\ &= 1,775 \end{aligned}$$

Step 4 SS Subjects. Square each participant's total score (column 5), add the squares, divide that total by the number of scores for each participant (4), and then subtract the results of Step 2.

$$\begin{aligned} SS \text{ Subject} &= 47,776/4 - \text{Step 2} \\ &= 11,944 - 11,449 \\ &= 495 \end{aligned}$$

Step 5 SS Rehearsal $= (363^2 + 493^2)/32 -$ Step 2
$$\begin{aligned} &= 374,818/32 - \text{Step 2} \\ &= 11,713.06 - 11,449 \\ &= 264.06 \end{aligned}$$

Step 6 MS Rehearsal. Divide the SS Rehearsal by the df for Rehearsal. The df Rehearsal $=$ the number of levels of Rehearsal $- 1$.

$$\begin{aligned} df \text{ Rehearsal} &= 2 - 1 \\ MS \text{ Rehearsal} &= 264.06/1 \\ &= 264.06 \end{aligned}$$

Box B–9   *(continued)*

Step 7   *SS* Error Rehearsal. The error term for Rehearsal is the interaction of participants with rehearsal. Square the subject totals for each level of Rehearsal (columns 6 and 7), add the squares, divide by the number of scores needed to get each sum (in this case, 2), then subtract C (Step 2), *SS* Subject (Step 4), and *SS* Rehearsal (Step 5).

$$SS \text{ Error Rehearsal} = \frac{18^2 + 22^2 + \ldots + 21^2 + 37^2}{2} - \text{Steps 2, 4, and 5}$$
$$= 24,820/2 - \text{Steps 2, 4, and 5}$$
$$= 12,410 - 11,449 - 495 - 264.06$$
$$= 201.94$$

Step 8   *MS* Error Rehearsal. Divide *SS* Error Rehearsal by *df* Error Rehearsal.

$$df = (\text{Subject} - 1)(df \text{ Rehearsal}) = (15)(1)$$
$$MS \text{ Error Rehearsal} = 201.94/15$$
$$= 13.46$$

Step 9   *F* Rehearsal = *MS* Rehearsal/*MS* Error Rehearsal
$$= \text{Step 6/Step 8}$$
$$= 264.06/13.46$$
$$= 19.62$$

Step 10   Repeat Steps 5–9 to find the F for Retention Interval (RI)

$$SS \text{ RI} = (512^2 + 344^2)/32 - \text{Step 2}$$
$$= 441.00$$
$$MS \text{ RI} = 441.00/(2 - 1)$$
$$= 441.00$$

$$SS \text{ Error RI} = \frac{26^2 + 14^2 + \ldots + 35^2 + 23^2}{2} - \text{Step 2, Step 4, and } SS \text{ RI}$$
$$= 24,910/2 - C - SS \text{ Subject} - SS \text{ RI}$$
$$= 12,455 - 11,449 - 495 - 441$$
$$= 70$$

$$MS \text{ Error RI} = SS \text{ Error RI}/(16 - 1)(2 - 1)$$
$$= 70/15$$
$$= 4.67$$

$$F \text{ RI} = 441.00/4.67$$
$$= 94.43$$

Step 11   *SS* Rehearsal × RI $= \dfrac{252^2 + 111^2 + 260^2 + 233^2}{16} - C$
$$- SS \text{ Reh} - SS \text{ RI}$$
$$= 12,357.13 - 11,449 - 264.06 - 441.00$$
$$= 203.07$$

Box B–9 *(continued)*

Step 12 MS Rehearsal $\times$ RI $= 203.07/(df$ Rehearsal$)(df$ RI$)$
$$= 203.07/1$$
$$= 203.07$$

Step 13 SS Error Rehearsal $\times$ RI. Calculate this triple interaction by subtracting all the SS you have calculated from SS Total.

SS Error Rehearsal $\times$ RI $= SS$ Total $- SS$ Subject $- SS$ Rehearsal $- SS$ RI
$\phantom{SS \text{ Error Rehearsal} \times \text{RI} =}$ $- SS$ Rehearsal $\times$ RI $- SS$ Error Rehearsal
$\phantom{SS \text{ Error Rehearsal} \times \text{RI} =}$ $- SS$ Error RI
$\phantom{SS \text{ Error Rehearsal} \times \text{RI} }= 1{,}775 - 495 - 264.06 - 441 - 203.07$
$\phantom{SS \text{ Error Rehearsal} \times \text{RI} =} -204.94 - 70$
$\phantom{SS \text{ Error Rehearsal} \times \text{RI} }= 99.93$

Step 14 MS Error Rehearsal $\times$ RI $= 99.93/($Subject $- 1)(df$ Rehearsal$)$
$\phantom{MS \text{ Error Rehearsal} \times \text{RI} =}(df$ RI$)$
$\phantom{MS \text{ Error Rehearsal} \times \text{RI} }= 99.93/15$
$\phantom{MS \text{ Error Rehearsal} \times \text{RI} }= 6.66$

Step 15 F Rehearsal $\times$ RI $= MS$ Rehearsal $\times$ RI$/MS$ Error Rehearsal $\times$ RI
$\phantom{F \text{ Rehearsal} \times \text{RI} }= 203.07/6.66$
$\phantom{F \text{ Rehearsal} \times \text{RI} }= 30.49$

Step 16 Summary table of 2×2 within-subjects ANOVA

Source	SS	df	MS	F
Subjects	495.00	15		
Rehearsal	264.06	1	264.06	19.62
Error Rehearsal	201.94	15	13.46	
Retention Interval	441.00	1	441.00	94.43
Error RI	70.00	15	4.67	
Rehearsal $\times$ RI	203.07	1	203.07	30.49
Error Rehearsal $\times$ RI	99.93	15	6.66	
Total	1,775.00	63		

To determine significance, enter Table C–6 with the appropriate degrees of freedom for each F ratio. (In this case, the $df = 1$ and 15). Note that both rehearsal and retention interval had significant effects on recall, and that the effects of type of rehearsal are dependent on the length of the retention interval.

χ^2 **Test for Independence**   Table B–5 is a repetition of Table 5–2 and shows the frequencies with which animal activists and nonactivists thought which kinds of research cause more animal suffering. The null hypothesis would be that level of activism would be independent of (not contingent on) the choice of "cruelest" research. That is, we would see roughly equivalent frequencies in

---

Table B–5   A 2 × 3 contingency table adapted from data presented by Plous (1991)

Group	Which kind of research causes more animal suffering?			
	Psychological	Medical	Equal	Total
Activists	64	56	281	401
	16.0%	14.0%	70.0%	100.0%
Nonactivists	8	20	25	53
	15.1%	37.7%	47.2%	100.0%
Total	72	76	306	454
	15.9%	16.7%	67.4%	100.0%

each of the cells of Table B–5. Obviously, the frequencies in the cells are different, and we can use χ^2 to determine whether being an activist determines how one responds.

The formula for determining χ^2 is

$$\chi^2 = \Sigma(O - E)^2/E \tag{B–10}$$

where O refers to the observed frequencies (the ones shown in each cell of Table B–5) and E refers to the expected frequencies for each cell. As shown in Box B–10, where χ^2 is calculated, the expected frequencies are calculated by multiplying together the row and column totals for a particular cell and then dividing that multiplicand by the total number of frequencies in the table. So, for animal activists who thought that psychological research caused the most suffering, the expected frequencies would be $(72 \times 401)/454 = 63.59$. The complete calculation is shown in Box B–10.

Box B–10   Calculation for χ^2 for the Data in Table B–5

Step 1   Calculate the expected frequencies for each main data cell.

Activists (A) × Psychological	$(72 \times 401)/454 = 63.59$
A × Medical	$(76 \times 401)/454 = 67.13$
A × Equal (E)	$(306 \times 401)/454 = 270.28$
Nonactivist (NA) × P	$(72 \times 53)/454 = 8.41$
NA × M	$(76 \times 53)/454 = 8.90$
NA × E	$(306 \times 53)/454 = 35.72$

Step 2   Subtract the expected frequencies from the observed, and square each difference, which is divided by the expected frequency for that cell.

A × P	$(64 - 63.59)^2 = .17/63.69 = .003$
A × M	$(67 - 56)^2 = 121/56 = 2.16$

Box B–10 *(continued)*

A × E	$(281 - 270.28)^2 = 114.92/270.28 = .43$
NA × P	$(8 - 8.41)^2 = .17/8.41 = .02$
NA × M	$(20 - 8.9)^2 = 123.21/8.9 = 13.8$
NA × E	$(25 - 35.7)^2 = 114.91/35.7 = 3.22$

Step 3 Sum the numbers from Step 2 to obtain χ^2.

$$\chi^2 = .003 + 2.16 + .43 + .02 + 13.8 + 3.22 + 19.63$$

Step 4 Check the significance of χ^2 in Table C–7 of Appendix C. The degrees of freedom for χ^2 are the number of rows less one times the number of columns less one $(2 - 1)(3 - 1) = 2$. To be significant at $p < .05$, a χ^2 with two degrees of freedom must be equal to or greater than 5.99. Because our χ^2 exceeds the critical value, we have a significant χ^2.

 Additional Information on Inferential Statistics

Explore the step-by-step presentation of standard error, hypothesis testing, *t* test for one sample, and *t*-test for between-groups and related-groups on the Wadsworth Psychology Resource Center, Statistics and Research Methods activities at *http://psychology.wadsworth.com/workshops/ workshops.html*

Statistical Tables

Statistical Tables

Table C–1   Proportions of area under the normal curve

Column A gives the positive *z* score.

Column B gives the area between the mean and *z*. Because the curve is symmetrical, areas for negative *z* scores are the same as for positive ones.

Column C gives the area that is beyond *z*.

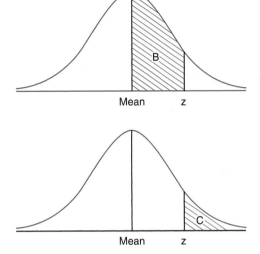

How to Use Table C–1: The values in this table represent the proportion of areas in the standard normal curve, which has a mean of 0, a standard deviation of 1.00, and a total area equal to 1.00. The raw scores must first be transformed into a *z* score. Column A represents this *z* score, Column B represents the distance between the mean of the standard normal distribution (0) and the *z* score, and Column C represents the proportion of the area beyond a given *z*.

(continued)

Table C–1 *(continued)*

(A) z	(B) area between mean and z	(C) area beyond z	(A) z	(B) area between mean and z	(C) area beyond z	(A) z	(B) area between mean and z	(C) area beyond z
0.00	.0000	.5000	0.45	.1736	.3264	0.90	.3159	.1841
0.01	.0040	.4960	0.46	.1772	.3228	0.91	.3186	.1814
0.02	.0080	.4920	0.47	.1808	.3192	0.92	.3212	.1788
0.03	.0120	.4880	0.48	.1844	.3156	0.93	.3238	.1762
0.04	.0160	.4840	0.49	.1879	.3121	0.94	.3264	.1736
0.05	.0199	.4801	0.50	.1915	.3085	0.95	.3289	.1711
0.06	.0239	.4761	0.51	.1950	.3050	0.96	.3315	.1685
0.07	.0279	.4721	0.52	.1985	.3015	0.97	.3340	.1660
0.08	.0319	.4681	0.53	.2019	.2981	0.98	.3365	.1635
0.09	.0359	.4641	0.54	.2054	.2946	0.99	.3389	.1611
0.10	.0398	.4602	0.55	.2088	.2912	1.00	.3413	.1587
0.11	.0438	.4562	0.56	.2123	.2877	1.01	.3438	.1562
0.12	.0478	.4522	0.57	.2157	.2843	1.02	.3461	.1539
0.13	.0517	.4483	0.58	.2190	.2810	1.03	.3485	.1515
0.14	.0557	.4443	0.59	.2224	.2776	1.04	.3508	.1492
0.15	.0596	.4404	0.60	.2257	.2743	1.05	.3531	.1469
0.16	.0636	.4364	0.61	.2291	.2709	1.06	.3554	.1446
0.17	.0675	.4325	0.62	.2324	.2676	1.07	.3577	.1423
0.18	.0714	.4286	0.63	.2357	.2643	1.08	.3599	.1401
0.19	.0753	.4247	0.64	.2389	.2611	1.09	.3621	.1379
0.20	.0793	.4207	0.65	.2422	.2578	1.10	.3643	.1357
0.21	.0832	.4168	0.66	.2454	.2546	1.11	.3665	.1335
0.22	.0871	.4129	0.67	.2486	.2514	1.12	.3686	.1314
0.23	.0910	.4090	0.68	.2517	.2483	1.13	.3708	.1292
0.24	.0948	.4052	0.69	.2549	.2451	1.14	.3729	.1271
0.25	.0987	.4013	0.70	.2580	.2420	1.15	.3749	.1251
0.26	.1026	.3974	0.71	.2611	.2389	1.16	.3770	.1230
0.27	.1064	.3936	0.72	.2642	.2358	1.17	.3790	.1210
0.28	.1103	.3897	0.73	.2673	.2327	1.18	.3810	.1190
0.29	.1141	.3859	0.74	.2704	.2296	1.19	.3830	.1170
0.30	.1179	.3821	0.75	.2734	.2266	1.20	.3849	.1151
0.31	.1217	.3783	0.76	.2764	.2236	1.21	.3869	.1131
0.32	.1255	.3745	0.77	.2794	.2206	1.22	.3888	.1112
0.33	.1293	.3707	0.78	.2823	.2177	1.23	.3907	.1093
0.34	.1331	.3669	0.79	.2852	.2148	1.24	.3925	.1075
0.35	.1368	.3632	0.80	.2881	.2119	1.25	.3944	.1056
0.36	.1406	.3594	0.81	.2910	.2090	1.26	.3962	.1038
0.37	.1443	.3557	0.82	.2939	.2061	1.27	.3980	.1020
0.38	.1480	.3520	0.83	.2967	.2033	1.28	.3997	.1003
0.39	.1517	.3483	0.84	.2995	.2005	1.29	.4015	.0985
0.40	.1554	.3446	0.85	.3023	.1977	1.30	.4032	.0968
0.41	.1591	.3409	0.86	.3051	.1949	1.31	.4049	.0951
0.42	.1628	.3372	0.87	.3078	.1922	1.32	.4066	.0934
0.43	.1664	.3336	0.88	.3106	.1894	1.33	.4082	.0918
0.44	.1700	.3300	0.89	.3133	.1867	1.34	.4099	.0901

Table C–1 *(continued)*

(A) z	(B) area between mean and z	(C) area beyond z	(A) z	(B) area between mean and z	(C) area beyond z	(A) z	(B) area between mean and z	(C) area beyond z
1.35	.4115	.0885	1.80	.4641	.0359	2.25	.4878	.0122
1.36	.4131	.0869	1.81	.4649	.0351	2.26	.4881	.0119
1.37	.4147	.0853	1.82	.4656	.0344	2.27	.4884	.0116
1.38	.4162	.0838	1.83	.4664	.0336	2.28	.4887	.0113
1.39	.4177	.0823	1.84	.4671	.0329	2.29	.4890	.0110
1.40	.4192	.0808	1.85	.4678	.0322	2.30	.4893	.0107
1.41	.4207	.0793	1.86	.4686	.0314	2.31	.4896	.0104
1.42	.4222	.0778	1.87	.4693	.0307	2.32	.4898	.0102
1.43	.4236	.0764	1.88	.4699	.0301	2.33	.4901	.0099
1.44	.4251	.0749	1.89	.4706	.0294	2.34	.4904	.0096
1.45	.4265	.0735	1.90	.4713	.0287	2.35	.4906	.0094
1.46	.4279	.0721	1.91	.4719	.0281	2.36	.4909	.0091
1.47	.4292	.0708	1.92	.4726	.0274	2.37	.4911	.0089
1.48	.4306	.0694	1.93	.4732	.0268	2.38	.4913	.0087
1.49	.4319	.0681	1.94	.4738	.0262	2.39	.4916	.0084
1.50	.4332	.0668	1.95	.4744	.0256	2.40	.4918	.0082
1.51	.4345	.0655	1.96	.4750	.0250	2.41	.4920	.0080
1.52	.4357	.0643	1.97	.4756	.0244	2.42	.4922	.0078
1.53	.4370	.0630	1.98	.4761	.0239	2.43	.4925	.0075
1.54	.4382	.0618	1.99	.4767	.0233	2.44	.4927	.0073
1.55	.4394	.0606	2.00	.4772	.0228	2.45	.4929	.0071
1.56	.4406	.0594	2.01	.4778	.0222	2.46	.4931	.0069
1.57	.4418	.0582	2.02	.4783	.0217	2.47	.4932	.0068
1.58	.4429	.0571	2.03	.4788	.0212	2.48	.4934	.0066
1.59	.4441	.0559	2.04	.4793	.0207	2.49	.4936	.0064
1.60	.4452	.0548	2.05	.4798	.0202	2.50	.4938	.0062
1.61	.4463	.0537	2.06	.4803	.0197	2.51	.4940	.0060
1.62	.4474	.0526	2.07	.4808	.0192	2.52	.4941	.0059
1.63	.4484	.0516	2.08	.4812	.0188	2.53	.4943	.0057
1.64	.4495	.0505	2.09	.4817	.0183	2.54	.4945	.0055
1.65	.4505	.0495	2.10	.4821	.0179	2.55	.4946	.0054
1.66	.4515	.0485	2.11	.4826	.0174	2.56	.4948	.0052
1.67	.4525	.0475	2.12	.4830	.0170	2.57	.4949	.0051
1.68	.4535	.0465	2.13	.4834	.0166	2.58	.4951	.0049
1.69	.4545	.0455	2.14	.4838	.0162	2.59	.4952	.0048
1.70	.4554	.0446	2.15	.4842	.0158	2.60	.4953	.0047
1.71	.4564	.0436	2.16	.4846	.0154	2.61	.4955	.0045
1.72	.4573	.0427	2.17	.4850	.0150	2.62	.4956	.0044
1.73	.4582	.0418	2.18	.4854	.0146	2.63	.4957	.0043
1.74	.4591	.0409	2.19	.4857	.0143	2.64	.4959	.0041
1.75	.4599	.0401	2.20	.4861	.0139	2.65	.4960	.0040
1.76	.4608	.0392	2.21	.4864	.0136	2.66	.4961	.0039
1.77	.4616	.0384	2.22	.4868	.0132	2.67	.4962	.0038
1.78	.4625	.0375	2.23	.4871	.0129	2.68	.4963	.0037
1.79	.4633	.0367	2.24	.4875	.0125	2.69	.4964	.0036

(continued)

Table C–1 *(continued)*

(A) z	(B) area between mean and z	(C) area beyond z	(A) z	(B) area between mean and z	(C) area beyond z	(A) z	(B) area between mean and z	(C) area beyond z
2.70	.4965	.0035	2.95	.4984	.0016	3.20	.4993	.0007
2.71	.4966	.0034	2.96	.4985	.0015	3.21	.4993	.0007
2.72	.4967	.0033	2.97	.4985	.0015	3.22	.4994	.0006
2.73	.4968	.0032	2.98	.4986	.0014	3.23	.4994	.0006
2.74	.4969	.0031	2.99	.4986	.0014	3.24	.4994	.0006
2.75	.4970	.0030	3.00	.4987	.0013	3.25	.4994	.0006
2.76	.4971	.0029	3.01	.4987	.0013	3.30	.4995	.0005
2.77	.4972	.0028	3.02	.4987	.0013	3.35	.4996	.0004
2.78	.4973	.0027	3.03	.4988	.0012	3.40	.4997	.0003
2.79	.4974	.0026	3.04	.4988	.0012	3.45	.4997	.0003
2.80	.4974	.0026	3.05	.4989	.0011	3.50	.4998	.0002
2.81	.4975	.0025	3.06	.4989	.0011	3.60	.4998	.0002
2.82	.4976	.0024	3.07	.4989	.0011	3.70	.4999	.0001
2.83	.4977	.0023	3.08	.4990	.0010	3.80	.4999	.0001
2.84	.4977	.0023	3.09	.4990	.0010	3.90	.49995	.00005
2.85	.4978	.0022	3.10	.4990	.0010	4.00	.49997	.00003
2.86	.4979	.0021	3.11	.4991	.0009			
2.87	.4979	.0021	3.12	.4991	.0009			
2.88	.4980	.0020	3.13	.4991	.0009			
2.89	.4981	.0019	3.14	.4992	.0008			
2.90	.4981	.0019	3.15	.4992	.0008			
2.91	.4982	.0018	3.16	.4992	.0008			
2.92	.4982	.0018	3.17	.4992	.0008			
2.93	.4983	.0017	3.18	.4993	.0007			
2.94	.4984	.0016	3.19	.4993	.0007			

Table C–2 Critical values of the U statistic of the Mann-Whitney U test

To use these four subtables, first decide what level of significance you want with either a one- or a two-tailed test. For example, if you want $p = .05$, two-tailed, use subtable c. Then locate the number of cases or measures (n) in both groups in the particular subtable you have chosen. The U value you have calculated must be *less* than that at the appropriate place in the table. For example, if you had 18 subjects in each group of an experiment and calculated $U = 90$, you could conclude that the null hypothesis can be rejected, because the critical U value with groups of these sizes is 99 (see subtable c).

(a) **Critical values of U for a one-tailed test at .001 or for a two-tailed test at .002**

n_1 \ n_2	9	10	11	12	13	14	15	16	17	18	19	20
1												
2												
3										0	0	0	0
4		0	0	0	1	1	1	2	2	3	3	3
5	1	1	2	2	3	3	4	5	5	6	7	7
6	2	3	4	4	5	6	7	8	9	10	11	12
7	3	5	6	7	8	9	10	11	13	14	15	16
8	5	6	8	9	11	12	14	15	17	18	20	21
9	7	8	10	12	14	15	17	19	21	23	25	26
10	8	10	12	14	17	19	21	23	25	27	29	32
11	10	12	15	17	20	22	24	27	29	32	34	37
12	12	14	17	20	23	25	28	31	34	37	40	42
13	14	17	20	23	26	29	32	35	38	42	45	48
14	15	19	22	25	29	32	36	39	43	46	50	54
15	17	21	24	28	32	36	40	43	47	51	55	59
16	19	23	27	31	35	39	43	48	52	56	60	65
17	21	25	29	34	38	43	47	52	57	61	66	70
18	23	27	32	37	42	46	51	56	61	66	71	76
19	25	29	34	40	45	50	55	60	66	71	77	82
20	26	32	37	42	48	54	59	65	70	76	82	88

SOURCE Adapted from Tables 1, 3, 5, and 7 of Aube, D. (1953). Extended tables for the Mann-Whitney statistic. *Bulletin of the Institute of Educational Research at Indiana University, 1, No.* 2. Taken from Siegel, S. (1956). *Nonparametric statistics for the behavior sciences.* New York: McGraw-Hill. Reprinted by permission of the Institute of Educational Research and McGraw-Hill Book Company.

(continued)

Table C–2   *(continued)*

(b) Critical values of *U* for a one-tailed test at .01 or for a two-tailed test at .02

$n_1 \backslash n_2$	9	10	11	12	13	14	15	16	17	18	19	20
1												
2					0	0	0	0	0	0	1	1
3	1	1	1	2	2	2	3	3	4	4	4	5
4	3	3	4	5	5	6	7	7	8	9	9	10
5	5	6	7	8	9	10	11	12	13	14	15	16
6	7	8	9	11	12	13	15	16	18	19	20	22
7	9	11	12	14	16	17	19	21	23	24	26	28
8	11	13	15	17	20	22	24	26	28	30	32	34
9	14	16	18	21	23	26	28	31	33	36	38	40
10	16	19	22	24	27	30	33	36	38	41	44	47
11	18	22	25	28	31	34	37	41	44	47	50	53
12	21	24	28	31	35	38	42	46	49	53	56	60
13	23	27	31	35	39	43	47	51	55	59	63	67
14	26	30	34	38	43	47	51	56	60	65	69	73
15	28	33	37	42	47	51	56	61	66	70	75	80
16	31	36	41	46	51	56	61	66	71	76	82	87
17	33	38	44	49	55	60	66	71	77	82	88	93
18	36	41	47	53	59	65	70	76	82	88	94	100
19	38	44	50	56	63	69	75	82	88	94	101	107
20	40	47	53	60	67	73	80	87	93	100	107	114

Table C–2 *(continued)*

(c) Critical values of *U* for a one-tailed test at .025 or for a two-tailed test at .05

n_1\n_2	9	10	11	12	13	14	15	16	17	18	19	20
1												
2	0	0	1	1	1	1	1	1	2	2	2	2
3	2	3	3	4	4	5	5	6	6	7	7	8
4	4	5	6	7	8	9	10	11	11	12	13	13
5	7	8	9	11	12	13	14	15	17	18	19	20
6	10	11	13	14	16	17	19	21	22	24	25	27
7	12	14	16	18	20	22	24	26	28	30	32	34
8	15	17	19	22	24	26	29	31	34	36	38	41
9	17	20	23	26	28	31	34	37	39	42	45	48
10	20	23	26	29	33	36	39	42	45	48	52	55
11	23	26	30	33	37	40	44	47	51	55	58	62
12	26	29	33	37	41	45	49	53	57	61	65	69
13	28	33	37	41	45	50	54	59	63	67	72	76
14	31	36	40	45	50	55	59	64	67	74	78	83
15	34	39	44	49	54	59	64	70	75	80	85	90
16	37	42	47	53	59	64	70	75	81	86	92	98
17	39	45	51	57	63	67	75	81	87	93	99	105
18	42	48	55	61	67	74	80	86	93	99	106	112
19	45	52	58	65	72	78	85	92	99	106	113	119
20	48	55	62	69	76	83	90	98	105	112	119	127

(continued)

Table C–2   *(continued)*

(d) Critical values of U for a one-tailed test at .05 or for a two-tailed test at .10

n_1\\n_2	9	10	11	12	13	14	15	16	17	18	19	20
1											0	0
2	1	1	1	2	2	2	3	3	3	4	4	4
3	3	4	5	5	6	7	7	8	9	9	10	11
4	6	7	8	9	10	11	12	14	15	16	17	18
5	9	11	12	13	15	16	18	19	20	22	23	25
6	12	14	16	17	19	21	23	25	26	28	30	32
7	15	17	19	21	24	26	28	30	33	35	37	39
8	18	20	23	26	28	31	33	36	39	41	44	47
9	21	24	27	30	33	36	39	42	45	48	51	54
10	24	27	31	34	37	41	44	48	51	55	58	62
11	27	31	34	38	42	46	50	54	57	61	65	69
12	30	34	38	42	47	51	55	60	64	68	72	77
13	33	37	42	47	51	56	61	65	70	75	80	84
14	36	41	46	51	56	61	66	71	77	82	87	92
15	39	44	50	55	61	66	72	77	83	88	94	100
16	42	48	54	60	65	71	77	83	89	95	101	107
17	45	51	57	64	70	77	83	89	96	102	109	115
18	48	55	61	68	75	82	88	95	102	109	116	123
19	51	58	65	72	80	87	94	101	109	116	123	130
20	54	62	69	77	84	92	100	107	115	123	130	138

Table C-3 Distribution for the sign test

This table shows alpha levels of the sign test for pairs of observations ranging from 3 to 42. The symbol x denotes the number of exceptions (the number of times the difference between conditions is in the unexpected direction), and the p level indicates the probability that that number of exceptions could occur by chance. If, out of 28 paired observations, 20 are ordered in the expected direction and only 8 are exceptions, the probability that this could occur by chance is .018.

x	p	x	p	x	p	x	p	x	p	x	p
n = 3		**n = 12**		**n = 19**		**n = 25**		**n = 31**		**n = 37**	
0	.125	1	.003	3	.002	5	.002	7	.002	10	.004
n = 4		2	.019	4	.010	6	.007	8	.005	11	.010
0	.062	3	.073	5	.032	7	.022	9	.015	12	.024
1	.312	4	.194	6	.084	8	.051	10	.035	13	.049
n = 5		**n = 13**		7	.180	9	.115	11	.075	14	.094
0	.031	1	.002	**n = 20**		10	.212	12	.141	15	.162
1	.188	2	.011	3	.001	**n = 26**		**n = 32**		**n = 38**	
n = 6		3	.016	4	.006	6	.005	8	.004	10	.003
0	.016	4	.133	5	.021	7	.014	9	.010	11	.007
1	.109	**n = 14**		6	.058	8	.038	10	.025	12	.017
2	.344	1	.001	7	.132	9	.084	11	.055	13	.036
n = 7		2	.006	**n = 21**		10	.163	12	.108	14	.072
0	.008	3	.029	4	.004	**n = 27**		13	.189	15	.128
1	.062	4	.090	5	.013	6	.003	**n = 33**		**n = 39**	
2	.227	5	.212	6	.039	7	.010	8	.002	11	.005
n = 8		**n = 15**		7	.095	8	.026	9	.007	12	.012
0	.004	1	.000	8	.192	9	.061	10	.018	13	.027
1	.035	2	.004	**n = 22**		10	.124	11	.040	14	.054
2	.145	3	.018	4	.002	11	.221	12	.081	15	.100
n = 9		4	.059	5	.008	**n = 28**		13	.148	16	.168
0	.002	5	.151	6	.026	6	.002	**n = 34**		**n = 40**	
1	.020	**n = 16**		7	.067	7	.006	9	.005	11	.003
2	.090	2	.002	8	.143	8	.018	10	.012	12	.008
3	.254	3	.011	**n = 23**		9	.044	11	.029	13	.019
n = 10		4	.038	4	.001	10	.092	12	.061	14	.040
0	.001	5	.105	5	.005	11	.172	13	.115	15	.077
1	.011	6	.227	6	.017	**n = 29**		14	.196	16	.134
2	.055	**n = 17**		7	.047	7	.004	**n = 35**		**n = 41**	
3	.172	2	.001	8	.105	8	.012	9	.003	11	.002
n = 11		3	.006	9	.202	9	.031	10	.008	12	.006
0	.000	4	.025	**n = 24**		10	.068	11	.020	13	.014
1	.006	5	.072	5	.008	11	.132	12	.045	14	.030
2	.033	6	.166	6	.011	**n = 30**		13	.088	15	.059
3	.113	**n = 18**		7	.032	7	.003	14	.155	16	.106
4	.274	3	.004	8	.076	8	.008	**n = 36**		17	.174
		4	.015	9	.154	9	.021	9	.002	**n = 42**	
		5	.048			10	.049	10	.006	12	.004
		6	.119			11	.100	11	.014	13	.010
		7	.240			12	.181	12	.033	14	.022
								13	.066	15	.044
								14	.121	16	.082
								15	.203	17	.140

Table C–4   Critical values of Wilcoxon's *T* statistic for the matched-pairs signed-ranks test

In using this table, first locate the number of *pairs* of scores in the *n* column. The critical values for several levels of significance are listed in the columns to the right. For example, if *n* were 15 and the computed value 19, we could conclude that because 19 is less than 25, the difference between conditions is significant beyond the .02 level of significance for a two-tailed test.

	Level of Significance for One-Tailed Test		
	.025	.01	.005
	Level of Significance for Two-Tailed Test		
n	.05	.02	.01
6	1	—	—
7	2	0	—
8	4	2	0
9	6	3	2
10	8	5	3
11	11	7	5
12	14	10	7
13	17	13	10
14	21	16	13
15	25	20	16
16	30	24	19
17	35	28	23
18	40	33	28
19	46	38	32
20	52	43	37
21	59	49	43
22	66	56	49
23	73	62	55
24	81	69	61
25	90	77	68

SOURCE Adapted from Table 1 of Wilcoxon, F. (1964). *Some rapid appoximate statistical procedures* (Rev. ed.). New York: American Cyanamid Company. Taken from Siegel, S. (1956). *Nonparametric statistics for the behavioral sciences.* New York: McGraw-Hill. Reprinted by permission of the American Cyanamid Company and McGraw-Hill Book Company.

Table C–5 Critical values of *t*

To find the appropriate value of *t*, read across the row that contains the number of degrees of freedom in your experiment. The columns are determined by the level of significance you have chosen. The value of *t* you obtain must be *greater* than that in the table to be significant. For example, with *df* = 15 and *p* = .05 (two-tailed test), your *t* value must be greater than 2.131.

	Level of Significance for One-Tailed Test					
	.10	.05	.025	.01	.005	.0005
	Level of Significance for Two-Tailed Test					
df	.20	.10	.05	.02	.01	.001
1	3.078	6.314	12.706	31.821	63.657	636.619
2	1.886	2.920	4.303	6.965	9.925	31.598
3	1.638	2.353	3.182	4.541	5.841	12.941
4	1.533	2.132	2.776	3.747	4.604	8.610
5	1.476	2.015	2.571	3.365	4.032	6.859
6	1.440	1.943	2.447	3.143	3.707	5.959
7	1.415	1.895	2.365	2.998	3.449	5.405
8	1.397	1.860	2.306	2.896	3.355	5.041
9	1.383	1.833	2.262	2.821	3.250	4.781
10	1.372	1.812	2.228	2.764	3.169	4.587
11	1.363	1.796	2.201	2.718	3.106	4.437
12	1.356	1.782	2.179	2.681	3.055	4.318
13	1.350	1.771	2.160	2.650	3.012	4.221
14	1.345	1.761	2.145	2.624	2.977	4.140
15	1.341	1.753	2.131	2.602	2.947	4.073
16	1.337	1.746	2.120	2.583	2.921	4.015
17	1.333	1.740	2.110	2.567	2.898	3.965
18	1.330	1.734	2.101	2.552	2.878	3.922
19	1.328	1.729	2.093	2.539	2.861	3.883
20	1.325	1.725	2.086	2.528	2.845	3.850
21	1.323	1.721	2.080	2.518	2.831	3.819
22	1.321	1.717	2.074	2.508	2.819	3.792
23	1.319	1.714	2.069	2.500	2.807	3.767
24	1.318	1.711	2.064	2.492	2.797	3.745
25	1.316	1.708	2.060	2.485	2.787	3.725
26	1.315	1.706	2.056	2.479	2.779	3.707
27	1.314	1.703	2.052	2.473	2.771	3.690
28	1.313	1.701	2.048	2.467	2.763	3.674
29	1.311	1.699	2.045	2.462	2.756	3.659
30	1.310	1.697	2.042	2.457	2.750	3.646
40	1.303	1.684	2.021	2.423	2.704	3.551
60	1.296	1.671	2.000	2.390	2.660	3.460
120	1.289	1.658	1.980	2.358	2.617	3.373
∞	1.282	1.645	1.960	2.326	2.576	3.291

SOURCE From Federighi, E. T. (1959). Extended tables of the percentage points of Student's *t*-distribution. *Journal of the American Statistical Association, 54*, 683–688. Reproduced by permission of the American Statistical Association.

Table C–6 Critical values of the F distribution

Find the appropriate values in the table by looking up the degrees of freedom in the numerator and denominator of the F ratio. After you have decided on the level of significance desired, the obtained F ratio must be *greater* than that in the table. For example, with $p = .05$ and 9 df in the numerator and 28 in the denominator, your F value must be greater than 2.24 to be reliable.

df for denom.	α	\multicolumn{9}{c}{df for numerator}
		1	2	3	4	5	6	7	8	9
3	.25	2.02	2.28	2.36	2.39	2.41	2.42	2.43	2.44	2.44
	.10	5.54	5.46	5.39	5.34	5.31	5.28	5.27	5.25	5.24
	.05	10.1	9.55	9.28	9.12	9.01	8.94	8.89	8.85	8.81
	.025	17.4	16.0	15.4	15.1	14.9	14.7	14.6	14.5	14.5
	.01	34.1	30.8	29.5	28.7	28.2	27.9	27.7	27.5	27.4
	.001	167	148	141	137	135	133	132	131	130
4	.25	1.81	2.00	2.05	2.06	2.07	2.08	2.08	2.08	2.08
	.10	4.54	4.32	4.19	4.11	4.05	4.01	3.98	3.95	3.94
	.05	7.71	6.94	6.59	6.39	6.26	6.16	6.09	6.04	6.00
	.025	12.2	10.6	9.98	9.60	9.36	9.20	9.07	8.98	8.90
	.01	21.2	18.0	16.7	16.0	15.5	15.2	15.0	14.8	14.7
	.001	74.1	61.2	56.2	53.4	51.7	50.5	49.7	49.0	48.5
5	.25	1.69	1.85	1.88	1.89	1.89	1.89	1.89	1.89	1.89
	.10	4.06	3.78	3.62	3.52	3.45	3.40	3.37	3.34	3.32
	.05	6.61	5.79	5.41	5.19	5.05	4.95	4.88	4.82	4.77
	.025	10.0	8.43	7.76	7.39	7.15	6.98	6.85	6.76	6.68
	.01	16.3	13.3	12.1	11.4	11.0	10.7	10.5	10.3	10.2
	.001	47.2	37.1	33.2	31.1	29.8	28.8	28.2	27.6	27.2
6	.25	1.62	1.76	1.78	1.79	1.79	1.78	1.78	1.78	1.77
	.10	3.78	3.46	3.29	3.18	3.11	3.05	3.01	2.98	2.96
	.05	5.99	5.14	4.76	4.53	4.39	4.28	4.21	4.15	4.10
	.025	8.81	7.26	6.60	6.23	5.99	5.82	5.70	5.60	5.52
	.01	13.8	10.9	9.78	9.15	8.75	8.47	8.26	8.10	7.98
	.001	35.5	27.0	23.7	21.9	20.8	20.0	19.5	19.0	18.7
7	.25	1.57	1.70	1.72	1.72	1.71	1.71	1.70	1.70	1.69
	.10	3.59	3.26	3.07	2.96	2.88	2.83	2.78	2.75	2.72
	.05	5.59	4.74	4.35	4.12	3.97	3.87	3.79	3.73	3.68
	.025	8.07	6.54	5.89	5.52	5.29	5.12	4.99	4.90	4.82
	.01	12.2	9.55	8.45	7.85	7.46	7.19	6.99	6.84	6.72
	.001	29.2	21.7	18.8	17.2	16.2	15.5	15.0	14.6	14.3
8	.25	1.54	1.66	1.67	1.66	1.66	1.65	1.64	1.64	1.63
	.10	3.46	3.11	2.92	2.81	2.73	2.67	2.62	2.59	2.56
	.05	5.32	4.46	4.07	3.84	3.69	3.58	3.50	3.44	3.39
	.025	7.57	6.06	5.42	5.05	4.82	4.65	4.53	4.43	4.36
	.01	11.3	8.65	7.59	7.01	6.63	6.37	6.18	6.03	5.91
	.001	25.4	18.5	15.8	14.4	13.5	12.9	12.4	12.0	11.8
9	.25	1.51	1.62	1.63	1.63	1.62	1.61	1.60	1.60	1.59
	.10	3.36	3.01	2.81	2.69	2.61	2.55	2.51	2.47	2.44
	.05	5.12	4.26	3.86	3.63	3.48	3.37	3.29	3.23	3.18
	.025	7.21	5.71	5.08	4.72	4.48	4.32	4.20	4.10	4.03
	.01	10.6	8.02	6.99	6.42	6.06	5.80	5.61	5.47	5.35
	.001	22.9	16.4	13.9	12.6	11.7	11.1	10.7	10.4	10.1

(continued)

Table C–6 *(continued)*

df for denom.	α	1	2	3	4	5	6	7	8	9
						df for numerator				
10	.25	1.49	1.60	1.60	1.59	1.59	1.58	1.57	1.56	1.56
	.10	3.29	2.92	2.73	2.61	2.52	2.46	2.41	2.38	2.35
	.05	4.96	4.10	3.71	3.48	3.33	3.22	3.14	3.07	3.02
	.025	6.94	5.46	4.83	4.47	4.24	4.07	3.95	3.85	3.78
	.01	10.0	7.56	6.55	5.99	5.64	5.39	5.20	5.06	4.94
	.001	21.0	14.9	12.6	11.3	10.5	9.92	9.52	9.20	8.96
11	.25	1.47	1.58	1.58	1.57	1.56	1.55	1.54	1.53	1.53
	.10	3.23	2.86	2.66	2.54	2.45	2.39	2.34	2.30	2.27
	.05	4.84	3.98	3.59	3.36	3.20	3.09	3.01	2.95	2.90
	.025	6.72	5.26	4.63	4.28	4.04	3.88	3.76	3.66	3.59
	.01	9.65	7.21	6.22	5.67	5.32	5.07	4.89	4.74	4.63
	.001	19.7	13.8	11.6	10.4	9.58	9.05	8.66	8.35	8.12
12	.25	1.46	1.56	1.56	1.55	1.54	1.53	1.52	1.51	1.51
	.10	3.18	2.81	2.61	2.48	2.39	2.33	2.28	2.24	2.21
	.05	4.75	3.89	3.49	3.26	3.11	3.00	2.91	2.85	2.80
	.025	6.55	5.10	4.47	4.12	3.89	3.73	3.61	3.51	3.44
	.01	9.33	6.93	5.95	5.41	5.06	4.82	4.64	4.50	4.39
	.001	18.6	13.0	10.8	9.63	8.89	8.38	8.00	7.71	7.48
13	.25	1.45	1.55	1.55	1.53	1.52	1.51	1.50	1.49	1.49
	.10	3.14	2.76	2.56	2.43	2.35	2.28	2.23	2.20	2.16
	.05	4.67	3.81	3.41	3.18	3.03	2.92	2.83	2.77	2.71
	.025	6.41	4.97	4.35	4.00	3.77	3.60	3.48	3.39	3.31
	.01	9.07	6.70	5.74	5.21	4.86	4.62	4.44	4.30	4.19
	.001	17.8	12.3	10.2	9.07	8.35	7.86	7.49	7.21	6.98
14	.25	1.44	1.53	1.53	1.52	1.51	1.50	1.49	1.48	1.47
	.10	3.10	2.73	2.52	2.39	2.31	2.24	2.19	2.15	2.12
	.05	4.60	3.74	3.34	3.11	2.96	2.85	2.76	2.70	2.65
	.025	6.30	4.86	4.24	3.89	3.66	3.50	3.38	3.29	3.21
	.01	8.86	6.51	5.56	5.04	4.69	4.46	4.28	4.14	4.03
	.001	17.1	11.8	9.73	8.62	7.92	7.43	7.08	6.80	6.58
15	.25	1.43	1.52	1.52	1.51	1.49	1.48	1.47	1.46	1.46
	.10	3.07	2.70	2.49	2.36	2.27	2.21	2.16	2.12	2.09
	.05	4.54	3.68	3.29	3.06	2.90	2.79	2.71	2.64	2.59
	.025	6.20	4.77	4.15	3.80	3.58	3.41	3.29	3.20	3.12
	.01	8.68	6.36	5.42	4.89	4.56	4.32	4.14	4.00	3.89
	.001	16.6	11.3	9.34	8.25	7.57	7.09	6.74	6.47	6.26
16	.25	1.42	1.51	1.51	1.50	1.48	1.47	1.46	1.45	1.44
	.10	3.05	2.67	2.46	2.33	2.24	2.18	2.13	2.09	2.06
	.05	4.49	3.63	3.24	3.01	2.85	2.74	2.66	2.59	2.54
	.025	6.12	4.69	4.08	3.73	3.50	3.34	3.22	3.12	3.05
	.01	8.53	6.23	5.29	4.77	4.44	4.20	4.03	3.89	3.78
	.001	16.1	11.0	9.00	7.94	7.27	6.81	6.46	6.19	5.98
17	.25	1.42	1.51	1.50	1.49	1.47	1.46	1.45	1.44	1.43
	.10	3.03	2.64	2.44	2.31	2.22	2.15	2.10	2.06	2.03
	.05	4.45	3.59	3.20	2.96	2.81	2.70	2.61	2.55	2.49
	.025	6.04	4.62	4.01	3.66	3.44	3.28	3.16	3.06	2.98
	.01	8.40	6.11	5.18	4.67	4.34	4.10	3.93	3.79	3.68
	.001	15.7	10.7	8.73	7.68	7.02	6.56	6.22	5.96	5.75

(continued)

Table C–6 *(continued)*

df for denom.	α	df for numerator								
		1	2	3	4	5	6	7	8	9
18	.25	1.41	1.50	1.49	1.48	1.46	1.45	1.44	1.43	1.42
	.10	3.01	2.62	2.42	2.29	2.20	2.13	2.08	2.04	2.00
	.05	4.41	3.55	3.16	2.93	2.77	2.66	2.58	2.51	2.46
	.025	5.98	4.56	3.95	3.61	3.38	3.22	3.10	3.01	2.93
	.01	8.29	6.01	5.09	4.58	4.25	4.01	3.84	3.71	3.60
	.001	15.4	10.4	8.49	7.46	6.81	6.35	6.02	5.76	5.56
19	.25	1.41	1.49	1.49	1.47	1.46	1.44	1.43	1.42	1.41
	.10	2.99	2.61	2.40	2.27	2.18	2.11	2.06	2.02	1.98
	.05	4.38	3.52	3.13	2.90	2.74	2.63	2.54	2.48	2.42
	.025	5.92	4.51	3.90	3.56	3.33	3.17	3.05	2.96	2.88
	.01	8.18	5.93	5.01	4.50	4.17	3.94	3.77	3.63	3.52
	.001	15.1	10.2	8.28	7.26	6.62	6.18	5.85	5.59	5.39
20	.25	1.40	1.49	1.48	1.47	1.45	1.44	1.43	1.42	1.41
	.10	2.97	2.59	2.38	2.25	2.16	2.09	2.04	2.00	1.96
	.05	4.35	3.49	3.10	2.87	2.71	2.60	2.51	2.45	2.39
	.025	5.87	4.46	3.86	3.51	3.29	3.13	3.01	2.91	2.84
	.01	8.10	5.85	4.94	4.43	4.10	3.87	3.70	3.56	3.46
	.001	14.8	9.95	8.10	7.10	6.46	6.02	5.69	5.44	5.24
22	.25	1.40	1.48	1.47	1.45	1.44	1.42	1.41	1.40	1.39
	.10	2.95	2.56	2.35	2.22	2.13	2.06	2.01	1.97	1.93
	.05	4.30	3.44	3.05	2.82	2.66	2.55	2.46	2.40	2.34
	.025	5.79	4.38	3.78	3.44	3.22	3.05	2.93	2.84	2.76
	.01	7.95	5.72	4.82	4.31	3.99	3.76	3.59	3.45	3.35
	.001	14.4	9.61	7.80	6.81	6.19	5.76	5.44	5.19	4.99
24	.25	1.39	1.47	1.46	1.44	1.43	1.41	1.40	1.39	1.38
	.10	2.93	2.54	2.33	2.19	2.10	2.04	1.98	1.94	1.91
	.05	4.26	3.40	3.01	2.78	2.62	2.51	2.42	2.36	2.30
	.025	5.72	4.32	3.72	3.38	3.15	2.99	2.87	2.78	2.70
	.01	7.82	5.61	4.72	4.22	3.90	3.67	3.50	3.36	3.26
	.001	14.0	9.34	7.55	6.59	5.98	5.55	5.23	4.99	4.80
26	.25	1.38	1.46	1.45	1.44	1.42	1.41	1.39	1.38	1.37
	.10	2.91	2.52	2.31	2.17	2.08	2.01	1.96	1.92	1.88
	.05	4.23	3.37	2.98	2.74	2.59	2.47	2.39	2.32	2.27
	.025	5.66	4.27	3.67	3.33	3.10	2.94	2.82	2.73	2.65
	.01	7.72	5.53	4.64	4.14	3.82	3.59	3.42	3.29	3.18
	.001	13.7	9.12	7.36	6.41	5.80	5.38	5.07	4.83	4.64
28	.25	1.38	1.46	1.45	1.43	1.41	1.40	1.39	1.38	1.37
	.10	2.89	2.50	2.29	2.16	2.06	2.00	1.94	1.90	1.87
	.05	4.20	3.34	2.95	2.71	2.56	2.45	2.36	2.29	2.24
	.025	5.61	4.22	3.63	3.29	3.06	2.90	2.78	2.69	2.61
	.01	7.64	5.45	4.57	4.07	3.75	3.53	3.36	3.23	3.12
	.001	13.5	8.93	7.19	6.25	5.66	5.24	4.93	4.69	4.50
30	.25	1.38	1.45	1.44	1.42	1.41	1.39	1.38	1.37	1.36
	.10	2.88	2.49	2.28	2.14	2.05	1.98	1.93	1.88	1.85
	.05	4.17	3.32	2.92	2.69	2.53	2.42	2.33	2.27	2.21
	.025	5.57	4.18	3.59	3.25	3.03	2.87	2.75	2.65	2.57
	.01	7.56	5.39	4.51	4.02	3.70	3.47	3.30	3.17	3.07
	.001	13.3	8.77	7.05	6.12	5.53	5.12	4.82	4.58	4.39

(continued)

Table C–6 *(continued)*

df for denom.	α	1	2	3	4	5	6	7	8	9
						df for numerator				
40	.25	1.36	1.44	1.42	1.40	1.39	1.37	1.36	1.35	1.34
	.10	2.84	2.44	2.23	2.09	2.00	1.93	1.87	1.83	1.79
	.05	4.08	3.23	2.84	2.61	2.45	2.34	2.25	2.18	2.12
	.025	5.42	4.05	3.46	3.13	2.90	2.74	2.62	2.53	2.45
	.01	7.31	5.18	4.31	3.83	3.51	3.29	3.12	2.99	2.89
	.001	12.6	8.25	6.60	5.70	5.13	4.73	4.44	4.21	4.02
60	.25	1.35	1.42	1.41	1.38	1.37	1.35	1.33	1.32	1.31
	.10	2.79	2.39	2.18	2.04	1.95	1.87	1.82	1.77	1.74
	.05	4.00	3.15	2.76	2.53	2.37	2.25	2.17	2.10	2.04
	.025	5.29	3.93	3.34	3.01	2.79	2.63	2.51	2.41	2.33
	.01	7.08	4.98	4.13	3.65	3.34	3.12	2.95	2.82	2.72
	.001	12.0	7.76	6.17	5.31	4.76	4.37	4.09	3.87	3.69
120	.25	1.34	1.40	1.39	1.37	1.35	1.33	1.31	1.30	1.29
	.10	2.75	2.35	2.13	1.99	1.90	1.82	1.77	1.72	1.68
	.05	3.92	3.07	2.68	2.45	2.29	2.17	2.09	2.02	1.96
	.025	5.15	3.80	3.23	2.89	2.67	2.52	2.39	2.30	2.22
	.01	6.85	4.79	3.95	3.48	3.17	2.96	2.79	2.66	2.56
	.001	11.4	7.32	5.79	4.95	4.42	4.04	3.77	3.55	3.38
∞	.25	1.32	1.39	1.37	1.35	1.33	1.31	1.29	1.28	1.27
	.10	2.71	2.30	2.08	1.94	1.85	1.77	1.72	1.67	1.63
	.05	3.84	3.00	2.60	2.37	2.21	2.10	2.01	1.94	1.88
	.025	5.02	3.69	3.12	2.79	2.57	2.41	2.29	2.19	2.11
	.01	6.63	4.61	3.78	3.32	3.02	2.80	2.64	2.51	2.41
	.001	10.8	.91	5.42	4.62	4.10	3.74	3.47	3.27	3.10

Table C–7 Critical values of the Pearson product-moment correlation coefficient

To look up the appropriate values in the table, you should begin by looking up the degrees of freedom, which is the number of subjects minus 2 (df = N − 2). After you have decided on the level of significance desired, the obtained correlation coefficient must be greater than that in the table. For example, with p = .01 and 19 df, your correlation coefficient must be greater than .5487 to be reliable using a two-tailed test.

	Level of Significance for One-Tailed Test		
	.05	.025	.005
	Level of Significance for Two-Tailed Test		
df	.10	.05	.01
1	.9877	.9969	.9999
2	.9000	.9500	.9900
3	.8054	.8783	.9587
4	.7293	.8114	.9172
5	.6694	.7545	.8745
6	.6215	.7067	.8343
7	.5822	.6664	.7977
8	.5494	.6319	.7646
9	.5214	.6021	.7348
10	.4973	.5760	.7079
11	.4762	.5529	.6835
12	.4575	.5324	.6614
13	.4409	.5139	.6411
14	.4259	.4973	.6226
15	.4124	.4821	.6055
16	.4000	.4683	.5897
17	.3887	.4555	.5751
18	.3783	.4438	.5614
19	.3687	.4329	.5487
20	.3598	.4227	.5368
25	.3233	.3809	.4869
30	.2960	.3494	.4487
35	.2746	.3246	.4182
40	.2573	.3044	.3932
45	.2428	.2875	.3721
50	.2306	.2732	.3541
60	.2108	.2500	.3248
70	.1954	.2319	.3017
80	.1829	.2172	.2830
90	.1726	.2050	.2673
100	.1638	.1946	.2540

SOURCE: Abridged from table in Diekhoff, G. (1992). *Statistics for the social and behavioral sciences: Univariate, bivariate, and multivariate.* Belmont, CA: Duxbury.

Table C–8 Critical values of the χ^2 distribution

Find the critical value by entering the table with the number of degrees of freedom ([# Rows − 1][# Columns − 1]). A significant χ^2 must equal or exceed the value for a given significance level. For example, with $p = .05$ and $df = 9$, χ^2 must be greater than or equal to 16.92.

df	p = .10	p = .05	p = .01
1	2.71	3.84	6.63
2	4.61	5.99	9.21
3	6.25	7.82	11.35
4	7.78	9.49	13.28
5	9.24	11.07	15.09
6	10.64	12.59	16.81
7	12.02	14.07	18.48
8	13.36	15.51	20.09
9	14.68	16.92	21.66
10	15.99	18.31	23.21
11	17.28	19.68	24.72
12	18.55	21.03	26.21
13	19.81	22.36	27.69
14	21.06	23.69	29.14
15	22.31	25.00	30.58
16	23.54	26.30	32.00
17	24.77	27.59	33.41
18	25.99	28.87	34.81
19	27.20	30.14	36.19
20	28.41	31.41	37.56
21	29.62	32.67	38.93
22	30.81	33.93	40.29
23	32.01	35.17	41.64
24	33.20	36.42	42.98
25	34.38	37.65	44.32

SOURCE Abridged from table in Howell, D. C. (1995). *Fundamental statistics for the behavioral sciences* (3rd ed.). Belmont, CA: Duxbury.

Table C–9 Random numbers

	1	2	3	4	5	6	7	8	9
1	32942	95416	42339	59045	26693	49057	87496	20624	14819
2	07410	99859	83828	21409	29094	65114	36701	25762	12827
3	59981	68155	45673	76210	58219	45738	29550	24736	09574
4	46251	25437	69654	99716	11563	08803	86027	51867	12116
5	65558	51904	93123	27887	53138	21488	09095	78777	71240
6	99187	19258	86421	16401	19397	83297	40111	49326	81686
7	35641	00301	16096	34775	21562	97983	45040	19200	16383
8	14031	00936	81518	48440	02218	04756	19506	60695	88494
9	60677	15076	92554	26042	23472	69869	62877	19584	39576
10	66314	05212	67859	89356	20056	30648	87349	20389	53805
11	20416	87410	75646	64176	82752	63606	37011	57346	69512
12	28701	56992	70423	62415	40807	98086	58850	28968	45297
13	74579	33844	33426	07570	00728	07079	19322	56325	84819
14	62615	52342	82968	75540	80045	53069	20665	21282	07768
15	93945	06293	22879	08161	01442	75071	21427	94842	26210
16	75689	76131	96837	67450	44511	50424	82848	41975	71663
17	02921	16919	35424	93209	52133	87327	95897	65171	20376
18	14295	34969	14216	03191	61647	30296	66667	10101	63203
19	05303	91109	82403	40312	62191	67023	90073	83205	71344
20	57071	90357	12901	08899	91039	67251	28701	03846	94589
21	78471	57741	13599	84390	32146	00871	09354	22745	65806
22	89242	79337	59293	47481	07740	43345	25716	70020	54005
23	14955	59592	97035	80430	87220	06392	79028	57123	52872
24	42446	41880	37415	47472	04513	49494	08860	08038	43624
25	18534	22346	54556	17558	73689	14894	05030	19561	56517
26	39284	33737	42512	86411	23753	29690	26096	81361	93099
27	33922	37329	89911	55876	28379	81031	22058	21487	54613
28	78355	54013	50774	30666	61205	42574	47773	36027	27174
29	08845	99145	94316	88974	29828	97069	90327	61842	29604
30	01769	71825	55957	98271	02784	66731	40311	88495	18821
31	17639	38284	59478	90409	21997	56199	30068	82800	69692
32	05851	58653	99949	63505	40409	85551	90729	64938	52403
33	42396	40112	11469	03476	03328	84238	26570	51790	42122
34	13318	14192	98167	75631	74141	22369	36757	89117	54998
35	60571	54786	26281	01855	30706	66578	32019	65884	58485
36	09531	81853	59334	70929	03544	18510	89541	13555	21168
37	72865	16829	86542	00396	20363	13010	69645	49608	54738
38	56324	31093	77924	28622	83543	28912	15059	80192	83964
39	78192	21626	91399	07235	07104	73652	64425	85149	75409
40	64666	34767	97298	92708	01994	53188	78476	07804	62404
41	82201	75694	02808	65983	74373	66693	13094	74183	73020
42	15360	73776	40914	85190	54278	99054	62944	47351	89098
43	68142	67957	70896	37983	20487	95350	16371	03426	13895
44	19138	31200	30616	14639	44406	44236	57360	81644	94761
45	28155	03521	36415	78452	92359	81091	56513	88321	97910
46	87971	29031	51780	27376	81056	86155	55488	50590	74514
47	58147	68841	53625	02059	75223	16783	19272	61994	71090
48	18875	52809	70594	41649	32935	26430	82096	01605	65846
49	75109	56474	74111	31966	29969	70093	98901	84550	25769
50	35983	03742	76822	12073	59463	84420	15868	99505	11426

REFERENCES

Adams, J. A. (1972). Research and the future of engineering psychology. *American Psychologist, 27,* 615–622.

Altman, E. (2004). Advance preparation in task switching. *Psychological Science, 15,* 616–622.

American Psychiatric Association. (2000). *Diagnostic and statistical manual of mental disorders* (4th ed., revised). Washington, DC: Author.

American Psychological Association. (1982). *Ethical principles in the conduct of research with human behavior.* Washington, DC: Author.

———. (2001a). *Non-academic careers for scientific psychologists.* Washington, DC: Author. Retrieved October 10, 2004 from: http://www.apa.org/science/nonacad.html.

———. (2001b). *Publication manual of the American Psychological Association* (5th ed.). Washington, DC: Author.

———. (2002). Ethical principles of psychologists and code of conduct. *American Psychologist, 57,* 1060–1073.

———. (2003). Committee on Animal Research and Ethics. *Guidelines for ethical conduct in the care and use of animals.* Retrieved February 11, 2005 from http://www.apa.org/science/anguide.html.

———. (2004). Report of the Ethics Committee. *American Psychologist, 59,* 434–441.

———. (2005). *Ethics in plain English: An illustrative casebook for psychologists* (2nd ed.). Washington, DC: Author.

Anderson, C. A., & Bushman, B. J. (1997). External validity of "trivial" experiments: The case of laboratory aggression. *Review of General Psychology, 1,* 19–41.

Anderson, N. H. (1981). *Foundations of information integration theory.* New York: Academic Press.

Atkinson, R. C. (1975). Mnemotechnics and second language learning. *American Psychologist, 30,* 821–828.

Bachman, J. D., & Johnston, L. D. (1979). The freshman. *Psychology Today, 13,* 78–87.

Baker, S. R., & Stephenson, D. (2000). Prediction and control as determinants of behavioral uncertainty: Effect on task performance and heart rate reactivity. *Integrative Physiological and Behavioral Science, 35,* 235–250.

Baldwin, J. D., & Baldwin, J. I. (1998). *Behavior principles in everyday life* (3rd ed.). Upper Saddle River, NJ: Prentice Hall.

Banaji, M. R., & Crowder, R. G. (1989). The bankruptcy of everyday memory. *American Psychologist, 44,* 1185–1193.

Barber, T. X. (1976). *Pitfalls in human research: Ten pivotal points.* New York: Pergamon.

Barefoot, J. C., Hoople, H., & McClay, D. (1972). Avoidance of an act which would violate personal space. *Psychonomic Science, 28,* 205–206.

Barker, R. G. (1968). *Ecological psychology.* Palo Alto, CA: Stanford University Press.

Barker, R. G., & Wright, H. F. (1951). *One boy's day.* New York: Harper and Row.

Bartlett, F. C. (1932). *Remembering: A study in experimental and social psychology.* Cambridge: Cambridge University Press.

Beaulieu, C. M. J. (2004). Intercultural study of personal space: A case study. *Journal of Applied Social Psychology, 34,* 794–805.

Begg, I. M., Anas, A., & Farinacci, S. (1992). Dissociation of process in belief: Source recollection, statement familiarity, and the illusion of truth. *Journal of Experimental Psychology: General, 121,* 446–458.

Bem, D. J. (2004). Writing the empirical journal article. In Darley, J. M., Zanna, M. P., & Roediger, H. L., III (Eds.), *The compleat academic: A career guide* (2nd Ed., pp. 185–219).

Bergman, E. T., & Roediger, H. L., III (1999). Can Bartlett's repeated reproduction experiments be replicated? *Memory & Cognition, 27,* 937–947.

Berkowitz, L., & Donnerstein, E. (1982). External validity is more than skin deep. *American Psychologist, 37,* 245–257.

Best, J. B. (1999). *Cognitive psychology* (5th ed.). Belmont, CA: Wadsworth/Thompson Learning.

Blaney, R. H. (1986). Affect and memory: A review. *Psychological Bulletin, 99,* 229–246.

Blum, D. (2002). *Love at Goon Park: Harry Harlow and the science of affection.* New York: Basic Books.

Boice, R. (1983). Observational skills. *Psychological Bulletin, 93,* 3–29.

Boring, E. G. (1950). *A history of experimental psychology.* New York: Appleton Century-Crofts.

———. (1954). The nature and history of experimental control. *American Journal of Psychology, 67,* 573–589.

———. (1961). The beginning and growth of measurement in psychology, *Isis, 52,* 238–257.

Bowd, A. D. (1980). Ethical reservations about psychological research with animals. *Psychological Record, 30,* 201–210.

Bowd, A. D., & Shapiro, K. J. (1993). The case against laboratory animal research in psychology. *Journal of Social Issues, 49,* 133–142.

Bower, G. H. (1972). Mental imagery and associative learning. In L. Gregg (Ed.), *Cognition in learning and memory.* New York: Wiley.

Bower, G. H., & Forgas, J. P. (2000). Affect, memory, and social cognition. In E. Eich & J. F. Kilhstrom (Eds.), *Cognition and emotion.* New York: Oxford University Press.

Brady, J. V. (1958). Ulcers in "executive" monkeys. *Scientific American, 199,* 92–100.

Brady, J. V., Porter, R. W., Conrad, D. G., & Mason, J. W. (1958). Avoidance behavior and the development of gastroduodenal ulcers. *Journal of the Experimental Analysis of Behavior, 1,* 69–72.

Brennen, T., Baguley, T., Bright, J., & Bruce, V. (1990). Resolving semantically induced tip-of-the-tongue states. *Memory & Cognition, 18,* 339–347.

Brewer, C. L., Hopkins, J. R., Kimble, G. A., Matlin, M. W., McCann, L. I., McNeil, O. V., et al. (1993). Curriculum. In T. V. McGovern (Ed.), *Handbook for enhancing undergraduate education in psychology* (pp. 161–182). Washington, DC: American Psychological Association.

Bridgeman, B., McCamley-Jenkins, L., & Ervin, N. (2000). *Predictions of freshman grade-point average from the revised and recentered SAT®1: Reasoning test* (College Board Research Report No. 2000–1) New York: College Entrance Examination Board.

Broad, W., & Wade, N. (1982). *Betrayers of the truth.* New York: Simon and Schuster.

Broadbent, D. E. (1971). *Decision and stress.* London: Academic Press.

———. (1973). *In defence of empirical psychology.* London: Methuen.

Bröder, A. (1998). Deception can be acceptable. *American Psychologist, 53,* 805–806.

Brown, R., & Kulick, J. (1977). Flashbulb memories. *Cognition, 5,* 73-79.

Brown, R., & McNeill, D. (1966). The "tip-of-the-tongue" phenomenon. *Journal of Verbal Learning and Verbal Behavior, 5,* 325–327.

Butters, N., & Cermak, L. S. (1986). A case study of the forgetting of autobiographical knowledge: Implications for the study of retrograde amnesia. In D. Rubin (Ed.), *Autobiographical memory* (pp. 253–272). New York: Cambridge University Press.

Campbell, D. T., & Erlebacher, A. (1970a). How regression artifacts can mistakenly make compensatory education look harmful. In J. Helmuth (Ed.), *Compensatory education: A national debate: Vol. 3. Disadvantaged child.* New York: Brunner/Mazel.

———. (1970b). Reply to the replies. In J. Helmuth (Ed.), *Compensatory education: A national debate: Vol. 3. Disadvantaged child.* New York: Brunner/Mazel.

Campbell, D. T., & Stanley, J. C. (1966). *Experimental and quasi-experimental designs for research.* Chicago: Rand McNally.

Carver, C. S., Coleman, A. E., & Glass, D. C. (1976). The coronary-prone behavior pattern and the suppression of fatigue on a treadmill test. *Journal of Personality and Social Psychology, 33,* 460–466.

Chaplin, J. P. (1968). *Dictionary of psychology.* New York: Dell.

Chen, Z., & Mo, L. (2004). Schema induction in problem solving: A multidimensional analysis. *Journal of Experimental Psychology: Learning, Memory, & Cognition, 30,* 583–600.

Cicirelli, V. (1970). The relevance of the regression artifact problem to the Westinghouse-Ohio evaluation of Head Start: A reply to Campbell and Erlebacher. In J. Helmuth (Ed.), *Compensatory education: A national debate: Vol. 3. Disadvantaged child.* New York: Brunner/Mazel.

Cicirelli, V., & Granger, R. (1969, June). *The impact of Head Start: An evaluation of the effects of Head Start on children's cognitive and affective development.* A report presented to the Office of Economic Opportunity pursuant to Contract B89–4356. Westinghouse Learning Corporation, Ohio University. (Distributed by Clearinghouse for Federal Scientific and Technical Information, U. S. Department of Commerce, National Bureau of Standards, Institute for Applied Technology, PB 184–328.)

Cohen, C. F., & Cohen, M. S. (1993). Defending your life: When women complain about sexual harassment. *Employee Responsibilities and Rights Journal, 7,* 235–242.

Cohen, F., Solomon, S., Maxfield, M., Pyszczynski, T., & Greenberg, J. (2004). Fatal attraction: The effects of mortality salience on evaluations of charismatic, task-oriented, and relationship-oriented leaders. *Psychological Science, 15,* 846–851.

Cohen, J. D., Dunbar, K., & McClelland, J. L. (1990). On the control of automatic processes: A parallel distributed processing account of the Stroop effect. *Psychological Review, 97,* 332–361.

Cole, M., Gay, J., Glick, J. A., & Sharp, D. W. (1971). *The cultural context of learning and thinking.* New York: Basic Books.

Collins, R., Elliott, M., Berry, S., Kanouse, D., Kunkel, D., Hunter, S., et al. (2004). Watching sex on television predicts adolescent initiation of sexual behavior [Electronic version]. *Pediatrics, 114,* e280–e290. Retrieved October 12, 2004 from http://www.pediatrics.org/cgi/content/full/114/3/e280

Cook, T. D., & Campbell, D. T. (1979). *Quasi-experimentation: Design and analysis for field settings.* Chicago: Rand McNally.

Craik, F. I. M., & Lockhart, R. S. (1972). Levels of processing: A framework for memory research. *Journal of Verbal Learning and Verbal Behavior, 11,* 671–684.

Dalton, P. (2002). Olfaction. In H. Pashler & S. Yantis (Eds.), *Stevens' handbook of experimental psychology: Vol.1. Sensation and perception* (3rd ed., pp. 691–756). New York: Wiley.

Dalton, P., Doolittle, N., Nagata, H., & Breslin, P. A. S. (2000). The merging of the senses: Integration of subthreshold taste and smell. *Nature Neuroscience, 3,* 431–432.

Darley, J. M., & Zanna, M. P. (2004). The hiring process in academia. In M. P. Zanna, J. M. Darley, & H. L. Roediger (Eds.), *The compleat academic: A career guide* (2nd ed., pp. 31–56). Washington, DC: American Psychological Association.

DeLuca, R. V., & Holborn, S. W. (1992). Effects of a variable-ratio reinforcement schedule with changing criteria on exercise in obese and nonobese boys. *Journal of Applied Behavior Analysis, 25,* 671–679.

Dickerson, S. S., & Kemeny, M. E. (2004). Acute stressors and cortisol responses: A theoretical integration and synthesis of laboratory research. *Psychological Bulletin, 130,* 355–391.

Dipboye, R. L., & Flanagan, M. F. (1979). Research settings in industrial and organizational psychology. *American Psychologist, 34,* 141–150.

Dollard, J., & Miller, N. E. (1950). *Personality and psychotherapy.* New York: McGraw-Hill.

Dorahy, M. J. (2001). Dissociative identity disorder and memory dysfunction: The current state of experimental research and its future directions. *Clinical Psychology Review, 21,* 771–795.

Edwards, A. L. (1953). The relationship between the judged desirability of a trait and the probability that the trait will be endorsed. *Journal of Applied Psychology, 37,* 90–93.

———. (1957). *The social desirability variable in personality research.* New York: Dryden.

Eibl-Eibesfeldt, I. (1970). *Ethology: The biology of behavior.* New York: Holt, Rinehart & Winston.

———. (1972). Similarities and differences between cultures in expressive movements. In R. A. Hinde (Ed.), *Non-verbal communication.* Cambridge: Cambridge University Press.

Elmes, D. G. (1978). *Readings in experimental psychology.* Chicago: Rand McNally.

———. (1988, May 8). Cheap-shot prize goes to Proxmire. *Roanoke Times & World News,* p. F3.

Elmes, D. G., & Bjork, R. A. (1975). The interaction of encoding and rehearsal processes in the recall of repeated and non-repeated items. *Journal of Verbal Learning and Verbal Behavior, 14,* 30–42.

Elmes, D. G., Chapman, P. F., & Selig, C. W. (1984). Role of mood and connotation in the spacing effect. *Bulletin of the Psychonomic Society, 22,* 186–188.

Eron, L. D. (1982). Parent-child interaction, television violence, and aggression of children. *American Psychologist, 37,* 197–211.

Eron, L. D., Huesmann, L. R., Lefkowitz, M. M., & Walder, L. O. (1972). Does television violence cause aggression? *American Psychologist, 27,* 253–263.

Evans, J. W., & Schiller, J. (1970). How preoccupation with possible regression artifacts can lead to a faulty strategy for the evaluation of social action programs: A reply to Campbell and Erlebacher. In J. Helmuth (Ed.), *Compensatory education: A national debate: Vol. 3. Disadvantaged child.* New York: Brunner/Mazel.

Eysenck, H. J., & Eaves, L. J. (1981). *The cause and effects of smoking.* New York: Gage.

Fechner, G. (1860/1966). *Elements of psychophysics* (Vol. 1). (H. E. Adler, D. H. Howes, and E. G. Boring, Eds. and Trans.). New York: Holt, Rinehart & Winston.

Feingold, B. F. (1975). Hyperkinesis and learning disabilities linked to artificial food flavors and colors. *American Journal of Nursing, 75,* 797–803.

Festinger, L. (1957). *A theory of cognitive dissonance.* Palo Alto, CA: Stanford University Press.

Festinger, L., Riecken, H. W., & Schachter, S. (1956). *When prophecy fails.* Minneapolis: University of Minnesota Press.

Ficken, M. S., Rusch, K. M., Taylor, S. J., & Powers, D. R. (2000). Blue-throated hummingbird song: A pinnacle of nonoscine vocalizations, *Auk, 117,* 120–128.

Fossey, D. (1972). Living with mountain gorillas. In T. B. Allen (Ed.), *The marvels of animal behavior.* Washington, DC: National Geographic Society.

Freedle, R., & Kostin, I. (1994). Can multiple-choice reading tests be construct-valid? A reply to Katz, Lautenschlager, Blackburn, and Harris. *Psychological Science, 5,* 107–110.

Gabrenya, W. K., Latané, B., & Wang, Y. (1983). Social loafing in cross-cultural perspective: Chinese on Taiwan. *Journal of Cross-Cultural Psychology, 14,* 368–384.

Gallup, G. G., & Suarez, S. D. (1985). Alternatives to the use of animals in psychological research. *American Psychologist, 40,* 1104–1111.

Garner, W. R., Hake, H., & Eriksen, C. W. (1956). Operationism and the concept of perception. *Psychological Review, 63,* 149–159.

Garry, M., Manning, C. G., Loftus, E. F., & Sherman, S. J. (1996). Imagination inflation: Imagining a childhood event inflates confidence that it occurred. *Psychonomic Bulletin & Review, 3,* 208–214.

Glenberg, A. M. (1988). *Learning from data.* San Diego: Harcourt Brace Jovanovich.

Goldstein, G., & Hersen, M. (Eds.). (1990). *Handbook of psychological assessment* (2nd ed.). New York: Pergamon.

Graessle, O. A., Ahbel, K., & Porges, S. W. (1978). Effects of mild prenatal decompressions on growth and behavior in the rat. *Bulletin of the Psychonomic Society, 12,* 329–331.

Greene, R. L. (1996). The influence of experimental design: The example of the Brown-Peterson paradigm. *Canadian Journal of Experimental Psychology, 50,* 240–242.

Greenough, W. T. (1992). Animal rights replies distort(ed) and misinform(ed). *Psychological Science, 3,* 142.

Gregory, R. (1970). *The intelligent eye.* New York: McGraw-Hill.

Grice, G. R., & Hunter, J. J. (1964). Stimulus intensity effects dependent upon the type of experimental design. *Psychological Review, 71,* 247–256.

Guilford, J. P. (1967). *The nature of human intelligence.* New York: McGraw-Hill.

Haines, M. M., Stansfeld, S. A., Head, J., & Job, R. F. S. (2002). Multilevel modelling of aircraft noise on performance tests in schools around Heathrow Airport London. *Journal of Epidemiology and Community Health, 56,* 139–144.

Hallahan, D. P., Kauffman, J. M., & Lloyd, J. W. (1999). *Introduction to learning disabilities* (rev ed.). Needham Heights, MA: Allyn & Bacon.

Hanowski, R. J., & Kantowitz, B. H. (1997). Driver memory retention of in-vehicle information system messages. *Transportation Research Record, 1573,* 8–16. Washington, DC: Transportation Research Board.

Hanson, N. R. (1958). *Patterns of discovery.* Cambridge: Cambridge University Press.

Harkins, S. G., Latané, B., & Williams, K. (1980). Social loafing: Allocating effort or taking it easy? *Journal of Experimental Social Psychology, 16,* 457–465.

Harlow, H. F. (1959, June). Love in infant monkeys. *Scientific American, 200,* 68–74.

Harlow, H. F., Gluck, J. P., & Suomi, S. J. (1972). Generalization of behavioral data between nonhuman and human animals. *American Psychologist, 27,* 709–716.

Harré, R. (1983). *Great scientific experiments.* Oxford: Oxford University Press.

Hart, B. M., Allen, K. E., Buell, J. S., Harris, F. R., & Wolf, M. M. (1964). Effects of social reinforcement on operant crying. *Journal of Experimental Child Psychology, 1,* 145–153.

Heaps, C., & Nash, M. (1999). Individual differences in imagination inflation. *Psychonomic Bulletin & Review, 6,* 313–318.

Hicks, R. A., & Kilcourse, J. (1983). Habitual sleep duration and the incidence of headaches in college students. *Bulletin of the Psychonomic Society, 21,* 119.

Hintzman, D. L., Carre, F., Eskridge, V. L., Owens, A. M., Shaff, S. S., & Sparks, M. E. (1972) "Stroop" effect: Input or output phenomenon? *Journal of Experimental Psychology, 95,* 458–459.

Hoff, C. (1980). Immoral and moral uses of animals. *New England Journal of Medicine, 302,* 115–118.

Homans, G. C. (1965). Group factors in worker productivity. In H. Proshansky & L. Seidenberg (Eds.), *Basic studies in social psychology.* New York: Holt.

Horn, D. B. (2001). Confounding the effects of delay and interference on memory distortion: Commentary on Schmolck, Buffalo, and Squire. *Psychological Science, 12,* 180–181.

Horowitz, L. M. (1974). *Elements of statistics for psychology and education.* New York: McGraw-Hill.

Howard, D. V., & Wiggs, C. L. (1993). Aging and learning: Insights from implicit and explicit tests. In J. Cerella, W. J. Hoyer, J. Rybash, & M. Commons (Eds.), *Adult age differences: Limits on loss.* New York: Academic Press.

Huesmann, L. R., Eron, L., Leftkowitz, M., & Walder, L. (1973). Television violence and aggression: The causal effect remains. *American Psychologist, 28,* 617–620.

Huesmann, L. R., Moise-Titus, J., Podolski, C., & Eron, L. (2003). Longitudinal relations between children's exposure to TV violence and their aggressive and violent behavior in young adulthood: 1977–1992. *Developmental Psychology, 39,* 201–221.

Huff, D. (1954). *How to lie with statistics.* New York: Norton.

Huntjens, R. J. C., Postma, A., Peters, M. L., Woertman, L., & van der Hart, O. (2003). Interidentity amnesia for neutral, episodic information in dissociative identity disorder. *Journal of Abnormal Psychology, 112,* 290–297.

Hurlburt, R. L. (1994). *Comprehending behavioral statistics.* Pacific Grove, CA: Brooks/Cole.

Hygge, S., Evans, G., & Bullinger, M. (2002). A prospective study of some effects of aircraft noise on cognitive performance in school children. *Psychological Science, 13,* 469–474.

Hyman, R. (1964). *The nature of psychological inquiry.* Englewood Cliffs, NJ: Prentice-Hall.

Imber, S. D., Glanz, L., Elkin, I., Sotsky, S., Boyer, J., & Leber, W. (1986). Ethical issues in psychotherapy research: Problems in a collaborative clinical study. *American Psychologist, 41,* 137–146.

Jacoby, L. L., Bishara, A. J., Toth, J. P., & Hessels, S. (2005). Aging, subjective experience, and cognitive control: Dramatic false remembering by older adults. *Journal of Experiment Psychology: General, 34,* 131–148.

James, L. E., Burke, D. M., Austin, A., & Hulme, E. (1998). Production and perception of "verbosity" in younger and older adults. *Psychology and Aging, 13,* 355–367.

James, W. (1890). *The principles of psychology.* New York: Henry Holt.

Jarrard, L. E. (1963). Effects of d-lysergic acid diethylamide on operant behavior in the rat. *Psychopharmacologia, 5,* 39–46.

Jensen, A. R. (1969). How much can we boost I.Q. and scholastic achievement? *Harvard Educational Review, 39,* 1–123.

Johnson-Laird, P. N. (1988). *The computer and the mind: An introduction to cognitive science.* Cambridge: Harvard University Press.

Jones, R. F. (1982). *Ancients and moderns.* New York: Dover.

Judd, C. M., Smith, E. R., & Kidder, L. H. (1991). *Research methods in social relations* (6th ed.). Fort Worth, TX: Holt, Rinehart & Winston.

Kantowitz, B. H. (1990). Can cognitive theory guide human factors measurement? *Proceedings of the Human Factors Society, 34,* 1258–1262.

———. (1992a). Selecting measures for human factors research. *Human Factors, 34,* 387–398.

———. (1992b). Heavy vehicle driver workload assessment: Lessons from aviation. *Proceedings of the Human Factors Society, 36,* 1113–1117.

———. (1994, January). *Evaluating driver workload in a heavy vehicle simulator.* Paper presented at INEL Workload Transition Workshop.

———. (2001). In-vehicle information systems: Premises, promises, and pitfalls. *Transportation Human Factors.*

Kantowitz, B. H., & Casper, P. A. (1988). Human workload in aviation. In E. Weiner & D. Nagel (Eds.), *Human factors in aviation* (pp. 157–187). New York: Academic Press.

Kantowitz, B. H., Hanowski, R. J., & Kantowitz, S. C. (1997). Driver acceptance of unreliable traffic information in familiar and unfamiliar settings. *Human Factors, 39,* 164–176.

Katz, D. (1979, February 7). Paying the price for drug development. *Roanoke Times & World News.*

Katz, S., Lautenschlager, G., Blackburn, A., & Harris, F. (1990). Answering reading comprehension items without passages on the SAT. *Psychological Science, 1,* 122–127.

Kawai, N., & Imada, H. (1996). Between- and within-subject effects of US duration on conditioned suppression in rats: Contrast makes otherwise unnoticed duration dimension stand out. *Learning and Motivation, 27,* 92–111.

Kazdin, A. E. (2001). *Behavior modification in applied settings* (6th ed.). Belmont, CA: Wadsworth/Thomson Learning.

Kendler, H. H. (1981). *Psychology: A science in conflict.* New York: Oxford.

Kerlinger, F. N., & Lee, H. B. (2000). *Foundations of behavioral research* (4th ed.). Fort Worth, TX: Harcourt College Publishers.

Kimmel, A. J. (1998). In defense of deception. *American Psychologist, 53,* 803–805.

Kinsbourne, M. (1984). Hyperactivity management: The impact of special diets. In M. Levine & P. Satz (Eds.), *Middle childhood: Development and dysfunction* (pp. 487–500). Baltimore: University Park Press.

Kinsey, A. C., Pomeroy, W. B., & Martin, C. E. (1953). *Sexual behavior in the human female.* Philadelphia: Saunders.

Kinzel, A. F. (1970). Body-buffer zone in violent prisoners. *The American Journal of Psychiatry, 127,* 59–64.

Kirk, R. R. (1982). *Experimental design: Procedures for the behavioral sciences* (2nd ed.). Pacific Grove, CA: Brooks/Cole.

Klein, W. M., & Kunda, Z. (1993). Maintaining self-serving social comparisons: Biased reconstruction of one's past behaviors. *Personality & Social Psychology Bulletin, 19,* 732–739.

Kluger, A. N., & Tikochinsky, J. (2001). The error of accepting the "theoretical" null hypothesis: The rise, fall, and resurrection of commonsense hypotheses in psychology. *Psychological Bulletin, 127,* 408–423.

Koch, C. (1997). Learning the research process on the world wide web. *Council on Undergraduate Research Quarterly, 18,* 27–29, 48–49.

Kohn, A. (1986). *False prophets.* New York: Basil Blackwell.

Korn, J. H. (1997). *Illusions of reality: A history of deception in social psychology.* Albany, NY: State University of New York Press.

Korn, J. H. (1998). The reality of deception. *American Psychologist, 53,* 805.

Kravitz, D. A., & Martin, B. (1986). Ringelmann rediscovered: The original article. *Journal of Personality and Social Psychology, 50,* 936–941.

Kuhn, T. S. (1962). *The structure of scientific revolutions.* Chicago: University of Chicago Press.

Kunda, Z. (1990). The case for motivated reasoning. *Psychological Bulletin, 108,* 480–498.

Kunda, Z., & Sanitioso, R. (1989). Motivated changes in the self-concept. *Journal of Experimental Social Psychology, 25,* 272–285.

Langston, W. (2005). *Research methods laboratory manual for psychology* (2nd ed.). Pacific Grove, CA: Wadsworth Group.

Latané, B. (1981). The psychology of social impact. *American Psychologist, 36,* 343–356.

Latané, B., & Darley, J. M. (1970). *The unresponsive bystander: Why doesn't he help?* New York: Appleton Century-Crofts.

Latané, B., Williams, K., & Harkins, S. (1979). Many hands make light the work: Causes and consequences of social loafing. *Journal of Personality and Social Psychology, 37,* 822–832.

Lester, B. M., & Brazelton, T. B. (1982). Cross-cultural assessment of neonatal behavior. In D. A. Wagner & H. W. Stevenson (Eds.), *Cultural perspectives on child development.* San Francisco: Freeman.

Levin, I. P., Louviere, J. J., & Schepanski, A. A. (1983). External validity tests of laboratory studies of information integration. *Organizational Behavior and Human Performance, 31,* 173–193.

Likert, R. (1932). A technique for the measurement of attitudes. *Archives of Psychology, 140,* 44–53.

Lloyd, M. A. (1997, August). *Entry-level jobs for psychology majors.* Retrieved October 5, 2004 from http://www.psych.com/careers/jobs

Lorig, B. T. (1996). Undergraduate research in psychology: Skills to take to work. *Council on Undergraduate Research Quarterly, 16,* 145–149.

Lovelace, E. A., & Twohig, P. T. (1990). Healthy older adult's perception of their memory function and use of mnemonics. *Bulletin of the Psychonomic Society, 28,* 115–118.

Luchins, A. S. (1942). Mechanization in problem solving: The effect of Einstellung. *Psychological Monographs, 54* (6, Whole No. 181).

MacLeod, C. M. (1991). Half a century of research on the Stroop effect: An integrative review. *Psychological Bulletin, 109,* 163–203.

Malott, R. W., Whaley, D. L., & Malott, M. E. (1997). *Elementary principles of behavior* (3rd ed.). Upper Saddle River, NJ: Prentice Hall.

Mann, T. (1994). Informed consent for psychological research: Do subjects comprehend consent forms and understand their legal rights? *Psychological Science, 5,* 140–143.

Markus, H. R., & Kitayama, S. (1991). Culture and the self: Implications for cognition, emotion, and motivation. *Psychological Review, 98,* 224–253.

Marriot, P. (1949). Size of working groups and output. *Occupational Psychology, 23,* 47–57.

Marsh, R. L., Landau, J. D., & Hicks, J. L. (1996). How examples may (and may not) constrain creativity. *Memory & Cognition, 24,* 669–680.

Marsh, R. L., Landau, J. D., & Hicks, J. L. (1997). Contributions of inadequate source monitoring to unconscious plagiarism during idea generation. *Journal of Experimental Psychology: Learning, Memory, & Cognition, 23,* 866–897.

Marsh, R. L., Ward, T. B., & Landau, J. P. (1999). The inadvertent use of prior knowledge in a generative cognitive test. *Memory & Cognition, 27,* 94–105.

Martin, G., & Pear, J. (1999). *Behavior modification: What it is and how to do it* (6th ed.). Upper Saddle River, NJ: Prentice Hall.

Martin, P., & Bateson, P. (1993). *Measuring behaviour: An introductory guide* (2nd ed.). Cambridge: Cambridge University Press.

Masling, J. (1966). Role-related behavior of the subject and psychologist and its effects upon psychological data. *Nebraska symposium on motivation* (Vol. 14). Lincoln, NE: University of Nebraska Press.

Mayer, R. E. (1977). Problem-solving performance with task overload: Effects of self-pacing and trait anxiety. *Bulletin of the Psychonomic Society, 9,* 283–286.

Mayr, E. (1982). *The growth of biological thought.* Cambridge, MA: Belknap Press.

McCall, R. B. (1990). *Fundamental statistics for the behavioral sciences* (5th ed.). San Diego: Harcourt Brace.

McGovern, T. V. (1993). *Handbook for enhancing undergraduate education in psychology.* Washington, DC: American Psychological Association.

McHugh, P. R. (1992). Psychiatric misadventures. *American Scholar, 61,* 497–510.

McSweeny, A. J. (1978). The effects of response cost on the behavior of a million persons: Charging for directory assistance in Cincinnati. *Journal of Applied Behavior Analysis, 11,* 47–51.

Melton, G., & Gray, J. (1988). Ethical dilemmas in AIDS research: Individual privacy and public health. *American Psychologist, 43,* 60–64.

Midgley, J. P., Matthew, A. G., Greenwood, C. M., & Logan, A. G. (1996). Effect of reduced dietary sodium on blood pressure: A meta-analysis of randomized controlled trials. *Journal of the American Medical Association (KFR), 275,* 1590–1597.

Milgram, S. (1963). Behavioral study of obedience. *Journal of Abnormal and Social Psychology, 67,* 371–378.

———. (1977). Ethical issues in the study of obedience. In B. Milgram (Ed.), *The individual in a social world* (pp. 188–199). Reading, MA: Addison-Wesley.

Mill, J. S. (1843/1930). *A system of logic.* London: Longmans Green.

Miller, D. B. (1977). Roles of naturalistic observation in comparative psychology. *American Psychologist, 32,* 211–219.

Miller, N. E. (1985). The value of behavioral research on animals. *American Psychologist, 40,* 423–440.

Monsell, S. (2003). Task switching. *Trends in Cognitive Science, 7,* 134–140.

Mook, D. G. (1983). In defense of external invalidity. *American Psychologist, 38,* 379–387.

Moscovitch, M. (1982). Multiple dissociations of functions in the amnesiac syndrome. In L. Cermak (Ed.), *Human memory and amnesia.* Hillsdale, NJ: Erlbaum.

Nantais, K. M., & Schellenberg, E. G. (1999). The Mozart effect: An artifact of preference. *Psychological Science, 10,* 370–373.

Neisser, U. (1976). *Cognition and reality: Principles and implications of cognitive psychology.* San Francisco: Freeman.

———. (1978). Memory: What are the important questions? In M. M. Gruneberg, P. E. Morris, & R. N. Sykes (Eds.), *Practical aspects of memory* (pp. 3–24). London: Academic Press.

———. (1981). John Dean's memory. *Cognition, 9,* 1–22.

———. (1982). *Memory observed: Remembering in natural contexts.* San Francisco: Freeman.

Ng, C. F. (2000). Effects of building construction noise on residents: A quasi-experiment. *Journal of Environmental Psychology, 20,* 375–385.

Nisbett, R. E., Peng, K., Choi, E., & Norenzayan, A. (2001). Culture and systems of thought: Holistic versus analytical cognition. *Psychological Review, 108,* 291–310.

Nissen, M. J., Ross, J. L., & Schacter, D. L. (1988). Memory and awareness in a patient with multiple personality disorder. *Brain and Cognition, 8,* 117–134.

Norcross, J. C., Hanych, J. M., & Terranova, R. D. (1996). Graduate study in psychology: 1992–1993. *American Psychologist, 51,* 631–643.

Notterman, J. M., & Mintz, D. E. (1965). *Dynamics of response.* New York: Wiley.

Oltmanns, T. F., Neale, J. M., & Davison, G. C. (1999). *Case studies in abnormal behavior* (5th ed., pp. 1–16). New York: Wiley.

Orne, M. T. (1962). On the social psychology of the psychological experiment: With particular reference to demand characteristics and their implications. *American Psychologist, 17,* 776–783.

———. (1969). Demand characteristics and the concept of quasi-controls. In R. Rosenthal & R. L. Rosnow (Eds.), *Artifact in behavioral research.* New York: Academic Press.

Orne, M. T., & Evans, T. J. (1965). Social control in the psychological experiment: Antisocial behavior and hypnosis. *Journal of Personality and Social Psychology, 1,* 189–200.

Ortmann, A., & Hertwig, R. (1997). Is deception acceptable? *American Psychologist, 52,* 746–747.

———. (1998). The question remains: Is deception acceptable? *American Psychologist, 53,* 806–807.

Overmier, B., & Carroll, M.E. (2001). Basic issues in the use of animals in health research. In M. E. Carroll & B. Overmier (Eds.), *Animal research in human health: Advancing human welfare through behavioral science* (pp. 3–13). Washington, DC: American Psychological Association.

Paik, H., & Comstock, G. (1994). The effects of television violence on antisocial behavior: A meta-analysis. *Communication Research, 21,* 516–546.

Paivio, A. (1975). Perceptual comparisons through the mind's eye. *Memory & Cognition, 3,* 635–647.

Parsons, H. M. (1974). What happened at Hawthorne? *Science, 183,* 922–931.

Pasupathi, M. (1999). Age differences in response to conformity pressure for emotional and nonemotional material. *Psychology & Aging 14,* 170–174.

Pavlov, I. P. (1963). *Lectures on conditioned reflexes.* New York: International Publishers.

Peirce, C. S. (1877). The fixation of belief. *Popular Science Monthly, 12,* 1–15. Reprinted in E. C. Moore (Ed.) (1972), *Charles S. Peirce: The essential writings.* New York: Harper & Row.

Perlmutter, M., & Myers, N. A. (1979). Development of recall in two- to four-year-old children. *Developmental Psychology, 15,* 73–83.

Phillips, D. P. (1972). Deathday and birthday: An unexpected connection. In J. Tanur, F. Mosteller, W. H. Kruskal, R. F. Link, R. S. Peters, & G. R. Rising (Eds.), *Statistics: A guide to the unknown.* San Francisco: Holden Day.

———. (1977). Motor vehicle fatalities increase just after publicized suicide stories. *Science, 196,* 1464–1465.

———. (1978). Airplane accident fatalities increase just after stories about murder and suicide. *Science, 201,* 148–150.

———. (1983). The impact of mass media violence on U. S. homicides. *American Sociological Review, 48,* 560–568.

Piaget, J., & Inhelder, B. (1969). *The psychology of the child.* London: Routledge & Kegan Paul.

Piliavin, I. M., Piliavin, J. A., & Rodin, J. (1975). Costs, diffusion and the stigmatized victim. *Journal of Personality and Social Psychology, 32,* 429–438.

Pittenger, D. J. (2002). Deception in research: Distinctions and solutions from the perspective of utilitarianism. *Ethics and Behavior, 12,* 117–142.

Platt, J. R. (1964). Strong inference. *Science, 146,* 347–353.

Plous, S. (1991). An attitude survey of animal rights activists. *Psychological Science, 2,* 194–196.

———. (1996a). Attitudes towards the use of animals in psychological research and education. *American Psychologist, 51,* 1167–1180.

———. (1996b). Attitudes towards the use of animals in psychological research and education: Results from a national survey of psychology majors. *Psychological Science, 7,* 352–358.

Popper, K. R. (1961). *The logic of scientific discovery.* New York: Basic Books.

Poulton, E. C. (1982). Influential companions: Effects of one strategy on another in the within-subjects designs of cognitive psychology. *Psychological Bulletin, 9,* 673–690.

Powers, D. E., & Rock, D. A. (1998). *Effects of coaching on SAT 1: Reasoning scores.* New York: College Board Publications.

Pratkanis, A. R., Greenwald, A. G., Leippe, M. R., & Baumgardner, M. H. (1988). In search of reliable persuasion effects: The sleeper effect is dead. Long live the sleeper effect. *Journal of Personality and Social Psychology, 54,* 203–218.

Putnam, F. W., Guroff, J. J., Silberman, E. K., Barban, L., & Post, R. M. (1986). The clinical phenomenology of multiple personality disorder: 100 recent cases. *Journal of Clinical Psychiatry, 47,* 285–293.

Rauscher, F. H., Shaw, G. L., & Ky, K. N. (1993). Music and spatial task performance. *Nature, 365,* 611.

———. (1995). Listening to Mozart enhances spatial-temporal reasoning: Towards a neurophysiological basis. *Neuroscience Letters, 185,* 44–47.

Rayner, K., & Pollatsek, A. (1995) *The psychology of reading.* Hillsdale, NJ: Erlbaum.

Read, J. D. (1983). Detection of *F*s in a single statement: The role of phonetic recoding. *Memory & Cognition, 11,* 390–399.

Reichardt, C. S., & Mark, M. M. (1998). Quasi-experimentation. In L. Bickman & D. J. Rigg (Eds.), *Handbook of applied social research methods.* Thousand Oaks, CA: Sage.

Responsible Science. (1992). *Ensuring the integrity of the research process* (Vol. 1). Washington, DC: National Academy Press.

Riccio, D. C., Ackil, J., & Burch-Vernon, A. (1992). Forgetting of stimulus attributes: Methodological implications for assessing associative phenomena. *Psychological Bulletin, 112,* 433–445.

Richman, C. L., Mitchell, D. B., & Reznick, J. S. (1979). Mental travel: Some reservations. *Journal of Experimental Psychology: Human Perception and Performance, 5,* 13–18.

Ringelmann, M. (1913). Recherches sur les moteurs animes: Travail de l'homme. *Annales de l'Institut National Agronomique,* 2e series-tome XII, 1–40.

Roberts, C. (1971). Debate I. Animal experimentation and evolution. *American Scholar, 40,* 497–503.

Roebers, C. M., & Schneider, W. (2000). The impact of misleading questions on eyewitness memory in children and adults. *Applied Cognitive Psychology, 14,* 509–526.

Roediger, H. L., & Neely, J. H. (1982). Retrieval blocks in episodic and semantic memory. *Canadian Journal of Psychology, 36,* 213–242.

Rollin, B. E. (1985). The moral status of research animals in psychology. *American Psychologist, 40,* 920–926.

Rose, T. L. (1978). The functional relationship between artificial food colors and hyperactivity. *Journal of Applied Behavior Analysis, 11,* 439–446.

Rosenbaum, P. R., (1995). *Observational studies.* New York: Springer-Verlag.

Rosenberg, M. J. (1969). The conditions and consequences of evaluation apprehension. In R. Rosenthal & R. L. Rosnow (Eds.), *Artifact in behavioral research.* New York: Academic Press.

Rosnow, R. L., & Rosenthal, R. (1970). Volunteer effects in behavioral research. In *New directions in psychology 4.* New York: Holt, Rinehart & Winston.

Rotton, J., & Kelly, I. W. (1985). Much ado about the full moon: A meta-analysis of lunar-lunacy research. *Psychological Bulletin, 97,* 286–306.

Rowan, A. N., & Loew, F. M. (1995). *The animal research controversy: Protest, process, and public policy.* North Grafton, MA: Tufts University, Center for Animals and Public Policy.

Rowland, L. W. (1939). Will hypnotized persons try to harm themselves or others? *Journal of Abnormal and Social Psychology, 34,* 114–117.

Ruback, R. B., & Snow, J. N. (1993). Territoriality and nonconscious racism at water fountains: Intruders and drinkers (blacks and whites) are affected by race. *Environment and Behavior, 25,* 250–267.

Rushton, J. P. (1997). Cranial size and IQ in Asian Americans from birth to age seven. *Intelligence, 25,* 7–20.

Rushton, J. P., & Ankney, C. D. (1996). Brain size and cognitive ability. Correlations with age, sex, social class, and race. *Psychonomic Bulletin & Review, 3,* 21–36.

Saari, L. M., & Latham, G. P. (1982). Employee reactions to continuous and variable ratio reinforcement schedules involving a monetary incentive. *Journal of Applied Psychology, 67,* 506–508.

Sanitioso, R. Kunda, Z., & Fong, G. T. (1990). Motivated recruitment of autobiographical memories. *Journal of Personality Social Psychology, 59,* 229–241.

Scarr, S. (1988). Race and gender as psychological variables: Social and ethical issues. *American Psychologist, 43,* 56–59.

Schachter, S. (1982). Don't sell habit-breakers short. *Psychology Today, 16,* 27–33.

Schaie, K. W. (1977). Quasi-experimental designs in the psychology of aging. In J. E. Birren & K. W. Schaie (Eds.), *Handbook of the psychology of aging.* New York: Van Nostrand.

Schmolck, H., Buffalo, E., & Squire, L. R. (2000). Memory distortions develop over time: Recollections of the O. J. Simpson trial verdict after 15 and 32 months. *Psychological Science, 11,* 39–45.

Schneider, D. J. (1988). *Introduction to social psychology.* New York: Harcourt Brace Jovanovich.

Schooler, J. W., Ohlsson, S., & Brooks, K. (1993). Thoughts beyond words: When language overshadows insight. *Journal of Experimental Psychology: General, 122,* 166–183.

Schreibman, L., O'Neill, R. E., & Koegel, R. L. (1983). Behavioral training for siblings of autistic children. *Journal of Applied Behavioral Analysis, 16,* 129–138.

Schwarz, N. (1999). Self-reports: How the questions shape the answers. *American Psychologist 54,* 93–105.

Schwarz, N., Knäuper, B., Hippler, H. J., Noelle-Neumann, E., & Clark, F. (1991). Rating scales: Numeric values may change the meaning of scale labels. *Public Opinion Quarterly, 55,* 570–582.

Sidman, M. (1960). *Tactics of scientific research.* New York: Basic Books.

Sieber, J. E., & Stanley, B. (1988). Ethical and professional dimensions of socially sensitive research. *American Psychologist, 43,* 49–55.

Simmons, W. W. (2000, December). One in six Americans admit to drinking too much. *The Gallup Poll Monthly, 423,* 42–45.

Singer, P. (1978). Animal experimentation: Philosophical perspectives. In W. T. Reich (Ed.), *Encyclopedia of bioethics.* New York: Free Press.

Skinner, B. F. (1963). The flight from the laboratory. In M. Marx (Ed.), *Theories in contemporary psychology.* New York: Macmillan.

Slife, B. D., & Williams, R. N. (1995). *What's behind the research?* Thousand Oaks, CA: Sage.

Smith, S.M. (1995). Getting into and out of mental ruts: A theory of fixation, incubation, and insight. In R.J. Sternberg & J. E. Davidson (Eds.), *The nature of insight* (pp. 229–251). Cambridge, MA: MIT Press.

Spanos, N. P. (1996). *Multiple identities and false memories: A sociocognitive perspective.* Washington, DC: American Psychological Association.

Squire, L. R., Schmolck, H., & Buffalo, E. A. (2001). Memory distortions develop over time: A reply to Horn. *Psychological Science, 12,* 182.

Steele, K. M., Bass, K. E., & Crook, M. D. (1999). The mystery of the Mozart effect: Failure to replicate. *Psychological Science, 10,* 366–369.

Sternberg, R. J. (2000). Article writing 101: A crib sheet of 50 tips for the final exam. In R. J. Sternberg (Ed.), *Guide to publishing in psychology journals* (pp. 199–206). New York: Cambridge University Press.

———. (1992). How to win acceptances by psychology journals: 21 Tips for better writing. *APS Observer, 5,* 12–14.

———. (2003). *The psychologist's companion* (4th ed.). New York: Cambridge University Press.

Sternberg, R. J., Grigorenko, E. L., & Kalmar, D. A. (2001). The role of theory in unified psychology. *Journal of Theoretical and Philosophical Psychology, 21,* 100–117.

Strayer, D. L., & Johnson, W. A. (2001). Driven to distraction: Dual-task studies of simulated driving and conversing on a cellular phone. *Psychological Science, 12,* 462–466.

Stroop, J. R. (1935). Studies of interference in serial verbal reactions. *Journal of Experimental Psychology, 18,* 643–662.

Swazey, J. P., Anderson, M. S., & Lewis, K. S. (1993). Ethical problems in academic research. *American Scientist, 81,* 542–553.

Talarico, J. M., & Rubin, D. C. (2003). Confidence, not consistency, characterizes flashbulb memories. *Psychological Science, 14,* 455–461.

Thios, S. J., & D'Agostino, P. R. (1976). Effects of repetition as a function of study-phase retrieval. *Journal of Verbal Learning and Verbal Behavior, 15,* 529–536.

Thompson, J. B., & Buchanan, W. (1979). *Analyzing psychological data.* New York: Scribner's.

Timberlake, W., & Silva, F. J. (1994). Observation of behavior, inference of function, and the study of learning. *Psychonomic Bulletin & Review, 1,* 73–88.

Todd, C. M., & Perlmutter, M. (1980). Reality recalled by school children. In M. Perlmutter (Ed.), *Children's memory: New directions for child development, 10* (pp. 69–85). San Francisco: Jossey-Bass.

Tsang, P. S., & Vidulich, M. A. (2003) *Principles and practices of aviation psychology.* Mahwah, NJ: Erlbaum.

Tversky, B., & Teiffer, E. (1976). Development of strategies for recall and recognition. *Developmental Psychology, 12,* 406–410.

Underwood, B. (1957). *Psychological research.* New York: Appleton.

———. (1975). Individual differences as a crucible in theory construction. *American Psychologist, 30,* 128–134.

Uttal, W. R. (1978). *The psychology of mind.* Hillsdale, NJ: Erlbaum.

Velten, E. A. (1968). A laboratory task for the induction of mood states. *Behavior Research and Therapy, 6,* 473–478.

Wagenaar, A. C. (1981). Effects of the raised legal drinking age on motor vehicle accidents in Michigan. *HSRI Research Review, 11,* 1–8.

Walsh, L. (2004). *Welcome to the pursuing psychology career page.* Retrieved February 11, 2005, from http://www.uni.edu/walsh/linda1.html

Walters, C., Shurley, J. T., & Parsons, O. A. (1962). Differences in male and female responses to underwater sensory deprivation: An exploratory study. *Journal of Nervous and Mental Disease, 135,* 302–310.

Wason, P. C. (1977). On the failure to eliminate hypotheses—a second look. In P. N. Johnson-Laird & P. C. Wason (Eds.), *Thinking: Readings in cognitive science.* Cambridge: Cambridge University Press.

Watson, D., Clark, L. A., & Tellegen, A. (1988). Development and validation of brief measures of positive and negative affect: The PANAS scales. *Journal of Personality and Social Psychology, 54,* 1063–1070.

Webb, E. J., Campbell, D. T., Schwartz, R. D., & Sechrist, L. (1981). *Unobtrusive measures: Nonreactive research in the social sciences.* Chicago: Rand McNally.

Weber, E. H. (1846/1948). The sense of touch and common feeling. In W. Dennis (Ed.), *Readings in the history of psychology.* New York: Appleton Century-Crofts.

Weber, S. J., & Cook, T. D. (1972). Subject effects in laboratory research: An examination of subject roles, demand characteristics, and valid inference. *Psychological Bulletin, 77,* 273–295.

Weisberg, H. F., Krosnick, J. A., & Bowen, B. D. (1989). *An introduction to survey research and data analysis* (2nd ed.). Glenview, IL: Scott, Foresman.

Weiss, J. M. (1968). Effects of coping responses on stress. *Journal of Comparative and Physiological Psychology, 65,* 251–260.

———. (1971). Effects of coping behavior in different warning signal conditions on stress pathology in rats. *Journal of Comparative and Physiological Psychology, 77,* 1–13.

White, R. J. (1971). Debate II. Antivivisection: The reluctant hydra. *American Scholar, 40,* 503–512.

Wildman, B. G., & Erickson, M. T. (1977). Methodological problems in behavioral observation. In J. D. Coe & R. P. Hawkins (Eds.), *Behavioral assessment.* New York: Brunner/Mazel.

Willerman, L., Schultz, R., Rutledge, J. N., & Bigler, E. D. (1991). *In vivo* brain size and intelligence. *Intelligence, 15,* 223–228.

Williams, K., Harkins, S., & Latané, B. (1981). Identifiability as a deterrent to social loafing: Two cheering experiments. *Journal of Personality and Social Psychology, 40,* 303–311.

Windes, J. D. (1968). Reaction time for numerical coding and naming of numerals. *Journal of Experimental Psychology, 78,* 318–322.

Wixted, J. T., & Squire, L. R. (2004). Recall and recognition are equally impaired in patients with selective hippocampal damage. *Cognitive, Affective and Behavioral Neuroscience, 4,* 58–66.

Wohwill, J. F. (1970). Methodology and research strategy in the study of developmental change. In L. R. Goulet & P. B. Baltes (Eds.), *Life-span developmental psychology: Research and theory.* New York: Academic Press.

Wolf, M. M., & Risley, T. R. (1971). Reinforcement: Applied research. In R. Glaser (Ed.), *The nature of reinforcement.* New York: Academic Press.

Wood, W., Wong, F. Y., & Chachere, J. G. (1991). Effects of media violence on viewers' aggression in unconstrained social interaction. *Psychological Bulletin, 109,* 371–383.

Woodzicka, J. A., & LaFrance, M. (2001). Real versus imagined gender harassment. *Journal of Social Issues, 57,* 15–30.

Woolfolk, M. E. (1981). The eye of the beholder: Methodological considerations when observers assess nonverbal communication. *Journal of Nonverbal Behavior, 5,* 199–204.

Woolfolk, M. E., Castellan, W., & Brooks, C. I. (1983). Pepsi versus Coke: Labels, not tastes, prevail. *Psychological Reports, 52,* 185–186.

Wright, L. (1988). The Type A behavior pattern and coronary artery disease. *American Psychologist, 43,* 2–14.

Wu, P., & Campbell, D.T. (1996). Extending latent variable LISREL analyses of the 1969 Westinghouse Head Start evaluation to Blacks and full year Whites. *Evaluation and Program Planning, 19,* 183–191.

Yonelinas, A. P., Kroll, N. E., Quamme, J. R., Lazzara, M. M., Sauve, M. J., Widamean, K. F., et al. (2002). Effects of extensive temporal lobe damage or mild hypoxia on recollection and familiarity. *Nature Neuroscience, 5,* 1236–1241.

Young, P. C. (1952). Antisocial uses of hypnosis. In L. M. LeCron (Ed.), *Experimental hypnosis.* New York: Macmillan.

Young, P. T. (1928). Precautions in animal experimentation. *Psychological Bulletin, 25,* 487–489.

Zajonc, R. B., & Marcus, N. (1975). Birth order and intellectual development. *Psychological Review, 82,* 74–88.

Zimbardo, P. (2001). *Discovering psychology: Updated edition (tape 19): The power of the situation* [VHS videotape]. Available from: Annenberg/CPB Collection at: http://www.learner.org/resources/series138.html#program_des. Retrieved February 11, 2005.

Zuckerman, M. (1996). Notes and shorter communications: Item revisions in the Sensation Seeking Scale Form V (SSS-V). *Personality and Individual Differences, 20,* 515.

AB design A frequently used design in which a therapy (*B*) is instituted after measuring a particular behavior (*A*); a poor research design

ABA and ABAB designs See *reversal (ABA) design*

Abscissa The horizontal axis (or *X*-axis) in a graph

Absolute threshold The average point on a sensory continuum (such as light intensity) at which an observer detects a stimulus

Abstract Short summary at the beginning of a journal article that informs the reader about the results

Alpha (a) level See *level of significance*

Alternating-treatments design A small-*n* design in which two or more independent variables alternate

Analysis of variance A statistical test appropriate for analyzing reliability from experiments with any number of levels on one or more independent variables

Anthropomorphizing Attributing human characteristics or emotions (such as happiness) to animals

APA American Psychological Association

APA format The journal article format specified by the APA

Apparatus A subsection of the Method portion of a technical paper that describes any special equipment used in the research to test participants.

Applied research Research focused on solving a practical problem

A priori method According to Peirce, a way of fixing belief due to the reasonableness of the event (see *method of tenacity, method of authority,* and *empirical*)

Apprehensive-subject role A presumed role taken by a research subject who dislikes being evaluated; see *evaluation apprehension* and *reactivity*

Author The person or persons responsible for a technical paper; a literature search via an author's name can be profitable

Balanced Latin square Counterbalancing scheme in which each condition is preceded and followed equally often by every other condition

Baseline The "normal" or typical behavior used as a standard of comparison in an experiment

Basic research Research in which the focus is on understanding rather than on the immediate solution to a problem

Behavior The basic dependent variable of psychology

Between-groups variance A measure of the dispersion among groups in an experiment

Between-subjects design An experimental design in which each subject is tested under only one level of each independent variable

Blind experiment Experiment in which subjects do not know whether they are in the treatment condition; see *double-blind design*

Block randomization A counterbalancing technique in which the treatment orders are randomized in successive blocks of presenting those conditions

Carryover effect Relatively permanent effect that testing subjects in one condition has on their later behavior in another condition

Case study Intensive investigation of a particular instance, or cases, of some behavior; does not allow inferences of cause and effect; is merely descriptive

Ceiling effect See *scale-attenuation effects*

Cell An entry in a data table defined by a particular row/column combination

Central tendency Descriptive statistics indicating the center of a distribution of scores; see *mean, median,* and *mode*

Changing-criterion design A small-*n* design in which the criterion behavior needed to produce an outcome changes

Computerized literature search A method of searching the database in a library that uses a computer

Conceptual replication Attempt to demonstrate an experimental phenomenon with an entirely new paradigm or set of experimental conditions; see *converging operations*

Confidence level See *level of significance*

Confidentiality Information obtained about subjects should remain confidential unless otherwise agreed

Confounding Simultaneous variation of a second variable with an independent variable of interest so that any effect on the dependent variable cannot be attributed with certainty to the independent variable; inherent in correlational research

Construct validity When several measures fit sensibly with other results, we are measuring an underlying psychological concept

Contingency table A relational research design in which the frequencies of all combinations of two variables are assessed to determine the relationship between them

Control The technique of producing comparisons and holding other variables constant

Control condition The comparison condition in a within-subjects design; compare *control group*

Control group The group in a between-subjects experiment that receives a comparison level of the independent variable

Control variable A potential independent variable that is held constant in an experiment

Converging operations A set of related lines of investigation that all bolster a common conclusion

Copy manuscript The preprint version of a research report; that is, it is a manuscript that has not yet been printed in a technical journal

Correlation A measure of the extent to which two variables are related, but not necessarily causally

Correlation coefficient A number that can vary from -1.00 to $+1.00$ and indicates the degree of relation between two variables

Correlational research Relational research that shows both the degree and the direction of the relationship between two variables

Counterbalancing Refers to any technique used to vary systematically the order of conditions in an experiment to distribute the effects of time of testing (e.g., practice and fatigue) so they are not confounded with conditions

Covariates Variables that covary with a target in statistical analyses, such as regression, that are accounted for in the analysis of the target

Criterion An independent means of determining the validity of an observation, experiment, or judgment

Critic A person who makes an informed judgment

Critical thinker A person who approaches scientific procedures and results with a critical attitude

Cross-lagged-panel correlation Calculating several correlation coefficients across time on the same participants to increase the internal validity of correlational research

Crossover interaction When the effect of one independent variable on a dependent variable reverses at different levels of a second independent variable

Cross-sectional method Taking a large sample of the population of various ages at one time and testing them; contrast with *longitudinal method*

Cross-sequential design A quasi-experimental design used when age is a subject variable to try to control for cohort and time-of-testing effects; involves testing several different age groups at several different time periods; see *longitudinal method* and *cross-sectional method*

Data The scores obtained on a dependent variable

Debriefing When subjects are told all details of an experiment after they have participated; an ethical obligation of the researcher

Deception A research technique in which the participant is misled about some aspect of the project; may be unethical; see *double-blind design*

Deduction Reasoning from the general to the particular

Degrees of freedom The number of values free to vary if the total number of values and their sum are fixed

Demand characteristics Those cues available to participants in an experiment that may enable them to determine the purpose of the experiment or what is expected by the experimenter

Dependent variable The variable measured and recorded by the experimenter

Descriptive observation A determination of the quantity (frequency, magnitude) of behavior resulting from observation, case study, survey, and testing methods

Descriptive statistics Methods of organizing and summarizing data

Deviant-case analysis Investigation of similar cases that differ in outcome in an attempt to specify the reasons for the different outcomes

Difference A basic property of all measurement scales, such that objects or their attributes can be categorized as different from each other

Difference threshold The average point at which two stimuli are judged to be different (half of the interval of uncertainty)

Diffusion of responsibility The tendency for individuals to assume less responsibility to act in a group situation

Direct replication Repeating an experiment as closely as possible to determine whether the same results will be obtained

Directional/nondirectional statistical tests See *one-* and *two-tailed tests*

Discounting cue A message, signal, or pertinent fact that makes you doubt the accuracy or credibility of a persuasive message

Discussion A section of a technical paper in which the author draws theoretical conclusions by examining, interpreting, and qualifying the results

Dispersion The amount of spread in a distribution of scores

Distribution A set of values of a variable

Double-blind design Experimental technique in which neither the participant nor the experimenter knows which participants are in which treatment condition

Ecological function The role of behaviors in adapting an organism to the environment

Ecological validity The extent to which a research setting matches the environment of the problem under investigation; a threat to the external validity of experiments

Effect size See *magnitude of effect*

Einstellung The effect of expectancy on cognition; for example, if people solve problems in one particular way, they will often approach new problems in the same way even when the original strategy is no longer effective

Empirical Relying on or derived from observation or experiment

Equal interval A property of measurement scales such that a one-unit change is equivalent throughout the range of the scale

η (eta) The effect size measure for F test

Ethical issues Stress on the well-being of the participants in research—avoiding physical and mental harm

Ethogram A data sheet providing categories for making naturalistic observations

Ethology The systematic study of behavior; usually animal behavior in natural settings

Evaluation apprehension A source of reactivity in which participants are uneasy about being evaluated in an experiment; see *reactivity*

Ex post facto Literally, "after the fact"; refers to conditions in an experiment that are not determined prior to the experiment, but only after some manipulation has occurred naturally

Experiment The systematic manipulation of some environment in order to observe the effect of this manipulation on behavior; a particular comparison is produced

Experimental control Holding constant extraneous variables in an experiment so that any effect on the dependent variable can be attributed to manipulation of the independent variable

Experimental group The group in an experiment that receives the level of interest of the independent variable

Experimental hypothesis The independent variable or a specific level of the independent variable that will have an effect on the dependent variable

Experimental reliability The extent to which the experimental results can be replicated

Explanation A causal statement about why or when a particular event occurs resulting from experimental methods (see *joint method of agreement and difference*)

External validity Refers to the generality of research; externally valid research is representative of real life and does not distort the question under investigation

Factorial design An experimental design in which each level of every independent variable occurs with all levels of the other independent variable

Faithful-subject role When participants do their utmost to follow the demands of the experimenter; see *reactivity*

Falsifiability view The assertion by Popper that negative results are more informative than positive results

Field research Research conducted in natural settings in which subjects typically do not know that they are in an experiment

Figure captions Descriptions of figures that appear on a page separate from the figures in a copy manuscript

Figures Graphical presentations of data in the Results sections of a research report

Floor effect See *scale-attenuation effects*

Forced-choice tests Tests in which the participant must select between two or more statements; often used to control response styles

***F* ratio** A ratio of between-groups variance to within-groups variance; forms the basis of the analysis of variance

Fraud Deliberate bias, in the research process, that includes fabrication of data and plagiarism

Freedom to withdraw Experimenter is ethically obligated to allow subjects to discontinue participation in the research

Frequency distribution A set of scores arranged in order along a distribution indicating the number of times each score occurs

Frequency polygon A frequency distribution in which the height of the curve indicates the frequency of scores; see *histogram*

Functional analysis An analysis of the antecedents and consequences of a particular behavior; usually undertaken before the implementation of a behavioral treatment

Generalizability The issue of whether a particular experimental result will be obtained under different circumstances, such as with a different subject population or in a different experimental setting

Generalization A broad statement derived from a theory that cannot be tested directly

Good-subject role When a subject attempts to determine the purposes of an experiment and reacts accordingly; see *demand characteristics* and *reactivity*

Hawthorne effect Refers to conditions under which performance in an experiment is affected by the knowledge of participants that they are in an experiment; see *demand characteristics*

Histogram A frequency distribution in which the height of bars in the graph indicates the frequency of a class of scores; also called a bar graph

History A possible confound in research that inadvertently takes place between measurements because of historical changes in the participant

Hypothesis A very specific testable statement derived from a theory that can be evaluated from observable data

Inadvertent researcher bias Unplanned bias owing to the characteristics of the researcher, including political beliefs, training, and other sources of individual differences

Independent variable The variable manipulated by the experimenter

Individual differences A problem that may confound the results of a between-subjects experiment

Induction Reasoning from the particular to the general

Inferential statistics Procedures for determining the reliability and generality of a particular experimental finding

Informed consent Potential subjects must be in a position to decide whether to participate in an experiment

Institutional review board (IRB) A board in nearly every United States institution conducting research that oversees the protection of human participants

Interactions Experimental results that occur when the effects of one independent variable depend on the levels of other independent variables

Internal validity Allows straightforward statements about causality; experiments are usually internally valid because the joint method of agreement and difference is employed

Interobserver reliability The degree to which two or more observers can accurately categorize naturalistic observations

Interrupted-time-series design A quasi-experiment that involves examination of a naturally occurring treatment on the behavior of a large number of participants

Interval scale A scale with equal intervals but without a true zero point (e.g., temperature)

Intervening variable An abstract concept that links independent variables to dependent variables

Introduction The portion of a technical paper that specifies the problem to be studied and tells why it is important

Joint method of agreement and difference In Mill's system a situation, such as an experiment, in which X always follows A and never occurs when A is not present

Large-*n* designs Designs in which inferential statistics are used to determine whether two or more groups differ reliably

Latin-square design A counterbalancing procedure in which each conditioning occurs equally often during each time period of the experiment; see *balanced Latin square*

Level of significance Probability that an experimental finding is due to chance, or random fluctuation, operating in the data

Likert scale See *summated rating (Likert) scale*

Longitudinal method Testing one group of people repeatedly as they age; contrast with *cross-sectional method*

Magnitude A property of measurement scales having to do with the fact that scale values can be ordered on the basis of magnitude—if $A > B$ and $B > C$, then $A > C$

Magnitude of effect A calculation such as r_{pb} that reveals the magnitude of the effect of the independent variable—how wrong the null hypothesis is

Main effect When the effect of one independent variable is the same at all levels of another independent variable

Mann-Whitney *U* test A nonparametric test to determine whether the behavior of two independent groups is statistically different

Matched-groups design Experimental design in which subjects are matched on some variable assumed to be correlated with the dependent variable and then randomly assigned to conditions

Matching See *subject variable* and *matched-groups design*

Materials A part of the method section in which elements other than the apparatus used to test participants are described, including surveys, videos, words presented for memorization, and the like

Maturation Changes in people over time because of growth and other historical factors; may be a source of confounding in quasi-experiments

Mean Measure of central tendency; the sum of all the scores divided by the number of scores

Measurement The systematic assignment of numbers to objects or attributes of objects

Measurement scales In order in increasing power; nominal, ordinal, interval, and ratio

Median Measure of central tendency; the middle score of a distribution, or the one that divides a distribution in half

Meta-analysis A relatively objective technique for summarizing across many studies investigating a single topic

Method A section of a technical paper that describes in detail the operations performed by the experimenter

Method of authority A method of fixing belief in which an authority's word is taken on faith; contrast with *empirical*

Method of tenacity A way of fixing belief involving a steadfast adherence to a particular belief, regardless of contrary arguments; see *empirical*

Mixed design An experimental design that contains both between-subjects and within-subjects manipulations of the independent variables

Mode A measure of central tendency; the most frequent score

Mortality A possible source of confounding in research resulting from participants dropping out either because they will not participate or because they cannot participate

Motivated forgetting Distortions of past events reported retrospectively because of the emotional nature of those events

Mozart effect The finding of better performance on spatial-temporal tasks following exposure to music composed by Mozart; the exact mechanisms underlying the effect (including whether it may be due to an experimental artifact) are still under debate

Multiple-baseline design A small-*n* design in which different behaviors (or different participants) receive baseline periods of varying lengths prior to the introduction of the independent variable

Multiple regression A type of regression analysis that uses more than one predictor variable

Naturalistic observation Description of naturally occurring events without intervention on the part of the investigator

Negativistic-subject role When a participant deliberately attempts to sabotage an experiment

Nominal scale A scale in which objects are named or categorized—the weakest measurement scale

Nonequivalent control group In quasi-experiments, a control group that is not determined by random assignment but is usually selected after the fact and is supposed to be equivalent to the naturally treated group

Nonparametric statistics Statistical tests that do not make any assumptions about the underlying distribution of scores; ordinarily require just ordinal-level data; see *parametric statistics*

Normal curve A distribution of events that, when plotted, results in a bell-shaped curve; in a normal curve the mean, the median, and the mode are all equal

Normal distribution One producing a symmetric bell-shaped curve

Null hypothesis States that the independent variable will have no effect on the dependent variable

Null result An experimental outcome in which the dependent variable was not influenced by the independent variable

Observation-treatment-observation A quasi-experimental design; usually includes a nonequivalent control group

One-shot case study A quasi-experiment in which the behavior of a single individual is studied and "explained" in terms of life events; see *case study* and *deviant-case analysis*

One-tailed test Test that places the rejection area at one end of a distribution

Operational definition A definition of a concept in terms of the operations that must be performed to demonstrate the concept

Ordinal scale A measurement scale in which objects or attributes are ordered but in which the intervals between points are not equal

Ordinate The vertical axis (or *Y*-axis) in a graph

Organization The function of a theory that collects or organizes what is known into a coherent statement

Parallel forms Two alternative forms of a test

Parametric statistics Statistical tests that make assumptions about the distribution of scores (e.g., normally distributed); require interval or ratio data

Parsimony A good, powerful theory should explain many events with few statements or explanatory concepts; thus, refers to simplicity

Participant observation An observation procedure in which the observer participates with those being observed (e.g., living with gorillas in the wild)

Participant or subject representativeness Determination of generality of results across different subject populations

Participants/subjects In a journal article, a subsection of the Method section indicating the number and manner of selecting the participants (humans) or subjects (nonhuman animals) in the research

Part-task simulator A device that simulates only a portion of a system; see *simulator*

Pearson *r* One form of correlation coefficient

Pearson's product-moment correlation coefficient See *Pearson r*

Personal space The "invisible bubble" surrounding a person

Pilot research Preliminary research undertaken to discover problems of method and design for a subsequent full-scale project

Placebo A pill or an injection that is inert

Placebo effect Improvement often shown in drug-effectiveness studies in which patients believe they have received a drug when they actually received an inert substance

Plagiarism The uncredited use of another person's words or ideas

Point biserial *r* A correlation coefficient often used in two-group experiments to determine the magnitude of effect of the independent variable

Population The total set of potential observations from which a sample is drawn

Power (of a statistical test) The probability of rejecting the null hypothesis in a statistical test when it is in fact false

Precision A good theory should be precise in its predictions

Prediction A specification of relationships resulting from correlational methods; also one aim of a theory

Predictive validity When a test can predict a particular outcome

Procedure In a journal article, a subsection of the Method section that explains what happened to the participants/subjects and contains enough information that someone else could repeat the study exactly as it was done

Protection from harm Ethical researchers protect their participants from any harm

Protocol A recipe to be followed exactly in conducting a research project

Proximate cause The immediate causes of an event, such as the independent variable in an experiment; see *ultimate cause*

Psychological Abstracts A journal produced by the APA that lists abstracts of most of the journal articles relevant to psychological topics

Psychometric scaling Measurement of psychological concepts that do not have clearly specified inputs

Psychophysical methods Procedures (such as the method of limits) used to determine thresholds that provide the bases of psychophysical scaling

Psychophysical scaling Scales having well-specified inputs and outputs

Psychophysics Judgment of stimuli that are on a known physical dimension

PsycINFO A computerized database containing abstracts of most psychological journal articles

Quasi-experiment An experiment in which the independent variable occurs naturally and is not under direct control of the experimenter; see *ex post facto*

Random-groups design When subjects are randomly assigned to conditions in a between-subjects design

Random sample A sample from a population that has been selected in an unbiased way

Random sampling See *random sample*

Randomization The process of unbiased assignment of subjects to conditions or unbiased variation of condition order

Range Descriptive measure of dispersion; the difference between the largest and smallest score in a distribution

Ratio scale The highest form of scale in which there is a true zero and in which it is meaningful to consider multiplicative differences among attributes

Reactivity Term to describe observations that are influenced by (or may be, in part, a reaction to) the detected presence of the investigator

Realism The extent to which a research procedure matches the characteristics of the real world; contrast with *generalizability*

References Found at the end of a technical paper; only articles cited in the text of the paper are included in the Reference section

Regression Use of correlation coefficients to predict one variable given another

Regression artifacts An artifact in the measurement of change on a variable when groups of subjects who scored at the extremes on the variable are tested again; see *regression to the mean*

Regression to the mean Tendency for extreme measures on some variable to be closer to the group mean when remeasured, due to unreliability of measurement

Relational observations See *relational research*

Relational research Research that tries to determine how two or more observations are related

Reliability Refers to the repeatability of an experimental result; inferential statistics provide an estimation of how likely it is that a finding is repeatable; also refers to the consistency of a test or measuring instrument determined by computing a correlation between scores obtained by participants taking the test twice (test-retest reliability), or taking two different parallel forms of the test, or scores obtained on each half of the test (split-half reliability)

Removing harmful consequences Ethical researchers remove any harmful consequences that their participants may have incurred

Repeated-measures design Several measures are taken on the same participant, such as several learning trials or numerous psychophysical judgments; a type of within-subjects experiment

Replication The repetition of an earlier experiment to duplicate (and perhaps extend) its findings; see also *systematic replication*

Researcher bias Deliberate or inadvertent bias in which data are misanalyzed or participants are differentially treated over and above any planned differences in treatment

Response acquiescence A habitual way of responding on tests that involves frequently responding "yes"; see *response styles*

Response deviation A habitual way of responding on tests that involves frequently responding "no"; see *response styles*

Response styles Habitual ways of responding on a test that are independent of the particular test item; see *response deviation, response acquiescence,* and *social desirability*

Results A section of a technical paper that tells what happened in the research

Retrospective In case studies, when the person has to report on events that occurred in the distant past; subject to ordinary and motivated forgetting

Reversibility An assumption made in research that the characteristics of different populations and species of subjects have the same underlying process; the behavioral "equation" can be determined from the behavior that is observed

Reversal (ABA) design Small-*n* design in which a participant's behavior is measured under a baseline (A) condition, then an experimental treatment is applied during the B phase and any changes in behavior are observed; finally, the original baseline (A) conditions are reinstituted to ensure that the experimental treatment was responsible for any observed change during the B phase

Running head In a journal article, the heading that appears at the top of the page

Sample Observations selected from a population

Scale-attenuation effects Difficulties in interpreting results when performance on the dependent variable is either nearly perfect (a ceiling effect) or nearly lacking altogether (a floor effect)

Scatter diagrams A graphical relationship indicating degree of correlation between two variables made by plotting the scores of individuals on two variables

Scientific method According to Peirce, this method fixes belief on the basis of experience; see *empirical*

Selection bias Occurs when subjects are not selected randomly; see *subject attrition* and *matching*

Self-correcting Science is self-correcting because it relies on public, empirical observation; old beliefs are discarded if they do not fit the empirical data

Self-report methods Most psychometric scales and many psychophysical scales produce data based on a personal report by the respondent and not from observational measurements made directly by the researcher

Setting representativeness See *ecological validity*

Short title In a journal article, the first few words of the title, which appear at the top of each page of the copy manuscript

Significance level Probability that an experimental finding is due to chance, or random fluctuation, operating in the data

Significantly different A difference between conditions that would occur only 1 time in 20 by chance

Simulated experiment A fake experiment in which participants are told to simulate the behavior of real participants in a particular experiment

Simulator A device that duplicates the functions of a real system to allow controlled experiments to be performed

Sleeper effect An improvement in the effect of a persuasive message with the passage of time

Small-*n* design Research design using a small number of subjects

Social desirability A habitual way of responding on tests that involves making socially desirable responses; see *response styles*

Social loafing The decrease in individual effort that sometimes occurs when other people are present and when group performance is measured

Social Science Citation Index A journal containing lists of articles that cite a particular author or work

Speciesism A term used to describe the view that animal life is qualitatively different from human life; therefore, a form of bigotry

Split-half reliability Determining reliability of a test by dividing the test items into two arbitrary groups and correlating the scores obtained on the two halves of the test

Standard deviation Descriptive measure of dispersion; square root of the sum of squared deviations of each score from the mean divided by the number of scores

Standard error of the mean The standard deviation of the distribution of sample means

Standard normal distribution A distribution of events that, when plotted, results in a bell-shaped curve; in a standard normal distribution, the mean, the median, and the mode are all equal

Standard scores Also called *z* scores; differences between individual scores and the mean score expressed in units of standard deviations

Statistical reliability (significance) Rejecting the null hypothesis on the basis of a statistical test that yields an alpha level of less than .05

Stratified sample An alternative to a random sample in which the population is divided into units and random sampling is done from the units

Strong inference Platt's view that scientific progress comes about through a series of tests of alternative theoretical outcomes

Stroop effect Difficulty in naming the color of an object when the color conflicts with the name of the object (e.g., when the word *blue* is printed in red ink)

Subject attrition When a subject fails to complete an experiment, which may destroy the basis of matching subjects across groups

Subject roles How a participant reacts in an experiment; see *apprehensive-subject role, faithful-subject role, good subject role,* and *negativistic-subject role*

Subject variable Some characteristics of people that can be measured or described but cannot be varied experimentally (e.g., height, weight, sex, IQ)

Sum of squares (*SS*) Sum of the squared scores used to calculate effects via analysis of variance

Summated rating (Likert) scale The sum of ratings given to attitude statements, on which people typically respond to positively and negatively oriented statements on 5-point scales

Survey research The technique of obtaining a limited amount of information from a large number of people, usually through random sampling

Synergism A term used in medical research to describe an interaction; see *interactions*

Systematic replication Repeating an experiment while varying numerous factors considered to be irrelevant to the phenomenon to see if it will survive these changes

Tables A nongraphical way of summarizing data in a technical paper. Summary values of the dependent variable are presented under headings describing the levels of the independent variable

Test reliability See *test-retest reliability* and *split-half reliability*

Testability A good theory needs to be capable of disproof

Testable hypothesis A hypothesis that specifies what can be measured and manipulated to test a theory

Test-retest reliability Giving the same test twice in succession over a short interval to see if the scores are stable, or reliable; generally expressed as a correlation between scores on the tests

Theory A collection of ideas whose purpose is to describe and predict

Theoretical constructs See *intervening variables*

Time-lag design A quasi-experimental design used when age is a subject variable in order to control time of testing effects; subjects of a particular age (e.g., 19-year-olds) are tested at different time periods

Title Provides an idea of the contents of an article or technical paper and usually states only the dependent and independent variables

Treatment × treatment × subjects A within-subjects factorial design with two independent variables

True zero The absence of a physical property (zero weight in grams) as opposed to an arbitrary zero such as 0° centigrade

Truncated range A problem in interpreting low correlations; the amount of dispersion (or range) of scores on one variable may be small, thus leading to the low correlation found

t **Tests** Parametric tests for testing differences between two groups

2 × 2 Factorial design A design in which there are two levels of each of two independent variables, yielding four conditions

Two-tailed test Test that places the rejection area at both ends of a distribution

Type 1 error Probability that the null hypothesis is rejected when it is in fracture; equals the significance level

Type 2 error Failure to reject the null hypothesis when it is in fact false

Ultimate cause The basic or final cause of an event, such as a "big bang" or evolution; contrast with *proximate cause*

Unobtrusive measures Measures taken from the results of behavior, not the behavior itself

Unobtrusive observations Observations not resulting in reactivity

Validity Refers to whether an observation or procedure is sound or genuine

Variable representativeness Determination of generality of results across different manipulations of an independent variable or different dependent variables

Variance Measure of dispersion; the standard deviation squared

Volunteer problem Volunteer subjects differ from those less eager to participate; may be a source of bias in research

Weber's law $\Delta I/I = K$ The just-noticeable difference is a constant fraction of the base intensity

Wilcoxon signed-ranks test A nonparametric test for two related groups

Within-groups variance A measure of the dispersion among subjects in the same group in an experiment

Within-subjects design An experimental design in which each subject is tested under more than one level of the independent variable

Workload The amount of attention-demanding effort imposed on a person

χ^2 Test for independence (chi-squared) A test that is often used to determine the statistical significance of the relationship between variables in a contingency table

NAME INDEX

SUBJECT INDEX

Psychophysics, 180
PsycINFO, 13, 15, 59, 84–85
*Publication Manual of the
    American Psychological
    Association,* 60, 325–326,
    351, 353
Publication of research reports,
    353–354

Quantitative versus qualitative
    variation, 403
Quasi-experimental design, 139
    defined, 254
    example, 276
    internal validity in, 254–274
    interrupted-time-series design,
        260–264
    natural treatments, 254–259
    one-shot case studies, 255–257
    regression in, 267–271
    subject variables, 264–271

rpb, 392, 396
Random error, 165–166
Random-groups design, 221
Randomization
    between-subjects design and,
        195
    within-subjects design and, 196–
        197
Random number table, 430
Random sample, 106
Random sampling, 172–174
Range, 363
Ratio scales, 66
Reactivity
    defined, 102
    in contingency table research,
        113
    in correlation research, 120–
        121
    in descriptive observations, 102–
        106
    in experimentation, 149–154
Realism, experimentation and, 50–
    52, 157–159
References, in an article, 67, 327
    format, 327
Regression, 121–122
Regression artifacts, 267, 305–309
Regression in compensatory
    education, 307–309
Regression to the mean, 267–271,
    305–309
Related-measures design, 389
Relational observations
    contingency table research, 111–
        113
    correlational research, 114
    defined, 111

Relational research, defined, 111,
    160
Reliability
    in communication, 20–21
    defined, 169
    experimental, 310–314
    interobserver, 93
    parallel forms, 171
    replication and, 310–314
    split-half, 171
    statistical, 171–172, 382
    test-retest, 171
Removing harmful consequences,
    ethics and, 285
Replications, 168, 293, 311
    conceptual, 313–314
    direct, 313
    Einstellung (set) experiments,
        311–314
    failure of, example, 315
    systematic, 313
Research
    applied and basic, 48–50
    biased, 17–18
Research careers in psychology, 8–
    9
Research design, external validity
    and, 154–159; *see also*
    Experimental design
Research project, steps in, 11
Research reports
    format, 325–328
    sample manuscript, 328–349
    sources of information on, 325
    style, 350–353
Research reports, publication of,
    353–354
Research with contingency table
    data, 111–113
Response acquiescence, 105
Response deviation, 105
Response sets, 105
Response styles, 105–106
Responsibility, diffusion of, 31 38,
    41
Results, interpreting
    converging operations, 273–274,
        314–320
    Einstellung (set) experiments,
        311–314
    regression artifacts and, 267,
        305–309
    reliability and replication, use
        of, 311–314
    scale-attenuation problem and,
        301–305
    temporal lobe damage
        experiment, 302–305
Results section, of an article, 61–
    67, 69, 326

Retrospective reports, 104
Reversal design, 237–241
Reversibility, 155
Reviewing the literature, 14–15,
    57–60, 84–85
Route guidance, 226–228
Running head, 325

Sample, 172, 375
Sampling
    description of, 172–174, 375–
        380
    stratified, 173–174
SAT, truncated range and, 119–120
Scale-attenuation effect, 301
Scale-attenuation problem, 301–
    305
Scatter diagrams, 116–117, 121
Schedule of reinforcement, 250–
    252
Scheffé test, 403
Scientific explanation
    defining a theory, 34–35
    evaluating a theory, 46–47
    induction versus deduction, 35–
        38
    intervening variables, 42–45, 55
    psychology and, 48–53
Scientific fraud, 292–294
Scientific method, 33
Segmented (fox) approach to
    theory, 47–48
Selection bias, 255
Self-correcting basis for fixing
    belief, 33–34
Self-report methods, 183
Setting representativeness, 157–159
Short title, 325
Significantly different, 382
Sign test, 389–390
    distribution for, 421
Simulated experimentation, 154
Simulator, 226–228
Sized sign test, 390
Sleep and tension headaches,
    relationship between, 130,
    276
Sleeper effect, 212–217
Small-*n* design in clinical
    psychology, 247–249
Small-*n* designs, 235–247
    ABA (reversal design), 237–241
    AB design, 236–237, 255
    alternating treatments design,
        241–242
    changing criterion design, 246–
        247
    multiple-baseline design, 242–
        246
Social desirability, 105

TO THE OWNER OF THIS BOOK:

I hope that you have found *Research Methods in Psychology*, Eighth Edition useful. So that this book can be improved in a future edition, would you take the time to complete this sheet and return it? Thank you.

School and address: _____

Department: _____

Instructor's name: _____

1. What I like most about this book is: _____

_____

_____

2. What I like least about this book is: _____

_____

_____

3. My general reaction to this book is:

_____

_____

4. The name of the course in which I used this book is

_____

5. Were all of the chapters of the book assigned for you to read? _____

   If not, which ones weren't? _____

6. In the space below, or on a separate sheet of paper, please write specific suggestions for improving this book and anything else you'd care to share about your experience in using this book.

_____

_____

_____

FOLD HERE

BUSINESS REPLY MAIL
FIRST-CLASS MAIL   PERMIT NO. 102   MONTEREY CA

POSTAGE WILL BE PAID BY ADDRESSEE

Attn: David G. Elmes

Wadsworth/Thomson Learning
60 Garden Ct Ste 205
Monterey CA 93940-9967

FOLD HERE

OPTIONAL:

Your name:_____ Date: _____

May we quote you, either in promotion for *Research Methods in Pyschology*, Eighth
Edition, or in future publishing ventures?

Yes: _____   No: _____

Sincerely yours,

David G. Elmes
Barry H. Kantowitz
Henry L. Roediger III

The Roman Catholic Church

AN ILLUSTRATED HISTORY